PeopleSoft for the Oracle DBA

David Kurtz

Apress®

PeopleSoft for the Oracle DBA

ISBN-13 (pbk): 978-1-4302-3707-5

ISBN-13 (electronic): 978-1-4302-3708-2

Trademarked names, logos, and images may appear in this book. Rather than use a trademark symbol with every occurrence of a trademarked name, logo, or image we use the names, logos, and images only in an editorial fashion and to the benefit of the trademark owner, with no intention of infringement of the trademark.

The use in this publication of trade names, trademarks, service marks, and similar terms, even if they are not identified as such, is not to be taken as an expression of opinion as to whether or not they are subject to proprietary rights.

While the advice and information in this book are believed to be true and accurate at the date of publication, neither the authors nor the editors nor the publisher can accept any legal responsibility for any errors or omissions that may be made. The publisher makes no warranty, express or implied, with respect to the material contained herein.

President and Publisher: Paul Manning
Lead Editor: Jonathan Gennick
Technical Reviewer: Wolfgang Breitling and Tim Gorman
Editorial Board: Steve Anglin, Mark Beckner, Ewan Buckingham, Gary Cornell, Morgan Ertel, Jonathan Gennick, Jonathan Hassell, Robert Hutchinson, Michelle Lowman, James Markham, Matthew Moodie, Jeff Olson, Jeffrey Pepper, Douglas Pundick, Ben Renow-Clarke, Dominic Shakeshaft, Gwenan Spearing, Matt Wade, Tom Welsh
Coordinating Editor: Anita Castro
Copy Editor: Tiffany Taylor
Compositor: Bytheway Publishing Services
Indexer: SPI Global
Artist: SPI Global
Cover Designer: Anna Ishchenko

Distributed to the book trade worldwide by Springer Science+Business Media New York, 233 Spring Street, 6th Floor, New York, NY 10013. Phone 1-800-SPRINGER, fax (201) 348-4505, e-mail orders-ny@springer-sbm.com, or visit www.springeronline.com.

For information on translations, please e-mail rights@apress.com, or visit www.apress.com.

Apress and friends of ED books may be purchased in bulk for academic, corporate, or promotional use. eBook versions and licenses are also available for most titles. For more information, reference our Special Bulk Sales–eBook Licensing web page at www.apress.com/bulk-sales.

Any source code or other supplementary materials referenced by the author in this text is available to readers at www.apress.com. For detailed information about how to locate your book's source code, go to www.apress.com/source-code/.

Contents at a Glance

Contents

Author's Preface to the Second Edition

Within a year of the publication of the first edition, I was regularly being asked when I would produce a second edition. For a long time, I said that nothing had really changed for the DBA. But it has! In seven years, there have been seven major releases of PeopleTools. So many little things had changed that not only was there enough to justify a revision, but it had become essential.

In fact, when it came to actually revising the book, I was surprised by just how much I had to change. Some material has been removed because it is no longer relevant in PeopleTools 8.4. Some things have been amended because they are no longer completely true.

There is a lot of new material throughout this edition. Some of the new material has been discussed on my blog, but this new edition has allowed me to organize it coherently and put it into context. Two very significant additions relate to performance measurement:

- When I wrote the first edition, I had not used PeopleSoft's built-in Performance Monitor on a live production system. I have now been using it for several years, and it has become an important tool for analyzing the performance of the on-line part of PeopleSoft applications. I have developed various techniques for working with the data it collects.

- PeopleTools has used the Oracle database instrumentation package dbms_application_info since PeopleTools 8.50. At first glance, this might seem to be a very minor change, but it has huge implications. It is now possible to bring a variety of Oracle database performance-analysis techniques to bear on PeopleSoft systems.

Even if you already have the first edition, there are still plenty of new ideas to read in this edition. Seven years ago, I wrote the first edition of this book while Oracle was trying to acquire PeopleSoft, and the deal was finally done at about the same time the book was published. Oracle has honored its commitment to continue to develop both PeopleSoft applications and PeopleTools. Today, although some Oracle Fusion Applications are available, companies are still installing and upgrading PeopleSoft systems.

It has never been more important than it is today to get the best possible value out of your PeopleSoft system. That requires a fundamental understanding of the underlying technologies. My objective remains not just to tell you what to do, but also why to do it.

David Kurtz
2011

Foreword to the First Edition

This book should have been written years ago, but then it would not have been as comprehensive as it is today. It bridges the gap between the worlds of PeopleSoft and Oracle, explaining where and how the two sides meet.

My own experience with PeopleSoft began in 1992 as the DBA on a GL 1.1/PeopleTools 2.1 implementation project. The DBA is often the only "technology-savvy" person on such a project, with the rest of the team consisting of functional experts, developers, and, of course, management. As such, the DBA often is tasked with helping to investigate and solve any technology-related problems, even if they have nothing to do with the database. In those early days, one of the big problems was to shoehorn all the pieces of the then client/server application into the first 640KB of a Windows 3.1 client. As a consultant on another implementation project, by now PeopleSoft 5.1, I learned firsthand the performance penalty of the client/server model in a wide area network (WAN) over frame relay, and the distinction between bandwidth and latency. The purchased bandwidth was sufficient for the demand, and that had been all the capacity planners were interested in. However, the accumulated latency of the frame relay network wreaked havoc with the performance. Of course, we were not alone in experiencing this, and in response PeopleSoft added the Tuxedo Application Server as a middle tier.

That was when I first encountered David's name. He was the author of a paper titled "Advanced Tuxedo" that went a long way toward improving my knowledge of the application server and my ability to fine-tune its configuration and administration. The application server is another piece of the growing technology stack in a PeopleSoft implementation that the DBA is tasked with administering simply because he or she is the most knowledgeable person around. Of course, with all the improvements Oracle continually makes to its software, databases these days manage themselves, and it is therefore high time to find something else for the DBA to do.

It is interesting how, in this time of the Internet and instant and constant communication, you get to know a person through his work expressed in papers or simply in contributions in newsgroups without ever meeting him. I have not (yet) met David in person, but when I received an e-mail asking me if I would consider being a technical reviewer for the book he was writing, I was honored—and eager, since I knew it would be a great book. I have only a slight disagreement over the title of the book because I believe it is a bit misleading. PeopleSoft is, by design, "database agnostic." Therefore, much of what David explains about how PeopleSoft works with Oracle is also applicable to any other database back-end. DBAs with PeopleSoft on DB2 or Microsoft SQL Server, for example, will get many of the same benefits from reading this book. So much for the "Oracle" part of the title.

As I said at the beginning of this foreword, this book bridges the gap between the PeopleSoft and the database worlds. For that reason, I am convinced that PeopleSoft administrators and developers also can learn a lot from what David lays out in this book and discover how some of the decisions they make affect what is happening at the database end. While readers who are new to PeopleSoft will gain the most from the material David presents, even seasoned users will benefit, particularly since the book is up-to-date with PeopleTools 8.44. What I like most about the book is that it is not a dry rehash of PeopleSoft manuals; rather, it is filled with solid advice and helpful scripts from David's many years of experience.

Wolfgang Breitling
2004

About the Author

David Kurtz has worked with the Oracle database since 1989, as an Oracle developer and DBA working on assurance, insurance, and actuarial software.

In 1996, he joined PeopleSoft, starting out in support. This gave him the opportunity to work out how PeopleTools works and how it interacts with the database. David moved to the PeopleSoft consultancy practice and worked on PeopleSoft customer sites across Europe.

In 2000, he set up Go-Faster Consultancy Ltd. (`www.go-faster.co.uk`), a company that provides specialist performance and technical consultancy to PeopleSoft users.

David is a member of the Oak Table network (`www.oaktable.net`) and an Oracle ACE Director. He is a regular presenter at UK Oracle User Group conferences and meetings.

About the Technical Reviewers

 **Wolfgang Breitling,** born in Stuttgart, Germany, studied mathematics, physics, and computer sciences at the University of Stuttgart. He joined IBM Germany in 1974 in the development laboratory, where he worked in the QA department. One of his tasks was to co-develop an operating system to test the hardware of the /370 model machines developed in Boeblingen, Germany, and Poughkeepsie and Endicott, New York. His first direct foray into performance-related tasks was a program to test the speed of individual operating codes. After IBM Germany, he worked as a systems programmer on IBM's hierarchical databases DL/1 and IMS for a company in Switzerland before emigrating to his current home in Calgary, Canada. After several years as a systems programmer for IMS and then DB2 on IBM mainframes, he became an independent consultant specializing in administering and tuning PeopleSoft, particularly on Oracle. In the past 20 years, he has been involved in several PeopleSoft installation and upgrade projects. The particular challenges in tuning PeopleSoft caused him to delve into the Oracle cost-based optimizer in an effort to better understand how it works and to use that knowledge in tuning. He has shared his findings in papers and presentations at Oracle user groups and conferences dedicated to Oracle performance topics.

 **Tim Gorman** has worked in IT with relational databases since 1984, as an Oracle PRO*C and PL/SQL application developer since 1990, as an Oracle DBA since 1993, and managing/designing very large data warehouses on Oracle since 1994. He is an independent contractor (www.EvDBT.com) specializing in performance tuning, database administration (particularly performance and availability), and data warehousing. Mr. Gorman has been a member of the Rocky Mountain Oracle Users Group (www.RMOUG.org) since 1993 and is currently president; has coauthored five books (three with Oak Table Press); has performed technical reviews on seven more books; is an Oracle ACE; has been a member of the Oak Table Network since 2002; and has presented at Oracle Open World, Collaborate, Hotsos, and local Oracle user groups in lots of wonderful places around the world.

Acknowledgments

You don't get to put your name on the cover of a book without a great deal of help from a lot of other people.

My thanks to my technical reviewers, Wolfgang Breitling and Tim Gorman, for reprising their roles in this second edition. Once again their probing questions have led to days of research and experimentation, and many of their insightful comments have been incorporated into the text. Their contribution has been huge.

Most important, I want to thank my wife, Angela, for her continuing support and patience while I have found yet another excuse to spend even more time than usual in front of a computer.

David Kurtz

Introduction

This book is aimed at helping Oracle DBAs understand and use PeopleSoft technology. For the typical DBA, the introduction to PeopleSoft is likely to include some surprises, not all of them agreeable. Many—if not most—DBAs have to deal with many different databases, usually supporting different applications. Often they will want to be able to administer all databases in a standard fashion. However, this is not always possible with a PeopleSoft system.

Most surprising to Oracle DBAs may be what is missing. In a vanilla PeopleSoft database, there is only minimal use of Oracle-specific features and Oracle-specific SQL constructions. There are no referential constraints. Very few optimizer hints are used, and only where there is no alternative. All PeopleSoft processes connect to the one database schema that contains all the database objects, so security is maintained by the application, not the database. Oracle sequences are never used; instead, sequence numbers are generated using ordinary tables.

In order to avoid the use of platform-specific SQL constructions, most of the delivered SQL conforms to a lowest common denominator subset of SQL accepted by the supported RDBMS platforms (Oracle, Microsoft SQL Server, DB2, Sybase, and Informix). The data model is kept uniform across all platforms, although there are variations in the column data types between platforms. There can be some differences in the indexing between platforms. There is some capability for different code on different platforms in PeopleSoft, but its use in the delivered product is kept to an absolute minimum.

Hence, PeopleSoft is sometimes described as a *platform-agnostic* product. It is my experience that this approach generally does not produce optimal performance. It may have assisted PeopleSoft to manufacture and maintain a single product on many platforms, but it does not help PeopleSoft customers to achieve optimal performance from their systems on their chosen database platform.

In PeopleTools 8, there has been some expansion of the areas in which it is possible to introduce database-specific features and code. From PeopleTools 8.1, database triggers were used to write audit records, although these have to be enabled by customization. Database instrumentation was added to PeopleTools 8.50. Active Data Guard is supported from PeopleTools 8.51.

The other area of confusion for typical Oracle DBAs, particularly those familiar with Oracle's management tools, is that unless certain DBA tasks are incorporated into the application with PeopleSoft's Application Designer, they may be lost. Consequently, this can restrict the effectiveness of generic Oracle administration and monitoring tools.

In short, to be effective, DBAs must become PeopleSoft aware. They must work with the PeopleSoft development tools and the application, rather than continually fighting against it—otherwise it will bite back! One of the goals of this book is to outline these areas for DBAs, providing workaround techniques where possible.

Who Should Read This Book?

Though primarily aimed at the Oracle DBA who is responsible for maintaining PeopleSoft databases, this book can justifiably claim a wider audience. It bridges the gap between the worlds of PeopleSoft and

Oracle, explaining where and how the two sides meet. There is plenty of material to interest the PeopleSoft developer.

The chapters dealing with the general PeopleSoft architecture and its evolution, and with Tuxedo and WebLogic, will also be of interest to PeopleSoft administrators. Also, is not uncommon for Tuxedo and web server installation, administration, tuning, and troubleshooting to fall to the DBA for lack of other qualified resources.

What Does This Book Cover?

The following is a chapter-by-chapter breakdown summarizing some of the key topics that we will cover:

- **Chapter 1: An Overview**. This chapter presents a brief history of the evolution of PeopleSoft and its technology.

- **Chapter 2: BEA Tuxedo: PeopleSoft's Application Server Technology**. This chapter explains what Tuxedo is, how it works, and how PeopleSoft introduced Tuxedo into its product. Of all the people concerned with a system, the DBA is most likely to have the skills needed to assimilate this technology.

- **Chapter 3: Database Connectivity**. Nearly all the objects in a PeopleSoft database are in a single schema in an Oracle database. This chapter explains how a PeopleSoft database is structured, and how PeopleSoft processes securely authenticate the user and connect to the database.

- **Chapter 4: PeopleSoft Database Structure: A Tale of Two Data Dictionaries**. In order to deliver the same application to different database platforms, PeopleSoft maintains its own data dictionary and then uses it to dynamically generate application SQL. This chapter examines the relationship between the PeopleSoft data dictionary and the Oracle database catalogue.

- **Chapter 5: Keys and Indexing**. This chapter describes how indexes are defined in the PeopleSoft Application Designer and how that definition is stored in the PeopleSoft data dictionary.

- **Chapter 6: PeopleSoft DDL**. This chapter shows how the PeopleSoft Application Designer generates DDL to build and analyze tables and indexes. It also explains to what extent the DBA can adjust that DDL to introduce Oracle-specific features, and when it is necessary to work outside the PeopleSoft design tools.

- **Chapter 7: Tablespaces**. This chapter discusses the tablespaces that are created when PeopleSoft is installed in an Oracle database. It also explains how to introduce some modern Oracle tablespace features.

- **Chapter 8: Locking, Transactions, and Concurrency**. This chapter explains how PeopleSoft maintains consistency of data without holding database locks for long periods. It also shows how PeopleSoft creates sequences without using Oracle sequences.

- **Chapter 9: Performance Metrics**. This chapter explains the various sources of performance metrics in both PeopleSoft and the Oracle database, and how to harvest them.

- **Chapter 10: PeopleSoft Performance Utilities**. This chapter describes the additional performance instrumentation that has been added to PeopleTools, including the Performance Monitor, which provides a sophisticated wait interface.

- **Chapter 11: SQL Optimization Techniques in PeopleSoft**. This chapter describes how to enable Oracle's SQL trace on PeopleSoft processes and, once the DBA has identified SQL bottlenecks, how to apply tuning techniques through PeopleSoft development tools.

- **Chapter 12: Configuring the Application Server**. The application server has an intimate relationship with the database, which can affect database and system performance; therefore, the DBA needs to know how to configure the application server.

- **Chapter 13: Tuning the Application Server**. This chapter explains how to appropriately size the application server. It also covers other features that can affect system performance.

- **Chapter 14: The Process Scheduler**. This chapter describes how the PeopleSoft Process Scheduler is used to initiate batch and report processes. Regulating the batch load has implications for overall system performance.

Software Versions

The rate at which new versions of software appear can be bewildering and terrifying. On completion of work on this book, I am using the following software versions:

- PeopleTools 8.51

- Tuxedo 8.1

- WebLogic 8.1

- Oracle 10.2.0.5 and 11.2.0.2

The good news is that PeopleSoft, and now Oracle, has built progressively on the structures established in previous versions, and many of the underlying principles have not changed.

Other Resources

This book does not seek to explain how to administer or tune an Oracle database. Many excellent books and other sources are available on these subjects. Also, if read in isolation, this book will not tell you absolutely everything that a DBA needs to know about PeopleSoft. There are other resources that you should also make use of:

- **My Oracle Support** (https://supporthtml.oracle.com): This is Oracle's support web site. It gives you access to product support, patches, and additional documentation for all Oracle products including PeopleSoft, Tuxedo, and WebLogic. You will need an account and a password to access this site.

- **PeopleBooks**: The PeopleSoft production documentation can be downloaded from http://edelivery.oracle.com. Documentation for all Oracle products is also available on-line at www.oracle.com/technetwork/indexes/documentation/index.html.

- **PeopleSoft Red Papers**: These are technical documents available on the Oracle Support site that discuss how to optimally configure various aspects of PeopleSoft technology. This documentation is good at telling you what to do, but not always why you should do it.

- **PeopleSoft DBA Forum** (http://groups.yahoo.com/group/psftdba): This Yahoo group is where PeopleSoft DBAs and other interested technicians discuss ideas, ask questions, and share information.

- **PeopleSoft DBA Blog** (http://blog.psftdba.com): This is my PeopleSoft technical blog.

- **Go-Faster Consultancy** (www.go-faster.co.uk): My web site contains a variety of presentations, papers, and scripts.

Online Resources for This Book

You've read the book, now surf the web site. This book has its own web site, www.psftdba.com, which includes the scripts and code examples in the text and any necessary corrections and additions.

I started the PeopleSoft DBA Forum (http://groups.yahoo.com/group/psftdba) after a roundtable discussion group at the PeopleSoft EMEA User Conference in 2002. It is a moderated forum aimed at the needs of DBAs who administer PeopleSoft systems. It is therefore the perfect place to discuss the subject matter of this book and ask related questions.

Contacting the Author

From time to time in the course of this book, I express my opinions about various things. Those opinions are purely my own and are not necessarily the opinions of any other person or organization.

Despite every effort to the contrary, there is no guarantee that the content in this book is error-free. If you find any errors, please contact me via e-mail at info@psftdba.com.

CHAPTER 1

An Overview

PeopleSoft is packaged business application software for larger companies. This chapter provides an introduction and overview of PeopleSoft, its technology, and its history. We take a very high-level look at some of the major parts that make up today's PeopleSoft systems: the database (in this case, Oracle) that stores both the PeopleSoft application data and much of the application code, the Tuxedo Application Server, and the PeopleTools integrated development environment that is used for most aspects of developing and administering PeopleSoft applications.

We then step through the overall architecture of a PeopleSoft system and see how it has evolved from the initial client/server architecture to the modern four-tier Internet architecture.

Finally, we look at what all this means to the database administrator (DBA) charged with maintaining a PeopleSoft application, and we consider the implications it has for the relationship between developers and DBAs on PeopleSoft systems. This introduction helps to put some of the following chapters into context.

What Is PeopleSoft?

PeopleSoft Inc. was founded by Dave Duffield and Ken Morris in 1985. It developed a suite of packaged business applications for larger companies based on its proprietary PeopleTools software. Reuters' abridged business summary for PeopleSoft began with this statement:

> *PeopleSoft, Inc. designs, develops, markets and supports enterprise application software products for use throughout large and medium-sized organizations worldwide. (...) The Company provides enterprise application software for customer relationship management, human capital management, financial management and supply chain management, each with a range of industry-specific features and functions.*[1]

In 2003, PeopleSoft acquired J.D. Edwards. The products that were formerly PeopleSoft are now referred to as *PeopleSoft Enterprise.* The products that were formerly J.D. Edwards were called *PeopleSoft EnterpriseOne* and *PeopleSoft World.* Oracle restored the original names after its acquisition of PeopleSoft.

In December 2004, Oracle Corp. acquired PeopleSoft Inc. after a protracted and contested takeover. Since then, Oracle Corporation has continued to develop PeopleSoft Enterprise Applications and the

---

[1] From http://web.archive.org/web/20031013071803/http://finance.yahoo.com/q/pr?s=PSFT.

1

PeopleTools technologies alongside Oracle's other applications. Oracle's Applications Unlimited commitment assures PeopleSoft of a continuing future beyond the release of Oracle's Fusion applications.

In 2008, Oracle also acquired BEA Systems Inc., which developed Tuxedo middleware and the WebLogic application server. WebLogic is the basis of Oracle Fusion Middleware.

This book is about PeopleSoft Enterprise Tools and Technology, which is generally referred to as *PeopleTools*. I refer to PeopleTools, the applications, and the embedded technologies collectively as *PeopleSoft*. I use the term *Oracle* to refer to either the database or the Oracle corporation.

There are currently 11 Enterprise product lines[2] that contain various modules:

- *Asset Lifecycle Management:* This product contains three applications for the management of the facilities and equipment of an organization.

- *Campus Solutions:* This product is designed for universities and other higher-education institutions.

- *Customer Relationship Management (CRM)*: PeopleSoft started to use Vantive CRM internally in the Global Support Center (GSC) in 1997. PeopleSoft liked the product so much that it purchased the Vantive Corporation in October 1999 and sold the Vantive product alongside PeopleSoft 7.5 products. Vantive CRM was rewritten to run under PeopleTools and was re-released as PeopleSoft CRM 8.

- *Enterprise Performance Management:* This product contains a number of applications that analyze data from other modules.

- *Enterprise Service Automation*: This product provides self-service access to various modules. From PeopleTools 8.44, offline mobile clients are also available for some modules.

- *Financial Management*: This is a complete financial management and accounting package.

- *Human Capital Management (HCM)*: This product was referred to as Human Resource Management (HRMS) until release 8.1. Traditionally, it has been PeopleSoft's strongest product. There are various modules including Time and Labor, Benefits, and Student Administration. There is a North American local payroll, and there are other payroll interfaces for various countries. A separate Global Payroll (GP) module was released with version 8.1, and Oracle delivers Global Payroll Country Extensions for certain countries.

- *Supplier Relationship Management*: This product supports purchase and procurement processes.

- *Supply Chain Management*: This product supports business-to-business interaction along the supply chain.

- *Solution for the Staffing Industry:* This is a selection of modules from HCM, CRM, Financials, and Project Management.

---

[2] See **www.oracle.com/us/products/applications/peoplesoft-enterprise/index.html**.

- *Enterprise Tools and Technology*: This product contains all the PeopleSoft proprietary technology and development tools (often referred to simply as *PeopleTools*) that are used by to develop PeopleSoft applications. The development tools are included in all the other products so that companies can customize and extend the delivered products to match their own requirements. However, it is also possible to license PeopleTools separately to develop a system from scratch.

There is no unique master-detail relationship between product lines and modules. Some modules are included in more than one product line. For example, there are HRMS and Payroll modules from HCM, and there are also Receivables and General Ledger modules from Financials in Service Automation.

Components of a PeopleSoft System

PeopleSoft installations have evolved over the years into a combination of technologies that are used to develop and deliver PeopleSoft applications to desktop Internet (HTML) browsers. PeopleSoft called this its *Pure Internet Architecture (PIA)*.[3]

When we step through the overall architecture, you will see more clearly that PeopleSoft is a chain of linked technologies that stretch between the user and the database. The database is fundamental to the entire structure, but the technology stack stretches out through the BEA Tuxedo Application Server and the Java servlet to the user's browser. PeopleSoft has also developed its own in-house development tools. All of this is collectively referred to as *PeopleTools*. Figure 1-1 shows, in a simplified fashion, how these pieces interact.

---

[3] In some PeopleSoft material, PIA is said to stand for PeopleSoft Internet Architecture.

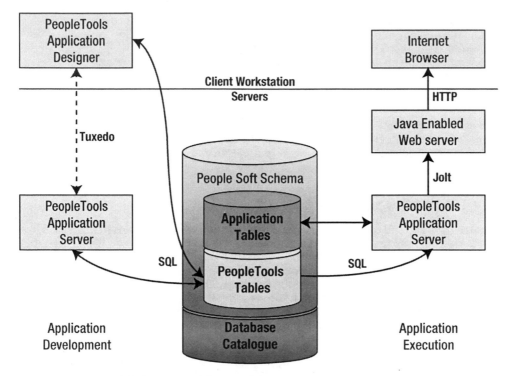

Figure 1-1. A simplified version of the PeopleTools architecture

The Database

From the beginning, PeopleSoft was designed to run on various database platforms. The majority of installations are on Oracle, but there are also many companies using IBM's DB2 and Microsoft SQL Server, and a few still use Sybase and Informix. Therefore, as far as possible, PeopleSoft delivers the same SQL code to all database platforms.

Both the PeopleSoft application and the application data are stored in the database:

- The database catalogue describes the all objects in the database.

- The PeopleTools tables describe the application data and contain the source code for much of the PeopleSoft application.

- The application tables contain the users' data.

The PeopleTools tables and the application tables all coexist in the same database schema.

When the Application Designer saves a development object, it writes to the PeopleTools tables. When the application is executed, that information is interpreted by the application server. Upon execution, much of the application SQL is generated dynamically, based on the contents of the PeopleTools tables.

The Application Designer is also responsible for defining data structures in PeopleSoft applications and for building database objects, so it is inevitable that some of the PeopleTools tables that describe data structures correspond closely to the Oracle database catalogue views. This means that in a

PeopleSoft database, we are dealing with two data dictionaries rather than one: the database's catalogue defines all the objects that do exist in the database, and the PeopleSoft dictionary defines all the objects that should exist in the PeopleSoft schema and that can therefore be referenced by the application. The interrelationship between these data dictionaries is discussed in detail in Chapter 3.

Tuxedo Application Server

PeopleSoft selected various "best of breed" solutions for its system architecture, including BEA Tuxedo for their application server.

At run time, the application server interprets the application data in the PeopleTools tables, executes the business logic of the application, and even generates the HTML pages that are served up to the browser. The "publish and subscribe" technology that generates and accepts XML messages has also been incorporated into the application server.

The middleware and batch processes run on the major Unix platforms, Linux and Windows . However, some components only run on Windows. Chapters 2 and 12 discuss the inner workings of the application server in more detail.

PeopleTools

All the PeopleSoft products listed so far are developed using PeopleSoft's proprietary development tools, namely PeopleTools. The development tools are also available to PeopleSoft customers so they can develop their own customizations and apply PeopleSoft upgrades and patches.

Since PeopleTools 7, many of the formerly separate development utilities have been consolidated into the Application Designer utility, and it is this PeopleTools utility that we'll encounter most often in this book. These are some of its functions:

- *Defining records*: The data model for the application is defined in the Application Designer. A record in PeopleSoft can correspond to a table or view on the database, or to a set of working storage variables (see Chapter 3). The indexes on the table are defined (Chapter 5). The Application Designer also generates the data definition language (DDL) to build the database objects (see Chapter 6). Column definitions in the DDL differ on different database platforms. Different databases also specify different physical attributes for objects.

- *Creating PeopleCode*: PeopleCode is PeopleSoft's proprietary programming language. It is used to perform additional processing in the PIA and in some Application Engine batch processes. PeopleCode is specified on records in the Application Designer. In PeopleTools 8, the Application Designer can also be used as an interactive debugging tool in which you can step through PeopleCode programs as they are executed.

- *Defining pages* (formerly called *panels*): Originally, panels were drawn in the graphical design tool, and they corresponded exactly with how they appeared in the Windows client. In PeopleTools 8, pages are developed in much the same way. Then, at run time, HTML pages are generated by the application server and are served up to the web browser. Thus, the developer can produce a web application without having to code any HTML or JavaScript, although additional HTML and Java can be included in a PeopleSoft application.

- *Defining menus*: The Application Designer also maintains the menu navigation for the application.

- *Upgrading:* The Application Designer is used to migrate sets of source code, called *projects,* between PeopleSoft systems. In version 8, projects can be exported to and imported from flat files. PeopleSoft also uses this mechanism during initial installation and to deliver patches.

PeopleSoft also delivers a number of other development tools and utilities:

- *Data Mover* is capable of exporting and importing data to and from a PeopleSoft database. It is used during installation to import all the objects and the data they contain into the database. PeopleSoft also uses Data Mover to deliver standing data to go with patches.[4] The same Data Mover export file can be imported into any database platform. Therefore, it can be used to migrate a PeopleSoft database from one platform to another, although it may not be fast enough for large databases. It is also capable of running some SQL scripts. Data Mover can only connect directly to the database in two-tier mode. It cannot connect to the application server.

- The *Upgrade Assistant* was introduced in PeopleTools 8 to assist with the automation of PeopleSoft upgrade and patch processes.

Batch and report processing is provided by a number of technologies:

- *Application Engine* is PeopleSoft's proprietary batch-processing utility. In PeopleTools 8, it was rewritten in C+ so that it could also execute PeopleSoft, and it is now developed in the Application Designer. This means Application Engine programs can also be migrated by Application Designer.

- *SQR* (also known as *Hyperion Production Reporting*) was licensed by SQRIBE to PeopleSoft some time around 2000. SQRIBE was acquired by Hyperion in 2003, which was in turn acquired by Oracle in 2007. SQR is used to perform some reporting and batch processing. It is a procedural language into which SQL statements can be embedded.

- The *PeopleSoft Query* tool (Query) still exists as a Windows client utility, although this functionality is also available in the PIA. Users can use this tool to develop and run ad hoc SQL queries without knowledge of SQL. Queries can be migrated with the Application Designer.

- *BI Publisher* (formerly known as *XML Publisher*) was introduced into PeopleSoft in PeopleTools 8.48 and used in version 9 applications. This product is Oracle's chosen enterprise reporting solution. It is used in various Oracle applications including Fusion Applications. Application Engine generates the XML data structure that is then formatted by Publisher into the final report.

---

[4] Until PeopleTools 7.x, Data Mover was used to import patches and their projects directly into the PeopleTools tables. As of PeopleTools 8, the Application Designer exports and imports projects directly to and from disk. In PeopleTools 8.4, these project files are in XML format.

- *Crystal Reports*[5] has been used for reports that require a sophisticated look and that include graphics. Crystal is capable of connecting directly to the database via an ODBC driver. Within PeopleTools, it connects via a PeopleSoft ODBC driver that presents PeopleSoft queries as database procedures. The ODBC driver can connect in either two- or three-tier mode. Crystal Reports only runs on Windows, so reports can only be scheduled on a Windows process scheduler.

- *nVision* is a reporting utility that plugs into Microsoft Excel. Although it can be used in any PeopleSoft module, it is most extensively used in General Ledger reporting. A user can drill down into a report, unrolling hierarchical data, such as a chart of accounts. In PeopleTools 8.4, nVision reports are defined via the PIA and stored in the database, rather than in Excel workbook files. They can be executed and viewed in the PIA,[6] or nVision can be installed on the client and executed in two- or three-tier mode.

Evolution of the PeopleSoft Architecture

Over the years and releases, PeopleSoft has progressively built on its previous achievements. I think that the easiest way to understand the current PeopleSoft architecture is to review how it evolved.

PeopleSoft was founded in 1985 and was launched on the crest of the client/server technology wave. Some of us can still remember a time when personal computers were just starting to appear in the workplace. Bill Gates' vision of a computer on every desktop was still a radical idea. Before then, the typical model for business computing was to use a monolithic mainframe. The following sections describe how computing models have evolved.

Single-Tier Monolithic Mainframe Architecture

Traditionally, the mainframe was a beast that lived deep in the bowels of the data center, tended by surly white-coated technicians. As depicted in Figure 1-2, the mainframe was responsible for all aspects of the application; data access, business logic, and presentation layers were all handled centrally. The users accessed the system via completely dumb green-screen terminals that were often wired directly to a serial port on the back of the mainframe.

---

[5] Crystal Services Inc. was acquired by Seagate in 1994. Ultimately, Seagate was acquired by Business Objects in 2003, which was in turn acquired by SAP in 2007.

[6] It has always been possible to schedule nVision reports to run on a process scheduler, but only on a Windows server. In PeopleTools 8, the generated reports are retrieved from the report repository. When a user drills down into an nVision report in the PIA, the drill-down is scheduled to run on a Windows process scheduler, and the user must wait for the report to execute and complete.

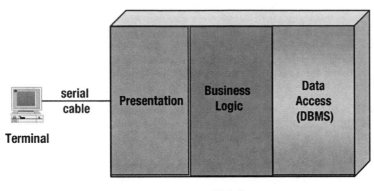

Figure 1-2. *Monolithic mainfram model*

Today, the most obvious legacy of this model on a PC is the choice of mode in a terminal emulator.

Two-Tier Client/Server Architecture

The appearance of the Apple II in 1977 and the IBM Personal Computer (PC) in 1981 brought processing power to the desktop, and the original killer desktop application was VisiCalc, a spreadsheet package released in 1979. By the end of the 1980s, PCs were becoming common in the workplace. When they were also connected to networks, client/server applications started to appear.

In a typical client/server program, depicted in Figure 1-3, all the business logic, as well as the presentation layer, is contained within the client program and executes on the client machine. Only the database remains central.

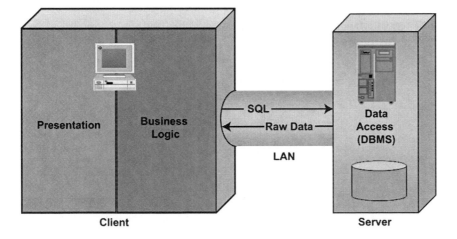

Figure 1-3. *The original client/server model*

This two-tier model started to show strain in a number of areas. The traffic across the network was mostly SQL conversations with the database; and because a relatively simple action in an application could generate many messages, network latency became a problem. Another issue was rolling out new clients and synchronizing the rollout with changes to the database.

Until version 6, PeopleSoft was a fairly typical two-tier client/server application. PeopleTools and the database connectivity software (SQL*Net in the case of Oracle) had to be installed on every desktop.

The online parts of PeopleSoft applications were stored as metadata in the PeopleTools tables in the database. The client program loaded, interpreted, and executed the instructions in these tables, and the development tools manipulated this metadata. This approach mitigated, but did not eliminate, the problem of rolling out new versions of the client every time the slightest application change was made. However, the act of querying the PeopleTools tables in turn created significant amounts of database activity and network traffic, so the PeopleTools client cached the information that it retrieved from the PeopleTools tables to the local disk of the Windows PC. If the cache was up to date, the PeopleTools client did not query the PeopleTools tables. This approach is still used in current version of PeopleTools.

Three-Tier Application Server Architecture

Three-tier computing models emerged to deal with the limitations of the two-tier model. As much as possible of the business logic layer was moved back into the data center, close to the database (see Figure 1-4). This reduced the size of the client and the volume and number of messages that needed to travel between client and server.

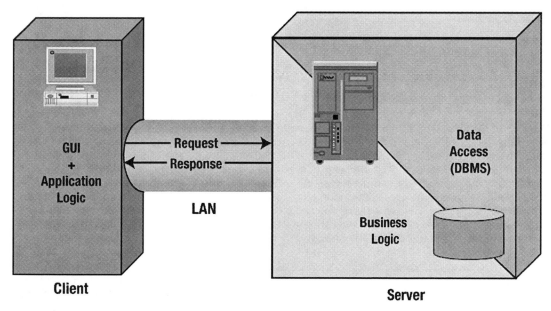

Figure 1-4. A first-generation three-tier client/server model

Oracle developed PL/SQL (Procedural SQL) to make it possible to write procedural program code that could either be stored and executed within the database or within Oracle applications or bespoke applications written with Oracle development tools. In this scenario, some of the business logic was moved inside the database server itself.

However, PeopleSoft's platform-independent approach precludes the use of database server–based code. None of the PeopleSoft application is executed within the database, although much of it is stored in the database in the form of metadata. However, in version 8, PeopleSoft started to make limited use of database triggers for populating audit tables and the now-discontinued Mobile Agents.

When PeopleSoft introduced a three-tier client with an application sever in PeopleTools 7.0, it chose to use BEA's Tuxedo product. The application server is a completely separate tier from the database, and it is normally placed on a different machine. This model (see Figure 1-5) can therefore be scaled horizontally by using multiple application servers on different nodes.

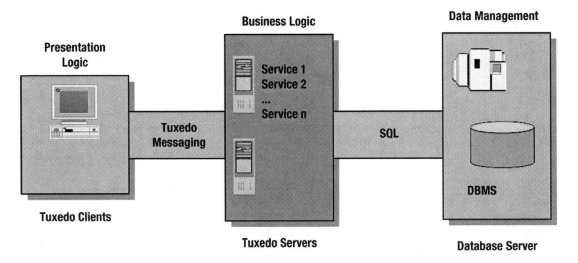

Figure 1-5. *The Tuxedo second-generation three-tier client/server model*

PeopleSoft developed its own procedural language, PeopleCode, in which it codes additional business logic. Pieces of PeopleCode are defined on certain columns in the application, and that code is executed when certain events in the client occur. In the two-tier client, PeopleCode was executed on the client, but in three-tier mode most of the PeopleCode is executed by the application server.

As a result, it is now the application server, rather than the client, that makes the connection to the database. The server loads the application metadata from the PeopleTools tables, executes most of the application code, and retrieves and updates the application data. Both the client and the application server cache the application code retrieved from the PeopleTools tables. The end result is that there are fewer connections to the database, easing memory management.

■ **Note** Only application code (metadata) is cached by client processes. This includes the application server, and Application Engine from PeopleTools 8. Since PeopleTools 7, application data is never cached by the client processes, although in earlier versions the PeopleTools client could optionally cache static application data.

Not only is the total volume of network traffic between the client and the application server reduced in the three-tier model, but the number of network messages is also greatly reduced. There are fewer, although individually larger, messages in three-tier mode. Every time a two-tier client fetches a row from a SQL cursor, a message is sent to the database, and the client must wait for a response. In a three-tier application, all of the data, possibly from many cursors, is returned to the client in a single message. Thus, three-tier clients are less susceptible to network latency.

Four-Tier Internet Architecture

In PeopleTools version 8, the Windows client was replaced by the PeopleSoft Internet architecture. The client is now just a web browser. There is no longer a problem rolling out PeopleSoft software or packaging it into a corporate desktop. Now you can use PeopleSoft from something other than a Windows PC.

This change has been achieved by building on the existing PeopleSoft three-tier model. PeopleSoft now delivers a Java servlet that runs on the web server (see Figure 1-6), and this servlet is the client of the application server. The web server can be placed on the same or a different physical server from the application server.

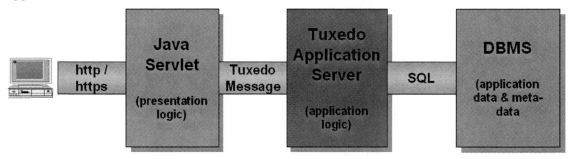

Figure 1-6. *The PeopleSoft Internet Architecture (PIA)*

"No code on the client" was the mantra of every PeopleSoft presentation I saw when version 8 was introduced. PeopleSoft code does execute on the client, but you don't have to preinstall it. The HTML pages include JavaScript, which is generated by the application server and then served up to the browser via the servlet. The JavaScript is executed when certain buttons are pushed or fields are navigated. Some output formats require Microsoft Excel or Adobe Acrobat to be installed on the client.

Release History

PeopleSoft's applications and PeopleTools have different version numbers that change independently. The first digit for both of them, sometimes called the Enterprise Release Number, is usually, but not always, the same. Some Enterprise releases have also had major upgrades (PeopleTools 7.5 and 8.4, for example) to both the application and PeopleTools that must effectively be treated as if they were new Enterprise releases. It is confusing, so it is important to specify whether a version number refers to an application or to PeopleTools.

PeopleTools versions 3.x and 5.x were 16-bit Windows applications.[7] They only connected directly to the database via the database API, which on Oracle is SQL*Net. Since it was a 16-bit application, it was

---

[7] There was no PeopleTools version 4 because it is considered to be an unlucky number in some Asian countries. Financials 3 and HRMS 4 ran on PeopleTools 3.

only possible to use 16-bit SQL*Net. PeopleTools 5.x saw a major overhaul in the interface, replacing pushbuttons with a menu. PeopleTools 5.1 has not been supported since 1999, and it was never certified for Y2K.

PeopleTools 6 was a 32-bit Windows application. It corresponded to the introduction of Windows 95, the first 32-bit Windows release. However, it was still almost exclusively a two-tier application. I say "almost" because this release saw the first appearance of the BEA Tuxedo application server, although it was only used for Remote Call functionality. This allowed batch processes to be initiated from the client, apparently synchronously, but to be executed on the application server. Within the delivered PeopleSoft applications, Remote Call was only used in Financials for online voucher editing and posting.

PeopleTools 7.0 was released in September 1997. This release introduced the full three-tier model in PeopleSoft. The Windows client was also able to connect to the BEA Tuxedo application server, which in turn connected to the database as the client did in two-tier mode. In this version, the separate development utilities (record designer, panel designer, and menu designer) were consolidated in the new Application Designer.

PeopleTools 7.5 was released in May 1998. It saw the consolidation of the application server—new application-server services were introduced to combine several service calls into one. This release also saw the introduction of the Java client, a Java applet that was downloaded to the browser on a client PC. It ran in the Java Virtual Machine (JVM) within the browser and connected to the application server. Java-enabled browsers were, at that time, still relatively new, and this client was never particularly popular, mainly due to the size of the applet download and memory leaks in some JVMs.

PeopleTools 8.0 was released at the very end of 1999, and it introduced a new and radical concept: a purely Internet client. Each screen or panel in the PeopleTools applications was a page in this iClient. This meant that the only software now needed on the user's PC was a standard web browser. The pages were rendered with JavaScript to enable the buttons on the page, and the client's session is a thread within a Java servlet that runs in a JVM that is either in or close to the web server. The servlet connects to the application server, just as the Java client did in the previous release.

In August 2000, PeopleTools version 8.1 was introduced. The iClient was renamed as the PeopleSoft Internet Architecture (PIA). Although the Windows client was still delivered, it was no longer a supported runtime environment. PS/Query (the ad hoc reporting tool) and the nVision reporting plug-in for Excel still exist as Windows executable applications to provide an alternative to the PIA functionality. Application development is still done via a Windows client that connects in both two- and three-tier modes.

PeopleTools 8.4 was the second release of the PIA, and there have been some changes to the look and feel of the products. The breadcrumb navigation of version 8.1 was replaced with a menu portlet. This release also no longer includes the Windows client, `pstools.exe`. With the exception of Query and nVision, the PeopleSoft application is only available via the PIA.

Since acquisition, Oracle has continued to maintain and enhance both PeopleTools and the PeopleSoft Applications. In 2006, Oracle's Applications Unlimited commitment explicitly promised indefinite "sustaining support" for PeopleSoft and announced a roadmap for version 9 applications. However, Oracle cancelled the planned PeopleTools 9 release. There probably will never be a PeopleTools 9, but each annual release of PeopleTools has brought enhancements and new features.

Generally, PeopleSoft remains platform agnostic, but Oracle has introduced features to help manage PeopleSoft running on an Oracle database, and to use some Oracle database features. There is a PeopleSoft plug-in to Oracle Enterprise Manager.

PeopleTools 8.50 uses the Oracle session instrumentation package (see Chapter 9).

PeopleTools 8.51 can perform read-only processing on an Active Data Guard standby database and has support for Transparent Application Failover and Fast Application Notification. Application Designer preserves any table or index partitioning.

■ **Note** PeopleTools 8.5x is not a new Enterprise version. PeopleTools 8.50 is merely the next major release after 8.49.

Oracle Corp. acquired Hyperion in 2007, and so SQR became owned by Oracle. Oracle bought BEA, makers of Tuxedo and WebLogic, in 2008. It also acquired Sun Microsystems, the ultimate owners of Java, in 2010. Oracle now owns all of the various third-party technologies used in PeopleTools.

Component Connectivity

Table 1-1 sets out the various PeopleSoft components and shows how they have connected to the database in different releases.

Table 1-1. PeopleSoft Component Connectivity

PeopleTools Version	5	6	7.0	7.5	8.0	8.1	8.4
Windows client	Two-tier	Two-tier (except remote call)	Two-tier and three-tier			Delivered but not supported—two-tier and three-tier	Not delivered
nVision & Query	Two-tier		Two-tier and three-tier				Two-tier, three-tier, or PIA
Crystal Reports	Two-tier only		Two-tier or via PeopleSoft ODBC driver, which connects in either two-tier or three-tier mode				
Data Mover	Two-tier only						
Application Designer	Two-tier only		Two-tier and three-tier				
Application upgrade	Two-tier only						
Java client	n/a		Three-tier only	n/a			
IClient/PIA	n/a			Via application server			

As a result of the evolutionary development of PeopleSoft, different components require different types of connections:

- Database connectivity from client workstation PCs to the database server is a prerequisite for a PeopleSoft installation. It is required for two-tier connections.

- The Data Mover utility, used to import PeopleSoft objects into the database, only works in two-tier mode.

- PeopleTools client programs connected in three-tier mode do not require database connectivity.

- The Application Designer can connect in both two-tier and three-tier modes. However, the application upgrade process within the Application Designer, which copies objects from one database to another, only works in two-tier mode.

- Crystal Reports is capable of connecting directly to the database via an Oracle ODBC driver, but within PeopleTools it connects via a PeopleSoft ODBC-style connection. This driver connects to the database in the same way as the Windows client. It can connect in either two- or three-tier mode.

- Cobol batch programs and SQR reports can only connect to the database in two-tier mode.

Developing and Administering PeopleSoft Systems

The diagram of the PIA (Figure 1-6) illustrates the most important point about PeopleSoft systems: they comprise a chain of linked technologies that stretch between the user and the database.

The database is fundamental to the entire structure. It must function efficiently, and it must itself be built upon solid foundations. However, as the PeopleSoft technology has evolved, additional tiers and various layers of software and infrastructure have been inserted between the user and the database. If any of these layers do not function efficiently, the users will be affected.

Developers and DBAs have different perspectives on the system and its technologies.

The Developer

The PeopleSoft development tools provide an environment in which to manage development and upgrading that is consistent across all platforms. This is both a strength and a weakness. The advantage is that PeopleSoft delivers and supports a single set of tools and procedures for all database platforms. This means that a PeopleSoft developer needs one set of skills, regardless of the database that is used.

The disadvantage of this consistency is that although the developer defines the basic application components, much of the SQL in a PeopleSoft application is generated dynamically and does not appear in its final form in the application. This has the effect of isolating the developer from the database. When processes are migrated to a test or production database, the DBA may show some of the resulting SQL to the developer, who may then struggle to relate it to its source. (This is discussed in Chapter 11.)

The DBA

The disadvantage of the PeopleSoft development tools for DBAs is that the application is hidden from them. Some of the tasks that are properly a part of their job must be managed from PeopleSoft utilities, or at least the change must be retrofitted back into PeopleSoft.

Usually, DBAs have many different databases to manage, and most of that work is done with standard Oracle tools, so (they claim) they do not have sufficient time to manage a PeopleSoft database differently. However, DBAs need to take the time to get sufficiently acquainted with the PeopleSoft tools, or they will be in for some nasty surprises.

Following are just a few of the main idiosyncrasies that a PeopleSoft DBA can expect to encounter (with references to where they are covered in more detail in this book):

- If a DBA decides to add an index to a table to improve the performance of a query, that index should be specified in and built with the Application Designer, or it could be lost (see Chapters 5 and 6).

- Changes to schema passwords must either be done with PeopleSoft utilities or be synchronized with PeopleSoft configuration changes (see Chapter 4).

- Referential integrity is enforced by the application not the database (also in Chapter 4).

- DBAs always want to know who is running a particular piece of SQL code (presumably so they can have a friendly word). The application server concentrates connections so that a database session does not correspond to a single user (see Chapter 2), but PeopleSoft can track which user's service request is on the server (see Chapter 9).

While it is helpful for DBAs to understand the application running on the database, it is essential that they at least understand the underlying technology. This book focuses heavily on how the PeopleSoft technology relates to the database.

Relationship Between the Developer and DBA

I believe that it is important for DBAs and developers to work closely together. The DBA needs to know what administrative tasks should be performed within PeopleTools and how to manage them. Developers, in turn, need to know what effect they are having on the database. In my experience, some of the most successful and efficient PeopleSoft implementations are those where a DBA is dedicated to, if not fully integrated into, the PeopleSoft project.

It is almost inevitable that when a user reports a problem with the system, the finger of blame is instinctively pointed at the database, and the DBA becomes embroiled in the resolution (and blame-allocation) process. That alone is reason enough for both DBAs and PeopleSoft developers to work together to understand the relationship between the database and PeopleTools.

Chapter 9 looks at the metrics that can be obtained from the various PeopleTools tiers and that help determine whether a performance problem is a database problem or not. Chapter 10 looks at the performance monitoring utilities that PeopleSoft introduced in release 8.4.

For a DBA to say that poor performance is a result of poor SQL and that there is nothing they can do about it is simply not an adequate response. If poor SQL is the problem, it needs to be addressed. PeopleSoft supplies packaged applications, but the majority of the SQL in those applications can be customized if necessary. Chapter 11 explains how to locate and adjust problem SQL.

Summary

This chapter has provided a high-level introduction to the PeopleSoft Enterprise technology. PeopleSoft is a chain of linked technologies that stretch between the user and the database, as was pointed out in Figure 1-6.

The database is fundamental to the entire structure, and it must function efficiently and be built on solid foundations. However, as the technology has evolved, additional software tiers and infrastructure have been introduced between the user and the database. If any of these layers do not function efficiently, users will be affected.

In a PeopleSoft environment, developers are so far removed from the system that the DBA is likely to be the only member of the team who can appreciate the whole picture. It is essential that the DBA know what PeopleSoft is doing to their database and how it is doing it.

## CHAPTER 2

BEA Tuxedo: PeopleSoft's Application Server Technology

DBAs might be forgiven for wondering what a chapter about middleware is doing in this book. They may initially think that the application server has nothing to do with them. However, it is a fundamental component in the PeopleSoft architecture, and it has an intimate relationship with the database. The sizing and configuration of the application server or servers can have a significant effect on the database and on the flow of work from the end user to the database, and therefore on the performance of the whole system. The DBA must at least have an appreciation of Tuxedo.

This chapter provides an overview of the parts of Tuxedo that PeopleSoft utilizes. I have always found the Tuxedo documentation to be impressive and useful, and this chapter should provide sufficient background for you to start using that documentation.[1] PeopleSoft's product documentation, PeopleBooks, also includes a section on the application server.

What Is Tuxedo?

Tuxedo,[2] in its own documentation, describes itself as "middleware for building scalable multi-tier client/server applications in heterogeneous distributed environments." The name Tuxedo is an acronym standing for Transactions under Unix Extended for Distributed Operations, which is a fair description of how Tuxedo works.

When a program executes a subroutine, it simply executes code in the same executable, or it dynamically loads a library. Tuxedo allows that subroutine to execute synchronously on a different physical machine. It passes the parameters to the subroutine and the return codes back from it. Hence, Tuxedo is sometimes referred to as a *messaging protocol*. It is much more than that, but PeopleSoft only uses a part of what Tuxedo provides—the part referred to as the Application-to-Transaction Monitor Interface (ATMI). This book deals only with that part of Tuxedo.

Every child has at some time made a telephone from two tin cans and a piece of string (see Figure 2-1). If you imagine that the string is the network and the tin cans are the client- and server-side programs, Tuxedo is the knots that hold the ends of the string to the cans. Tuxedo links the client and server sides of an application across a network.

---

[1] The Tuxedo documentation is freely available on the Oracle documentation web site (http://download.oracle.com/docs/cd/E13161_01/tuxedo/index.html).

[2] Tuxedo was originally developed in the Bell Laboratories in 1983, and in 1993 it was transferred to Novell. In 1996, BEA Systems entered into an exclusive agreement with Novell to distribute and continue developing the Tuxedo system. BEA Inc. was acquired by Oracle Corporation in 2008 (http://download. oracle.com/docs/cd/E18050_01/tuxedo/docs11gr1/overview/overview.html#wp1023066).

Figure 2-1. *Tuxedo is the knots in a tin-cans-and-string telephone.*

Conceptually, the PeopleTools Windows client in PeopleTools 7.x was the same in two-tier mode as in three-tier mode. However, when it was used in three-tier mode, the client had been effectively cut in half, as shown in Figure 2-2. The front half consisted of the presentation layer and some of the application logic processing. The back half included the rest of the application logic layer, and this part makes the connection to the database.

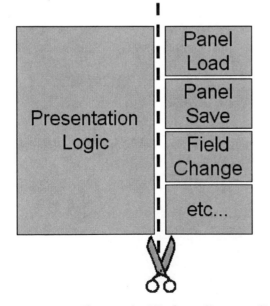

Figure 2-2. *The two-tier Windows client was divided in two when three-tier mode was used.*

These two halves were reconnected by Tuxedo, as shown in Figure 2-3.

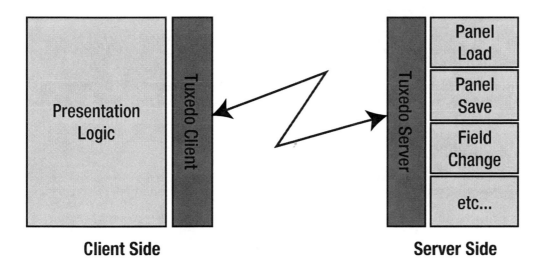

Client Side   **Server Side**

Figure 2-3. Tuxedo connects the client to the functions in the server process.

When this division was carried out, PeopleSoft had over 30 functions on the server side that executed at the request of the client, such as loading a panel, executing PeopleCode, executing particular SQL queries, saving the panels, and so on. Each of these functions became a Tuxedo service in the application server.

The application server consists of a number of server processes that communicate with the client via shared memory segments and queues. Some of those processes are delivered by Tuxedo to manage the communication within the application server, but most were developed by PeopleSoft to service the requests from the PeopleTools clients and include some libraries provided by BEA. The service requests correspond to subroutines in the application server processes that execute the application. Tuxedo provides the infrastructure to route the messages to the appropriate server process and back to the client.

The structure of the application server has not changed significantly with the introduction of the PeopleSoft Internet Architecture (PIA) in PeopleTools 8, although the balance of the workload has shifted. Another tier has been added, and a Java servlet is now the client to the application server, instead of a Windows application. These are the principal changes:

- The application server performs more of the work in PeopleTools 8. There is a new set of PIA services, reflecting the fact that the PeopleTools client was heavily rewritten in PeopleTools 8. There are fewer services overall, but they are more generic.

- The application server still executes all the PeopleCode and submits SQL to the database, and now it also generates all the HTML, JavaScript, and images. It packages them into messages and passes them to the servlet.

- The Java servlet is a thinner presentation layer than the previous Java client applet was. It unpacks the messages, writing the JavaScript and images to the web server file system and passing the HTML directly back to the browser.

- The PeopleSoft application server's processes make persistent connections to the database. All of the online activities from real live users, some of the reporting activity, and some of the interfaces to and from other systems are provided via the application server.

Not surprisingly, the version of Tuxedo shipped with PeopleTools has changed with the version of PeopleTools. However, the way PeopleTools uses Tuxedo has not changed. All of the material in this chapter is applicable to all versions of Tuxedo.

The Simple Application Server

PeopleSoft delivers fully compiled client and server processes, and it defines and develops all the services. The source code is not revealed to the user, and there is neither opportunity nor reason to make changes. However, PeopleSoft also ships a full development version of Tuxedo as part of the PeopleSoft distribution, and this includes a number of sample applications. One of these, the Simple application (shown in Figure 2-4), gives some insight into how Tuxedo works. It illustrates how a call to a subroutine can be distributed between two processes. All the source files can be found in $TUXDIR/samples/atmi/simpapp.

I want to stress that when working with PeopleSoft, you will never see PeopleSoft source code, nor is it ever necessary to recompile server or client processes.

The Simple application has only one function: to convert a string to uppercase. A function called TOUPPER has been placed in an application server, and a service called TOUPPER has also been defined and is called from the client.

The Simple client can be called from the command line. The string that is to be converted to uppercase is specified as the first parameter to the command, as shown in Listing 2-1.

Listing 2-1. Simple Application Command Line

```
simpcl "Hello World"
```

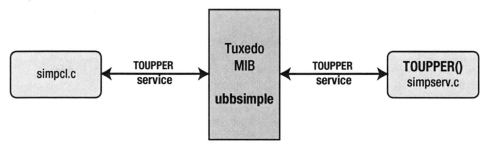

Figure 2-4. The Simple client and application server

The Simple Client

The C code examples in this section are taken from the Simple client, simpcl.c, and they illustrate the actions that a Tuxedo client must perform.

The client process must first connect to the Tuxedo Management Information Base (MIB) with the tpinit() function, as shown in Listing 2-2. The MIB is a shared memory segment that describes the application server. It is also referred to as the Bulletin Board.

Listing 2-2. Client Attaches to the Tuxedo MIB

```
/* Attach to System/T as a Client Process */
if (tpinit((TPINIT *) NULL) == -1) {
    (void) fprintf(stderr, "Tpinit failed\n");
    exit(1);
}
```

Memory is allocated by the tpalloc() function for the outgoing and incoming return message, the locations being assigned to pointers sendbuf and rcvbuf respectively, as shown in Listing 2-3. The length of the message is derived from the length of the string specified on the command line, argv[1].

Listing 2-3. Client Allocates Memory for Tuxedo Messages

```
sendlen = strlen(argv[1]);
if((sendbuf = (char *) tpalloc("STRING", NULL, sendlen+1)) == NULL) {
    (void) fprintf(stderr,"Error allocating send buffer\n");
    tpterm();
    exit(1);
}
if((rcvbuf = (char *) tpalloc("STRING", NULL, sendlen+1)) == NULL) {
    (void) fprintf(stderr,"Error allocating receive buffer\n");
    tpfree(sendbuf);
    tpterm();
    exit(1);
}
```

The string to be converted to uppercase is copied from the first command-line parameter to the send buffer, and the service call is made by the tpcall() function (see Listing 2-4). Pointers to the buffers are then passed to this function. It is a synchronous call, so tpcall() waits until it gets a response from the server, or times out.

Listing 2-4. Client Submits the TOUPPER Service Request

```
(void) strcpy(sendbuf, argv[1]);
ret = tpcall("TOUPPER", (char *)sendbuf, 0, (char **)&rcvbuf, &rcvlen, (long)0);
...
```

The return message from the service call is placed in the receive buffer by tpcall(); see Listing 2-5.

Listing 2-5. Client Prints the Return Message

```
(void) fprintf(stdout, "Returned string is: %s\n", rcvbuf);
```

Finally, the client releases the memory that it allocated for the service call, and it disconnects from the application server (see Listing 2-6).

Listing 2-6. Client Releases Memory, Disconnects, and Terminates

```
/* Free Buffers & Detach from System/T */
tpfree(sendbuf);
tpfree(rcvbuf);
tpterm();
return(0);
```

The Simple Server

The Simple server, `simpserv.c`, is little more than a function that has the same name as the service. The parameter to the function is a pointer to a Tuxedo-defined memory structure, and incoming data is retrieved from that structure. The structure is defined as shown in Listing 2-7.

Listing 2-7. An Extract from %TUXDIR%/include/atmi.h

```
/* interface to service routines */
struct tpsvcinfo {
#define XATMI_SERVICE_NAME_LENGTH   32
    char    name[XATMI_SERVICE_NAME_LENGTH]; /* service name invoked */
    long    flags;              /* describes service attributes */
    char    *data;              /* pointer to data */
    long    len;                /* request data length */
    int     cd;                 /* connection descriptor */
    long    appkey;             /* application authentication client key */
    CLIENTID cltid;             /* client identifier for originating client */
};
typedef struct tpsvcinfo TPSVCINFO;
```

Listing 2-8 shows the TOUPPER service. When it is compiled, a Tuxedo stub is added. When the server process is started, the Tuxedo stub connects the server to the MIB, and it polls for incoming service requests. When it finds one, it takes the message, populates the `tpsvcinfo` structure, calls the service routine, and returns the result via the structure.

Listing 2-8. An Excerpt from simpserv.c

```
TOUPPER(TPSVCINFO *rqst)
{
    int i;
    for(i = 0; i < rqst->len-1; i++)
        rqst->data[i] = toupper(rqst->data[i]);
    /* Return the transformed buffer to the requestor. */
    tpreturn(TPSUCCESS, 0, rqst->data, 0L, 0);
}
```

The Simple Tuxedo Domain

Between the client and the server is the Tuxedo MIB. The Tuxedo configuration file is compiled from the source file ubbsimple, shown in Listing 2-9. It specifies that a single server advertises a single service. When the service request is received, it is routed to the server process that handles it.

Listing 2-9. *An Excerpt from* ubbsimple

```
*SERVERS
DEFAULT:
    CLOPT="-A"

Simpserv    SRVGRP=GROUP1 SRVID=1

*SERVICES
TOUPPER
```

More information about the sample applications can be found in the Tuxedo documentation on the Oracle web site.[3]

Anatomy of the Application Server

PeopleSoft works in exactly the same way as the Simple application. Tuxedo passes parameters to certain functions between client and server. The only difference is that there are more server processes and more services, and the Simple application example did not include the Tuxedo listener processes.

Processes, Memory, and Messages

A Tuxedo application server domain consists of a number of server processes that communicate via shared memory segments and message queues. These structures are a part of the Unix Interprocess Communication (IPC) model. They are created and administered using Unix system functions that are supplied as a standard part of the operating system.

There is no concept of protected and shared memory on Windows, so BEA developed provided tuxipc.exe, the BEA Process Manager service (also referred to as the Tuxedo IPC Helper service in earlier versions), which supports the Unix IPC system call functions required by Tuxedo.[4] BEA also implemented the ipcs and ipcrm commands on Windows. The Tuxedo documentation does not explain these commands because they are standard Unix commands, common to all flavors.

When any Tuxedo application server domain is booted, the first process to be started is the Bulletin Board Liaison process (BBL). This process is the heart of the application server. It reads the configuration of the domain from a binary configuration file, which in a PeopleSoft domain is called PSTUXCFG (see Figure 2-5). The BBL then establishes a shared memory segment, referred to as the Bulletin Board (BB) or Management Information Base (MIB), some message queues (determined by the specifications set out in the configuration file), and two semaphores.

The Bulletin Board holds all the information about the rest of application server domain. It is used as a form of database by the application server processes to determine how they should behave.

---

[3] http://download.oracle.com/docs/cd/E18050_01/tuxedo/docs11gr1/tutor/tutsi.html#wp1112066
[4] This means your Windows server now has a Unix kernel to tune! See Chapter 13 for more on this.

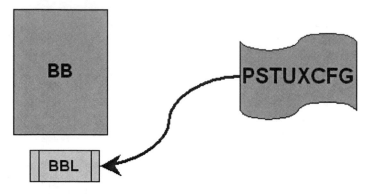

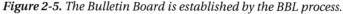

Figure 2-5. *The Bulletin Board is established by the BBL process.*

I'll start by describing the Tuxedo structure required for the Windows three-tier client processes, and add the PIA structure later.

The Workstation Listener (WSL) is a Tuxedo process in the application server domain. It is configured to listen on a specified IP address and port for incoming connections from Tuxedo client processes, which are any of the PeopleTools Windows client processes that operate in three-tier mode.

The WSL spawns at least one Workstation Handler (WSH) process, and it can be configured to start further handlers on demand. The WSHs listen for incoming service requests on the same IP address as the WSL and, unless they are configured to use a specific range of ports, use the next available port after the WSL port.

Initially the client contacts the WSL on the port specified in the configuration. The WSL then assigns the client to one of the WSH processes. The client then closes the connection to the WSL and thereafter only communicates with the WSH. This initial communication process is outlined in Figure 2-6.

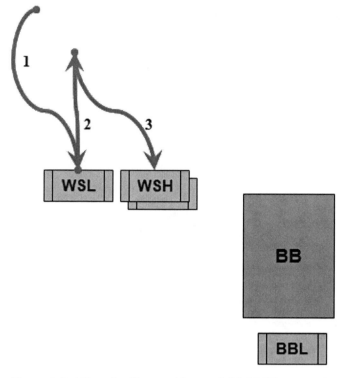

Figure 2-6. *A Tuxedo client making an initial WSL connection*

The client processes must be told where to find a WSL. They can be configured to load balance or fail over between multiple WSLs. WSL addresses and ports are configured in the Workstation Configuration Manager (Figure 2-7).

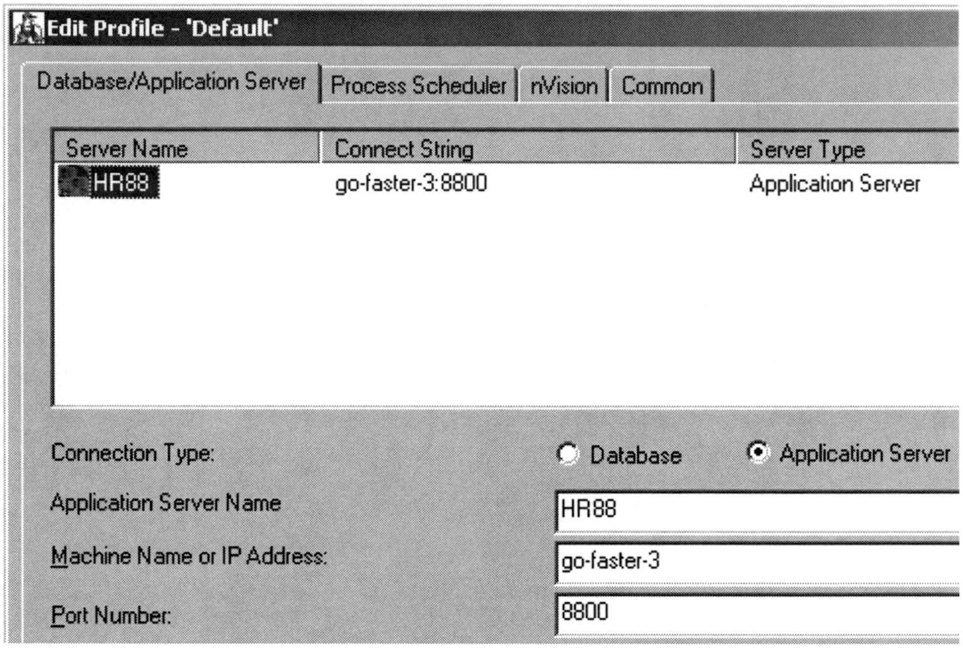

Figure 2-7. *Configuring a workstation listener for a Windows client*

PeopleSoft delivers various server processes, and each new release of PeopleTools has introduced more. Some server processes are optional and need only be configured when particular functions are required.

In PeopleTools 8.4, there must be at least one instance of each of the following three servers: PSSAMSRV, PSMONITORSRV, and PSWATCHSRV. There should be at least two instances of PSAPPSRV because it recycles. When the application server is booted, the minimum number of instances of the specified servers are started. Tuxedo can also be configured to spawn more instances of these servers on demand. All of the PeopleSoft server processes (except PSWATCHSRV) make a persistent connection to the database on startup.

Whenever a message passes between any two processes in the application server, it is sent via a queue to which the receiving process listens. Other information can pass between processes by being written to a shared memory segment.

The following simplified steps (illustrated in Figure 2-8) describe the activity in the application server during a transaction with a Windows client:

1. The service request is sent by the client to the WSH process to which it is connected.

2. The WSH looks up the service on the BB to determine which server or servers are advertising the service and which queues lead to those servers.

3. The WSH enqueues the message requesting that service on an appropriate queue. In this case, the service is placed on the queue called APPQ. Note that not all the queues are explicitly named in Tuxedo.

4. The PSAPPSRV polls for service requests on APPQ, dequeues that request, and executes the PeopleSoft code associated with that service.

5. Processing the service request may involve several interactions with the data. The PSAPPSRV server may need to read or update the physical files that cache PeopleTools objects, as shown in this example.

6. Each WSH process has a return message queue. When the service is complete, the PSAPPSRV server enqueues the return message on the queue (WSHQ in this example) that leads back to the WSH process that sent the request.

7. The WSH process polls and dequeues the return message from the WSHQ.

8. The WSH sends the return message back to the client that has been waiting for a response.

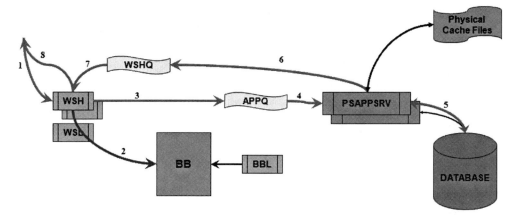

Figure 2-8. *A simplified three-tier Windows client transaction*

The PIA servlet in PeopleTools 8.4 runs in a JVM in the web server. Each PeopleSoft operator is assigned to a thread in the JVM, which is the operator's PeopleSoft session. The thread connects to the application server domain via the Jolt Server Listener (JSL), and the thread is then assigned to a Jolt Server Handler (JSH). The JSL and JSH are very similar to the WSL and WSH, except that they receive Java class requests.

Figure 2-9 illustrates what happens when a PIA transaction is processed by the application server. The steps in the figure are as follows:

1. A Java class request is received from the servlet.

2. The JSH needs to know which Tuxedo service corresponds to the Java class, so it enqueues a request for the JREPSVR.

3. JREPSVR picks up the request from the JSH.

4. JREPSVR looks up the Java class in the JREPOSITORY database (a flat file) to find the Tuxedo service that maps to the Java class.

5-6. JREPSVR returns the Tuxedo service name to the JSH via the queue JSHQ.

7. The JSH interrogates the BB to determine which queue the request should be placed on.

8-13. From this point, the transaction is the same as the three-tier transaction. The Tuxedo service request is sent to the appropriate server, and the response is transmitted back via the same JSH to the servlet.

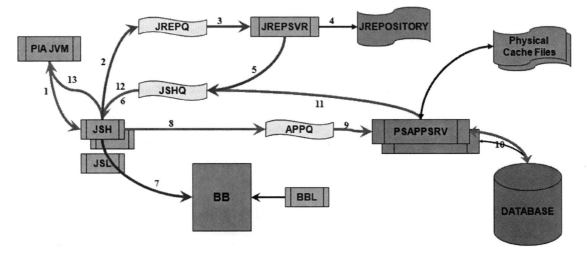

Figure 2-9. *A simplified PIA transaction*

IPC Resources

If you use the Unix `ipcs` command to examine all the IPC resources in use, you see that the full picture is rather more complicated than shown in Figure 2-8.

The report in Listing 2-10 was produced on Windows with the version of `ipcs` supplied by BEA with Tuxedo 8.1. It provides a snapshot of a PeopleSoft 8.44 application server domain. On Windows, the OWNER, GROUP, CREATOR, and CGROUP columns always have a value of 0. They have been removed from the following example for clarity.

Listing 2-10. *Typical `ipcs` Output*

```
ipcs -a
IPCS status from BEA_segV8.1 as of Mon May 10 14:39:08 2004
T    ID    KEY       MODE      CBYTES QNUM QBYTES LSPID LRPID   STIME    RTIME    CTIME
Message Queues:
q   5632 0x00000000 --rw-rw-rw-     0    0  65536     0     0 no-entry no-entry 14:38:42
q    257 0x0000bbe2 -Rrw-rw-rw-     0    0  65536  4072  1716 14:39:00 14:39:00 12:10:42
q    515 0x00000000 -Rrw-rw-rw-     0    0  65536     0     0 no-entry no-entry 12:26:14
q    516 0x00000000 -Rrw-rw-rw-     0    0  65536  2904  3952 13:12:51 13:12:51 12:26:14
q    517 0x00000000 -Rrw-rw-rw-     0    0  65536  2904  3544 12:37:30 12:37:30 12:26:14
q    518 0x00000000 --rw-rw-rw-     0    0  65536     0     0 no-entry no-entry 12:28:11
q    519 0x00000000 --rw-rw-rw-     0    0  65536  1716   688 14:37:14 14:37:14 12:28:11
q    520 0x00000000 --rw-rw-rw-     0    0  65536     0     0 no-entry no-entry 12:28:46
q    521 0x00000000 --rw-rw-rw-     0    0  65536     0     0 no-entry no-entry 12:28:46
```

```
q    522 0x00000000 -Rrw-rw-rw-      0     0  65536  3544  2548 12:37:26 12:37:26 12:30:13
q    523 0x00000000 --rw-rw-rw-      0     0  65536  3544  2548 12:37:26 12:37:26 12:30:13
q    524 0x00000000 -Rrw-rw-rw-      0     0  65536     0     0 no-entry no-entry 12:30:59
q    525 0x00000000 -Rrw-rw-rw-      0     0  65536  1132  3648 14:39:07 14:39:07 12:30:59
q    526 0x00000000 -Rrw-rw-rw-      0     0  65536  1132  2616 14:39:07 14:39:07 12:30:59
q    783 0x00000000 -Rrw-rw-rw-      0     0  65536  2616  1708 12:46:04 12:46:04 12:32:22
q    784 0x00000000 --rw-rw-rw- 13608     1  65536  2616  1132 14:39:08 14:39:07 12:33:04
q   1297 0x00000000 --rw-rw-rw-      0     0  65536  1716  2904 12:37:30 12:37:30 12:33:04
q   3602 0x00000000 --rw-rw-rw-      0     0  65536     0     0 no-entry no-entry 12:37:26
q    532 0x00000000 --rw-rw-rw-      0     0  65536  1716  1132 14:38:53 14:38:53 14:38:51
T    ID   KEY         MODE    NATTCH SEGSZ  CPID  LPID  ATIME    DTIME    CTIME
Shared Memory:
m     50 0x0000bbe2 --rw-rw-rw-    27 646432  1716  4072 14:39:00 14:39:00 12:10:40
m    101 0x00000000 --rw-rw-rw-     3    504  2196  3544 12:26:14 no-entry 12:26:14
m    102 0x00000000 --rw-rw-rw-     3   1112   260  2616 12:30:59 no-entry 12:30:59
T    ID   KEY         MODE     NSEMS  OTIME   CTIME
Semaphores:
s   1024 0x0000bbe2 --ra-ra-ra-     5 14:39:07 12:10:40
s   3073 0x00000000 --ra-ra-ra-    52 13:34:04 12:10:40
```

If you start the application server processes one by one and watch the changes in the ipcs output, you can determine which queues are associated with which processes. The LSPID and LRPID columns show the IDs of the processes that last sent a message to and retrieved a message from the relevant queue. Hence, it is possible to determine the flow of messages between servers and queues.

Figure 2-10 shows the full picture. The process, queue, and segment IDs in the figure correspond to the preceding ipcs report.

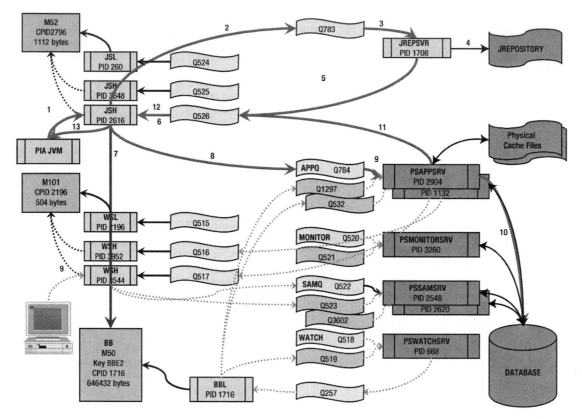

Figure 2-10. *A PIA transaction showing the full IPC model*

Various additional queues are created as each process starts. Each is used to send messages to a specific server. You should think of the queues as being associated with the process that receives the message via the queue. These are the queues you see:

- A queue is created for each instance of the Tuxedo command-line utility tmadmin when it is running, and the related queue is deleted when the instance is terminated.

- The BBL process has one queue. It receives messages from PSWATCHSRV and tmadmin.

- A queue is created for each Tuxedo message queue (APPQ, SAMQ, and so on). These queues are used to send service request messages from the handler processes to the server processes, and they are revealed in tmadmin with the printqueue (or pq) command.

- A queue is created for each PeopleSoft server process (PSAPPSRV, PSSAMSRV, PSWATCHSRV, and so on). This is an administrative queue for receiving instructions from the BBL.

- There is one queue for each WSL and each WSH. The WSH queues are used to receive return messages from the application server processes after the service requests have been processed. The queue to the WSL process appears not to be used.

- There is a queue for each JSL and JSH process (as for the WSL and WSH processes).

There are three shared memory segments:

- The Bulletin Board is created by the BBL process.

- A small shared memory segment is created by the WSL. It is used to permit the WSL and WSH processes to communicate.

- The JSL process similarly creates a small shared memory segment for interprocess communication.

tmadmin and ipcs

The printqueue command in the tmadmin utility reports only on the status of the queues that carry inbound service-request messages to the application server processes.

In the example shown in Listing 2-11, printqueue (pq) reports that the APPQ that serves requests to two PSAPPSRV processes has a message queued on it.

Listing 2-11. Tuxedo printqueue Output

```
> pq
Prog Name       Queue Name   # Serve Wk Queued  # Queued  Ave. Len    Machine
---------       ----------   ------- ---------  --------  --------    -------
PSSAMSRV.exe    SAMQ            2        -          0         -  GO-FASTER+
JSL.exe         00095.00200     1        -          0         -  GO-FASTER+
WSL.exe         00001.00020     1        -          0         -  GO-FASTER+
JREPSVR.exe     00094.00250     1        -          0         -  GO-FASTER+
PSMONITORSRV.e  MONITOR         1        -          0         -  GO-FASTER+
PSAPPSRV.exe    APPQ            2        -          1         -  GO-FASTER+
BBL.exe         48098           1        -          0         -  GO-FASTER+
PSWATCHSRV.exe  WATCH           1        -          0         -  GO-FASTER+
```

The output in Listing 2-11 corresponds to the entry in the ipcs report in Listing 2-12 that provides this information:

- One message of 13,608 bytes is on queue 784.

- The last message sent to the queue was placed by process 2616, a JSH.

- Process 1132, a PSAPPSRV, was the last process to receive a message from this queue.

Listing 2-12. ipcs Report

```
ipcs -a
IPCS status from BEA_segV8.1 as of Mon May 10 14:39:08 2004
T    ID     KEY      MODE     CBYTES QNUM QBYTES LSPID LRPID   STIME    RTIME    CTIME
Message Queues:
...
q   784 0x00000000 --rw-rw-rw- 13608    1  65536  2616  1132 14:39:08 14:39:07 12:33:04
...
```

PIA Servlets

The PIA servlets are not part of the application server; they are its clients. It is important to understand their relationship with the application server.

When you boot a WebLogic server, you are effectively starting a JVM that runs a servlet engine. Various PIA servlets are then registered with this servlet engine. The WebLogic server is not really a web server at all—it is simply shipped with a servlet that acts as a web server.

The PIA connects to the application server as illustrated in Figure 2-11 and outlined in the following steps:

1-2. HTTP requests for the PeopleSoft servlet are received by the web server listener and routed to the servlet. When a PIA session is established, a new servlet thread is created. That thread is the operator's session, and it is stateful. HTTP messages are not stateful, but an in-memory cookie is sent back to the browser, and that cookie is then sent to the web server with subsequent HTTP requests to identify the user's servlet thread.

3. Each servlet thread makes a persistent connection to the application server via one of the JSH processes. The JSL ports are specified in the servlet configuration file, `configuration.properties`. All of the HTML, JavaScript, and graphics are generated by application server and are sent back to the servlet in a single message from Tuxedo.

4. The servlet unpacks the message, writing the static files (JavaScript and graphics) to the physical file system that is referenced by the web server. The main HTML page is sent back via the web server thread to the client.

5-6. The main HTML page sent back to the client contains references to the static files. If those files have not already been cached locally, the browser makes further HTTP requests for those files that are served by the web server without further reference to the servlet.

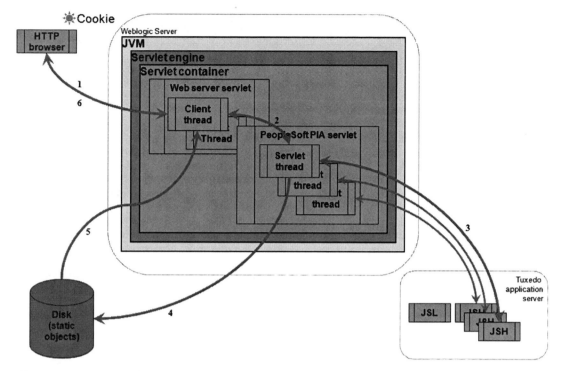

Figure 2-11. *A PIA servlet transaction*

PeopleSoft supported Apache HTTP Server 1.3, but only with PeopleTools 8.1. PeopleTools 8.4 does not support Apache, but it does support IBM WebSphere. In these servers, the web server itself is a separate process distinct from the JVM. Otherwise the function of the PIA is the same on all web servers.

Integration Broker

The Integration Broker is the foundation of PeopleSoft's Service Orientated Architecture. It was introduced in PeopleTools 8.4 to provide a mechanism to offer elements of PeopleSoft applications as a web service and to consume other web services. It can send messages between PeopleSoft systems or between PeopleSoft and other applications. These messages may be processed either synchronously or asynchronously.

The use of this technology has become more common as PeopleSoft systems are interfaced to each other or to other systems, as has the use of the PeopleSoft Portal to create a seamless environment between PeopleSoft systems. Oracle emphasized the importance of this technology with its Application Integration Architecture statement in 2007. Other enterprise resource planning (ERP) vendors, not just Oracle, are delivering APIs to permit integration with messaging between their systems. Application upgrade doesn't have to be done in a single big bang, but can be achieved in a series of smaller bangs. For example, I have seen a site where different versions of PeopleSoft Human Capital Management (HCM) are installed and presented via Portal to permit use of a new piece of functionality without the need for a full upgrade.

Probably the most common use of messaging is to replicate data from one system to another, usually asynchronously. For example, messaging can be used to synchronize operator passwords between PeopleSoft systems or post payroll data from Global Payroll in HCM to General Ledger in a PeopleSoft or other Financials system.

An example of synchronous messaging is to invoke a web server to obtain real-time information from another system. PeopleSoft's favorite demonstration of this displayed real-time tracking information for a shipment, obtained from the courier's web service, and presented that information in the PeopleSoft session, but without storing it in the PeopleSoft database.

Inbound messages into a PeopleSoft system are sent to the Integration Gateway. This is another servlet in the web server, although it is often used in a separate web server. However, one gateway can be shared by many PeopleSoft databases. The gateway maps PeopleSoft nodes to Application Server domains and communicates with the JSL/JSH processes in much the same way as the other servlets. Synchronous service requests are handled by the PSAPPSRV processes in the same way as on-line users. Asynchronous messages are stored in the application message subscription queue tables in the database, where they are picked up and handled by the subscription processes that poll for new messages.

Outbound messages are generated by the application server or Application Engine batch process that generates the message. Asynchronous messages are placed on application message-publication queues tables where they are picked up and handled by the publication server processes.

Figure 2-12 shows an application server domain with publish and subscribe servers. I haven't shown the JREPSVR processing depicted in Figure 2-9. Nor have I shown the physical cache files used by all PeopleSoft server processes.

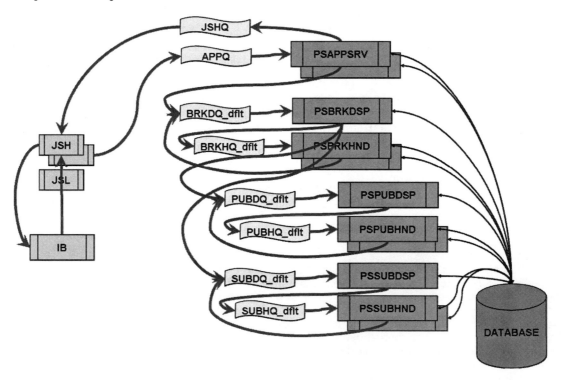

Figure 2-12. Part of an application server with publish and subscribe server processes

There are three pairs of process types: Broker, Publication, and Subscription Dispatchers and Handlers. The dispatcher processes (PSBRKDSP, PSPUBDSP, and PSSUBDSP) look for unprocessed asynchronous messages by periodically polling the message queue tables in the database. They submit asynchronous Tuxedo service requests to their corresponding handler queue, which is handled by one of the handler processes that service that queue. Only one of each kind of dispatcher runs in a single domain. Like the PSAPPSRV process, the handler processes (PSBRKHND, PSPUBHND, and PSSUBHND) handle service requests, but here the service requests come from the dispatcher processes instead of via the JSH. There should be at least two instances of each type of handler process because they recycle and more may be necessary to handle the workload.

Summary

This chapter has discussed the architecture of the Tuxedo application server in some detail. The client and server processes, written by PeopleSoft, communicate with each other via the infrastructure provided by Tuxedo and using shared memory segments and queues provided by the Unix IPC system. Tuxedo passes the parameters in the function calls to the functions in the server, and it passes the return values back again. The application server also provides a degree of connection concentration so that relatively few server processes can handle many client sessions.

## CHAPTER 3

Database Connectivity

All but one of the database objects in a standard PeopleSoft database are contained in a single Oracle schema. All PeopleSoft processes that connect directly to the database via SQL*Net go through the standard PeopleSoft signon processing, negotiating security and ending up connected to that schema. (Thereafter, security is handled by PeopleTools, not the database.)

This chapter describes the database schemas that PeopleSoft creates, their privileges, and how those privileges are used by the signon process, explaining what this reveals about the structure of PeopleSoft databases.

PeopleSoft Database versus Oracle Database

It is not uncommon in the IT industry for different vendors to use the same word to mean very different things. *Database* is one of those words.

The word *database* is often used by PeopleSoft to refer to the collection of tables in the PeopleSoft administrative schema within an Oracle (or other) database. In contrast, Oracle would describe a database as the collection of physical data, log files, and control files. An Oracle *instance* is the collection of intercommunicating processes that administer the database. The importance of these distinctions will become apparent as I describe the signon process.

Sometimes even DBAs are guilty of using terminology carelessly. Unless you are running Real Application Clusters (RAC), there is a one-to-one relationship between instances and databases. You may hear DBAs talking about starting the database when really they mean starting the instance.

Oracle recommends that each PeopleSoft database be created in a separate Oracle database. Thus, each instance can be started, shut down, backed up, and tuned independently. Nevertheless, it is possible to have more than one PeopleSoft database in a single Oracle database, in which case each PeopleSoft database resides in a different Oracle schema, and the signon process has to connect accordingly.

On the rare occasions where I have seen this arrangement, a number of PeopleSoft development databases have been co-located. With the exception of customizations or patches that have not yet been migrated, each of the PeopleSoft databases contains the same tables with the same structures. Unless the tablespace model is explicitly overridden, the same table in different PeopleSoft databases, and therefore in different Oracle schemas, is built in the same tablespace. Thus, each tablespace contains objects for all the PeopleSoft databases that reside in the same Oracle database.

I consider that the administrative complexity of co-locating PeopleSoft databases far outweighs the additional memory, disk, and CPU overhead in having additional Oracle databases and instances.

Oracle Database Users

Every process that makes a two-tier connection to the database identifies itself with a PeopleSoft user or operator ID. The purpose of this signon processing is to securely validate that the PeopleSoft operator, authenticated by password, is permitted to access the PeopleSoft application.

As such, it will be useful to quickly review the database user accounts available in a PeopleSoft database before walking through the actual signon process. From version 8 onward, a PeopleSoft database requires only three Oracle database schemas:

- *Owner ID:* This schema contains most of the database objects, and it is as this database user that PeopleSoft processes access the database.

- *Connect ID:* This low-security database user is used by the signon process until the password is validated.

- *PS:* This schema contains a table that describes which PeopleSoft databases are in the Oracle database.

Owner ID (SYSADM)

Once the signon process is complete, a PeopleSoft process (such as a two-tier client or an application server process) is connected to the database via the administrative schema, which is referred to as the *Owner ID* because it contains nearly all of the database objects. This schema can access any table or view in the PeopleSoft database. Access to objects in the database is controlled within the PeopleSoft application, rather than by the database.

■ **Note** The Owner ID is also referred to as the *Access ID* because the PeopleSoft processes use this user to access the database. However, it is possible to have other Access IDs, as discussed later in this chapter in the section "Using PeopleSoft Access Profiles and Oracle Resource Profiles."

By convention, the administrative schema is usually called SYSADM, although there is nothing to prevent you from using a different name. The password to this account is the key to the kingdom. It should be treated with the same respect as the password to the superuser (root) account, the accounts in the dba group on Unix, and the passwords to the SYS and SYSTEM accounts on an Oracle database.

The Owner ID has certain privileges granted by a role called PSADMIN (discussed shortly in the "Oracle Database Roles" section).

Connect ID (PEOPLE)

From PeopleTools 8 on, the first connection that each process makes to the database is via a low-security user account, referred to as the *Connect ID* and usually named PEOPLE. It is only granted CREATE SESSION privilege via the PSUSER role and three explicit SELECT privileges (see Listing 3-1).

Listing 3-1. Extract from `grant.sql`: *SELECT Privileges Being Granted to the PEOPLE Account*

```
GRANT SELECT ON PSSTATUS TO PEOPLE;
GRANT SELECT ON PSOPRDEFN TO PEOPLE;
GRANT SELECT ON PSACCESSPRFL TO PEOPLE;
```

The Connect ID provides only the bare minimum of access to the PeopleTools tables in order to permit authentication by the signon process. Later, after successful validation of the password, the process reconnects as the Access ID.

Up to PeopleTools 7.x, instead of a single Connect ID, there was a database user corresponding to each PeopleSoft operator. Every time a PeopleSoft operator was created in the application, the PSUSER role was granted to that PeopleSoft operator ID. The PSUSER role contains only the CREATE SESSION privilege, and granting this privilege implicitly creates the database user, as shown in Listing 3-2.

Listing 3-2. A PeopleTools Trace Showing a User Being Created in PeopleTools 7.5

```
5-312   0.961 Cur#1 RC=0 Dur=0.310 COM Stmt=GRANT PSUSER TO NEWOP
5-313   0.811 Cur#1 RC=0 Dur=0.811 COM Stmt=GRANT SELECT ON PSLOCK TO NEWOP
5-314   0.531 Cur#1 RC=0 Dur=0.531 COM Stmt=GRANT SELECT ON PSOPRDEFN TO NEWOP
```

When an operator was deleted from the application under version 7.x, the grants were revoked, but this leaves the empty schema without any privileges.

When a PeopleSoft system has been upgraded from PeopleTools 7, it is common to find these empty schemas left behind because there is no step in the upgrade procedure to remove them. This is not a security risk, because no one can connect to these schemas. However, I still recommend that they be removed.

PS Schema

The PS schema is used to hold only the table PSDBOWNER, which maps the name of the PeopleSoft database to the schema in the database that holds it. PS.PSDBOWNER is the only table in a PeopleSoft database that is in a different schema from the rest of the objects.

The PS schema and PS.PSDBOWNER table are created during the installation procedure by the `dbowner.sql` script shown in Listing 3-3. All privileges are revoked from the schema after the table has been created.

Listing 3-3. An Extract from `dbowner.sql`

```
GRANT CONNECT, RESOURCE, DBA TO PS IDENTIFIED BY PS;
CONNECT PS/PS;
CREATE TABLE PSDBOWNER (DBNAME VARCHAR2(8) NOT NULL
, OWNERID VARCHAR2(8) NOT NULL ) TABLESPACE PSDEFAULT;
CREATE UNIQUE INDEX PS_PSDBOWNER ON PSDBOWNER (DBNAME) TABLESPACE PSDEFAULT;
CREATE PUBLIC SYNONYM PSDBOWNER FOR PSDBOWNER;
GRANT SELECT ON PSDBOWNER TO PUBLIC;
CONNECT SYSTEM/MANAGER;
REVOKE CONNECT, RESOURCE, DBA FROM PS;
ALTER USER PS QUOTA UNLIMITED ON PSDEFAULT;
```

As shown later in Listing 3-12, the PeopleTools 8.x signon procedure explicitly references the table and schema as PS.PSDBOWNER. The "PS" is hard-coded into the process, so you cannot choose a different name for this schema.

The creation of a public synonym in the dbowner.sql script is a throwback to earlier versions of PeopleTools where the signon procedure did not explicitly specify the schema. The synonym still permits the table to be referenced from the application, but this table can also be queried by any user connected to the database. It would be more appropriate to create a user synonym in the Owner ID schema and only grant SELECT privilege to that user.

When a PeopleSoft database is created, a Data Mover script is generated to import the PeopleSoft objects into the Oracle database. An extract of that script is shown in Listing 3-4; it also populates PS.PSDBOWNER with one row that describes that PeopleSoft database.

Listing 3-4. An Excerpt from the Script that Builds a PeopleSoft Database

```
REM - Final Database cleanup
REM -
REM - Based on your inputs to Database Setup, you will be using
REM - ConnectID's to connect to your PeopleSoft Application
REM -
/
INSERT INTO PS.PSDBOWNER VALUES('HCM91', 'SYSADM');
UPDATE PSSTATUS SET OWNERID = 'SYSADM';
```

■ **Note** SYSADM can populate the PS.PSDBOWNER table because it has been granted IMP_FULL_DATABASE via the PSADMIN role (see Listing 3-5), which in turn includes INSERT ANY TABLE and UPDATE ANY TABLE. SYSADM has no privilege to delete those rows. PS does not even have CONNECT privilege after installation.

If you duplicate a PeopleSoft database by performing a full Oracle export and import, the PS.PSDBOWNER table must exist in the target database before the import is run. Otherwise, the import process cannot create the table, because the PS schema does not have RESOURCE privilege any more.

Oracle Database Roles

Two Oracle database roles, PSUSER and PSADMIN, are created during the installation of the PeopleSoft database, as shown in Listing 3-5. These two roles are discussed in the following sections.

Listing 3-5. An Extract from PSADMIN.SQL

```
CREATE ROLE PSUSER;
GRANT CREATE SESSION TO PSUSER;

CREATE ROLE PSADMIN;
GRANT
ANALYZE ANY,
ALTER SESSION, ALTER TABLESPACE, ALTER ROLLBACK SEGMENT,
CREATE CLUSTER, CREATE DATABASE LINK, CREATE PUBLIC DATABASE LINK,
```

```
CREATE PUBLIC SYNONYM, CREATE SEQUENCE, CREATE SNAPSHOT,
CREATE SESSION, CREATE SYNONYM, CREATE TABLE, CREATE VIEW,
CREATE PROCEDURE, CREATE TRIGGER, CREATE TABLESPACE, CREATE USER,
CREATE ROLLBACK SEGMENT,
DROP PUBLIC DATABASE LINK, DROP PUBLIC SYNONYM, DROP ROLLBACK SEGMENT,
DROP TABLESPACE, DROP USER, MANAGE TABLESPACE, RESOURCE,
EXP_FULL_DATABASE, IMP_FULL_DATABASE,
GRANT ANY ROLE, ALTER USER, BECOME USER
TO PSADMIN WITH ADMIN OPTION;

EXEC DBMS_RESOURCE_MANAGER_PRIVS.GRANT_SYSTEM_PRIVILEGE -
    (GRANTEE_NAME => 'PSADMIN', -
    PRIVILEGE_NAME => 'ADMINISTER_RESOURCE_MANAGER', -
    ADMIN_OPTION => TRUE);

conn / as sysdba;

GRANT SELECT ON V_$MYSTAT to PSADMIN;
```

The privilege to use the Oracle Resource Manager was added in PeopleTools 8.51.

PSUSER Role

The PSUSER role was introduced in PeopleTools 7, where it was granted to each of the database users that corresponded to PeopleSoft operators. However, in PeopleTools 8, the role is never granted to anyone. Instead, the CREATE SESSION privilege is explicitly granted to the Connect ID (usually PEOPLE), as shown Listing 3-6.

Listing 3-6. An Extract from `connect.sql`

```
CREATE USER people IDENTIFIED BY people DEFAULT TABLESPACE psdefault
TEMPORARY TABLESPACE pstemp;

GRANT CREATE SESSION to people;
```

PSADMIN Role

The PSADMIN role is granted to the Access ID (usually SYSADM). PeopleSoft describes the privileges defined by this role as the minimum for running PeopleSoft. The Access ID is an administrative account, so there needs to be a degree of trust and cooperation between the DBA and the PeopleSoft administrator (if they are not the same person).

However, not all of the privileges in the PSADMIN role are absolutely essential to the operation of PeopleSoft, and I have come across some sites where the DBAs want to limit the privileges granted by this role even further. Table 3-1 explains the purpose of the various privileges granted to PSADMIN.

Table 3-1. *PSADMIN Role Privileges*

Privilege	Comments	Removable?
ANALYZE ANY	From PeopleTools 8.48, the DDL models call `dbms_stats` (see Chapter 6) instead of the `ANALYZE` command, whereas COBOL processes still use `ANALYZE`. However, PeopleSoft processes collect statistics on objects in the schema to which they are connected, so they don't need this privilege.	Yes
ALTER SESSION	This privilege is required during some SQR processing, and it is also necessary to enable SQL tracing during performance tuning.	No
ALTER TABLESPACE	This is required only if Data Mover creates the tablespace during an import; otherwise, PeopleSoft does not alter the tablespaces directly. This is a job for the DBA instead.	Yes
ALTER ROLLBACK SEGMENT	In the installation process, the rollback segments are created by the Access ID. However, they should generally be managed by the DBA. From Oracle 9i on, if you use system-managed undo, the question does not arise.	Yes
CREATE CLUSTER	PeopleSoft does not cluster any objects—PeopleTools cannot generate the DDL to create them. It is just conceivable, but highly unlikely, that a DBA might choose to introduce a cluster in the course of performance tuning.	Yes
CREATE DATABASE LINK	Private database links are no longer used. They were used during the upgrade-compare process in PeopleTools 7.x and earlier. In PeopleTools 8, this function has been brought into the Application Designer, which connects directly to the two databases.	Yes
CREATE PUBLIC DATABASE LINK	Public database links are not used by PeopleSoft.	Yes
CREATE PUBLIC SYNONYM	A public synonym is created for PS.PSDBOWNER at installation time (see Listing 3-3), but while connected to database user PS.	Yes
CREATE SEQUENCE	Sequences are not used by PeopleSoft.	Yes
CREATE SNAPSHOT	PeopleSoft does not use snapshots or materialized views.	Yes
CREATE SESSION	This privilege allows connection to the database and is essential.	No

Privilege	Comments	Removable?
CREATE SYNONYM	This is no longer required. In PeopleTools 6.x and earlier, private synonyms were created for use by the upgrade-compare processes.	Yes
CREATE TABLE	Application Designer can create tables online, and Data Mover creates tables during the initial database build. If this privilege is revoked, all DDL generated by Application Designer must be executed as another schema, and it has to be amended to include the owner of the object.	No
CREATE VIEW	Application Designer can create views online, and Data Mover does create views during the initial database build.	No
CREATE PROCEDURE	This privilege is not used by PeopleSoft.	Yes
CREATE TRIGGER	From PeopleTools 8.1 on, triggers are used for auditing. Beginning with PeopleTools 8.4, the Application Designer can also generate triggers used for synchronizing with mobile clients.	No
CREATE TABLESPACE	This privilege is only required if Data Mover creates the tablespace during an import, which the default installation process does not attempt. This is a job for the DBA instead.	Yes
CREATE USER	From PeopleTools 8 on, only three schemas are required. After installation, this privilege is no longer used. It is really left over from PeopleTools 7.x and earlier versions, in which a new database user was created for each PeopleSoft operator ID.	Yes (after installation)
CREATE ROLLBACK SEGMENT	Rollback segments should be maintained by the DBA.	Yes
DROP PUBLIC DATABASE LINK	Public database links are not used by PeopleSoft.	Yes
DROP PUBLIC SYNONYM	There is only one public synonym, and it should not be dropped.	Yes
DROP ROLLBACK SEGMENT	The rollback segments should be completely maintained by the DBA.	Yes
DROP TABLESPACE	PeopleSoft never attempts to drop tablespaces. This is a job for the DBA.	Yes

Privilege	Comments	Removable?
DROP USER	PeopleTools never drops any users. Even in PeopleTools 7.x and earlier versions, when a PeopleSoft operator was deleted, the privileges were revoked from the corresponding schema but the database user was not dropped.	Yes
MANAGE TABLESPACE	This privilege allows tablespaces to be taken online and offline during a backup. This is a job for the DBA.	Yes
RESOURCE	This provides a number of system privileges, including CREATE CLUSTER, CREATE PROCEDURE, CREATE SEQUENCE, CREATE TABLE, and CREATE TRIGGER. It is used for compatibility with previous versions of Oracle. This privilege is not required.	Yes
EXP_FULL_DATABASE	This provides a range of privileges required to perform full and incremental exports, and the DBA rather than the PeopleSoft system administrator can perform the exports. However, this role also provides SELECT_CATALOG_ROLE, which is required when generating DDL scripts in Application Designer.	Only if replaced with SELECT_ CATALOG_ ROLE
IMP_FULL_DATABASE	This provides a range of privileges required to perform full imports, and the DBA rather than the PeopleSoft system administrator can perform the imports. However, this role also provides SELECT_CATALOG_ROLE, which is required when generating DDL scripts.	Only if replaced with SELECT_ CATALOG_ ROLE
GRANT ANY ROLE	This privilege is no longer required because schemas are not created when operators are created. This, like any ANY privilege, is dangerous because it opens the door to the entire Oracle database. Since it is no longer necessary in PeopleTools 8, I recommend removing it.	Yes
ALTER USER	This privilege allows the database user to change passwords. It is required when the PeopleSoft administrator changes the password of the Access ID. Up to PeopleTools 7.5, it was also required when an operator password was changed.	No
BECOME USER	This privilege is required by and implicit in IMP_FULL_USER, but it is not otherwise required by PeopleTools.	Yes

Signing On to a PeopleSoft 8 Database

Having covered the available database users, I am now going to step through the processing that a PeopleTools program performs when it makes a two-tier connection to the database. When PeopleSoft Windows client processes, such as the Application Designer, make a three-tier connection, they connect to the application server; each application server process has already made a two-tier connection to the database when it was started. (The Pure Internet Architecture [PIA] is sometimes referred to as a fourth tier. As described in Chapter 2, the browser connects the servlet, which in turn connects to the application server.)

As discussed earlier in this chapter, any process wishing to connect to the database must identify itself with a PeopleSoft user or operator ID. The purpose of the signon processing is to securely validate that the PeopleSoft operator, authenticated by password, is permitted to access the PeopleSoft database. When a PeopleSoft Windows client process is started, a signon dialog box is presented, as shown in Figure 3-1.

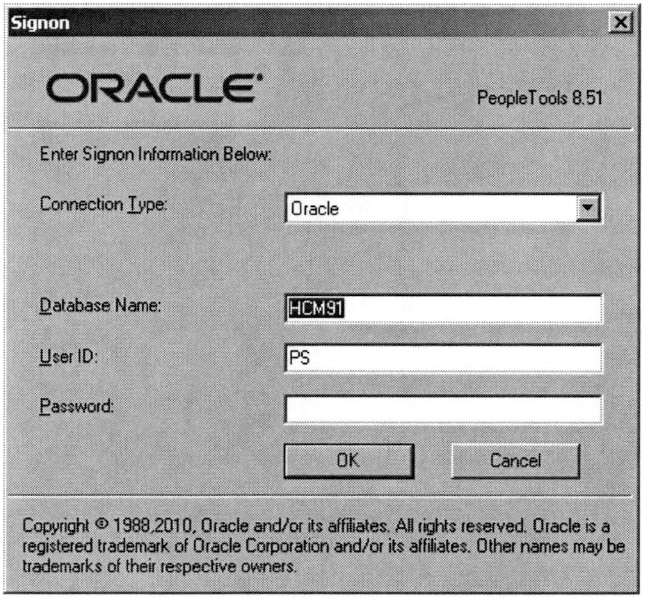

Figure 3-1. The PeopleSoft signon dialog box for the Windows client

This signon dialog box can be suppressed if the signon options are supplied as command-line options, as follows:

```
pside.exe -ct ORACLE -cd HCM91 -co PS -cp PS
```

The full set of command-line options is specified in PeopleBooks.

To best see what happens when a PeopleTools program makes a two-tier connection to the database, I will walk through a PeopleSoft trace of the process in the following sections.

Making the Initial Connection

As discussed earlier, the nature of the very first connection to the database has changed in PeopleTools 8, compared to version 7.5x. As of version 8, all PeopleSoft processes, regardless of the PeopleSoft operator, connect to the same low-security database user, referred to as the Connect ID.

For Windows client programs, various settings, including the name and password for the Connect ID user, are set with the Configuration Manager (see Figure 3-2). The database name and user ID are used as default values in the login screen for Windows client programs. This utility also encrypts the Connect ID password.

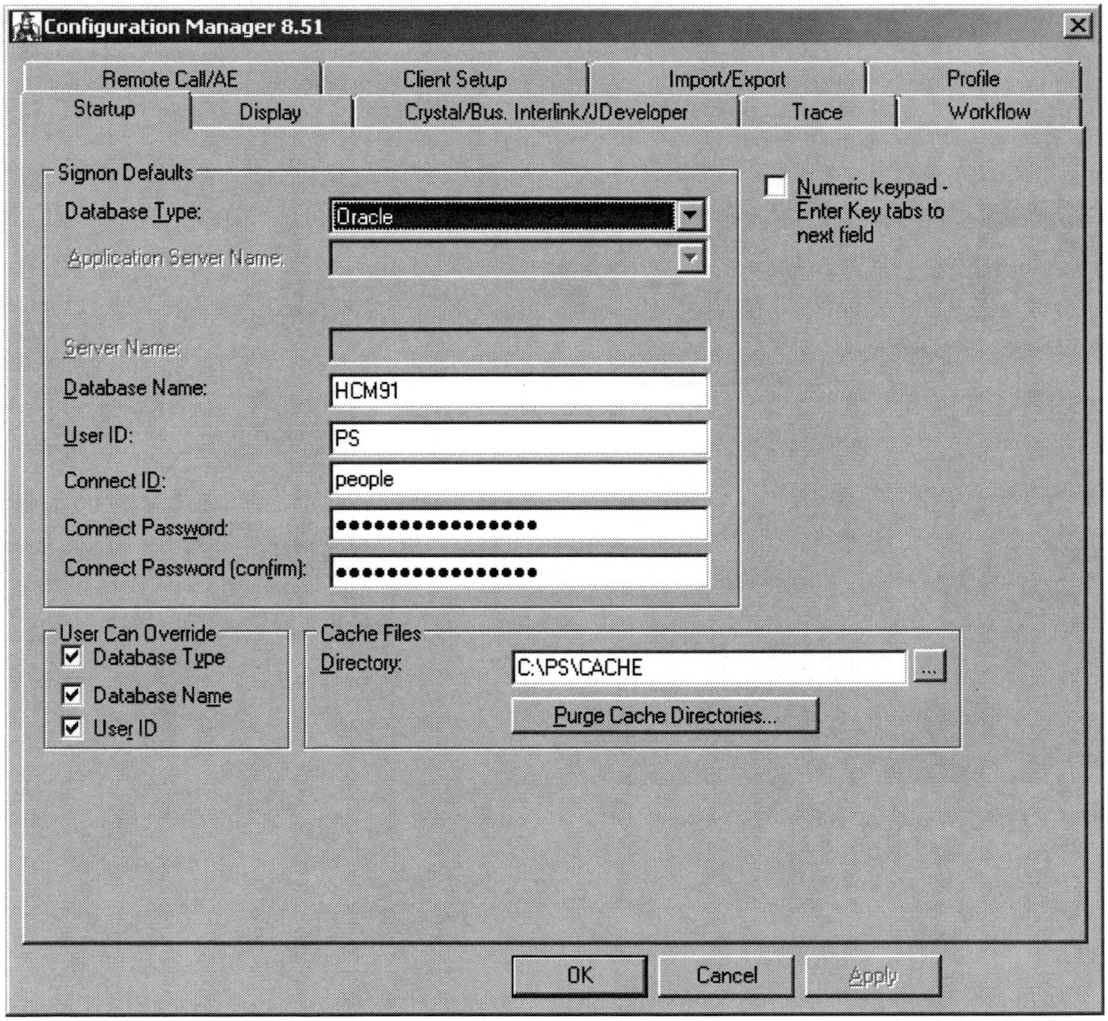

Figure 3-2. The Configuration Manager for the PeopleSoft Windows client allows you to set the Connect ID password.

The Configuration Manager is essentially a tool for setting registry values on the client (see Figure 3-3). A Windows client process, such as Application Designer, reads these registry settings.

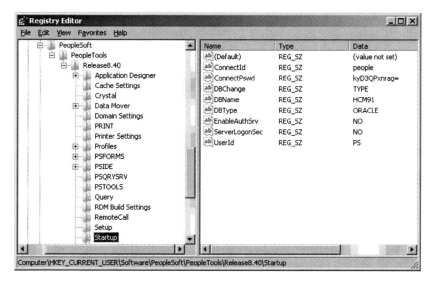

Figure 3-3. *PeopleTools 8.4 registry entries in Windows, set by the Configuration Manager*

If you do not use the same Connect ID and password across all your databases, the Windows client processes (mainly Application Designer) cannot connect to all the databases in two-tier mode without changing those registry keys. In particular, you cannot migrate Application Designer projects directly between databases because Application Designer must log on to both databases in two-tier mode, and it will try to use the same Connect ID for both. The workaround for this problem is to export the project from the source database to a flat file and then import that file into the target database.

The Configuration Manager is also used to install or remove the PeopleSoft shortcuts in the Windows Start menu, the ODBC driver, and a local installation of the PeopleTools executables.

■ **Note** PeopleSoft places registry settings in both the HKEY_CURRENT_USER and HKEY_LOCAL_MACHINE files. Therefore, the configuration for Windows clients needs to be set up separately for each user who needs it, unlike Oracle, which only puts registry entries into HKEY_LOCAL_MACHINE.

The PeopleSoft application server processes, COBOL programs, and Application Engine processes perform similar logon procedures. Their connection details are stored in either the application server configuration file psappsrv.cfg or the Process Scheduler configuration file psprcs.cfg, as shown in Listing 3-7.

■ **Note** Application server and Process Scheduler processes running on a Windows server do not use the registry settings. Instead, all their settings are read from the configuration files, just as on other operating systems.

Listing 3-7. An Extract from the Process Scheduler Configuration File `psprcs.cfg`

```
[Startup]
;========================================================================
; Database Signon settings
;========================================================================
DBName=HCM91
DBType=ORACLE
UserId=PS
UserPswd=sxaYMMOCrai26F3R14mO+JWdoXJsSHVovUxlKDaxFDM=
ConnectId=people
ConnectPswd=kyD3QPxnrag=
ServerName=
```

The PeopleTools client trace (discussed in detail in Chapter 9) can show all the SQL operations performed during the signon process. As shown in Listing 3-8, the first action of any PeopleSoft process is to connect to the ConnectId with the ConnectPswd (both of which are shown in bold in the listing).

Listing 3-8. The Start of a PeopleTools Client Trace

```
PID-Line   Time         Elapsed    Trace Data...
--------   --------     ----------  -------------------->
 1-1       09.51.31                 Tuxedo session opened {oprid='PS', appname='TwoTier',
addr='//TwoTier:7000', open at 057C00DO, pid=1064}
 1-2       09.51.33     2.330000 Cur#0.1064.HCM91 RC=0 Dur=2.267000 Create Connection
Info=Primary/HCM91/people/ Handle=057E7BC8
```

In Oracle terms, the SQL*Net connect string is people/peop1e@HCM91 (although for obvious reasons the trace does not show the password). The TNS service name in the connect string, HCM91, is taken from the PeopleSoft database name entered on the signon screen. If an Oracle database contains more than one PeopleSoft database, there must be a TNS service name for each of the PeopleSoft database names, and they should all point to the same Oracle connection descriptor.

The TNS service must also exist in the default SQL*Net domain, because PeopleSoft does not specify any domain in the connect string. In the example in Listing 3-9, an Oracle database contains two PeopleSoft databases, so the TNS service has two names.

Listing 3-9. An Extract from `tnsnames.ora`

```
HCM91, HCM91REP =
  (DESCRIPTION =
    (ADDRESS_LIST =
      (ADDRESS = (PROTOCOL = TCP)(HOST = go-faster-6)(PORT = 1521))
    )
    (CONNECT_DATA =
      (SERVICE_NAME = hcm91)
    )
  )
```

Although not specified in Oracle's documentation, SQL*Net supports the syntax in the preceding example, where more than one service name can be mapped to a single connection descriptor.

Using Direct Shared Memory Connections (UseLocalOracleDB)

When a SQL*Net client process is on the same physical server as the database, it can connect directly to the database via shared memory, without using the Oracle Listener or any network protocols. This should provide better performance and consume less CPU time.

This connection through shared memory is sometimes called an Interprocess Communication (IPC) connection, because on Unix it uses IPC resources and the IPC protocol is specified in the SQL*Net configuration files. In earlier versions of Oracle, the IPC protocol was called the *bequeath* protocol.

If the TNS service name is not appended to the user ID and password in the connect string, SQL*Net makes a shared memory connection. The database instance is specified by the ORACLE_SID environment variable.

If the UseLocalOracleDB option in the application server configuration files is set to 1, as shown in Listing 3-10, the SQL*Net connect string used by PeopleSoft is simply the username and password. PeopleSoft does not append the TNS service name. The tnsnames.ora file is not used in this case.

Listing 3-10. An Extract from psappsrv.cfg

```
[Database Options]
;========================================================================
; Database-specific configuration options
;========================================================================
SybasePacketSize=
UseLocalOracleDB=1
ORACLE_SID=HR88
```

The Process Scheduler (which initiates batch and report processes and is discussed in more detail in Chapter 14) can be similarly configured, in which case it and any COBOL or Application Engine processes that it spawns also make a direct shared-memory connection.

▪ **Note** It has become very rare to find either the application server or Process Scheduler co-located with the database. One very good reason is that Oracle database licensing is usually based on the number of CPUs on the database server. If the database server is also running PeopleSoft middleware, then it is consuming CPU for which you are paying to license the database.

PeopleSoft recommends setting UseLocalOracleDB to 1 for performance reasons. This way, an Oracle Listener is not required in order to make the connection, and therefore the connection to the database should be slightly faster than using an IPC key. However, the improvement is tiny in proportion to the overall response time.

This setting also makes the application server and Process Scheduler sensitive to the value of the ORACLE_SID variable in the environment, although this can also be set in the configuration files (psappsrv.cfg and psprcs.cfg).

Instead, I prefer to keep the UseLocalOracleDB=0 setting and specify an IPC key in the tnsnames.ora file, as shown previously in Listing 3-9, and to use a corresponding entry in the listener.ora file, as shown in Listing 3-11. Then all SQL*Net clients that run on the database server make IPC connections.

Listing 3-11. An Extract from `listener.ora`

```
LISTENER =
  (DESCRIPTION_LIST =
    (DESCRIPTION =
      (ADDRESS = (PROTOCOL = IPC)(KEY = ORA11gR2))
    )
    (DESCRIPTION =
      (ADDRESS = (PROTOCOL = TCP)(HOST = go-faster-6)(PORT = 1522))
    )
  )
```

Occasionally, if a client process connected to the database terminates without disconnecting from the database, especially while waiting for a response from the database, the Oracle shadow process can continue to run. This situation can happen when PSAPPSRV or PSQRYSRV processes crash or exceed the Tuxedo service timeout while waiting for a long-running SQL query to return. A query timeout can also be set in the PeopleSoft operator security profile, after which time the PeopleSoft process running the query terminate. PeopleSoft does not do anything to clean up the database session. Therefore Oracle Terminated Connection Timeout should always be enabled by setting SQLNET.EXPIRE_TIME in the sqlnet.ora file. Although this mechanism is not foolproof, it helps to clean up disconnected shadow processes.

Determining the PeopleSoft Schema

Having connected to Oracle, the first action of the signon process is to determine which database schema contains the PeopleSoft database. The next few lines in the PeopleTools client trace (shown in Listing 3-12) show how the PSDBOWNER table is used to map the database to the schema.

Listing 3-12. An Excerpt from a PeopleTools Client Trace Showing the Mapping of Database to Schema

```
1-4      09.51.33    0.000000 Cur#1.1064.HCM91 RC=0 Dur=0.000000 COM Stmt=SELECT OWNERID FROM
PS.PSDBOWNER WHERE DBNAME=:1
1-5      09.51.33    0.000000 Cur#1.1064.HCM91 RC=0 Dur=0.000000 Bind-1 type=2 length=5
value=HCM91
```

The schema that contains the PeopleSoft database is referred to as the Owner ID. The signon process explicitly references three objects in that schema until it connects directly when the signon process completes successfully. Therefore, SELECT privilege is explicitly granted on those tables during the installation process by the Data Mover script, as shown in Listing 3-13. The installation process itself connects to the schema that will contain the PeopleSoft database, so there is no schema name in the GRANT commands in the script.

Listing 3-13. An Excerpt from the Data Mover Script that Builds a PeopleSoft Database

```
GRANT SELECT ON PSSTATUS TO PEOPLE;
GRANT SELECT ON PSOPRDEFN TO PEOPLE;
GRANT SELECT ON PSACCESSPRFL TO PEOPLE;
```

The PS.PSDBOWNER table allows PeopleSoft to manage multiple PeopleSoft databases in one Oracle database. It contains a row to map each PeopleSoft database name to the Oracle schema that holds it.

It is also possible to give two names to the same PeopleSoft database by adding rows that map to the same OWNERID. There are a few situations where this can be useful, such as these:

- If you are changing the name of a PeopleSoft database, both names can be valid during the transitional period.

- If the production database is copied to a read-only reporting database, you may wish to query that database without making any changes to it.

Either way, for every database name (DBNAME) specified in PS.PSDBOWNER, there must also be a corresponding SQL*Net TNS service in the default SQL*Net domain that maps to the database instance.

■ **Note** If there is no entry in PS.PSDBOWNER matching the TNS connect string, the error pop-up says "Invalid User ID and password for signon." That is actually a catch-all error message for any problem during signon, so don't limit your diagnostic to only investigating the user ID and password.

Checking the PeopleTools Release

The next job is to ensure that the signon process is attempting to connect to a PeopleSoft database that is at the same PeopleTools version as the client. The structure of the PeopleTools tables has always changed between major PeopleTools releases (8.1 to 8.4). From PeopleTools 8.x on, there can now be structural changes between minor releases (for example, from 8.50 to 8.51). There may also be new functionality and therefore new objects or messages that are delivered.

The major and minor release numbers are stored in the database in PSSTATUS.TOOLSREL, as shown in Listing 3-14.

Listing 3-14. An Extract from the PSSTATUS Table

```
OWNERID                 TOOLSREL
----------------------- -------------------------------
TO_CHAR(LASTREFRESHDTTM,'YYYY-MM-DDHH24:MI:SS')
-------------------------------------------------------
TO_CHAR(LASTCHANGEDTTM,'YYYY-MM-DDHH24:MI:SS')
-------------------------------------------------------
SYSADM                  8.51
2011-09-29 13:54:22
2011-09-29 13:54:22
```

The PeopleTools client trace in Listing 3-15 shows the client querying the PeopleTools release from PSSTATUS.

Listing 3-15. An Excerpt from a PeopleTools Client Trace Showing the Client Getting the Version Release Number

```
1-6     09.51.33    0.001000 Cur#1.1064.HCM91 RC=0 Dur=0.000000 COM Stmt=SELECT OWNERID,
TOOLSREL, TO_CHAR(LASTREFRESHDTTM,'YYYY-MM-DD HH24:MI:SS'), TO_CHAR(LASTCHANGEDTTM,'YYYY-MM-DD
HH24:MI:SS') FROM SYSADM.PSSTATUS
1-7     09.51.33    0.001000 Cur#1.1064.HCM91 RC=0 Dur=0.001000 COM Stmt=SELECT DBID FROM
SYSADM.PSSTATUS
```

The column DBID was added to PSSTATUS in PeopleTools 8.46. I don't know why Oracle created a second query to obtain this value rather that just add it to the first.

One step in the process of upgrading PeopleTools from one version to another is to run a "rel" script supplied by PeopleSoft. This script (see Listing 3-16) rebuilds the PeopleTools tables whose structures have changed and also updates the PeopleTools version number in the column TOOLSREL.

Listing 3-16. An Extract from rel850.sql

```
UPDATE PSSTATUS SET TOOLSREL='8.51',
                    LASTREFRESHDTTM = SYSDATE
;
```

This test of the PeopleTools release is not sensitive to the patch level of PeopleTools. Any patch of release 8.50 (for example, 8.50.09) successfully connects to the database.[1] PeopleSoft does not change the structure of PeopleTools in patch releases.

If the version numbers do not match during the signon process, an error dialog box appears on the client PC (see Figure 3-4). It indicates either that the installation process has not been completed correctly or that the wrong executables are being used.

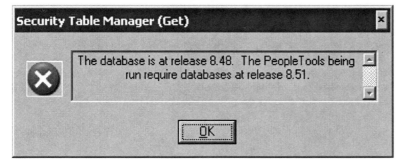

Figure 3-4. PeopleTools version-mismatch error message

---

[1]The version of the PIA servlet must exactly match that of the Application Server, or the connection will fail. An 8.50.09 servlet cannot connect to an 8.50.08 application server. The same applies to Windows client programs, such as the Application Designer or nVision, in three-tier mode.

Within the application server, the PeopleTools version test is performed by each PeopleSoft application server process as it starts. The exception to this is the PSWATCHSRV server process that was introduced in PeopleTools 8.43, which detects and kills application server processes that have become zombies (see Chapter 11 for details). This process does not connect to the database at all.

As the application server processes start, they write messages to APPSRV.LOG, an example of which is shown in Listing 3-17.

Listing 3-17. An Extract from APPSRV_<mmdd>.LOG

```
PSAPPSRV.6812 (0) [10/15/11 10:12:28](0) PeopleTools Release 8.51 (WinX86) starting. Tuxedo
server is APPSRV(99)/2
PSAPPSRV.6812 (0) [10/15/11 10:12:28](1) GenMessageBox(0, 0, M): Security Table Manager (Get):
The database is at release 8.48.  The PeopleTools being run require databases at release 8.51.
PSAPPSRV.6812 (0) [10/15/11 10:12:28](0) Server failed to start
```

Checking the Operator Password

The next stage in the signon process is to retrieve the PeopleSoft user's encrypted password stored on the operator definition table PSOPRDEFN, as shown in the next part of the trace file in Listing 3-18; the data retrieved is shown in Listing 3-19.

Listing 3-18. An Excerpt from a PeopleTools Client Trace Showing the Checking of the Operator Password

```
1-8     09.51.33    0.000000 Cur#1.1064.HCM91 RC=0 Dur=0.000000 COM Stmt=SELECT VERSION,
OPERPSWD, ENCRYPTED, SYMBOLICID, ACCTLOCK FROM SYSADM.PSOPRDEFN WHERE OPRID = :1
1-9     09.51.33    0.000000 Cur#1.1064.HCM91 RC=0 Dur=0.000000 Bind-1 type=2 length=2
value=PS
```

Listing 3-19. An Encrypted Operator Password on PSOPRDEFN

VERSION	OPERPSWD	ENCRYPTED	SYMBOLICID	ACCTLOCK
165	5iCGeTd2aRl/N+E3E8ZUz72qEe4=	1	SYSADM1	0

The query in Listing 3-18 shows that PeopleTools verifies the password entered by the operator or provided in the configuration file against the database.

Obtaining the Access Password

The operator's access profile, read from PSOPRDEFN.SYMBOLICID in the previous step, is used to look up the ACCESSID and ACCESSPSWD in PSACCESSPRFL, as shown in Listing 3-20.

Listing 3-20. An Excerpt from a PeopleTools Client Trace Showing the Access Profile Being Looked Up

```
1-10    09.51.33    0.001000 Cur#1.1064.HCM91 RC=0 Dur=0.000000 COM Stmt=SELECT ACCESSID,
ACCESSPSWD, ENCRYPTED FROM SYSADM.PSACCESSPRFL WHERE SYMBOLICID = :1
1-11    09.51.33    0.000000 Cur#1.1064.HCM91 RC=0 Dur=0.000000 Bind-1 type=2 length=7
value=SYSADM1
```

The PSACCESSPRFL table existed in PeopleTools 7.5, but it was not checked during the signon process because the encrypted access password was also on PSOPRDEFN. In PeopleTools 8, the access password exists only on PSACCESSPRFL, as shown in Listing 3-21.

Listing 3-21. Access Profile

```
ACCESSID                ACCESSPSWD              ENCRYPTED
--------------------    --------------------    ----------
sBzLcYlPrag=            sBzLcYlPrag=                     1
```

■ **Note** In this example, I am using the default Access ID SYSADM, whose password is also SYSADM. In general, it is not a good idea to have the same value for ACCESSID and ACCESSPSWD because their encrypted values are also the same.

Reconnecting as Access ID

Having determined the Access ID schema and its password in the previous step, the process disconnects from the database and reconnects to the schema specified by the Access ID, which is SYSADM in Listing 3-22.

Listing 3-22. An Excerpt from a PeopleTools Client Trace Showing the Connection to the Schema Specified by Access ID

```
1-12     09.51.33    0.001000 Cur#1.1064.HCM91 RC=0 Dur=0.000000 Disconnect
1-13     09.51.33    0.002000 Cur#0.1064.notSamTran RC=0 Dur=0.002000 Destroy Connection
Handle=057E7BC8
1-14     09.51.35    2.267000 Cur#0.1064.HCM91 RC=0 Dur=2.267000 Create Connection
Info=Primary/HCM91/SYSADM/ Handle=057E7BC8
1-15     09.51.35    0.003000 Cur#1.1064.notSamTran RC=0 Dur=0.002000 Open Cursor
Handle=057E7BC8
1-16     09.51.36    0.003000 Cur#1.1064.HCM91 RC=0 Dur=0.000000 CEX Stmt=select
pt_tde_encrypt_alg from psoptions
1-17     09.51.36    0.001000 TDE Encryption Algorithm: ''
1-18     09.51.36    0.000000 Cur#1.1064.HCM91 RC=0 Dur=0.000000 COM Stmt=SELECT
TO_CHAR(SYSTIMESTAMP,'YYYY-MM-DD-HH24.MI.SS.FF') FROM PSCLOCK
```

The application performs many more checks to determine whether the operator is allowed to connect, and to determine how much they are permitted do in either the application or the design tools; but from here on, everything is done with the process connected to the schema that contains the PeopleSoft database.

This can make it difficult to identify which operator is responsible for which piece of SQL, or to use Oracle's Resource Manager or resource profiles to set different resource-usage thresholds for different classes of users. Since PeopleTools 7.53, PeopleSoft has used DBMS_APPLICATION_INFO to help identify operators' sessions (see Chapter 9 for more details).

■ **Note** The name of the Access ID schema does not come from PS.PSDBOWNER.OWNERID, but from PSACCESSPRFL.ACCESS_ID, although they are usually the same. The following sections show what happens when these tables have different values.

Using PeopleSoft Access Profiles and Oracle Resource Profiles

So far, I have shown how PeopleSoft processes all connect to the same Access ID. However, PeopleSoft provided a way to make its processes connect to the same PeopleSoft database via a different Oracle user. One of the stated reasons for this feature was to permit the use of Oracle Database Resource Manager.

Having all user processes connected to the database as the same database user effectively prevented the use of Oracle's Resource Manager up to Oracle 9i. In that version, it was only possible to automatically allocate a resource plan to a user; otherwise, commands would have had to be issued by the application. Having the application issue those commands was not something PeopleSoft wanted to do.

However, from Oracle 10g onward, Consumer Groups can be mapped to sessions not only by user but also by service name, operating system user, client program name, client machine name, module, and action. This is enough to identify specific application servers or just the server processes that handle ad hoc queries. Module and Action are automatically populated from PeopleTools 8.50, so different resource profiles can even be applied for specific parts of the online application or specific batch processes. This is much easier to configure and maintain than creating the additional schema and all of the grants required to make the addition Access Profile work. Nonetheless, Access Profiles still exist in PeopleTools and have some uses I discuss in the next section after I have explained how they work.

At the beginning of the signon processing, the schema containing the PeopleSoft database is read from the column OWNERID on the table PS.PSDBOWNER. The signon process references PSSTATUS, PSOPRDEFN, and PSACCESSPRFL from that schema. But then, at the end, it connects to the schema specified in ACCESSID on the PSACCESSPRFL table.

During the default PeopleSoft installation process, a Data Mover script imports all the tables into the database and populates PS.PSDBOWNER. It then updates the single row on PSACCESSPRFL with a SYMBOLICID and the name and password of the PeopleSoft schema, as shown in Listing 3-23. All PeopleSoft operators are assigned to that SYMBOLICID. Hence, the value of ACCESSID on PSACCESSPRFL is the same as OWNERID on PS.PSDBOWNER, and all PeopleSoft processes connect to that schema, no matter which operator ID they use.

Listing 3-23. An Excerpt from the Data Mover Script that Builds a PeopleSoft Database

```
UPDATE PSOPRDEFN SET SYMBOLICID = 'SYSADM1'
, OPERPSWD = OPRID, ENCRYPTED = 0;
UPDATE PSACCESSPRFL SET ACCESSID = 'SYSADM'
, SYMBOLICID = 'SYSADM1', ACCESSPSWD = 'SYSADM'
, VERSION = 0, ENCRYPTED = 0;
```

However, it is possible to create another SYMBOLICID in Application Designer, as shown in Figure 3-5. You have to create the corresponding database user yourself, though. Application Designer will not do it for you.

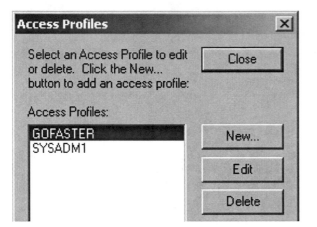

Figure 3-5. Creating another symbolic ID in Application Designer

The result is an additional row on PSACCESSPRFL, shown in Listing 3-24. The symbolic ID is specified as part of the user profile, as shown in Figure 3-6. Now, when a PeopleSoft process signs in as operator PS, it ultimately connects to the database as database user GOFASTER.

Listing 3-24. Two Access Profiles in the PSACCESSPRFL Table

```
SYMBOLICID    VERSION ACCESSID              ACCESSPSWD            ENCRYPTED
----------  ---------- --------------------  --------------------  ----------
SYSADM1            1 sBzLcYlPrag=          sBzLcYlPrag=                   1
GOFASTER           8 pArecZ5W6Po=          pArecZ5W6Po=                   1
```

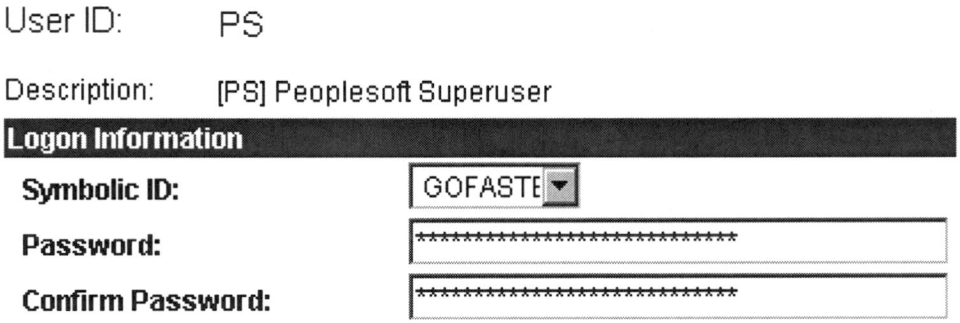

User ID: PS

Description: [PS] Peoplesoft Superuser

Logon Information

Symbolic ID: GOFASTE▼

Password: ****************************

Confirm Password: ****************************

Figure 3-6. Definiton of a user profile in PIA

At this point, though, the schema GOFASTER is empty. There is only a single PeopleSoft database in the Oracle database, and it is in the SYSADM schema. An on-connect trigger changes the current schema to SYSADM for users connecting as GOFASTER (see Listing 3-25).

Listing 3-25. connect.sql, an On-connect Trigger to set CURRENT_SCHEMA

```
CREATE OR REPLACE TRIGGER gofaster.current_schema_sysadm
AFTER LOGON ON gofaster.schema
BEGIN
    EXECUTE IMMEDIATE 'ALTER SESSION SET CURRENT_SCHEMA = SYSADM';
    EXCEPTION WHEN OTHERS THEN NULL;
END;
/
```

Database sessions connecting as GOFASTER now reference objects in the SYSADM schema by default. All privileges on all tables in SYSADM also have to be granted to GOFASTER, so that PeopleSoft processes connecting to GOFASTER will execute properly.

Now there is a way to make a particular PeopleSoft operator connect to the database as a particular database user. As an example, I set up an application server that connects with operator PSAPPS, whose SYMBOLICID is SYSADM1, which connects to the database as user SYSADM. I also set up a Process Scheduler that connects with operator PS, whose SYMBOLICID is GOFASTER, which connects to the database as user SYSADM.

This was verified by querying V$SESSION (see Listing 3-26). This proves that it is the Access ID that determines the schema to which PeopleSoft connects.

Listing 3-26. PeopleSoft Database Sessions

```
SELECT sid, program, username FROM v$session;

  SID PROGRAM              USERNAME
----- -------------------- ------------------
    7 PSPPMSRV.exe         SYSADM
    8 PSSAMSRV.exe         SYSADM
    9 PSMONITORSRV.exe     SYSADM
   11 PSAPPSRV.exe         SYSADM
   12 PSMSTPRC.exe         GOFASTER
   13 PSDSTSRV.exe         GOFASTER
   14 PSAESRV.exe          GOFASTER
   15 PSAESRV.exe          GOFASTER
   16 PSMONITORSRV.exe     GOFASTER
   18 PSPRCSRV.exe         GOFASTER
```

Thus, it is possible to have different Oracle users in operation within your PeopleSoft application, but there are some additional considerations:

- This technique cannot be used for the Application Designer and Data Mover tools because they reference USER data-dictionary views, such as USER_TABLES, to determine what database objects exist before creating them. This technique would cause them to do this while signed into a user that does not own the tables.

- In PeopleTools 8, only Query or nVision Windows clients make two-tier runtime connections to the database. Otherwise, all connections are via the application server or Process Scheduler. Using the delivered configuration files, you can only set the operator ID for the whole of a particular application server or Process Scheduler, not just for some of the server processes. This means all of the operators that connect via an application server connect to the Access ID of the SYMBOLICID of the operator ID used to start the application server, and not the Access ID of their own SYMBOLICID.

- This technique should not be used to switch between different PeopleSoft databases in the same Oracle database (which you should not be creating anyway), because doing so would only lead to confusion.

SPECIFYING AN ALTERNATIVE CONFIGURATION FILE FOR SOME APPLICATION SERVER PROCESSES

It is possible to make some application server process use a different configuration file (psappsrv.cfg). For example, the PSQRYSRV process can connect with a different database name, and hence a different TNS service, so that queries can be directed to particular instances of a RAC cluster, or even against a different database. A different PeopleSoft user can be specified that has a different SYMBOLICID so the process connects to the database as a different user and uses a different Oracle Resource Profile.

A shell script can be created in the same directory as the rest of the domain configuration files that sets the environment variable PS_SERVER_CFG to the name of the alternative configuration file and then calls the application server executable. However, this technique can only be implemented on Unix because Tuxedo cannot call a Windows batch file:

```
export PS_SERVER_CFG=psappsrv2.cfg
${PS_HOME}/bin/PSQRYSRV $*
```

I called my shell script GFCQRYSRV and then referenced it in the Tuxedo template:

```
{QUERYSRV}
GFCQRYSRV        SRVGRP=APPSRV
                 SRVID=70
                 MIN={$PSQRYSRV\Min Instances}
                 MAX={$PSQRYSRV\Max Instances}
                 RQADDR="QRYQ"
                 REPLYQ=Y
                 CLOPT="{$PSQRYSRV\Spawn Server} -sICQuery -sSqlQuery:SqlRequest -- -C
{CFGFILE} -D {$Domain Settings\Domain ID} -S PSQRYSRV"
{QUERYSRV}
```

From PeopleTools 8.51, the second connection provided to support Active Data Guard can be used to achieve the same effect for specific read-only components and batch processes, rather than all the server process that serve a particular queue.

PeopleSoft Support for Oracle Active Data Guard

Data Guard is an Oracle database mechanism to maintain either a physical or logical standby copy of a database. A physical copy is maintained by applying redo from the primary database to a standby that is in recovery mode. A logical copy is maintained by applying SQL mined from the redo log. A physical standby database can be opened in read-only mode and put back into recovery mode.

Active Data Guard is a new and separately licensed feature in Oracle 11g. The physical standby database is open for read-only access while redo is applied. Oracle has added support for this feature to PeopleTools 8.51. Application servers and Process Schedulers can be configured to make a second database connection to the read-only standby database (as shown in Listing 3-27)..An additional access profile is part of the implementation.

Listing 3-27. PeopleTools 8.51 Database Signon Section of psappsrv.cfg

```
[Startup]
;========================================================================
; Database Signon settings
;========================================================================
DBName=HCM91
DBType=ORACLE
UserId=PS
UserPswd=PS
ConnectId=people
ConnectPswd=peop1e
ServerName=
StandbyDBName=HCM91REP
StandbyDBType=ORACLE
StandbyUserId=PSREP
StandbyUserPswd=PSREP
```

This second connection connects to a second schema in the database using a different access profile. This second schema contains synonyms that point back to the original tables and views. The second schema is created in the primary database. The standby database is a physical copy, so the second schema appears in the standby database. All of the application server and Process Scheduler server processes maintain an additional connection to the standby database.

Online components can be specified as read-only, and then the application server directs database traffic for those components to the second database connection. Batch processes marked as read-only are connected to the standby database at startup. A few tables are updated by otherwise read-only batch-report processes, and these tables have synonyms in the second schema that point back across a database link to the table in the primary database. This still works properly should the standby become the primary, because the destination of the database link also fails over.

If you don't have Active Data Guard but maintain a set of reporting tables with a different technology, in either a different database or a different schema, then it is possible to use this feature to direct specific processes or components to run against those tables.[2]

---

[2]"PeopleTools 8.51 PeopleBook: Data Management" contains more information (see http://download.oracle.com/docs/cd/E18083_01/pt851pbr0/eng/psbooks/tadm/htm/tadm01.htm).

59

Connecting Third-Party Applications

PeopleSoft also supplies reporting and batch functionality via two third-party reporting packages (Crystal Reports and SQR), as well as through its own COBOL and Application Engine programs.

Crystal Reports

The version of Crystal Reports shipped with PeopleSoft has been specially modified to use PeopleSoft signon security. It is closely bound to the PeopleSoft Query tool and connects via the PeopleSoft ODBC driver. This provides logon and row-level security. The ODBC driver presents the queries, which are defined through the application, as stored procedures.

SQR Reports

SQR, originally from SQRIBE, but now owned by Oracle, simply connects directly to the PeopleSoft schema (usually SYSADM) just like SQL*Plus or any other two-tier client. SQR is run via a PeopleTools process named pssqr. This process is a wrapper for SQR that performs the same security checks as other PeopleTools processes, and it will also pass other parameters to SQR to control report formatting.

In PeopleTools 7.x, the Process Scheduler supplied the user ID and password directly to SQR, via a short-lived file that could only be read by the Unix user who owned the Process Scheduler process.

Changing Database Passwords

It is good practice on any system to regularly change passwords. However, as the description of the PeopleSoft signon processing shows, encrypted passwords are stored by PeopleTools in ordinary tables. If these values are not synchronized with actual schema passwords, your application will fail to connect to the database.

Connect ID Password

Connect ID passwords are stored in two places:

- *Windows registry:* The password can be set and encrypted with the PeopleSoft configuration manager. The registry must be set on every PC that makes a two-tier connection to the database.

- *Application server and Process Scheduler configuration files:* The password can be set by editing the configuration files directly, but only the interactive configuration dialog box encrypts the Connect password (see Chapter 12).

The Connect ID is not stored in the database. The main challenge of changing the Connect ID password is to synchronize the PeopleSoft configuration change to the change of the database password. Realistically, it requires system downtime. However, bear in mind that it is a low-security account.

Owner ID Password

In PeopleTools 8, the password to the Owner ID schema should be changed with the CHANGE_ACCESS_PASSWORD command in Data Mover, as shown in Listing 3-28.

Listing 3-28. Data Mover Command to Change Access Password

```
CHANGE_ACCESS_PASSWORD <SymbolicID> <newAccessPswd>
```

This updates both the schema password and the encrypted value on PSACCESSPRFL.

If for some reason you cannot set the password in Data Mover, it is also possible to set the schema password and the Access ID and password on PSACCESSPRFL to the unencrypted values as shown in Listing 3-29.

Listing 3-29. SQL to Manually Set Access ID and Password

```
ALTER USER sysadm IDENTIFIED BY sysadm
/
UPDATE psaccessprfl
SET    accessid = 'SYSADM'
,      accesspswd = 'SYSADM'
,      encrypted = 0
,      version = 0
WHERE  symbolicid = 'SYSADM1'
/
```

The Access ID password on the profile must then be encrypted with the `encrypt_password` command in Data Mover. Otherwise, PeopleSoft processes cannot connect to the database:

```
encrypt_password *;
```

Summary

PeopleSoft and Oracle use the term *database* differently. A PeopleSoft database exists in a schema within an Oracle database. That schema has certain privileges that permit PeopleSoft to function.

The signon processing securely authenticates an operator before permitting them to connect to the PeopleSoft database, but without using any database-specific security features and without revealing database passwords to the user.

CHAPTER 4

PeopleSoft Database Structure: A Tale of Two Data Dictionaries

One of the ways that PeopleSoft is able to deliver the same application to any platform is by having its own data dictionary. Different database platforms structure their data dictionaries differently, and platform independence is an overriding principle in PeopleSoft. Except when building DDL scripts and executing audit reports, PeopleTools never interrogates the database's data dictionary, but instead relies on its own. PeopleTools is also a development environment, so it is necessary to have a way of defining a table before it is actually created in the database—the PeopleSoft data dictionary serves this function.

As introduced briefly in Chapter 1, a PeopleSoft database on any platform is usually described as having the following three sections, which are shown in Figure 4-1:

- The database data dictionary, which is sometimes referred to as the data dictionary, describes all the objects in the database. The structure of the database's data dictionary varies from platform to platform, but the concept is common to all. In Oracle, the data dictionary is exposed through the underlying fixed objects (tab$, col$, and so on) and is visible in a more user-friendly format through views (such as DBA_TABLES and DBA_TAB_COLUMNS)

- The PeopleTools tables contain most of the source code for the PeopleSoft application. This includes certain tables that hold information about the structure of all the PeopleTools and application tables and their indexes. This subset is PeopleSoft's data dictionary.

- Application tables contain the users' data. The PeopleTools tables and the application tables all exist in the same database schema.

Figure 4-1. The three sections of a PeopleSoft database

This chapter discusses the function and interrelationship of the Oracle and PeopleSoft dictionaries, focusing on how the PeopleTools tables specify the data model to PeopleSoft. Chapter 5 looks at how indexes are defined, and Chapter 6 explains how Application Designer defines physical storage parameters and then combines all this information to generate the SQL to create the tables and indexes.

Application and PeopleTools Tables

Application and PeopleTools tables are mixed up together in the same database schema. DBAs and developers often want to know which is which. In general, PeopleTools record names begin with "PS", and the SQLTABLENAME is explicitly set in PSRECDEFN to be the same as the record name. PeopleTools records can be of any type.

Application tables generally do not have their names overridden; the record name does not begin with "PS", and so the table name is the record name prefixed with "PS_". However, some tables do not follow this standard, and some tables are not quite PeopleTools tables and not quite application tables either. Table 4-1 shows some examples of different table names.

Table 4-1. Application and PeopleTools Tables

Record Name	Table Name	Comment
JOB	PS_JOB	Typical application data table.
JOB_VW	PS_JOB_VW	Typical application view.
PSRECDEFN	PSRECDEFN	Typical PeopleTools table.
PSRECFLDKEYSVW	PSRECFLDKEYSVW	Typical PeopleTools views.

PRCSDEFN	PS_PRCSDEFN	This is actually a PeopleTools table. It defines the processes that can be run on the Process Scheduler. It is one of seven delivered records where the SQLTABLENAME is explicitly set to the name the table would have been given anyway.
XLATTABLE_VW	XLATTABLE_VW	This view is also a PeopleTools object, but the record name does not start with PS. It is a view of PSXLATITEM and PSXLATDEFN, which hold translate values used in drop-down lists in the PIA.

The PeopleSoft Definition Security utility contains a PeopleTools group that contains a list of all types PeopleTools objects. As delivered, these objects cannot be altered in Application Designer because the PeopleTools group is marked as read-only in all Permission Lists. The security group is stored in the PeopleTools table PSOBJGROUP. The list of PeopleTools records defined in Definition Security can be obtained with the following query:

```
SELECT r.recname, r.rectype, r.objectownerid
FROM    psrecdefn r
,       psobjgroup o
WHERE   o.objgroupid = 'PEOPLETOOLS'
AND     o.enttype = 'R'
AND     o.entname = r.recname
```

Many PeopleTools tables have the column OBJECTOWNERID. The value PPT indicates that it is a PeopleTools object. So you can use this second query to identify a PeopleTools object:

```
SELECT r.recname, r.rectype, r.objectownerid
FROM    psrecdefn r
WHERE   r.objectownerid = 'PPT'
```

All of the tables in the PeopleTools object group have an Owner ID of PeopleTools. However, some tables with an Owner ID of PeopleTools that are not part of the PeopleTools object group including PeopleTools.

Nonetheless, I consider the PeopleTools object group, rather than the object Owner ID, to be the definitive list of PeopleTools tables because it controls the behavior of Application Designer.

Two Data Dictionaries

This section examines some of the PeopleTools tables that correspond to the Oracle data dictionary. It is useful for the both DBAs and developers to be familiar with these tables. While the Oracle data dictionary tells you what actually exists in the database, the PeopleSoft data dictionary tells you what should be there. Table 4-2 lists the principal PeopleTools tables that correspond to the Oracle data dictionary.

Table 4-2. Corresponding PeopleTools and Oracle Data Dictionary Tables

Table Description	Oracle Data Dictionary View	PeopleTools Table (version 7.x or earlier)	PeopleTools Table (from version 8)
1 row per table or view	DBA_TABLES DBA_VIEWS	PSRECDEFN	PSRECDEFN and PSRECTBLSPC
1 row per column	DBA_TAB_COLUMNS	PSRECFIELD	PSRECFIELDDB and PSRECFIELD
1 row per distinct column name	n/a	PSDBFIELD	
1 row per view	DBA_VIEWS	PSVIEWTEXT	PSSQLDEFN and PSSQLTEXTDEFN
1 row per index	DBA_INDEXES	PSINDEXDEFN	
1 row per index column	DBA_IND_COLUMNS	PSKEYDEFN	
1 row per user	DBA_USERS	PSOPRDEFN	

PeopleSoft does not create or use database privileges, synonyms, or referential constraints. All the PeopleTools and application tables are in the same database schema. All object- and row-level security issues are handled in the application. Only UNIQUE and NOT NULL constraints are enforced by the database. All other validation is handled by the application.

Although there is good PeopleSoft documentation and training on how to develop and customize a PeopleSoft application, PeopleSoft does not officially explain the meaning and use of the PeopleTools tables.[1] Their structure and meaning can change from release to release, as it has in the past. However, by investigating the contents of the PeopleTools tables, by trying to relate settings in Application Designer to values on the PeopleTools tables, and by investigating the PeopleTools recursive SQL, it is possible to discover some of the meaning of these tables.

■ **Caution** One of the reasons PeopleSoft did not provide detailed documentation for the PeopleTools tables is to discourage people from updating them directly. While these tables are a valuable source of information about a PeopleSoft system, you are cautioned not to alter them yourself. If you do, you are on your own.

---

[1] However, see www.go-faster.co.uk/peopletools

The following sections describe these PeopleTools tables in more detail. Only some of the columns on these tables correspond to columns in the Oracle data dictionary views. The other columns control the behavior of the PeopleSoft application; they are shown for completeness but are not described in this chapter. The primary key columns of the PeopleTools tables are indicated with a key icon.

PSRECDEFN: Record Definition

This table contains one row for each PeopleSoft record, and it is described in Table 4-4. One of the attributes of a record set in Application Designer (see Figure 4-2) is the record type. A record can correspond to a table or view, depending on the record type, as set out in Table 4-3, although some record types do not correspond to any database object.

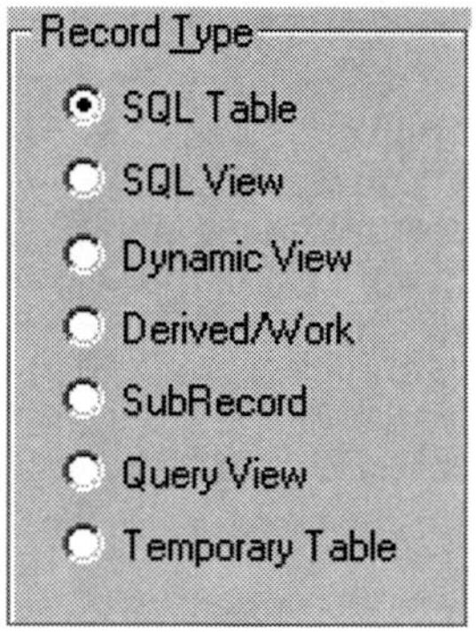

Figure 4-2. Record types in Application Designer

Table 4-3. Record Types in PeopleTools

Record Type	Type Description	Comment
0	SQL table	The record is built as a table, and there is a corresponding row on DBA_TABLES.
1	SQL view	The record is built as a view, and there is a corresponding row on DBA_VIEWS.
2	Derived/Work	This provides working storage in the component. It does not correspond to any database object.
3	Subrecord	This is a group of columns or other subrecords that is referenced by other records. It does not correspond to a database object.
4		Not used.

Record Type	Type Description	Comment
5	Dynamic view	This does not correspond to any database object. A database view is a query executed by the database; this is a query executed by PeopleTools to populate a page.
6	Query view	The record is also built as a database view. The difference between this and record type 2 is that the query is defined via the PeopleTools Query utility, rather than with free-format text in Application Designer.
7	Temporary Table	This record type is new in PeopleTools 8. One temporary table record can correspond to a number of database tables. They are used by the Application Engine to temporarily hold data. If multiple instances of the same Application Engine process execute simultaneously, each instance can use a different temporary table. The number of instances of the table is defined both globally and on the Application Engine program. If, for example, there are 10 instances of record XXX, then there are 11 tables, PS_XXX, PS_XXX_1, through PS_XXX_10.

The PSRECDEFN table contains one row per PeopleTools record.

Table 4-4. *Records vs. Tables and Views*

PeopleTools PSRECDEFN	Oracle DBA_TABLES	Description of PeopleTools Column
☞RECNAME		Unique name of a record in PeopleSoft (see SQLTABLENAME).
FIELDCOUNT		Number of fields on a record before expanding any subrecords; this does not therefore equate to the number of columns on a table.
INDEXCOUNT		Number of keys on a record, including those implied by the PeopleTools record key definition. Note that views can also have PeopleTools keys, because PeopleSoft queries a record by its primary key columns, although it is not possible to build an index on a view.
DDLCOUNT		Number of DDL override parameters specified.
VERSION		Internal PeopleTools version for controlling caching of object.

PeopleTools PSRECDEFN	Oracle DBA_TABLES	Description of PeopleTools Column
AUDITRECNAME		Name of an audit record. The PIA writes audit information about this record to the audit record.
RECUSE		One of the following audit options: 1 = Add 2 = Change 4 = Delete 8 = Selective
RECTYPE		See Table 4-3.
SETCNTRLFLD		Multi-company row-level security feature.
RELLANGRECNAME		Related language record that contains translated values.
OPTDELRECNAME		Optimization delete record (new in PeopleTools 8.4).
RECDESCR		Short description of the record.
PARENTRECNAME		Name of the parent record for use in Query utility.
QRYSECRECNAME		Name of the query security record.
DDLSPACENAME	TABLESPACE_NAME	In PeopleTools 8.1, this column specifies the tablespace in which the table is to be built. In PeopleTools 8.4, the tablespace is stored on PSRECTBLSPC instead (see Chapter 6), and this column has been dropped.

SQLTABLENAME	TABLE_NAME or VIEW_NAME	Name of any table or view that is built in the database. If this column is blank, the table name is "PS_" followed by the RECNAME.
		`DBA_TABLES.TABLE_NAME`
		`= DECODE(PSRECDEFN.SQLTABLENAME`
		`,' ','PS_'||PSRECDEFN.RECNAME`
		`,PSRECDEFN.SQLTABLENAME)`

BUILDSEQNO		Controls the order in which objects are built by Application Designer. For instance, a table must be built before a view that references it, so the view has a higher build sequence number.

PeopleTools PSRECDEFN	Oracle DBA_TABLES	Description of PeopleTools Column
OPTTRIGFLAG		Set to Y if a trigger is to be built to maintain the system ID field (new in PeopleTools 8.4).
OBJECTOWNERID		Short code indicating the functional area that owns the record. There are more than 250 codes, and the translations are on PSXLATITEM. For example: PPT: PeopleTools HCR: HR Core Objects HG: Global Payroll Core Application
LASTUPDDTTM		Timestamp of the last update in Application Designer.
LASTUPDOPRID		Operator (developer) who last updated this record.
SYSTEMIDFIELDNAME		Field on the record to be updated by a database trigger with a sequence number obtained from record PSSYSTEMID (new in PeopleTools 8.4).
TIMESTAMPFIELD-NAME		Field on the record to be updated by a database trigger with a timestamp (new in PeopleTools 8.4).
AUXFLAGMASK		Auxiliary flag mask (new in PeopleTools 8.4).
DESCRLONG		Long description of the record.

PSRECFIELD: Record Field Definition

This table contains one row for each field, or subrecord, in each record. In PeopleSoft, a *subrecord* is a group of fields or other subrecords. For example, Figure 4-3 shows the NAMES record from Human Capital Management (HCM). It includes a subrecord called NAMEGBL_SBR.

In PeopleSoft, a subrecord defines a group of fields. It is used in many records, or even in other subrecords, so that the same group of fields is included in each record. For example, NAMEGBL_SBR contains all the fields required to hold a name.

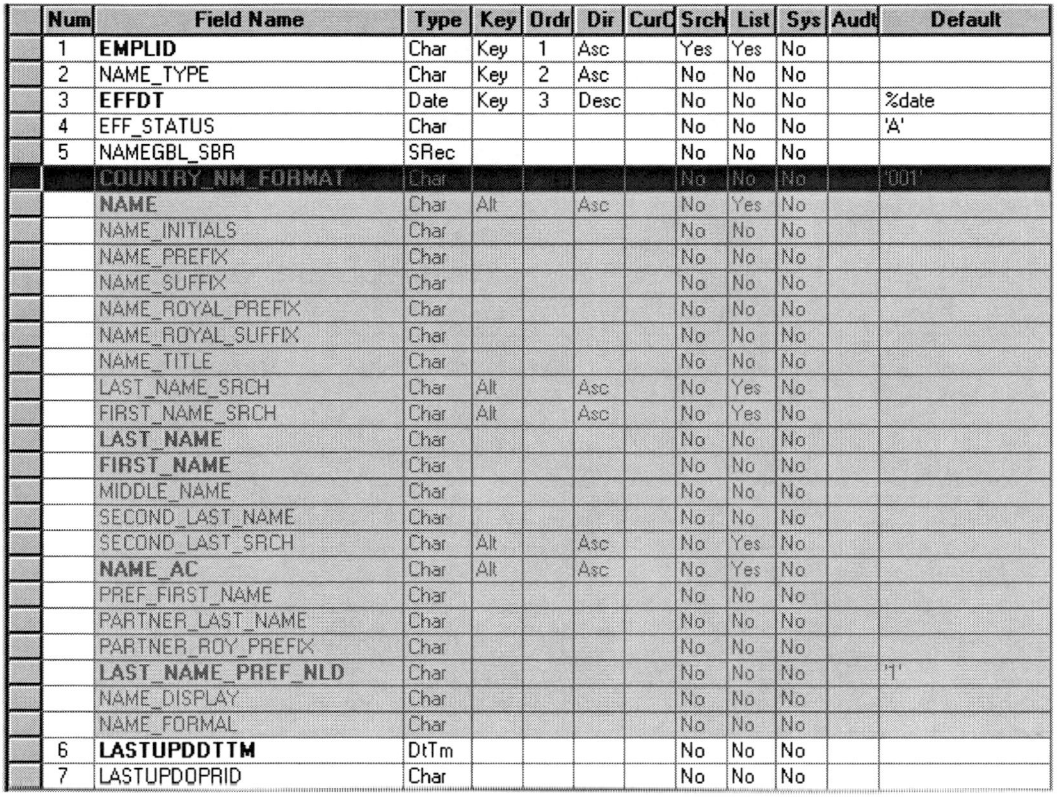

Num	Field Name	Type	Key	Ordr	Dir	CurC	Srch	List	Sys	Audt	Default
1	EMPLID	Char	Key	1	Asc		Yes	Yes	No		
2	NAME_TYPE	Char	Key	2	Asc		No	No	No		
3	EFFDT	Date	Key	3	Desc		No	No	No		%date
4	EFF_STATUS	Char					No	No	No		'A'
5	NAMEGBL_SBR	SRec					No	No	No		
	COUNTRY_NM_FORMAT	Char					No	No	No		'001'
	NAME	Char	Alt		Asc		No	Yes	No		
	NAME_INITIALS	Char					No	No	No		
	NAME_PREFIX	Char					No	No	No		
	NAME_SUFFIX	Char					No	No	No		
	NAME_ROYAL_PREFIX	Char					No	No	No		
	NAME_ROYAL_SUFFIX	Char					No	No	No		
	NAME_TITLE	Char					No	No	No		
	LAST_NAME_SRCH	Char	Alt		Asc		No	Yes	No		
	FIRST_NAME_SRCH	Char	Alt		Asc		No	Yes	No		
	LAST_NAME	Char					No	No	No		
	FIRST_NAME	Char					No	No	No		
	MIDDLE_NAME	Char					No	No	No		
	SECOND_LAST_NAME	Char					No	No	No		
	SECOND_LAST_SRCH	Char	Alt		Asc		No	Yes	No		
	NAME_AC	Char	Alt		Asc		No	Yes	No		
	PREF_FIRST_NAME	Char					No	No	No		
	PARTNER_LAST_NAME	Char					No	No	No		
	PARTNER_ROY_PREFIX	Char					No	No	No		
	LAST_NAME_PREF_NLD	Char					No	No	No		'1'
	NAME_DISPLAY	Char					No	No	No		
	NAME_FORMAL	Char					No	No	No		
6	LASTUPDDTTM	DtTm					No	No	No		
7	LASTUPDOPRID	Char					No	No	No		

Figure 4-3. *The NAMES record with expanded subrecord*

Where a PeopleSoft record corresponds to a table or view in the database, each field in the record corresponds to a column in that object, as shown in Table 4-5.

Table 4-5. *Fields vs. Columns*

PeopleTools PSRECFIELD	Oracle DBA_TAB_COLUMNS	Description of PeopleTools Column
☞RECNAME	TABLE_NAME	Not an exact match (see PSRECDEFN.SQLTABLENAME).
☞FIELDNAME	COLUMN_NAME	Column or subrecord name.
FIELDNUM	COLUMN_ID	Controls order of fields in the record or subrecord.
DEFRECNAME		Default value from DEFFIELDNAME on the record DEFRECNAME.

71

PeopleTools PSRECFIELD	Oracle DBA_TAB_COLUMNS	Description of PeopleTools Column
DEFFIELDNAME		Default value from DEFFIELDNAME on the record DEFRECNAME.
CURCTLFIELDNAME		
EDITTABLE		Prompt table: a lookup table to provide a list of values and to validate entry.
USEEDIT		See Table 4-6; contains 0 if the column is a subrecord.
USEEDIT2		New in PeopleTools 8.4.
SUBRECORD		Y/N: Is this column is a subrecord?
SUBRECORDVER		
SETCNTRLFLD		Tree Structure Node User Key Field Name
DEFGUICONTROL		
LABEL_ID		LABEL_ID identifies uniqueness of DB Field Labels.
LASTUPDDTTM		Timestamp of the last update in Application Designer.
LASTUPDOPRID		Operator (developer) who last updated this record.
TIMEZONEUSE		
TIMEZONEFIELDNAME		
RELTMDTFIELDNAME		
CURRCTLUSE		

The USEEDIT Field

The USEEDIT field on PSRECFIELD is an integer value. When converted to a binary number, each digit defines whether a certain attribute in PeopleTools is enabled for the field. Table 4-6 describes the meanings of these bits.

Table 4-6. USEEDIT Bit Values

Bit Number	USEEDIT Bit Value	Set (Not Set) Value	Comment
0	1	Key value	This column is a part of the PeopleSoft key index (PS_<recname>).
1	2	Duplicate (unique) key	The PeopleSoft key index is NONUNIQUE if any one field in the key is given a duplicate attribute.
2	4	System-maintained field	
3	8	Audit field—add	
4	16	Alternate search key	This field is not part of the primary key but can be used to query the data in a record locator. The field appears in the alternate search-key indexes.
5	32	List box item	This column appears in the result set of the component record locator dialog or list of values. Up to PeopleTools 7.x, an index was created on all list columns.
6	64	Ascending (descending) key field	Controls the order of the columns in the ORDER BY clauses of SQL generated by the PIA. Up to PeopleTools 8.14 and again from PeopleTools 8.48, the indexes are also built with the order specified on the field.
7	128	Audit field—change	
8	256	Required field	Date and Long columns have NOT NULL constraints. The PeopleSoft application does not allow 0 for Number columns or blank character fields.
9	512	X/Lat	Lookup value for fields in table XLATTABLE.
10	1024	Audit field—delete	
11	2048	Keys—Search	

Bit Number	USEEDIT Bit Value	Set (Not Set) Value	Comment
12	4096	Edits—Reasonable Date	
13	8192	Y/N	Field only accepts a Y/N response that is mapped to specified database values.
14	16384	Table edit enabled	
15	32768	Auto Update	
18	262144	From search field	
19	514288	To search field	
20	1048576	1/0 Table Edit	
21	2097152	Disable advanced search options	
23	8388608	Regular field (subrecord)	Not a subrecord.
24	16777216	Default search field	
28	268435456	Keys—Search Edit	

PSRECFIELDDB: Expanded Record Field Definition

One of the difficulties of working with PSRECFIELD is that subrecords are not expanded, and in some places PeopleSoft delivers subrecords nested within subrecords. PSRECFIELDDB was introduced in PeopleTools 8 and contains the fully expanded record definitions. Thus, this table is a much closer match for USER_TAB_COLUMNS.

As a result of the subrecord expansion, the field numbers (FIELDNUM) are not the same as in PSRECFIELD when a record contains a subrecord. They may not be the same as the COLUMN_ID on USER_TAB_COLUMNS either, because PeopleSoft moves long columns to be the last column in the table definition.

As you see later in this chapter, PeopleSoft does not use PSRECFIELDDB during run time; the table is only maintained as a reporting table by Application Designer from PeopleTools 8.4.

The structure of PSRECFIELDDB is identical to PSRECFIELD except it has one extra field: RECNAME_PARENT. This column contains the same value as RECNAME unless the field is defined via a subrecord, in which case it contains the name of the subrecord.

PSDBFIELD: Field Definition

This table contains one row for each distinct field name. As well as containing some descriptive and display information, it defines the data type of the fields (see Table 4-7). It doesn't correspond directly to any object in the Oracle data dictionary, but when joined with PSRECFIELD, it provides additional information about how a column should be defined.

This table indicates how, in PeopleTools, fields with the same names are always created with the same attributes, regardless of the record or table on which they are created. There is a single definition for each field in PeopleSoft that is held on a single row in PSDBFIELD.

Table 4-7. *Data Type Definitions*

PeopleTools PSDBFIELD	Oracle (DBA_TAB_COLUMNS)	Description of PeopleTools Column
⌀▻FIELDNAME	COLUMN_NAME	Column or subrecord name.
VERSION		Internal PeopleTools version to control caching of the object.
FIELDTYPE		See Table 4-8.
LENGTH	DATA_LENGTH or DATA_PRECISION	See comments in Table 4-8.
DECIMALPOS	DATA_SCALE	Only for FIELDTYPE 2 (Number) and FIELDTYPE 3 (Signed Number); see Table 4-8.
FORMAT		
FORMATLENGTH		
IMAGE_FMT		
FORMATFAMILY		
DISPFMTNAME		
DEFCNTRYYR		
IMEMODE		
KBLAYOUT		
OBJECTOWNERID		Short code indicating the functional area that owns the field (see PSRECDEFN.OBJECTOWNERID).

PeopleTools PSDBFIELD	Oracle (DBA_TAB_COLUMNS)	Description of PeopleTools Column
LASTUPDDTTM		Timestamp of the last update in Application Designer.
LASTUPDOPRID		Operator (developer) who last updated this record.
FLDNOTUSED		New in PeopleTools 8.4.
AUXFLAGMASK		New in PeopleTools 8.4.
DESCRLONG		Long description of the record.

Field Types and Lengths

The FIELDTYPE column on PSDBFIELD specifies the data type of the field, and hence the data type of the column when the record is built. The field types are set out in Table 4-8. Some PeopleSoft field types correspond to more than one Oracle data type, depending on the length and precision of the field. The LENGTH column on PSDBFIELD corresponds differently with the columns DATA_LENGTH and DATA_PRECISION on USER_TAB_COLUMNS, depending on the PeopleTools FIELDTYPE.

All character, numeric, and required fields in PeopleSoft have a NOT NULL constraint.

Table 4-8. Field Types and Column Definitions

Value of FIELDTYPE	PeopleSoft Data Type	Oracle Data Type	Comment
0	Character	VARCHAR2	Maximum length 255 characters imposed by PeopleTools
1	Long Character	VARCHAR2	If LENGTH between 1 and 2000
		LONG	Up to PeopleTools 8.1, if LENGTH = 0 or LENGTH > 2000
		LONG VARCHAR	From PeopleTools 8.4, if LENGTH = 0 or LENGTH > 2000 and from PeopleTools 8.48 if PSSTATUS.DATABASE_OPTIONS = 0
		CLOB	From PeopleTools 8.48 if LENGTH = 0 or LENGTH > 2000 and PSSTATUS.DATABASE_OPTIONS = 2
2	Number	DECIMAL(precision,scale)	If DECIMALPOS > 0

			Or if PeopleTools >= 8.47 and LENGTH > 8 Where precision = LENGTH-1 and scale = DECIMALPOS
		SMALLINT	If DECIMALPOS = 0 and LENGTH <= 4
		INTEGER	If DECIMALPOS = 0 and LENGTH > 4
3	Signed Number	DECIMAL(precision,scale)	If DECIMALPOS > 0 Where precision = LENGTH–2 and scale = DECIMALPOS
		NUMBER	If DECIMALPOS = 0
4	Date	DATE	LENGTH=10
5	Time	DATE	LENGTH=15
6	DateTime	DATE	LENGTH=26
8	Image	LONG RAW	If PeopleTools < 8.48 Or if PeopleTools >= 8.48 and PSSTATUS.DATABASE_OPTIONS = 0
		BLOB	From PeopleTools 8.48 if PSSTATUS.DATABASE_OPTIONS = 2
9	ImageRef	VARCHAR2(30)	LENGTH=30 Contains a reference to a file

The replacement of long columns with CLOBs from PeopleTools 8.48 (and Application version 9) has some advantages. For example:

- It is not possible to partition a table with a LONG, but it is permitted with a CLOB.

- SQL string functions can be used on CLOBs but not on LONGs.

■ **Note** If you are building a PeopleTools–only system database—for example, to be a Performance Monitor monitoring database—remember to set PSSTATUS.DATABASE_OPTIONS=2 yourself before you import the database with Data Mover. Otherwise, you will have LONG columns instead of CLOBs. That would prevent you from partitioning tables.

Unicode in PeopleSoft

If you need to support a language other than the Western European languages or just Japanese, then you cannot use a single-byte character set and must use Unicode. PeopleSoft only supports certain single-byte character sets,[2] as shown in Table 4-9.

Table 4-9. PeopleSoft-Supported Single-Byte Character Sets

Character Set	Description
WE8ISO8859P1	All Western European characters
WE8ISO8859P15	All Western European characters and the Euro symbol (€)
WE8MSWIN1252	Microsoft Windows 8-bit code page 1252
US7ASCII	7-bit Roman characters (no accented characters)
JA16SJIS	16-bit Japanese characters

So if, for example, you operate in Poland, Czech Republic, Slovakia, and Hungary, you are forced to use Unicode because PeopleSoft does not support EE8ISO8859P1, the single-byte codepage that covers those countries.

■ **Note** If you choose to use Unicode and you also need to run PeopleSoft Cobol programs, then Oracle delivers alternate versions of the Cobol programs that allocate three bytes per character in internal string variables.

Unicode from PeopleTools 8.48 and Application Version 9

Oracle changed the way PeopleTools handles Unicode from PeopleTools 8.48. That version did not support Oracle 8i, and so it could use character semantics in the database, meaning the length of character columns was defined in terms of characters rather than bytes. The initialization parameter nls_length_semantics must be set to char instead of byte before the PeopleSoft database is imported, and it is no longer necessary to create the length-checking constraint. However, the new method was only supported from application version 9 because Oracle did not retest and certify previous versions under Unicode. Therefore, character semantics are not supported on a version 8.x application that has been upgraded to PeopleTools 8.48 or higher.

A new column, PSSTATUS.DATABASE_OPTION, was added to control how character columns are created. Table 4-10 illustrates how the DDL generated by Application Designer changes depending on how UNICODE_ENABLED and DATABASE_OPTION are set.

---

[2] See Oracle support document 654171.1

Table 4-10. Unicode DDL

PSSTATUS. DATABASE_OPTION	PSSTATUS. UNICODE_ENABLED	Create Table DDL
| 0 | 0 | ```
CREATE TABLE PS_DMK
(EMPLID VARCHAR2(11) NOT NULL
,EMPL_RCD SMALLINT NOT NULL
,EFFDT DATE
,DESCRLONG LONG VARCHAR) ...
``` |
| 0 | 1 | ```
CREATE TABLE PS_DMK
(EMPLID VARCHAR2(33) NOT NULL
CHECK(LENGTH(EMPLID)<=11)
,EMPL_RCD SMALLINT NOT NULL
,EFFDT DATE
,DESCRLONG LONG VARCHAR) ...
``` |
| 2 | Either 0 or 1 | ```
CREATE TABLE PS_DMK
(EMPLID VARCHAR2(11) NOT NULL
,EMPL_RCD SMALLINT NOT NULL
,EFFDT DATE
,DESCRLONG CLOB) ...
``` |

From version 9 applications, DATABASE_OPTIONS is always set to 2. This setting has two effects. CLOBs are used instead of LONGs, and character semantics are used for Unicode. Thus, Application Designer builds exactly the same DDL whether Unicode is used or not.

Unicode in Application Version 8.x

PeopleSoft first introduced support for Unicode in PeopleTools 8.1. This version of PeopleTools is also supported on Oracle 8i, so PeopleSoft is not able to use character semantics, which was only introduced in Oracle 9i. However, there are some interesting and unfortunate implications for the way columns are specified on tables created by PeopleTools.

On a database with a non-Unicode, single-byte character set, character columns between 1 and 1,999 characters in length have the same length as the field in PeopleSoft. EMPLID is an 11-character field in PeopleSoft, so it is built as an 11-byte field in Oracle, as shown in Listing 4-1.

Listing 4-1. Creating the PS_JOB Table in a Database with a Single-Byte Codepage

```
CREATE TABLE PS_JOB
(EMPLID VARCHAR2(11) NOT NULL,...
```

However, if the database uses Unicode (indicated to PeopleTools by PSSTATUS.UNICODE_ENABLED=1), Application Designer builds character columns three times as long and adds a constraint to enforce the original length in characters, as shown in Listing 4-2.
```

Listing 4-2. Creating the PS_JOB Table in a Unicode Database

```
CREATE TABLE PS_JOB
(EMPLID VARCHAR2(33) NOT NULL CHECK(LENGTH(EMPLID)<=11),...
```

The result is approximately 165,000 length-checking constraints in a vanilla HCM database, and over 500,000 in a Financials database. There are two problems with this approach:

- The constraints have to be loaded into the library cache with the rest of the information about the table, with additional recursive SQL at parse time. Tests indicate up to four times as much time is spent parsing, which consumes CPU resources on the database server.[3] The performance of the Financials application is particularly badly affected by this problem.

- The constraints are not explicitly named and so are given system-generated names. It is possible that an Oracle import process could duplicate the constraints without warning.

If you create a long character field in Application Designer of between 1,334 and 1,999 characters in length, it is always built in Oracle as a 4,000 byte VARCHAR2 column with a maximum length of 1,333 characters, as shown in Listing 4-3. The maximum length for a VARCHAR2 column from Oracle 8 onward is 4,000 bytes. The PeopleSoft application permits you to enter more than 1,333 characters in the field without warning or error. Only when PeopleSoft attempts to save the data to the database does the resulting SQL INSERT or UPDATE statement then error.

Listing 4-3. Oracle Restricts VARCHAR2 Columns to 4,000 Bytes

```
CREATE TABLE PS_MYTABLE
(MY_CHAR VARCHAR2(4000) CHECK(LENGTH(MY_CHAR)<=1333),...
```

If you have to use Unicode, there are no supported options available to deal with the constraint problem. Probably the simplest option is just to drop the constraints. There is a risk that a 10-character field could end up with 30 Roman characters; but the Pure Internet Architecture (PIA) does not let the user type in more characters than are defined in PeopleSoft, so the main risk comes from batch processes, and few of those process strings.

---

[3] See www.go-faster.co.uk/bugs.htm#unicode_oddity.pps.

PSSQLDEFN: Definition of SQL Objects

This table is the parent of PSSQLTEXTDEFN. It holds SQL object definitions, and these objects are used widely in PeopleTools (see Table 4-11). Only rows where SQLTYPE = 2 correspond to DBA_VIEWS.

Until version 7.x of PeopleTools, the definition of SQL Views in PeopleTools was held in PSVIEWTEXT, and that table corresponded directly with DBA_VIEWS.

Table 4-11. *PSSQLDEFN: SQL Definitions*

PeopleTools PSSQLDEFN	Oracle DBA_VIEWS	Description of PeopleTools Column
SQLID	(VIEW_NAME)	SQL Object Identifier
		Not an exact match. This column has different meanings depending upon value of SQLTYPE
		SQLTYPE = 0: SQL object name
		SQLTYPE = 1: Application Engine Step Identifier
		SQLTYPE = 2: RECNAME
		SQLTYPE = 6: Application Engine XSLT (XML definition)
SQLTYPE		SQL Object Type
		0=SQL Object referenced from elsewhere
		1=Application Engine Step
		2=SQL View
		5=Queries for DDDAUDIT and SYSAUDIT
		6= Application Engine Step XSLT
VERSION		Internal PeopleTools version to control caching of object
LASTUPDDTTM		Timestamp of last update in Application Designer
LASTUPDOPRID		Operator (developer) who last updated this record
ENABLEEFFDT		
OBJECTOWNERID		Short code of functional area that owns the SQL (see PSRECDEFN.OBJECTOWNERID).

PSSQLTEXTDEFN

This table is the child of PSSQLDEFN. It specifies the SQL text for the object so that PeopleTools can specify different SQL strings for different platforms (see Table 4-12). This table corresponds to DBA_VIEWS for SQLTYPE = 2.

Table 4-12. *PSSQLTEXTDEFN: SQL Text Definitions*

PeopleTools PSSQLTEXTDEFN	Oracle DBA_VIEWS	Description of PeopleTools Column
☞SQLID		See PSSQLDEFN.SQLID.
☞SQLTYPE		See PSSQLDEFN.SQLTYPE.
☞MARKET		Market. GBL: Global product USF: U.S. Federal product
☞DBTYPE		0 = SQLBase 1 = DB2 2 = Oracle 3 = Informix 4 = DB2/Unix 5 = AllBase 6 = Sybase 7 = Microsoft 8 = DB2/400
☞EFFDT		Date from which the definition is effective. Only used on SQLTYPE 0 (SQL objects) and 1 (Application Engine steps).
SQLTEXT	TEXT	Text of the SQL query part of the view. However, SQLTEXT can contain PeopleSoft %functions that either reference other SQL objects or expand to database-specific functions.

PSINDEXDEFN: Index Definition

This table corresponds to DBA_INDEXES. The specification of certain column attributes on PSRECFIELD implies the creation of certain indexes (see also Chapter 5 for more information on keys and indexing). Additional indexes can then be specified in Application Designer. See Table 4-13.

Up to PeopleTools 7.x, PSINDEXDEFN and PSKEYDEFN were maintained for all record types, not just SQL tables, despite the fact that indexes cannot be built for the other object types, such as views!

Indexes can be suppressed or enabled on either all or certain platforms. Thus PeopleSoft can deliver different indexes on Oracle and DB2.

Table 4-13. PSINDEXDEFN: Index Definitions

PeopleTools PSINDEXDEFN	Oracle DBA_INDEXES	Description of PeopleTools Column
☞*RECNAME*	TABLE_NAME	Not an exact match. (see PSRECDEFN.SQLTABLENAME)
☞INDEXID	INDEX_NAME	Not an exact match INDEX_NAME = 'PS'‖INDEXID‖RECNAME _ = PeopleSoft Key Index. Implied from record definition. 1-9 = Alternate Search Key Indexes. Implied from record definition. (# = List Index. Implied from record definition. Only applicable in PeopleTools 7.5 and earlier, not used in PeopleTools 8) A-Z = User Specified Index
INDEXTYPE		1 = PeopleSoft Key Index 2 = List Index 3 = Alternate Search Key Index 4 = User Specified Index
UNIQUEFLAG	UNIQUENESS	1 = UNIQUE 0 = NONUNIQUE
CLUSTERFLAG		No meaning in Oracle. In Microsoft SQL Server and Sybase a clustered index is similar to an Oracle Index Organized Table.

		0=Build Index as a normal index 1=Build Index as a Clusters Index
ACTIVEFLAG		1 = Index to be built on at least one platform 0 = Index not to be built on any platform
CUSTKEYORDER		0 = Order of columns in PeopleTools generated index is the same as in the record 1 = Developer specified order of columns in PeopleTools generated index. Indexes with columns on a subrecord cannot have a custom key order.
KEYCOUNT		Number of columns in an PeopleTools index. A subrecord counts as one, so this does not correspond to the number of columns in the database index
DDLCOUNT		Number of distinct DDL override parameters specified on index across all platforms.
PLATFORM_SBS		1 = Index to be built on SQL Base 0 = Index not to be built on SQL Base Not used from PeopleTools 8. Database platform no longer supported.
PLATFORM_DB2		1 = Index to be built on DB2 0 = Index not to be built on DB2
PLATFORM_ORA		1 = Index to be built on Oracle 0 = Index not to be built on Oracle
PLATFORM_INF		1 = Index to be built on Informix 0 = Index not to be built on Informix
PLATFORM_DBX		1 = Index to be built on DB2/Unix 0 = Index not to be built on DB2/Unix
PLATFORM_ALB		1 = Index to be built on AllBase 0 = Index not to be built on AllBase Not used from PeopleTools 8. Database platform no longer supported.

PLATFORM_SYB		1 = Index to be built on Sybase
		0 = Index not to be built on Sybase
PLATFORM_MSS		1 = Index to be built on Microsoft SQL Server
		0 = Index not to be built on Microsoft SQL Server
PLATFORM_DB4		1 = Index to be built on DB2/AS400
		0 = Index not to be built on DB2/AS400
		Not used from PeopleTools 8. Database platform no longer supported.
IDXCOMMENTS		Holds comment added by developer on user indexes only. Added in PeopleTools 8.4.

PSKEYDEFN: Index definition

This table contains one row for each column in each index specified in PeopleTools, so it corresponds to DBA_IND_COLUMNS (see Table 4-14).

Table 4-14. PSKEYDEFN: Index Key Definition

PeopleTools PSKEYDEFN	Oracle DBA_IND_COLUMNS	Description of PeopleTools Column
☞*RECNAME*	TABLE_NAME	Not an exact match. (see PSRECDEFN.SQLTABLENAME)
☞*INDEXID*	INDEX_NAME	Not an exact match See PSINDEXDEFN.INDEXID
☞*KEYPOSN*	COLUMN_POSITION	Order of column or subrecord in index
FIELDNAME	COLUMN_NAME	Name of field or subrecord on PeopleTools record.
ASCDESC	DESCEND	Ordering of column in index 1 = Ascending order 0 = Descending order

---

■ **Note** From PeopleTools 8.15, PeopleSoft stopped building indexes in descending order because of Oracle Bug #869177. This affected descending indexes on most versions of Oracle 8.1.x. However, this behavior was reintroduced in PeopleTools 8.48, as the bug has been resolved in Oracle 9i. There is no way in PeopleTools to disable this behavior. If you do not want to build descending indexes at all in your Oracle database, you can set this undocumented initialization parameter: `_ignore_desc_in_index = TRUE`.

Recursive PeopleTools SQL

When a SQL statement that is not in the library cache is submitted to Oracle, the instance must parse the SQL in order to determine whether the SQL is valid, and if so how to execute it. During the parse process, the instance queries the data dictionary in order to obtain information about the tables and columns in the statement. The SQL generated by the parsing that queries the data dictionary is called *recursive SQL* and can be seen in an Oracle SQL*Trace.[4]

PeopleSoft uses its own data dictionary in a similar way. All of the application objects in a PeopleSoft application are stored in the PeopleTools tables. When a component is executed, the component processor in the PIA must load the objects, if they are not already cached and up to date, by querying the PeopleTools tables. Application Engine, Query, and nVision also query PeopleTools tables in order to execute.

COMPONENT PROCESSOR

Up to PeopleTools 7.x, the term *Panel Processor* referred to the code in the Windows client and application server programs that was responsible for parsing the content of the PeopleTools tables, executing the application, and referencing the application data.

In PeopleTools 8, panel groups became components and panels became pages (although the names of the underlying PeopleTools tables did not change). Now, PeopleSoft talks about the component processor, which is additionally responsible for rendering the HTML pages, graphics, and JavaScript that are sent to the browser.

This section steps through some of the recursive SQL issued by PeopleTools to load a component in the PIA. The examples are taken from the PERSONAL_DATA component, where employee name and address information is entered into the HCM application. Figure 4-4 shows a page from this component.

When DDL is executed in Oracle, recursive SQL is issued to maintain the data dictionary. Similarly, the PeopleTools tables are administered via Application Designer, and when an object is saved in Application Designer, rows are inserted into or deleted from the Tools tables.

---

[4] Oracle support Note 39817.1 explains the content of the extended trace file. However, in *Optimizing Oracle Performance* (O'Reilly, 2003), Cary Millsap with Jeff Holt gives a very clear and detailed explanation of this trace.

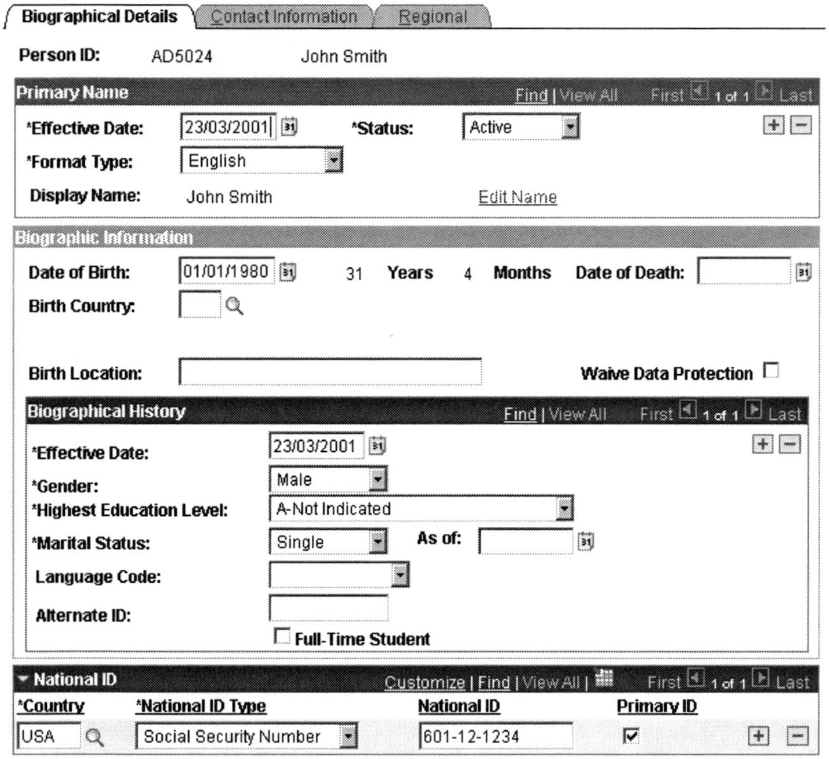

Figure 4-4. Personal Data component of HCM

Page definitions are held in various rows on various PeopleTools tables. There are tables for each of the design elements within the component, including these:

- *Components:* PSPNLGRPDEFN, PSPNLGROUP

- *Menus:* PSMENUDEFN, PSMENUITEM

- *Pages:* PSPNLDEFN

- *Objects and positions within the page (including fields, scroll bars, graphics, and push buttons):* PSPNLFIELD, PSPNLCNTRLDATA, PSPNLBTNDATA

- *Records within which the fields exist:* PSRECFIELD

- *Data types of the field:* PSDBFIELD

- *PeopleCode that executes when certain events occur:* PSPCMPROG

The PeopleTools trace that is discussed over the following pages was obtained from an HCM 9.0 database.[5] The user entered the PERSONAL_DATA component, which had not previously been cached by PeopleTools. To load and open the component, the processor went through a number of stages:

- Check the PeopleTools object version numbers for caching.

- Load the component definition.

- Load the menu item.

- Perform the component search dialog.

- Identify and load pages in the component.

- Load any component PeopleCode.

- Load the page definitions.

- Load the fields on each page.

- Load the record definitions.

- Load the field definitions.

- Identify any subrecords.

- Load the field labels.

- Load the record DDL definitions.

- Recursively load the subrecord definitions.

- Load the application data.

Some stages may have been executed more than once for different objects. In general, not all components require all these stages; for example, a record may not have subrecords.

Navigating from signon to the page generated 38,000 lines of trace, so I only show some extracts. I also only show the SQL statements and bind variable values from the trace.

Version Numbers and Caching

A system of version numbering is used on PeopleTools objects to enable the caching algorithm to determine whether a cached object is up to date. The table PSVERSION holds a global version number (object type SYS) and a version number for each of the PeopleTools object types (records, panels, and so on).

When an object is changed and saved by Application Designer, the version number on PSVERSION for that object type is incremented and allocated to the object. The global version number is also incremented.[6] By comparing version numbers on the database and in the local caches, PeopleTools processes can determine whether the cached objects are up to date or have changed.

In a PeopleSoft trace, you frequently see queries of the PSVERSION table like the one shown in Listing 4-4.

---

[5] Enabling PIA trace is described in Chapter 9.
[6] PeopleSoft uses ordinary tables rather than Oracle sequences. This is discussed in Chapter 8.

Listing 4-4. PeopleTools Version-Number Check

```
Stmt=SELECT VERSION FROM PSVERSION WHERE OBJECTTYPENAME = 'SYS'
```

PeopleTools uses this query to determine whether any new objects have been added to any Tools table. If the global version number on the database is higher than the cached version, then something must have been added, and PeopleTools goes on to examine version numbers for the PeopleTools object types. Where these version numbers have incremented, the Tools tables are queried, as shown next.

Component Definition

When the Modify a Person link on the menu is clicked in the PIA, the application server starts to load the component, beginning with the component definition on PSPNLGRPDEFN; see Listing 4-5.

Listing 4-5. Loading the Panel Group Definition

```
Stmt=SELECT DESCR, ACTIONS, VERSION, SEARCHRECNAME, ADDSRCHRECNAME, SEARCHPNLNAME, LOADLOC,
SAVELOC, DISABLESAVE, PRIMARYACTION, DFLTACTION, DFLTSRCHTYPE, DEFERPROC, EXPENTRYPROC,
WSRPCOMPLIANT, REQSECURESSL, INCLNAVIGATION, FORCESEARCH, ALLOWACTMODESEL, PNLNAVFLAGS,
TBARBTNS, SHOWTBAR, ADDLINKMSGSET, ADDLINKMSGNUM, SRCHLINKMSGSET, SRCHLINKMSGNUM,
SRCHTEXTMSGSET, SRCHTEXTMSGNUM, OBJECTOWNERID, TO_CHAR(LASTUPDDTTM,'YYYY-MM-DD-
HH24.MI.SS."000000"'), LASTUPDOPRID, DESCRLONG  FROM PSPNLGRPDEFN WHERE PNLGRPNAME = :1 AND
MARKET = :2
Bind-1 type=2 length=13 value=PERSONAL_DATA
Bind-2 type=2 length=3 value=GBL
```

Search Record

A search record imposes row-level security on the data that can be seen in a component. It lists the key values of the data that the operator is allowed to retrieve in the component. Search records are often database views that query several other security tables and may contain business logic.

The search record is specified for the component on the PeopleTools table PSPNLGRPDEFN in the column SEARCHRECNAME but can be overridden in the menu-item definition on PSMENUITEM (see Listing 4-6). Thus the same component can be used in different places and retrieve different data according to different row-level security.

Listing 4-6. Loading the Menu-Item Definition

```
Stmt=SELECT BARNAME, ITEMNAME, BARLABEL, ITEMLABEL, MARKET, ITEMTYPE, PNLGRPNAME,
SEARCHRECNAME, ITEMNUM, XFERCOUNT FROM PSMENUITEM WHERE MENUNAME = :1 ORDER BY ITEMNUM
Bind-1 type=2 length=26 value=ADMINISTER_WORKFORCE_(GBL)
```

The layout of the search dialog is controlled by the specification of the component search record, in this case PS_PERALL_SEC_SRCH. It identifies the data to be retrieved into the component by primary key, the columns against which search criteria can be specified, and the columns listed in the search results (see Figure 4-5).

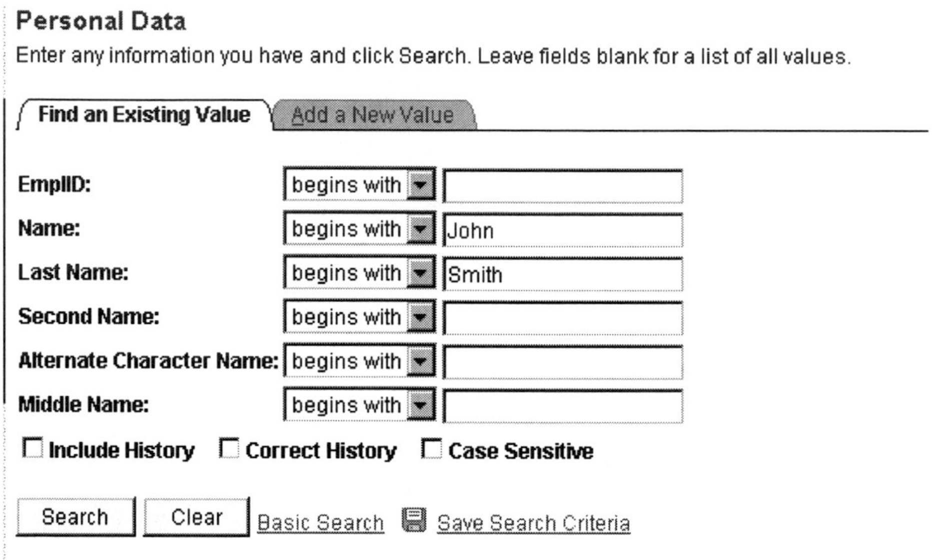

Personal Data

Enter any information you have and click Search. Leave fields blank for a list of all values.

| Find an Existing Value | Add a New Value |

EmplID:	begins with ▼	
Name:	begins with ▼	John
Last Name:	begins with ▼	Smith
Second Name:	begins with ▼	
Alternate Character Name:	begins with ▼	
Middle Name:	begins with ▼	

☐ **Include History** ☐ **Correct History** ☐ **Case Sensitive**

| Search | Clear | Basic Search 💾 Save Search Criteria |

Figure 4-5. Personal search dialog before executing search

The operator ID is a criterion in the query on the search record. The criteria specified in the dialog in Figure 4-5 also become criteria in SQL query (see Listing 4-7).

Listing 4-7. Component Search Dialog

```
Stmt=SELECT DISTINCT EMPLID, NAME, NAME_DISPLAY_SRCH, LAST_NAME_SRCH, SECOND_LAST_SRCH,
NAME_AC, MIDDLE_NAME, BUSINESS_UNIT, DEPTID, EMPL_STATUS FROM PS_PERALL_SEC_SRCH WHERE
OPRID=:1 AND NAME_DISPLAY_SRCH LIKE 'JOHN%' AND LAST_NAME_SRCH LIKE 'SMITH%'  ORDER BY
NAME_DISPLAY_SRCH, LAST_NAME_SRCH, EMPL_STATUS, EMPLID
Bind-1 type=2 length=8 value=KURTZ
```

Strictly speaking, the query generated by the search dialog is not a recursive statement because it is referencing an application record, but the search dialog is not explicitly coded by the developer. It is automatically generated by PeopleTools because a search record has been specified in the component definition (PSPNLGRPDEFN).

Note that although the OPRID condition uses a bind variable, the content of the search fields in the page appears as a literal string in the trace. Every time any operator enters a different search string, a different SQL statement is generated. The database treats it as a new SQL statement and has to parse it. This is one reason there is so much parsing on a PeopleSoft database.

Case-Insensitive Searching

In Figure 4-5, the operator has searched for employees whose surnames begin with "Smith" and whose name begins with "John". When the results are returned (see Figure 4-6) the search terms have become uppercase. They also appear in the SQL (and Listing 4-7) in uppercase.

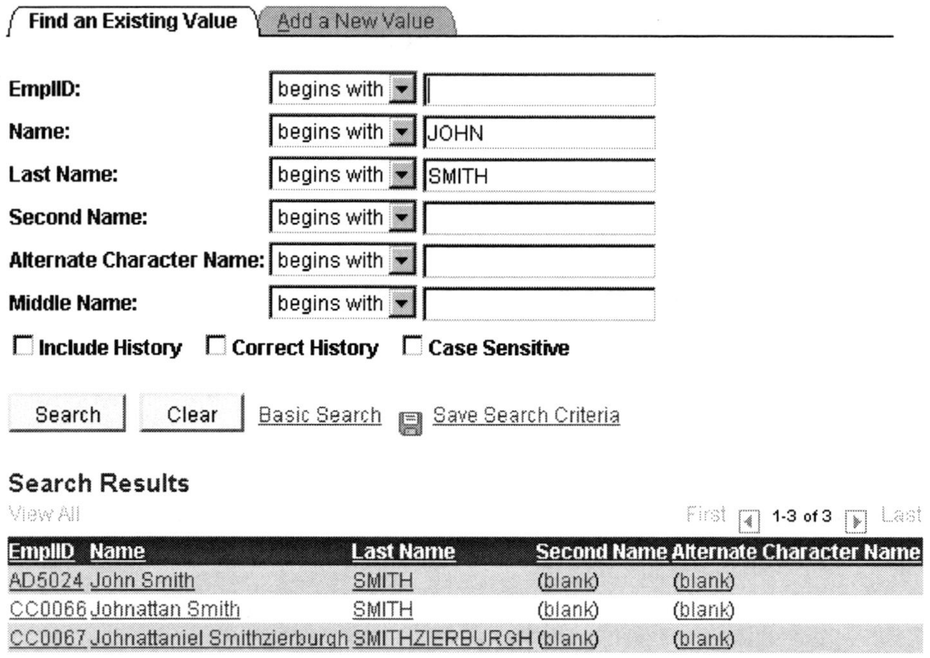

Figure 4-6. Personal search dialog after executing a search with results

The query in Listing 4-7 was not case-sensitive because the PeopleSoft application also maintains uppercase copies of the name and last name in the columns NAME_DISPLAY_SRCH and LAST_NAME_SRCH. The advantage of this approach is that the additional columns can simply be indexed from within Application Designer like any other column, and the solution can be applied to any database platform. The disadvantage is that you have to store the data twice, and something has to update the uppercase copy whenever the mixed-case value changes.

However, if you search on a mixed-case field, such as MIDDLE_NAME in the example in Listing 4-8, the SQL is a little different.

Listing 4-8. Case-Insensitive Query During Component Search Dialog

```
Stmt=SELECT DISTINCT EMPLID, NAME, NAME_DISPLAY_SRCH, LAST_NAME_SRCH, SECOND_LAST_SRCH,
NAME_AC, MIDDLE_NAME, BUSINESS_UNIT, DEPTID, EMPL_STATUS FROM PS_PERALL_SEC_SRCH WHERE
OPRID=:1 AND UPPER(MIDDLE_NAME) LIKE UPPER('Leopold') || '%' ESCAPE '\' ORDER BY MIDDLE_NAME,
BUSINESS_UNIT, EMPL_STATUS, EMPLID
Bind-1 type=2 length=8 value=SYSDEVPG
```

PeopleTools makes the search on the mixed-case column case-insensitive by putting the UPPER() function around the name and the search string. This has the effect of preventing any index on the column being used effectively, and it can cause performance problems. There are two ways to address this:

- Case-insensitive searching can be disabled globally in PeopleTools Options. This option rarely finds favor with users.

- Function-based indexes can be created on the case-sensitive columns, but Application Designer is not capable of generating them automatically, so they have to be managed manually, as in Listing 4-9.

Listing 4-9. Creating a Function-Based Index

```
CREATE INDEX psznames ON ps_names (UPPER(middle_name), EMPLID);
```

Component Pages

Pages exist within a component, and all of the pages within a component are loaded simultaneously. PSPNLGROUP specifies all the pages within the components, whether they appear to the user or not, the order in which they appear, and the details on the tabs. The pages within a component are retrieved with the query in Listing 4-10.

Listing 4-10. Determining Pages in Component

```
Stmt=SELECT PNLNAME, ITEMNAME, HIDDEN, ITEMLABEL, FOLDERTABLABEL, SUBITEMNUM FROM PSPNLGROUP
WHERE PNLGRPNAME = :1 AND MARKET = :2 ORDER BY SUBITEMNUM
Bind-1 type=2 length=13 value=PERSONAL_DATA
Bind-2 type=2 length=3 value=GBL
```

In Figure 4-4, three tabs are visible; these are the pages in the PERSONAL_DATA component. Listing 4-11 shows the contents of PSPNLGROUP for this component.

Listing 4-11. Contents of PSPNLGROUP

```
PNLNAME             ITEMNAME            HIDDEN ITEMLABEL                        SUBITEMNUM
-----------------   -----------------   ------ ------------------------------   ----------
PERSONAL_DATA1      PERSONAL_DATA1           0 &Biographical Details                     1
PERSONAL_DATA2      PERSONAL_DATA2           0 &Contact Information                       2
PERSONAL_DATA3      PERSONAL_DATA3           0 &Regional                                  3
PERSONAL_DATA4      PERSONAL_DATA4           0 &Organizational Relationships             4
PERSONAL_DATA_WRK PERSONAL_DATA_WRK          1 Personal Data Wrk5
```

The query actually returns five rows. PERSONAL_DATA_WRK is a hidden page that contains working storage fields referenced by PeopleCode. PERSONAL_DATA4 was programmatically hidden by component PeopleCode. The hidden pages are also loaded by the component processor.

Component PeopleCode

The last stage in loading the component is to find any component-level PeopleCode (see Listing 4-12).

Listing 4-12. Loading Component-Level PeopleCode

```
Stmt=SELECT OBJECTID1,OBJECTVALUE1, OBJECTID2,OBJECTVALUE2, OBJECTID3,OBJECTVALUE3,
OBJECTID4,OBJECTVALUE4, OBJECTID5,OBJECTVALUE5, OBJECTID6,OBJECTVALUE6, OBJECTID7,OBJECTVALUE7
FROM PSPCMPROG WHERE OBJECTID1 = :1 AND OBJECTVALUE1 = :2 AND  OBJECTID2 = :3 AND OBJECTVALUE2
= :4 ORDER BY OBJECTID1,OBJECTVALUE1, OBJECTID2,OBJECTVALUE2, OBJECTID3,OBJECTVALUE3,
OBJECTID4,OBJECTVALUE4, OBJECTID5,OBJECTVALUE5, OBJECTID6,OBJECTVALUE6, OBJECTID7,OBJECTVALUE7
Bind-1 type=8 length=4 value=10
Bind-2 type=2 length=13 value=PERSONAL_DATA
Bind-3 type=8 length=4 value=39
Bind-4 type=2 length=3 value=GBL
```

Listing 4-13 shows that there are 13 pieces of PeopleCode on the PERSONAL_DATA component.

Listing 4-13. Component-Level PeopleCode

OBJECTID1	OBJECTVALUE1	OBJECTID2	OBJECTVALUE2	OBJECTID3	OBJECTVALUE3	OBJECTID4	OBJECTVALUE4
OBJECTID5	OBJECTVALUE5	OBJECTID6	OBJECTVALUE6	OBJECTID7	OBJECTVALUE7		
10	PERSONAL_DATA	39	GBL	1	ADDRESSES	12	RowInsert
0		0		0			
10	PERSONAL_DATA	39	GBL	1	DERIVED_ADDR	12	RowInit
0		0		0			
10	PERSONAL_DATA	39	GBL	1	DIVERS_ETHNIC	2	REG_REGION
12	FieldChange	0		0			
10	PERSONAL_DATA	39	GBL	1	DIVERS_ETHNIC	2	REG_REGION
12	FieldEdit	0		0			
10	PERSONAL_DATA	39	GBL	1	NAMES	12	RowInit
0		0		0			
10	PERSONAL_DATA	39	GBL	1	PERSON	12	SaveEdit
0		0		0			
10	PERSONAL_DATA	39	GBL	1	PERS_SRCH_ALL	12	SearchInit
0		0		0			
10	PERSONAL_DATA	39	GBL	1	PERS_SRCH_ALL	12	SearchSave
0		0		0			
10	PERSONAL_DATA	39	GBL	1	PERS_WRKLV_CHN	12	SaveEdit
0		0		0			
10	PERSONAL_DATA	39	GBL	12	PostBuild	0	
0		0		0			
10	PERSONAL_DATA	39	GBL	12	PreBuild	0	
0		0		0			

```
10 PERSONAL_DATA      39 GBL              12 SavePostChange      0
 0                     0                   0

10 PERSONAL_DATA      39 GBL              12 SavePreChange       0
 0                     0                   0
```

Page Definition

A component can consist of a number of pages. Each page within the component is loaded, starting with the page definition stored on the table PSPNLDEFN (see Listing 4-14).

Listing 4-14. Loading the Page Definition

```
Stmt=SELECT VERSION, PNLTYPE, GRIDHORZ, GRIDVERT, FIELDCOUNT, MAXPNLFLDID, HELPCONTEXTNUM,
PANELLEFT, PANELTOP, PANELRIGHT, PANELBOTTOM, PNLSTYLE, STYLESHEETNAME, PNLUSE, DEFERPROC,
DESCR, POPUPMENU, LICENSE_CODE, TO_CHAR(LASTUPDDTTM,'YYYY-MM-DD-HH24.MI.SS."000000"'),
LASTUPDOPRID, OBJECTOWNERID, DESCRLONG FROM PSPNLDEFN WHERE PNLNAME = :1
Bind-1 type=2 length=14 value=PERSONAL_DATA1
```

Page Fields

Each field on the page is then loaded (see Listing 4-15).

Listing 4-15. Loading Fields on a Page

```
Stmt=SELECT PNLFLDID, FIELDTYPE, EDITSIZE, FIELDLEFT, FIELDTOP, FIELDRIGHT, FIELDBOTTOM,
EDITLBLLEFT, EDITLBLTOP, EDITLBLRIGHT, EDITLBLBOTTOM, DSPLFORMAT, DSPLFILL, LBLTYPE, LBLLOC,
LBLPADSIZE, LABEL_ID, LBLTEXT, FIELDUSE, FIELDUSETMP, DEFERPROC, OCCURSLEVEL, OCCURSCOUNT1,
OCCURSCOUNT2, OCCURSCOUNT3, OCCURSOFFSET1, OCCURSOFFSET2, OCCURSOFFSET3, PNLFIELDNAME,
RECNAME, FIELDNAME, SUBPNLNAME, ONVALUE, OFFVALUE, ASSOCFIELDNUM, FIELDSTYLE, LABELSTYLE,
FIELDSIZETYPE, LABELSIZETYPE, PRCSNAME, PRCSTYPE, FORMATFAMI?Y, DISPFMTNAME, PROMPTFIELD,
POPUPMENU, TREECTRLID, TREECTRLTYPE, MULTIRECTREE, NODECOUNT, GRDCOLUMNCOUNT, GRDSHOWCOLHDG,
GRDSHOWROWHDG, GRDODDROWSTYLE, GRDEVENROWSTYLE, GRDACTIVETABSTYLE, GRDINACTIVETABSTYL,
GRDNAVBARSTYLE, GRDLABELSTYLE, GRDLBLMSGSET, GRDLBLMSGNUM, GRDLBLALIGN, GRDACTTYPE, TABENABLE,
PBDISPLAYTYPE, OPENNEWWINDOW, URLDYNAMIC, URL_ID, GOTOPORTALNAME, GOTONODENAME, GOTOMENUNAME,
GOTOPNLGRPNAME, GOTOMKTNAME, GOTOPNLNAME, GOTOPNLACTION, SRCHBYPNLDATA, SCROLLACTION,
TOOLACTION, CONTNAME, CON?NAMEOVER, CONTNAMEDISABLE, PTLBLIMGCOLLAPSE, PTLBLIMGEXPAND,
SELINDICATORTYPE, PTADJHIDDENFIELDS, PTCOLLAPSEDATAAREA, PTDFLTVIEWEXPANDED, PTHIDEFIELDS,
SHOWCOLHIDEROWS, PTLEBEXPANDFIELD, SHOWTABCNTLBTN, SECUREINVISIBLE, ENABLEASANCHOR,
URLENCODEDBYAPP, USEDEFAULTLABEL, GRDALLOWCOLSORT, PNLNAME, FIELDNUM FROM PSPNLFIELD WHERE
PNLNAME = :1 ORDER BY FIELDNUM
Bind-1 type=2 length=14 value=PERSONAL_DATA1
```

Record Definition

The record definitions for all the records referenced on all the pages in the component are loaded (see Listing 4-16).

Listing 4-16. Loading Record Definitions

```
Stmt=SELECT VERSION, FIELDCOUNT, RECTYPE, RECUSE, OPTTRIGFLAG, AUDITRECNAME, SETCNTRLFLD,
RELLANGRECNAME, OPTDELRECNAME, PARENTRECNAME, QRYSECRECNAME, SQLTABLENAME, BUILDSEQNO,
OBJECTOWNERID, TO_CHAR(LASTUPDDTTM,'YYYY-MM-DD-HH24.MI.SS."000000"'), LASTUPDOPRID,
SYSTEMIDFIELDNAME, TIMESTAMPFIELDNAME, RECDESCR, AUXFLAGMASK, DESCRLONG  FROM PSRECDEFN WHERE
RECNAME = :1
Bind-1 type=2 length=6 value=PERSON
```

The record definition includes details such as the underlying SQLTABLENAME, which is the name of the table in the database that corresponds to the record.

Field Definitions

For each record that is loaded, all of the fields are also loaded. PeopleTools has the concept of subrecords, which are groups of fields or other subrecords that, for ease and consistency, can be included in a number of different records. Subrecords can contain other subrecords. The concept is similar to a parts explosion, or to a structure in a C program.

In this example, the record NAMES has a subrecord NAMEGBL_SBR. This subrecord is used in several other records in the HCM application.

PeopleTools starts by loading fields on a record that are not part of a subrecord (see Listing 4-17).

Listing 4-17. Loading Fields that Are Not Subrecords

```
Stmt=SELECT VERSION, A.FIELDNAME, FIELDTYPE, LENGTH, DECIMALPOS, FORMAT, FORMATLENGTH,
IMAGE_FMT, FORMATFAMILY, DISPFMTNAME, DEFCNTRYYR,IMEMODE,KBLAYOUT,OBJECTOWNERID, DEFRECNAME,
DEFFIELDNAME, CURCTLFIELDNAME, USEEDIT, USEEDIT2, EDITTABLE, DEFGUICONTROL, SETCNTRLFLD,
LABEL_ID, TIMEZONEUSE, TIMEZONEFIELDNAME, CURRCTLUSE, RELTMDTFIELDNAME,
TO_CHAR(B.LASTUPDDTTM,'YYYY-MM-DD-HH24.MI.SS."000000"'), B.LASTUPDOPRID, B.FIELDNUM,
A.FLDNOTUSED, A.AUXFLAGMASK, B.RECNAME FROM PSDBFIELD A, PSRECFIELD B WHERE B.RECNAME = :1 AND
A.FIELDNAME = B.FIELDNAME AND B.SUBRECORD = 'N' ORDER BY B.RECNAME, B.FIELDNUM
Bind-1 type=2 length=6 value=PERSON
```

Subrecords

Columns that are not subrecords are loaded first (see Listing 4-18) with information about their type, length, and how they are to be displayed. Then the subrecords on NAMES are loaded. PeopleSoft has not changed this algorithm in PeopleTools 8. It still loads the fields from PSRECFIELD and not PSRECFIELDDB.

Listing 4-18. Identifying Subrecords on the Record

```
Stmt=SELECT FIELDNUM, FIELDNAME, TO_CHAR(LASTUPDDTTM,'YYYY-MM-DD-HH24.MI.SS."000000"'),
LASTUPDOPRID, RECNAME FROM PSRECFIELD WHERE RECNAME = :1 AND SUBRECORD = 'Y' ORDER BY RECNAME,
FIELDNUM
Bind-1 type=2 length=11 value=PERSON_NAME
```

There is just one subrecord on the NAMES record (see Listing 4-19). It is loaded a little later, after all the records are loaded.

Listing 4-19. Subrecords on NAMEGBL_SBR

```
FIELDNUM FIELDNAME   TO_CHAR(LASTUPDDTTM,'YYYY- LASTUPDOPR RECNAME
-------- ----------- ------------------------- ---------- ---------------
       2 NAMEGBL_SBR 2001-04-16-21.44.26.000000 PPLSOFT    PERSON_NAME
```

Field Labels

Field *labels* are the prompts that appear by a field in a page. By default, whenever fields of the same name appear in pages, they have the same label next to them, although the developer can override this on the page when the field is added. This approach tends to make the labeling of a field consistent wherever it appears in the system, and simplifies translation of field prompts into other languages.

Field descriptions are loaded after the fields are loaded (see Listing 4-20). Due to the recursive nature of the component processor, the field labels for subrecords are loaded before the field labels for their parents because subrecords are loaded before field labels.

Listing 4-20. Loading Field Labels

```
Stmt=SELECT FIELDNAME, LABEL_ID, LONGNAME, SHORTNAME, DEFAULT_LABEL FROM PSDBFLDLABL WHERE
FIELDNAME IN (SELECT A.FIELDNAME FROM PSDBFIELD A, PSRECFIELD B WHERE B.RECNAME = :1 AND
A.FIELDNAME = B.FIELDNAME) ORDER BY FIELDNAME, LABEL_ID
Bind-1 type=2 length=5 value=NAMES
```

Record DDL

Part of the record definition describes how Application Designer should build the table and index or view on the database. Although the PIA never does that, this information is part of the record definition, and it is all loaded (see Listing 4-21) and cached at the same time.

Listing 4-21. Loading Index Definitions

```
Stmt=SELECT INDEXID, INDEXTYPE, UNIQUEFLAG, CLUSTERFLAG, ACTIVEFLAG, CUSTKEYORDER,
IDXCOMMENTS, PLATFORM_SBS, PLATFORM_DB2, PLATFORM_ORA, PLATFORM_INF, PLATFORM_DBX,
PLATFORM_ALB, PLATFORM_SYB, PLATFORM_MSS, PLATFORM_DB4, RECNAME FROM PSINDEXDEFN WHERE RECNAME
= :1 ORDER BY RECNAME, INDEXTYPE, INDEXID
Bind-1 type=2 length=5 value=NAMES
Stmt=SELECT INDEXID, KEYPOSN, FIELDNAME, ASCDESC, RECNAME FROM PSKEYDEFN WHERE RECNAME = :1
ORDER BY RECNAME, INDEXID, KEYPOSN
Bind-1 type=2 length=5 value=NAMES
Stmt=SELECT INDEXID, PLATFORMID, SIZINGSET, PARMNAME, PARMVALUE, RECNAME FROM PSIDXDDLPARM
WHERE RECNAME = :1 ORDER BY RECNAME, INDEXID, PLATFORMID, SIZINGSET, PARMNAME
Bind-1 type=2 length=5 value=NAMES
Stmt=SELECT PLATFORMID, SIZINGSET, PARMNAME, PARMVALUE, RECNAME FROM PSRECDDLPARM WHERE
RECNAME = :1 ORDER BY RECNAME, PLATFORMID, SIZINGSET, PARMNAME
Bind-1 type=2 length=5 value=NAMES
Stmt=SELECT DDLSPACENAME, DBNAME, DBTYPE FROM PSRECTBLSPC WHERE RECNAME = :1 ORDER BY DBTYPE
Bind-1 type=2 length=5 value=NAMES
```

Subrecord Definition

After the rest of the record is loaded, the subrecords are loaded (see Listing 4-22). The whole of the record-loading process is repeated recursively. This includes the DDL definition in the previous section, although it is meaningless for a subrecord.

Listing 4-22. Loading Subrecord Definitions

```
Stmt=SELECT VERSION, FIELDCOUNT, RECTYPE, RECUSE, OPTTRIGFLAG, AUDITRECNAME, SETCNTRLFLD,
RELLANGRECNAME, OPTDELRECNAME, PARENTRECNAME, QRYSECRECNAME, SQLTABLENAME, BUILDSEQNO,
OBJECTOWNERID, TO_CHAR(LASTUPDDTTM,'YYYY-MM-DD-HH24.MI.SS."000000"'), LASTUPDOPRID,
SYSTEMIDFIELDNAME, TIMESTAMPFIELDNAME, RECDESCR, AUXFLAGMASK, DESCRLONG  FROM PSRECDEFN WHERE
RECNAME = :1
Bind-1 type=2 length=11 value=NAMEGBL_SBR
```

Application SQL

Eventually, after all of the application components have been loaded, the application data is queried into the page. In Listing 4-23, the NAMES record for employee AD5024 is queried from the database, loaded into the component buffer, and displayed on the screen.

Listing 4-23. Loading the Application Data for Employee AD5024

```
Stmt=SELECT EMPLID, TO_CHAR(BIRTHDATE,'YYYY-MM-DD'), BIRTHPLACE, BIRTHCOUNTRY, BIRTHSTATE,
TO_CHAR(DT_OF_DEATH,'YYYY-MM-DD'), TO_CHAR(LAST_CHILD_UPDDTM,'YYYY-MM-DD') FROM PS_PERSON
WHERE EMPLID=:1 ORDER BY EMPLID
Bind-1 type=2 length=8 value=AD5024
```

There are a few things to note in the SQL in Listing 4-23:

- This query has been dynamically constructed by PeopleTools from the information loaded from the PeopleTools tables.

- The columns in the SELECT list were derived from the columns on the NAMES record and its subrecord. The field types are stored on PSDBFIELD. This indicates that EFFDT is a date, and the TO_CHAR function is added to convert it to a date string.

- The query on the record is by the primary key columns in common with the search record, so this query is only on EMPLID. The search key value was taken from the row selected on the search dialog. Whether a field is part of the unique key, the order in which it should be queried, and whether a field appears in a search dialog are all attributes of the field on that record and are queried from PSRECFIELD.

- The query is ordered by all the primary key columns in descending order where the key is specified as descending.

We have now seen how PeopleSoft retrieves the application and the data structures from the PeopleTools tables and then queries the application data. Queries on the Tools tables are effectively recursive queries, just as an Oracle database may recursively query its data dictionary when a SQL statement is parsed.

Data Dictionary Synchronization

I have demonstrated how PeopleTools dynamically generates SQL to reference the application data from information in the PeopleTools tables, in much the same way that a database recursively queries its own data dictionary. I have also described the relationship between certain PeopleTools tables and the Oracle database data dictionary.

DDL Changes

It is essential that, wherever possible, all DDL changes be specified via Application Designer, which is then also used to generate all of the DDL scripts. If any changes to the data model are not implemented in this way, they introduce discrepancies between the two data dictionaries. They are likely to cause errors because PeopleSoft builds invalid SQL or the changes are lost in a subsequent application upgrade or patch. If other parts of PeopleTools tables are not referentially integral, the application server or even Application Designer may simply crash. Here are two examples:

- If a developer removes a character or numeric column from a table and does not implement the ALTER TABLE script generated by Application Designer, the application fails when it tries to insert data into the table because the column is no longer in the generated insert SQL, the default value of the column is NULL, and the column has a NOT NULL constraint. The application fails with "ORA-1400: cannot insert NULL into …"

- If a DBA decides to add an index to a table, and then a developer makes a subsequent change, that record may get rebuilt. PeopleTools usually alters tables by building a copy, copying the data from the original table to the copy, renaming the tables, rebuilding the indexes, and dropping the original table. If PeopleTools doesn't know about the index that the DBA added, it does not rebuild it, and that index is lost.

There are, however, some Oracle-specific object types for which Application Designer cannot construct DDL. It is not possible to build partitioned, Global Temporary, or Index-Organized Tables (see Chapter 6). The columns must still be specified in Application Designer, but the actual creation of the objects must be handled manually.[7]

PeopleSoft provides two diagnostic SQR reports to help identify problems in the PeopleTools tables so they can be repaired:

- DDDAUDIT compares the two data dictionaries and reports on discrepancies between them.

- SYSAUDIT checks relational integrity within the PeopleTools tables.

Both reports run a series of queries that generate an exception report. The possible errors from this report and the recommended remedies are set out in the "Data Management" PeopleBook.[8]

---

[7] Some of these Oracle object types are discussed in Chapter 6. For Global Payroll, a PL/SQL script was developed to build partitioned result tables and the global temporary working storage tables according to the specifications in the PeopleTools tables.

[8] See http://download.oracle.com/docs/cd/E25688_01/pt852pbr0/eng/psbooks/tadm/htm/ tadm05.htm#g037ee99c9453fb39_ef90c_10c791ddc07__7b1a

Column Difference Audit Script

One significant limitation of PeopleSoft's DDDAUDIT is that this report does not check that columns are defined consistently on both data dictionaries. If a developer adds a column to a table and forgets to rebuild that table, it is not reported by DDDAUDIT, but PeopleTools adds that column to the SQL that it generates. The result is Oracle error "ORA-00904: <column name>: invalid identifier."

The colaudit.sql script was originally written to detect this and similar problems.[9] The script should simply be run in SQL*Plus while connected to the database schema in which the PeopleSoft database resides. It generates a report of exceptions, set out in Table 4-15, to the screen and a spool file. It also creates a project in Application Designer from which DDL scripts can be built to rebuild objects if necessary.

Table 4-15. *colaudit Report Sections*

Error Code	Error Description	Comments
COL-01	Object in PeopleSoft data dictionary, but not in Oracle.	DDDAUDIT also performs this test. It is included here for convenience.
COL-02	Object in Oracle data dictionary, but not in PeopleSoft. DDDAUDIT also performs this test. It is included here for convenience.	
COL-03	More instances of the PS temporary table exist in Oracle than are defined in PeopleSoft.	
COL-04	Corresponding PeopleSoft and Oracle tables and views with different numbers of columns.	This section summarizes COL-05 and COL-06.
COL-05	Columns in the PeopleSoft data dictionary, but not in the Oracle data dictionary.	
COL-06	Columns in the Oracle data dictionary, but not in PeopleSoft.	
COL-07	Columns in both Oracle and PeopleSoft, but with different definitions.	There are separate versions of this test for PeopleTools 8.1x and PeopleTools 8.4x to handle the new SYSTEMIDFIELD.
COL-08	Records referenced as but no longer defined as subrecords.	This doesn't cause a run-time error but can produce spurious messages in COL-01 and in DDDAUDIT.

---

[9] colaudit.sql is available for download from the Go-Faster Consultancy web site (www.go-faster.co.uk).

Error Code	Error Description	Comments
COL-09	Tables or views with the same number of columns in both Oracle and PeopleSoft, but in different positions.	This can be a problem if INSERT INTO statements do not explicitly list columns.
COL-10	Corresponding PeopleSoft and Oracle indexes with different numbers of columns.	
COL-11	Indexes in both Oracle and PeopleSoft, but with columns in different positions.	
COL-12	Warning: key columns not at the top of the record definition.	This is not an error, but it is contrary to PeopleTools development advice.

Mostly, the problems reported by colaudit.sql can be resolved by rebuilding the objects.

Summary

The chapter has described the PeopleTools data dictionary and its relationship to the Oracle data dictionary, and it has provided a reference for the PeopleTools tables that correspond to table structures.

On all database platforms, the data dictionary tells you what actually exists in the database, and it is used by the database to validate and execute SQL statements. The PeopleSoft data dictionary tells you what should exist in the database, and it is used by PeopleTools to dynamically generate SQL statements at run time.

Discrepancies in corresponding parts of the data dictionaries can cause PeopleTools to generate invalid SQL, leading to run-time errors. Hence, all changes to the database should, whenever possible, be implemented via the scripts built by the Application Designer.

CHAPTER 5

Keys and Indexing

This chapter discusses the use of keys and indexes in PeopleSoft, and how they translate into indexes and implicit constraints in Oracle (there is an almost total absence of explicit constraints in a PeopleSoft database). The previous chapter looked at how the two data dictionaries are related. Here, we look at how PeopleSoft uses the "keys"[1] defined in its data dictionary to generate SQL in the application and to create the indexes in the database to support that SQL.

We also examine the role of Application Designer in more detail. This Windows client program is a complete development environment for PeopleSoft online applications. In addition, it is used to specify Application Engine batch programs, to migrate functionality between PeopleSoft environments, and to apply PeopleSoft patches.

Application Designer is also a tool for the DBA. It is used to specify all the database objects, and it then generates and optionally executes the DDL scripts to build or alter them. I explain how the definition of PeopleSoft records controls which indexes are built, upon which columns, and whether the indexes are unique. The derivation of the generated DDL is explained in the next chapter.

First, I will recap some basic principles related to indexes, constraints, and keys.

What Is the Purpose of an Index?

This is the most succinct definition of the purpose of indexes that I have seen:

Indexes exist to reduce the cost of data retrieval.[2]

I will start by restating the obvious: databases store data in tables. That data can be queried back via a SQL statement:

```
SELECT column1
FROM   table1
WHERE  column2 = 'VALUE';
```

If the table has no indexes, when this statement is submitted, the database scans through the entire table and identifies all the rows where the condition is met. Every row in the table must be read from disk or, if you are lucky, the block buffer cache. Data that does not match the query is discarded. The

---

[1] "Key" is another word that means one thing in database terms and several different things when used by PeopleSoft.
[2] Jonathan Lewis, *Practical Oracle 8i* (Boston, MA: Addison-Wesley Professional, 2001).

time taken to perform this operation, of course, increases roughly in proportion to the number of rows on the table.

This is obviously not efficient for even moderately sized tables. Therefore, indexes exist to help the database find the data quickly. Indexes are really tables that, for each row in the table, contain the data for the indexed columns and the physical address of that row in the table.

If we go back to the example and assume that there is an index on COLUMN2 of TABLE1, then when the query is submitted, the database identifies COLUMN2 as an indexed column when it parses the SQL statement. It might use that index to find the rows for which the data matches the condition.

What Is a Constraint?

An *integrity* constraint restricts the values in one or more columns such that they conform to a condition. A *referential* or *foreign key* constraint verifies that data in the database is referentially integral, ensuring that a child record does not exist without a corresponding parent record.

If an enforced constraint is not met, it prevents a database update from taking place. Constraints can be made deferrable, and enforcement is deferred until commit time, in which case if the constraint is violated the entire transaction rolls back. Validation of the constraint can also be disabled without dropping the constraint, and subsequently enabled.

The benefit of using constraints is that processing occurs within the database engine and so does not have to be coded into every program that updates the database. In a client/server model, this also reduces SQL traffic across the network. However, the cost is some additional overhead on the database server.

PeopleSoft never uses explicitly defined constraints[3] because each database implements them differently. In PeopleTools, the validation of field values and referential integrity is defined in the PeopleSoft data dictionary in terms of the data model and is executed by the Pure Internet Architecture (PIA). Wherever the same record is used in the online system, the same validation is employed.

CAN I ADD EXPLICIT CONSTRAINTS TO PEOPLESOFT?

It has occasionally been suggested that it would be possible to use the information in the PeopleTools tables to generate a set of explicit constraints. I do not believe that this is either possible or advisable, for the following reasons:

---

[3] The length-checking constraints on character columns in a Unicode database, discussed in Chapter 4, are not used from application version 9.

- Some of the referential validation performed by the application involves effective dated logic that could not be coded within standard constraints.

- Parent records are not always defined in PeopleSoft where they could be.

- Since there is no way to turn off the PeopleSoft validation without significantly customizing the application, you would be doubling up on the work done to validate data.

- Some of the parent/child relationships and relationships to edit tables could be constructed as referential constraints. However, there is no guarantee that PeopleSoft inserts parents before children but deletes children before parents. Thus, the constraints would have to be deferred.

- There is no guarantee that batch programs only perform intermediate commits at times when the data is referentially integral. This could generate additional failures.

- PeopleSoft does not handle Oracle errors well. The end user would see an Oracle error rather than a meaningful message in their own language.

What Is the Purpose of a Unique Constraint?

A *unique* or *primary key* constraint specifies the columns whose values uniquely describe a single row on the table, and prevents more than one row from having that combination of values. A primary key constraint implies NOT NULL constraints on the primary key columns.

There are three ways to create a unique constraint on a table in Oracle:

- Explicitly create a unique index in a separate command.

- Specify a unique constraint within the CREATE TABLE command.

- Add a constraint to a table that uses a preexisting non-unique index.[4]

The three constructions are illustrated in Table 5-1.

---

[4]A unique index on the same columns as a non-unique index is slightly smaller and slightly more efficient because there is no need to provide for multiple rows with the same key values. However, this construction has the advantage of permitting additional columns in the index other than the unique key columns that might allow the index to satisfy a query without the need to visit the table. This could save an entire index.

Table 5-1. Unique Indexes vs. Unique Constraints

| ```
CREATE TABLE tab1
(a NUMBER
,b NUMBER
,c NUMBER
,d NUMBER
);

CREATE UNIQUE INDEX idx1
ON tab1(a,b,c);
``` | ```
CREATE TABLE tab1
(a NUMBER
,b NUMBER
,c NUMBER
,d NUMBER
,CONSTRAINT idx1
UNIQUE (a,b,c));
``` | ```
CREATE TABLE tab1
(a NUMBER
,b NUMBER
,c NUMBER
,d NUMBER
);

CREATE INDEX idx1
ON tab3(a,b,c,d);

ALTER TABLE tab1
ADD CONSTRAINT idx1
UNIQUE(a,b,c)
USING INDEX idx1;
``` |

The functional effect of these three methods is identical. It is not possible to insert duplicate rows into the table. A unique constraint violation error is produced:

```
ORA-00001: unique constraint (SYSADM.IDX1) violated
```

There is one minor difference. The unique constraint, unless it uses a preexisting non-unique index, implies a unique index, and you can see entries on both DBA_INDEXES and DBA_CONSTRAINTS. The index has the same name as the constraint. The unique index enforces uniqueness without creating a unique constraint, so there is no entry on DBA_CONSTRAINTS.

This excursion into unique constraints and their enforcement through unique or non-unique indexes is purely theoretical as far as this book goes. PeopleSoft never explicitly specifies any unique or referential constraints; it uses only the unique index syntax.

STAR TRANSFORMATIONS ON A PEOPLESOFT DATABASE?

I have encountered a few PeopleSoft customers running data-warehouse tools that generate star queries on their PeopleSoft Enterprise Performance Management (EPM) databases. Data is manipulated into one or more star schemas, and they use a data-warehouse tool such as Oracle Business Intelligence Enterprise Edition (OBIEE) that generates star queries.

The Oracle database has a feature called *star transformation*. This optimization technique is aimed at executing star queries efficiently. It relies on implicitly rewriting (or transforming) the SQL of the original query. Oracle's query optimizer automatically chooses to perform star transformation where it calculates that it is a cheaper way to execute the query.

Star transformation must be explicitly enabled by setting an initialization parameter, but it has some other prerequisites, including the following:
```

- Each dimension table is joined to the fact table using a primary key to foreign key join. So each dimension table must have a primary key, and each join column on the fact table must have a foreign key referencing the fact table.

- There must be a single-column bitmap index on every join column of the fact table. These join columns include all foreign key columns. Application Designer can create bitmap indexes. There is a delivered parameter in the index DDL model where the BITMAP keyword can be specified.

If you try to do this within a PeopleSoft schema, you run into some problems:

- Application Designer creates a unique index on the key columns of a record. You would have to manually add a primary key using the existing unique index. However, that is not possible if any of the keys are descending, because then the unique index would also be a function-based index.

- Application Designer cannot create any referential constraints; so again, you would have to add them manually. You might choose not to enforce the constraint in the database by specifying the NOVALIDATE option.

- Bitmap indexes are very dense structures that can behave badly if their underlying tables are subject to even fairly low levels of insert, update, or delete.[5] Some customers have written custom Application Engine programs to process data. These are sometimes complicated by the need to drop and re-create bitmap indexes and manipulate partitions.

---

[5] http://jonathanlewis.wordpress.com/2009/10/21/bitmap-updates/

Record Field Key Attributes

In Application Designer, the fields in a PeopleSoft record can be given certain key attributes (see Figure 5-1).

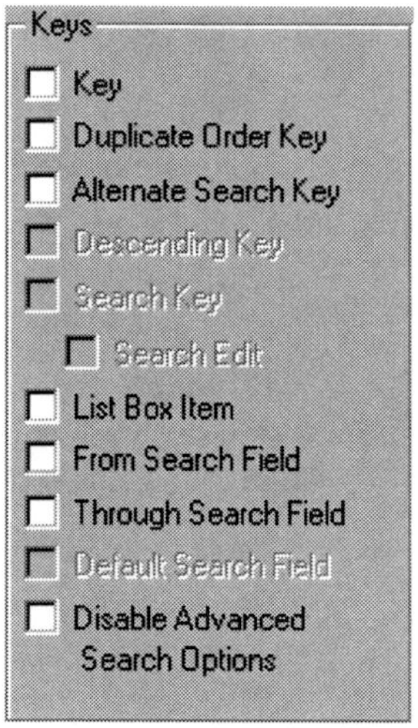

Figure 5-1. Key attributes

These key attributes have two main purposes:

- They control the behavior of the PeopleSoft application and therefore determine some of the SQL that is generated by the PIA and submitted to the database.

- The attributes with *key* in their names cause Application Designer to generate certain indexes to assist with the performance of the application. I refer to these as *system-generated* indexes to distinguish them from the additional *custom* or *user-defined* indexes that can be defined by developers.

Field Attributes and Application Behavior

This section looks at how key attributes on records control the behavior of the PeopleSoft application. The example used is the JOB_DATA component from the HCM 8.8 application.[6] It is one of the most heavily used parts of the HCM product.

---

[6] I have deliberately retained this example in the 2nd edition of this book, from what is now an old version of the application, because it brings together a number of PeopleTools behaviors in one example. This area changed in HCM 9.0. Additional uppercase fields hold uppercase copies of names, thus obviating the need for case-insensitive SQL queries. Row-level security has also changed.

Record Locator Dialog

In some places in the application, you may simply be able to insert a new key value, but usually you need to find existing data. In this case, before you enter a page in the PIA, you are presented with the record-locator dialog (see Figure 5-2), also known as the search dialog.

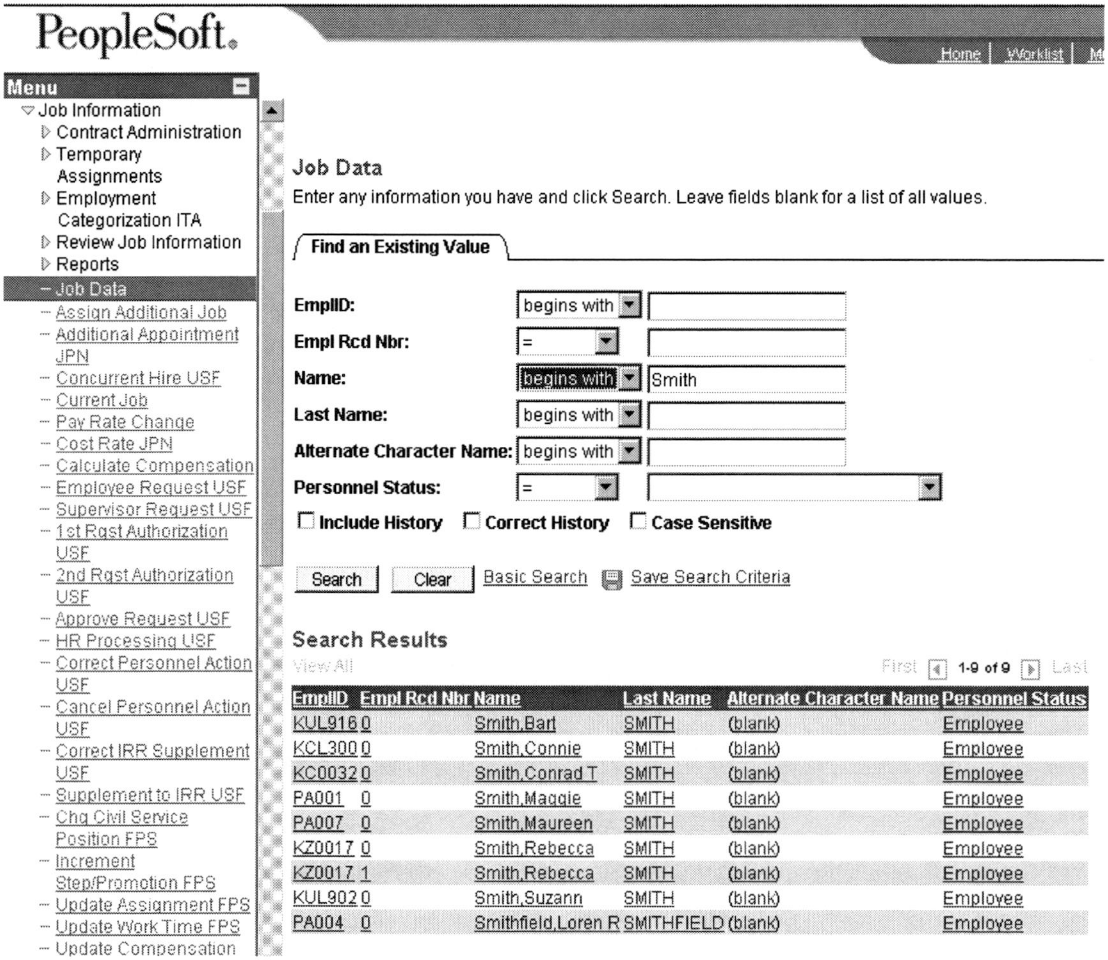

Figure 5-2. Record-locator or search dialog for the JOB_DATA component

The purpose of the search record is to permit the operator to identify the primary key values for the data to be retrieved into the component. Figure 5-3 shows that EMPLMT_SRCH_COR is specified in Application Designer as the search record for the JOB_DATA component.

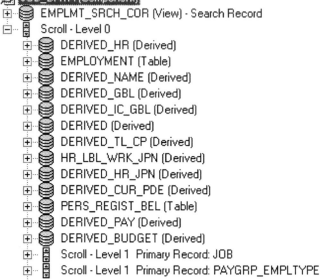

Figure 5-3. *JOB_DATA component structure from Application Designer*[7]

Figure 5-4 shows the definition of the EMPLMT_SRCH_COR record. EMPLID and EMPL_RCD are key fields. These two fields are also the first two key fields for each of the hierarchy of records, headed by EMPLOYMENT, that are queried by the component. It is the application developer's responsibility to ensure that these keys match; otherwise, the application does not function correctly.

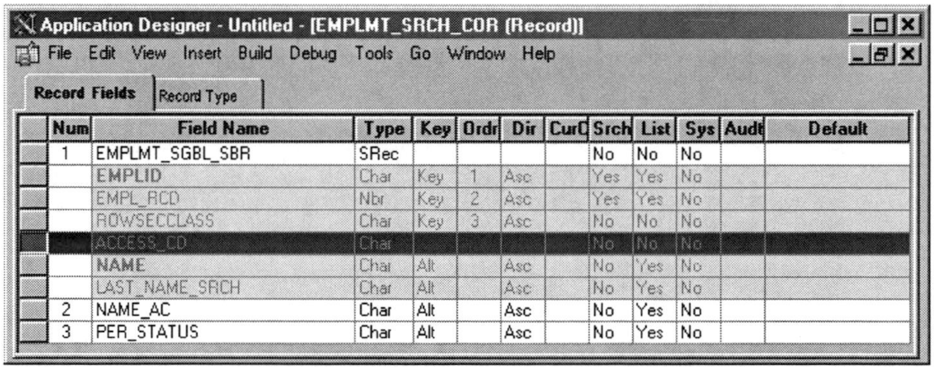

Num	Field Name	Type	Key	Ordr	Dir	CurD	Srch	List	Sys	Audt	Default
1	EMPLMT_SGBL_SBR	SRec					No	No	No		
	EMPLID	Char	Key	1	Asc		Yes	Yes	No		
	EMPL_RCD	Nbr	Key	2	Asc		Yes	Yes	No		
	ROWSECCLASS	Char	Key	3	Asc		No	No	No		
	ACCESS_CD	Char					No	No	No		
	NAME	Char	Alt		Asc		No	Yes	No		
	LAST_NAME_SRCH	Char	Alt		Asc		No	Yes	No		
2	NAME_AC	Char	Alt		Asc		No	Yes	No		
3	PER_STATUS	Char	Alt		Asc		No	Yes	No		

Figure 5-4. *Search record for the JOB_DATA component*

---

[7] The "derived" records are effectively groups of working storage variables used by the component.

The format of the search dialog page is determined by the key field attributes of the record specified as the component search record. The user can specify criteria for the fields in this dialog to restrict the search results, before eventually selecting one of the key values in the list.

The fields that appear under the Find an Existing Value tab in the search dialog (in Figure 5-2) are

- Key or duplicate key fields that also have the search attribute

- Alternate search fields

Only fields with key or alternate key attributes can be given the search attribute. ROWSECCLASS does not appear in the search dialog shown in Figure 5-2 because although it is also a key field, it does not have the search attribute.

In this example, the search record EMPLMT_SRCH_COR contains a subrecord EMPLMT_SGBL_SBR. A *subrecord* in PeopleTools is simply a group of fields that often appear together on various records or even other subrecords. They can be added to a record as a group by adding the subrecord. The attributes of the fields in the subrecord are inherited by the record in which the subrecord is used. The record definition shown in Figure 5-4 has been expanded to show the subrecord EMPLMT_SGBL_SBR. EMPLID is a key field in subrecord EMPLMT_SGBL_SBR; hence it is a key on record EMPLMT_SRCH_COR.

Behind the scenes, the search results were produced from the SQL in Listing 5-1. The SELECT clause was determined by the list of Key and List fields.

Listing 5-1. SQL Trace of the Search Dialog

```
PSAPPSRV.3608    1-31132   14.55.58     0.000 Cur#1.3608.HR88 RC=0 Dur=0.000
COM Stmt=
SELECT DISTINCT EMPLID, EMPL_RCD, NAME, LAST_NAME_SRCH, NAME_AC, PER_STATUS
FROM   PS_EMPLMT_SRCH_COR
WHERE  ROWSECCLASS=:1
AND    UPPER(NAME) LIKE UPPER('Smith') || '%' ESCAPE '\'
ORDER BY NAME, EMPLID, EMPL_RCD
PSAPPSRV.3608    1-31133   14.55.58     0.000 Cur#1.3608.HR88 RC=0
Dur=0.000 Bind-1 type=2 length=7 value=HCDPALL
```

There are several points of interest in the search dialog SQL:

- ROWSECCLASS is a field name that triggers special processing by PeopleTools. It is common for search records to be views that join application data with security data. Operators are allocated to security classes. In the preceding example, the primary security class for the user is HCDPALL. So when a column called ROWSECCLASS with the key attribute is encountered in the search record, the condition on ROWSECCLASS in the WHERE clause is automatically added. The query on PS_EMPLMT_SRCH_COR returns the employees that an operator with the specified security class is permitted to see in the application.

- The DISTINCT keyword is always added to the search dialog. The use of DISTINCT makes Oracle retrieve and sort the entire result set before a single row is fetched. Even though the search dialog only fetches up to the first 300 rows, all the data is fed to the SQL sort operation. This can be a cause of poor search dialog performance.

- Search records, as in this example, are often views. The DISTINCT keyword can alter the execution plan of the query, taking the tables in the view in the order encountered in the SELECT clause of the view. An ordered hint in the view can suppress undesirable execution plans. However, the scope of hints in views is not limited to the view. If the view is used elsewhere, the hint may cause undesirable effects.

- Note also that when the user types **Smith** into the Name field, the literal 'Smith' appears in the generated SQL statement. Every time a user searches for something different or searches by a different attribute, a different SQL statement is generated and parsed.

- The condition in the WHERE clause on the column NAME uses the LIKE operator because the operator specified is begins with (see Figure 5-5). Where the whole of a search string is entered, the operator can choose to use the = operator rather than begins with. The Component Processor generates the SQL with = instead of LIKE. Sometimes, if the search key column is indexed, this can result in better performance. There is an advantage in training the users to do this.

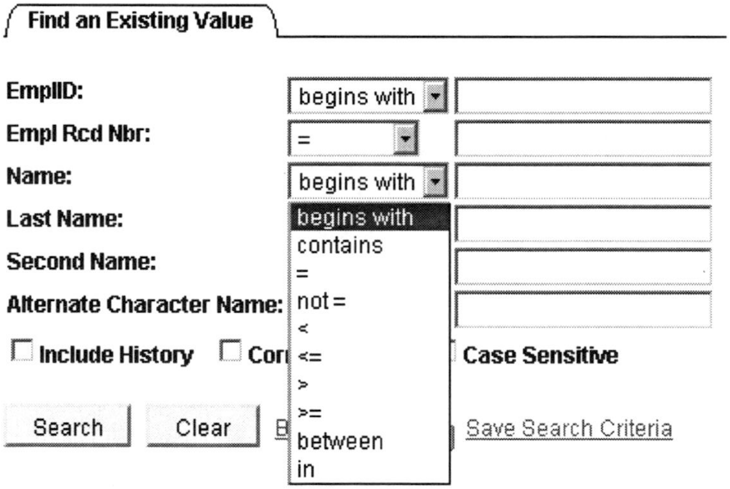

Find an Existing Value

EmplID:	begins with ▼	
Empl Rcd Nbr:	= ▼	
Name:	begins with ▼	
Last Name:	begins with	
Second Name:	contains	
Alternate Character Name:	=	
	not =	
☐ Include History ☐ Cor	<	Case Sensitive
	<=	
	>	
Search Clear B	>=	Save Search Criteria
	between	
	in	

Figure 5-5. Operators available in the search dialog

■ **Note** In earlier versions of PeopleTools, the LIKE operator was used when the string entered by the operator was shorter than the field defined in PeopleTools. If the string entered was the same length as the field, it used =. This is why PeopleSoft recommended that customers use five-character values for SETID and BUSINESS_UNIT, which are both five-character fields. This behavior changed somewhere between PeopleTools 8.44 and 8.47.

- This query was case-insensitive, so PeopleSoft searches for UPPER(NAME) LIKE UPPER('Smith'). This disables the use of the index on NAME on the underlying table and can be another cause of poor performance. There are two options in this situation: either globally disable the use of case-insensitive searching throughout PeopleSoft (set in PeopleTools ➤ Utilities ➤ PeopleTools Options) or create a function-based index leading on NAME.

Component Queries

The search dialog discussed in the previous section provides EMPLID and EMPL_RCD values as a key to query the component.

One of the records queried by the component is JOB. Figure 5-6 shows that this record has four fields defined with the key attribute. These key fields tell PeopleSoft what columns should be specified to uniquely identify a row in the record. With only two fields specified from the search dialog, the PIA expects to retrieve many rows.

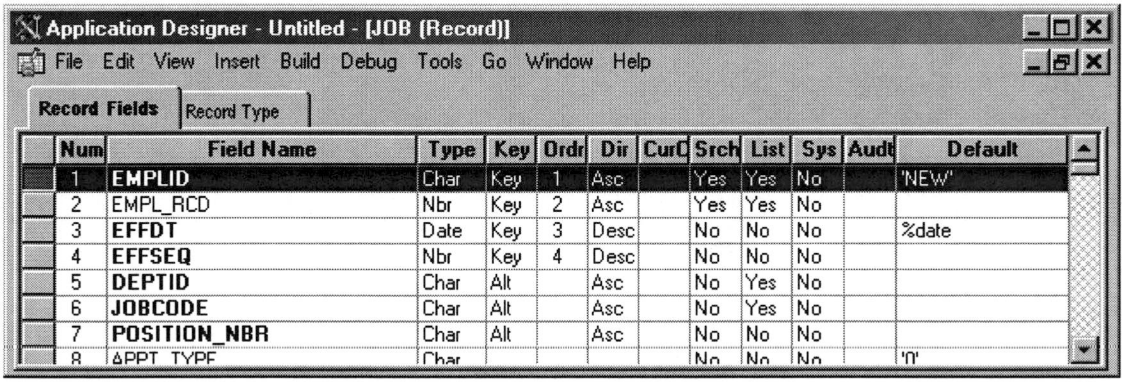

Num	Field Name	Type	Key	Ordr	Dir	CurD	Srch	List	Sys	Audt	Default
1	EMPLID	Char	Key	1	Asc		Yes	Yes	No		'NEW'
2	EMPL_RCD	Nbr	Key	2	Asc		Yes	Yes	No		
3	EFFDT	Date	Key	3	Desc		No	No	No		%date
4	EFFSEQ	Nbr	Key	4	Desc		No	No	No		
5	DEPTID	Char	Alt		Asc		No	Yes	No		
6	JOBCODE	Char	Alt		Asc		No	Yes	No		
7	POSITION_NBR	Char	Alt		Asc		No	No	No		
8	APPT_TYPE	Char					No	No	No		'0'

Figure 5-6. *The keys view of Application Designer, showing a record with a unique key*

On entering the JOB component, the PIA generates the following SQL to retrieve the job history for a particular employee. The two known keys are specified in the WHERE clause, but all the keys are used to generate the ORDER BY clause. EFFDT and EFFSEQ are descending keys on the JOB record, so the query is in descending order on those columns:

```
SELECT EMPLID,
...
FROM PS_JOB
WHERE EMPLID=:1
AND EMPL_RCD=:2
ORDER BY EMPLID, EMPL_RCD, EFFDT DESC, EFFSEQ DESC
```

EFFECTIVE DATE/SEQUENCE PROCESSING

Columns called EFFDT and EFFSEQ automatically trigger special effective date and sequence processing in PeopleTools. Effective dated rows are active from the EFFDT until superseded by a later row. PeopleSoft handles multiple effective dated records on the same day by having an effective sequence in the column EFFSEQ. The maximum effective sequence number is considered to supersede the other records for the same effective date.

As shown in Figure 5-6, the fields have a descending key attribute. When data is loaded into a page, the PIA queries the rows in descending order, and it only fetches rows until EFFDT is less than or equal to the current date. The last row fetched is the current effective dated row. The PIA only queries the historical rows if the Include History check box is selected.

In some places, such as the Query tool, PeopleTools automatically builds the subqueries to get the current effective row, or the maximum sequenced rows, as shown in the following example (see also Chapter 11):

```
SELECT A.EMPLID
  FROM PS_JOB B, PS_EMPLMT_SRCH_QRY B1
  WHERE A.EMPLID = A1.EMPLID
    AND A.EMPL_RCD = A1.EMPL_RCD
    AND A1.ROWSECCLASS = 'HCDPALL'
    AND (A.EFFDT =
        (SELECT MAX(A_ED.EFFDT) FROM PS_JOB A_ED
        WHERE A.EMPLID = A_ED.EMPLID
          AND A.EMPL_RCD = A_ED.EMPL_RCD
          AND A_ED.EFFDT <= SYSDATE)
    AND A.EFFSEQ =
        (SELECT MAX(A_ES.EFFSEQ) FROM PS_JOB A_ES
        WHERE A.EMPLID = A_ES.EMPLID
          AND A.EMPL_RCD = A_ES.EMPL_RCD
          AND A.EFFDT = A_ES.EFFDT) )
```

Field Attributes and System Index Definitions

We have seen so far how the key attributes on a record control some of the functionality of PeopleSoft applications, and hence the SQL that is created by the application. This approach produces indexes that generally result in good performance of the SQL generated by the online application. However, it also produces a large number of indexes. Typically in a PeopleSoft 8.x database, the volume of the indexes is about 5% larger than the volume of the tables.

Application Designer can build SQL scripts to build the tables, indexes, views, and triggers in a PeopleSoft database, and it can also build these objects directly. The exact format of the CREATE TABLE and CREATE INDEX commands can be customized to include some additional physical parameters (see Chapter 6).

Data Mover, another Windows client program, is PeopleSoft's import/export utility. Therefore, it also creates tables and indexes in the database. The DDL generated during import is written to the export file when it is exported. Data Mover provides a platform-independent environment in which to run scripts and perform certain administrative tasks during installation or upgrade.

The next sections examine how the same information is used to determine what indexes are necessary. I have created a record (see Figure 5-7) and gradually add various key field attributes to illustrate what indexes are built.

No Keys

Some tables have no key attributes defined on any fields (see Figure 5-7). Therefore, they are created without any system-defined indexes. Typically, these tables either contain only a single row or are used for batch working storage.

There is, of course, nothing stopping the developer from specifying a *user index*, which is described later in this chapter.

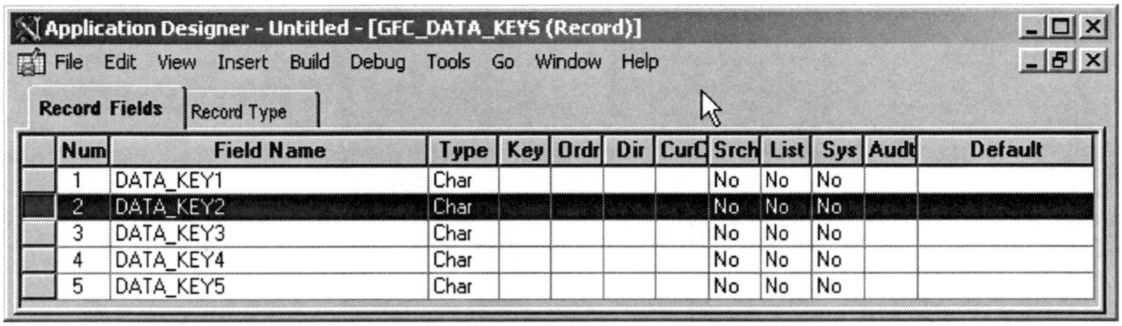
Application Designer - Untitled - [GFC_DATA_KEYS (Record)]
File Edit View Insert Build Debug Tools Go Window Help
Record Fields
Record Type
Num Field Name Type Key Ordr Dir CurC Srch List Sys Audt Default
1 DATA_KEY1 Char No No No
2 DATA_KEY2 Char No No No
3 DATA_KEY3 Char No No No
4 DATA_KEY4 Char No No No
5 DATA_KEY5 Char No No No

Figure 5-7. *A record with no keys*

Key

The key fields on a record are those that are used to uniquely identify a single row. Therefore, Application Designer builds a unique index for the key fields.

If a row in a table is queried by the primary key, then that particular key can be found in the primary key index. The row can be found with a single fetch operation, and no further searching is required. This is the most efficient possible use of an index.

Figure 5-8 shows a record in Application Designer with only two key fields.

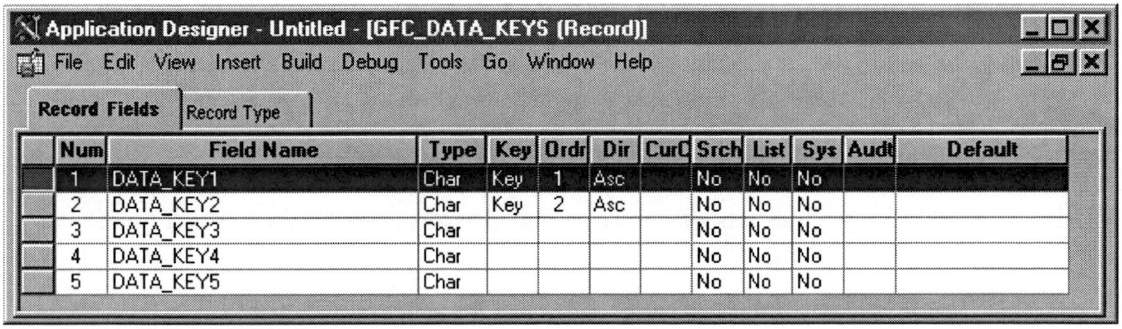
Application Designer - Untitled - [GFC_DATA_KEYS (Record)]
File Edit View Insert Build Debug Tools Go Window Help
Record Fields
Record Type
Num Field Name Type Key Ordr Dir CurC Srch List Sys Audt Default
1 DATA_KEY1 Char Key 1 Asc No No No
2 DATA_KEY2 Char Key 2 Asc No No No
3 DATA_KEY3 Char No No No
4 DATA_KEY4 Char No No No
5 DATA_KEY5 Char No No No

Figure 5-8. *A record with a unique key*

The key fields are used to build a unique index, which can then be seen in the Change Record Indexes dialog (Tools ➤ Data Administration ➤ Indexes) shown in Figure 5-9.

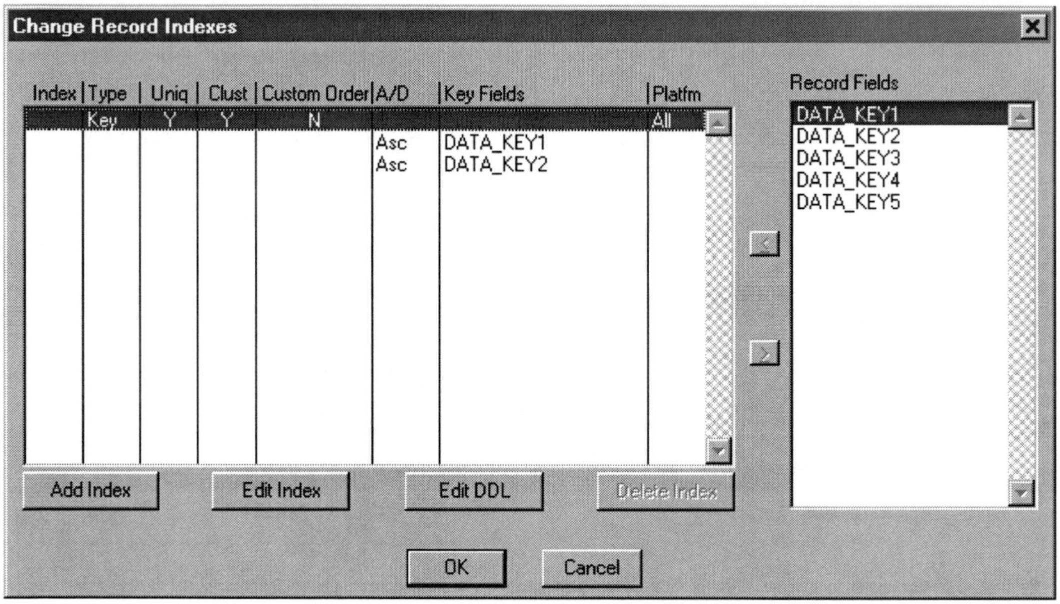

Figure 5-9. *Index definition*

As you can see in Figure 5-9, the Delete Index button is grayed out. System-generated indexes cannot be deleted other than by changing the field attributes. However, changing field attributes changes the application.

The indexes generated by Application Designer have the following naming convention:

```
INDEX_NAME = 'PS '||<index_id>||<peoplesoft record name>
```

The index ID, described in Table 5-2, indicates which kind of index it is.

Table 5-2. *Index IDs*

Index ID	Description
_	PeopleSoft key index. Implied from the record definition.
1–9	Alternate search key indexes. Implied from the record definition.
#	List index. Implied from the record definition. Only applicable up to PeopleTools 7.5x; not used in PeopleTools 8.
A–Z	User-specified index.

Thus, provided that a nonstandard table name has not been specified on the record definition, the primary key index generated by Application Designer has the same name as the table on which it is built.

The Edit DDL button on the Change Record Indexes dialog leads to the Maintain DDL dialog (not shown), where you can click the View DDL button to see the DDL that is generated by Application Designer, as shown in Figure 5-10.

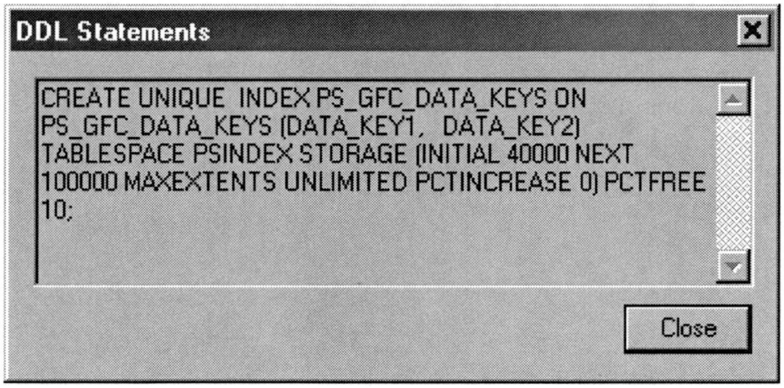
DDL Statements
CREATE UNIQUE INDEX PS_GFC_DATA_KEYS ON PS_GFC_DATA_KEYS (DATA_KEY1, DATA_KEY2) TABLESPACE PSINDEX STORAGE (INITIAL 40000 NEXT 100000 MAXEXTENTS UNLIMITED PCTINCREASE 0) PCTFREE 10;
Close

Figure 5-10. *Index DDL*

Descending Key

We have already seen how PeopleSoft uses descending keys to control the order in which data is queried into search dialogs and components. In Figure 5-11, the first key field is descending.

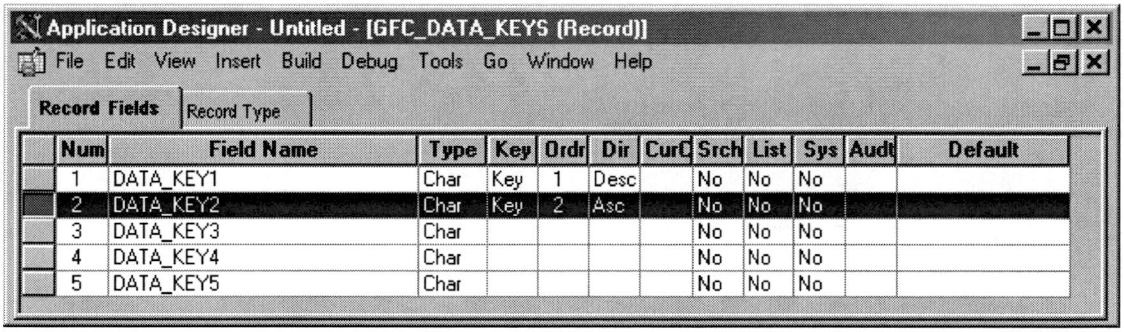
Application Designer - Untitled - [GFC_DATA_KEYS (Record)]
File Edit View Insert Build Debug Tools Go Window Help
Record Fields
Record Type
Num Field Name Type Key Ordr Dir CurC Srch List Sys Audt Default
1 DATA_KEY1 Char Key 1 Desc No No No
2 DATA_KEY2 Char Key 2 Asc No No No
3 DATA_KEY3 Char No No No
4 DATA_KEY4 Char No No No
5 DATA_KEY5 Char No No No

Figure 5-11. *A record with a descending key field*

The descending key attribute is carried forward into the index that is created (see Figure 5-12).

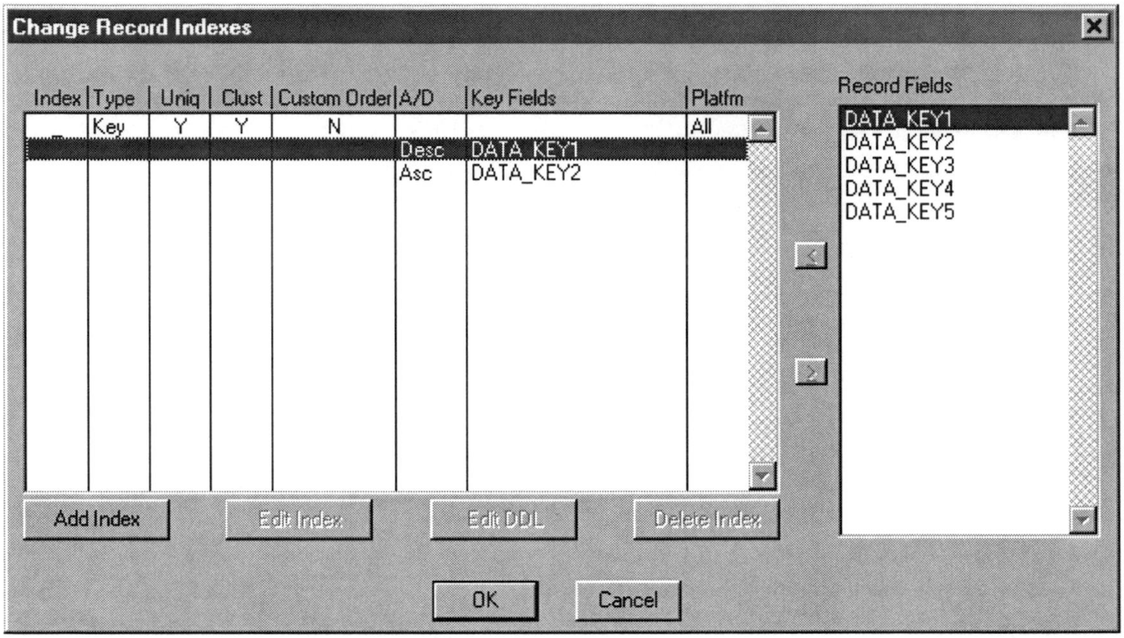

Figure 5-12. Change Record Indexes dialog for a record with a descending key field

Descending columns in the index are built in descending order in the index. A DESC keyword appears in the DDL after the column. This applies to indexes implied by the key definitions and any additional user-defined indexes. PeopleSoft removed this behavior in PeopleTools 8.15 but reintroduced it in 8.48 (see Figure 5-13).[8]

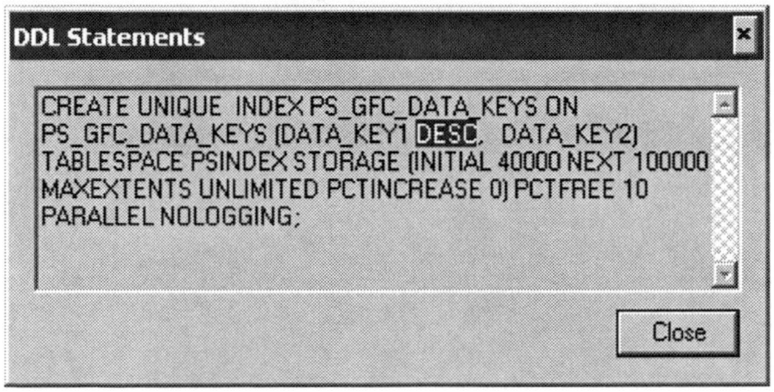

Figure 5-13. Index DDL for a record with a descending key field

---

[8] PeopleSoft removed the DESC keyword because Oracle Bug #869177, which affected most versions of Oracle 8.1.x, could cause the error ORA-3113 when accessing a descending index. It didn't come back until PeopleTools 8.48, which was not certified on Oracle 8*i*.

Duplicate Order Key

Even if a record does not have a field or group of fields that uniquely identify each row, PeopleTools still needs to know by which fields it should query the record. In this case, a duplicate key should be defined, as shown in Figure 5-14.

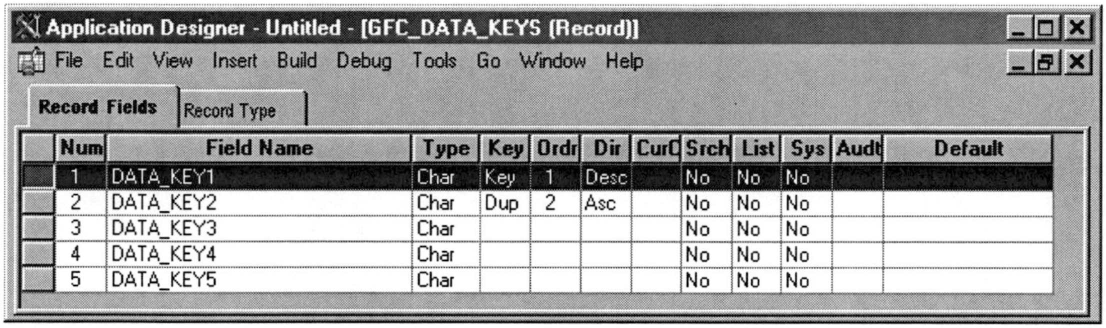
Application Designer - Untitled - [GFC_DATA_KEYS (Record)]
File Edit View Insert Build Debug Tools Go Window Help
Record Fields
Record Type
Num Field Name Type Key Ordr Dir CurC Srch List Sys Audt Default
1 DATA_KEY1 Char Key 1 Desc No No No
2 DATA_KEY2 Char Dup 2 Asc No No No
3 DATA_KEY3 Char No No No
4 DATA_KEY4 Char No No No
5 DATA_KEY5 Char No No No

Figure 5-14. *A record with a duplicate key*

Either Key or Duplicate Order Key can be specified in the field properties (see Figure 5-15), but not both.

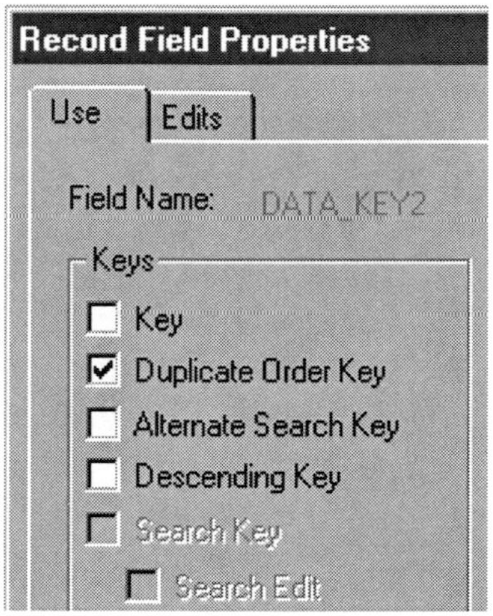
Record Field Properties
Use
Edits
Field Name: DATA_KEY2
Keys
Key
Duplicate Order Key
Alternate Search Key
Descending Key
Search Key
Search Edit

Figure 5-15. *Duplicate Order Key field attribute*

If any one of the key fields is specified as a Duplicate Order Key, then the key index is not built as a unique index. In Figure 5-16, the unique flag is set to N.

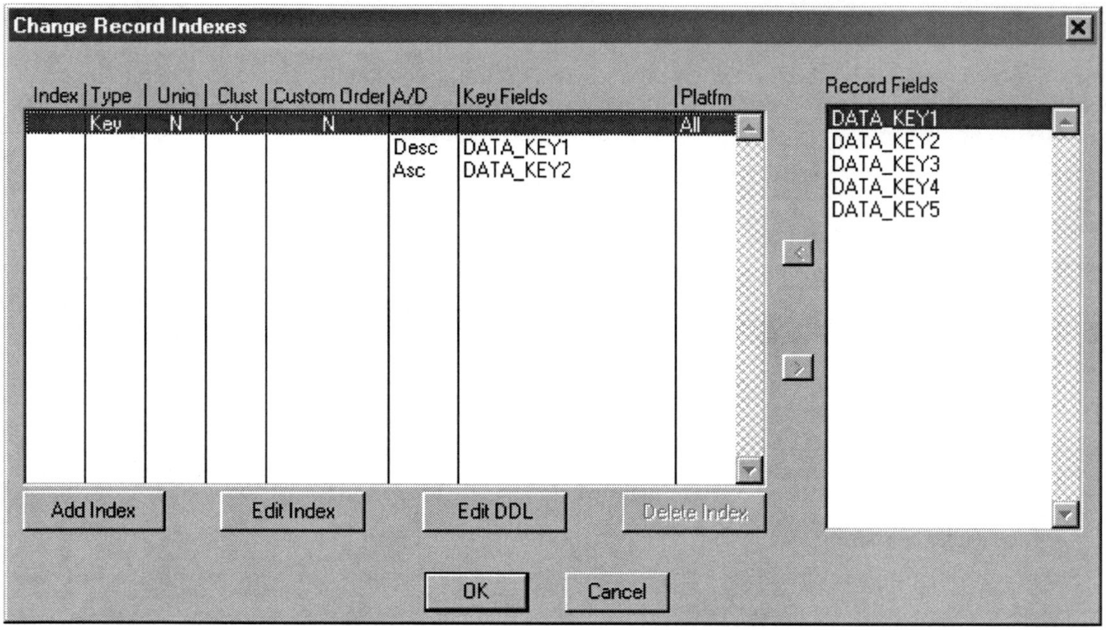

Figure 5-16. *A non-unique key index*

The UNIQUE keyword has disappeared from the index DDL in Figure 5-17 (but you may notice that there are two spaces between CREATE and INDEX).

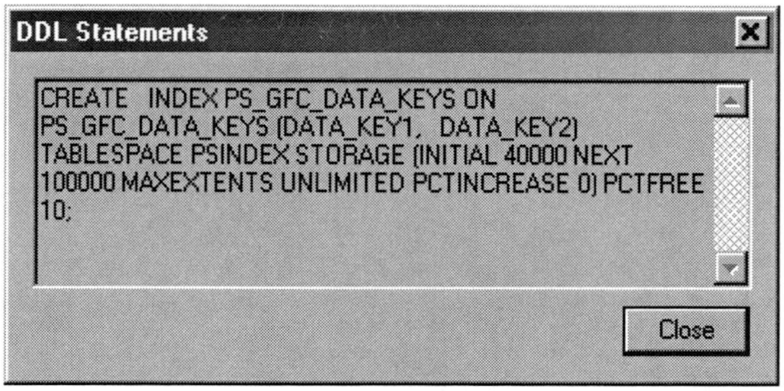

Figure 5-17. *DDL to create a non-unique key index*

Alternate Search Key

Alternate search keys are columns by which the data can be queried from the search dialog, but which are not part of the primary key. Figure 5-18 shows two alternate key fields in addition to the two key fields.

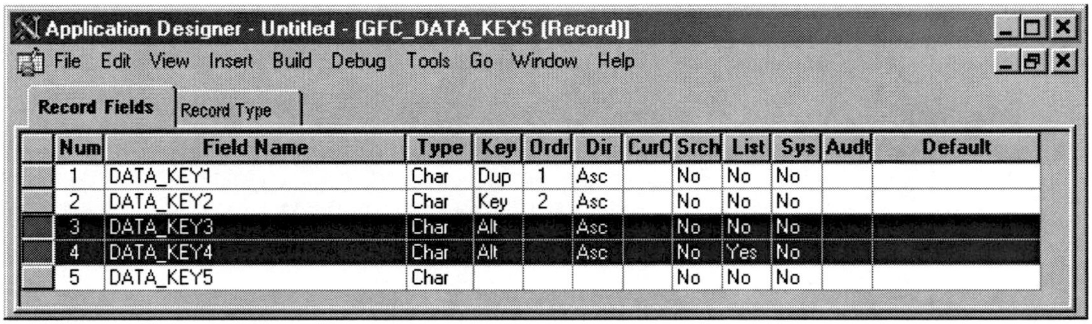

	Num	Field Name	Type	Key	Ordr	Dir	CurC	Srch	List	Sys	Audt	Default
	1	DATA_KEY1	Char	Dup	1	Asc		No	No	No		
	2	DATA_KEY2	Char	Key	2	Asc		No	No	No		
	3	DATA_KEY3	Char	Alt		Asc		No	No	No		
	4	DATA_KEY4	Char	Alt		Asc		No	Yes	No		
	5	DATA_KEY5	Char					No	No	No		

Figure 5-18. A record with two alternate search keys

To support search dialog queries on alternate search keys, PeopleSoft automatically creates an index for each alternate search field that is composed of that field followed by the primary (but not the duplicate) key fields (see Figure 5-19).

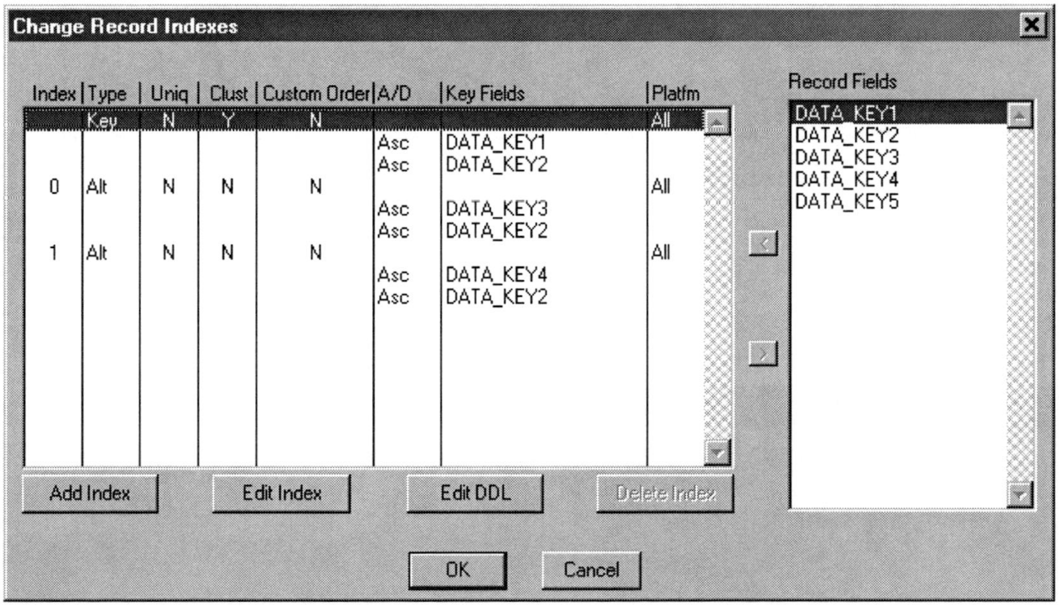

Figure 5-19. Alternate search key indexes

Uniqueness of Alternate Search Key Indexes

It follows that if a record has a unique key index, the unique key fields are included within the columns of each of the alternate search key indexes. Therefore, the composite alternate search keys are themselves unique.

For example, Figure 5-20 shows the indexes on the JOB record. The four key fields also appear in each of the alternate search key indexes.

Change Record Indexes

Index	Type	Uniq	Clust	Custom Order	A/D	Key Fields	Platfm
	Key	N	Y	N			All
					Asc	DATA_KEY1	
					Asc	DATA_KEY2	
0	Alt	N	N	N			All
					Asc	DATA_KEY3	
					Asc	DATA_KEY2	
1	Alt	N	N	N			All
					Asc	DATA_KEY4	
					Asc	DATA_KEY2	

Record Fields: DATA_KEY1, DATA_KEY2, DATA_KEY3, DATA_KEY4, DATA_KEY5

Add Index | Edit Index | Edit DDL | Delete Index | OK | Cancel

Figure 5-20. Key and alternate search key indexes

Unfortunately, PeopleSoft does not create these indexes as unique indexes. This nugget of information can be very valuable to the cost-based optimizer, which has special optimization when it is able to use a unique index.

Even more unfortunate is that the Unique check box in the Edit Index dialog is grayed out on all system-generated indexes, including alternate search key indexes (see Figure 5-21).

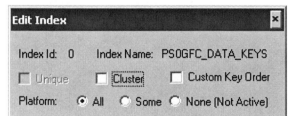

Edit Index

Index Id: 0   Index Name: PSOGFC_DATA_KEYS

☐ Unique   ☐ Cluster   ☐ Custom Key Order
Platform: ⦿ All   ○ Some   ○ None (Not Active)

Figure 5-21. Edit Index dialog

The DBA could simply edit the index-creation scripts generated by Application Designer to build the indexes as unique. However, the next time Application Designer is asked to build the create-index DDL for that table, it will detect that the index is unique when it should not be, and it will generate a script to drop and re-create the index.[9] There is a significant risk that the unique attribute may get lost in subsequent object-build operations.

The only way to make PeopleSoft generate these indexes as unique indexes is to update the PeopleTools table directly, as follows:

```
UPDATE psversion SET version = version + 1
WHERE objecttypename IN('SYS','RDM');

UPDATE pslock SET version = version + 1
WHERE objecttypename IN('SYS','RDM');

UPDATE psrecdefn
SET version = (
  SELECT version  FROM psversion WHERE objecttypename = 'RDM')
WHERE recname = '<record name>';

UPDATE psindexdefn a
SET    a.uniqueflag = 1
WHERE  a.uniqueflag = 0
AND    a.indextype = 3
AND    EXISTS(
           SELECT 'x'
           FROM   psindexdefn k
           WHERE  k.recname = a.recname
           AND    k.indexid = '_'
           AND    k.indextype = 1
           AND    k.uniqueflag = 1)
AND    a.recname = '<record name>'
;
```

The Unique check box is then selected, albeit still grayed out (see Figure 5-22), and the index-build process creates the desired unique indexes.

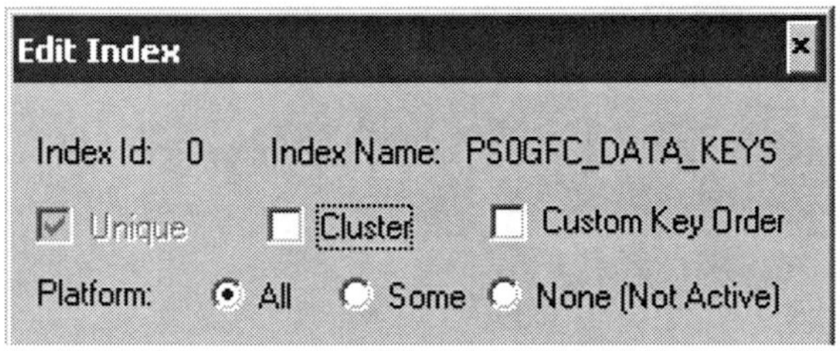

Figure 5-22. A unique alternate search key index

---

[9] The same problem occurs if the **BITMAP** variable in the DDL model is used to hold the UNIQUE keyword. Application Designer builds the correct DDL but keeps rebuilding it because the index is unique and PSINDEXDEFN.UNIQUEFLAG = 0.

■ **Caution** Updating the PeopleTools tables as described in this section is, of course, not supported by PeopleSoft. Nor does this section imply that you should make all the alternate search key indexes unique. As always, follow the principle of minimum intrusion, and make this change only where it brings a demonstrable benefit.

Alternate Search Key Indexes in PeopleTools 7.x

Up to PeopleTools 7.x, the alternate search key indexes consisted of the alternate search key, followed by the primary keys, followed by any other alternate search keys or list-box fields specified for the record. Thus, all of the alternate search key indexes contained the same columns, but in a different order.

The effect of removing the additional columns and the additional list index (see Figure 5-23) has reduced the volume of indexes in a typical PeopleSoft database by approximately 15%.

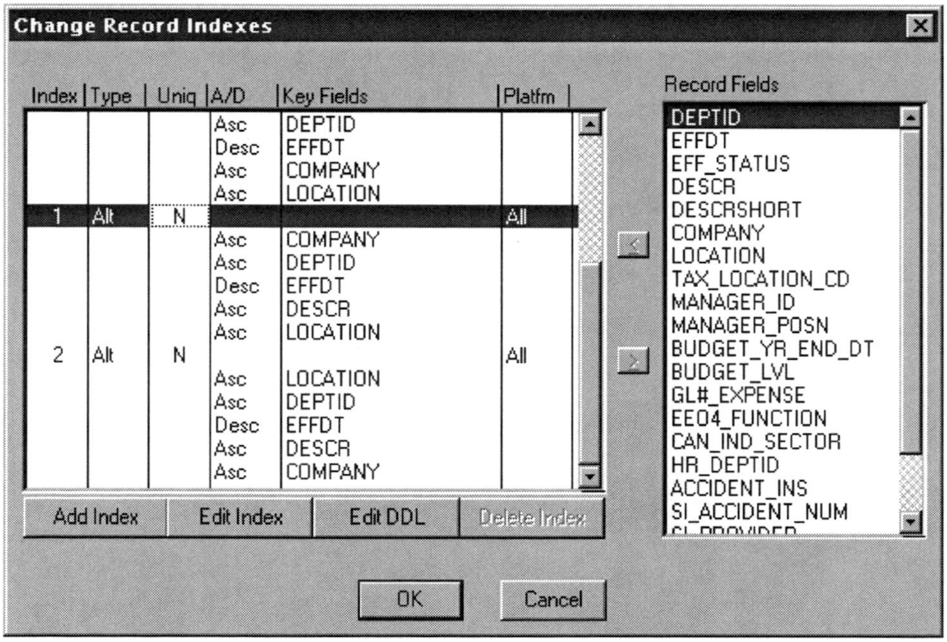

Figure 5-23. Alternate search keys in PeopleTools 7.x

List

The list-box attribute controls which fields from the component search record appear in the result set (see Figure 5-24).

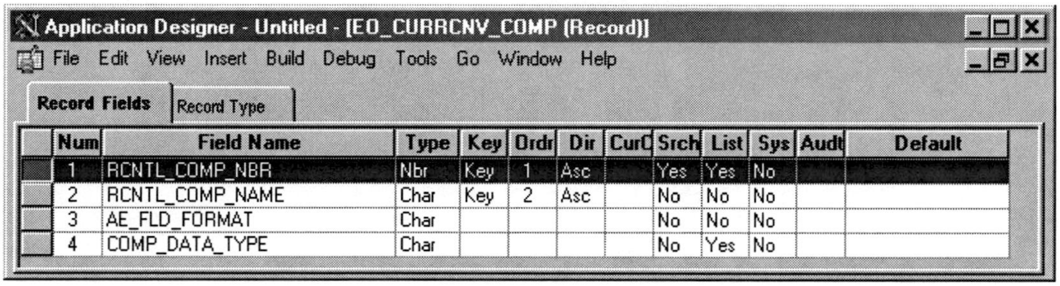

Application Designer - Untitled - [EO_CURRCNV_COMP (Record)]

File Edit View Insert Build Debug Tools Go Window Help

Record Fields | Record Type

Num	Field Name	Type	Key	Ordr	Dir	CurC	Srch	List	Sys	Audt	Default
1	RCNTL_COMP_NBR	Nbr	Key	1	Asc		Yes	Yes	No		
2	RCNTL_COMP_NAME	Char	Key	2	Asc		No	No	No		
3	AE_FLD_FORMAT	Char					No	No	No		
4	COMP_DATA_TYPE	Char					No	Yes	No		

Figure 5-24. A record with a list field

In PeopleTools 7.x and earlier, a separate index was built that contained each of the list-box columns (see Figure 5-25). The intention appeared to be that the list index would supply all the columns for the list box without visiting the table.

The list indexes consumed space in the database, generated additional redo logging, and degraded DML for very little benefit. Most list indexes were hardly ever used. Most of the panel-search records are actually views, which cannot be indexed. The rule-based optimizer, which was more likely to be used at this time, is predisposed to use the unique indexes. On the rare occasions when the list index was used, it did not significantly improve performance.

This index is no longer built from PeopleTools 8.

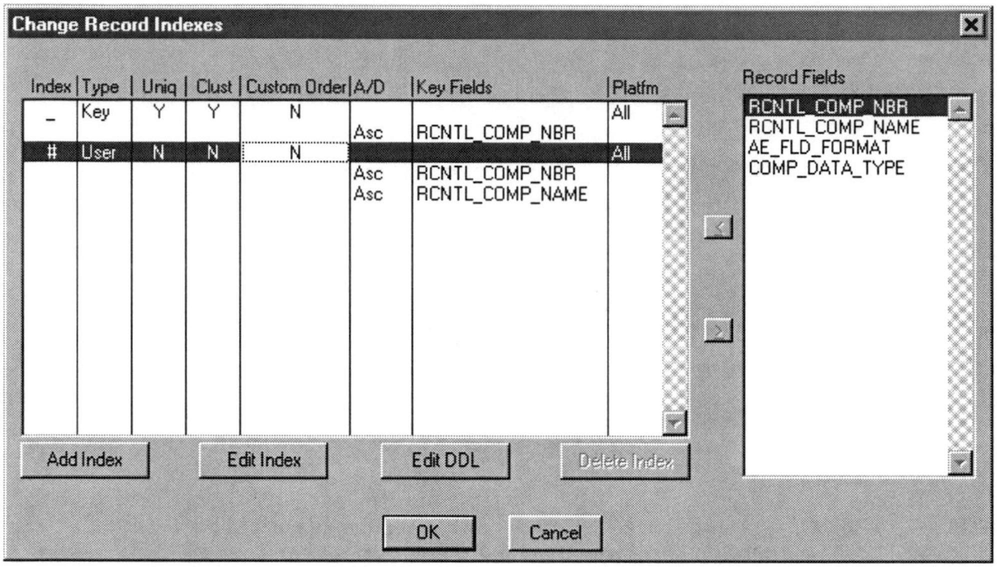

Figure 5-25. *List index in PeopleTools 7.5x[10]*

Custom Key Order

The order of the columns in the system-generated indexes follows the order of columns in the table. From PeopleTools 8, this can be overridden on specific indexes with the Custom Key Order attribute (see Figure 5-26).

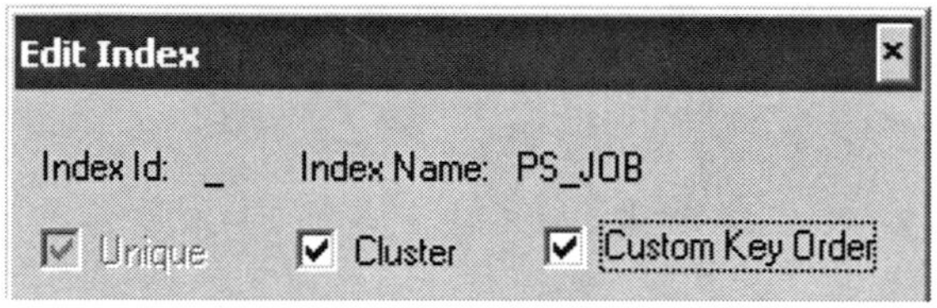

Figure 5-26. *Custom Key Order attribute*

Selecting the Custom Key Order check box enables drag-and drop-of columns in the Change Record Indexes dialog (see Figure 5-27) for system-generated indexes in exactly the same way that it has always been possible for user-defined indexes.

---

[10] This screenshot is actually from PeopleTools 8.18.10 running on the HR8 SP1 demo database. There was a step in the upgrade process from PeopleTools 7.5 to 8 to remove existing list indexes, because you can't delete them in Application Designer. Two of them have slipped through to this demo database: EO_CNV_CMP_LANG and EO_CURRCNV_COMP still have list (#) indexes, and you can still build them with Application Designer!

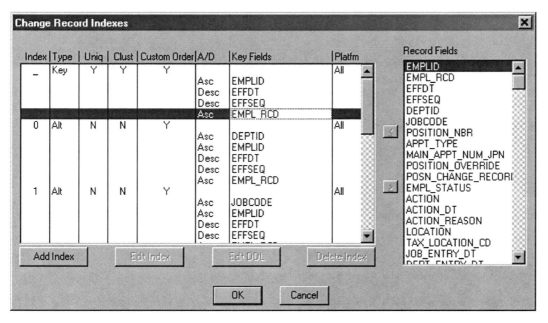

Figure 5-27. *Custom Key Order attribute on a primary key index*

On the JOB record, EMPL_RCD is delivered as the second key column. This column is used to handle the situation that occurs in some companies in which an employee can have two concurrent jobs or may be temporarily posted to another job, perhaps overseas. In companies that do not use this feature, all rows have an EMPL_RCD of zero. Even when concurrent job processing is used, only a very small proportion of employees normally have rows with a nonzero EMPL_RCD.

In this example (see Figure 5-27), I have demoted EMPL_RCD to be the last column in every index. I can't remove the column from the index without changing the field attributes, and that will change the application functionality. While the column is still part of the key, it will be referenced in the queries generated by PeopleTools, so it needs to be in the index. Otherwise, there are occasions when SQL queries will reference the table where previously they would have been fully satisfied from the index alone. So I have relegated the field EMPL_RCD to the bottom of the index because it does not help the selectivity of the queries. In this particular case, it made sense to do the same to all the indexes. Custom key order has been separately specified for each system-generated index.

In previous versions, the same effect was achieved by suppressing index creation for a PeopleTools-defined index and adding a user index to replace it. However, this created the potential for problems during upgrades and manual errors when specifying the alternate index.

Custom key order cannot be enabled on indexes where the key fields are on subrecords. In this case, the only option is to suppress and replace the index as described previously.

User-Defined Indexes

The automatically generated indexes derived from the field attributes are usually suitable for most of the SQL generated by PeopleTools. However, it is inevitable that some processing—particularly batch processing—requires additional indexes.

Additional indexes can be added by the developer via the Add Index dialog shown in Figure 5-28.

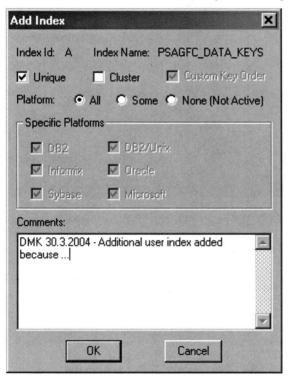

Figure 5-28. Add Index dialog

A user index can also be unique, as is the case in Figure 5-28. There is nothing to prevent the same table from having more than one unique index on different columns.

The Cluster option has no meaning when PeopleSoft is installed on an Oracle database. The variable does not appear in the Create Index DDL model for Oracle. On DB2, Microsoft SQL Server, and Sybase, it adds the CLUSTER keyword to the Create Index DDL. On these platforms, a clustered index is similar to an index-organized table in Oracle.

The Custom Key Order option is grayed out on user indexes (see Figure 5-28) because the choice and order of the columns is already entirely at the developer's discretion.

From PeopleTools 8.4x, separate comments can be recorded for user indexes only. User indexes can also be changed without changing the record, can be separately upgraded, and are recorded separately in an Application Designer upgrade project. Since system-generated indexes can only be changed by changing the record, comments can only be put in the comments for the record.

The developer can add columns to the index by selecting from the Record Fields list on the right side of the Change Records Indexes dialog, as shown in Figure 5-29.

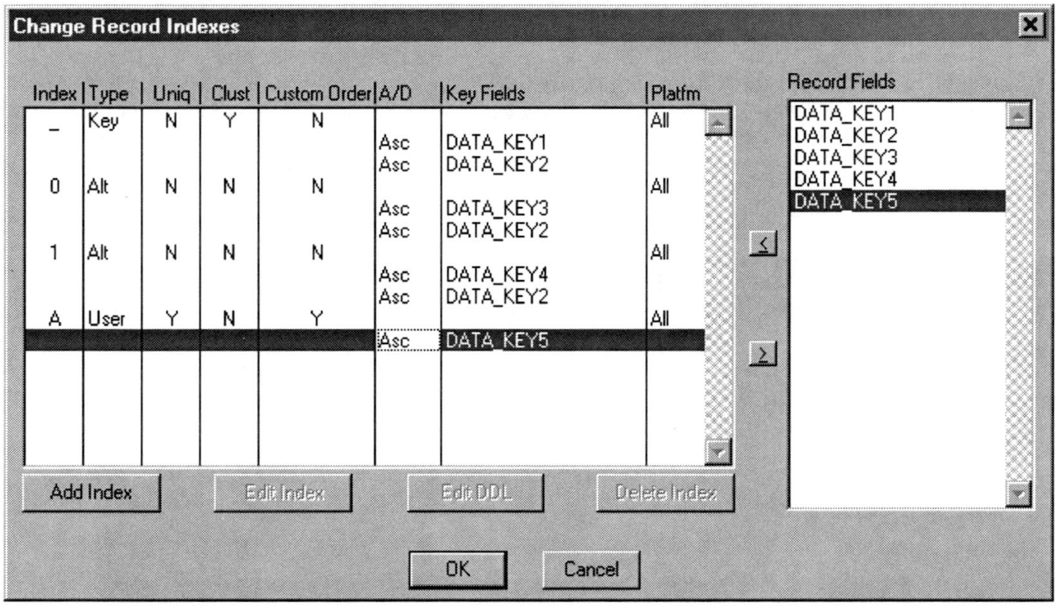

Figure 5-29. Adding columns to a user index

Other Index Issues

A number of other issues in PeopleSoft relate to the use of indexes. I detail some of these issues in the following sections.

Views, Keys, and Indexing

The various key attributes can be applied to fields on any type of record in PeopleTools. It follows that keys can be allocated to records that are views (see Figure 5-30), and that PeopleSoft generates SQL to reference them at run time, much as it does records that are tables.

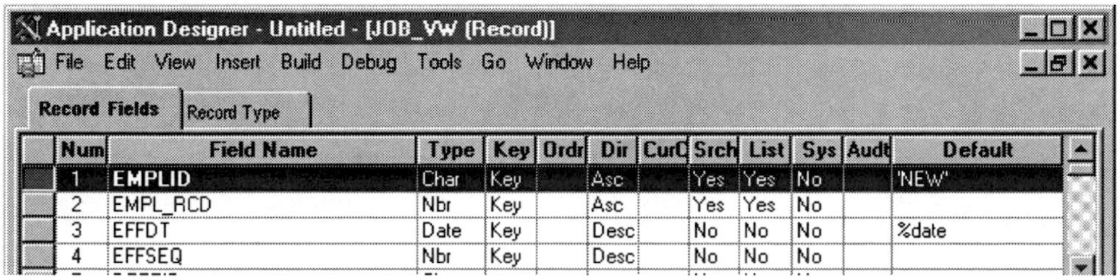

Figure 5-30. A view with a key

For records that do not correspond to tables, the Tools ➤ Data Administration ➤ Indexes option is not available[11] in PeopleTools 8.

It is usually beneficial if the columns on the tables referenced by views have indexes to support the allocation of key attributes on the view. If a column of a view is given a particular attribute in PeopleTools, then often the attribute should also exist on the underlying table. PeopleTools does not do this automatically; the developer must do this manually.

The default indexes tend to enable the queries generated by the record-locator dialog to obtain data from the index without a further need to read the table. The performance benefit of this is considerable.

Consider the record EMPLMT_SRCH_COR (see Figure 5-31). It is one of a family of almost identical records that are used in an HCM 8.8 application as component search records. Different countries use different, but similar, views.

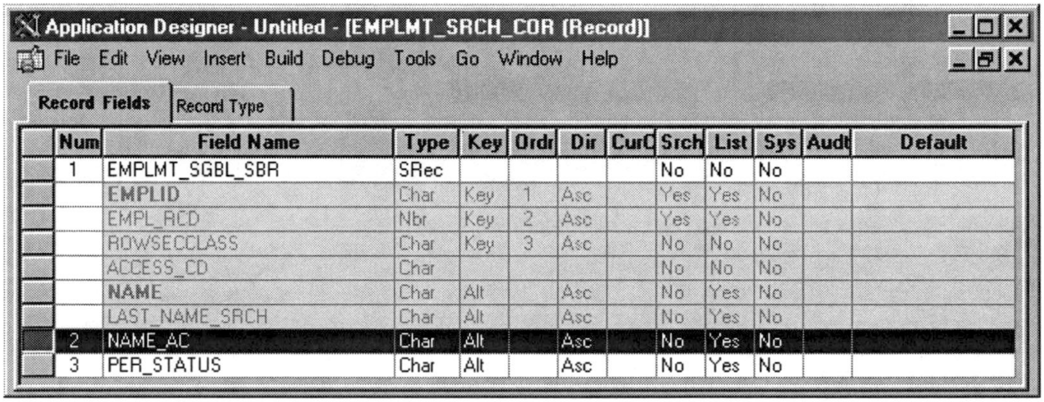
Application Designer - Untitled - [EMPLMT_SRCH_COR (Record)]
File Edit View Insert Build Debug Tools Go Window Help
Record Fields
Record Type
Num | Field Name | Type | Key | Ordr | Dir | CurC | Srch | List | Sys | Audt | Default
1 | EMPLMT_SGBL_SBR | SRec | | | | | No | No | No
EMPLID | Char | Key | 1 | Asc | | Yes | Yes | No
EMPL_RCD | Nbr | Key | 2 | Asc | | Yes | Yes | No
ROWSECCLASS | Char | Key | 3 | Asc | | No | No | No
ACCESS_CD | Char | | | | | No | No | No
NAME | Char | Alt | | Asc | | No | Yes | No
LAST_NAME_SRCH | Char | Alt | | Asc | | No | Yes | No
2 | NAME_AC | Char | Alt | | Asc | | No | Yes | No
3 | PER_STATUS | Char | Alt | | Asc | | No | Yes | No

Figure 5-31. *Component search record*

In the view EMPLMT_SRCH_COR, the field NAME_AC is an alternate search key. Ultimately, this column in the view is derived from the NAME_AC column on the table PS_NAMES (see Figure 5-32).

[11] In PeopleTools 7.x and earlier, this option was available. When a column on a view was given a key attribute, then PeopleTools 7.5 appeared to specify indexes in the Change Record Indexes dialog, although they could not be built.

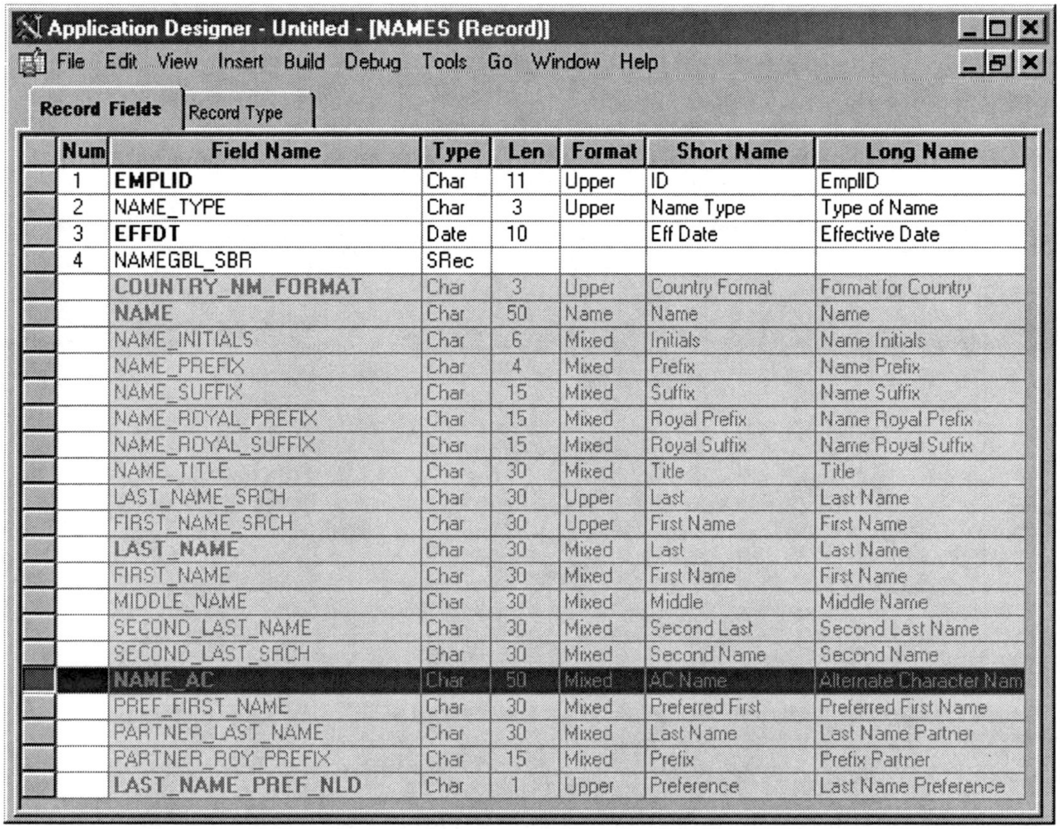

Num	Field Name	Type	Len	Format	Short Name	Long Name
1	**EMPLID**	Char	11	Upper	ID	EmplID
2	NAME_TYPE	Char	3	Upper	Name Type	Type of Name
3	**EFFDT**	Date	10		Eff Date	Effective Date
4	NAMEGBL_SBR	SRec				
	COUNTRY_NM_FORMAT	Char	3	Upper	Country Format	Format for Country
	NAME	Char	50	Name	Name	Name
	NAME_INITIALS	Char	6	Mixed	Initials	Name Initials
	NAME_PREFIX	Char	4	Mixed	Prefix	Name Prefix
	NAME_SUFFIX	Char	15	Mixed	Suffix	Name Suffix
	NAME_ROYAL_PREFIX	Char	15	Mixed	Royal Prefix	Name Royal Prefix
	NAME_ROYAL_SUFFIX	Char	15	Mixed	Royal Suffix	Name Royal Suffix
	NAME_TITLE	Char	30	Mixed	Title	Title
	LAST_NAME_SRCH	Char	30	Upper	Last	Last Name
	FIRST_NAME_SRCH	Char	30	Upper	First Name	First Name
	LAST_NAME	Char	30	Mixed	Last	Last Name
	FIRST_NAME	Char	30	Mixed	First Name	First Name
	MIDDLE_NAME	Char	30	Mixed	Middle	Middle Name
	SECOND_LAST_NAME	Char	30	Mixed	Second Last	Second Last Name
	SECOND_LAST_SRCH	Char	30	Mixed	Second Name	Second Name
	NAME_AC	Char	50	Mixed	AC Name	Alternate Character Nam
	PREF_FIRST_NAME	Char	30	Mixed	Preferred First	Preferred First Name
	PARTNER_LAST_NAME	Char	30	Mixed	Last Name	Last Name Partner
	PARTNER_ROY_PREFIX	Char	15	Mixed	Prefix	Prefix Partner
	LAST_NAME_PREF_NLD	Char	1	Upper	Preference	Last Name Preference

Figure 5-32. *The NAMES record*

However, on the NAMES record, NAME_AC is not an alternate search key, nor does it appear in a user index, and so the column is not indexed. The column is used to hold a name in an alternate character set. For example, a multinational company operating in Russia has a legal requirement to hold some employee data, include names, in Cyrillic characters. Most HCM customers do not populate this field and frequently remove the alternate search attribute from the view. However, if this column is going to be populated and frequently searched, then it would probably be advantageous to index it on PS_NAMES.

In this situation, you have two customization options:

- The NAME_AC field is on the subrecord NAMEGBL_SBR, which complicates the picture. It could be given the alternate search key attribute, which would then be inherited by EMPLMT_SRCH_COR. However, this would also affect every other record where this subrecord is referenced, and it could change the functionality of the application if any of those records are used as search records on any components. That may or may not be desirable, depending on the circumstances.

- A user index could be explicitly specified on the NAMES record.

Suppressing Index Creation

It is possible to suppress creation of a particular index by Application Designer for some or all platforms via the Add/Edit Index dialog.

There may be situations in which a field is made an alternate search key for functional reasons, so that the field appears in a search dialog, but it is not appropriate to build an index. An example of this is the CUST_MICR_TBL table in the Financials product (see Figure 5-33).

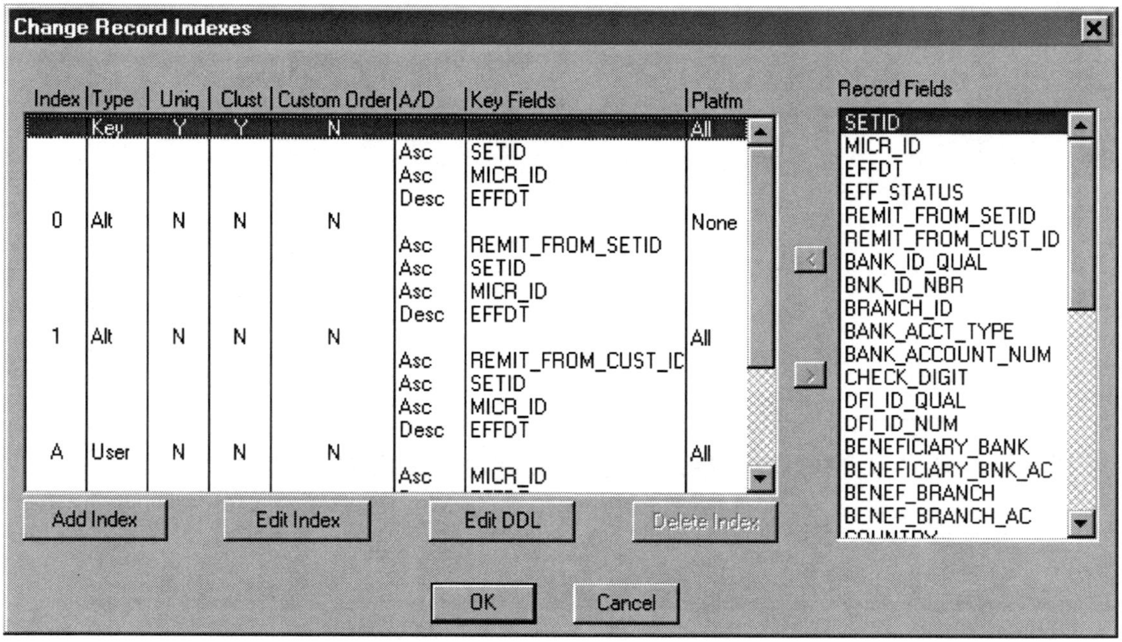

Figure 5-33. Alternate search index 0 is suppressed.

PeopleSoft uses this feature to deliver different indexes to different database platforms. In most cases, it specifies platforms on user indexes, but the feature can be applied to any index. In PeopleTools 8.44, index E on PSPMTRANSHIST has been suppressed on DB2 (see the left-hand image in Figure 5-34) and replaced with index H, which is only built on DB2 (see the right-hand image in Figure 5-34).

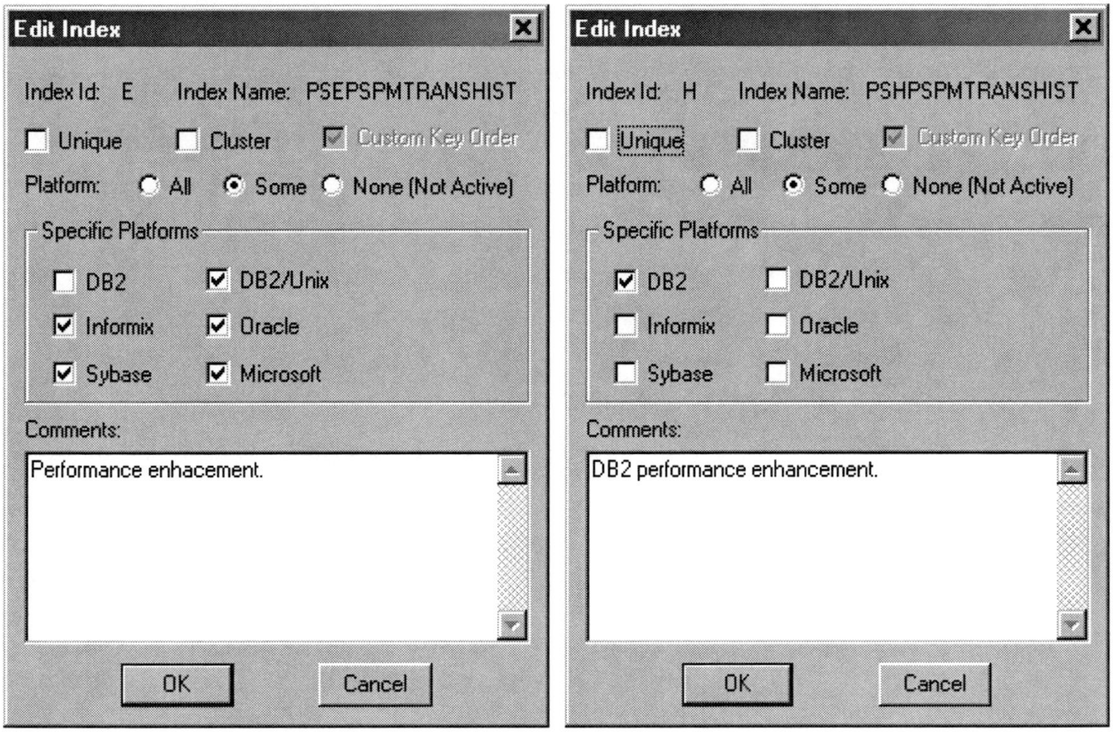

Figure 5-34. *Indexes for only some database platforms*

During performance tuning, you may decide that a particular index is not beneficial or perhaps is actually degrading performance. Instead of deleting the index definition from PeopleTools, you can suppress index creation and add an explanatory comment (see Figure 5-35). Thus, you can easily reverse the change.

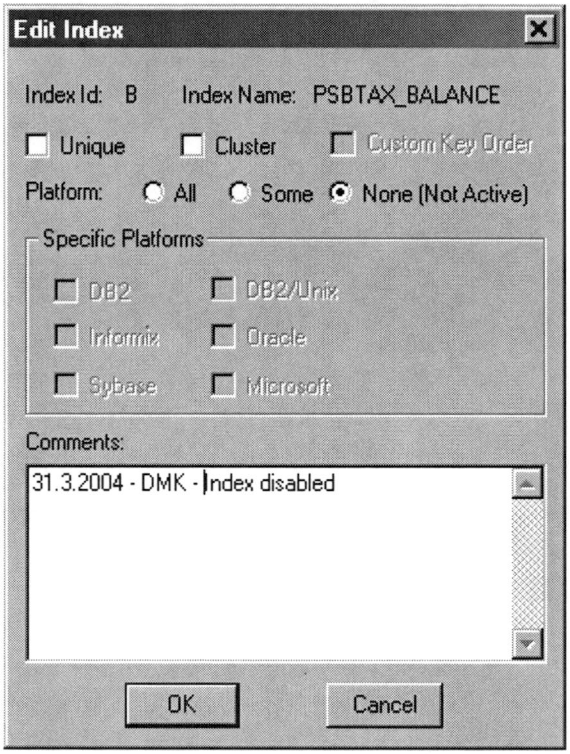

Figure 5-35. User index disabled on all platforms

The index always appears in the Change Record Indexes panel. The setting of the Platform radio button is also reported on this screen.

Discrepancy Between Platform Radio Button and Platform Flags

Since PeopleTools 8.45, I have often noticed that while the Platform radio button in the Edit Index dialog is set to Some (see Figure 5-37), all the specific platform check boxes are selected (see Figure 5-36). The confusion starts in the Change Record Indexes dialog. The platform column reports Some if the Platform radio button is set to Some. A developer sees that an index is only built on some platforms but doesn't know which.

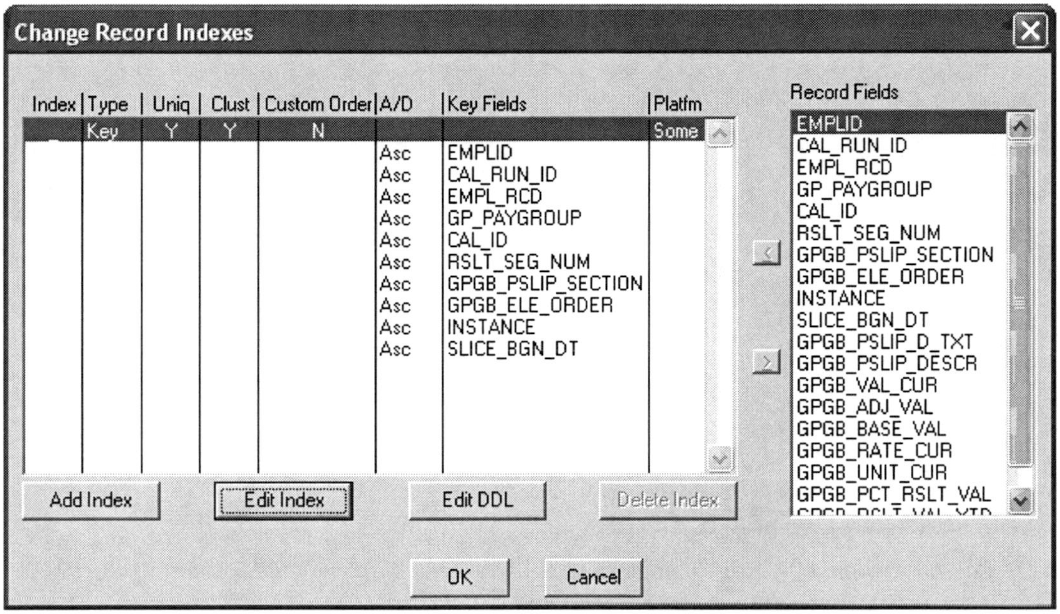

Figure 5-36. Change Record Indexes dialog showing an index to be built on Some platforms

Then, when you edit the index, you see that the Platform radio button is set to Some, yet all the specific platform boxes are selected.

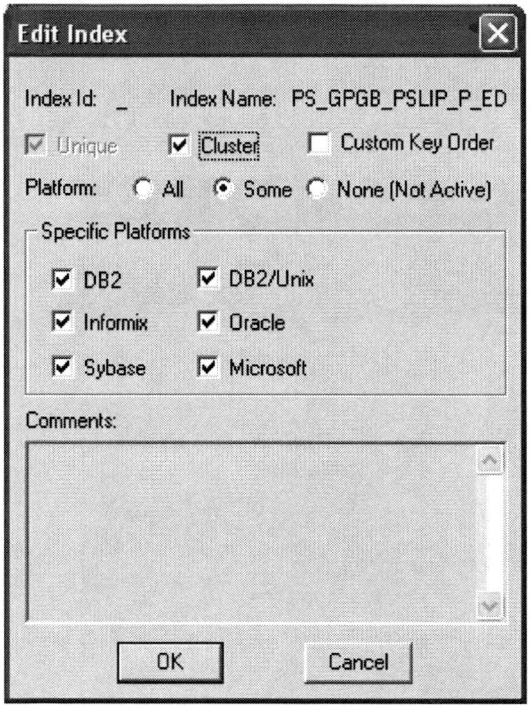

Figure 5-37. Edit Index dialog showing an index to be built on Some platforms, but all platforms selected

The cause of this behavior is that the table PSINDEXDEFN has nine columns that specify whether the index should be built on certain platforms (see Table 4-15). Six platforms are still supported by PeopleTools and shown in Application Designer. However, three columns remain for de-supported platforms:

- *PLATFORM_SBS:* SQL Base

- *PLATFORM_ALB:* Allbase

- *PLATFORM_DB4:* DB2/AS400

No column on PSINDEXDEFN corresponds to the Platform radio button. Instead, Application Designer checks the value of all nine platform columns, and if any of them are different from each other, the Platform radio button is set to None. This problem seems to affect records that were first defined prior to PeopleTools 8.45 and have since been upgraded.

The problem I've just described is a nuisance because sometimes indexes are released by PeopleSoft for platforms as described in the previous section, and it would be much better if Platform was set to All or None where the index is built on all or none of the supported platforms.

The affected indexes can be identified with the query in Listing 5-2.

Listing 5-2. SQL Query to Identify Mismatched Platform Flags

```
SELECT *
FROM psindexdefn
WHERE platform_db2=platform_dbx
AND platform_dbx=platform_inf
AND platform_inf=platform_ora
AND platform_ora=platform_syb
AND platform_syb=platform_mss
AND (platform_ora!=platform_sbs
  OR platform_ora!=platform_alb
  OR platform_ora!=platform_db4);
```

The platform flags can be set consistently with the sequence of commands in Listing 5-3.

Listing 5-3. SQL to Correct Mismatched Platform Flags

```
UPDATE psversion SET version = version + 1
WHERE objecttypename IN('SYS','RDM');

UPDATE pslock SET version = version + 1
WHERE objecttypename IN('SYS','RDM');

UPDATE psrecdefn
SET version = (
   SELECT version  FROM psversion WHERE objecttypename = 'RDM')
WHERE recname IN (
  SELECT recname
  FROM psindexdefn
  WHERE platform_db2=platform_dbx
  AND platform_dbx=platform_inf
  AND platform_inf=platform_ora
  AND platform_ora=platform_syb
  AND platform_syb=platform_mss
  AND (platform_ora!=platform_sbs
    OR platform_ora!=platform_alb
    OR platform_ora!=platform_db4);

UPDATE psindexdefn
SET platform_db4=platform_ora
, platform_alb=platform_ora
, platform_sbs=platform_ora
  WHERE platform_db2=platform_dbx
  AND platform_dbx=platform_inf
  AND platform_inf=platform_ora
  AND platform_ora=platform_syb
  AND platform_syb=platform_mss
  AND (platform_ora!=platform_sbs
    OR platform_ora!=platform_alb
    OR platform_ora!=platform_db4);
COMMIT;
```

The next time the record is opened in Application Designer, the platform flag will be All for these indexes.

Indexes and Histograms

In the Financials product in particular, much of the batch processing is status driven. Statuses are usually held in single-character columns. It is often useful to have an index on the status column only in order to enable the batches to find the rows for processing efficiently. There are usually only a few distinct values for each status column. The cost-based optimizer assumes that the distribution of data values is uniform and so does not use the index.

However, the usual scenario in a system that has been running for a while is that most of the rows have a completed status, and only a few have live statuses. Most batch processes are looking for the live statuses. Oracle will, almost certainly, use indexes on statuses only if there is also a histogram on the column.

The column PROCESS_INSTANCE is also used in some Application Engine processes to select rows for subsequent processing by that process. When the process is initiated by the Process Scheduler, it is given a unique instance number, and it writes that number on the rows to be processed. When the process completes, it sets the PROCESS_INSTANCE column back to zero.[12] An index on the PROCESS_INSTANCE column is often helpful, but again, the column is extremely skewed, and a histogram helps Oracle decide when not to use the index.

Problems can occasionally occur in General Ledger processing on the ACCOUNTING_PERIOD column. This column has values in the range 0 to 999. In a company with 12 monthly periods, there are only 15 distinct values. Most of the data is in the range 1 to 12. Values 13 to 997 are not used at all. Values 0, 998, and 999 are used in year-end processing.

On numeric columns, the cost-based optimizer assumes that there are data values evenly distributed between the minimum and maximum values for a column. The optimizer assumes that each value has 1/1,000 of the data and is likely to use an index where a full scan might be more appropriate. A histogram helps the optimizer make a more informed choice.

Null Columns in PeopleSoft

If a field is marked as required in PeopleSoft, then the corresponding column in the database is defined as NOT NULL. The online application validates that the operator has put an entry into required fields before updating the database and prevents a constraint error.

If a field is not required in PeopleSoft, these rules apply:

- Date columns are nullable. They are set to null if the field in the application is blank.

- Numeric columns are not null. PeopleSoft sets them to zero if the field is blank.[13]

---

[12] What about the additional overhead? What about the additional redo logging? What happens if the process crashes before setting the values back to zero? Good questions, but that's what PeopleSoft delivers!

[13] From PeopleTools 8.4x, if a column is specified as the SYSTEMIDFIELD, its value is populated with a database trigger that is generated by Application Designer, and the column on the database *is* nullable. This is a part of the now-discontinued Mobile Agents functionality.

- VARCHAR2 columns that correspond to character fields in PeopleSoft are not null. PeopleSoft sets them to a single space if the field is blank.

- However, long character fields in PeopleSoft that have a length specified between 1 and 2,000 characters are created as VARCHAR2 columns. These are nullable.

Table 5-3 shows a comparison of field validation in PeopleSoft and column constraints in Oracle.

Table 5-3. *Field Validation in PeopleSoft vs. Column Constraints in Oracle*

PeopleSoft Data Type	Not Required		Required	
	PeopleSoft	Oracle	PeopleSoft	Oracle
CHARACTER	Blank (single space in database)	Not Null	No Blanks	Not Null
NUMERIC	Zero	Not Null	No Zeros	Not Null
DATE	Blank	Null	Valid Date	Not Null
LONG	Blank	Null	No Blanks	Not Null

Prohibiting null data values has various implications:

- Table row lengths are longer than if nulls were permitted, and so tables are larger. However, chained rows are less common because the row does not expand as much as numeric data values are filled in.

- All columns need to be specified in INSERT statements because the default column values default to null, which would result in an error.

- Status and process instance columns cannot be set to null when the row reaches its final status. Thus, the row remains in the index. This makes sparse indexing difficult to implement in PeopleSoft.

SPARSE INDEXING

Oracle indexes do not include rows in which all the indexed columns are null:

```
CREATE TABLE dmk(a number,b number,c number,d number);
CREATE UNIQUE INDEX dmk ON dmk(a,b,c);
INSERT INTO dmk VALUES (null,null,0,1);
INSERT INTO dmk VALUES (null,null,0,2) /*this insert fails, no surprises*/;
INSERT INTO dmk VALUES (null,null,null,3);
INSERT INTO dmk VALUES (null,null,null,4) /*this insert succeeds!*/;
ANALYZE TABLE dmk COMPUTE STATISTICS;

SELECT * FROM dmk;
```

```
             A          B          C          D
         ---------- ---------- ---------- ----------
                                    0          1
                                               3
                                               4
```

```
SELECT num_rows FROM user_tables WHERE table_name = 'DMK';

  NUM_ROWS
----------
        3
```

```
SELECT num_rows FROM user_indexes WHERE index_name = 'DMK';

  NUM_ROWS
----------
        1
```

There are three rows on the table but only one in the index. Notice also that there are two duplicate unindexed rows in the table. These features enable a technique sometimes called *sparse indexing* to be used.

Suppose that a table contains many rows, that a process requires only a very few rows, and that there is no easy way to query those few rows without the database performing a full table scan. A possible approach would be to add a column to the table set to 1 for the rows that must be processed and set to null as they are processed. The column would effectively be a "request to process" flag. If an index were built on that column, then it would be used by a query looking for rows due to be processed. The index would remain small because only the rows with the flag set would ever be indexed. As the rows were processed and the flag set to null, the rows would drop out of the index.

However, all numeric and character fields in PeopleSoft become not-nullable columns in the database. Fixed-length long character fields do become nullable VARCHAR2 columns, but Application Designer does not let you add them to an index. Hence, the only way to implement a sparse index on a PeopleSoft system, using Application Designer, is to use a non-required date type column.

Index Organized Tables in PeopleSoft

In an index-organized table, the data is held in the index. This type of structure can provide much faster key-based access to data because there is only one object to access.

This book has a conventional index at the back, and the entries refer to the text via page numbers. However, a dictionary is its own index because the entries are arranged in order, and the definitions are stored next to the word. The same is true in a database. A conventional index holds the values of the indexed columns and the ROWID, the physical address of the block and row that holds the data to which you can navigate directly. In an index-organized table, the rest of the row is held with the key instead of the ROWID, saving that last lookup.

Index-organized tables are a database feature that you may want to employ on tables where most of the columns are in the unique key index, and generally the table is accessed by that key. However, Application Designer cannot generate the DDL to manage this type of object (see Chapter 6), so you have to implement this manually.

An index-organized table must have a primary key. Therefore, the PeopleSoft record must have a unique key. All of the columns in the primary key must be NOT NULL, so any date fields in the key must be defined as required in PeopleTools.[14]

Let's take an example from HCM. The BENEFIT_PARTIC record has five fields (see Figure 5-38), all of which are part of the unique key. There are no other indexes.

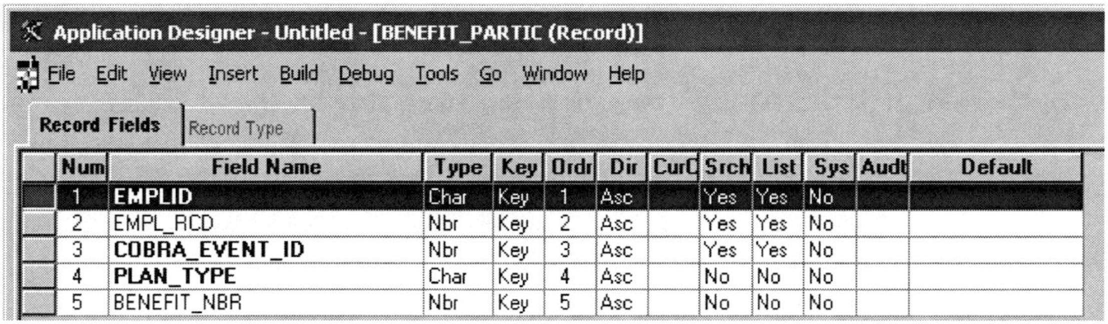

Figure 5-38. Key view of the BENEFIT_PARTIC record in Application Designer

Listing 5-4 shows how Application Designer rebuilds this table as a normal table and an index.

Listing 5-4. SQL Alter Script Generated by Application Designer

```
CREATE TABLE PSYBENEFIT_PARTIC (EMPLID VARCHAR2(11) NOT NULL,
   EMPL_RCD SMALLINT NOT NULL,
   COBRA_EVENT_ID SMALLINT NOT NULL,
   PLAN_TYPE VARCHAR2(2) NOT NULL,
   BENEFIT_NBR SMALLINT NOT NULL) TABLESPACE BNAPP STORAGE (INITIAL
146432 NEXT 100000 MAXEXTENTS UNLIMITED PCTINCREASE 0) PCTFREE 10
PCTUSED 80
/
INSERT INTO PSYBENEFIT_PARTIC (
   EMPLID,
   EMPL_RCD,
   COBRA_EVENT_ID,
   PLAN_TYPE,
   BENEFIT_NBR)
 SELECT
   EMPLID,
   EMPL_RCD,
   COBRA_EVENT_ID,
   PLAN_TYPE,
   BENEFIT_NBR
 FROM PS_BENEFIT_PARTIC
/
```

---

[14] Application Designer does not allow you to enable any key attributes on a long character field even if it corresponds to a VARCHAR2 column in the database.

```
DROP TABLE PS_BENEFIT_PARTIC
/
RENAME PSYBENEFIT_PARTIC TO PS_BENEFIT_PARTIC
/
CREATE UNIQUE  INDEX PS_BENEFIT_PARTIC ON PS_BENEFIT_PARTIC (EMPLID,
    EMPL_RCD,
    COBRA_EVENT_ID,
    PLAN_TYPE,
    BENEFIT_NBR) TABLESPACE PSINDEX STORAGE (INITIAL 315392 NEXT 100000
 MAXEXTENTS UNLIMITED PCTINCREASE 0) PCTFREE 10 PARALLEL NOLOGGING
/
ALTER INDEX PS_BENEFIT_PARTIC NOPARALLEL LOGGING
/
```

If you choose to rebuild PS_BENEFIT_PARTIC as an index-organized table it is relatively simple to edit the script as shown in Listing 5-5. Following are some things to note about that listing:

- The primary key is defined as a constraint at the end of the column list.

- The list of key columns can be taken from the unique index definition.

- The keywords ORGANIZATION INDEX must be added.

- I have chosen to store the index-organized table in the same tablespace where PeopleTools would have built the table.

- The PCTUSED option cannot be specified on an index and should be removed from the create table command generated by Application Designer.

- I have explicitly named the primary key constraint because this determines the name of the index reported in USER_INDEXES. Later in the script I must rename the index, and I need to know which index to rename.

- Rename both the table and the index so that Application Designer thinks both objects exist and does not generate scripts to rebuild either unless forced.

- For the sake of completeness, I have also renamed the constraint to match the final index name. Thus the next time the table is rebuilt, there will be no error because the constraint name has already been used.

Listing 5-5. SQL Alter Script to Create an Index-Organized Table

```
CREATE TABLE PSYBENEFIT_PARTIC (EMPLID VARCHAR2(11) NOT NULL,
    EMPL_RCD SMALLINT NOT NULL,
    COBRA_EVENT_ID SMALLINT NOT NULL,
    PLAN_TYPE VARCHAR2(2) NOT NULL,
    BENEFIT_NBR SMALLINT NOT NULL
, CONSTRAINT PSYBENEFIT_PARTIC PRIMARY KEY (EMPLID,
    EMPL_RCD,
    COBRA_EVENT_ID,
    PLAN_TYPE,
    BENEFIT_NBR))
ORGANIZATION INDEX
TABLESPACE BNAPP
```

```
STORAGE (INITIAL 146432 NEXT 100000 MAXEXTENTS UNLIMITED PCTINCREASE 0)
PCTFREE 1
/

INSERT /*+APPEND*/ INTO PSYBENEFIT_PARTIC (
    EMPLID,
    EMPL_RCD,
    COBRA_EVENT_ID,
    PLAN_TYPE,
    BENEFIT_NBR)
  SELECT
    EMPLID,
    EMPL_RCD,
    COBRA_EVENT_ID,
    PLAN_TYPE,
    BENEFIT_NBR
  FROM PS_BENEFIT_PARTIC
/
DROP TABLE PS_BENEFIT_PARTIC
/
ALTER TABLE PSYBENEFIT_PARTIC RENAME TO PS_BENEFIT_PARTIC
/
ALTER INDEX PSYBENEFIT_PARTIC RENAME TO PS_BENEFIT_PARTIC
/
ALTER TABLE PS_BENEFIT_PARTIC RENAME CONSTRAINT PSYBENEFIT_PARTIC TO PS_BENEFIT_PARTIC
/
ALTER TABLE PS_BENEFIT_PARTIC NOPARALLEL LOGGING
/
```

Summary

The majority of indexes in a PeopleSoft system are system generated. Their definition is derived directly from the definition of the application. As you learned in this chapter, using PeopleSoft's Application Designer, you can add, remove, or adjust index specifications. You use the same tool to generate and issue DDL to build those tables and indexes.

It is part of the DBA's role to resolve database performance issues, and this may well involve changes to indexing. These changes must be specified and should be implemented via Application Designer, or they are likely to be lost in a subsequent upgrade.

CHAPTER 6

PeopleSoft DDL

So far, I have described how the PeopleSoft and Oracle data dictionaries are related, and how the specification of keys on PeopleSoft records controls both the SQL that is generated by the panel processor and the indexes that are built.

This chapter describes how Application Designer dynamically builds DDL statements, and in particular where some of the physical attributes are defined and how these models can be enhanced to handle some, but not all, Oracle features. This chapter also covers additional PeopleTools tables that correspond to parts of the Oracle data dictionary.

PeopleSoft DDL and the DBA

DBAs usually have a range of responsibilities, including managing growth and change (capacity planning) and performance monitoring and tuning of the database and application. In an application development environment, the DBA's job may also include responsibility for the design or enhancement of the data model.

This may legitimately lead the DBA to want to adjust the physical properties of existing objects. Common reasons include the following:

- Add, remove, or change an index.

- Move an object to a different tablespace.

- Change the physical parameters (PCTUSED, PCTFREE, and so on).

Consider what happens if the DBA adjusts a table that is then altered by a PeopleSoft patch or some other customization. The upgrade process includes generating and applying a script to alter the table structure, usually by re-creating it.

If the new parameters introduced by the DBA are not placed in Application Designer, altering the table effectively erases the work performed by the DBA. Re-creating the table with the original parameters may reintroduce the original problem, or it may cause an error during the upgrade.

If the DBA moves a growing table to a larger tablespace, and that table continues to grow beyond the capacity of the old tablespace, then if that table is re-created by a PeopleSoft alter script, it is re-created in the original tablespace. It is not possible to repopulate the upgraded table with the application data, and the ALTER script fails. Worse still, if that space-management error is not caught immediately, it is possible to lose data if the script goes on to drop the original table. If the new tablespace was specified in PeopleTools, then not only would the error not occur during the upgrade, but the DBA wouldn't have had to write the script to move the table in the first place. It could have been generated by Application Designer.

Therefore, it is very important that object-level changes that the DBA makes to tables and indexes should at least be reflected in Application Designer, and preferably they are made in Application Designer in the first place.

At some PeopleSoft customer sites, the scripts that are produced by Application Designer must be reviewed by a DBA before they are applied. The DBA then edits them to conform to a local "standard." While it may be appropriate to have the DBA apply the DDL scripts, the sheer number of PeopleSoft tables and views makes this approach virtually impossible and introduces further opportunity for human error. I suggest that it is better to edit the PeopleSoft DDL models, set appropriate DDL model defaults and overrides, and restrict manual editing to Oracle features that Application Designer cannot handle.

DDL Models

The Application Designer and Data Mover utilities build the DDL statements to create the objects referenced by the PeopleSoft application. The formats for these statements are defined as *DDL models* (see Figure 6-1; this window is accessed by selecting PeopleTools ➤ Utilities ➤ Administration ➤ DDL Model Defaults), which are stored in the PeopleTools tables and maintained via the PeopleSoft Pure Internet Architecture (PIA). Each database platform builds objects in a slightly different way. Therefore, PeopleSoft maintains a separate DDL model for each of the database platforms it supports.

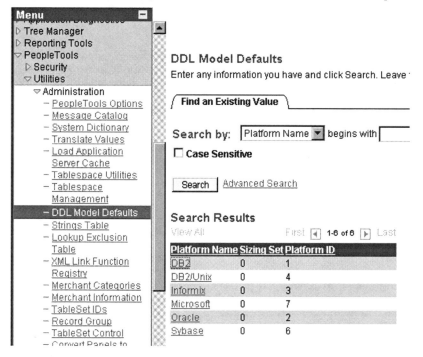

Figure 6-1. DDL Model Defaults window

PeopleSoft defines five DDL models:

- Create Table

- Create Index

- Create Tablespace

- Analyze Table Estimate Statistics (new in PeopleTools 8.1x)

- Analyze Table Compute Statistics (new in PeopleTools 8.1x)

Create Table

Each DDL model consists of a string containing an outline of a SQL command. For example, Figure 6-2 shows the CREATE TABLE command. Various parts of the command are built up using two classes of substitution variables.[1]

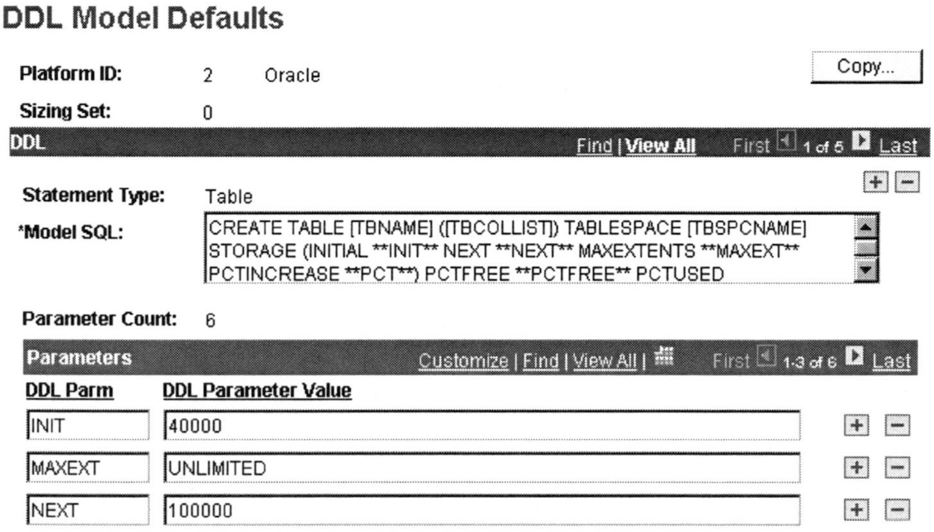

DDL Model Defaults

| Platform ID: | 2 | Oracle | Copy... |

| Sizing Set: | 0 | | |

DDL   Find | View All   First ◁ 1 of 5 ▷ Last

| Statement Type: | Table | | |

| *Model SQL: | CREATE TABLE [TBNAME] ([TBCOLLIST]) TABLESPACE [TBSPCNAME] STORAGE (INITIAL **INIT** NEXT **NEXT** MAXEXTENTS **MAXEXT** PCTINCREASE **PCT**) PCTFREE **PCTFREE** PCTUSED | |

| Parameter Count: | 6 | | |

Parameters   Customize | Find | View All | First ◁ 1-3 of 6 ▷ Last

DDL Parm	DDL Parameter Value	
INIT	40000	+ −
MAXEXT	UNLIMITED	+ −
NEXT	100000	+ −

Figure 6-2. Create Table DDL model

Variables delimited with square brackets ([]) are PeopleTools internal variables. The values of these variables are determined by code inside the Application Designer and Data Mover utilities, which is not revealed to the user and cannot be changed except by PeopleSoft's Tools development.

Variables delimited with double asterisks (**) are explicitly declared additional variables. They are defined independently for each DDL model on each RDBMS. Additional variables can be defined through these pages to enable additional features. The samples shown in this section are the PeopleSoft vanilla definitions. Each of these additional variables has a default value in the model that can be overridden in the object definition in Application Designer.

---

[1] PeopleSoft doesn't have official terms for these variables. I refer to them as *internal* and *additional* DDL variables.

Table Definition

Listing 6-1 shows the DDL model for creating a table.

Listing 6-1. Create Table DDL Model

```
CREATE TABLE [TBNAME] ([TBCOLLIST])
TABLESPACE [TBSPCNAME]
STORAGE (
    INITIAL **INIT**
    NEXT **NEXT**
    MAXEXTENTS **MAXEXT**
    PCTINCREASE **PCT**)
PCTFREE **PCTFREE**
PCTUSED **PCTUSED**;
```

There are four internal variables in the Create Table DDL model that are described in Table 6-1.

Table 6-1. Create Table Internal Variables

DDL Model Internal Variable	Description
[DBNAME]	Name of the PeopleSoft database. Not used in any Oracle DDL model. Evaluates to null on Oracle.
[TBNAME]	Name of the table: DECODE(PSRECDEFN.SQLTABLENAME, ' ', PS_'||PSRECDEFN.RECNAME, SQLTABLENAME)
[TBCOLLIST]	Column list. Includes the data type of the column, whether it is NOT NULL, and a length-checking constraint if this is a Unicode database using byte semantics.
[TBSPCNAME]	Tablespace in which table is to be built, an attribute of the record (PSRECTBLSPC.DDLSPACENAME). This parameter does not appear in the DDL models for Microsoft SQL Server and Sybase because it has no meaning on those platforms.

PeopleSoft delivers a number of additional variables (see Table 6-2) that correspond to the various physical table parameters.

Table 6-2. *Create Table Additional Variables*

Oracle Keyword	Variable	Default Value
INITIAL	**INIT**	40000
NEXT	**NEXT**	100000
MAXEXTENTS	**MAXEXT**	UNLIMITED
PCTINCREASE	**PCT**	0
PCTFREE	**PCTFREE**	10
PCTUSED	**PCTUSED**	80

Column Definitions

The variable [TBCOLLIST] in the Create Table DDL model specifies

- The columns that make up the table

- How the columns are defined

- The length-checking constraints if the database is set to use Unicode

This variable evaluates to different values on different database platforms. It is coded inside PeopleTools and cannot be altered by the user. It is one of the few examples of platform-sensitive coding in PeopleSoft.

Listing 6-2 shows the start of the [TBCOLLIST] variable for the JOB record on Oracle.

Listing 6-2. *Value of [TBCOLLIST] for the JOB Record*

```
EMPLID VARCHAR2(33) NOT NULL
,EMPL_RCD SMALLINT NOT NULL
,EFFDT DATE NOT NULL
,EFFSEQ SMALLINT NOT NULL
,DEPTID VARCHAR2(30) NOT NULL
...
```

The column definitions are based on the field definitions on PSDBFIELD, as described in Chapter 4.

Create Index

From PeopleTools 8, there is only a single DDL model, the Create Index DDL model (see Listing 6-3), that combines the separate DDL models for unique and nonunique indexes in previous versions.

Listing 6-3. *Create Index DDL Model*

```
CREATE [UNIQUE] **BITMAP** INDEX [IDXNAME] ON [TBNAME] ([IDXCOLLIST])
TABLESPACE **INDEXSPC**
STORAGE (
    INITIAL **INIT**
    NEXT **NEXT**
    MAXEXTENTS **MAXEXT**
    PCTINCREASE **PCT**)
PCTFREE **PCTFREE**;
```

There are four internal variables in the Create Index DDL model, as described in Table 6-3.

Table 6-3. *Internal Index Variables*

Internal DDL Model Variable	Description
[TBNAME]	Name of the table: DECODE(PSRECDEFN.SQLTABLENAME, ' ', PS_'||PSRECDEFN.RECNAME, SQLTABLENAME)
[IDXNAME]	Name of the index: 'PS'||INDEX_ID||RECNAME
[IDXCOLLIST]	Comma-separated list of columns in the index
[UNIQUE]	Set to UNIQUE for a unique index; otherwise NULL

As with the table DDL, the additional variables (shown in Table 6-4) handle the physical parameters.

Table 6-4. *Create Index Additional Variables*

Oracle Keyword	Variable	Default Value
BITMAP	**BITMAP**	NULL
TABLESPACE	**INDEXSPC**	PSINDEX
INITIAL	**INIT**	40000
NEXT	**NEXT**	100000

MAXEXTENTS	**MAXEXT**	UNLIMITED
PCTINCREASE	**PCT**	0
PCTFREE	**PCTFREE**	10

It is interesting to note that the `BITMAP` keyword is handled with an additional variable, whereas the `UNIQUE` keyword is from an internal variable. Both of these were introduced in PeopleTools 8. The reason for the difference in handling is that the `UNIQUE` keyword is common to `CREATE INDEX` commands on all database platforms, while the `BITMAP` keyword is specific to Oracle. Hence, the **BITMAP** parameter appears only in the DDL model for Oracle.

The specification of tablespace for tables and indexes is handled differently. For tables, it is an internal variable defined on the record until PeopleTools 8.1 or PSRECTBLSPC from PeopleTools 8.4. For indexes, there has always been an additional variable in the DDL model.

Create Tablespace

The Create Tablespace DDL model is only used by Data Mover when it creates an entire database including the tablespaces, either at installation time or if migrating a PeopleSoft database from another RDBMS to Oracle. However, not even the PeopleSoft documented installation process uses this feature. Instead, PeopleSoft supplies SQL scripts (`utlspace.sql` and `xxddl.sql`, where `xx` is the product code; so it is `hrddl.sql` for HCM) to create the default tablespaces, and the installation instructions require you to run these scripts before the Data Mover import. The database-import script, generated by Data Mover itself (see Listing 6-4), suppresses tablespace creation with the `SET NO SPACE` command. So, Data Mover normally never gets the opportunity to build a tablespace.

Listing 6-4. Script to Import a Data Mover Dump During Installation

```
REM - hr88ora.dms
REM - Created by Data Mover 8.44.05 Wed Mar 17 01:24:22 2004
REM -
REM - Database Platform: Oracle
REM - Non-Unicode Database
REM - Selected Character Set: WE8ISO8859P15 - Western European ISO 8859-15 (with Euro sign)
REM - Generate Latin-1 Code
REM -
/
REM - PeopleSoft HRMS Database - US English
/
SET LOG c:\temp\hcengs.log;
SET INPUT D:\ps\hr88\data\hcengs.db;
SET COMMIT 30000;
SET NO VIEW;
SET NO SPACE;
SET NO TRACE;
SET UNICODE OFF;
SET IGNORE_DUPS;
IMPORT *;
```

Even if PeopleSoft didn't do this, as a DBA I would insist on creating the tablespaces manually so that all the relevant options can be specified.

The Create Tablespace DDL model (see Listing 6-5) has only a single internal variable, which is the tablespace name. The tablespace name is also used to make up part of the data file name.

Listing 6-5. Create Tablespace DDL Model

```
CREATE TABLESPACE [TBSPCNAME]
DATAFILE '**DIR**[TBSPCNAME].DBF'
SIZE **SIZE**
DEFAULT STORAGE (
    INITIAL **INIT**
    NEXT **NEXT**
    MAXEXTENTS **MAXEXT**
    PCTINCREASE **PCT**);
```

The additional variables (see Table 6-5) specify the physical location of the data file and the default storage options.

Table 6-5. Create Tablespace Additional Variables

Oracle Keyword	Variable	Default Value
DATAFILE	**DIR**	/dir/
INITIAL	**INIT**	40000
NEXT	**NEXT**	100000
MAXEXTENTS	**MAXEXT**	UNLIMITED
PCTINCREASE	**PCT**	0
PCTFREE	**PCTFREE**	10

Maintaining Cost-Based Optimizer Statistics in Application Engine with %UpdateStats

PeopleSoft introduced two new DDL models in PeopleTools 8, but only for Oracle and DB2 (not DB2/Unix). They are only used by the %UpdateStats macro in Application Engine to collect cost-based optimizer statistics during execution, usually on working storage and reporting tables.

■ **Note** Although certain COBOL processes also gather statistics on some tables during execution, they do not use the DDL models.

Originally, the DDL models supplied for Oracle used the ANALYZE TABLE command. There are no additional parameters specified. Instead, PeopleSoft created two DDL models, one for ESTIMATE and one for COMPUTE. These are listed in Table 6-6.

Table 6-6. Statistics DDL Models Up to PeopleTools 8.47

Model	%UpdateStats Option	DDL Model Text
4	LOW	`ANALYZE TABLE [TBNAME] ESTIMATE STATISTICS;`
5	HIGH	`ANALYZE TABLE [TBNAME] COMPUTE STATISTICS;`

From PeopleTools 8.48, the DDL models were changed (by Oracle Corp.) to use the Oracle-supplied DBMS_STATS package. These are listed in Table 6-7.

Table 6-7. Statistics DDL Models from PeopleTools 8.48

Model	%UpdateStats Option	DDL Model text

4	LOW	`DBMS_STATS.GATHER_TABLE_STATS`
		`(ownname=> [DBNAME]`
		`, tabname=>[TBNAME]`
		`, estimate_percent=>1`
		`, method_opt=> 'FOR ALL COLUMNS SIZE 1'`
		`,cascade=>TRUE);`

5	HIGH	`DBMS_STATS.GATHER_TABLE_STATS`
		`(ownname=> [DBNAME]`
		`, tabname=>[TBNAME]`
		`, estimate_percent=> dbms_stats.auto_sample_size`
		`, method_opt=> 'FOR ALL INDEXED COLUMNS SIZE 1'`
		`,cascade=>TRUE);`

The format of the macro is %UpdateStats(record name ,[HIGH/LOW]). The default is LOW. The SQL generated by this macro is sourced from the DDL models, as shown in Table 6-8.

Table 6-8. %UpdateStats Examples on Oracle

Application Engine Code	Issued SQL (Default DDL models)
%UpdateStats(JOB)	DBMS_STATS.GATHER_TABLE_STATS(ownname=> 'SYSADM', tabname=>[TBNAME], estimate_percent=>1, method_opt=> 'FOR ALL COLUMNS SIZE 1',cascade=>TRUE);
%UpdateStats(JOB,LOW)	DBMS_STATS.GATHER_TABLE_STATS(ownname=> 'SYSADM', tabname=>[TBNAME], estimate_percent=>1, method_opt=> 'FOR ALL COLUMNS SIZE 1',cascade=>TRUE);
%UpdateStats(JOB,HIGH)	DBMS_STATS.GATHER_TABLE_STATS(ownname=> 'SYSADM', tabname=>[TBNAME], estimate_percent=>dbms_stats.auto_sample_size, method_opt=> 'FOR ALL COLUMNS SIZE 1',cascade=>TRUE);

However, I suspect that the models are back to front:

- Model 4 (low, formerly ESTIMATE STATISTICS) uses a fixed 1% sample size, whereas Model 5 (high, formerly COMPUTE STATISTICS) uses the default sample size. Typically, auto_sample_size produces a very low value, often less than 1%. Thus %UpdateStats LOW may result in a higher sample size that HIGH. I think this may be a typographical error: somebody meant to replace COMPUTE with a 100% sample size, and then the models were swapped.

- Model 4 specifies a method of FOR ALL INDEXED COLUMNS SIZE 1. It is perfectly reasonable not to collect histograms. SIZE 1 specifies a single bucket histogram, which is only the minimum and maximum value on the column. There is a body of opinion that says that histograms should not be collected unless you know they are helpful, because there is additional overhead to collecting them, storing them, and using them. SIZE 1 was the default value for the parameter in Oracle 9i, but in Oracle 10g the default became FOR ALL COLUMNS SIZE AUTO. The INDEXED keyword was added in PeopleTools 8.51. The minimum and maximum values on the index columns are updated, but the values on unindexed columns are unchanged. This could lead to incorrect calculation of the selectivity of predicates on unindexed columns. I think the INDEXED keyword should be removed.

- For Model 5, the method has been FOR ALL INDEXED COLUMNS SIZE 1 since PeopleTools 8.48.

%UpdateStats Limitations

Commits are suppressed in Application Engine programs when the program is called from PeopleCode, because the PIA that executes the PeopleCode is in the middle of a transaction. When inside a select/fetch loop, and when the program is restartable, they can be deferred until the loop ends.

PeopleSoft designed the %UpdateStats macro to issue the ANALYZE TABLE command on Oracle, which is DDL and so implies a commit. DBMS_STATS.GATHER_TABLE_STATISTICS also contains a commit. If commits are deferred, the %UpdateStats macro is ignored and the table is not analyzed.

Listing 6-6 shows an example of the warning that is written to the Application Engine trace file if step trace is enabled (although this trace does have a run-time overhead).

Listing 6-6. Part of an Application Engine Trace

```
11.30.18 ...(FS_VATUPDFS.BB000.BB000-3) (SQL)
RECSTATS PS_VAT_UPD_BU_TAO LOW
/
11.30.18 UpdateStats ignored - COMMIT required
```

A commit in the wrong place could jeopardize both data integrity and the ability to restart Application Engine programs from the last commit point.

Restricting the implied commit by placing DBMS_STATS inside an autonomous transaction is not an effective workaround. Some of the statistics are not correctly calculated, because the autonomous transaction cannot "see" the uncommitted data.

Optimizer Dynamic Sampling

Ideally, a working storage table should be truncated, populated, have statistics gathered, and used, and then the data should be disposed of. However, the DBA depends on the developer to code the %UpdateStats macro into the Application Engine program. Often, I find that it has not been used in a program when perhaps it should be.

This issue is clearly not unique to PeopleSoft applications. Oracle introduced Optimizer Dynamic Sampling into the database in version 9.2 to improve cardinality estimates used by the optimizer.

If there are no statistics on an object, the Optimizer samples some blocks in the object during the SQL parse so that it has statistics with which to work. In Oracle 9i, by default, this was only applied in very limited circumstances. From, Oracle 10g it is applied to all unanalyzed objects (level 2).

I have had considerable success by increasing this to level 4, where it also estimates selectivity on "all tables that have single-table predicates that reference 2 or more columns."[2] However, I have also encountered situations where Optimizer Dynamic Sampling, even at the maximum level, doesn't produce a suitable execution plan, but explicitly gathered statistics do.

It is a useful database feature that can be applied to PeopleSoft systems. I think it generally should be used. However, it is not a silver bullet!

Controlling How Application Engine Programs Collect Statistics

Having just two options for how to collects statistics on tables during Application Engine programs is better than none, but I have found that it is helpful to have more control. For each table that is populated or updated in a process, you need to consider a number of questions:

- Should statistics be collected? Perhaps they should be collected if the existing statistics are stale. Or, should they be removed and allow the optimizer to dynamically sample the object?

- What sample size should be used? Should dbms_stats sample rows or blocks in the table?

---

[2] http://download.oracle.com/docs/cd/B19306_01/server.102/b14211/stats.htm#i43032.

- Should histograms be collected, and if so on which columns and with how many buckets?

The answer for each table could easily be different.

In the first edition of this book I proposed a PL/SQL package that could be called so that %UpdateStats could invoke the dbms_stats package instead of the ANALYZE command. PeopleTools now does that by default. I have produced an enhanced version of the wrapper package.[3] I use a table (defined in Listing 6-7) to control whether and how to collect statistics on each table.

If there is no row in the control table for a specific record, the default behavior of the package is to gather statistics on normal tables, refresh stale statistics[4] if the table is partitioned, and not collect statistics on the shared instances of temporary records that have been built as Global Temporary Tables.

Listing 6-7. Control Table to Hold Metadata for Wrapper Package

```
CREATE TABLE ps_gfc_stats_ovrd
(  RECNAME           VARCHAR2(15)  NOT NULL, --peoplesoft record name
   GATHER_STATS      VARCHAR2(1)   NOT NULL,
                   --(G)ather Stats / Do(N)t Gather Stats / (R)efresh stale Stats
   ESTIMATE_PERCENT VARCHAR2(30)   NOT NULL,
                   --dbms_stats sample size - 0 implies automatic sample size
   BLOCK_SAMPLE      VARCHAR2(1)   NOT NULL, --(Y)es / (N)o (default)
   METHOD_OPT        VARCHAR2(1000) --same as dbms_stats method_opt parameter
) TABLESPACE PTTBL
PCTFREE 10 PCTUSED 80
/
```

The only parameters passed to the package (see Listing 6-8) are those that are specified in the DDL model. PeopleTools has variables that contain the owner and table name. The default sample size is specified as a literal. The verbose option has been provided for debugging.

Listing 6-8. Wrapper Package Specification

```
CREATE OR REPLACE PACKAGE wrapper AS
…
--------------------------------------------------------------------------------------
procedure called from DDL model for %UpdateStats
--------------------------------------------------------------------------------------
PROCEDURE ps_stats
(p_ownname       IN VARCHAR2 /*owner of table*/
,p_tabname       IN VARCHAR2 /*table name*/
,p_estpct        IN NUMBER  DEFAULT NULL /*size of sample: 0 or NULL means dbms_stats default*/
,p_verbose       IN BOOLEAN DEFAULT FALSE /*if true print SQL*/
);
```

---

[3] The book itself only contains excerpts from the package. However, the package and associated scripts are supplied with the book, but the latest version can be downloaded from www.go-faster.co.uk/scripts.htm#wrapper848meta.sql.

[4] For Oracle 10g, it has been necessary to write explicit code to detect segments where the number of changes in the table compared to the statistics exceeds the fixed 10% stale threshold. In Oracle 11g, the stale threshold can be specified globally and at the table level.

```
END wrapper;
/
```

The DDL models must be changed to call the PL/SQL package rather than the dbms_stats package directly (see Listing 6-9).

Listing 6-9. Data Mover Script to Create DDL Models to Call the Wrapper Package

```
--   ****************************************************************
--   ddlora-wrapper.dms (c) Go-Faster Consultancy 2008
--   ReLoads the PeopleTools DDL tables for Analyze statements for Oracle
--   ****************************************************************

SET LOG DDLORA.LOG;

DELETE FROM PSDDLMODEL
WHERE PLATFORMID=2 AND STATEMENT_TYPE IN (4,5);

INSERT INTO PSDDLMODEL (
STATEMENT_TYPE,
PLATFORMID,
SIZING_SET,
PARMCOUNT,
MODEL_STATEMENT)
VALUES(
:1,
:2,
:3,
:4,
:5)
\
$DATATYPES NUMERIC,NUMERIC,NUMERIC,NUMERIC,CHARACTER
4,2,0,0,$long
wrapper.ps_stats(p_ownname=>[DBNAME],p_tabname=>[TBNAME],p_estpct=>0);
//
5,2,0,0,$long
wrapper.ps_stats(p_ownname=>[DBNAME],p_tabname=>[TBNAME],p_estpct=>100);
//
/
```

I have also encountered situations where the %UpdateStats macro has been overused and collection of statistics has become a performance issue.

Controlling How PeopleSoft COBOL Programs Collect Statistics

Some of the stored statements used by PeopleSoft COBOL program use the %UPDATESTATS macro to instruct them to analyze optimizer statistics on certain tables during execution. The example in Listing 6-10 is used in the Global Payroll calculation program.

Listing 6-10. Stored Statement to Updates Statistics on a Table During a COBOL Program

```
STORE GPPSERVC_U_STATS
%UPDATESTATS(PS_GP_PYE_STAT_WRK)
;
```

The concept is identical to Application Engine, but the implementation is different. COBOL programs do not invoke the DDL models described earlier. The expansion is hard-coded in the COBOL. Even from PeopleTools 8.48, when the DDL models changed to using dbms_stats, the COBOL programs expand %UPDATESTATS to the analyze command:

```
ANALYZE TABLE PS_GP_PYE_STAT_WRK ESTIMATE STATISTICS
```

However, it is possible to change the stored statement to call the wrapper package described previously (see Listing 6-11).

Listing 6-11. Stored Statement Calling the Wrapper Package Directly

```
STORE GPPSERVC_U_STATS
BEGIN wrapper.ps_stats(p_ownname=>user, p_tabname=>'PS_GP_PYE_STAT_WRK'); END;;
```

I use the script in Listing 6-12 to generate all the stored statements where the delivered %UPDATESTATS statements can be replaced. I recommend that the delivered .dms scripts that contain the stored statements be updated with the new statements so you can perform a file compare when new versions are included in patches or bundles.

Listing 6-12. updatestats_after.sq

```
set head off feedback off long 5000
column stmt formata 200
spool updatestats_after.dms
select 'STORE '||pgm_name||'_'||stmt_type||'_'||stmt_name
||CHR(10)
||'BEGIN wrapper.ps_stats(p_ownname=>user,p_tabname=>'''
||substr(stmt_text
, INSTR(stmt_text,'(')+1
, INSTR(stmt_text,')')-INSTR(stmt_text,'(')-1
)
||'''); END;;' stmt
from ps_sqlstmt_tbl
where stmt_text like '%UPDATESTATS(%'
/
spool off
```

▨ **Note** This script only works on version 9.0 applications where long columns, including PS_SQLSTMT_TBL.STMT_TEXT, have become CLOBs.

Statistics Retention

From Oracle 10g, the database retains a copy of the previous statistics every time dbms_stats updates the statistics on an object. The default period of retention is 31 days. The idea is that should collecting fresh statistics on an object cause an undesirable change in an execution plan, then the old retained statistics can be restored at least temporarily until a longer-term solution can be worked out.

If statistics were only collected by a nightly maintenance job, this wouldn't be a problem. However, I have seen some PeopleSoft systems that run thousands of processes per day, some of which repeatedly collect statistics on working storage tables. I found some tables with many thousands of versions of previous statistics because the batch process has used the %UpdateStats macro that many times.

This can cause two problems:

- The retained statistics are stored in the SYS.WRI$_OPTSTAT%HISTORY tables, which are located in the SYSAUX tablespace. Retaining lots of statistics causes this tablespace to grow. If histograms are also stored, the growth is greater.

- dbms_stats also appears to be responsible for purging history older than the retention limit. The default retention period is 31 days. I have seen concurrent calls to dbms_stats blocked on row-level locks on the statistics history tables. For me, this occurred 31 days after the system went live on a significantly increased volume!

An option to mitigate this effect would be to suppress collection of statistics on these tables with the wrapper package, then also delete and lock optimizer statistics to prevent the maintenance window from collecting statistics, and rely instead on Optimizer Dynamic Sampling. However, you may find that some tables need real statistics.

The one certain way to prevent this is to disable statistics retention, but this can only be specified globally. It cannot be disabled for individual tables. This disadvantage is that you must give up the ability to restore statistics to any table:

EXECUTE dbms_stats.alter_stats_history_retention(retention=>0);

Statistics Collection Strategy in PeopleSoft

To paraphrase an old joke, where there are two DBAs there shall be three opinions about how to collect optimizer statistics. Whole books[5] have been written about Oracle's cost-based optimizer. I am only going to make a couple of suggestions on how to collect statistics, because every system is different and your mileage will vary.

Many DBAs leave statistics collection to the Oracle-delivered maintenance window. By default, it collects histograms on all columns that are rarely helpful. Nonetheless, this works well for many tables, but in some cases the DBA needs to take control. I suggest that statistics on these tables should be locked, to remove them from schema-wide and database-wide statistics jobs. I have written PL/SQL procedures that call the wrapper package for specific tables. The wrapper package then calls the dbms_stats package with the force option to override the lock on the statistics.

Statistics on working storage tables should only be collected by the process that populates them. The %UpdateStats macro should be used in Application Engine programs. An overnight batch program is

---

[5] The most dog-eared one on my shelves is *Cost-Based Oracle Fundamentals* by Jonathan Lewis (Apress, 2005).

certain to collect statistics that are out of date by the next time they are used because the data in the table (usually the process instance column) is different. Again, I recommend locking the statistics on these tables so they are not analyzed by schema-wide or database-wise statistics processes. Optimizer Dynamic Sampling is usually effective, and where it is I also suggest deleting existing statistics and suppressing collection with the wrapper package.

Sizing Sets

It is possible to define different sets of DDL models for the same platform. These are called *sizing sets*. However, they are used only by Data Mover. For example, a particular sizing set can be used to build and import a development database with one sizing set and a production database with another. The DDL models in different sizing sets can be completely different.

I have never seen this feature used, because most databases are created by cloning other databases, and most objects are created by DDL scripts generated by Application Designer. PeopleSoft does not deliver multiple sizing sets.

Overriding DDL Model Defaults

The default DDL model parameters can be overridden for specific objects in both Application Designer and Data Mover. I explain how to do so in the following sections.

Application Designer

The DDL model and additional variables with their default values can be viewed in Application Designer. The values of the additional variables can be overridden in Application Designer on each record and index. Figure 6-3 shows the DDL parameter values for the CREATE TABLE statement for the JOB record. The initial extent size of 40000 has been overridden with 957440. This particular override is delivered in the vanilla database.

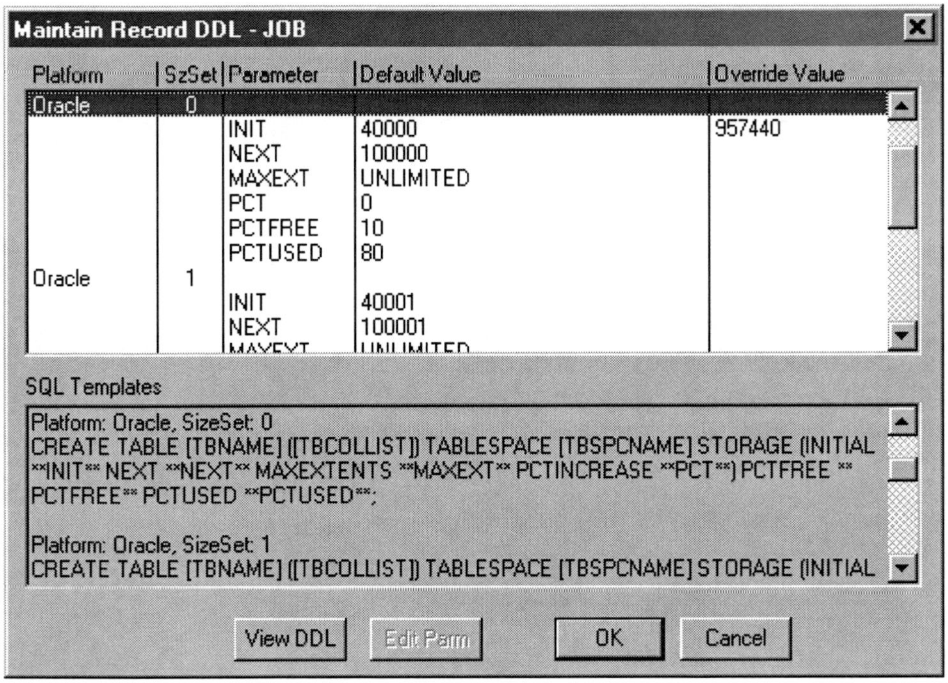

Figure 6-3. DDL override

In Oracle, the units for the INIT parameter are bytes unless explicitly specified otherwise. Since the DDL default and override values are character strings, there is nothing to stop these overrides from being specified in K (kilobytes) or M (megabytes) where appropriate, as shown in Figure 6-4.

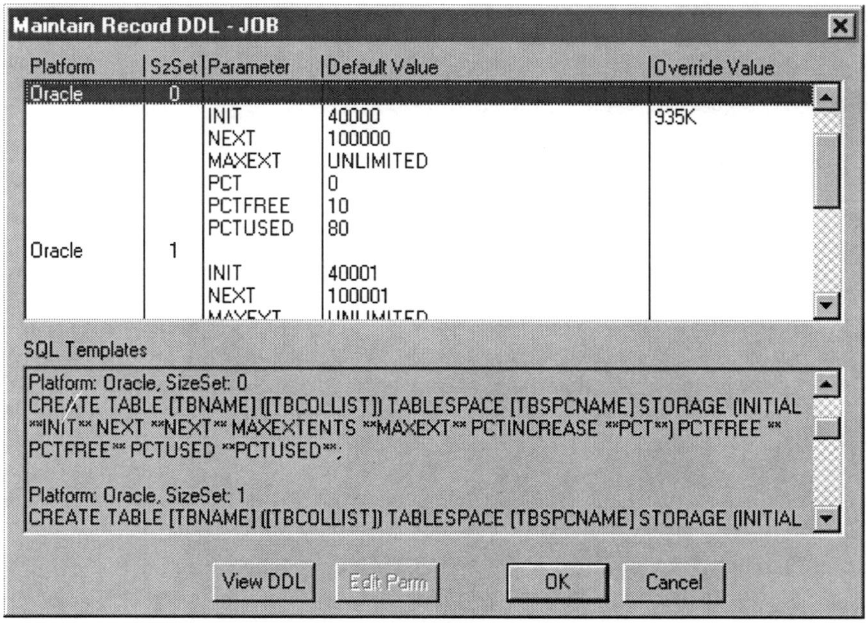

Figure 6-4. *DDL override specified in kilobytes*

The resulting CREATE statement can be viewed in Application Designer (see Figure 6-5) after the record has been saved. Both sizing sets can be viewed depending on which one is selected, but Application Designer only builds DDL scripts for sizing set 0.

The variables in the DDL models are simply replaced with their string values to produce a DDL statement.

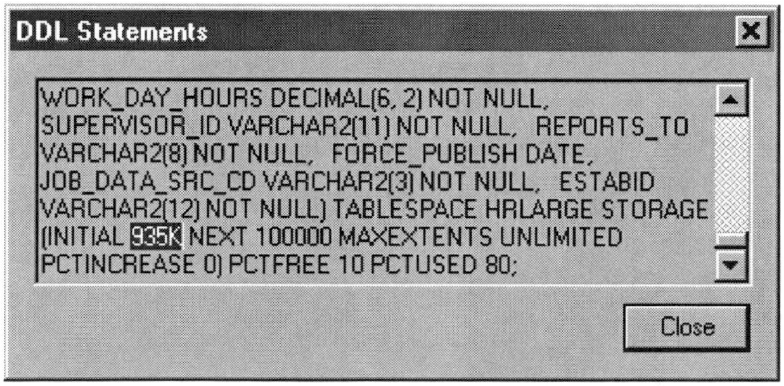

Figure 6-5. *Record DDL with DDL override*

Like any other object or attribute defined in Application Designer, the DDL overrides can be migrated between environments. However, their migration is optional. This is controlled by a radio button in the general upgrade options (see Figure 6-6). The default setting for this button is Keep Target DDL, which means DDL overrides are not migrated.

However, I think DDL overrides should be defined in the development environment, rather than anywhere else, and be migrated via test environments to production. To introduce them at any intermediate point along the migration path would risk losing them due to subsequent migrations or refreshing environments. I think Take DDL from Source should always be selected.

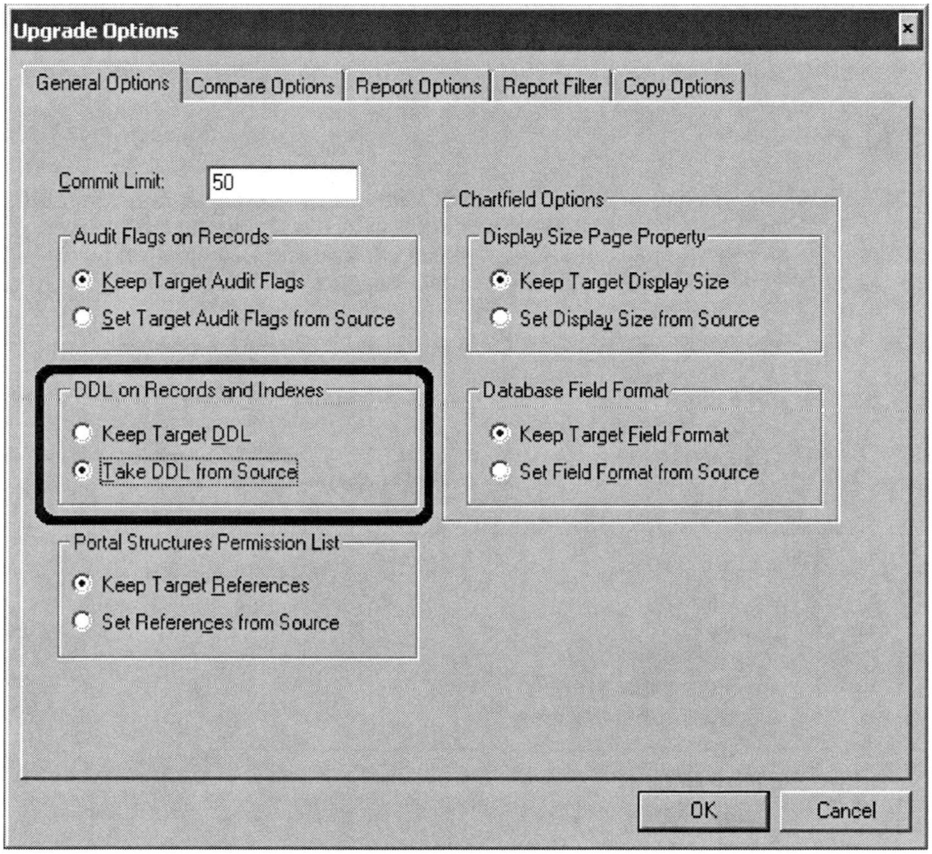

Figure 6-6. General Upgrade Options

Data Mover

The DDL models and their defaults are encoded into the top of Data Mover export files, and so are read in during an import. This is similar to Oracle's export and import utilities. Although you cannot override the DDL model during a Data Mover import, it is possible to override individual DDL model variables for one or more tables:

```
SET DDL {RECORD | INDEX | UNIQUE INDEX | SPACE} {object_name | *} INPUT parm AS value;
```

For example, if you are installing a PeopleSoft database in which all the tablespaces are locally managed, the number of extents that are used by the table when it is created but before any rows are inserted is still determined by the INITIAL, NEXT, and MINEXTENTS parameters in the STORAGE clause (although by default PeopleSoft does not specify MINEXTENTS). The table has as many extents as are required to allocate at least the same volume as would have been allocated if the table were dictionary managed. But you might decide that you only ever want one extent allocated when the table is built, and then let it expand as it is populated. To do so, you add the following commands to the top of the Data Mover import:

```
SET DDL RECORD * INPUT INIT AS 2K;
SET DDL INDEX * INPUT INIT AS 2K;
SET DDL UNIQUE INDEX * INPUT INIT AS 2K;
```

PeopleTools Tables

The following PeopleTools tables are used to store the DDL statement models, storage parameters, and override values. Only the additional parameters, delimited by double asterisks (**) in the DDL model, are stored on these tables. The internal variables, delimited by square brackets ([ ]), are placed in the DDL model, but their values are generated code inside Application Designer and Data Mover.

PSDDLMODEL (or PS_DDLMODEL_VW): DDL Model Statement

The PSDDLMODEL table, shown in Table 6-9, defines the SQL statement for the DDL model.

Table 6-9. PSDDLMODEL

Field Name	Description
STATEMENT_TYPE	Statement Type 1 = Table 2 = Index 3 = Tablespace 4 = Analyze Table Estimate 5 = Analyze Table Compute
PLATFORMID	Platform ID 0 = SQLBase 1 = DB2 2 = Oracle 3 = Informix 4 = DB2/Unix 5 = ALLBASE (not supported from PeopleTools 8.x) 6 = Sybase 7 = Microsoft 8 = DB2/400 (not supported from PeopleTools 8)
SIZING_SET	Sizing Set
PARMCOUNT	The number of parameters defined in this model.

Field Name	Description
MODEL_STATEMENT	Long column that holds the model SQL statement as seen in the panels.

PSDDLDEFPARMS (or PS_DDLDEFPARMS_VW): DDL Model Parameter

This PSDDLDEFPARMS table, shown in Table 6-10, defines the default values for the additional parameters in the DDL model. It contains one row for each parameter in each DDL model.

Table 6-10. PSDDLDEFPARMS

Field Name	Description
STATEMENT_TYPE	Statement type (see PSDDLMODEL)
PLATFORMID	Platform ID (see PSDDLMODEL)
SIZING_SET	Sizing set (see PSDDLMODEL)
PARMNAME	DDL parameter name
PARMVALUE	DDL parameter value

PSRECDDLPARM: Record DDL Parameter

The PSRECDDLPARM table, shown in Table 6-11, holds the DDL parameter overrides for CREATE TABLE statements. It contains one row for each override on a table entered in Application Designer. If a parameter is not overridden, there is not a row on this table.

Table 6-11. PSRECDDLPARM

Field Name	Description
RECNAME	PeopleTools record name
PLATFORMID	Platform ID (see PSDDLMODEL)
SIZINGSET	Sizing set (see PSDDLMODEL)
PARMNAME	DDL parameter name (see PSDDLDEFPARMS)
PARMVALUE	DDL parameter value

PSTBLSPCCAT: Tablespace Catalogue

The PSTBLSPCCAT table, shown in Table 6-12, was introduced in PeopleTools 8.4. It provides a list of available tablespaces, and it contains at least one row for every tablespace referenced by PeopleTools.

Table 6-12. PSTBLSPCCAT

Field Name	Description
DDLSPACENAME	Name of the tablespace.
DBNAME	Name of the database in which the tablespace occurs. If blank (single space), then the tablespace is in all databases.
TSTYPE	Tablespace type. A = Audit G = Large L = LOB R = Regular S = Small
DBXTSTYPE	DB2 Unix tablespace type.
COMMENTS	Comment.

PSRECTBLSPC: Record Tablespace Allocation

From PeopleTools 8.4, the tablespace for a table is no longer defined on the record definition on PSRECDEFN—it has been moved to PSRECTBLSPC (see Table 6-13). This table contains at least one row for every table. A record can be assigned to different tablespaces on different databases.

Table 6-13. PSRECTBLSPC

Field Name	Description
DDLSPACENAME	Name of the tablespace.
DBNAME	Name of the database. If blank (single space), then the record appears in this tablespace in all databases.
RECNAME	PeopleTools record name.
DBTYPE	Database platform. It has the same values and meanings as PLATFORMID (see PSDDLMODEL).
TEMPTBLINST	

PSIDXDDLPARM: Index DDL Parameters

This table (see Table 6-14) holds the DDL parameter overrides for CREATE INDEX statements. It contains one row for each override on an index entered in Application Designer.

Table 6-14. PSIDXDDLPARM

Field Name	Description
RECNAME	PeopleTools record name
INDEXID	Index identifier _ = Primary key index # = List columns index (no longer used in PeopleTools 8 0–9 = Alternate search key indexes A–Z = User-specified indexes
PLATFORMID	Platform ID (see PSDDLMODEL)
SIZINGSET	Sizing set (see PSDDLMODEL)
PARMNAME	DDL parameter name (see PSDDLDEFPARMS)
PARMVALUE	DDL parameter value

DDL Model Enhancements

The flexibility of the DDL model provides many possibilities. The overriding principle is that PeopleSoft should generate the correct DDL in the first place, although there are some exceptional situations in which this cannot be done.

This section covers a number of possible DDL model enhancements, such as the ability to add physical parameters, Key-Compressed Indexes, and Global Temporary Tables.

Additional DDL Parameters

Not only can you alter the values of the existing DDL parameters, but you can also add additional variables. PeopleSoft added PCTFREE and PCTUSED to the table and index models from PeopleTools 8.

The following could also be specified, although they are, perhaps, less likely to be used. I am not recommending that you add any or all of these, but if you need to, you can:

- MINEXTENTS
- FREELISTS
- BUFFER_POOL
- CACHE/NOCACHE
- LOGGING/NOLOGGING
- INITRANS
- PARALLEL/NOPARALLEL

Figure 6-7 shows how the DDL model and default can be set up.

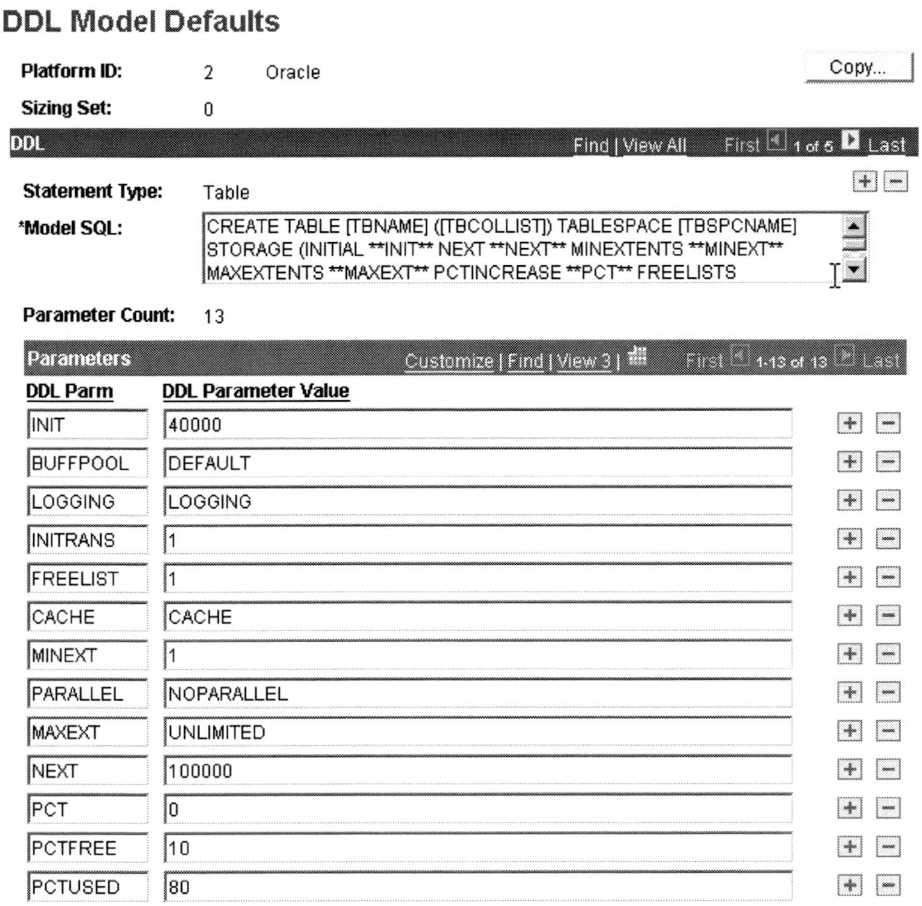

DDL Model Defaults

Platform ID:	2	Oracle
Sizing Set:	0	

DDL Find | View All   First ◄ 1 of 5 ► Last

Statement Type:	Table
*Model SQL:	CREATE TABLE [TBNAME] ([TBCOLLIST]) TABLESPACE [TBSPCNAME] STORAGE (INITIAL **INIT** NEXT **NEXT** MINEXTENTS **MINEXT** MAXEXTENTS **MAXEXT** PCTINCREASE **PCT** FREELISTS

Parameter Count: 13

Parameters Customize | Find | View 3 | 🎛   First ◄ 1-13 of 13 ► Last

DDL Parm	DDL Parameter Value		
INIT	40000	+	−
BUFFPOOL	DEFAULT	+	−
LOGGING	LOGGING	+	−
INITRANS	1	+	−
FREELIST	1	+	−
CACHE	CACHE	+	−
MINEXT	1	+	−
PARALLEL	NOPARALLEL	+	−
MAXEXT	UNLIMITED	+	−
NEXT	100000	+	−
PCT	0	+	−
PCTFREE	10	+	−
PCTUSED	80	+	−

Figure 6-7. Enhanced DDL model default

All that is needed is to edit the DDL statement in the DDL Model Defaults component for the relevant statement and to insert the extra parameters in the scroll, as shown in Listing 6-13.

Listing 6-13. Enhanced Create Table DDL Model

```
CREATE TABLE [TBNAME] ([TBCOLLIST]) TABLESPACE [TBSPCNAME]
STORAGE (INITIAL **INIT** NEXT **NEXT** MINEXTENTS **MINEXT** MAXEXTENTS
**MAXEXT** PCTINCREASE **PCT** FREELISTS **FREELIST** BUFFER_POOL **BUFFPOOL**
PCTFREE **PCTFREE** PCTUSED **PCTUSED**
;
```

If any variables in the DDL model do not match any of either the internal or additional variables, you get the following error message:

```
Error: Inconsistent statement type Create Table, platform 2, sizing set 0,
reason code 1. (76,39)
```

If you do create additional variables, you may wish to customize settable.sqr and setindex.sqr. These SQR processes feed the real values of the Oracle physical storage variables back from USER_TABLES and USER_INDEXES into PeopleTools. I discuss the issues surrounding synchronizing physical parameters in the data dictionaries later in this chapter.

■ **Note** The number of extents allocated when the table is created in a locally managed tablespace is the number that provides the same space as if the table had been created in a dictionary managed tablespace. If you choose to add MINEXTENTS to the DDL models for tables and indexes, and if you are using locally managed tablespaces, then set the default values for INITIAL and NEXT in the DDL model to the uniform extent size of the tablespace. Thus, the actual number of extents matches the number specified in the STORAGE clause.

At the very least, following this procedure makes space calculations easier. It is helpful if you also feed back the MIN_EXTENTS from USER_TABLES into PeopleTools. This requires customization of settable.sqr and setindex.sqr, or an alternative script.

If the locally managed tablespace uses automatic extent sizing, set INITIAL and NEXT to the minimum allocation size (usually 64KB), but the number of extents may not match.

You can see the effect of the changes in the Maintain Record DDL dialog (see Figure 6-8) in Application Designer (after you have restarted it and the application server also if you are developing in three-tier mode).

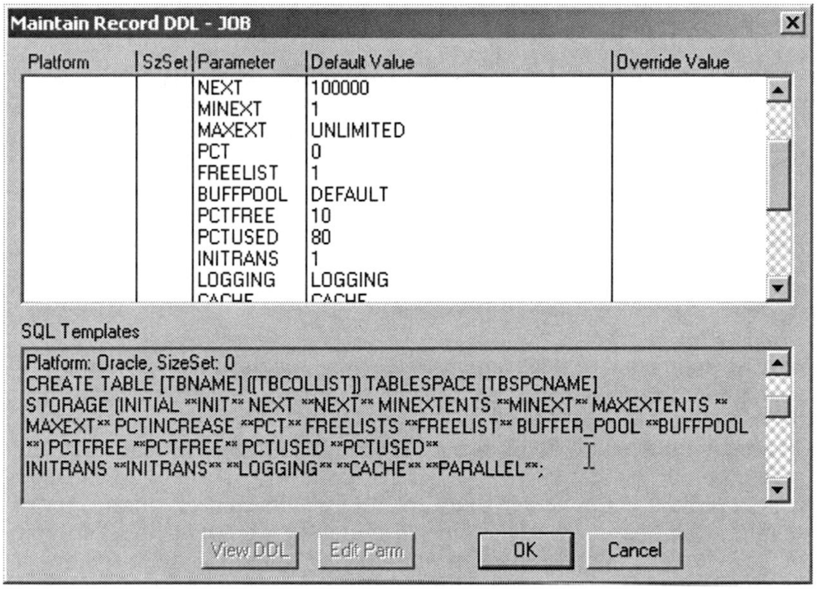

Figure 6-8. Additional parameters can be overridden

You can also see the effect on the DDL statement in the DDL window shown in Figure 6-9.

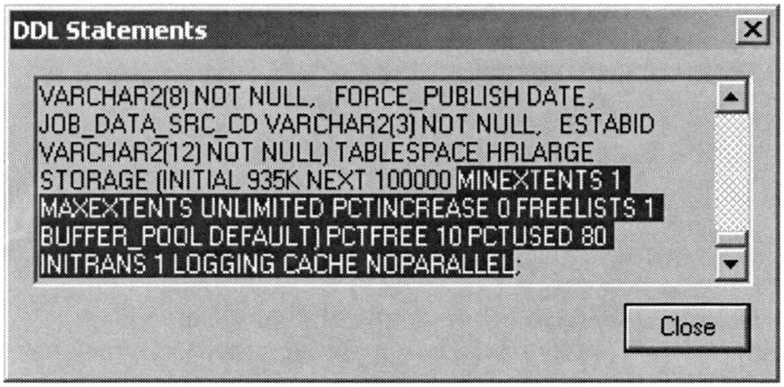

Figure 6-9. Enhanced DDL statement

■ **Caution** If you do customize the DDL models, be aware that during the PeopleTools upgrade process on an Oracle database is an instruction to run the Data Mover script `ddlora.dms` (there is a similar script for each database platform), which sets up the default DDL models. This deletes all sizing sets and reinstates the vanilla configuration. Any changes you make to the DDL model or any additional sizing sets are lost. Therefore, you may choose not to run this script.

Deferred Segment Creation

From Oracle 11g, it is possible to create a table but defer creation of the physical segments until data is inserted into the table. This is a useful database feature for PeopleSoft because there are often many thousands of empty tables. There is a new clause in the create table command for this feature:

```
CREATE TABLE ... SEGMENT CREATION DEFERRED;
```

From Oracle 11.2.0.2, this becomes the default, so there is no need to take any action. However, as an interim measure while using 11gR1, I recommend adding this clause to the create table DDL model.

Fewer DDL Parameters

Locally managed tablespaces were introduced in Oracle8*i* and have become the default in Oracle9*i*. PeopleSoft's delivered scripts now create locally managed tablespaces by default. You might decide it would be better if the PeopleSoft DDL did not include INITIAL, NEXT, or MAXEXTENTS. It may look simple to just delete them from the DDL model in the PIA, but doing so causes problems. If you completely delete the variables and the default values, then the processes to feed sizing information back into PeopleTools (settable.sqr or setindex.sqr) creates overrides for which there are not defaults, and so causes errors to be generated in Application Designer when viewing or generating DDL. It appears that all the additional variables that have defined defaults in the model must also appear in the DDL model; otherwise, this also causes errors in Application Designer.

I suggest commenting out the unwanted parameters in the DDL model string, as shown in Listing 6-14.

Listing 6-14. *Create Table DDL Model with Physical Storage Parameters Commented Out*

```
CREATE TABLE [TBNAME] ([TBCOLLIST]) TABLESPACE [TBSPCNAME]
/*STORAGE (INITIAL **INIT** NEXT **NEXT** MINEXTENTS **MINEXT** MAXEXTENTS
**MAXEXT** PCTINCREASE **PCT**)*/
PCTFREE **PCTFREE** PCTUSED **PCTUSED**;
```

Global Temporary Tables

It is possible to make Application Designer implement Global Temporary Tables, although the solution is a bit untidy.

The problem is that you cannot specify any physical parameters in the DDL statements, but in Application Designer you cannot add parameters to or remove them from the DDL model for some records and not others, nor can you specify a different sizing set for a particular record. Therefore, the existing physical parameters in the PeopleSoft DDL model must be hidden inside comments.

Creating Global Temporary Tables

The DDL model can be amended as shown in Listing 6-15 with three new parameters. The default values for the new parameters are all blank.

Listing 6-15. *DDL Model to Create Global Temporary Tables and Indexes*

```
CREATE **GLOBTEMP** TABLE [TBNAME] ([TBCOLLIST])
**STRING1**
```

```
TABLESPACE [TBSPCNAME]
STORAGE (
    INITIAL **INIT** NEXT **NEXT**
    MAXEXTENTS **MAXEXT** PCTINCREASE **PCT**) PCTFREE **PCTFREE** PCTUSED **PCTUSED**
**STRING3**;

CREATE [UNIQUE] **BITMAP** INDEX [IDXNAME] ON [TBNAME] ([IDXCOLLIST])
**STRING1**
TABLESPACE **INDEXSPC**
STORAGE (
    INITIAL **INIT** NEXT **NEXT**
    MAXEXTENTS **MAXEXT** PCTINCREASE **PCT**)
PCTFREE **PCTFREE**
**STRING2**;
```

Three new additional variables are set out on Table 6-15 that are needed in both the Create Table and Create Index DDL models.

Table 6-15. *New Variables to Handle Global Temporary Objects in the DDL Model*

DDL Model	DDL Model Parameter	DDL Override (for Global Temporary Table)	Description
TABLE	GLOBTEMP	GLOBAL TEMPORARY	Introduce GLOBAL TEMPORARY keyword in CREATE TABLE statement.
TABLE	STRING1	ON COMMIT PRESERVE ROWS /*	Specify preserve clause and open comment before storage clause
TABLE	STRING3	*/	Close comment after storage clause
INDEX	STRING1	/*	Open comment before storage clause
INDEX	STRING2	*/	Close comment after storage clause

Figure 6-10 shows the DDL overrides after they have been entered in the Maintain Record DDL dialog.

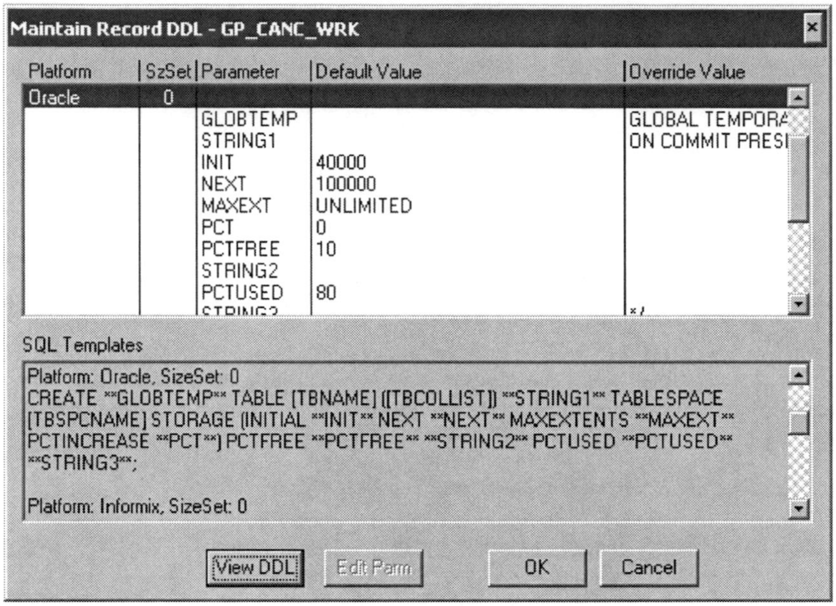

Figure 6-10. *DDL overrides for a Global Temporary Table*

Application Designer generates the SQL shown in Listing 6-16. The storage parameters are still generated, but they are now within multiline comments.

Listing 6-16. *DDL to Create a Global Temporary Table and Index*

```
DROP TABLE PS_GP_CANC_WRK
/
CREATE GLOBAL TEMPORARY TABLE PS_GP_CANC_WRK (EMPLID VARCHAR2(11) NOT NULL,
   CAL_RUN_ID VARCHAR2(18) NOT NULL,
   GP_PAYGROUP VARCHAR2(10) NOT NULL,
   CAL_ID VARCHAR2(18) NOT NULL) ON COMMIT PRESERVE ROWS /* TABLESPACE GPAPP STORAGE
(INITIAL 40000 NEXT 100000 MAXEXTENTS UNLIMITEDPCTINCREASE 0) PCTFREE 10 PCTUSED 80 */
/

CREATE UNIQUE  INDEX PS_GP_CANC_WRK ON PS_GP_CANC_WRK (EMPLID,
   CAL_RUN_ID,
   GP_PAYGROUP,
   CAL_ID) /* TABLESPACE PSINDEX STORAGE (INITIAL 40000 NEXT 100000  MAXEXTENTS UNLIMITED
PCTINCREASE 0) PCTFREE 10 */
/
ALTER INDEX PS_GP_CANC_WRK NOPARALLEL LOGGING
/
```

Since at least PeopleTools 8.48, indexes are built with the PARALLEL NOLOGGING option and then explicitly altered to NOPARALLEL LOGGING. Neither of these options is valid for Global Temporary Tables. It is not possible to suppress the explicit alter command. It is not part of the Index DDL model; instead, it is hard-coded into Application Designer. If you let Application Designer execute the script, no error is reported. However, if you run the generated script in SQL*Plus, it produces an error that can be ignored:

```
ORA-14451: unsupported feature with temporary table
```

Global Temporary Tables can be used very effectively in PeopleSoft applications. Although you can implement a Global Temporary Table in Application Designer, I recommend handling this type of table manually because of the potential for making errors in the override values.

Issues with Global Temporary Tables

Global Temporary Tables are an attractive solution to some problems; however, there are some issues you need to consider before implementing them.

From Oracle9*i*, it is possible to collect optimizer statistics for a Global Temporary Table[6] with either the `ANALYZE` command or `DBMS_STATS`, but there is only a single place for statistics in the Oracle data dictionary, so the statistics are common to all sessions that reference a table. Therefore, analyzing a Global Temporary Table in one session could impact another. From Oracle 10g, I have found that deleting and locking statistics on Global Temporary Tables and relying instead on Optimizer Dynamic Sampling is generally helpful.

From PeopleTools 8.4, Application Engine can be run as a persistent server process within a Tuxedo Process Scheduler domain (see Chapter 14). Like other PeopleSoft application server processes, it makes a persistent connection to the database. Thus, one session may run several Application Engine programs. Global Temporary Tables must be defined to preserve rows on commit. When they are referenced by a session, they consume physical space in the temporary segment, unless truncated, until the database session terminates, which happens only when the Process Scheduler domain is shut down.

Preserve On Commit Global Temporary Tables cannot be dropped until all the database sessions that have referenced them have terminated. If you use Application Engine server processes, you may have to shut down the Process Scheduler in order to alter any Global Temporary Tables that have been used.

PeopleSoft Application Engine programs automatically truncate temporary records associated with the program as it starts. Some programs are additionally coded to explicitly truncate temporary working storage tables at the start and/or the end of a process. I have seen the `REUSE STORAGE` option used in some programs. If you truncate a Global Temporary Table with the `REUSE STORAGE` option, the command completes without raising an error, but it does not truncate the table—it doesn't do anything at all:[7]

```
TRUNCATE TABLE my_gtt REUSE STORAGE
```

This another reason to configure the Process Scheduler to use stand-alone Application Engine programs rather than the persistent server processes.

---

[6] In Oracle 8i, `ANALYZE` didn't collect any statistics on a Global Temporary Table, and `DBMS_STATS.GATHER_STATISTICS` raised an "unsupported feature" error, although it was possible to set statistics with specific values.

[7] I reproduced this on Oracle 8.1.7.4, 9.2.0.5, and 10.1.0.2.

Extra Parameters with the Default DDL Model

Although it is quite easy to customize the DDL models to provide additional parameters, I find that many PeopleSoft administrators shy away from making this change. Fortunately, there is a workaround for a feature I use quite often.

Index Compression

You can choose to compress some or all of the columns in an index with the COMPRESS keyword. As I said earlier (and demonstrated in Figures 6-4 and 6-5), the override values are just strings. They can hold up to 128 characters. That is enough room to specify a value for PCTFREE, even if only the default, and then to add the COMPRESS keyword and the number of columns (as shown in Figure 6-11).

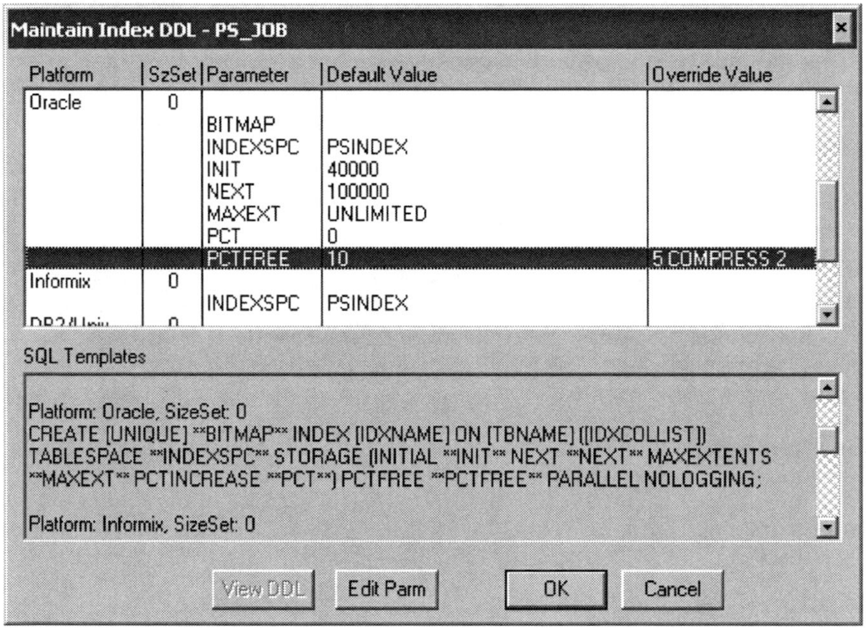

Figure 6-11. Specifying index compression in the PCTFREE override

The result (see Figure 6-12) is the COMPRESS keyword in the generated DDL string. Now, whenever the index is built or rebuilt by Application Designer, it is built with the compression option

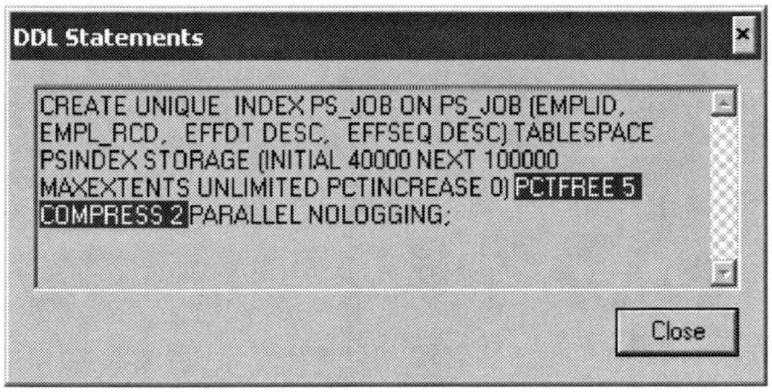

Figure 6-12. Index compression in Generated DDL

Limitations of PeopleSoft DDL Models

Application Designer is principally a tool for PeopleSoft developers, not DBAs. I think DBAs should use it as far as it is reasonably possible. However, certain Oracle features cannot reasonably be introduced and managed via the PeopleSoft DDL models, as I explain in this section.

Grants

Sometimes it is necessary to allow other Oracle users to access tables in the PeopleSoft schema. This might be to allow access to an interface process or to developers. Usual Oracle practice would be to create database roles and grant the privileges to the roles.

In the first edition of this book, I suggested that it would be possible to grant privileges on newly built tables by adding an additional grant command to the create table DDL model as suggested in Listing 6-17.

Listing 6-17. Create Table DDL Model with Additional Grants

```
CREATE TABLE [TBNAME] ([TBCOLLIST])
TABLESPACE [TBSPCNAME]
STORAGE (
    INITIAL **INIT** NEXT **NEXT**
    MAXEXTENTS **MAXEXT** PCTINCREASE **PCT**)
PCTFREE **PCTFREE** PCTUSED **PCTUSED**;
GRANT SELECT ON [TBNAME] TO **READROLE**;
GRANT SELECT, INSERT, UPDATE, DELETE ON [TBNAME] TO **WRITROLL**;
```

However, as I also pointed out, there is a limitation with this technique. When altering a table by re-creation, only the first command in the Create Table model is used in the generated script. When the table is altered by re-creation, the grants are lost.

Instead, I have a way to implement such privileges automatically using a DDL trigger. The DDL trigger cannot directly grant the privilege because it would have to issue DDL, which is prohibited:

```
ORA-30511: invalid DDL operation in system triggers
```

Instead, I have created a PL/SQL procedure that executes a DDL statement passed in a string; the trigger submits a request to the job scheduler to execute that procedure. Listing 6-18 shows this procedure.

Listing 6-18. PL/SQL Procedure and DDL Trigger to Grant Privileges

```
CREATE OR REPLACE PROCEDURE myddl (p_ddl IN VARCHAR2) IS
BEGIN
 EXECUTE IMMEDIATE p_ddl;
END;
/

CREATE OR REPLACE TRIGGER gfc_grant
AFTER CREATE ON sysadm.schema
DECLARE
 l_jobno NUMBER;
BEGIN
 IF ora_dict_obj_type = 'TABLE' THEN
 dbms_job.submit(l_jobno,'myddl(''GRANT SELECT ON '
||ora_dict_obj_owner||'.'||ora_dict_obj_name||' TO gofaster'');');
END IF;
END;
/
```

This trigger simply grants SELECT privilege on every table in the SYSADM schema to a role called GOFASTER; more complex logic could easily be built into the trigger. The privilege is not granted immediately, but the request to the job scheduler is submitted synchronously with the DDL. The job should then execute within a minute of the triggering DDL, which should be soon enough for nearly all practical purposes.

Partitioned Tables

Application Designer cannot generate partitioned tables because of the variable length of the PARTITION clause, depending on the number of partitions. It would be possible to add a number of additional variables to the DDL model and type the PARTITION clauses in as a number of overrides, but this would be very hard to manage, and the DDL overrides can only hold 128 characters.

CASE STUDY: PARTITIONED AND GLOBAL TEMPORARY TABLES

Manually managing objects that Application Designer cannot generate is an issue I encounter in many PeopleSoft systems, but particularly in Global Payroll (GP). To enable efficient parallel batch processing, approximately 40 tables all need to be similarly range-partitioned to match the payroll processing. The largest tables are also subpartitioned. In addition, the range partitions are placed in different tablespaces; the number of partitions can change, as well as the range partition boundary values; and patches can add additional columns. More than 50 other tables have been made Global Temporary Tables. It is simply not possible to implement all this in Application Designer in a manageable fashion.

My solution was to write a PL/SQL package that uses the information in the PeopleTools tables, some of the GP application tables, and some additional metadata tables of my own to build SQL scripts that build

---

the tables and indexes, including the extra keywords and partitioning clauses.[8] The result is a utility that can be easily maintained. When changes are made in either the GP application or its configuration that require the tables to be altered, the script is used to generate the DDL instead of Application Designer.

The overhead of developing the utility was set against the time spent manually editing and debugging Application Designer–generated DDL scripts. The cost of making configuration changes that would improve performance was greatly reduced because the manual editing of DDL scripts was removed.

All that is necessary is to remember which tables should be built with the utility and not Application Designer.

Preserving Partitioning in Application Designer from PeopleTools 8.51

Oracle introduced limited support for partitioned objects into Application Designer in PeopleTools 8.51 for customers running on Oracle database. Application Designer does not help you partition in the first instance; you have to generate the scripts to do that yourself.

However, if you already have partitioned tables and indexes, then if you need to alter the table, Application Designer uses the Oracle-supplied dbms_metadata package to generate the DDL after the column list instead of the DDL model. Listing 6-19 shows a portion of a script generated from Application Designer:

- The CREATE TABLE and CREATE INDEX options in Application Designer generate scripts that are entirely generated from the DDL models, and if used remove any partitioning.

- Table partitioning is not preserved by the Alter Table script. That also comes only from the DDL model.

- If Application Designer detects any change in the column list in an index, it uses the DDL model, not dbms_metadata, and that index is rebuilt as a single segment.

[8] See the papers "Configuring and Operating Streamed Processing in PeopleSoft Global Payroll" and "Managing Oracle Table Partitioning in PeopleSoft Applications with GFC_PSPART Package" on www.go-faster.co.uk.

Listing 6-19. Part of the Alter Table Script Generated by Application Designer PT8.51

```
CREATE    INDEX PSDPSPMTRANSHIST ON PSPMTRANSHIST (PM_TOP_INST_ID,
    PM_TRANS_DEFN_SET,
    PM_TRANS_DEFN_ID) TABLESPACE PSINDEX STORAGE (INITIAL 40000 NEXT
 100000 MAXEXTENTS UNLIMITED PCTINCREASE 0) PCTFREE 1 COMPRESS 3
 PARALLEL NOLOGGING
/
ALTER INDEX PSDPSPMTRANSHIST NOPARALLEL LOGGING
/
CREATE    INDEX PSEPSPMTRANSHIST ON PSPMTRANSHIST (PM_CONTEXT_VALUE1,
    PM_AGENTID,
    PM_MON_STRT_DTTM)
 PCTFREE 10 INITRANS 2 MAXTRANS 255  LOGGING
 STORAGE(
 BUFFER_POOL DEFAULT) LOCAL
 (PARTITION "PSPMTRANSHISTETRANS101"
 PCTFREE 10 INITRANS 2 MAXTRANS 255
 STORAGE(INITIAL 65536 NEXT 1048576 MINEXTENTS 1 MAXEXTENTS
2147483645
 PCTINCREASE 0 FREELISTS 1 FREELIST GROUPS 1 BUFFER_POOL DEFAULT)
 TABLESPACE "PSDEFAULT" ,
...
 PARTITION "PSPMTRANSHISTEOTHERS"
 PCTFREE 10 INITRANS 2 MAXTRANS 255
 STORAGE(INITIAL 65536 NEXT 1048576 MINEXTENTS 1 MAXEXTENTS
2147483645
 PCTINCREASE 0 FREELISTS 1 FREELIST GROUPS 1 BUFFER_POOL DEFAULT)
 TABLESPACE "PSDEFAULT" )
/
ALTER INDEX PSEPSPMTRANSHIST NOPARALLEL LOGGING
/
```

Constraints

It is inappropriate to add constraints to a PeopleSoft database (as discussed in Chapter 5). In addition, they cannot be added to tables at create time because the syntax is inside the column list, which is generated by the internal PeopleTools variable [TBCOLLIST], which cannot be altered (see Listing 6-20).

Listing 6-20. PeopleSoft Doesn't Create a Table with a Constraint

```
CREATE  TABLE PS_PERSONAL_DATA
(EMPLID VARCHAR2(11) NOT NULL,
...
   SEX VARCHAR2(1) NOT NULL CONSTRAINT sex_check CHECK SEX IN('M','F','U');
...
```

Function-Based Indexes

We saw in Chapter 5 that searches on character fields in the record locator dialog are, by default, case-insensitive. When PeopleTools builds the query for the search dialog, it adds the UPPER() functions to the query that it constructs, as shown in Listing 6-21.

Listing 6-21. Case-insensitive Search Dialog Query

```
SELECT DISTINCT EMPLID, EMPL_RCD, NAME, LAST_NAME_SRCH, NAME_AC, PER_STATUS
FROM    PS_EMPLMT_SRCH_COR
WHERE   ROWSECCLASS=:1
AND     UPPER(NAME) LIKE UPPER('Smith') || '%' ESCAPE '\'
ORDER BY NAME, EMPLID, EMPL_RCD
```

However, placing a function on a column prevents Oracle from scanning an index by that column. If you don't want to suppress the functionality, an alternative is to build a function-based index on the columns that are frequently the subject of case-insensitive searches. If the function in the index matches the function on the column, then the index can be used. Experience has shown that this generally works well in PeopleSoft. There are only a few columns, usually name and address fields, where such an index is necessary.

The CREATE INDEX syntax is simple. You merely specify an expression instead of a column:

```
CREATE INDEX sysadm.PSZCUSTOMER_FBI ON sysadm.PS_CUSTOMER (UPPER(NAME1));
```

There is an administrative drawback to this approach. The PeopleSoft Application Designer cannot generate the DDL for function-based indexes. The list of indexed columns comes from an internal variable that cannot be altered other than by specifying columns in the index. Therefore, function-based indexes must be maintained manually outside of PeopleSoft. They also appear in the DDDAUDIT exception report because they are not defined in PeopleSoft.

■ **Tip** In the example above, I have given the function-based index a non-standard name to prevent Application Designer dropping the index. The third letter of the index name is Z, so Application Designer will try to drop index PSZCUSTOMER. It is very unlikely that a developer will try to add enough indexes to need Z, and if they do, they probably shouldn't.

Index Organized Tables

It is possible to make Application Designer generate the DDL to create an Index Organized Table. The Create Table DDL model can be extended as I demonstrated earlier for Global Temporary Tables, and parts of the DDL can be specified as DDL overrides in Application Designer (as shown in Figure 6-13).

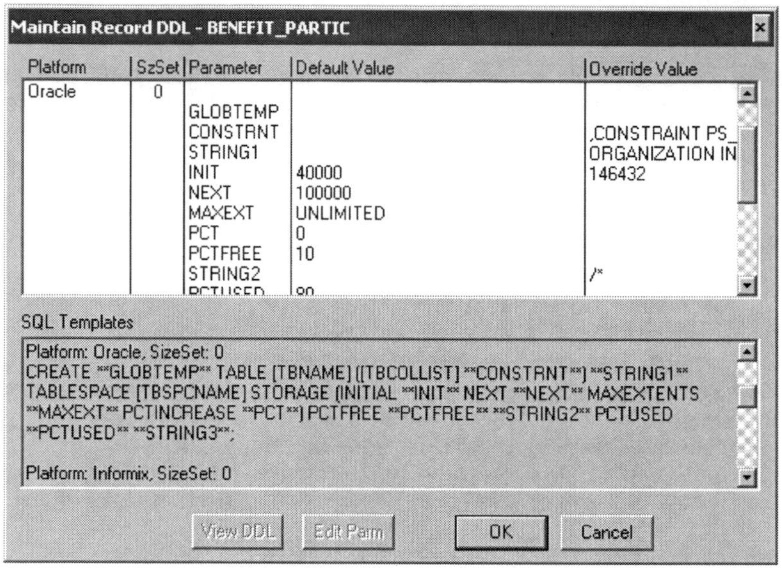

Figure 6-13. DDL overrides for an Index Organized Table

However, the alter-table script generated by Application Designer fails as it attempts to create a second table with the same constraint name (see Listing 6-22).

Listing 6-22. Excerpt of Application Designer Alter-Table Script

```
>CREATE TABLE PSYBENEFIT_PARTIC (EMPLID VARCHAR2(11) NOT NULL,
 2      EMPL_RCD SMALLINT NOT NULL,
 3      COBRA_EVENT_ID SMALLINT NOT NULL,
 4      PLAN_TYPE VARCHAR2(2) NOT NULL,
 5      BENEFIT_NBR SMALLINT NOT NULL ,CONSTRAINT PS_BENEFIT_PARTIC PRIMARY
 6   KEY (EMPLID, EMPL_RCD, COBRA_EVENT_ID, PLAN_TYPE, BENEFIT_NBR))
 7   ORGANIZATION INDEX TABLESPACE BNAPP STORAGE (INITIAL 146432 NEXT
 8   100000 MAXEXTENTS UNLIMITED PCTINCREASE 0) PCTFREE 10 /* PCTUSED 80 */
 9   /
  BENEFIT_NBR SMALLINT NOT NULL ,CONSTRAINT PS_BENEFIT_PARTIC PRIMARY
                                 *
ERROR at line 5:
ORA-02264: name already used by an existing constraint
```

Index Organized Tables can be used in PeopleSoft applications, but once again, they should be handled manually outside Application Designer.

Other DDL

Other DDL statements are generated by Application Designer that do not, either wholly or partly, use the DDL models. The following sections cover these statements.

Alter Table in Place

The Application Designer can generate the ALTER statements to add columns to a table without re-creating it, although it drops and re-creates the index. Only the CREATE INDEX command is generated from a DDL model; the rest is hard-coded in Application Designer.

A table cannot always be altered in place. In such a case, it is altered by re-creation, as shown in Listing 6-23.

Listing 6-23. Script to Alter a Table in Place

```
-- Alters for record PS_GFC_DATA_KEYS
--          DATA_KEY5 - add
-- Add Columns
ALTER TABLE PS_GFC_DATA_KEYS ADD DATA_KEY5 VARCHAR2(18)
/
-- Set Default Values
UPDATE PS_GFC_DATA_KEYS SET DATA_KEY5 = ' '
/
-- Modify NULLability

ALTER TABLE PS_GFC_DATA_KEYS MODIFY DATA_KEY5 NOT NULL
/
-- Done
DROP INDEX PS_GFC_DATA_KEYS
/
CREATE UNIQUE  INDEX PS_GFC_DATA_KEYS ON PS_GFC_DATA_KEYS (DATA_KEY1,
   DATA_KEY2) TABLESPACE PSINDEX STORAGE (INITIAL 40000 NEXT 100000
 MAXEXTENTS UNLIMITED PCTINCREASE 0) PCTFREE 10
/
```

■ **Caution** If columns are added to a table in a production-like environment and subsequently populated, the rows can consume all the free space in the block, causing the rows to migrate to a second block. This can cause performance problems.

Alter Table by Re-creation

Most table alterations are done by building, populating, and renaming a copy of the original table. The DDL models are used to create the temporary table and the indexes at the end of the script.

Alter-table scripts cannot be run directly by Application Designer; rather, they must be run manually in SQL*Plus. Listing 6-24 shows another script to alter a table by re-creation.

Listing 6-24. Script to Alter a Table by Re-creation

```
-- Create temporary table
CREATE TABLE PSYGFC_DATA_KEYS (DATA_KEY1 VARCHAR2(18) NOT NULL,
   DATA_KEY2 VARCHAR2(18) NOT NULL,
```

```
      DATA_KEY3 VARCHAR2(18) NOT NULL,
      DATA_KEY4 VARCHAR2(18) NOT NULL,
      DATA_KEY5 VARCHAR2(18) NOT NULL) TABLESPACE USERS STORAGE (INITIAL
  40000 NEXT 100000 MAXEXTENTS UNLIMITED PCTINCREASE 0) PCTFREE 10
  PCTUSED 80
/
-- Copy from source to temp table
INSERT INTO PSYGFC_DATA_KEYS (
        DATA_KEY1,
    DATA_KEY2,
    DATA_KEY3,
    DATA_KEY4,
    DATA_KEY5)
  SELECT
        DATA_KEY1,
    DATA_KEY2,
    DATA_KEY3,
    DATA_KEY4,
    ' '
  FROM PS_GFC_DATA_KEYS
/
-- CAUTION: Drop Original Table
DROP TABLE PS_GFC_DATA_KEYS
/
-- Rename Table
RENAME PSYGFC_DATA_KEYS TO PS_GFC_DATA_KEYS
/
-- Done
CREATE UNIQUE  INDEX PS_GFC_DATA_KEYS ON PS_GFC_DATA_KEYS (DATA_KEY1,
    DATA_KEY2) TABLESPACE PSINDEX STORAGE (INITIAL 40000 NEXT 100000
  MAXEXTENTS UNLIMITED PCTINCREASE 0) PCTFREE 10
/
```

■ **Caution** This script is not without risks. If the creation or population of the temporary table fails for any reason, the script continues and drops the original table, and the data is lost. To stop the SQL*Plus session if an error occurs, add this command:

```
WHENEVER SOLERROR EXIT FAILURE
```

It is not until Oracle 10 that you can "undrop" a table using the flashback facility.

Views

The CREATE VIEW commands are entirely hard-coded. It is not possible, for instance, to change the command to CREATE OR REPLACE. Listing 6-25 shows how to drop and re-create a view.

Listing 6-25. Dropping and Re-creating a View

```
DROP VIEW PS_NAME_TYPE_VW
/
CREATE VIEW PS_NAME_TYPE_VW (EMPLID, ORDER_BY_SEQ, NAME_TYPE) AS
 SELECT DISTINCT A.EMPLID ,B.ORDER_BY_SEQ ,A.NAME_TYPE FROM PS_NAMES A
 , PS_NAME_TYPE_TBL B WHERE A.NAME_TYPE = B.NAME_TYPE
/
COMMIT
/
```

PeopleSoft Temporary Tables

These are regular permanent tables that are used for temporary working storage by Application Engine processes. Do not confuse them with Oracle Global Temporary Tables!

In order to permit multiple instances of the same Application Engine process to run concurrently without contention on working storage tables, PeopleSoft creates temporary tables. Additional copies of each table are created in the database, and each instance of the Application Engine process is allocated to a different copy of the table.

A table named according to the usual conventions is always built along with a number of copies of that table, with the instance number of the table added as a suffix. The number of additional copies of the table is determined by the sum of the following:

- A global number of temporary table instances (PSOPTIONS.TEMTBLINSTANCES). This can be set via the PIA on PeopleTools Options.

- The number of instances for each Application Engine process that references a particular table (PSTEMPTBLCNTVW.TEMPTBLINSTANCES).

If the table is not referenced by any Application Engine program, no additional copies are built. Each copy of the table and its indexes are built with the DDL model in the usual way (as shown in Listing 6-26).

Listing 6-26. DDL Script to Create All Copies of a PeopleSoft Temporary Table

```
DROP TABLE PS_GPJP_YSS4_TAO
/
CREATE TABLE PS_GPJP_YSS4_TAO (PROCESS_INSTANCE DECIMAL(10) NOT NULL,
   EMPLID VARCHAR2(11) NOT NULL,
   GPJP_YEA_NONLIF DECIMAL(18, 6) NOT NULL,
   GPJP_YEA_LTNONL DECIMAL(18, 6) NOT NULL) TABLESPACE GPAPP STORAGE
 (INITIAL 40000 NEXT 100000 MAXEXTENTS UNLIMITED PCTINCREASE 0)
 PCTFREE 10 PCTUSED 80
/
CREATE UNIQUE  INDEX PS_GPJP_YSS4_TAO ON PS_GPJP_YSS4_TAO
 (PROCESS_INSTANCE,
   EMPLID) TABLESPACE PSINDEX STORAGE (INITIAL 40000 NEXT 100000
```

```
  MAXEXTENTS UNLIMITED PCTINCREASE 0) PCTFREE 10 PARALLEL NOLOGGING
/
ALTER INDEX PS_GPJP_YSS4_TAO NOPARALLEL LOGGING
/
DROP TABLE PS_GPJP_YSS4_TAO1
/
CREATE TABLE PS_GPJP_YSS4_TAO1 (PROCESS_INSTANCE DECIMAL(10) NOT NULL,
    EMPLID VARCHAR2(11) NOT NULL,
    GPJP_YEA_NONLIF DECIMAL(18, 6) NOT NULL,
    GPJP_YEA_LTNONL DECIMAL(18, 6) NOT NULL) TABLESPACE GPAPP STORAGE
 (INITIAL 40000 NEXT 100000 MAXEXTENTS UNLIMITED PCTINCREASE 0)
 PCTFREE 10 PCTUSED 80
/
CREATE UNIQUE  INDEX PS_GPJP_YSS4_TAO1 ON PS_GPJP_YSS4_TAO1
 (PROCESS_INSTANCE,
   EMPLID) TABLESPACE PSINDEX STORAGE (INITIAL 40000 NEXT 100000
 MAXEXTENTS UNLIMITED PCTINCREASE 0) PCTFREE 10 PARALLEL NOLOGGING
/
ALTER INDEX PS_GPJP_YSS4_TAO1 NOPARALLEL LOGGING
/
…
DROP TABLE PS_GPJP_YSS4_TAO4
/
CREATE TABLE PS_GPJP_YSS4_TAO4 (PROCESS_INSTANCE DECIMAL(10) NOT NULL,
    EMPLID VARCHAR2(11) NOT NULL,
    GPJP_YEA_NONLIF DECIMAL(18, 6) NOT NULL,
    GPJP_YEA_LTNONL DECIMAL(18, 6) NOT NULL) TABLESPACE GPAPP STORAGE
 (INITIAL 40000 NEXT 100000 MAXEXTENTS UNLIMITED PCTINCREASE 0)
 PCTFREE 10 PCTUSED 80
/
CREATE UNIQUE  INDEX PS_GPJP_YSS4_TAO4 ON PS_GPJP_YSS4_TAO4
 (PROCESS_INSTANCE,
   EMPLID) TABLESPACE PSINDEX STORAGE (INITIAL 40000 NEXT 100000
 MAXEXTENTS UNLIMITED PCTINCREASE 0) PCTFREE 10 PARALLEL NOLOGGING
/
ALTER INDEX PS_GPJP_YSS4_TAO4 NOPARALLEL LOGGING
/
```

The temporary tables can also be built by Data Mover using the CREATE_TEMP_TABLE command.

Triggers

PeopleSoft Mobile Agents was introduced in 2001 into PeopleTools. To support the incremental replication of data between the central database to offline and mobile devices, trigger-maintained sequence numbers and timestamps were added to tables that were replicated. From PeopleTools 8.4, Application Designer builds a trigger (like the one in Listing 6-27) in either one or both of two situations. There is no DDL model for this trigger; it is generated directly by Application Designer:

- *If a system ID field is defined on a record definition:* When a row is inserted, it is set to the maximum value that exists on the table. Alternatively, if the key does not already exist, it takes a new value from the PSSYSID table.

- *If a timestamp field is specified on a record definition:* The trigger sets the value of that column the current system date.

Listing 6-27. PeopleTools Trigger for Mobile Agent Synchronization

```
CREATE OR REPLACE TRIGGER PSUCURRENCY_CD_TBL BEFORE INSERT OR UPDATE
 OF  CURRENCY_CD,EFFDT,EFF_STATUS,DESCR,DESCRSHORT,COUNTRY,CUR_SYMBOL
,DECIMAL_POSITIONS,SCALE_POSITIONS ON PS_CURRENCY_CD_TBL FOR EACH ROW
 DECLARE PSSYSID  NUMBER (31,0);
BEGIN
IF INSERTING THEN
SELECT MAX(SYNCID) INTO PSSYSID FROM PS_CURRENCY_CD_TBL WHERE
 :NEW.CURRENCY_CD = PS_CURRENCY_CD_TBL.CURRENCY_CD;
IF PSSYSID <= 0 OR PSSYSID IS NULL THEN
UPDATE PSSYSTEMID SET PTNEXTSYSTEMID = PTNEXTSYSTEMID + 1 WHERE
 RECNAME = 'CURRENCY_CD_TBL';
SELECT PTNEXTSYSTEMID INTO PSSYSID FROM PSSYSTEMID WHERE
 RECNAME='CURRENCY_CD_TBL';
:NEW.SYNCID:= PSSYSID;
ELSE
:NEW.SYNCID:= PSSYSID;
END IF;
END IF;
:NEW.LASTUPDDTTM := SYSDATE;
END;
/
COMMIT
/
```

Mobile Agents have been deprecated since PeopleTools 8.50,[9] but the capability to generate the triggers remains for backward compatibility only. If you are not using Mobile Agents, the trigger is an unnecessary overhead. There is also a risk that row-level locking on the table used as a sequence could lead to locking. I suggest dropping the trigger.

Protecting Database Objects Not Managed by Application Designer

If you have gone to the time and trouble to manually implement database objects for which Application Designer cannot generate the necessary DDL, such as partitioning, you don't want Application Designer to then drop and re-create objects and destroy that work.

To protect against this, I have written a DDL trigger[10] that executes before a DROP, ALTER, or RENAME command. It performs a number of checks and raises a custom error (see Table 6-16) if it detects a problem that prevents the triggering DDL from executing.

---

[9] See PeopleTools 8.50 PeopleBook: PeopleSoft Application Designer Developer's Guide ä Administering Data (`http://download.oracle.com/docs/cd/E15645_01/pt850pbr0/eng/psbooks/tapd/chapter.htm?File=tapd /htm/tapd10.htm%236e392b55_12acea23682__5b45`).

[10] PSFT_DDL_TRIGGER can be download from `www.go-faster.co.uk/scripts.htm#psft_ddl_lock.sql`.

Table 6-16. Custom Errors in PSFT_DDL_LOCK trigger

Error Number	Message and Description
20002	DDL on Index on Global Temporary Table
20003	DDL on Partitioned Index
20004	DDL on Function Based Index
20005	DDL on Index not defined in PeopleSoft
20006	Cannot alter PSRECDEFN because PSFT_DDL_LOCK trigger references it
20007	DDL on Global Temporary Table
20008	DDL on Partitioned Table
20009	DDL on Table that is part of Cluster
20010	DDL on Index Organized Table
20011	DDL on Table where an index not defined in PeopleSoft
20012	DDL on Table with Function Based Index
20013	DDL on Table with Non-PSU Trigger
20014	DDL on Table with Primary Key Constraint
20015	DDL on Table with Materialized View Log
20016	DDL on Table that is a Materialized View
20017	DDL on Table with shadow Global Temporary Table[11]
20018	DDL on Index of Table with shadow Global Temporary Table

---

[11] Errors 20017 and 20018 relate to use of another trigger, GFC_TEMP_TABLE_TYPE. It switches a non-shared instance of a temporary record from a normal table to a Global Temporary Table if restart is disabled on an Application Engine program or switches it back to a normal table if restart is enabled. The trigger creates the Global Temporary Table and any indexes on it if necessary and renames the tables as needed. This can be downloaded from www.go-faster.co.uk/scripts.htm#gfc_temp_table_type.sql.

■ **Note** Naturally, the indexes on a table are also dropped when the table is dropped. The DDL trigger only fires once for the drop table and does not fire for each additional index that is dropped. Hence there are additional tests, which raise different messages, for indexes that are executed when attempting to drop a table.

Of course, there are times when you really do want to drop and re-create these objects. The trigger reads a package global variable to determine whether to apply the checks. Thus the trigger can be disabled for just the current session by setting that variable:

```
EXECUTE psft_ddl_lock.set_ddl_permitted(TRUE);
```

Application Designer and the Oracle Recycle Bin

The Recycle Bin was introduced in Oracle 10g and is enabled by default. It works just like the Windows Recycle Bin. You can drop a table and then flash it back:

```
FLASHBACK TABLE employees TO BEFORE DROP RENAME TO employees_old;
```

When you drop a table, Oracle marks it as dropped and renames it with a system-generated name beginning with BIN$. If you drop the table with the PURGE option, the Recycle Bin is not used; the behavior is as in previous versions of Oracle.

Scripts generated by Application Designer that drop tables do not use the PURGE option. If I rebuild a table with an alter script as generated by Application Designer, such as the script in Listing 6-26, I see the entries from Listing 6-28 in the Recycle Bin using the USER_RECYCLEBIN view.

Listing 6-28. Contents of the Recycle Bin after PeopleTools Alter Script

```
SELECT * FROM user_recyclebin ORDER BY droptime, purge_object;

OBJECT_NAME                         ORIGINAL_NAME      OPERATION TYPE
--------------------------------    ----------------   ---------  -------------------------
TS_NAME                             CREATETIME         DROPTIME             DROPSCN
--------------------------------    ----------------   -------------------  ----------
                                    CAN_   CAN_
PARTITION_NAME                      UNDROP PURGE   RELATED BASE_OBJECT PURGE_OBJECT    SPACE
--------------------------------    ------ -----   ---------- ----------- ------------ ----------
BIN$RPoc1eIiSGuRufOHB6IG6Q==$0 PS_GPJP_YSS4_TAO   DROP      TABLE
GPAPP                               2011-06-12:23:23:25 2011-06-12:23:29:29   57454098
                                    YES    YES     225237     225237        225237          8

BIN$P+IvvzIkTYKNuK3UJSNroQ==$0 PS_GPJP_YSS4_TAO   DROP      INDEX
PSINDEX                             2011-06-12:23:23:25 2011-06-12:23:29:29   57454096
                                    NO     YES     225237     225237        225238          8
```

Use of the DROP TABLE command in generated scripts is hard-coded within Application Designer. The purge option can only be introduced by manually editing the script before executing it.

PeopleSoft alter scripts usually drop and re-create tables. In a production system, this is often the best option; otherwise you run the risk of causing rows to migrate to other blocks when you add new columns. However, in one system, I found over 17,000 objects in the Recycle Bin, occupying 1.3GB!

Personally, I would disable the Recycle Bin by setting the initialization parameter `RECYCLEBIN = OFF` in all PeopleSoft environments, with the possible exception of the development environment.

The `RECYCLEBIN` parameter can be set dynamically at the session or system level. You could perhaps turn it on prior to upgrade/data-migration procedures and then, when satisfied, turn it off again and manually purge the Recycle Bin. However, you are not guaranteed to be able to recover a table from the Recycle Bin. If there isn't enough free space in the tablespace, it may be purged. Instead, you might use the Flashback database with a guaranteed restore point set at the start of the maintenance outage. Then you would know you could revert the entire database to the state when you started.

I think Oracle features should be used knowingly. It doesn't matter whether you decide to use a feature or not. It *is* important that in making that decision, you have thought about how to deal with the implications, rather than be surprised later.

Synchronizing PeopleSoft with the Oracle Data Dictionary

Chapter 4 discussed the importance of keeping the definition of table and index structures in the PeopleSoft data dictionary synchronized with the Oracle catalogue. To some extent, the same is true of storage options and other physical attributes. However, these vary across the PeopleSoft-supported database platforms and hence are not reported by DDDAUDIT.

What Tools Are Available?

Ideally, all changes to segment attributes should, as far as possible, be managed within Application Designer. However, changes may be made directly to the database objects, in which case it is important to feed these back into the PeopleSoft data dictionary so that the next time Application Designer rebuilds them, these settings are not lost.

PeopleTools is delivered with three SQR reports that update the PeopleSoft data dictionary with the actual values as reported by the Oracle catalogue views. Thus, when an object is re-created by a script generated by Application Designer, any values set by the DBA directly are preserved. There is no delivered process definition for these SQR reports, but it is an easy matter to create one for each process.

`Settable.sqr` and `Setindex.sqr` copy the physical attributes on tables and indexes from the USER_TABLES and USER_INDEXES views and, where they differ from the default values, create or replace DDL overrides on records and indexes. This includes the tablespace for indexes, which is held as a DDL override in PeopleTools.

On both partitioned and Global Temporary Tables, `MAX_EXTENTS` is null on USER_TABLES. `settable.sqr` writes 0 into the MAXEXT DDL override. The Create Table DDL statements then generated by Application Design fail because 0 is an invalid value for `MAX_EXTENTS`. The same issue on USER_INDEXES causes `setindex.sqr` to fail with a NOT NULL constraint error when it attempts to insert a blank DDL override. I suggest customizing these processes to exclude partitioned and Global Temporary objects.

`Setspace.sqr` copies the tablespace of the table into the PeopleSoft record definition. Again, partitioned and Global Temporary objects present a problem. The tablespace is blank in USER_TABLES, so `setspace.sqr` allocates the record to tablespace PTTBL.

What Should Be Fed Back Into PeopleTools?

The DDL models for Oracle have three groups of parameters that are synchronized by these SQR programs:

- *Segment attributes:* TABLESPACE

- *Physical attributes:* PCTFREE, PCTUSED, INITRANS
- *Storage clause attributes:* INITIAL, NEXT, MAXEXTENTS, PCTINCREASE

Segment Attributes

If you choose to move away from the default tablespace configuration in PeopleSoft, then it is important to make sure that thereafter, objects are rebuilt in the correct tablespace. If the DBA moves the tables or indexes without updating Application Designer, the new tablespaces need to be fed back into the PeopleTools tables.

Physical Attributes

Many PeopleSoft programs populate reporting and temporary working storage tables by first inserting rows and then updating the other columns. This can lead to row migration as the updates consume and exhaust the free space in the data blocks. The problem can be prevented by reserving more free space in the block for updates, by setting a higher PCTFREE value. Therefore, it is important to feed this attribute back into PeopleTools.

The introduction of Automatic Segment Space Management in Oracle 9i effectively rendered PCTUSED, INITRANS, and other physical attributes obsolete.

Storage Clause Attributes

One of the great Oracle urban legends was that DML operations performed better on objects with fewer extents. DBAs spent many happy hours exporting and reimporting databases, or writing and executing scripts to resize tables and indexes into single extents.

The legend was always and is still false on both dictionary and locally managed tablespaces. There is no provable link between DML performance and the number of extents that exist in a table.

A lot of people expended a lot of effort on papers and presentations to debunk the legend. Since at least 1990, when Oracle version 6.0 was current and long before locally managed tablespaces were invented, Oracle has recommended using uniform extent sizes in tablespaces to eliminate fragmentation.[12] The legend only died when locally managed tablespaces became the standard and took management of segments away from DBAs!

The INIT and NEXT storage-clause parameters do not change the size of extents that are created in a locally managed tablespaces, but in conjunction with MINEXTENTS they can affect how many extents are created (see Chapter 7).

There is no real point in feeding back these parameters from Oracle into PeopleTools, but settable.sqr and setindex.sqr copy these and other attributes together. As discussed earlier in this chapter, it is not appropriate to the remove these parameters from the DDL model. Instead, I suggest commenting out the storage clause (as shown in Listing 6-14) so that it has no effect.

---

[12] Bhaskar Himatsingka and Juan Loaiza, Oracle Paper #711: "How to Stop Defragmenting and Start Living: The Definitive Word on Fragmentation,"1997. This paper no longer appears on Oracle's public website, but can be obtained from http://web.archive.org/web/20061231020749/http://www.oracle.com/technology/deploy/availability/pdf/defrag.pdf. It is also attached to Oracle support note 10640.1

Summary

This chapter revealed the mechanism that PeopleSoft uses to generate the DDL to create tables and indexes based on information stored in its own data dictionary. In addition, this chapter covered how to gather statistics for the cost-based optimizer.

The objective should always be to work with the PeopleSoft tools and, where possible, make them work for you, rather than continuously fighting against them. If you know how this mechanism works, then you can intercept it in order to enhance the DDL to include additional database features, such as additional attributes and optimizer statistics.

However, the DDL models have their limitations, and although it is always preferable to manage object parameters from within PeopleSoft, there are times when there really is no alternative but to manage them manually outside. In these cases, such as partitioning in Global Payroll, the benefit of using a feature must outweigh the overhead of managing it manually.

CHAPTER 7

Tablespaces

This chapter looks at the various tablespaces that PeopleSoft creates in an Oracle database and how they are used. Some of the choices that PeopleSoft has made are a little surprising, such as the decision to have many tablespaces for tables but only one for indexes. So, I also discuss some of the options you have to make life a little easier when managing tablespaces.

In the PeopleSoft installation procedure, the default tablespaces in the database are created immediately after the database is created. Therefore, this is also a suitable place to consider how to create the database in the first place.

Database Creation

Creating a new PeopleSoft database from scratch is not something that DBAs need to do very often. Mostly, databases are created by cloning another environment. Fortunately, the procedure for creating a PeopleSoft database is described in the PeopleSoft installation guides. There are separate versions for each database platform, which are reissued for each PeopleTools release, and they can be downloaded from the My Oracle Support web site. In this section, I focus on how, during the PeopleSoft installation procedure, the Oracle database itself is created.

Supplied Database Creation Scripts

PeopleSoft has always provided, and continues to provide, SQL scripts with which to create an Oracle database. They are a starting point, and Oracle expects customer DBAs to review and adjust these scripts as necessary.

Create Database

A separate create database script, `createdb10.sql` for Oracle 10g, has been shipped with PeopleTools since it was first certified on that version and is still shipped with PeopleTools 8.51, although it is no longer certified on Oracle 9i. The significant differences are that it creates the following:

- An explicitly locally managed SYSTEM tablespace

- The SYSAUX tablespace

- A default temporary tablespace, called TEMP, with a temp file

Listing 7-1 shows the `CREATE DATABASE` command from the script.

Listing 7-1. createdb10.sql: *Creating the Database*

```
CREATE DATABASE    <SID>
    maxdatafiles  1021
    maxinstances  1
    maxlogfiles   8
    maxlogmembers 4
    CHARACTER SET WE8ISO8859P15
    NATIONAL CHARACTER SET UTF8
DATAFILE '<drive>:\oradata\<SID>\system01.dbf' SIZE 2000M REUSE AUTOEXTEND ON NEXT 10240K
MAXSIZE UNLIMITED
EXTENT MANAGEMENT LOCAL
SYSAUX DATAFILE '<drive>:\oradata\<SID>\sysaux01.dbf' SIZE 120M REUSE AUTOEXTEND ON NEXT
10240K MAXSIZE UNLIMITED
DEFAULT TEMPORARY TABLESPACE TEMP TEMPFILE '<drive>:\oradata\<SID>\temp01.dbf' SIZE 20M REUSE
AUTOEXTEND ON NEXT  640K MAXSIZE UNLIMITED
UNDO TABLESPACE "PSUNDOTS" DATAFILE '<drive>:\oradata\<SID>\psundots01.dbf' SIZE 300M REUSE
AUTOEXTEND ON NEXT  5120K MAXSIZE UNLIMITED
LOGFILE GROUP 1 ('<drive>:\oradata\<SID>\redo01.log') SIZE 100M,
        GROUP 2 ('<drive>:\oradata\<SID>\redo02.log') SIZE 100M,
        GROUP 3 ('<drive>:\oradata\<SID>\redo03.log') SIZE 100M;
spool off
```

The script utlspace.sql runs the Oracle catalogue scripts, creates a system rollback segment, and creates a number of utility tablespaces.

Temporary Tablespace

The temporary tablespace for the users on a PeopleSoft database has always been PSTEMP. The tablespace is usually created with the database (see Listing 7-1), although it can also be created manually using the delivered utlspace.sql script (see Listing 7-2).

Listing 7-2. utlspace.sql: *Creating the PSTEMP Tablespace*

```
CREATE TEMPORARY TABLESPACE PSTEMP
TEMPFILE                    '<drive>:\oradata\<SID>\pstemp01.dbf'      SIZE 300M
EXTENT MANAGEMENT LOCAL UNIFORM SIZE 128K
;
```

The create tablespace commands still explicitly specify local extent management, although that has always been the default since it was introduced into the Oracle database. If the system tablespace is locally managed, dictionary management cannot be used at all.

The Connect ID, the database user to whom the PeopleSoft processes ultimately connect, is created by the script psadmin.sql (see Listing 7-3). It assigns the PSTEMP tablespace as the temporary tablespace for that user.

Listing 7-3. An Extract from psadmin.sql

```
ACCEPT ADMIN CHAR FORMAT 'A8' -
PROMPT 'Enter name of PeopleSoft Owner ID(max. 8 characters): '
ACCEPT PASSWORD CHAR FORMAT 'A8' -
PROMPT 'Enter PeopleSoft Owner ID password(max. 8 characters): '
PROMPT
PROMPT Enter a desired default tablespace for this user.
PROMPT
PROMPT Please Note:  The tablespace must already exist
PROMPT                  If you are unsure, enter PSDEFAULT or SYSTEM
PROMPT
ACCEPT TSPACE CHAR PROMPT 'Enter desired default tablespace:'


REMARK -- Create the PeopleSoft Administrator schema.

create user &ADMIN identified by &PASSWORD default tablespace &TSPACE
temporary tablespace pstemp;
grant PSADMIN TO &ADMIN;

REMARK -- PeopleSoft Administrator needs unlimited tablespace in order to
REMARK -- create the PeopleSoft application tablespaces and tables in Data
REMARK -- Mover.  This system privilege can only be granted to schemas, not
REMARK -- Oracle roles.

grant unlimited tablespace to &ADMIN;

REMARK -- Run the commands below to create database synonyms.
REMARK -- Modify the connect string appropriately for your organization.
```

Undo Segments

Undo is another area of the database where Oracle has taken control of management. An undo tablespace must be specified when the database is created, as shown in Listing 7-1. Oracle manages the undo segments according to the amount of time that undo information should be retained, which is specified by the UNDO_RETENTION parameter. Now, instead of the sizing the rollback segments and the tablespaces that hold them, the DBA needs to consider for what period of time undo needs to remain available in the undo segments to support consistent reads.

It is still possible to use manually managed rollback segments, and the script to create the rollback segments is still shipped with PeopleTools. However, automatic (or system managed) undo is the default, and I can't imagine any reason not to use it.

Default Tablespace

The tablespace PSDEFAULT is created for use as the default tablespace, as shown in Listing 7-4. From PeopleTools 8.4, it is also locally managed.

Listing 7-4. utlspace.sql: Creating the PSDEFAULT Tablespace

```
CREATE TABLESPACE      PSDEFAULT
DATAFILE               '<drive>:\oradata\<SID>\psdefault.dbf'    SIZE 100M
EXTENT MANAGEMENT LOCAL AUTOALLOCATE
;
```

The comment at the top of the psadmin.sql script (in Listing 7-3) supplied by PeopleSoft suggests making SYSTEM the temporary tablespace for the Connect ID. **This is not a good idea**. In any database, the SYSTEM tablespace should be reserved exclusively for use by Oracle-supplied administrative scripts. If you are not sure, do not proceed further.

Tablespace PSDEFAULT was introduced at the same time PSTEMP was created as type temporary. The comment in psadmin.sql changed at the same time to recommend PSDEFAULT as a possible default tablespace. This is a sensible suggestion[1] and is also appropriate for earlier versions of PeopleTools.

Oracle Database Configuration Assistant

The PeopleSoft installation guide no longer recommends using the Oracle Database Configuration Assistant (DBCA). In the past, PeopleSoft made DBCA templates available on the Customer Support web site, but they are not available on the My Oracle Support web site. Instead of DBCA, use the PeopleSoft wizard described next.

---

[1] In fact, I think the script should not ask for a default tablespace. The default tablespace should be specified as PSDEFAULT just as the temporary tablespace is specified as PSTEMP!

PeopleSoft Database Configuration Wizard

In PeopleTools 8.4, PeopleSoft introduced its own Database Configuration Wizard, shown in Figure 7-1, to provide a consistent method of creating a PeopleSoft database on all database platforms. The documented process no longer suggests using the Oracle DBCA.

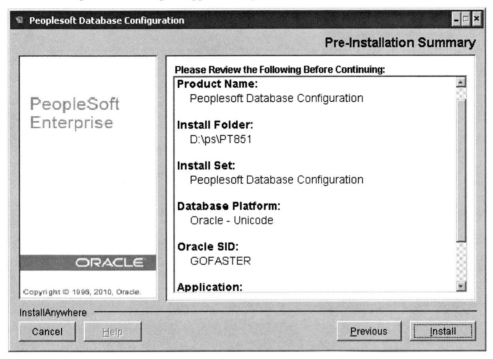

Figure 7-1. PeopleSoft Database Configuration Wizard on Windows

The PeopleSoft wizard is a Java process, and it can be run on any of the supported operating systems. The graphical interface shown in Figure 7-2 only runs on Windows. The wizard provides a text-only version on Unix systems.

The PeopleSoft wizard appears to be a wrapper for the same actions described in the manual database-creation process. It requires to be told where the Oracle database software, and specifically the SQL*Plus executable, is located. It creates a new Oracle instance and database, and populates it with the PeopleSoft database objects. The Data Mover import facility appears to have been incorporated for this purpose.

My chief objection to using this wizard is that there is no way of reviewing or controlling what it is going to do, before it does it. I, for one, will be sticking to the manual script-based database creation process described in the next section. The wizard is probably better suited to other database platforms, such as Microsoft's SQL Server, where the database server is established and then a database is created within that server.

Managing Tablespaces for PeopleSoft

PeopleSoft's approach to tablespaces has not significantly changed since at least PeopleTools 5.0, which was released in 1996, although each successive release has added to it.

The PeopleSoft application product lines or modules are given two-character mnemonics, which are used as the first two characters for most of the tablespaces that contain tables. Table 7-1 does not present an exhaustive list—just a few examples.

Table 7-1. *Product Line Mnemonics*

Mnemonic	Product Line
BN	Base Benefits
EO	Enterprise Components
EP	Enterprise Planning
FS	Financials
GP	Global Payroll
HR	Human Resources
IN	Inventory
PA	Pension Administration
PC	Projects
PI	Payroll Interface
PO	Purchasing
PS	Portal Solutions
PT	People Tools
PY	Payroll for North America
ST	Stock Administration
TL	Time and Labor

PeopleSoft usually creates a number of tablespaces for each product line. The rest of each tablespace name is made up by appending APP, LARGE, or WORK (or something similar; PeopleSoft is not always consistent) to the product-line mnemonic. By default, all tablespaces are dictionary managed:

- Tablespaces whose names end with APP or APP*n* (where *n* is a single digit) are where most of the application data tables are held. Nearly all product modules have at least one APP tablespace. Some have more (for example, HRAPP, HRAPP1 through HRAPP6).

- Tablespaces whose names end with LARGE, LRG, or LARG*n* (where *n* is a single digit) generally hold the larger tables for a project module.

- Tablespaces whose names end in WORK, WRK, or WK are generally used to store tables used for working storage.

- Other tables whose names begin with PT or PS hold PeopleTools tables.

- The tablespaces SYSTEM, SYSAUX, TEMP, TOOLS, USERS, INDX, CWMLITE, PSTEMP, and PSRBS should not be considered PeopleSoft tablespaces. The DBA can safely adjust these as necessary.

- PSINDEX is the tablespace where, by default, all indexes on all the PeopleTools and application data tables are created.

PeopleSoft seems to have two completely different attitudes toward the use of tablespaces. On the one hand, all the tables are split into different tablespaces. Nominally, they are grouped by functional area and by size. In a vanilla HCM database, there are 92 such tablespaces. It is almost at the point at which there may be so many tablespaces that the administration is becoming complicated. However, if the need arises, it is an easy matter to place tablespaces for different modules on different disk subsystems.

On the other hand, all the indexes for the tables in those 92 tablespaces are thrown together in a single tablespace, PSINDEX, as described next.

A Single Index Tablespace: PSINDEX

I can think of absolutely no reason why PeopleSoft should have chosen to place all indexes in a single tablespace. It is as if two distinct and different groups of developers had responsibility for tables and indexes.

You can typically expect the total volume of index segments to be greater than the total volume of table segments in a PeopleSoft database. So, the index tablespace can be larger than all the table tablespaces put together. As such, a monolithic index tablespace can produce administrative problems and risks. For example, if you have a file corruption to a database in this tablespace, the scope of the recovery operation is much wider and more complex.

Creating Multiple Index Tablespaces

There are a number of options for breaking up the monolithic PSINDEX tablespace, which I describe in this section. Breaking up this tablespace does not, in itself, improve performance, but it may help relieve some of the administrative difficulties and risk associated with backup, recovery, and so on, as described in the previous section.

Manual Adjustment

The DBA could simply move indexes to new tablespaces by rebuilding them manually, and rely on setindex.sqr (discussed in Chapter 6) to update the new tablespace name in the PeopleTools tables. The downside of this approach is that every time a new index is created, or an existing index is updated by a PeopleSoft patch, the index is likely to be recreated in PSINDEX again. It will result in a continual process of making changes to PeopleSoft objects.

One Index Tablespace per Table Tablespace

An easier strategy to break up the index tablespaces is to have one tablespace for indexes per table tablespace, and to place the index accordingly. This can be easily enforced by changing the DDL model for index creation (discussed in Chapter 6).

Listing 7-5 shows the Create Index DDL model. The addition variable **INDEXSPC**, which defaults to PSINDEX from the DDL Model Defaults, has been commented out and replaced with the internal variable [TBSPCNAME],[2] which is the tablespace name to which the table is allocated.

■ **Note** The original index tablespace variable **INDEXSPC** cannot be removed because it is populated with the setindex.sqr process. If the variable is defined by specifying a DDL model default and does not appear in the DDL model, then Application Designer produces errors when the DDL is either viewed or generated.

Listing 7-5. Alternative Index DDL Model

```
CREATE [UNIQUE] **BITMAP** INDEX [IDXNAME]
ON [TBNAME] ([IDXCOLLIST])
TABLESPACE [TBSPCNAME]_IDX /* **INDEXSPC** */
STORAGE (
    INITIAL **INIT** NEXT **NEXT**
    MAXEXTENTS **MAXEXT** PCTINCREASE **PCT**)
PCTFREE **PCTFREE**;
```

You see that I have added a fixed suffix of _IDX, so the tablespaces I create for indexes must be named accordingly. For example, the table PS_JOB is stored in the tablespace HRLARGE. The index is now created in the tablespace HRLARGE_IDX, as shown in Listing 7-6.

---

[2] Internal variables from the Create Table DDL model are available to the Create Index DDL model, but not vice versa.

Listing 7-6. *Creating the PS1JOB Index*

```
CREATE   INDEX PS1JOB ON PS_JOB (JOBCODE, EMPLID, EMPL_RCD, EFFDT, EFFSEQ)
TABLESPACE HRLARGE_IDX /* PSINDEX */
STORAGE (INITIAL 123904 NEXT 100000 MAXEXTENTS UNLIMITED PCTINCREASE 0)
PCTFREE 10;
```

Each index must be rebuilt to move it into its new tablespace. The build script can be generated by Application Designer by building the Create Index DDL for an Application Designer project containing every record in the database.

This has the limitation of permitting no flexibility. The location of the index always follows the table. If the DBA attempts to move an index manually and runs `setindex.sqr`, the new tablespace value goes into **PSINDEX**, which is commented out in the DDL model. The PeopleSoft script builds the index only in the tablespace that corresponds to the tablespace for the table. However, this is also a benefit. When a new index is created, it does not, by default, go into PSINDEX, but into the index tablespace that corresponds to the table's tablespace.

This arrangement also permits tablespaces to be moved or copied to other databases using the transportable tablespaces mechanism. The monolithic index tablespace prevents transport of individual table tablespaces. Transportable tablespaces can be effective during testing or when moving data to a reporting database.

Storage Options

Since the introduction of locally managed tablespace in Oracle 10g, storage options have become much less important. Initial and next extent sizes are overridden by the extent size of the tablespace.

EFFECT OF STORAGE OPTIONS ON OBJECTS IN LOCALLY MANAGED TABLESPACES

In my test, HRAPP is a locally managed tablespace with automatic allocation of extent sizing. The block size is 8KB

```
SELECT tablespace_name, block_size, initial_extent, extent_management
FROM dba_tablespaces WHERE tablespace_name = 'HRAPP';
```

TABLESPACE_NAME	BLOCK_SIZE	INITIAL_EXTENT	EXTENT_MAN
HRAPP	8192	65536	LOCAL

Now I try to create a table with an initial and next extent size, and two extents:

```
CREATE TABLE dmk (a NUMBER) TABLESPACE hrapp
STORAGE (INITIAL 100K NEXT 50K MINEXTENTS 2);
```

On a dictionary managed tablespace, the extents would total 150KB. However, in a locally managed tablespace, I get three extents of 64KB, totaling 192KB:

```
SELECT   extent_id, bytes, blocks, tablespace_name
FROM     user_extents
```

```
WHERE    segment_name = 'DMK' AND segment_type = 'TABLE';

EXTENT_ID       BYTES     BLOCKS TABLESPACE_NAME
---------- ----------- ---------- ------------------------------
        0       65536          8 HRAPP
        1       65536          8 HRAPP
        2       65536          8 HRAPP
                ----------- ----------
sum            196608         24
```

In a locally managed tablespace, Oracle allocates extents such that there is as much space in the table as if it had been created in a dictionary managed tablespace. In AUTOALLOCATE tablespaces, extents start at 64KB and follow a progression becoming 8 or 16 times larger (1MB after 16 extents, 8MB after a further 63 extents, and so on). Oracle omits the smaller extent sizes and starts with the largest extent size in the progression that is less that the amount of space to be allocated to the table.

The same behavior occurs in Oracle 11gR2 if segment creation is deferred. All of these extents are created, but only when data is first inserted into the table.

By default, the PeopleSoft DDL model doesn't specify MINEXTENTS, so only the initial extent size determines how many extents Oracle creates.

It seems to me that the main questions left for the DBA to consider about storage options are these:

- Should a large table/index be moved to a separate tablespace, and if so should that tablespace be created with a sensible uniform extent size?

- If not, should the table be created/re-created with a large initial extent size (1MB or 8MB), thus skipping over the smaller extent sizes?

Summary

This chapter looked at tablespaces in PeopleSoft. They are created when the database is created, so we also examined database creation procedures. Oracle no longer provides a template for its Database Configuration Assistant. It does deliver a PeopleSoft Database Configuration Assistant, but this does not allow the DBA to review the process. I recommend creating the database by script.

Remember that any change to either the tablespace or the storage options of a table or index should be made via the PeopleSoft Application Designer so that the change is not lost if the object is re-created for another reason.

CHAPTER 8

Locking, Transactions, and Concurrency

This chapter discusses some of the methods that PeopleSoft uses to maintain data integrity in a multiuser environment while at the same time avoiding techniques that are specific to a particular database platform.

This chapter begins with a discussion of locking in PeopleSoft. It is useful to understand how and where PeopleSoft locks tables, because this can have implications for the performance and scalability of your applications. I then examine how PeopleSoft uses tables to generate sequence numbers instead of Oracle sequences, in order to maintain platform independence. However, this platform independence has implications for concurrency and scalability. Finally, I cover the row-level locking that occurs during PIA transactions, and how by holding locks for as short a time as possible, PeopleSoft minimizes the impact of the table-based sequences.

Locking

PeopleSoft, like most database applications, relies mostly on implicit row-level locking to protect data being updated by one transaction from being corrupted by another. However, there are times when it is necessary to deliberately serialize some processing so that only one thing can happen at a time. In such cases, it would be normal to exclusively lock a table, and if necessary wait to acquire the lock.

The Oracle database itself also has mechanisms that must be serialized. For example, during a TRUNCATE operation, the shadow process writes to the data file (this is called a *local write*), and the local write is protected by the Reuse Object (RO) enqueue. Only one process can acquire the enqueue at one time, so only one process can truncate at any one time, and in extreme cases this can be a cause of contention.

▒ **Note** PeopleSoft systems can suffer batch-process performance problems due to multiple concurrent Application Engine programs issuing many competing TRUNCATE commands. In such a case, the Application Engine sessions report significant amounts of time spent waiting on the *local write wait* and *enq: RO - fast object reuse* events.

A possible option is to allocate the temporary tables that are truncated to a separate tablespace with a different blocksize than the main buffer pool. The use of a tablespace with a different blocksize requires a separate buffer pool with a matching block size. This buffer pool can be kept smaller than the main buffer pool, which reduces the various wait and enqueue times, thus improving overall performance and throughput.[1]

PeopleSoft applications do not use the LOCK TABLE command because it is Oracle-specific, and corresponding platform-specific code would be required for all the other databases. Instead, PeopleSoft updates a row on a table, sometimes the only row on the table, and possibly without changing the data value.

For example, an Application Engine process may use a PeopleSoft temporary table in which a single record in PeopleSoft corresponds to a number of copies of the table (as described in Chapter 4, PSRECDEFN, Record Type 7). Each copy is referred to in PeopleTools as an *instance*. When the Application Engine process starts, it must determine which instance of the temporary table is available, and then it allocates that instance to itself by inserting a row into the table PS_AETEMPTBLMGR.

It must make sure that no other Application Engine process is trying to allocate an instance of that record at the same time, so it locks the table PS_AELOCKMGR by updating the only row in it. Doing so deliberately serializes this processing, as shown in Listing 8-1. A row-level lock on a table with only a single row has the same functional behavior as a table-level lock.

Listing 8-1. Processing Serialized by a Lock on Table PS_AELOCKMGR

```
UPDATE PS_AELOCKMGR SET AE_LOCK = :1
;
SELECT MIN(B.CURTEMPINSTANCE)
FROM    PS_AEINSTANCENBR B
,       PSTEMPTBLCNTVW C
WHERE   C.RECNAME = :1
AND     B.CURTEMPINSTANCE > :2
AND     (B.CURTEMPINSTANCE - C.TEMPTBLINSTANCES) <= :3
AND     B.CURTEMPINSTANCE NOT IN (
            SELECT D.CURTEMPINSTANCE
            FROM   PS_AETEMPTBLMGR D
            WHERE  D.RECNAME = C.RECNAME)
;
INSERT INTO PS_AETEMPTBLMGR (PROCESS_INSTANCE, RECNAME, CURTEMPINSTANCE,
   OPRID, RUN_CNTL_ID, AE_APPLID, RUN_DTTM, AE_DISABLE_RESTART, AE_DEDICATED)
VALUES(:1, :2, :3, :4, :5, :6, SYSDATE, :7, :8)
;
COMMIT
;
```

---

[1] See Oracle Support Note 334822.1 and my technical note "Factors Affecting Concurrent Truncate During Batch Processes" at www.go-faster.co.uk/docs.htm#local_write_wait.

PIA Transactions

This section examines what happens when you change an existing value in a PIA component and save the new value to the database. I want to draw attention to how PeopleSoft manages consistency of data without holding database locks for a long time while the operator enters data. The approach is sometimes called *optimistic locking*. Instead of locking the data when it is first queried into a component, PeopleTools requeries it during save-time processing. If the Component Processor detects a difference in the results of these two queries, an error is generated. However, PeopleSoft's optimism that this will only happen very rarely is well founded in practice.

Figure 8-1 shows the Edit Name subpage called from the Personal Data component in the HCM product (accessed by selecting Workforce Administration ➤ Personal Information ➤ Modify a Person and then selecting the Add Name link). A person's name is an effective-dated attribute—for example, a name may change on marriage, effective from the date of marriage. In this case, PeopleSoft, when in normal add/update mode, adds a new row to a table with that effective date. However, the following example uses "correction" mode to change the middle name on an existing name record, not add a name change.

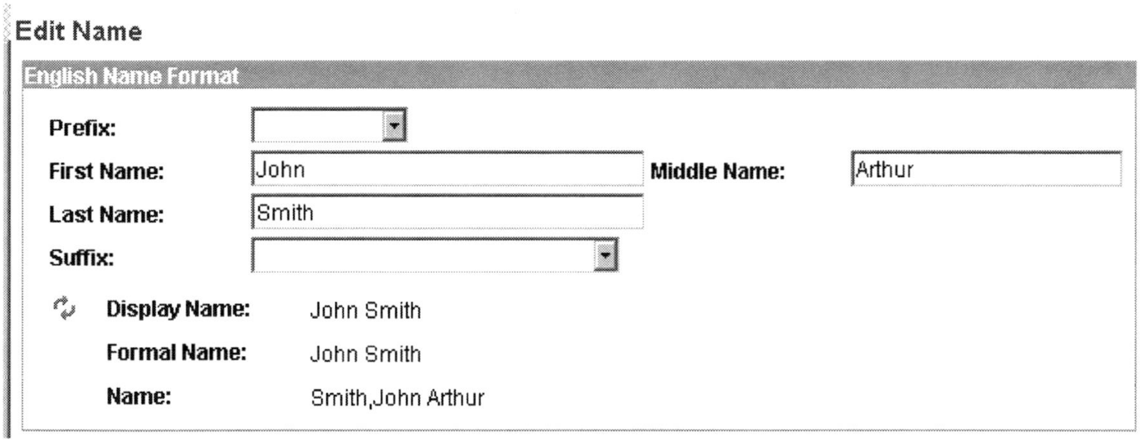

Figure 8-1. Edit Name Subpage

Listings 8-2 and 8-3 show the SQL generated by the PIA as captured by the PeopleTools trace. I only show the SQL that references the PS_NAMES table where names are stored.

When the Modify a Person component is opened, the PS_NAMES table is queried from the database, as shown in Listing 8-2, into the component buffer for the requested employee ID (EMPLID). Note that all of the name history for the employee is loaded. There may be only a few rows per employee on PS_NAMES, but this is generic PIA behavior; other tables such as the job and absence histories will grow more quickly.

Listing 8-2. PS_NAMES Loaded into the Component Buffer[2]

```
RC=0 Stmt=SELECT EMPLID, NAME_TYPE, EFFDT, TO_CHAR(EFFDT,'YYYY-MM-DD'), EFF_STATUS,
COUNTRY_NM_FORMAT, NAME, NAME_INITIALS, NAME_PREFIX, NAME_SUFFIX, NAME_ROYAL_PREFIX,
NAME_ROYAL_SUFFIX, NAME_TITLE, LAST_NAME_SRCH, FIRST_NAME_SRCH, LAST_NAME, FIRST_NAME,
MIDDLE_NAME, SECOND_LAST_NAME, SECOND_LAST_SRCH, NAME_AC, PREF_FIRST_NAME, PARTNER_LAST_NAME,
PARTNER_ROY_PREFIX, LAST_NAME_PREF_NLD, NAME_DISPLAY, NAME_FORMAL, TO_CHAR(LASTUPDDTTM,'YYYY-
MM-DD-HH24.MI.SS."000000"'), LASTUPDOPRID FROM PS_NAMES WHERE EMPLID=:1 ORDER BY EMPLID,
NAME_TYPE, EFFDT DESC
RC=0 Bind-1 type=2 length=4 value=0036
RC=0 Fetch
RC=1 Fetch
```

The query in Listing 8-2 could have returned more than one row into the scroll area, although in this case we know it did not because only the first fetch has a zero return code.

A little later, after I updated the MIDDLE_NAME field in the subpage and returned to the parent component, I clicked the Save button. Listing 8-3 shows that the PIA requeried the data to make sure it hadn't been changed by another process in the intervening period.

This time, the PS_NAMES table was queried by all three primary key fields. Only a single row could be returned, so PeopleTools only performed a single fetch. The key values came from the row I updated.

Listing 8-3. PS_NAMES Requeried, Locked, and Updated

```
Stmt=SELECT EMPLID, NAME_TYPE, EFFDT, TO_CHAR(EFFDT,'YYYY-MM-DD'), EFF_STATUS,
COUNTRY_NM_FORMAT, NAME, NAME_INITIALS, NAME_PREFIX, NAME_SUFFIX, NAME_ROYAL_PREFIX,
NAME_ROYAL_SUFFIX, NAME_TITLE, LAST_NAME_SRCH, FIRST_NAME_SRCH, LAST_NAME, FIRST_NAME,
MIDDLE_NAME, SECOND_LAST_NAME, SECOND_LAST_SRCH, NAME_AC, PREF_FIRST_NAME, PARTNER_LAST_NAME,
PARTNER_ROY_PREFIX, LAST_NAME_PREF_NLD, NAME_DISPLAY, NAME_FORMAL, TO_CHAR(LASTUPDDTTM,'YYYY-
MM-DD-HH24.MI.SS."000000"'), LASTUPDOPRID FROM PS_NAMES WHERE EMPLID=:1 AND NAME_TYPE=:2 AND
EFFDT=TO_DATE(:3,'YYYY-MM-DD') FOR UPDATE OF NAME, MIDDLE_NAME, LASTUPDDTTM
Bind-1 type=2 length=4 value=0036
Bind-2 type=2 length=3 value=PRI
Bind-3 type=26 length=10 value=2011-07-12
Fetch
Connect=Primary/HCM89/SYSADM/
Stmt=UPDATE PS_NAMES SET NAME=:1,MIDDLE_NAME=:2
,LASTUPDDTTM=TO_DATE(SUBSTR(:3, 0, 19),'YYYY-MM-DD-HH24.MI.SS')
WHERE EMPLID=:4 AND NAME_TYPE=:5 AND EFFDT=TO_DATE(:6,'YYYY-MM-DD')
Bind-1 type=2 length=17 value=Smith,John Arthur
Bind-2 type=2 length=6 value=Arthur
Bind-3 type=25 length=26 value=2011-07-12-17.57.52.000000
Bind-4 type=2 length=4 value=0036
Bind-5 type=2 length=3 value=PRI
Bind-6 type=26 length=10 value=2011-07-12
Dur=0.000000 Disconnect
```

Notice that the row is selected FOR UPDATE OF, thus taking out a lock on this row,. This has certain implications:

---

[2] The extracts from trace files in this and other listings in this chapter have been edited for readability.

- The row is not locked while the user is working in the component. The lock is only requested within the save-time processing.

- Once I have acquired the lock on this row, nobody else can update this row until my transaction has been committed.

- If somebody else has a lock on this row, my transaction waits to be able to complete. This appears to extend the time taken to save the component, during which the "processing" message is displayed.

- The transaction is short-lived, because it does not wait for the user at any point. It starts when the row is requeried for update, thus locking the row, and it commits the update at the end. In this case, all the save-time PeopleCode and SQL processing have the same clock time in the trace in Listing 8-3, and so take less than a second to complete.

The same columns that are updated in the UPDATE statement also appear in the FOR UPDATE OF clause. This is a little unfortunate because the database has to parse a different SQL statement depending upon which columns are updated by the component. The row would be just as locked if the OF sub-clause was simply omitted[3].

If the second query detects that the data has changed since it was first loaded into the component buffer, the PIA raises the error "(18,1) Page data is inconsistent with database." The help text for the message (see Listing 8-4) points out that the problem can also be generated by SQL updates issued from within the save-time PeopleCode.

Listing 8-4. Additional Explanation for the "Page data is inconsistent with database" Error Message

```
Page data is inconsistent with database. (18,1)

When trying to save your page data, the system found that the information currently in the
database did not match what was expected.

This problem can happen if another user has changed the same information while you were making
your changes. Note the changes you have made, then cancel the page.  Reload the page and view
any changes made by the other user.  Ensure your changes are compatible and retry, if
appropriate.

If the problem persists, it may be a result of an application or other programming error and
should be reported to technical support staff.

Possible application errors that can cause this message include:
- changing page data from SavePostChange PeopleCode, without making a corresponding change to
the database.
- changing the database via SqlExec at various points, for data that is also in the component
buffers.
```

---

[3] The OF clause is used to lock rows only for particular tables or views in a join. The columns in the OF clause only indicate which table or view rows are locked. The specific columns are not significant. If the OF clause is not specified all selected rows on all tables in the query are locked even if no columns are referenced in the select clause.

- database auto-update fields maintained by triggers didn't get defined correctly in Record Field definition or in Record Properties definition.

Different SQL statements are generated to save component data, depending on which columns are updated by either the operator or any PeopleCode that executes. The code in Listing 8-5 was generated by the same component when I updated the employee's middle name again, and this time the surname also.

Listing 8-5. PS_NAMES Requeried, Locked, and Updated Again

```
tmt=SELECT EMPLID, NAME_TYPE, EFFDT, TO_CHAR(EFFDT,'YYYY-MM-DD'), EFF_STATUS,
COUNTRY_NM_FORMAT, NAME, NAME_INITIALS, NAME_PREFIX, NAME_SUFFIX, NAME_ROYAL_PREFIX,
NAME_ROYAL_SUFFIX, NAME_TITLE, LAST_NAME_SRCH, FIRST_NAME_SRCH, LAST_NAME, FIRST_NAME,
MIDDLE_NAME, SECOND_LAST_NAME, SECOND_LAST_SRCH, NAME_AC, PREF_FIRST_NAME, PARTNER_LAST_NAME,
PARTNER_ROY_PREFIX, LAST_NAME_PREF_NLD, NAME_DISPLAY, NAME_FORMAL, TO_CHAR(LASTUPDDTTM,'YYYY-
MM-DD-HH24.MI.SS."000000"'), LASTUPDOPRID FROM PS_NAMES WHERE EMPLID=:1 AND NAME_TYPE=:2 AND
EFFDT=TO_DATE(:3,'YYYY-MM-DD') FOR UPDATE OF NAME, LAST_NAME_SRCH, LAST_NAME, MIDDLE_NAME,
NAME_DISPLAY, NAME_FORMAL, LASTUPDDTTM
Bind-1 type=2 length=4 value=0036
Bind-2 type=2 length=3 value=PRI
Bind-3 type=26 length=10 value=2011-07-12
EXE
Fetch
Connect=Primary/HCM89/SYSADM/
Stmt=UPDATE PS_NAMES SET NAME=:1,LAST_NAME_SRCH=:2,LAST_NAME=:3,MIDDLE_NAME=:4
,NAME_DISPLAY=:5
,NAME_FORMAL=:6,LASTUPDDTTM=TO_DATE(SUBSTR(:7, 0, 19),'YYYY-MM-DD-HH24.MI.SS')
WHERE EMPLID=:8 AND NAME_TYPE=:9 AND EFFDT=TO_DATE(:10,'YYYY-MM-DD')
Bind-1 type=2 length=20 value=Smithson,John Philip
Bind-2 type=2 length=8 value=SMITHSON
Bind-3 type=2 length=8 value=Smithson
Bind-4 type=2 length=6 value=Philip
Bind-5 type=2 length=13 value=John Smithson
Bind-6 type=2 length=13 value=John Smithson
Bind-7 type=25 length=26 value=2011-07-13-07.23.13.000000
Bind-8 type=2 length=4 value=0036
Bind-9 type=2 length=3 value=PRI
Bind-10 type=26 length=10 value=2011-07-12
```

NAME, LAST_NAME_SRCH, NAME_DISPLAY, NAME_FORMAL, and LASTUPDDTTM are updated by PeopleCode, and so also appear in the FOR UPDATE OF clause of the query and in the SET clause of the UPDATE statement. FIRST_NAME was not updated and so does not appear in either statement.

This shows that PeopleSoft updates only the columns that have changed rather than the whole row. Although this does reduce redo logging, there are a greater number of different SQL statements, each of which has to be parsed.

Sequence Numbers and Concurrency

PeopleSoft does not use Oracle sequences. This is mainly because it would require widespread use of platform-specific code in the PIA. While this is not completely unprecedented, PeopleSoft generally avoids it.

The platform-agnostic alternative that PeopleSoft has chosen is to store a sequence number in a table and increment it as a part of the transaction. For example, in HCM, when a new employee is hired, the employee ID is shown as NEW (see Figure 8-2) until the transaction is saved.

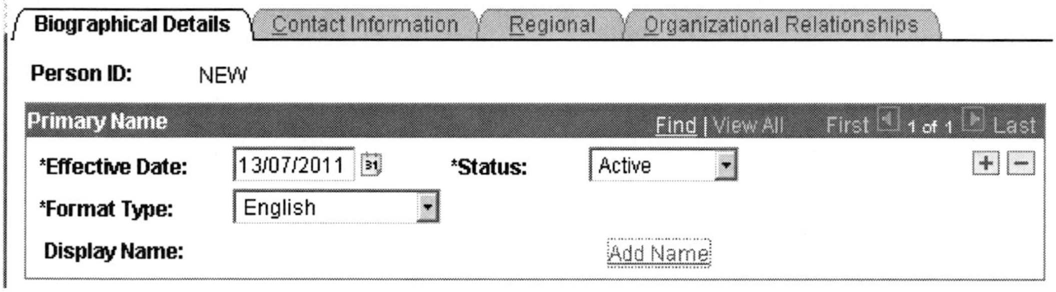

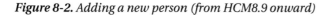

Figure 8-2. Adding a new person (from HCM8.9 onward)

Up to version 8.8 of HCM, during the save-time processing, the PeopleCode function assign_employee_id() (see Listing 8-6) executes explicit code to increment the value of EMPLID_LAST_EMPL on the table PS_INSTALLATION (which contains only a single row). The new value is then selected and used as the new employee's number. From PeopleTools 8.44, this behavior is also packaged inside the PeopleCode function GetNextNumber().

Listing 8-6. Incrementing the EMPLID Sequence Number (HCM8.8)

```
[FUNCLIB_HR.EMPLID.FieldFormula]
…
SQLExec("Update PS_INSTALLATION Set EMPLID_LAST_EMPL = EMPLID_LAST_EMPL +  1");
SQLExec("Select EMPLID_LAST_EMPL From PS_INSTALLATION", &EMPLID);
```

From the point in the save-time processing at which the new employee ID is obtained up to the point at which the transaction is committed, the single row on the PS_INSTALLATION table is locked and nobody else can allocate a sequence number. So, this method effectively serializes allocation of sequence numbers.

The amount of time for which this lock is held is a function of the amount of save-time processing in the application. In the case of the employee hire processing, it can be several seconds, so only one employee-hire transaction can be saved at any one time.

PeopleSoft applications derive sequence numbers from various tables, but in HCM8.9 the situation is compounded because 24 sequence numbers are derived from the single row on the table PS_INSTALLATION (see Table 8-1). Incrementing any one of these columns locks the row and prevents another process from allocating a sequence number for any column, even a different one.

Table 8-1. Sequence Numbers on PS_INSTALLATION

Column Name	Description
ACCT_CD_LAST	Account code
AP_INVNO_LAST	Last AP invoice number
CAR_LAST	Car number
CLAIM_NBR_LAST	H&S claim number
COBRA_EMPLID_LAST	COBRA employee
CPS_TRANS_ID_LAST	Last CPS transmission ID number
DEMAND_ID_LAST	Demand ID
EMPLID_LAST_EMPL	Employee ID
FILE_CREATE_LAST	Last file-creation number
FSA_CLAIM_NBR_LAST	FSA claim number
FSA_CRY_CLAIM_LAST	Last FSA carry-forward claim number
GRIEVANCE_NBR_LAST	Grievance number
ILL_NBR_LAST_GER	Illness number (Germany)
ILL_NBR_LAST_NLD	Illness number (Netherlands)
INCIDENT_NBR_LAST	H&S incident number
LAST_OSHA_CASE_NBR	Last OSHA case number assigned
LAST_TL_CONTRCTR	T&L contractor ID
NON_EMPLOYEE_LAST	H&S non-employee number
PIN_NUM_LAST	Last used GP element number
POSN_NBR_LAST	Position number

RETRODED_SEQ_LAST	Payroll retro deduction sequence
RETROPAY_SEQ_LAST	Payroll retro payment sequence
ROE_NBR_LAST	Last ROE number used (Canadian)
TEMP_ASSGN_ID_LAST	Temporary job assignment ID

Although most systems are unlikely to use anything like all 24 sequences, they generally use several. It is easy to see how a moderately active system could start to experience contention on sequence-number allocation.

If you must generate sequence numbers from a table, then you should at least have different sequences on different rows, so they can be updated independently. For example, when PeopleSoft applications are developed, version numbers are allocated to objects to control the caching. There is a sequence of version numbers for each object type. Until PeopleTools 7, these numbers came from different columns in the single row on PSLOCK. In PeopleTools 8, PSLOCK has just two columns and one row for each of the 46 PeopleTools object types, as shown in Listing 8-7. Each sequence number can be allocated independently.

Listing 8-7. PeopleTools Version Number Sequences

```
OBJECTTY   VERSION
--------   ----------
ACM             2
AEM             2
AES             2
BCM             2
BPM             2

...
```

Autonomous Transactions

Another PeopleCode function GetNextNumberWithGapsCommit()[4] was introduced in PeopleTools 8.44 but was not generally used until version 8.9 applications. This function performs exactly the same updates as described previously and shown in Listing 8-6, but PeopleTools does something similar to an Autonomous Transaction in the Oracle database by executing the update and query in a second database connection created by the PSAPPSRV process. This update is committed immediately and does not affect the activity in the first connection, thus minimizing the time for which the database lock is held.

Listing 8-8 shows part of AssignNextId function in the FUNCLIB_HR.FieldFormula PeopleCode from HCM8.9 that obtains the next employee ID using GetNextNumberWithGapsCommit().

---

[4]GetNextNumberWithGapsCommit PeopleCode:
http://download.oracle.com/docs/cd/E18083_01/pt851pbr0/eng/psbooks/tpcl/book.htm?File=tpcl/htm
/tpcl02.htm#H4387.

Listing 8-8. Incrementing the EMPLID Sequence Number (HCM8.9)

```
Function AssignNextId(&Recname As string, &Fieldname As string
, &Length As number, &Prefix As string) Returns string
…
    &NextIdNbr = GetNextNumberWithGapsCommit(@(&RecFieldName), &MaxId, 1);
…

    SQLExec("SELECT EMPLID FROM PS_PERSON WHERE EMPLID = :1", &NextId, &DuplicateId);
```

Listing 8-9 shows part of the PeopleTools trace when the code in Listing 8-8 executes. CUR#2 indicates that the update is done in the second connection. The SQL issued by the PeopleCode is effectively the same as previously hard coded (see Listing 8-6).

Listing 8-9. Incrementing the EMPLID with the GetNextNumberWithGapsCommit() Function

```
1-1693081 >>> start     Nest=00  PERSON.EMPLID.SavePreChange
1-1693082 >>> start-ext Nest=01 assign_employee_id FUNCLIB_HR.EMPLID.FieldFormula
1-1693083 Cur#2.4316.HCM89 RC=0 Dur=0.000000 COM Stmt=UPDATE PS_INSTALLATION SET
EMPLID_LAST_EMPL = EMPLID_LAST_EMPL + 1
1-1693084 Cur#2.4316.HCM89 RC=0 Dur=0.000000 COM Stmt=SELECT EMPLID_LAST_EMPL FROM
PS_INSTALLATION
1-1693085 Cur#2.4316.HCM89 RC=0 Dur=0.000000 Fetch
1-1693086 Cur#2.4316.HCM89 RC=0 Dur=0.028000 Commit
1-1693087 > GetNextNumberWithGapsCommit info ( INSTALLATION, EMPLID_LAST_EMPL, (null) )
1-1693088 Cur#1.4316.HCM89 RC=0 Dur=0.000000 COM Stmt=SELECT EMPLID FROM PS_PERSON WHERE
EMPLID = :1
1-1693089 Cur#1.4316.HCM89 RC=0 Dur=0.000000 Bind-1 type=2 length=4 value=0038
1-1693090 Cur#1.4316.HCM89 RC=1 Dur=0.000000 Fetch
```

The behavior is like that of a NOCACHE Oracle sequence that updates SYS.SEQ$ in an autonomous transaction, but without the advantage of caching the next values in the SGA. There is still a possibility of blocking locks, but it is very much reduced because the lock is not held while the rest of the save-time processing happens.

Like Oracle sequences, and as the name of the PeopleCode function suggests, the function admits the possibility of gaps in the sequence of numbers generated. If, for some reason, a transaction that called the function does not complete successfully but rolls back any update, then the update to the sequence is not rolled back, and so the number is never used in the application.

However, that may not be acceptable in some applications. Unexplained gaps in a sequence of invoice numbers could give rise to concern among accountants and auditors. In these situations, the GetNextNumber() PeopleCode function can be used instead.

Summary

This chapter covered locking, transactions, and concurrency in PeopleSoft. As discussed in the first part of this chapter, when a PeopleSoft application does require a database lock, it usually does so by creating a row-level lock by updating a table that has only a single row.

Database transactions generated by PIA activity should usually be short-lived because they never wait for user response. In that respect, they can be thought of as very small batch processes. Thus, any locks that they hold are held only for a short time. It is unusual to find PIA save-time processing locked on other PIA save-time processing.

Care must be taken when making customizations—especially in SaveEdit, FieldChange, FieldEdit, and SavePreChg PeopleCode, which fire at save-time—that these changes do not introduce locking or significantly extend the length of the transaction because of poorly performing SQL. A single, isolated transaction may be affected by "only" a fraction of a second, which may escape unnoticed in unit testing. However, in a high-concurrency situation, the holding of a row lock for an extended period can easily translate into many seconds or even minutes of performance degradation to the business function (I've seen it), ultimately to the point at which the system becomes effectively unusable.

PeopleSoft derives sequence numbers from tables. This serializes processing that allocates new sequence numbers and can lead to performance problems. In online processing, the effect is mitigated because the locks are held for only a short time, and the new GetNextNumberWithGapsCommit() function further reduces the duration of the lock. However, batch processes can hold locks for a longer time, and this can impact other batch processes and online activity.

There is not much DBAs can do about the issues discussed in the chapter—this is the way PeopleSoft applications work—but DBAs should at least be aware of them.

CHAPTER 9

Performance Metrics

Performance tuning is a search for lost time.

Performance improvements are achieved by reducing response time.[1] Therefore, I am always looking for the processes or parts of processes that take the most time. These places are where it is most efficient to direct the tuning effort, and where the minimum amount of tuning effort can have the maximum amount of performance effect. This is the first of three chapters that look at sources of performance metrics and techniques that can help you find out what is going on in a PeopleSoft system.

The Oracle database provides various sources of information about how long SQL statements took to execute, how they were executed, and how long they spent waiting for which database resources. Active Session History and Extended SQL Trace are two such sources, and I look at those in Chapter 11.

However, what if a performance problem is not the database? If it isn't the database, the SQL trace file reports an idle wait time. There is no ASH data because the session is not active. That time could be client process busy time, but it could also be waiting for a user to respond. You also need to be able to obtain measurements for other parts of the PeopleSoft technology.

The only place that it is reasonable to measure the performance of the PeopleSoft Pure Internet Architecture (PIA) is standing behind the user with a stopwatch in hand. The response time that the user experiences is the sum of the response times for the database, application server, Java servlet, web server, network, and browser.

From PeopleTools 8.43 to 8.45, PeopleSoft added instrumentation to PeopleTools that give a much fuller picture of what is happening in the middleware. I look at that in the next chapter.

This chapter details the other various sources of performance metrics and monitoring facilities in PeopleSoft, specifically online monitoring and metrics, batch metrics, and trace files. Some of these are physical log files, whereas others are stored in the database. While none of them exactly measures the user experience, they are certainly closer to the user than the database. From these, it is possible to obtain better information about how well a particular piece of the technology chain or a particular process is performing.

If data isn't already in the database, I sometimes load it with SQL*Loader. Then I can process it with SQL and relate different time-based sets of data, query it from Microsoft Excel via an ODBC link, and present the data graphically. Excel charts can be easily incorporated into documents or presentations.

The techniques described in this chapter require a certain amount of time and effort to implement and operate, and they cannot easily be completely automated. They are not an industrial-strength solution, and I do not suggest that they are a suitable long-term solution to performance monitoring of a

---

[1] See Anjo Kolk, Shari Yamaguchi, and Jim Viscusi, "Yet Another Performance Profiling Method," www.oraperf.com/whitepapers.html, 1999.

PeopleSoft system. For that, you may need to look at the commercial packages that are available, some of which have PeopleSoft-specific modules.

However, the techniques I outline here do have the merit of not requiring any additional software. They can quickly be brought to bear on a current performance problem, which is perhaps not the best time to procure, install, and "bed in" another sophisticated software package.

PeopleSoft started to address the problem of performance measurement[2] with the introduction of PeopleSoft Ping in PeopleTools 8.4 and with the PeopleSoft Performance Monitor (PPM) utility in PeopleTools 8.44. These tools work by instrumenting PIA service requests from the browser to the database and back again. I look at them more closely in the next chapter.

Online Monitoring and Metrics

When an operator logs into PeopleSoft via the PIA, that operator is at one end of a chain of technology that stretches across the enterprise to the core of the IT infrastructure. By measuring the performance of the chain at various points along that chain, as shown in Figure 9-1, it is possible to isolate the performance of each section and, by extension, performance problems in each section.

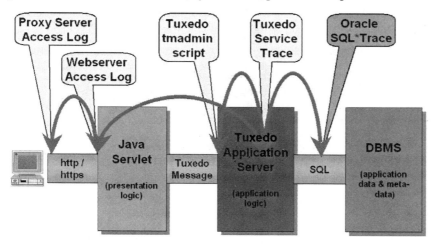

Figure 9-1. PeopleSoft Internet Architecture with sources of metrics

For instance, by deducting the sum of the Tuxedo service times from the sum of the service times for servlet requests for a given period, it is possible to calculate how much time is spent in the Java servlet and queuing.[3] A tmadmin script can determine how much queuing occurred in the application server.

In this section, I discuss each of the sources of on-line performance metrics in the web and application server tiers, including how they can be configured and analyzed.

---

[2] Don't confuse the term *performance measurement* with the PeopleSoft Enterprise Performance Measurement (EPM) product. I am talking only about measuring the performance of the technology.
[3] It is effectively impossible to do this for individual servlet requests because the requests can only be matched on the basis of time, and in some cases, one servlet request can correspond to more than one Tuxedo service request.

Application Server

Most of the performance metrics for online activity are generated from the Tuxedo Application Server, although later you see that the web server access log is also useful. The following sections cover the various sources of performance information in the application server.

EnableDBMonitoring

It is always useful to know which user is responsible for issuing a particular SQL statement to the database. Oracle provided the dbms_application_info PL/SQL package[4] to supply a mechanism to register information about the client, module, and current action with the database.

In PeopleTools 7.53, PeopleSoft introduced the parameter EnableDBMonitoring to both the application server configuration file, psappsrv.cfg (see Listing 9-1), and the Process Scheduler configuration file, psprcs.cfg. From PeopleTools 8.4, this parameter is enabled by default.

Listing 9-1. Extract from psappsrv.cfg

```
[Database Options]
;========================================================================
; Database-specific configuration options
;========================================================================

SybasePacketSize=
UseLocalOracleDB=0
;ORACLE_SID=
EnableDBMonitoring=1
```

If this parameter is enabled the application server writes a string to the session information using the Oracle supplied PL/SQL package subprogram dbms_application_info.set_client_info. The value can be read back with dbms_application_info.read_client_info, or it can be queried from v$session.client_info (see Listing 9-2).

▓ **Note** Unfortunately, the application server does not call dbms_application_info but
sys.dbms_application_info. Otherwise you could create a **sysadm**.dbms_application_info wrapper that could capture additional information or insert the fact with time information into a table for analysis later.

Listing 9-2. Database Sessions of PeopleSoft Processes

```
SELECT client_info, program
FROM   v$session
WHERE  client_info IS NOT NULL
```

---

[4] See http://download.oracle.com/docs/cd/E11882_01/appdev.112/e25788/d_appinf.htm

```
CLIENT_INFO                                        PROGRAM
---------------------------------------------      --------------------
PS,6856                                            sqrw.exe
PS,David,GO-FASTER-4,,psae.exe,                    psae.exe
PSAPPS,David,GO-FASTER-4,,PSMONITORSRV.exe,        PSMONITORSRV.exe
PSAPPS,David,GO-FASTER-4,,PSMONITORSRV.exe,        PSMONITORSRV.exe
PSAPPS,David,GO-FASTER-4,,PSSAMSRV.exe,            PSSAMSRV.exe
PSAPPS,David,GO-FASTER-4,,PSPRCSRV.exe,            PSPRCSRV.exe
PSAPPS,David,GO-FASTER-4,,PSMSTPRC.exe,            PSMSTPRC.exe
PSAPPS,David,GO-FASTER-4,,PSDSTSRV.exe,            PSDSTSRV.exe
PS,,go-faster-4,HCM90,PSAPPSRV.exe,                PSAPPSRV.exe
PSAPPS,David,GO-FASTER-4,,PSPPMSRV.exe,            PSPPMSRV.exe
```

The CLIENT_INFO string reports the PeopleSoft Operator ID, the operating system user who started the process, the IP address of the browser that made the request (or the physical machine name if it can be resolved), the database name, and the program name. When the application server processes a service request, it first rewrites this string with the operator who made the current request. Thus the DBA can see the Operator ID who requested the currently active SQL. In Listing 9-2, all the application server and process scheduler processes were started by PSAPPS, but PSAPPSRV is processing, or just processed, a request from the operator PS.

This is not really a performance metric, but it is useful to identify which PeopleSoft Operator ID is responsible for what SQL, so this information can be incorporated into other scripts.

If database triggers are used to perform record-level auditing, then the triggers obtain the operator ID for the audit record from the CLIENT_INFO string (see Listing 9-3).

Listing 9-3. *Extract from PeopleTools-Generated Database Trigger to Audit Record TL_RPTD_TIME*

```
CREATE OR REPLACE TRIGGER TL_RPTD_TIME_TR
 AFTER INSERT OR UPDATE OR DELETE ON PS_TL_RPTD_TIME
 FOR EACH ROW
DECLARE
 V_AUDIT_OPRID VARCHAR2(64);
BEGIN
 DBMS_APPLICATION_INFO.READ_CLIENT_INFO(V_AUDIT_OPRID);
 IF INSERTING THEN
  INSERT INTO PS_AUDIT_TLRPTTIME
  VALUES(GET_PS_OPRID(V_AUDIT_OPRID),SYSDATE,'A', ...
  ...
 END IF;
END TL_RPTD_TIME_TR;
/
```

tmadmin

tmadmin is the administrative utility for Tuxedo. It is a command-line interface that can be used to administer or monitor a Tuxedo system, and it can also be used within scripts.

Commands can be piped in as keyboard input, and the output captured as standard output, as shown in Listing 9-4.

Listing 9-4. tmadmin.bat

```
REM tmadmin.bat
REM (c) Go-Faster Consultancy Ltd. 2004-2011

set TUXDIR=d:\ps\bea\tuxedo
set PS_SERVDIR=D:\ps\hcm8.9\appserv\HCM89
set PS_SERVER_CFG=%PS_SERVDIR%\psappsrv.cfg
set TUXCONFIG=%PS_SERVDIR%\PSTUXCFG

%TUXDIR%\bin\tmadmin -r <tmadmin.in >tmadmin.out
```

■ **Tip** Monitoring scripts should always use the -r switch (as shown in Listing 9-4) to run the tmadmin utility in read-only mode. It prevents them from issuing any administrative commands. Only one instance of tmadmin can connect to a Tuxedo domain in administrative mode at the same time.

A full description of the tmadmin commands can be found in the Tuxedo documentation on the Oracle web site.[5] The most useful commands for monitoring are presented in Listing 9-5.

In a Unix script, the commands can be piped directly into the tmadmin command, but on Windows you need to put them in a separate file (as shown in Listing 9-5) and pipe the file into tmadmin (as shown in Listing 9-4).[6]

Listing 9-5. tmadmin.in

```
pclt
pq
psr
q
```

Listing 9-5 includes the following commands:

- pclt or printclient: Lists clients of the bulletin board. However, if Jolt pooling is enabled, you merely get a list of the pools.

- pq or printqueue: Lists queues within the application server and the number of requests queued.

- psr or printserver: Lists application server processes and how many service requests they have processed.

---

[5] See www.oracle.com/technetwork/middleware/tuxedo/documentation/index.html.
[6] www.go-faster.co.uk/scripts/tuxmon.zip is an example of a Unix shell script that can be used to periodically collect metrics from a Tuxedo domain.

- q or quit: Scripts that call tmadmin must manually quit from the utility or hang indefinitely.

Listing 9-6 shows the output from the script in Listing 9-4.

Listing 9-6. `tmadmin.out`

```
>     LMID           User Name          Client Name     Time     Status   Bgn/Cmmt/Abrt
---------------   ----------------    --------------  --------  -------  -------------
GO-FASTER-4       NT                  JSH             0:18:28  IDLE     0/0/0
GO-FASTER-4       NT                  tmadmin         0:00:00  IDLE     0/0/0
GO-FASTER-4       PTWEBSERVER         GO-FASTER-4     0:17:46  IDLE/W   0/0/0
GO-FASTER-4       PTWEBSERVER         GO-FASTER-4     0:17:40  IDLE/W   0/0/0
GO-FASTER-4       PS                  go-faster-4     0:01:51  IDLE/W   0/0/0

> Prog Name       Queue Name     # Serve Wk Queued   # Queued  Ave. Len    Machine
---------        ------------------  ----------  ---------  --------  -------
BBL.exe          61375               1           -          0         - GO-FASTER+
PSSAMSRV.exe     SAMQ                1           -          0         - GO-FASTER+
JSL.exe          00095.00200         1           -          0         - GO-FASTER+
JREPSVR.exe      00094.00250         1           -          0         - GO-FASTER+
PSMONITORSRV.e   MONITOR             1           -          0         - GO-FASTER+
PSAPPSRV.exe     APPQ                1           -          0         - GO-FASTER+
PSWATCHSRV.exe   WATCH               1           -          0         - GO-FASTER+

> Prog Name       Queue Name  Grp Name      ID RqDone Load Done Current Service
---------        ----------  --------      -- ------ --------- ----------------
BBL.exe          61375       GO-FAST+        0    37     1850 (   IDLE )
PSMONITORSRV.e   MONITOR     MONITOR         1     0        0 (   IDLE )
PSAPPSRV.exe     APPQ        APPSRV          1   141     7050 (   IDLE )
PSWATCHSRV.exe   WATCH       WATCH           1     0        0 (   IDLE )
PSPPMSRV.exe     PPMQ2       PPMGRP        100     0        0 (   IDLE )
PSSAMSRV.exe     SAMQ        APPSRV        100     0        0 (   IDLE )
JSL.exe          00095.00200 JSLGRP        200     0        0 (   IDLE )
JREPSVR.exe      00094.00250 JREPGRP       250     9      450 (   IDLE )
```

Tuxedo Service Trace (-r Option)

If the application server process is started with the -r option (see Listing 9-7), then Tuxedo logs every service request that passes through the server, noting the start and end times.

Listing 9-7. Extract from `psappsrv.ubb`: *Application Server Process Command Line*

```
CLOPT="-r -o \"./LOGS/APPQ.stdout\" -e \"./LOGS/APPQ.stderr\" -p 1,600:1,1 -s@psappsrv.lst --
-D CSPROD1A -S PSAPPSRV"
```

To incorporate this into the Tuxedo configuration, I usually add a new variable to the trace section of the application configuration file `psappsrv.cfg` (see Listing 9-8).

Listing 9-8. Extract from psappsrv.ubb

```
[Trace]
…
;-------------------------------------------------------------------------
; when set to -r enables Tuxedo service trace, else set to a single space
TuxedoServiceTrace=-r
```

The new variable can then be referenced in the Tuxedo configuration template file psappsrv.ubx (as shown in Listing 9-9).

Listing 9-9. Extract from psappsrv.ubx

```
CLOPT="{$Trace\TuxedoServiceTrace} -o \"{REL_LOG}{FS}APPQ1.stdout\"
-e \"{REL_LOG}{FS}APPQ1.stderr\" {$PSAPPSRV\Spawn Server} -s@psappsrv.lst
-- -D {$Domain Settings\Domain ID} -S PSAPPSRV"
```

The output is written to the standard error file, which by default is in the current working directory for the server process, $PS_HOME/appserv/<domain name>, and is called *stderr*. The output file name can be specified explicitly with the -e option, so servers on different queues can write to different files. In Listing 9-7, I have chosen to call the file APPQ.stderr.

The overhead of the Tuxedo service trace is low. It is safe to enable it on production systems for long periods. However, this trace cannot be enabled or disabled dynamically via tmadmin. The application server domain must be shut down, reconfigured, and restarted.[7] If they are not managed, the trace files simply continue to grow. There is no file rotation in Tuxedo; trace files must be administered manually.

■ **Note** Tuxedo server command lines can be edited directly with the Tuxedo Administrative Console (see Chapter 13), but changes do not take effect until the individual server processes are restarted.

For each service, there are two pairs of numbers (see Listing 9-10). The date and time at the start and end of the service are logged. The dates are in whole seconds, and the origin is 00:00hrs GMT on January 1, 1970. The units of the time columns are operating-system dependent. On Windows, they are milliseconds, whereas on Unix platforms they are centiseconds.

Listing 9-10. Tuxedo Service Trace Entries

SERVICE	PID	SDATE	STIME	EDATE	ETIME
@PortalRegistry	29079	1312808847	389950803	1312808848	389950897
@FileAttach	29079	1312808848	389950897	1312808848	389950927
@PortalRegistry	29079	1312808848	389950901	1312808848	389950969
@ICPanel	29079	1312808848	389950929	1312808870	389953142

---

[7] It is possible to do this with the Tuxedo Administration Console without shutting down the domain (see Chapter 13).

```
@JavaMgrGetObj  29079   1312808870   389953147   1312808870   389953160
@PortalRegistry 29079   1312808870   389953159   1312808870   389953180
@ICScript       29079   1312808871   389953181   1312808884   389954528
@ICScript       29079   1312808884   389954531   1312808903   389956390
@ICScript       29079   1312808903   389956394   1312808907   389956873
@ICScript       29079   1312808907   389956876   1312808912   389957281
@ICPanel        29079   1312808914   389957504   1312808916   389957721
@ICPanel        29079   1312808916   389957724   1312808927   389958820
```

You can tell that Listing 9-10 is taken from a Unix system. The difference in SDATE and EDATE for the last entry is 11 seconds, but the difference in STIME and EDATE is 1096. Therefore the timings are in centiseconds, and the service took 10.96 seconds to execute.

The times are 32-bit integers that recycle when they reach the maximum value (in approximately 50 days on Windows and 500 days on Unix). It is not possible to directly determine the time at which the service began from this value. The times can be used only to determine the duration of the service request. I have noticed on some platforms that the times lose a few time units per day against the date column, although I have no explanation for this.

The log file is written by the Tuxedo libraries that are compiled into each application server program. It records the time at which the service message reaches the server and the time it leaves the server. Therefore, the difference is the time spent inside the server process, and it does not include any queuing time. The entry is written only when the service completes. If the service times out or the server crashes for some reason, the service is not logged.

Tuxedo provides a simple command-line utility, txrpt, to process the stderr file. This utility is fully described in the Tuxedo documentation. In the example in Listing 9-11, I am going to process the trace file for a specific time period: 6 a.m. to 8 a.m. on August 17.

Listing 9-11. Running txrpt

```
txrpt -d 08/17 -s 06 -e 08 <APPQ.stderr >txrpt.out
```

The txrpt utility produces an hour-by-hour summary of the performance of each service on the application server, showing the number of services processed and the average service execution time, as shown in Listing 9-12.

Listing 9-12. txrpt.out

```
START AFTER:    17 August 2011 06:00:00 BST
END BEFORE:     17 August 2011 08:00:00 BST
        SERVICE SUMMARY REPORT


SVCNAME          6a-7a       7a-8a                TOTALS
                 Num/Avg     Num/Avg              Num/Avg
---------------- --------    --------             -------
ICPanel          300/0.59    380/0.62             680/0.61
ICScript         94/0.17     132/0.16             226/0.16
PortalRegistry   35/0.02     32/0.01              67/0.02
GetCertificate   21/0.07     15/0.09              36/0.08
JavaMgrGetObj    8/0.01      5/0.01               13/0.01
FileAttach       4/0.13      3/0.05               7/0.10
GetAppImages     3/0.01      2/0.01               5/0.01
HomepageT        1/0.07      2/0.05               3/0.05
```

```
--------------- -------    -------          -------
TOTALS           466/0.42  571/0.45         1037/0.44
```

Although txrpt is a good "quick and dirty" way to find out how the application server is performing, it reports only average execution times, which can hide a great deal of information. If the standard error file is loaded into a table (see Listing 9-13) in the database, it is possible to ask more sophisticated questions and correlate them with other metrics to produce graphs.

Listing 9-13. Script to Create a Table to Hold Tuxedo Service Trace Information

```
CREATE TABLE txrpt
(service     VARCHAR2(20)                     NOT NULL
,pid         NUMBER(6)                        NOT NULL
,stimestamp DATE                              NOT NULL
,stime       NUMBER(10,3)                     NOT NULL
,etime       NUMBER(10,3)                     NOT NULL
,queue       VARCHAR2(5)  DEFAULT 'XXXXX' NOT NULL
,concurrent  NUMBER(2)    DEFAULT 0      NOT NULL
,scenario    NUMBER(2)    DEFAULT 0      NOT NULL
);

CREATE unique index txrpt
ON txrpt(service,pid,stimestamp,stime,etime);
```

Extra analysis columns, concurrent and queue, have been added to the table. They can be updated later (see Listing 13-2).

It is then easy to load the stderr file into the table using Oracle's SQL*Loader utility, using the control file described in Listing 9-14. You could also use external tables to load this data.

*Listing 9-14. SQL*Loader Control File*

```
LOAD DATA
INFILE 'APPQ.stderr'
REPLACE
INTO TABLE txrpt
WHEN (1) = '@'
FIELDS TERMINATED BY WHITESPACE
TRAILING NULLCOLS
(service     "SUBSTR(:service,2)"        -- remove leading @
,pid
,stimestamp ":stimestamp/86400+1/24+TO_DATE('01011970','DDMMYYYY')"
                                         -- convert to Oracle data (GMT+1)
,stime       ":stime/100"               -- convert to seconds (Unix)
,queue       "'APPQ'"                    -- do not remove this line
,etime       ":etime/100"               -- convert to seconds (Unix)
)
```

In this example control file

- The stimestamp column in the table is converted to an Oracle date using a function string.

- The function includes +1/24 to convert the time from GMT to the local time zone. On Unix systems, the time zone variable can be set to GMT instead:

  ```
  set TZ=GMT0; export TZ
  ```

- The stime and etime columns are converted on load from operating-system times to seconds. On Windows, the raw data is 1/1,000 of a second; on Unix platforms, the raw data is 1/100 of a second.

- The queue name is defaulted to APPQ because APPQ.stderr is being loaded, and this was produced by server processes on the APPQ queue. Do not change the position of the queue directive in the loader file because it is used to skip the etimestamp column in the stderr file.

- The data cannot be loaded in direct path mode in conjunction with the SQL operator strings.

Application Server Log

The LogFence parameter in the application server configuration file, psappsrv.cfg (see Listing 9-15), controls the amount of information written to the application server log file, APPSRV_mmdd.log (where mmdd is the month and day). If LogFence is set to 4, the additional trace information includes some performance metrics.

Listing 9-15. Extract from psappsrv.cfg

```
[Domain Settings]
;---------------------------------------------------------------------
; Logging detail level
;
; Level      Type of information
; -----      -------------------
;  -100      - Suppress logging
;  -1        - Protocol, memory errors
;   0        - Status information
;   1        - General errors
;   2        - Warnings
;   3        - Tracing Level 1 (default)
;   4        - Tracing Level 2
;   5        - Tracing Level 3
; Dynamic change allowed for LogFence
LogFence=4
```

Listing 9-16 is a sample of the additional trace information generated with LogFence set to a value of 4. It shows that PeopleSoft operator PS logged in and opened component JOB_DATA in the Administer Workforce menu, and the ICPanel service took 0.421 seconds to execute. Note also that the LogFence value of the message appears in brackets on every line in the trace.

Listing 9-16. Application server log APPSRV_0820.log

```
PSAPPSRV.6076 (46) [08/20/11 20:51:59 PS@go-faster-4 ICPanel](4) Starting Service
PSAPPSRV.6076 (46) [08/20/11 20:51:59 PS@go-faster-4 (NETSCAPE 7.0; WINXP) ICPanel](4)
Executing component JOB_DATA/GBL in menu ADMINISTER_WORKFORCE_(GBL)
PSAPPSRV.6076 (46) [08/20/11 20:52:03 PS@go-faster-4](4) Service ICPanel completed: elapsed
time=3.5630
```

Listing 9-17 is the Tuxedo service trace output that corresponds to the entries in Listing 9-16. This reports that the ICPanel services took 3.672 seconds.

Listing 9-17. Tuxedo Service Trace APPQ.stderr

```
@ICPanel     5376        1313869919   50710562    1313869923   50714234
```

Note that there is a discrepancy between the two trace files. The Tuxedo server process was busy for 3.672 seconds, but the PeopleSoft code took 3.563 seconds to execute. This is not surprising, as these traces are generated by different instrumentation at different points in the technology chain and so mean slightly different things. This also implies that in this case, the Tuxedo code took 0.109 seconds to handle the service messages.

While the application server log tells you which operator accessed which part of the application, the Tuxedo service trace gives more accurate timing for the duration of the service. Setting LogFence to 4 also generates a lot of additional information, but there is only a small overhead on service time for so doing.

WebLogic Server Access Log

The WebLogic server supports the standard extended log file format, which permits additional information to be recorded in the web server's access log file.

However, access logging must first be enabled and the extended format selected in the WebLogic configuration file. A custom enhanced access log format can be specified by directives in the access log itself, as I discuss in the sections that follow.

WebLogic Configuration

The WebLogic configuration is held the file called config.xml in an XML format, as shown in Listing 9-18.

Listing 9-18. Extract from config.xml

```
<?xml version='1.0' encoding='UTF-8'?>
...
  <name>HCM91</name>
  <domain-version>10.3.3.0</domain-version>
  <security-configuration>
    <name>HCM91</name>
...
  </security-configuration>
  <server>
    <name>PIA</name>
...
```

```
      <listen-port>80</listen-port>
      <web-server>
        <name>PIA</name>
        <web-server-log>
          <name>PIA</name>
          <file-name>./logs/PIA_access.log</file-name>
          <rotation-type>byTime</rotation-type>
          <number-of-files-limited>true</number-of-files-limited>
          <file-count>7</file-count>
          <file-time-span>24</file-time-span>
          <rotation-time>00:00</rotation-time>
          <file-min-size>500</file-min-size>
          <rotate-log-on-startup>false</rotate-log-on-startup>
          <logging-enabled>true</logging-enabled>
          <elf-fields>date time time-taken bytes c-ip c-dns cs-method sc-status cs-uri-stem cs-
uri-query cs(User-Agent)</elf-fields>
          <log-file-format>extended</log-file-format>
          <log-time-in-gmt>false</log-time-in-gmt>
        </web-server-log>
        <https-keep-alive-secs>120</https-keep-alive-secs>
      </web-server>
...
    </server>
...
</domain>
```

However, it is not advisable to edit this file directly. All configuration changes to the server should be made via WebLogic console, as shown in Figure 9-2.

The access log file is called PIA_access.log by default.

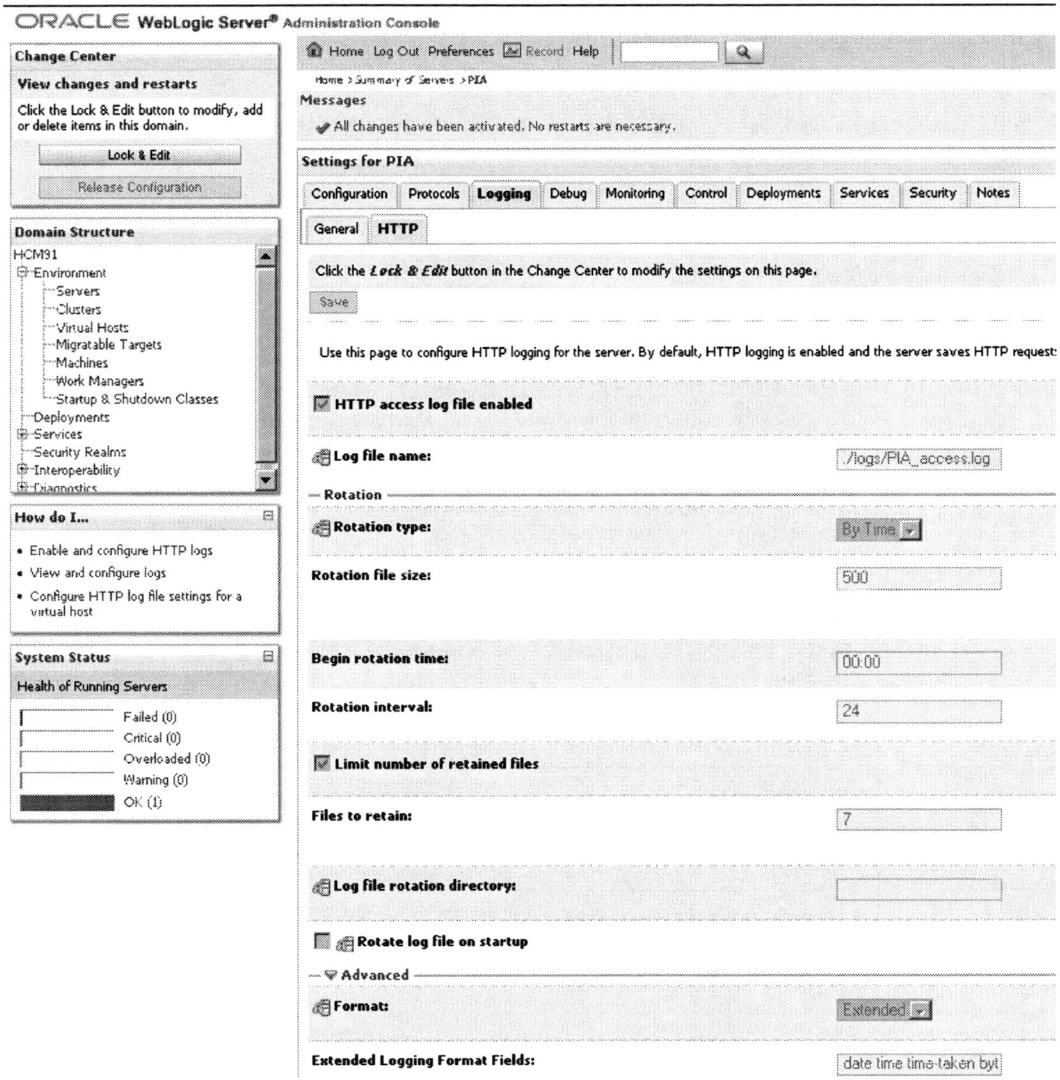

Figure 9-2. WebLogic console

Defining the Access Log Format

In all versions of WebLogic, the format of the log file can be defined by directives in the log file itself. The directives can be appended to the end of the log file. I normally create a seed log file and copy that to the access log file. When a log file rotates, the directives are rewritten at the top of the new file by WebLogic (see Listing 9-19).

Listing 9-19. Seed access.log

```
#Version: 1.0
#Fields: date time time-taken bytes c-ip c-dns cs-method sc-status cs(User-Agent) cs-uri-stem
cs-uri-query
```

Table 9-1 describes the directives used in Listing 9-19. It is not an exhaustive list. The directives are described in the Oracle Fusion Middleware documentation.[8]

Table 9-1. W3C Extended Log-File Formats

Custom Log Format	Description
date	Date at which the transaction completed. The format is fixed as YYYY-MM-DD, where YYYY, MM, and DD stand for the numeric year, month, and day, respectively.
time	Time at which the transaction completed. The format is fixed as HH:MM:SS, where HH is the hour in 24-hour format, MM is minutes, and SS is seconds. All times are specified in GMT.
time-taken	Time taken for the transaction to complete in seconds. This is accurate to the limit of the operating system. On Windows NT, this is in thousandths of a second.
bytes	Number of bytes transferred.
c-ip	Client IP address and port.
c-dns	DNS name of the client.
sc-status	Server-to-client status code.
cs-status	Client-to-server status code.
cs-method	Client-to-server method.
cs(User-Agent)	The user-agent string in the HTTP header in the message from the client.
cs-uri-stem	The stem portion of the URI requested by the client, omitting the query.

---

[8] See http://download.oracle.com/docs/cd/E14571_01/web.1111/e13701/web_server.htm#CNFGD207, although this also references the World Wide Web Consortium (W3C) draft specification at www.w3.org/TR/WD-logfile.html.

Custom Log Format	Description
cs-uri-query	The query portion of the URI requested by the client.

The variables are fully described in the W3C standard to which the WebLogic documentation refers. Listing 9-20 shows a sample of the resulting log for a PeopleTools 8.4 system.

Listing 9-20. Extract of PIA_access.log

```
#Version:
#Version:    1.0
#Fields:    date time time-taken bytes c-ip c-dns cs-method sc-status cs(User-Agent) cs-uri-
stem cs-uri-query
#Software:    WebLogic
#Start-Date:    2011-09-29    20:24:09
...
2011-09-29    20:31:17    0.516    5517    192.168.1.84    go-faster-6.london.go-faster.co.uk
POST    200    "Mozilla/5.0 (Windows NT 6.1; WOW64; rv:6.0) Gecko/20100101 Firefox/6.0"
/psc/HCM91_3/EMPLOYEE/HRMS/c/HRS_HRPM.HRS_JO_360.GBL    -
2011-09-29    20:31:33    2.155    1032    192.168.1.84    go-faster-6.london.go-faster.co.uk
GET    200    "Mozilla/5.0 (Windows NT 6.1; WOW64; rv:6.0) Gecko/20100101 Firefox/6.0"
/psc/HCM91_3/EMPLOYEE/HRMS/s/WEBLIB_PT_NAV.ISCRIPT1.FieldFormula.IScript_PT_NAV_INFRAME
navtype=dropdown&pt_fname=HC_WORKFORCE_ADMINISTRATION&FolderPath=PORTAL_ROOT_OBJECT.HC_WORKFOR
CE_ADMINISTRATION&mode=x&templatetype=IFRM&templateid=DEFAULT_TEMPLATE&c=PfDKxdOQe8E%2fR8xQKXo
Cng%3d%3d
2011-09-29    20:31:34    0.28    2679    192.168.1.84    go-faster-6.london.go-faster.co.uk
GET    200    "Mozilla/5.0 (Windows NT 6.1; WOW64; rv:6.0) Gecko/20100101 Firefox/6.0"
/psc/HCM91_3/EMPLOYEE/HRMS/s/WEBLIB_PT_NAV.ISCRIPT1.FieldFormula.IScript_PT_NAV_INFRAME
navtype=dropdown&pt_fname=HC_WORKFORCE_INFO&FolderPath=PORTAL_ROOT_OBJECT.HC_WORKFORCE_ADMINIS
TRATION.HC_WORKFORCE_INFO&mode=x&templatetype=IFRM&templateid=DEFAULT_TEMPLATE&c=PfDKxdOQe8E%2
fR8xQKXoCng%3d%3d
2011-09-29    20:31:36    0.021    656    192.168.1.84    go-faster-6.london.go-faster.co.uk
GET    200    "Mozilla/5.0 (Windows NT 6.1; WOW64; rv:6.0) Gecko/20100101 Firefox/6.0"
/psc/HCM91_3/EMPLOYEE/HRMS/s/WEBLIB_PT_NAV.ISCRIPT1.FieldFormula.IScript_PT_NAV_INFRAME
navtype=dropdown&mode=bc&isfldr=false&objname=HC_JOB_DATA_GBL&c=PfDKxdOQe8E%2fR8xQKXoCng%3d%3d
2011-09-29    20:31:38    2.191    66550    192.168.1.84    go-faster-6.london.go-faster.co.uk
GET    200    "Mozilla/5.0 (Windows NT 6.1; WOW64; rv:6.0) Gecko/20100101 Firefox/6.0"
/psc/HCM91_3/EMPLOYEE/HRMS/c/ADMINISTER_WORKFORCE_(GBL).JOB_DATA.GBL
FolderPath=PORTAL_ROOT_OBJECT.HC_WORKFORCE_ADMINISTRATION.HC_WORKFORCE_INFO.HC_JOB_DATA_GBL&Is
Folder=false&IgnoreParamTempl=FolderPath%2cIsFolder
2011-09-29    20:31:43    0.149    2356    192.168.1.84    go-faster-6.london.go-faster.co.uk
POST    200    "Mozilla/5.0 (Windows NT 6.1; WOW64; rv:6.0) Gecko/20100101 Firefox/6.0"
/psc/HCM91_3/EMPLOYEE/HRMS/c/ADMINISTER_WORKFORCE_(GBL).JOB_DATA.GBL    -
```

The fields in the log file are tab-separated. The W3C standard states the following:

Each logfile entry consists of a sequence of fields separated by whitespace and terminated by a CR or CRLF sequence. The meanings of the fields are defined by a preceding #Fields directive. If a field is omitted for a particular entry a single dash "-" is substituted.[9]

This log can be loaded into a table in the database that is created as shown in Listing 9-21.

Listing 9-21. `wl_pre.sql`

```
CREATE TABLE weblogic
(timestamp       DATE              NOT NULL
,duration        NUMBER(9,3)       NOT NULL
,bytes_sent      NUMBER(7)         NOT NULL
,return_status   NUMBER(3)
,remote_host1    VARCHAR2(3)       NOT NULL
,remote_host2    VARCHAR2(3)       NOT NULL
,remote_host3    VARCHAR2(3)       NOT NULL
,remote_host4    VARCHAR2(3)       NOT NULL
,remote_dns      VARCHAR2(100)
,user_agent      VARCHAR2(1000)
,request_method  VARCHAR2(8)
,request_status  NUMBER(4)
,url             VARCHAR2(4000)    NOT NULL
,query_string1   VARCHAR2(4000)
,query_string2   VARCHAR2(4000)
,query_string3   VARCHAR2(4000)
,query_string4   VARCHAR2(4000)
,query_string5   VARCHAR2(4000)
,query_string6   VARCHAR2(4000)
,query_string7   VARCHAR2(4000)
,query_string8   VARCHAR2(4000)
,scenario        NUMBER DEFAULT 0
,domain          VARCHAR2(10)
);
```

The WebLogic access log can then be imported into the table with the SQL*Loader control file shown in Listing 9-22.

*Listing 9-22. SQL*Loader Control File* `wl.ldr`

```
LOAD DATA
INFILE 'PIA_access.log'
REPLACE
INTO TABLE weblogic
WHEN (1) != '#'
FIELDS TERMINATED BY WHITESPACE
TRAILING NULLCOLS
```

---

[9] See www.w3.org/TR/WD-logfile.html.

```
(timestamp        position(1:19) "TO_DATE(:timestamp,'YYYY-MM-DD HH24:MI:ss')"
,duration
,bytes_sent
,remote_host1    TERMINATED BY '.'
,remote_host2    TERMINATED BY '.'
,remote_host3    TERMINATED BY '.'
,remote_host4
,request_method
,return_status   NULLIF (return_status="-")
,user_agent
,url
,query_string1   TERMINATED BY '&' "SUBSTR(:query_string1,2)"
,query_string2   TERMINATED BY '&'
,query_string3   TERMINATED BY '&'
,query_string4   TERMINATED BY '&'
,query_string5   TERMINATED BY '&'
,query_string6   TERMINATED BY '&'
,query_string7   TERMINATED BY '&'
,query_string8   TERMINATED BY '&'
)
```

The query string is broken up into up to eight strings delimited by the ampersand character (&). The different parts of the query string contain information about which component and action are in use (although the query strings are very different in PeopleTools 8.1 and 8.4). Hence, it is possible to analyze PIA performance for different panels in the system.

HANDLING HEXADECIMAL CODES IN WEB SERVER ACCESS LOGS

From PeopleTools 8.4, the access log converts special characters back to their ASCII values in hexadecimal, so you get "%3a" instead of ":", for example. I find the data is easier to read if it is converted back to the characters. I do this with a trigger and a packaged function that executes as the rows are inserted into the table with SQL*Loader.[10]

```
CREATE OR REPLACE PACKAGE dehex AS
FUNCTION dehex(p_string VARCHAR2) RETURN VARCHAR2;
PRAGMA restrict_references(dehex,wnds,wnps);
END dehex;
/

CREATE OR REPLACE PACKAGE BODY dehex AS
FUNCTION dehex(p_string VARCHAR2) RETURN VARCHAR2 IS
    l_string VARCHAR2(4000);
BEGIN
    l_string := p_string;
    WHILE INSTR(l_string,'%')>0 LOOP
        l_string :=
```

---

[10] See dehex.sql

```
        SUBSTR(l_string,
            1,
            INSTR(l_string,'%')-1
        )
        ||CHR(
          TO_NUMBER(
            SUBSTR(l_string
                ,   INSTR(l_string,'%')+1
                ,     2
                )
            ,    'XXXXXXXX'
          )
        )
        ||SUBSTR(l_string
        ,    INSTR(l_string,'%')+3
        );
    END LOOP;
    RETURN l_string;
    END dehex;
END dehex;
/

CREATE OR REPLACE TRIGGER weblogic_query_string_dehex
BEFORE INSERT OR UPDATE ON weblogic
FOR EACH ROW
BEGIN
    :new.query_string1 := dehex.dehex(:new.query_String1);
    :new.query_string2 := dehex.dehex(:new.query_String2);
    :new.query_string3 := dehex.dehex(:new.query_String3);
    :new.query_string4 := dehex.dehex(:new.query_String4);
    :new.query_string5 := dehex.dehex(:new.query_String5);
    :new.query_string6 := dehex.dehex(:new.query_String6);
    :new.query_string7 := dehex.dehex(:new.query_String7);
    :new.query_string8 := dehex.dehex(:new.query_String8);
END;
/
;
```

The result is that the data loaded into the table is much easier to read. Here is the access log after conversion by the dehex procedure:

```
17:26:07 20/04/2004    .39    7930    200 10  0   0    8
go-faster-3
Mozilla/4.0 (compatible; MSIE 6.0; Windows NT 5.1)
GET /psc/ps/EMPLOYEE/HRMS/s/WEBLIB_PT_NAV.ISCRIPT1.FieldFormula.IScript_PT_NAV_INFRA
ME
=PfDKxdOQe8E/R8xQKXoCng==
PortalActualURL=https://go-faster-3:7202/psc/ps/EMPLOYEE/HRMS/c/ADMINISTER_WORKF
ORCE_(GBL).JOB_DATA.GBL
PortalContentURL=https://go-faster-3:7202/psc/ps/EMPLOYEE/HRMS/c/ADMINISTER_WORK
FORCE_(GBL).JOB_DATA.GBL
PortalContentProvider=HRMS
```

```
PortalRegistryName=EMPLOYEE
PortalServletURI=https://go-faster-3:7202/psp/ps/
```

For example, in Figure 9-3, I have looked at the cumulative execution time for different panels in the system and produced a graph of the top ten components. This required that I group the data by the first three parts of the query string.

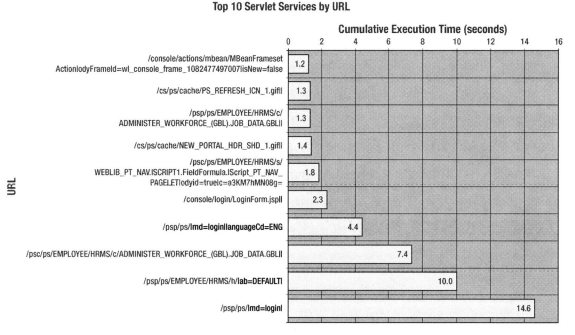

Figure 9-3. Top ten operations by cumulative execution time

Query Metrics

On more than one occasion, I have encountered PeopleSoft systems that have been brought to their knees by unrestricted use of the ad hoc Query tool. It is relatively easy to write a query that functions correctly, but it is often more challenging to write one that also executes efficiently. Queries are also used as the data source by Crystal and nVision reports and for database agent queries.

The question that needs to be answered is, "Which queries are consuming the most time?" This section provides information on a number of techniques to obtain query metrics that can help you answer this question. PeopleSoft has added additional instrumentation to PeopleTools 8.4 to aggregate query execution time and to optionally log each query execution to the database. This new functionality is discussed in Chapter 10. Otherwise, this question has always been difficult to answer.

SQL Tracing Queries

If the Windows client PS/Query, Crystal, or nVision is run in two-tier mode, and it is possible to enable Oracle session trace with an AFTER LOGON database trigger, then the trace files could be processed with tkprof. However, you usually end up with a huge number of trace files to go through manually. I discuss methods of enabling SQL trace with PeopleTools in Chapter 11.

From PeopleTools 7.53, ad hoc queries from PeopleTools programs connecting to the application server in three-tier mode, including the PIA, are routed via a separate dedicated application server process, PSQRYSRV. Oracle session trace can be enabled on the database sessions for these servers. Now there are a limited number of trace files to be processed and examined.

However, SQL trace only gives you the SQL statement. If you have enabled EnableDBMonitoring in the application server, you can also find the call to dbms_application_info before the query in the trace, and so identify the user who submitted it. To identify the query defined in PeopleSoft, you need to query the PeopleTools tables (this method is described in Chapter 11). So it is still a lot of manual work.

Web Server Access Log

The web server access log provides some information about query performance, as detailed in the following sections.

In PeopleTools 8.4, the ad hoc query designer was incorporated into the PIA, although the Windows-based version is still available. Queries can be developed and then run directly from the Query Manager component. A new browser window is spawned, as shown in Figure 9-4.

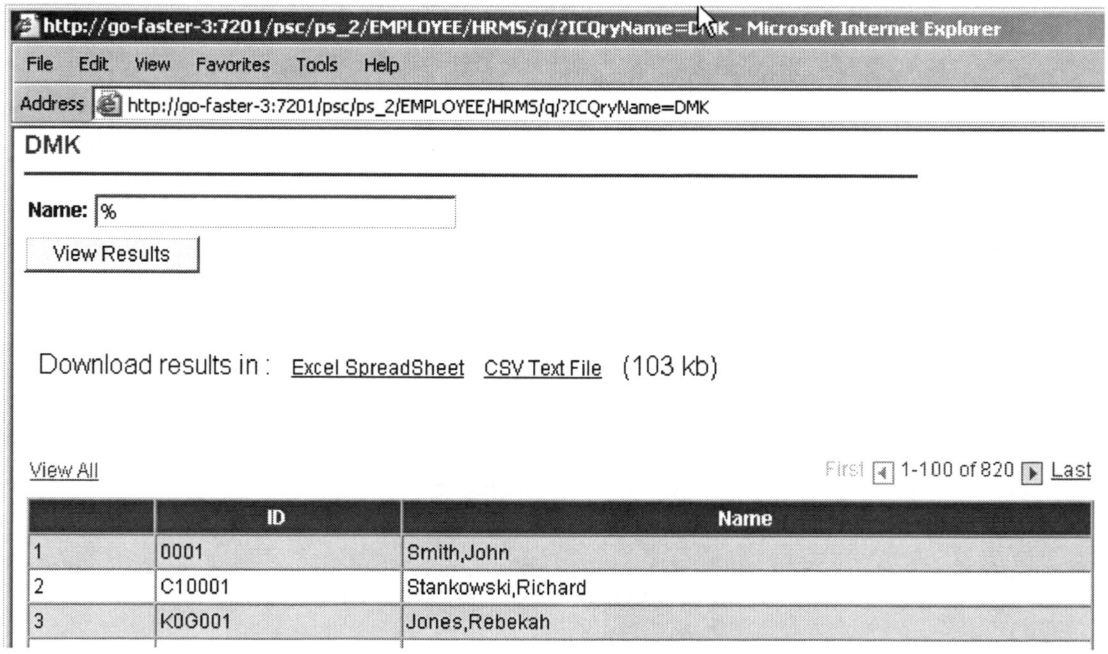

Figure 9-4. Query results

When the query is first run, and the data is actually selected from the database by the ICQuery service, there are two servlet requests. The query name is embedded in the URL query string, but it is prefixed with PUBLIC or PRIVATE depending on the query type.

In Listing 9-23, the access log shows that a private query called DMK was executed, but the name of the Operator ID that owns it is not shown. Figure 9-4 shows that the query has a run-time parameter. The first entry in Listing 9-23 is for the parameter dialog; the second is to execute the query. If there is a parameter dialog before the query is executed, this activity also generates similar access-log entries. Therefore, if different users execute their own private queries that happen to have the same name, you cannot distinguish between them, except by the IP address of the client.

Listing 9-23. The owner of a private query does not appear in the access log

```
2004-05-21 16:41:49 0.01 361 10.0.0.8 go-faster-3 GET 302 "Mozilla/4.0
(compatible; MSIE 6.0; Windows NT 5.1)" /psc/ps_newwin/EMPLOYEE/HRMS/q/
ICAction=ICQryNameURL=PRIVATE.DMK
2004-05-21 16:41:51 1.773 37274 10.0.0.8 go-faster-3 GET 200 "Mozilla/4.0
(compatible; MSIE 6.0; Windows NT 5.1)" /psc/ps_7/EMPLOYEE/HRMS/q/
ICAction=ICQryNameURL=PRIVATE.DMK
```

When the user navigates around the query results, there are still additional entries in the access log. For example, in Figure 9-4, only the first 100 rows of the result set are shown, and the user could navigate to the next 100 rows. The access-log entries have the name of the query in the URL query string, but this time without the query-type prefix (see Listing 9-24).

Users often take a public query and clone it as a private query, but keep the same name. You cannot tell from the access log which one the user is running.

Listing 9-24. Access-Log Entries for Navigating Results but Not Executing the Query

```
2004-05-21 16:41:55 0.481 53383 10.0.0.8 go-faster-3 POST 200 "Mozilla/4.0 (compatible; MSIE
6.0; Windows NT 5.1)" /psc/ps_7/EMPLOYEE/HRMS/q/ ICQryName=DMK
2004-05-21 16:41:57 0.16 41523 10.0.0.8 go-faster-3 POST 200 "Mozilla/4.0 (compatible; MSIE
6.0; Windows NT 5.1)" /psc/ps_7/EMPLOYEE/HRMS/q/ ICQryName=DMK
```

However, if a user is in the Query Manager developing an ad hoc query, and they run the query by navigating to the Preview tab, then all that is reported in the access log is the component name (see Listing 9-25); the specific query cannot be determined. So, the access log does not provide any specific information about the performance of queries run in the Query Manager.

Listing 9-25. A Query Run in the Query Manager Component—But Which One?

```
2004-05-21 16:37:18 0.35 86748 10.0.0.8 go-faster-3 POST 200 "Mozilla/4.0
(compatible; MSIE 6.0; Windows NT 5.1)"
/psc/ps/EMPLOYEE/HRMS/c/QUERY_MANAGER.QUERY_MANAGER.GBL -
```

The web server access log does not provide a complete picture of query activity, although you can compute, for each query, the total amount of time spent entering parameters, executing the query, and navigating the results online. However, in PeopleTools 8.4, PeopleSoft instrumented the Query Manager to collect query-execution statistics and put them in the database (see Chapter 10).

Batch Metrics

Various sources of time-based statistics are available from PeopleSoft batch and report processing that can be collected and analyzed. I describe these sources in this section of the chapter.

Process Scheduler

The Process Scheduler agent is responsible for initiating most batch and report processes in PeopleTools.

Every time a process is scheduled to run via the Process Scheduler, a request record is created on a pair of tables. PSPRCSQUE is tells the Process Scheduler which processes to run and when. Its sibling PSPRCSRQST is used to report the status of each job to the Process Monitor component. These two tables have many columns in common. In earlier versions of PeopleTools, only PSPRCSRQST was used to control the Process Scheduler. I suspect that PSPRCSQUE was introduced to avoid locking problems experienced in databases other than Oracle that run in the Read Committed isolation level.

Request Table

Processes initiated by the Process Scheduler update their run status on their request record in the table PSPRCSRQST as they start and finish. They also log the start and end times as they do this. Thus it is possible to determine who ran what process and when, and how long it took; therefore, this table is a rich source of performance data within PeopleSoft. The Process Monitor component shown in Figure 9-5 queries this table.

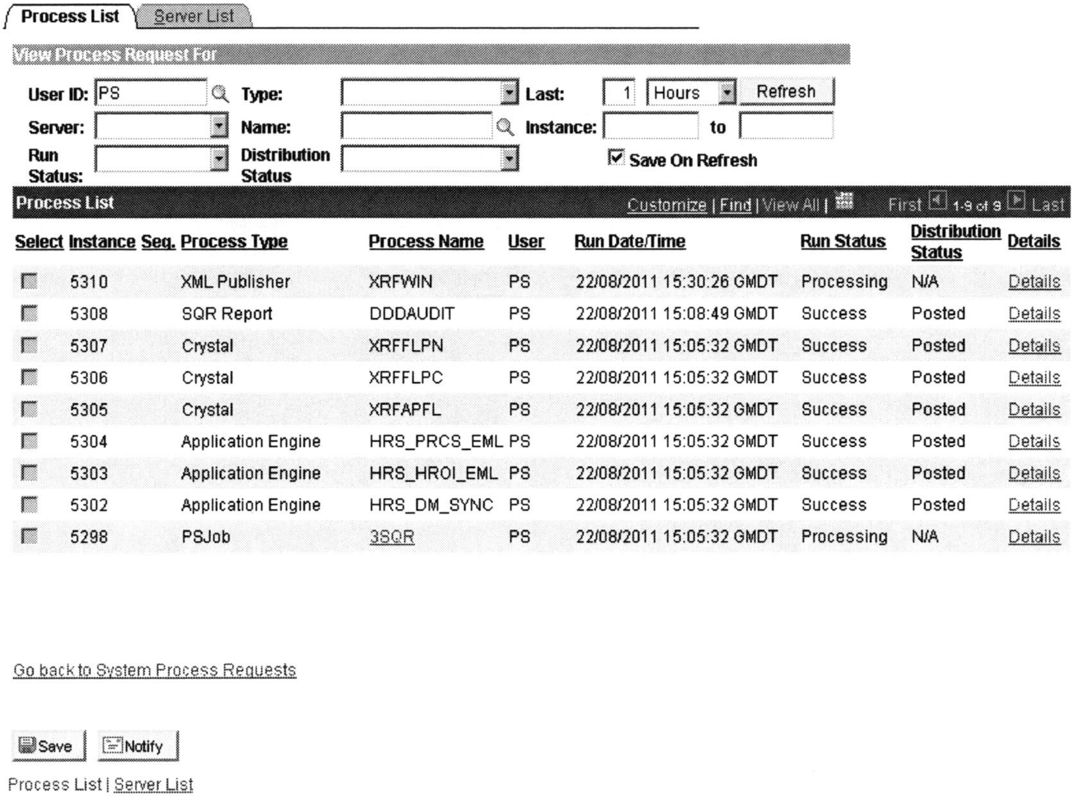

Process List	Server List

View Process Request For

User ID:	PS	🔍	Type:		▾	Last:	1	Hours	▾	Refresh
Server:		▾	Name:		🔍	Instance:		to		
Run Status:		▾	Distribution Status		▾		☑ Save On Refresh			

Process List   Customize | Find | View All | 🏢   First ◀ 1-9 of 9 ▶ Last

Select	Instance	Seq.	Process Type	Process Name	User	Run Date/Time	Run Status	Distribution Status	Details
☐	5310		XML Publisher	XRFWIN	PS	22/08/2011 15:30:26 GMDT	Processing	N/A	Details
☐	5308		SQR Report	DDDAUDIT	PS	22/08/2011 15:08:49 GMDT	Success	Posted	Details
☐	5307		Crystal	XRFFLPN	PS	22/08/2011 15:05:32 GMDT	Success	Posted	Details
☐	5306		Crystal	XRFFLPC	PS	22/08/2011 15:05:32 GMDT	Success	Posted	Details
☐	5305		Crystal	XRFAPFL	PS	22/08/2011 15:05:32 GMDT	Success	Posted	Details
☐	5304		Application Engine	HRS_PRCS_EML	PS	22/08/2011 15:05:32 GMDT	Success	Posted	Details
☐	5303		Application Engine	HRS_HROI_EML	PS	22/08/2011 15:05:32 GMDT	Success	Posted	Details
☐	5302		Application Engine	HRS_DM_SYNC	PS	22/08/2011 15:05:32 GMDT	Success	Posted	Details
☐	5298		PSJob	3SQR	PS	22/08/2011 15:05:32 GMDT	Processing	N/A	Details

Go back to System Process Requests

💾 Save   ✉ Notify

Process List | Server List

Figure 9-5. *Process Monitor component*

Within the Process Monitor, you can drill into a single process, as shown in Figure 9-6.

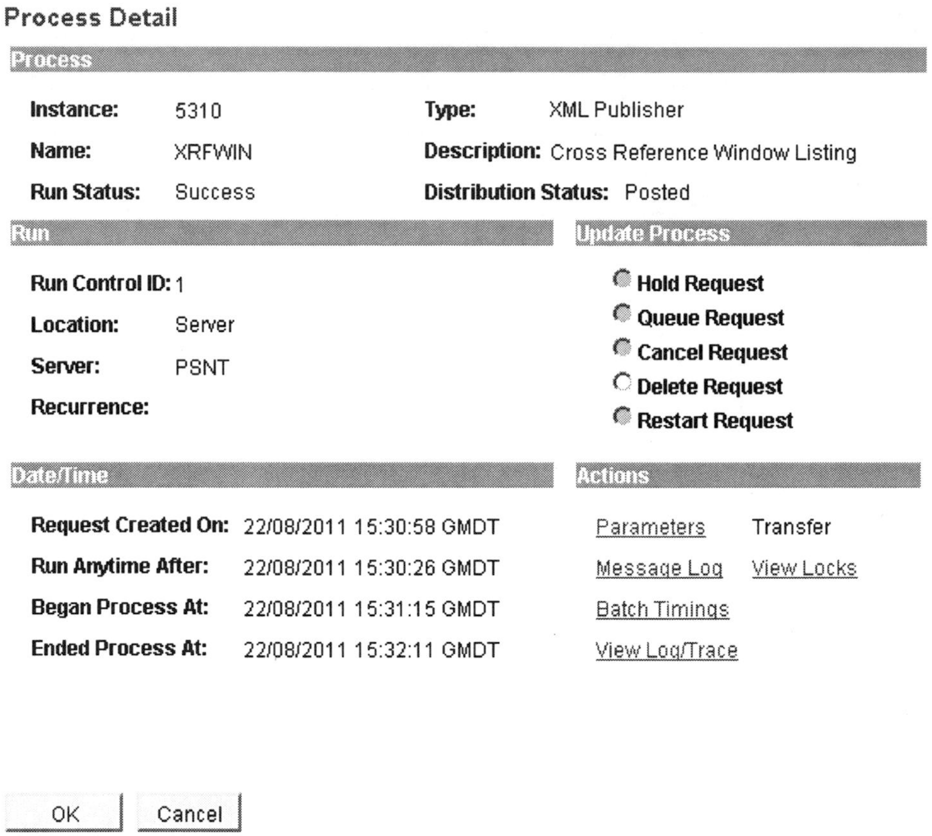

Process Detail

Process

Instance:	5310	**Type:**	XML Publisher
Name:	XRFWIN	**Description:**	Cross Reference Window Listing
Run Status:	Success	**Distribution Status:**	Posted

Run

Run Control ID: 1

Location: Server

Server: PSNT

Recurrence:

Update Process

○ **Hold Request**
○ **Queue Request**
○ **Cancel Request**
○ **Delete Request**
○ **Restart Request**

Date/Time

Request Created On:	22/08/2011 15:30:58 GMDT
Run Anytime After:	22/08/2011 15:30:26 GMDT
Began Process At:	22/08/2011 15:31:15 GMDT
Ended Process At:	22/08/2011 15:32:11 GMDT

Actions

Parameters   Transfer

Message Log   View Locks

Batch Timings

View Log/Trace

[OK]   [Cancel]

Figure 9-6. Process Monitor detail page

From PeopleTools 8.4, jobs are displayed differently in the Process Monitor. There are still separate rows on PSPRCSRQST for the job and the processes within the job, but the job can no longer be expanded within the Process Monitor. The job name is now a link that expands into another page, as shown in Figure 9-7.

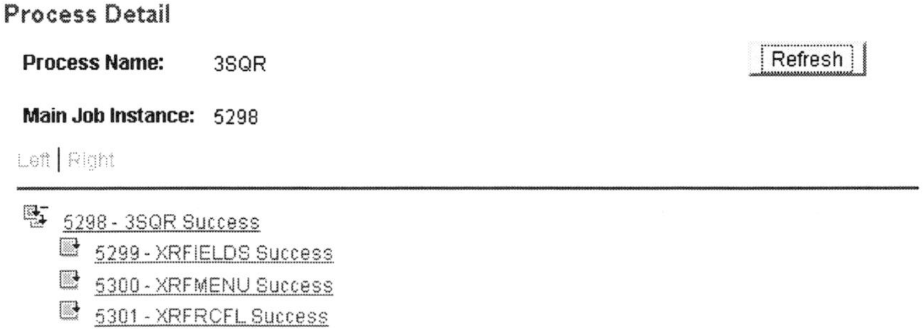

Process Detail

Process Name: 3SQR

Main Job Instance: 5298

[Refresh]

Left | Right

 5298 - 3SQR Success
    5299 - XRFIELDS Success
    5300 - XRFMENU Success
    5301 - XRFRCFL Success

Figure 9-7. Job detail

All the information in the preceding three figures comes from the PSPRCSRQST table. Table 9-2 describes some of the more useful columns on that table.

Table 9-2. PSPRCSRQST Columns

Column Name	Description
PRCSINSTANCE	Process instance number. This uniquely identifies each process run through any process scheduler. This number is allocated sequentially.
JOBINSTANCE	Process instance number of parent job. If the process is not part of a job, this is set to 0.
PRCSTYPE	Type of process.
PRCSNAME	Name of the process.
SERVERNAMERUN	Name of the Process Scheduler on which the process is run.
OPRID	ID of the operator who requested the process. This can be looked up against PSOPRDEFN.
RUNSTATUS	Status of the process request. When a process request is created, it is first given a status of 5 (Queued); then, when the Process Scheduler picks up the request and initiates it, the Process Scheduler updates the status to 6 (Initiated). When the process is started, the status is updated to 7 (Processing). When the process terminates, the status changes again to 9 (Success) or 2 (Error).
RUNDTTM	Date and time at which the process should be initiated.
RQSTDTTM	Date and time at which the request was submitted.
BEGINDTTM	Date and time at which the process began.
ENDDTTM	Date and time at which the process terminated.

▨ **Note** From PeopleTools 8.50, PeopleSoft datetime fields are created as Oracle timestamp columns. In previous versions of PeopleTools, they were date columns. The difference between two Oracle dates is a number of days, but the difference between two Oracle timestamps is an Oracle interval. The easiest way to deal with this is to cast the two timestamps to dates before subtracting one from the other.

More statuses have been added with successive releases. PeopleSoft has created translate values for the column RUNSTATUS that can be seen in Application Designer or can be queried directly from

PSXLATITEM, as shown in Listing 9-26. Some values are no longer used, and their status has been changed to Inactive, since the DISTSTATUS column was added to separately manage posting files to the report repository.

Listing 9-26. *Translate Values for RUNSTATUS[11]*

```
SELECT fieldvalue, eff_status, xlatlongname
FROM psxlatitem i
WHERE fieldname = 'RUNSTATUS'
AND effdt = (
    SELECT max(effdt)
    FROM   psxlatitem i1
    WHERE  i1.fieldname = i.fieldname
    AND    i1.fieldvalue = i.fieldvalue
    AND    i1.effdt <= SYSDATE)
ORDER BY TO_NUMBER(fieldvalue)
/


FIELDVALUE EFF_STATUS XLATLONGNAME
---------- ---------- --------------------
1          A          Cancel
2          A          Delete
3          A          Error
4          A          Hold
5          A          Queued
6          A          Initiated
7          A          Processing
8          A          Cancelled
9          A          Success
10         A          Not Successful
11         I          Posted
12         I          Unable to post
13         I          Resend
14         I          Posting
15         I          Content Generated
16         A          Pending
17         A          Success With Warning
18         A          Blocked
19         A          Restart
```

In SQL, if one date is subtracted from another, the result is the difference in days. The difference between ENDDTTM and BEGINDTTM is the execution time of the process in days. This can easily be converted to hours, minutes, or seconds in a simple SQL query, such as the example in Listing 9-27.

---

[11] The inactive statuses for RUNSTATUS were used when posting content to the report repository in PeopleTools 8.1. DISTSTATUS was added to PSPRCSQUE and PSPRCSRQST in PeopleTools 8.4.

Listing 9-27. Performance metrics from the Process Scheduler request table

```
column exec_time format a8
column prcsname format a12
column prcstype format a20
SELECT r.prcsinstance, r.prcstype, r.prcsname
,      TO_CHAR(TRUNC(SYSDATE)+(CAST(r.enddttm AS DATE)-r.begindttm),'HH24:MI:SS') exec_time
,      (CAST(r.enddttm AS DATE)-CAST(r.begindttm AS DATE)) exec_days
,      (CAST(r.enddttm AS DATE)-CAST(r.begindttm AS DATE))*24 exec_hrs
,      (CAST(r.enddttm AS DATE)-CAST(r.begindttm AS DATE))*1440 exec_mins
,      (CAST(r.enddttm AS DATE)-CAST(r.begindttm AS DATE))*86400 exec_secs
FROM   psprcsrqst r
…
/
Process
Instance PRCSTYPE            PRCSNAME      EXEC_TIM  EXEC_DAYS  EXEC_HRS   EXEC_MINS   EXEC_SECS
-------- -------------------- ------------- --------  ---------- ---------- ----------- ---------
-
    5307 Crystal              XRFFLPN       00:02:17  .001585648 .038055556 2.28333333        137
    5308 SQR Report           DDDAUDIT      00:03:10  .002199074 .052777778 3.16666667        190
    5309 Application Engine    AEMINITEST    00:00:13  .000150463 .003611111 .216666667         13
    5310 XML Publisher        XRFWIN        00:00:56  .000648148 .015555556 .933333333         56
```

■ **Note** When a failed process is restarted, BEGINDTTM is updated, although this was not the case in earlier versions of PeopleTools. When a restarted process terminates, successfully or otherwise, ENDDTTM is updated. ENDDTTM is updated to the system date again when the distribution agent posts output files to the report repository. This causes a small error in the calculation of execution time. You may notice that execution times tend to be greater than a multiple of the Process Scheduler sleep time. You can see this additional update in the result of the flashback query in Listing 9-28. For Application Engine programs, the ENDDTTM recorded in the batch timings log (PS_BAT_TIMING_LOG) is the time at which the process finished.

Listing 9-28. Flashback Query to Illustrate the Second Update of ENDDTTM

```
column prcsinstance heading 'Process|Instance' format 999999
column runstatus heading 'Run|Status' format a4
column diststatus heading 'Dist|Status' format a4
column versions_endscn heading 'Versions|End SCN' format 99999999
column versions_operation heading 'Versions|Op' format a3
SELECT prcsinstance, begindttm, enddttm, runstatus, diststatus
, versions_starttime
, versions_operation
, versions_endscn
FROM psprcsrqst
 VERSIONS BETWEEN timestamp
```

```
    systimestamp - INTERVAL '15' MINUTE AND
    systimestamp
WHERE versions_starttime IS NOT NULL
AND prcsinstance = 5313
ORDER BY 1, versions_endscn
/
```

Process Instance	BEGINDTTM	ENDDTTM	Run Stat	Dist Stat	VERSIONS_STARTTIME	Ver Op	Versions End SCN
5313			5	1	22-AUG-11 16.19.46	I	59488516
			6	1	22-AUG-11 16.20.01	U	59488548
	16:20:06 22/08/2011		7	1	22-AUG-11 16.20.04	U	59488561
	16:20:06 22/08/2011	16:20:21 22/08/2011	9	1	22-AUG-11 16.20.19	U	59488655
	16:20:06 22/08/2011	16:20:34 22/08/2011	9	1	22-AUG-11 16.20.30	U	59488660
	16:20:06 22/08/2011	16:20:34 22/08/2011	9	7	22-AUG-11 16.20.34	U	59488680
	16:20:06 22/08/2011	16:20:34 22/08/2011	9	5	22-AUG-11 16.20.34	U	59488700
	16:20:06 22/08/2011	16:20:34 22/08/2011	9	5	22-AUG-11 16.20.34	U	

It is possible to write more sophisticated queries making use of SQL analytic functions. Listing 9-29 is an example query that reports the five processes that have the longest cumulative execution time on successful completions in the last 30 days.

Listing 9-29. Top Five Processes in the Last 30 Days

```
SELECT x.*
,    d.descr
FROM    (
     SELECT prcstype, prcsname
     ,        dur
     ,        avg_dur
     ,        freq
     ,        RANK() OVER (ORDER BY dur DESC) prcrnk
     FROM    (
          SELECT prcstype, prcsname
          ,        COUNT(*) freq
          ,        SUM(CAST(r.enddttm AS DATE)-CAST(r.begindttm AS DATE))*86400 dur
          ,        AVG(CAST(r.enddttm AS DATE)-CAST(r.begindttm AS DATE))*86400 avg_dur
          FROM    psprcsrqst r
          WHERE   begindttm < enddttm /*have completed*/
          AND     runstatus IN(9,11,12,13,14,15,16,17) /*successful proc*/
          AND     begindttm > SYSDATE - 30 /*in the last 30 days*/
          AND     prcstype != 'PSJob' /*omit job records*/
          GROUP BY prcstype, prcsname
          )
     ) x
LEFT OUTER JOIN ps_prcsdefn d
        ON    d.prcstype = x.prcstype
        AND   d.prcsname = x.prcsname
WHERE   x.prcrnk <= 5
ORDER BY x.prcrnk
```

```
/
PRCSTYPE              PRCSNAME        DUR  AVG_DUR  FREQ  PRCRNK
--------------------  -------------   ----  --------  -----  -------
SQR Report            XRFFLRC          770      770     1       1
SQR Report            DDDAUDIT         672      336     2       2
SQR Report            XRFRCFL          618      618     1       3
Application Engine    HRS_DM_SYNC      510      255     2       4
SQR Report            XRFIELDS         456      152     3       5
```

Purging the Process Scheduler Tables

The Process Scheduler request table can grow at a significant rate; in some busy systems, I have seen thousands of requests per day. As the table grows, the performance of the Process Monitor and the Process Scheduler degrades. Therefore, it is important to purge this table of completed requests as aggressively as possible. Purging is vanilla PeopleSoft functionality.

If you are purging for the first time, or if you change the purge parameters so that you delete an unusually large amount of data, it may be advisable to rebuild the tables from which you have deleted data in order to reset their high-water marks. One option is to use Application Designer to build an Alter Table script where the build options are set to "Alter even if no changes" and "Alter by table rename". Alternatively, you can rebuild the table with the ALTER TABLE MOVE command and then rebuild the indexes that would have become unusable. Either method requires system downtime: not only must all Process Schedulers be stopped, but also the users must be prevented from scheduling new requests.

Delivered Purge Process

From PeopleTools 8.4, there is a new Application Engine process called PRCSYSPURGE that replaces the SQR process used in previous versions. The details of the purge process are hidden within the PurgeProcessRequest() and ArchiveReportMgr() PeopleCode functions called from this process. However, the SQL commands can be revealed by a PeopleTools trace.

At the same time, a new table, PSPRCSRQSTARCH, was introduced. There was also a new option on the Process Scheduler Purge Settings page: Archive Process Requests. The PRCSYSPURGE process does copy rows to be purged from PSPRCSRQST into PSPRCSRQSTARCH, but it also deletes rows that were inserted by the previous execution of the purge process. So despite the name, this table does not form a long-term archive of Process Scheduler request data.

Archiving Trigger

The data that is, and should be, purged by the Process Scheduler is the same data that I described earlier as a rich the source of batch performance metrics, so it needs to be retained in a different table.

I suggest creating a copy of the PSPRCSRQST record in Application Designer and building this as an archive table, in this case called PS_PRCSRQSTARCH. It is advisable to have at least the same unique key index on both tables. The easiest way is simply to duplicate the record in Application Designer. Then, create a trigger that copies the record into the archive table when it is deleted from the request table.

Over the years, new columns have been added to PSPRCSRQST. Rather than supply a script that creates the trigger, I have provided a script in Listing 9-30 that dynamically builds a script to create the trigger. Thus all the columns in PSPRCSRQST are built into the INSERT statement in the trigger.

Listing 9-30. prcsarch.sql: Script to Generate a Script to Create an Archiving Trigger

```
rem prcsarch.sql
set head off trimout on trimspool on message off feedback off timi off echo off
spool prcsarch0.sql
SELECT 'CREATE OR REPLACE TRIGGER '||user||'.psprcsrqst_archive'
FROM    dual
;
SELECT 'BEFORE DELETE ON '||user||'.psprcsrqst'
FROM    dual
;
SELECT 'FOR EACH ROW'
FROM    dual
;
SELECT 'BEGIN'
FROM    dual
;
SELECT '   INSERT INTO '||user||'.ps_prcsrqstarch'
FROM    dual
;
SELECT '   '||DECODE(column_id,1,'(',',')||column_name
FROM    user_tab_columns
WHERE   table_name = 'PSPRCSRQST'
ORDER BY column_id
;
SELECT '   ) VALUES'
FROM    dual
;
SELECT '   '||DECODE(column_id,1,'(',',')||':old.'||column_name
FROM    user_tab_columns
WHERE   table_name = 'PSPRCSRQST'
ORDER BY column_id
;
SELECT '   );'
FROM    dual
;
SELECT 'end;'
FROM    dual
;
SELECT '/'
FROM    dual
;
spool off
set head on message on feedback on echo on
spool prcsarch
@prcsarch0
show errors
set echo off
SELECT COUNT(*) psprcsrqst      FROM psprcsrqst;
DELETE                          FROM psprcsrqst WHERE runstatus=2;
SELECT COUNT(*) psprcsrqst      FROM psprcsrqst;
```

```
SELECT COUNT(*) ps_prcsrqstarch FROM ps_prcsrqstarch;
ROLLBACK;
spool off
```

The output of this script is shown in Listing 9-31.

Listing 9-31. `prcsarch0.sql`*: Script to Create an Archiving Trigger*

```
CREATE OR REPLACE TRIGGER SYSADM.psprcsrqst_archive
BEFORE DELETE ON SYSADM.psprcsrqst
FOR EACH ROW
BEGIN
    INSERT INTO SYSADM.ps_prcsrqstarch
    (PRCSINSTANCE
...
    ,TIMEZONE
    ) VALUES
    (:old.PRCSINSTANCE
...
    ,:old.TIMEZONE
    );
end;
/
```

Queries on the performance data should now be run on the combination of both tables in order to get a complete view of performance. The tables can be combined within a query using an inline view, as shown in Listing 9-32.

Listing 9-32. *Querying the Live and Reporting Tables with an Inline UNION ALL View*

```
SELECT ...
FROM    (
        SELECT * FROM psprcsrqst
        UNION ALL
        SELECT * FROM ps_prcsrqstarch
        )
/
```

Purging Application Engine Batch Timings

The Batch Timings tables, populated as Application Engine programs complete successfully, are not automatically purged during the Process Scheduler tables. They are also a valuable source of performance metrics. PS_BAT_TIMINGS_DTL contains a row for each step of each process. Hence, it is possible to trend the run time of particular steps within an Application Engine, not just the whole program. However, on systems that run many Application Engine processes, the volume of data can build up quickly, and it can become difficult to work with the data.

I have written an Application Engine program[12] to aggregate and purge the data in the batch timings table by day and by program into other tables. The batch timings are purged in line with the Process Scheduler retention policy so that batch timings can still be seen in the Process Monitor.

Message Log

The Application Engine and COBOL processes also write timestamped records to the message log table, PS_MESSAGE_LOG. These messages can be seen in the Process Monitor. When a process terminates abnormally, the Process Scheduler may write rows on behalf of the processes.

When a COBOL process is initiated by the remote-call facility, it does not have a process instance, and there is no row on the process request table, PSPRCSRQST. However, the process still writes rows to the message log table, so this can be used to measure the execution time of remote call processes.

Process Scheduler Configuration

Two settings in the Process Scheduler configuration file ($PS_HOME/appserv/prcs/<process scheduler name>/psprcs.cfg) cause PeopleSoft COBOL and Application Engine processes to generate additional trace information. I describe these settings in the sections that follow.

COBOL Statement Timings

PeopleSoft still uses COBOL for some of its batch processing. There are COBOL processes in the Financials and Campus Solutions products and the Global Payroll & Absence calculation process.

SQL statements generated by PeopleSoft COBOL are termed either *static* or *dynamic*:

- Static statements are read into the COBOL read from the stored-statements table, PS_SQLSTMT_TBL, and are then executed dynamically.

- Dynamic statements are assembled at run time from static fragments that are hard-coded into the COBOL

Setting the TraceSQL flag in the Process Scheduler configuration file to 128 (see Listing 9-33) causes the COBOL process to produce a report detailing the aggregated elapsed time for each stored statement.

Listing 9-33. Trace-File Settings: Extract from psprcs.cfg

```
;-----------------------------------------------------------------------
; SQL Tracing Bitfield
;
; Bit       Type of tracing
; ---       ---------------
; 1         - SQL statements
; 2         - SQL statement variables
; 4         - SQL connect, disconnect, commit and rollback
; 8         - Row Fetch (indicates that it occurred, not data)
```

---

[12] An Application Designer project can be downloaded from www.go-faster.co.uk/scripts.htm#gfc_timings_arch.

```
; 16           - All other API calls except ssb
; 32           - Set Select Buffers (identifies the attributes of columns
;                 to be selected).
; 64           - Database API specific calls
; 128          - COBOL statement timings
; 256          - Sybase Bind information
; 512          - Sybase Fetch information
; 1024         - SQL Informational Trace
; 4096         - Manager information
; 8192         - Mapcore information
; Dynamic change allowed for TraceSql and TraceSqlMask
TraceSQL=128
```

There are some version differences to be aware of:

- This parameter can be dynamically changed from PeopleTools 8.4, so that trace settings can be modified without restarting the process scheduler or the Application Engine server processes.

- In PeopleTools 8.44, the options for bit values 1024, 4096, and 8192 were added.

Each COBOL process produces its own trace file. The path and name of the file are of the following form

```
<$PS_HOME>\appserv\prcs\<process scheduler name>\log_output\
<short process type>_<prcsname>_<prcsinstance>\
<long process type>_<prcsname>_<prcsinstance>.trc
```

where

- $PS_HOME is the root of the PeopleSoft installation, as chosen during the installation.

- <process scheduler name> is the name of the Process Scheduler, for which there is a directory of the same name.

- <short process type> is a two- or three-letter code indicating the type of program: CBL for COBOL, SQR, or Application Engine.

- <long process type> is a another string indicating the type of program: COBSQL for COBOL, SQR, or Application Engine.

- <prcsname> is the name of the process. This is up to eight characters.

- <prcsinstance> is the unique number that identifies each process request.

The report, shown in Listing 9-34, displays the amount of time taken by each stored and dynamic SQL statement in the process. Hence, you can determine where the most execution time was expended and direct any tuning effort accordingly.

Listing 9-34. *Extract from a Cobol Batch Timings Report*

```
PeopleSoft Batch Timings Report: cobsql_81282.trc

Encoding Scheme Used: Ansi
```

PeopleSoft Batch Statistics
(All timings in seconds)

Encoding Scheme Used: Ansi

Statement	Retrieve Count	Retrieve Time	Compile Count	Compile Time	Execute Count	Execute Time	Fetch Count	Fetch Time	STMT Time	TOTALS % SQL
(Unknown)	0	0.00	0	0.00	197989	852.19	0	0.00	852.19	10.23
COMMIT	0	0.00	0	0.00	112	1.03	0	0.00	1.03	0.01
CONNECT	0	0.00	0	0.00	188	0.26	0	0.00	0.26	0.00
DISCONNECT	0	0.00	0	0.00	188	0.05	0	0.00	0.05	0.00
DYNAMIC	0	0.00	0	0.00	0	0.00	7004	0.08	0.08	0.00
...										
GPPDPDM2_S_ABSDATR	1	0.01	1	0.00	1	110.39	414209	44.80	155.20	1.86
GPPDPDM2_S_ACHST	1	0.00	1	0.01	1	171.14	304964	9.94	181.09	2.17
GPPDPDM2_S_ACSEG	1	0.01	1	0.00	1	70.09	27357	1.12	71.22	0.85
GPPDPDM2_S_ED	1	0.00	1	0.01	1	11.29	9338	0.38	11.68	0.14
GPPDPDM2_S_RPIN	1	0.01	1	0.00	1	27.42	107865	2.59	30.02	0.36
GPPDPDM3_S_OLDADJ	1	0.01	1	0.00	3	0.08	7	0.00	0.09	0.00
GPPDPDM3_S_PLEFFDT	1	0.00	1	0.00	24094	9.97	24094	0.10	10.07	0.12
GPPDPDM3_S_PSADJ	1	0.00	1	0.01	4002	6.82	4002	0.00	6.83	0.08
GPPDPDM3_S_PSSADJ	1	0.00	1	0.00	4002	3.54	4002	0.00	3.54	0.04
GPPDPDM3_S_RSADJ	1	0.01	1	0.00	4002	14.14	4206	0.00	14.15	0.17
GPPDPDM3_S_SSADJ	1	0.01	1	0.00	4002	2.38	4002	0.00	2.39	0.03
GPPDPDM3_U_RSADJ	1	0.01	1	0.00	71	0.04	0	0.00	0.05	0.00
GPPDPDM4_S_PSECDTL	1	0.01	1	0.00	1	0.00	1	0.00	0.01	0.00
GPPDPDM4_S_TRGRMBR	1	0.00	1	0.00	1	0.01	108	0.00	0.01	0.00
GPPDPDM4_S_TRIGGER	1	0.00	1	0.00	1	4.21	289	0.01	4.22	0.05
GPPDPDM4_U_TRIGGER	4830	0.21	4830	1.60	23330	17.31	0	0.00	19.12	0.23
...										
PTPUSTAT_S_JOBINST	2	0.00	2	0.00	2	0.00	2	0.00	0.00	0.00
PTPUSTAT_U_PRCQUE	1	0.01	1	0.00	2	0.00	0	0.00	0.01	0.00
PTPUSTAT_U_PRCRQSB	1	0.00	1	0.00	1	0.00	0	0.00	0.00	0.00
PTPUSTAT_U_PRCRQSE	1	0.00	1	0.00	1	0.02	0	0.00	0.02	0.00
Total:	11655	1.50	11705	3.56	3319770	8165.87	9063444	159.67		
Percent of Total:		0.02%		0.04%		98.02%		1.92%		

	Time	% Total
Total in SQL:	8330.60	68.77
Total in Application:	3783.37	31.23
Total Run Time:	12113.97	

Total Statements:	345
Max Cursors Connected:	164

From PeopleTools 8, most dynamic statements are given a unique name of a format similar to the stored statements, and reported separately in the trace file. It is not possible to distinguish static from dynamic statements from just the batch timings report.

Application Engine Batch Timings

The TraceAE flag has a similar effect on Application Engine processes as TraceSQL does on PeopleSoft COBOL processes. It is also set in the Process Scheduler configuration file psprcs.cfg (see Listing 9-35).

Listing 9-35. Extract from psprcs.cfg

```
;-------------------------------------------------------------------------
; AE Tracing Bitfield
;
; Bit        Type of tracing
; ---        ---------------
; 1          - Trace STEP execution sequence to AET file
; 2          - Trace Application SQL statements to AET file
; 4          - Trace Dedicated Temp Table Allocation to AET file
; 8          - not yet allocated
; 16         - not yet allocated
; 32         - not yet allocated
; 64         - not yet allocated
; 128        - Timings Report to AET file
; 256        - Method/BuiltIn detail instead of summary in AET Timings Report
; 512        - not yet allocated
; 1024       - Timings Report to tables
; 2048       - DB optimizer trace to file
; 4096       - DB optimizer trace to tables
TraceAE=1152
```

TraceAE and the other PeopleTools trace parameters can be set on the Application Engine command line. Command-line settings override the setting in the Process Scheduler configuration file. For example, you might want to generate an Application Engine SQL trace for a particular Application Engine program. In Figure 9-8, I have enabled three forms of trace for the AEMINITEST program only:

- TRACE overrides the value of TraceAE in psprcs.cfg. I want to set the first three trace flags. However, if I had only set the value to 7, I would have disabled the batch timings reports. Therefore, whenever I specify trace this way, I also set the batch timings flags.

- TOOLSTRACESQL enables PeopleTools SQL trace. The bit values are shown in Listing 9-33.

- TOOLSTRACEPC emits additional PeopleCode information into the PeopleTools trace file. If bit 64 is set, the start and end of PeopleCode programs are written to the trace file. This can be helpful if you want to know which PeopleCode program issues a particular piece of SQL.

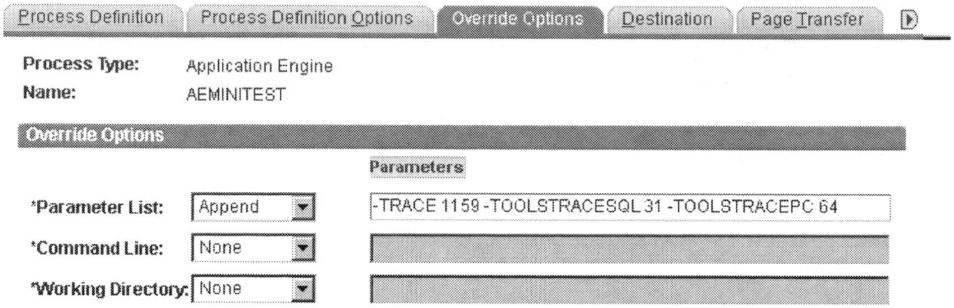

Figure 9-8. Example of appending command-line options for a specific AE program

Setting TraceAE to 128 causes the Application Engine to produce a report of step timings, similar to that produced by the COBOL processes. Listing 9-36 shows a sample of this report. It shows how much time has been spent in each operation on each step, and how many times that operation has been executed. It also contains an analysis of the time spent in PeopleCode.

■ **Note** Remember, the timings in PeopleSoft reports are elapsed times for the operations as measured in the client process. Therefore, they also include any database waits.

Listing 9-36. AE_PER099_181.AET: Application Engine Trace File with Batch Timings[13]

```
-- PeopleTools 8.44.09 -- Application Engine
-- Copyright (c) 1988-2004 PeopleSoft, Inc.
-- All Rights Reserved
-- Database: HR88 (Oracle)


                  PeopleSoft Application Engine Timings
                        (All timings in seconds)
                        2004-05-04   23.59.06

                     C o m p i l e   E x e c u t e   F e t c h       Total
SQL Statement        Count   Time    Count   Time    Count   Time    Time
------------------   ------- -------- ------- -------- ------- -------- --------

Application Engine

COMMIT                  0     0.0      78     4.1       0     0.0      4.1
                                                                    --------
                                                                       4.1
```

---

[13] This listing has been edited slightly for readability.

AE Program: PERO99

COPY.Step01.S	5	0.0	5	0.7	0	0.0	0.7
COPY.Step02.S	5	0.0	5	2.1	0	0.0	2.1
COPY.Step03.S	5	0.0	5	3.3	0	0.0	3.3
COPY_LNG.Step01.S	54	0.0	54	0.3	0	0.0	0.3
COPY_LNG.Step02.S	54	0.0	54	0.0	0	0.0	0.0
COPY_LNG.Step03.S	54	0.0	54	0.0	0	0.0	0.0
DELETES.Step01.S	1	0.0	1	2.6	0	0.0	2.6
DELETES.Step02.S	1	0.0	1	0.3	0	0.0	0.3
DELETES.Step03.S	1	0.0	1	0.2	0	0.0	0.2
DELETES.Step04.S	1	0.0	1	0.1	0	0.0	0.1
INIT.Step02.S	1	0.0	1	0.0	1	0.0	0.0
INSERT.Step01.S	1	0.0	1	3.8	0	0.0	3.8
RELLANG.Step02.D	1	0.0	1	0.1	19	0.0	0.1
UPDATE.Step01.S	1	0.0	1	1.2	0	0.0	1.2
UPDATE.Step03.S	1	0.0	1	0.9	0	0.0	0.9
UPDATE.Step05.S	1	0.0	1	3.1	0	0.0	3.1
UPDATE.Step09.S	1	0.0	1	1.1	0	0.0	1.1
UPDATE.Step11.S	1	0.0	1	1.1	0	0.0	1.1
UPD_LNG.DELETE.S	18	0.0	18	0.5	0	0.0	0.5
UPD_LNG.DEPT.S	18	0.0	18	0.8	0	0.0	0.8
UPD_LNG.EMPLMT.S	18	0.0	18	0.2	0	0.0	0.2
UPD_LNG.INITROWS.S	18	0.0	18	0.5	0	0.0	0.5
UPD_LNG.JOBCODE.S	18	0.0	18	0.4	0	0.0	0.4

```
                                                              --------
                                                                23.5
```

PeopleCode	Call Count	Non-SQL Time	SQL Time	Total Time

AE Program: PERO99

INIT.Step03	1	0.0	0.0	0.0
		0.0	0.0	0.0

PEOPLECODE Builtin/Method	Execute Count	Time
Boolean(Type 5) BuiltIns	1	0.0

Total run time   :   48.4

```
Total time in application SQL :      27.7   Percent time in application SQL :       57.1%

Total time in PeopleCode      :       0.0   Percent time in PeopleCode      :        0.0%

Total time in cache           :       4.0   Number of calls to cache        :          11
```

```
PeopleTools SQL Trace value: 128 (0x80)
PeopleTools PeopleCode Trace value: 0 (0)
Application Engine Trace value: 1152 (0x480)
Application Engine DbFlags value: 0 (0)
```

However, if TraceAE is set to 1024, then this information is stored on three tables in the database: PS_BAT_TIMINGS_DTL, PS_BAT_TIMINGS_FN, and PS_BAT_TIMINGS_LOG. Data is only inserted into these tables when a process completes successfully. If you want both the trace file and the batch timings enabled, set TraceAE to 1152, and both bits are set. These statistics can then be viewed in the Process Monitor (see Figure 9-9) for a given process instance.

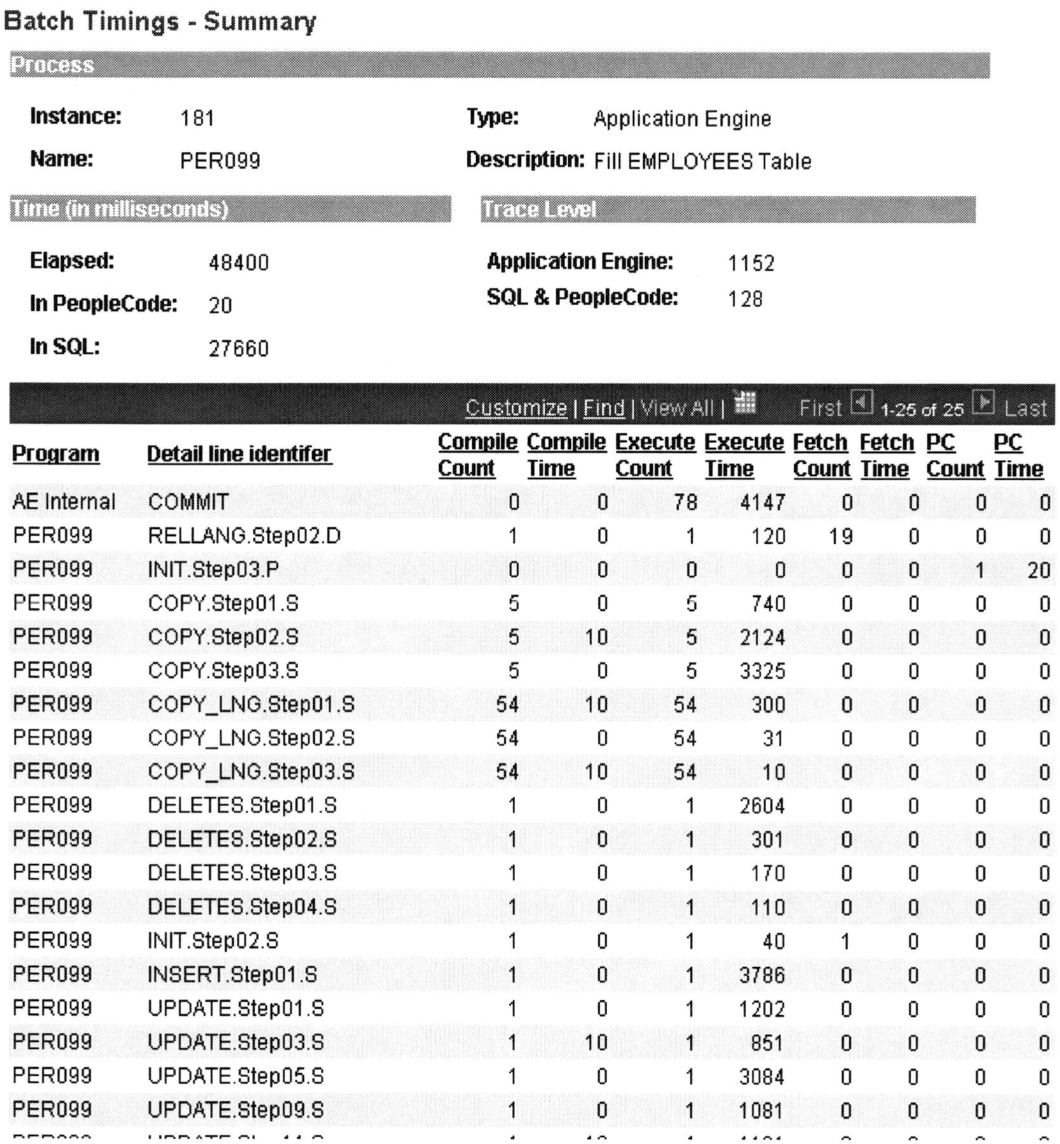

Batch Timings - Summary

Process

Instance:	181	Type:	Application Engine
Name:	PER099	Description:	Fill EMPLOYEES Table

Time (in milliseconds)

Elapsed:	48400
In PeopleCode:	20
In SQL:	27660

Trace Level

Application Engine:	1152
SQL & PeopleCode:	128

Customize | Find | View All | First ◄ 1-25 of 25 ► Last

Program	Detail line identifer	Compile Count	Compile Time	Execute Count	Execute Time	Fetch Count	Fetch Time	PC Count	PC Time
AE Internal	COMMIT	0	0	78	4147	0	0	0	0
PER099	RELLANG.Step02.D	1	0	1	120	19	0	0	0
PER099	INIT.Step03.P	0	0	0	0	0	0	1	20
PER099	COPY.Step01.S	5	0	5	740	0	0	0	0
PER099	COPY.Step02.S	5	10	5	2124	0	0	0	0
PER099	COPY.Step03.S	5	0	5	3325	0	0	0	0
PER099	COPY_LNG.Step01.S	54	10	54	300	0	0	0	0
PER099	COPY_LNG.Step02.S	54	0	54	31	0	0	0	0
PER099	COPY_LNG.Step03.S	54	10	54	10	0	0	0	0
PER099	DELETES.Step01.S	1	0	1	2604	0	0	0	0
PER099	DELETES.Step02.S	1	0	1	301	0	0	0	0
PER099	DELETES.Step03.S	1	0	1	170	0	0	0	0
PER099	DELETES.Step04.S	1	0	1	110	0	0	0	0
PER099	INIT.Step02.S	1	0	1	40	1	0	0	0
PER099	INSERT.Step01.S	1	0	1	3786	0	0	0	0
PER099	UPDATE.Step01.S	1	0	1	1202	0	0	0	0
PER099	UPDATE.Step03.S	1	10	1	851	0	0	0	0
PER099	UPDATE.Step05.S	1	0	1	3084	0	0	0	0
PER099	UPDATE.Step09.S	1	0	1	1081	0	0	0	0

Figure 9-9. Batch timings in the Process Monitor

However, this data can also be queried directly from the database, as shown in Listing 9-37. This query aggregates the timing data from all executions and reports the top 20 Application Engine steps by their cumulative execution time.

Once the TraceAE flag is set, a set of metrics begins to build up that describes the performance of all the Application Engine processing. Hence, it is possible to determine which steps are consuming the most time across the whole system.

Listing 9-37. topae.sql: Top 20 Application Engine Steps by Cumulative Total Execution Time

```
SET PAUSE OFF AUTOTRACE OFF ECHO OFF PAGES 40 LINES 80
COLUMN stmtrank              HEADING 'Stmt|Rank'         FORMAT 99
COLUMN detail_id             HEADING 'Statement ID'      FORMAT a21
COLUMN pct_sqltime           HEADING '%|SQL|Time'        FORMAT 90.0
COLUMN pct_total_time        HEADING '%|Total|Time'      FORMAT 90.0
COLUMN cum_pc_sqltime        HEADING 'Cum %|SQL|Time'    FORMAT 90.0
COLUMN cum_pc_total_time HEADING 'Cum %|Total|Time' FORMAT 90.0
COLUMN executions            HEADING 'Execs'             FORMAT 9990
COLUMN compile_time          HEADING 'Compile|Time'      FORMAT 9990.0
COLUMN compile_count         HEADING 'Compile|Count'     FORMAT 9990
COLUMN fetch_time            HEADING 'Fetch|Time'        FORMAT 9990.0
COLUMN fetch_count           HEADING 'Fetch|Count'       FORMAT 9990
COLUMN retrieve_time         HEADING 'Retrieve|Time'     FORMAT 9990.0
COLUMN retrieve_count        HEADING 'Retrieve|Count'    FORMAT 9990
COLUMN execute_time          HEADING 'Exec|Time'         FORMAT 9990.0
COLUMN execute_count         HEADING 'Exec|Count'        FORMAT 9990
COLUMN ae_sqltime            HEADING 'AE|SQL|Time'       FORMAT 9990.0
COLUMN pc_sqltime            HEADING 'PC|SQL|Time'       FORMAT 9990.0
COLUMN pc_time               HEADING 'PC|Time'           FORMAT 990.0
COLUMN pc_count              HEADING 'PC|Count'          FORMAT 9990
spool topae
SELECT stmtrank
,       detail_id
,       execute_count
,       ae_sqltime
,       pc_sqltime
,       pc_time
,       ratio_sqltime*100 pct_sqltime
,       SUM(ratio_sqltime*100)
            OVER (ORDER BY stmtrank RANGE UNBOUNDED PRECEDING) cum_pc_sqltime
,       ratio_total_time*100 pct_total_time
,       SUM(ratio_total_time*100)
            OVER (ORDER BY stmtrank RANGE UNBOUNDED PRECEDING) cum_pc_total_time
FROM    (
        SELECT rank() OVER (ORDER BY sqltime desc) as stmtrank
        ,       a.*
        ,       RATIO_TO_REPORT(sqltime) OVER () as ratio_sqltime
        ,       RATIO_TO_REPORT(total_time) OVER () as ratio_total_time
        FROM    (
                SELECT bat_program_name||'.'||detail_id detail_id
                ,       COUNT(distinct process_instance) executions
--              ,       SUM(compile_time)/1000 compile_time
--              ,       SUM(compile_count) compile_count
--              ,       SUM(fetch_time)/1000 fetch_time
--              ,       SUM(fetch_count) fetch_count
--              ,       SUM(retrieve_time)/1000 retrieve_time
--              ,       SUM(retrieve_count) retrieve_count
                ,       SUM(execute_time)/1000 execute_time
                ,       SUM(execute_count) execute_count
```

```
        ,        SUM(peoplecodesqltime)/1000 pc_sqltime
        ,        SUM(peoplecodetime)/1000 pc_time
        ,        SUM(peoplecodecount) pc_count
        ,        SUM(execute_time +compile_time +fetch_time +retrieve_time)
                   /1000 ae_sqltime
        ,        SUM(execute_time +compile_time +fetch_time +retrieve_time
                   +peoplecodesqltime)/1000 sqltime
        ,        SUM(execute_time +compile_time +fetch_time +retrieve_time
                   +peoplecodesqltime +peoplecodetime)/1000 total_time
        FROM   ps_bat_timings_dtl a
        GROUP BY bat_program_name, detail_id
        ) a
      )
WHERE   stmtrank <= 20
/
spool off
```

The result is a simple report (see Listing 9-38) that tells you which Application Engine steps are consuming the most processing time.

Listing 9-38. `topae.lst:` *Report of Top Application Engine Statements*

Stmt Rank	Statement ID	Exec Count	AE SQL Time	PC SQL Time	PC Time	% SQL Time	Cum % SQL Time	% Total Time	Cum % Total Time
1	HR_FASTVIEW.SEC_UPD.S tep01.D	39	6.4	0.0	0.0	16.4	16.4	4.8	4.8
2	AE Internal.COMMIT	101	4.8	0.0	0.0	12.3	28.7	3.6	8.5
3	PER099.INSERT.Step01. S	1	3.8	0.0	0.0	9.7	38.5	2.9	11.4
4	PER099.COPY.Step03.S	5	3.3	0.0	0.0	8.6	47.0	2.5	13.9
5	PER099.UPDATE.Step05.	1	3.1	0.0	0.0	7.9	54.9	2.3	16.2

...

NEGATIVE TIMINGS IN BATCH-TIMING REPORTS

Sometimes you can get negative times reported for a single line in a batch timings report. Both COBOL and Application Engine exhibit this behavior. I believe this occurs when the timer used to calculate step durations wraps round to 0. Hence only one line in the report is affected:

```
              PeopleSoft Application Engine Timings
                    (All timings in seconds)
                     2011-09-26  02.28.20

                  C o m p i l e  E x e c u t e  F e t c h     Total
SQL Statement        Count Time    Count Time   Count Time      Time
---------------------- ----- -------- ----- -------- ----- -------- --------
```

```
AE Program: TL_TA001300
...
TA001300.Step013B.S          53     0.0     53  -42838.9    0      0.0 -42838.8
...
-----------------------------------------------------------------------------

Total run time               :-34564.4

Total time in application SQL:-34592.9  Percent time in application SQL:100.1%

Total time in PeopleCode     :     0.5  Percent time in PeopleCode     : -0.0%

Total time in cache          :     2.0  Number of calls to cache       :  6042
```

It is possible to calculate the overall run time from the begin and end timestamps on PS_BAT_TIMINGS_LOG and hence reconstruct the corrupted data:

```
SELECT begindttm, enddttm FROM ps_bat_timings_log
WHERE process_instance = 6781529
```

```
BEGINDTTM              ENDDTTM              TIME_ELAPSED
-------------------    -------------------  ------------
00:08:35 26/09/2011 02:28:20 26/09/2011    -34564453
```

The process actually ran for 8385 seconds, and I can calculate a correction:

```
Correction = 8385-(-34564.453)=42949.453
```

The correction can be added to each of the negative numbers:

```
                       C o m p i l e  E x e c u t e  F e t c h     Total
SQL Statement          Count Time     Count Time     Count Time    Time
---------------------- ----- -------- ----- -------- ----- ------- --------
TA001300.Step013B.S       53     0.0    53    110.5     0     0.0    110.6
```

Enhanced Application Engine Batch Timings

From PeopleTools 8.50, bit 16384 on TraceAE enables batch timings to be written to two new tables PS_AE_TIMINGS_LG and PS_AE_TIMINGS_DT. This setting is not mentioned in the comments in any of the configuration file (shown in Listing 9-35), but it is described in PeopleBooks.

   PS_AE_TIMINGS_LG has the same structure as PS_BAT_TIMINGS_LOG. It seems to hold the same data, though I have noticed small discrepancies in the timings.

   PS_AE_TIMINGS_DT has a structure similar to PS_BAT_TIMINGS_DTL but with some additional columns that hold more detail that identifies source code. An important difference is the reporting of SQL issued from within PeopleCode steps. Listing 9-39 shows the contents of PS_BAT_TIMINGS_DTL for the four long-running SQL statements from the Performance Monitor Archive process. I have also shown the line that indicates that the PeopleCode step PSPM_ARCHIVE.ARCHIVE.ARCPCODE.P took 233.229s. I happen to know that these four SQL statements were all issued by the one PeopleCode step, but nothing in the batch timings indicates that.

Listing 9-39. *Entries from PS_BAT_TIMINGS_DTL*

```
      BAT  BAT          BAT
      PROC PROGRAM      DTL  DETAIL                                      COMPILE COMPILE
P.I.  TYPE NAME         TYPE ID                                          COUNT   TIME
----- ---- ------------ ---- ------------------------------------------- ------- -------
EXECUTE EXECUTE  FETCH  FETCH RETRIEVE RETRIEVE BULK  PCode  PCode   PCode CURR EXEC
COUNT   TIME     COUNT  TIME  COUNT    TIME INSE Count SQLTime Time  ROUN EDIT
------- ------- ------- ----- -------- -------- ---- ------- ------- ------- ---- ----
 911 A    PSPM_ARCHIVE   3 ARCHIVE.ARCPCODE.P                              0       0
   0      0       0      0       0        0 N       1  233229    5702 N    N

 911 A    PeopleCode     9 INSERT PSPMEVENTARCH(PM_INSTANCE_ID,           0       0
57963  183221     0      0       0        0 Y       0       0       0 N    N

 911 A    PeopleCode     9 INSERT PSPMTRANSARCH(PM_INSTANCE_ID,           0       0
 8087   41865     0      0       0        0 Y       0       0       0 N    N

 911 A    PeopleCode     9 SELECT PSPMEVENTHIST                           0       0
   58      31   57964   5294      0        0 N       0       0       0 N    N

 911 A    PeopleCode     9 DELETE PSPMEVENTHIST                           0       0
   58    1435     0      0       0        0 N       0       0       0 N    N
```

Listing 9-40 shows the corresponding rows from PS_BAT_TIMINGS_DT that relate to the same step and the same four SQL statements. Now I can see which PeopleCode step submitted the SQL.

Listing 9-40. *Entries from PS_AE_TIMINGS_DT*

```
      BAT  BAT          BAT
      PROC PROGRAM      DTL  DETAIL                DETAIL
P.I.  TYPE NAME         TYPE ID                    ID2
----- ---- ------------ ---- -------------------- --------------------------------------------
DETAIL                                       PTPC     PTPC COMPILE COMPILE EXECUTE
ID3                                          SQLLINE EXECLINE COUNT   TIME    COUNT
-------------------------------------------- ------- -------- ------- ------- -------
EXECUTE  FETCH  FETCH RETRIEVE RETRIEVE BULK  PCode  PCode   PCode CURR EXEC
TIME     COUNT  TIME  COUNT    TIME INSE Count SQLTime Time  ROUN EDIT
-------  -----  ----- -------- -------- ---- ------- ------- ------- ---- ----
 911 A    PSPM_ARCHIVE    3 ARCHIVE.ARCPCODE.P
                                              0        0       0       0       0
   0       0      0       0        0 N       1  233229    5702 N    N

 911 A    PSPM_ARCHIVE    9 ARCHIVE.ARCPCODE.P   INSERT PSPMEVENTARCH(PM_INSTANCE_ID,
AEAPPLICATIONID.PSPM_ARCHIVE.AESECTION.A...   37      -1       0       0       57963
183221    0      0       0        0 Y       0       0       0 N    N

 911 A    PSPM_ARCHIVE    9 ARCHIVE.ARCPCODE.P   INSERT PSPMTRANSARCH(PM_INSTANCE_ID,
AEAPPLICATIONID.PSPM_ARCHIVE.AESECTION.A...    9      -1       0       0       8087
 41865    0      0       0        0 Y       0       0       0 N    N
```

```
   911 A     PSPM_ARCHIVE    9 ARCHIVE.ARCPCODE.P    SELECT PSPMEVENTHIST
AEAPPLICATIONID.PSPM_ARCHIVE.AESECTION.A...        -1      35     0        0        0
     0   57964    5294       0        0 N         0       0      0 N      N

   911 A     PSPM_ARCHIVE    9 ARCHIVE.ARCPCODE.P    DELETE PSPMEVENTHIST
AEAPPLICATIONID.PSPM_ARCHIVE.AESECTION.A...        50      -1     0        0       58
  1435      0       0        0        0 N         0       0      0 N      N
```

PeopleSoft Trace Files

All PeopleTools client and application server processes that connect to the database can produce PeopleTools trace files. The level of detail can be controlled, but they can show the following:

- The SQL submitted by the process

- Any PeopleCode executed

- The duration of the SQL execute or fetch operations

- The time since the last trace line was emitted

In this section, I discuss how PeopleTools trace can be enabled for various components in the PeopleSoft architecture, and I show how the trace files can be analyzed.

Application Designer and Client

The Configuration Manager, shown in Figure 9-10, enables the user to set trace flags that are picked up by the PS/Query and nVision Windows clients, the Application Designer tool, and Data Mover.

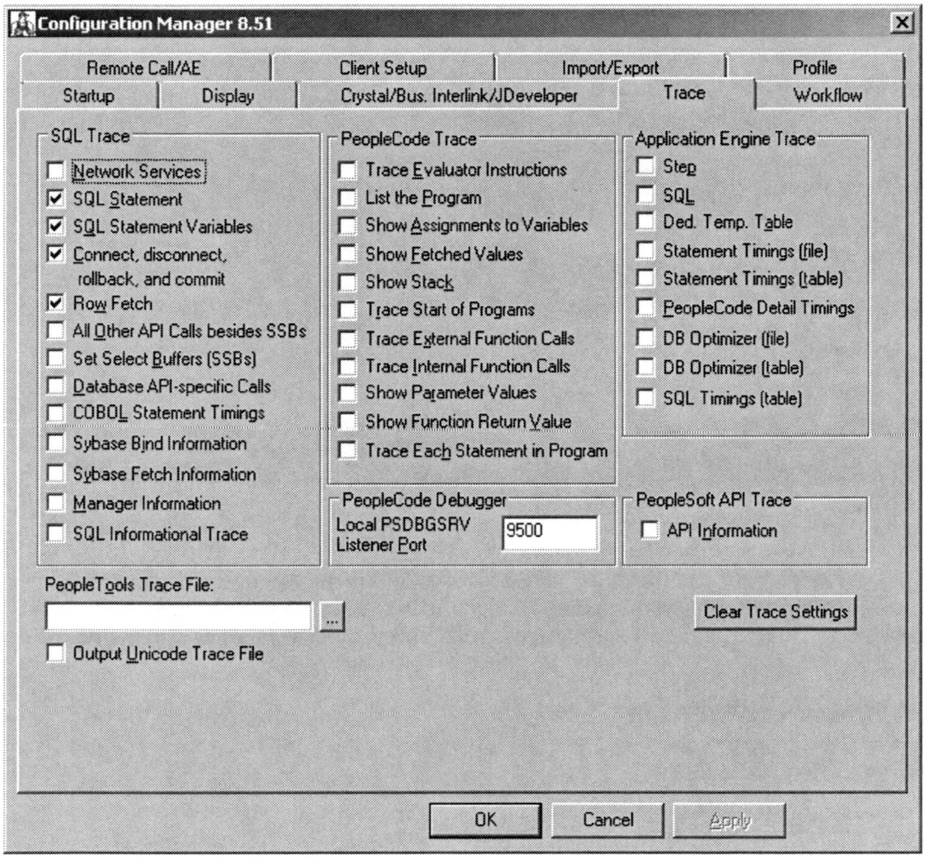

Figure 9-10. Configuration Manager

It is effectively a method of setting some registry keys that invoke the trace. Different Enterprise release versions of PeopleTools write to different registry keys and so can coexist. The three registry keys shown in Figure 9-11 correspond to the three sets of trace flags in Figure 9-9. Each check box corresponds to a bit in a binary number, and that number is stored in the registry.

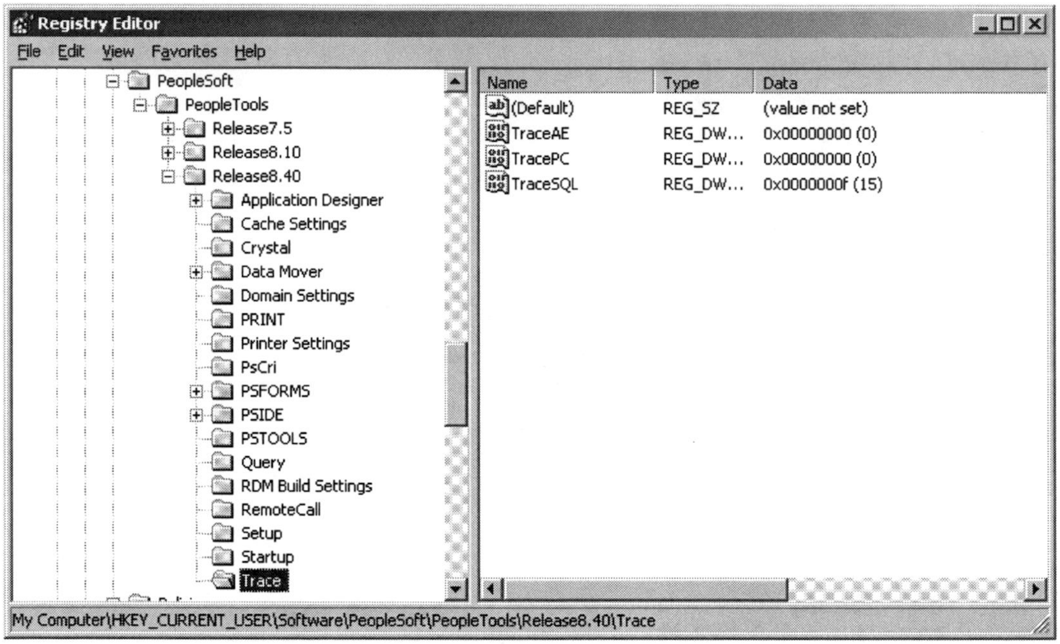

Figure 9-11. PeopleTools trace registry settings

The trace file that is subsequently produced is called DBG1.tmp and is written to the directory indicated by the Windows environment variable %TEMP%. Each line in the trace (see Listing 9-41) has an elapsed duration in seconds. This can be used to find the parts of the processing that are taking the most time.

Listing 9-41. Extract of Windows Client Trace DBG1.tmp

```
PeopleTools 8.51 Client Trace - 2011-10-25

PID-Line  Time       Elapsed   Trace Data...
--------  --------   ---------- -------------------->
 1-1      10.24.12             Tuxedo session opened {oprid='PS', appname='TwoTier',
addr='//TwoTier:7000', open at 059200D0, pid=9540}
 1-2      10.24.14   2.332000 Cur#0.9540.HCM91 RC=0 Dur=2.270000 Create Connection
Info=Primary/HCM91/people/ Handle=0593FBC8
 1-3      10.24.14   0.002000 Cur#1.9540.notSamTran RC=0 Dur=0.002000 Open Cursor
Handle=0593FBC8
...
1-865    10.24.21   2.492000 Cur#1.9540.notSamTran RC=0 Dur=0.000000 Open Cursor
Handle=0593FBC8
1-866    10.24.21   0.000000 Cur#1.9540.HCM91 RC=0 Dur=0.000000 COM Stmt=SELECT DISPLAYONLY
FROM PSOPROBJ A, PSOBJGROUP B WHERE B.ENTTYPE = :1 AND B.ENTNAME = :2 AND A.CLASSID = :3 AND
(A.OBJGROUPID = '*ALL DEFINITIONS*'   OR A.OBJGROUPID = B.OBJGROUPID) UNION SELECT 2 FROM
PSOBJGROUP WHERE ENTTYPE = :4 AND ENTNAME = :5 ORDER BY 1
```

```
1-867    10.24.21    0.000000 Cur#1.9540.HCM91 RC=0 Dur=0.000000 Bind-1 type=1 length=1
value=J
1-868    10.24.21    0.000000 Cur#1.9540.HCM91 RC=0 Dur=0.000000 Bind-2 type=2 length=1
value=
1-869    10.24.21    0.000000 Cur#1.9540.HCM91 RC=0 Dur=0.000000 Bind-3 type=2 length=7
value=HCPPALL
1-870    10.24.21    0.000000 Cur#1.9540.HCM91 RC=0 Dur=0.000000 Bind-4 type=1 length=1
value=J
1-871    10.24.21    0.000000 Cur#1.9540.HCM91 RC=0 Dur=0.000000 Bind-5 type=2 length=1
value=
1-872    10.24.21    0.001000 Cur#1.9540.HCM91 RC=1 Dur=0.000000 Fetch
1-873    10.24.21    0.000000 Cur#1.9540.HCM91 RC=0 Dur=0.000000 Commit
```

Application Server

The application server can be traced in a similar way. The TraceSQL flag in the application server configuration file psappsrv.cfg (see Listing 9-42) enables trace for all server processes.

Listing 9-42. Extract from psappsrv.cfg

```
;-------------------------------------------------------------------------
; SQL Tracing Bitfield
;
; Bit        Type of tracing
; ---        ---------------
; 1          - SQL statements
; 2          - SQL statement variables
; 4          - SQL connect, disconnect, commit and rollback
; 8          - Row Fetch (indicates that it occurred, not data)
; 16         - All other API calls except ssb
; 32         - Set Select Buffers (identifies the attributes of columns
;                to be selected).
; 64         - Database API specific calls
; 128        - COBOL statement timings
; 256        - Sybase Bind information
; 512        - Sybase Fetch information
; 1024       - SQL Informational Trace
; 4096       - Manager information
; 8192       - Mapcore information
; Dynamic change allowed for TraceSql and TraceSqlMask
TraceSql=15
TraceSqlMask=12319
```

When the server is started, the trace file is generated as <operator ID>_<server name>.tracesql, where operator ID is the operator used to start the application server, specified in the Startup section of the configuration file. As each service request is received by the server process, the trace is switched to a new file called <operator ID>_<client machine name>.tracesql (see Listing 9-43). If the machine name cannot be determined, the IP address is used instead. So, a trace file is produced for each operator/machine combination.

Listing 9-43. Extract of Client Trace File PS_go-faster-3.tracesql

```
PSAPPSRV.4060   1-1853   19.52.52   0.060 Cur#1.4060.HR88 RC=0 Dur=0.030 COM Stmt=Select
COUNTRY, STATE from PS_PERSON_ADDRESS where ADDRESS_TYPE = 'HOME' and EMPLID = :1
PSAPPSRV.4060   1-1854   19.52.52   0.000 Cur#1.4060.HR88 RC=0 Dur=0.000 Bind-1 type=2
length=1 value=
PSAPPSRV.4060   1-1855   19.52.52   0.541 Cur#1.4060.HR88 RC=1 Dur=0.000 Fetch
```

There is no heading on the application server log as there is on the client log, but the structure is essentially the same. Additional columns identify the server process name and process ID.

Enabling server-wide trace this way is a very blunt instrument. You generate a lot of trace, it has a significant overhead on performance, and the trace files are fairly difficult to process. I would be much more likely to enable Oracle SQL trace for all of the PSAPPSRV processes than PeopleTools SQL trace.

■ **Caution** There is also a significant performance overhead to this trace. Tracing fetches considerably increases the amount and overhead of trace. I have experienced up to a 20% increase in response times. Trace should be used sparingly in a production environment, and only the elements of interest should be traced.

PIA Trace

Occasionally you want to get metrics for a particular transaction. One method is to configure an application server with just a single PSAPPSRV process. You also need a PIA domain that references only that application server. Then you know that all the activity goes through that application server process, and you can enable SQL trace for that database session. It is not always possible to implement this quickly—or at all—in a production environment.

The alternative is to enable PeopleTools SQL trace for that session. This can be done in two ways. First, the operator can enable trace for their session at login. There is a link to an alternative login page from which trace options can be set, as shown in Figure 9-12.

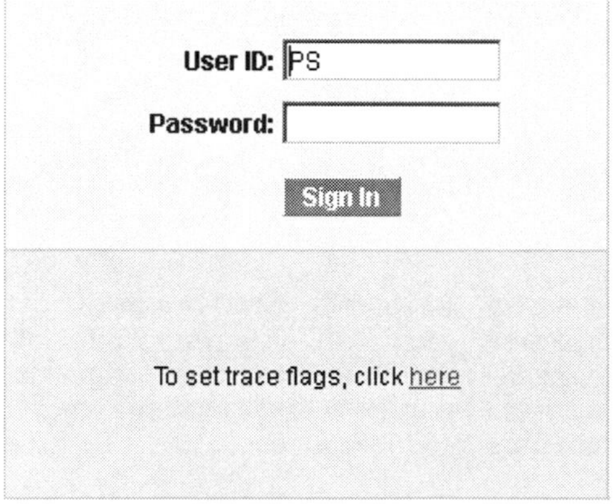

Figure 9-12. PIA login challenge

SUPPRESSING THE TRACE LINK ON THE PIA SIGN-ON PAGE

From PeopleTools 8.44 onward, the link to the trace options on the login screen can be suppressed in the web profile by choosing PeopleTools Web Profile Web Profile Configuration.

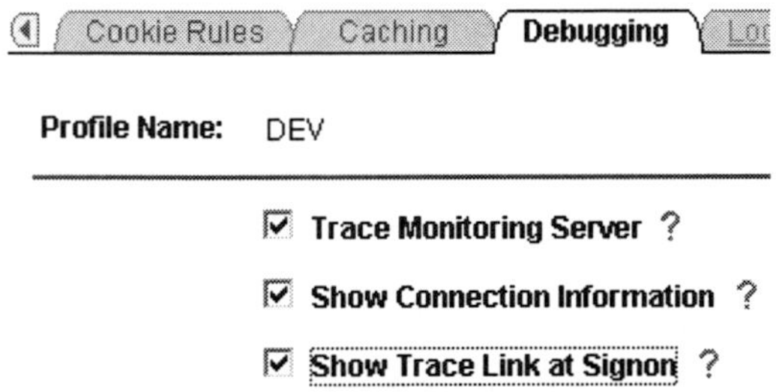

| ◄ | Cookie Rules | Caching | **Debugging** | Lo |

Profile Name: DEV

☑ **Trace Monitoring Server** ?

☑ **Show Connection Information** ?

☑ **Show Trace Link at Signon** ?

If the trace link has been suppressed, you can get to the trace-configuration page by manually adding &trace=y to the URL of the sign-on page:

```
http://go-faster-4:8400/psp/hcm/?cmd=login&trace=y
```

A large number of diagnostic trace options are available in PeopleTools. In the following example (see Figure 9-13), I have chosen to trace all SQL statements, including fetch and commit operations. Bind variable values are also logged. Then all the SQL issued by this user's session is logged to a file in the application server log directory.

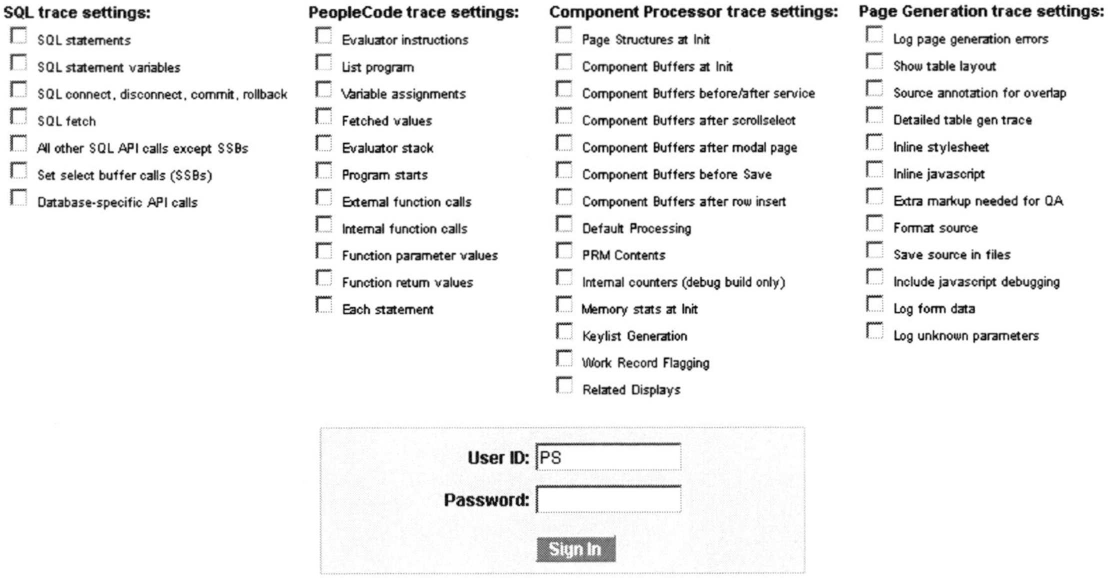

SQL trace settings:	PeopleCode trace settings:	Component Processor trace settings:	Page Generation trace settings:
☐ SQL statements	☐ Evaluator instructions	☐ Page Structures at Init	☐ Log page generation errors
☐ SQL statement variables	☐ List program	☐ Component Buffers at Init	☐ Show table layout
☐ SQL connect, disconnect, commit, rollback	☐ Variable assignments	☐ Component Buffers before/after service	☐ Source annotation for overlap
☐ SQL fetch	☐ Fetched values	☐ Component Buffers after scrollselect	☐ Detailed table gen trace
☐ All other SQL API calls except SSBs	☐ Evaluator stack	☐ Component Buffers after modal page	☐ Inline stylesheet
☐ Set select buffer calls (SSBs)	☐ Program starts	☐ Component Buffers before Save	☐ Inline javascript
☐ Database-specific API calls	☐ External function calls	☐ Component Buffers after row insert	☐ Extra markup needed for QA
	☐ Internal function calls	☐ Default Processing	☐ Format source
	☐ Function parameter values	☐ PRM Contents	☐ Save source in files
	☐ Function return values	☐ Internal counters (debug build only)	☐ Include javascript debugging
	☐ Each statement	☐ Memory stats at Init	☐ Log form data
		☐ Keylist Generation	☐ Log unknown parameters
		☐ Work Record Flagging	
		☐ Related Displays	

User ID: PS

Password:

Sign In

Figure 9-13. PIA sign-on trace option

> ■ **Tip** If you are not sure which application server you are connected to, press Ctrl+J to get the address and port number of the Jolt Listener.[14] You need access to the application server's log directory in order to obtain the trace file.

Trace can be also enabled or disabled midsession by opening a new window, navigating to PeopleTools ▸ Utilities ▸ Debug ▸ Trace SQL (see Figure 9-14), and setting the trace flags as required. There is a separate page on the same menu to enable PeopleCode traces.

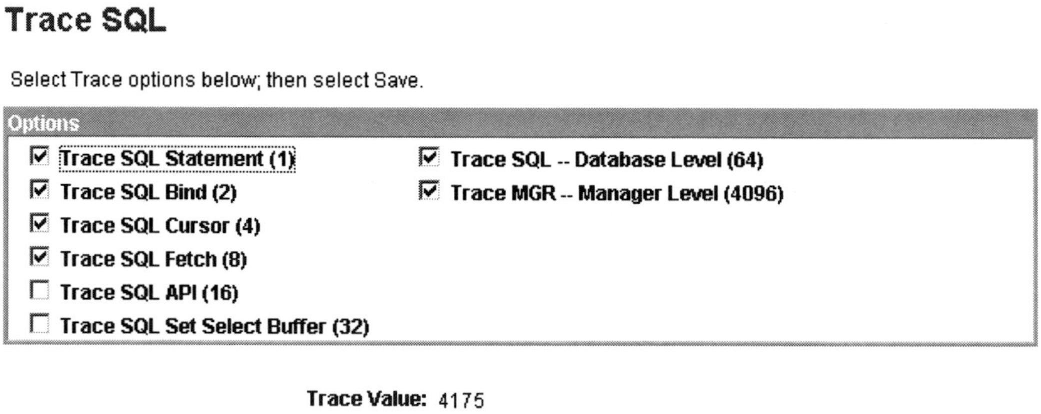

Trace SQL

Select Trace options below; then select Save.

Figure 9-14. Selecting trace options

The earlier warnings about the impact on performance still apply. PeopleTools trace can seriously degrade application server performance. The resulting trace file is shown in Listing 9-44.

Listing 9-44. Extract of the PeopleTools Trace File `PS_go-faster-3.tracesql`

```
PSAPPSRV.4060   1-1853   19.52.52  0.060 Cur#1.4060.HR88 RC=0 Dur=0.030 COM Stmt=Select
COUNTRY, STATE from PS_PERSON_ADDRESS where ADDRESS_TYPE = 'HOME' and EMPLID = :1
PSAPPSRV.4060   1-1854   19.52.52  0.000 Cur#1.4060.HR88 RC=0 Dur=0.000 Bind-1 type=2 length=1
value=
PSAPPSRV.4060   1-1855   19.52.52  0.541 Cur#1.4060.HR88 RC=1 Dur=0.000 Fetch
```

---

[14] This functionality can be disabled in the Web Profile. Some browsers use the same keystroke as a shortcut to their own features.

Two times are recorded in the trace:

- The duration of the logged operation is recorded and prefixed with Dur=. This measures only in centiseconds on most platforms, although the number is formatted with three decimal places.

- The time since the last trace line was emitted is recorded after the time at which the line was emitted. It is accurate to milliseconds on Windows and centiseconds on most Unix systems. Idle time since the last service also seems to be accurate to milliseconds, even on Unix platforms.

The SQL statement in line 1853 took 0.03 seconds to parse and execute, but it was 0.06 seconds since the last trace line was emitted. The difference suggests the time taken by processing in the application server process itself. The fetch operation at line 1855 reports a duration of 0, so it took less than 1 millisecond to execute, but it was 0.541 seconds since the last trace line was emitted. Therefore, this was time consumed in the PSAPPSRV process, handling the result of the fetch. The return code of 1 indicates that nothing was returned by the fetch.

Be aware that sometimes the duration is incorrectly reported as zero in the PeopleTools trace, as in the following example, where a rowset is populated by PeopleCode:

```
&PnlField_Rs = CreateRowset(Record.CO_PNLFIELD_VW);
&PnlField_Rs.Flush();
&PnlField_Rs.Fill("WHERE PNLNAME = :1 and FIELDTYPE = 16 and LBLTYPE = 7 AND RECNAME =
:2 and FIELDNAME = :3", %Page, &LinkRecName, &LinkFieldName);
```

The resulting SQL query has the alias FILL. The duration of the statement is reported as zero. The first SQL in any application service is a query on the PSVERSION table, so a rowset FILL command is unlikely to be the first SQL in a service. Therefore, there is no pause waiting for user action, so the duration can safely be assumed to be equal to the time since the last trace line was emitted:

```
PSAPPSRV.2564    1-4321    01.52.36    0.551 Cur#1.2564.HR88 RC=0 Dur=0.000 COM Stmt=SELECT
FILL.PNLNAME,FILL.PNLFLDID,FILL.FIELDNUM,FILL.PNLFIELDNAME,FILL.FIELDTYPE,FILL.RECNAME,FILL.FI
ELDNAME,FILL.LBLTYPE,FILL.GOTOPORTALNAME,FILL.GOTONODENAME,FILL.GOTOMENUNAME,FILL.GOTOPNLGRPNA
ME,FILL.GOTOMKTNAME,FILL.GOTOPNLNAME,FILL.GOTOPNLACTION FROM PS_CO_PNLFIELD_VW FILL   WHERE
PNLNAME = :1 and FIELDTYPE = 16 and LBLTYPE = 7 AND RECNAME = :2 and FIELDNAME = :3
```

In this example, it took 0.551 seconds for PeopleSoft to generate and execute the SQL statement and load the results into memory structures in the application server.

Analyzing PeopleSoft Trace Files

Sometimes, to help find long-running statements, it can be useful to load the trace file into a table in the database (created by Listing 9-45).

Listing 9-45. Extract from `tracesql_pre.sql`

```
CREATE TABLE tracesql
(program         VARCHAR2(12)    DEFAULT 'Client' NOT NULL
,pid             NUMBER          DEFAULT 0        NOT NULL
,line_id         NUMBER                           NOT NULL
,line_num        NUMBER                           NOT NULL
,timestamp       DATE                             NOT NULL
,time_since_last NUMBER                           NOT NULL
```

```
,cursor          NUMBER                          NOT NULL
,database        VARCHAR2(10)                    NOT NULL
,return_code     NUMBER                          NOT NULL
,duration        NUMBER                          NOT NULL
,operation       VARCHAR2(4000)                  NOT NULL
,CONSTRAINT nonzero CHECK (duration>0 OR time_since_last>0)
);
```

The constraint can be used to prevent from being loaded lines that do not account for any time. The SQL*Loader control file in Listing 9-46 can be used.

Listing 9-46. SQL*Loader Control File `tracesql.ldr`

```
LOAD DATA
INFILE 'PS_go-faster-3.tracesql'
REPLACE
INTO TABLE tracesql
FIELDS TERMINATED BY WHITESPACE
TRAILING NULLCOLS
(program                  TERMINATED BY '.'
,pid
,line_id                  TERMINATED BY '-'
,line_num
,timestamp        "TO_DATE(REPLACE(:timestamp,'.',':'),'HH24:MI:SS')"
,time_since_last
,cursor_lead      FILLER  TERMINATED BY '#'
,cursor                   TERMINATED BY '.'
,pid2                     FILLER TERMINATED BY '.'
,database
,return_lead      FILLER  TERMINATED BY '='
,return_code
,duration_lead    FILLER  TERMINATED BY '='
,duration
,operation        CHAR(4000) TERMINATED BY '&' "SUBSTR(:operation,1,4000)"
--,tracesql_seq SEQUENCE(MAX,1)
)
```

Traces from Windows client processes do not have a program name and process ID. Therefore, these columns should be removed from the SQL*Loader file when loading client trace files.

Aggregating SQL Statements with Different Literal Values

When working with nVision or Application Engine traces, it can be useful to remove literal values from SQL statements so that time can be aggregated across SQL statements that are identical except for the literal values (the same principle as CURSOR_SHARING=FORCE in Oracle).

The packaged function shown in Listing 9-47 replaces all literal values with a colon (:).

Listing 9-47. Extract from `tracesql_pre.sql`

```
CREATE OR REPLACE PACKAGE cleansql AS
FUNCTION cleansql(p_operation VARCHAR2) RETURN VARCHAR2;
PRAGMA restrict_references(cleansql,wnds,wnps);
```

```
END cleansql;
/

CREATE OR REPLACE PACKAGE BODY cleansql AS
FUNCTION cleansql(p_operation VARCHAR2) RETURN VARCHAR2 IS
    l_newop      VARCHAR2(4000) := '';            --output string
    l_char       VARCHAR2(1)    := '';            --current char in input string
    l_inquote    BOOLEAN        := FALSE;         --are we in a quoted string
    l_inlitnum   BOOLEAN        := FALSE;         --are we in literal number
    l_lastchar   VARCHAR2(1)    := '';            --last char in output string
    l_len        INTEGER;                         --length of input string
    l_opsym      VARCHAR2(20)   := ' =<>+-*/,';   --string of symbols
    l_nextchar   VARCHAR2(1);                     --next character
    l_numbers    VARCHAR2(20)   := '1234567890'; --string of symbols
    l_pos        INTEGER        := 1;             --current pos in input string
BEGIN
    l_len := LENGTH(p_operation);
    WHILE (l_pos <= l_len) LOOP
        l_lastchar := l_char;
        l_char := SUBSTR(p_operation,l_pos,1);
        l_nextchar := SUBSTR(p_operation,l_pos+1,1);
        l_pos := l_pos+1;
        IF l_char = CHR(39) THEN -- we are on a quote mark
            IF l_inquote THEN -- coming out of quote
                l_inquote := FALSE;
            ELSE --going into quote
                l_inquote := TRUE;
                l_newop := l_newop||':';
            END IF;
            l_char := '';
        END IF;
        IF l_inquote THEN
            l_char := '';
        ELSIF (l_char = ' '
            AND INSTR(l_opsym,l_lastchar)>0) THEN --after symbol suppress space
            l_char := '';
        ELSIF (l_lastchar = ' '
            AND INSTR(l_opsym,l_char)>0) THEN -- suppress space before symbol
            l_newop := SUBSTR(l_newop,1,LENGTH(l_newop)-1)||l_char;
            l_char := '';
        END IF;

        IF (l_inlitnum) THEN --in a number
            IF (l_char = '.'
                AND INSTR(l_numbers,l_lastchar)>0
                AND INSTR(l_numbers,l_nextchar)>0) THEN
                l_inlitnum := TRUE; --still a number if a decimal point
            ELSIF (INSTR(l_numbers,l_char)=0) THEN -- number has finished
                l_inlitnum := FALSE;
            ELSE -- number continues
                l_char := '';
            END IF;
```

265

```
        ELSIF (NOT l_inlitnum
                AND INSTR(l_opsym,l_lastchar)>0
                AND INSTR(l_numbers,l_char)>0) THEN --start literal
            l_newop := l_newop||':';
            l_char := '';
            l_inlitnum := TRUE;
        END IF;

        l_newop := l_newop||l_char;

        IF l_newop = 'CEX Stmt=' THEN
            l_newop := '';
        END IF;
    END LOOP;
    RETURN l_newop;
END cleansql;
END cleansql;
/
show errors

CREATE OR REPLACE TRIGGER tracesql
BEFORE INSERT on tracesql
FOR EACH ROW
BEGIN
    :new.operation := cleansql.cleansql(:new.operation);
END;
/
;
```

For example, the SQL queries in Listing 9-48 generated by nVision are the same but have different literal values.

Listing 9-48. Raw PeopleTools Trace Generated by an nVision Report

```
CEX Stmt=SELECT L.TREE_NODE_NUM,A.PROJECT_ID,SUM(A.POSTED_TOTAL_AMT) FROM
PS_LEDGER_BUDG A, PSTREESELECT10 L, PSTREESELECT15 L1 WHERE A.LEDGER='BUDGET'
AND A.FISCAL_YEAR=2005 AND (A.ACCOUNTING_PERIOD BETWEEN 0 AND 1 OR
A.ACCOUNTING_PERIOD=998) AND A.BUSINESS_UNIT='XXXXX' AND  L.SELECTOR_NUM=143 AND
A.ACCOUNT>= L.RANGE_FROM_10 AND A.ACCOUNT <= L.RANGE_TO_10 AND (L.TREE_NODE_NUM
BETWEEN 511278162 AND 1548872078 OR L.TREE_NODE_NUM BETWEEN 1578947265 AND
1989974894) AND  L1.SELECTOR_NUM=140 AND A.PROJECT_ID>= L1.RANGE_FROM_15 AND
A.PROJECT_ID <= L1.RANGE_TO_15 AND L1.TREE_NODE_NUM BETWEEN 38461539 AND
2000000000 AND A.CURRENCY_CD='GBP' AND A.STATISTICS_CODE=' ' GROUP BY
L.TREE_NODE_NUM,A.PROJECT_ID
CEX Stmt=SELECT L.TREE_NODE_NUM,A.PROJECT_ID,SUM(A.POSTED_TOTAL_AMT) FROM
PS_LEDGER_BUDG A, PSTREESELECT10 L, PSTREESELECT15 L1 WHERE A.LEDGER='BUDAPP'
AND A.FISCAL_YEAR=2005 AND (A.ACCOUNTING_PERIOD BETWEEN 0 AND 1 OR
A.ACCOUNTING_PERIOD=998) AND A.BUSINESS_UNIT='XXXXX' AND  L.SELECTOR_NUM=143 AND
A.ACCOUNT>= L.RANGE_FROM_10 AND A.ACCOUNT <= L.RANGE_TO_10 AND (L.TREE_NODE_NUM
BETWEEN 511278162 AND 1548872078 OR L.TREE_NODE_NUM BETWEEN 1578947265 AND
b1989974894) AND  L1.SELECTOR_NUM=140 AND A.PROJECT_ID>= L1.RANGE_FROM_15 AND
A.PROJECT_ID <= L1.RANGE_TO_15 AND L1.TREE_NODE_NUM BETWEEN 38461539 AND
```

2000000000 AND A.CURRENCY_CD='GBP' AND A.STATISTICS_CODE=' ' GROUP BY
L.TREE_NODE_NUM,A.PROJECT_ID

However, the package function removed all the literals and any unnecessary spaces when the trace file was imported by SQL*Loader. So now you can aggregate time with a simple SQL query, as shown in Listing 9-49.

Listing 9-49. *Aggregated Execution Time for a SQL Statement*

```
SELECT    operation, SUM(duration), MAX(duration), AVG(duration), COUNT(*)
FROM      tracesql
GROUP BY operation
HAVING SUM(duration)>300
/
OPERATION
--------------------------------------------------------------------------------SUM(DURATION)
MAX(DURATION) AVG(DURATION)    COUNT(*)
------------- -------------- -------------- ----------
SELECT L.TREE_NODE_NUM,A.PROJECT_ID,SUM(A.POSTED_TOTAL_AMT) FROM PS_LEDGER_BUDG
A,PSTREESELECT10 L,PSTREESELECT15 L1 WHERE A.LEDGER=: AND A.FISCAL_YEAR=: AND (A
.ACCOUNTING_PERIOD BETWEEN : AND : OR A.ACCOUNTING_PERIOD=:) AND A.BUSINESS_UNIT
=: AND L.SELECTOR_NUM=: AND A.ACCOUNT>=L.RANGE_FROM_10 AND A.ACCOUNT<=L.RANGE_TO
_10 AND (L.TREE_NODE_NUM BETWEEN : AND : OR L.TREE_NODE_NUM BETWEEN : AND :) AND
 L1.SELECTOR_NUM=: AND A.PROJECT_ID>=L1.RANGE_FROM_15 AND A.PROJECT_ID<=L1.RANGE
_TO_15 AND L1.TREE_NODE_NUM BETWEEN : AND : AND A.CURRENCY_CD=: AND A.STATISTICS
_CODE=: GROUP BY L.TREE_NODE_NUM,A.PROJECT_ID
     1468.509      965.003     112.962231             13
```

Summary

If performance tuning is a search for lost time, then you need ways to determine where time is being lost. Instrumentation in the Oracle database is very effective for diagnosing SQL performance problems, but PeopleSoft delivers a huge stack of technology that sits between the database and the user.

The metrics described in this chapter can identify which parts of the application, in which tier, are consuming the most time. Some problems are not caused by SQL performance, in which case trace tells you that the performance bottleneck is not the database, and you are not much further forward.

Fortunately, many problems do come down to SQL performance, in which case PeopleSoft metrics indicate which processes, and sometimes which step within a process, you should examine in more detail. You can then choose a specific process or transaction to trace. Chapter 11 looks in more detail at how to use database instrumentation in PeopleSoft.

CHAPTER 10

PeopleTools Performance Utilities

In PeopleTools 8.4, PeopleSoft has started to introduce some utilities to help detect and identify performance problems in the online part of the application. This chapter discusses some aspects of these utilities.

This chapter does not seek to replace PeopleSoft's documentation. Instead, you are advised to read this chapter in conjunction with PeopleBooks.

Query Metrics in PeopleTools 8.4

In PeopleTools 8.4, PeopleSoft introduced two new methods of collecting query execution times: query statistics and query logging.

Query Statistics

Whenever a query is executed via the Pure Internet Architecture (PIA), the new average execution time, fetch time, and number of rows for that query across all executions are either inserted into or updated on the table PSQRYSTATS, as shown in Listing 10-1.

Listing 10-1. How PeopleSoft Updates Query Statistics

```
UPDATE PSQRYSTATS
SET    AVGEXECTIME = (AVGEXECTIME * EXECCOUNT + :4)/(EXECCOUNT + 1)
,      AVGFETCHTIME = (AVGFETCHTIME * EXECCOUNT + :5)/(EXECCOUNT + 1)
,      AVGNUMROWS = (AVGNUMROWS * EXECCOUNT + 0)/(EXECCOUNT + 1)
,      LASTEXECDTTM = TO_DATE(SUBSTR(:3, 0, 19),'YYYY-MM-DD-HH24.MI.SS')
,      EXECCOUNT = EXECCOUNT + 1
WHERE  OPRID = :1
AND    QRYNAME = :2
```

The limitation of this technique is that you can only see an average for a query since the averages were last deleted from the table. Query logging, described in the next section, provides information about each query execution.

The content of this table can be queried via the PeopleTools ➤ Utilities ➤ Administration ➤ Query Administration component (see Figure 10-1).

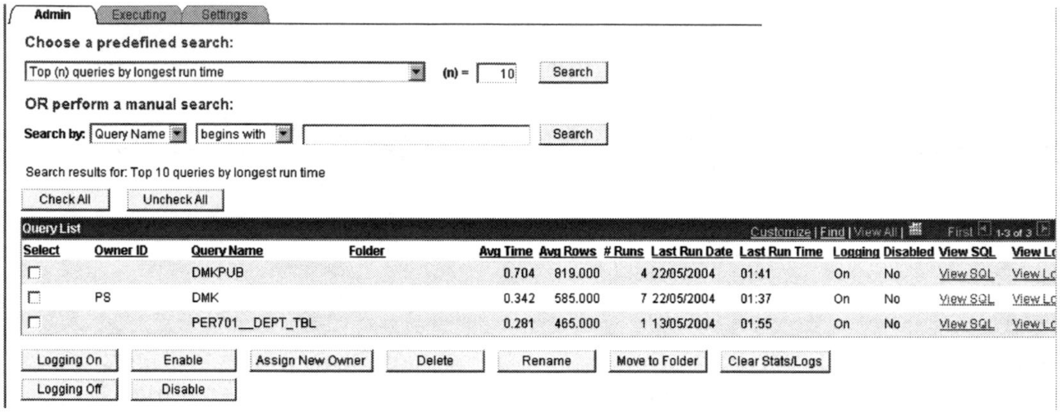

Figure 10-1. *Query Administration component*

Although the component can list the top *n* queries by cumulative execution time, it does not calculate total execution time. Queries are listed by average rather than cumulative execution time. However, it is easy to query this table in SQL, as shown in Listing 10-2.

Listing 10-2. *Top Ten Queries by Cumulative Execution Time (top10qry.sql)*

```
SELECT *
FROM    (
        SELECT RANK() OVER (ORDER BY tottime DESC ) as qryrank
        ,       oprid, qryname, totexec, tottime
        ,       100*RATIO_TO_REPORT(tottime) OVER () as pcttime
        FROM    (SELECT oprid, qryname
                ,        SUM(execcount) totexec
                ,        SUM(execcount*avgexectime) tottime
                FROM     psqrystats
                GROUP BY oprid, qryname
                ) a
        )
WHERE   qryrank <= 10
/
```

The results of the query are shown in Listing 10-3.

Listing 10-3. *Top Queries by Cumulative Execution Time (top10qry.lst)*

```
QRYRANK OPRID      QRYNAME                         TOTEXEC    TOTTIME PCTTIME
------- ---------- ------------------------------- ---------- ---------- -------
      1            DMKPUB                                4        2.8    51.3
      2 PS         DMK                                   7        2.4    43.6
      3            PER701__DEPT_TBL                      1        0.3     5.1
```

Query Logging

Also from PeopleTools 8.4, you can choose to log each execution of particular queries. Logging can be enabled for selected queries in the Query Administration component (shown in Figure 10-1). Every time the query runs, a row is written to the table PSQRYEXECLOG, as shown in Figure 10-2.

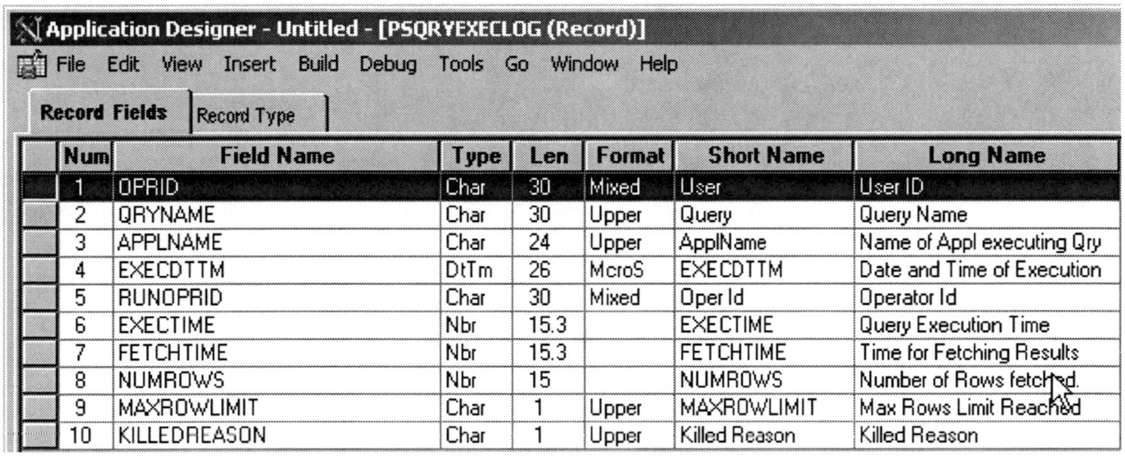
Application Designer - Untitled - [PSQRYEXECLOG (Record)]
File Edit View Insert Build Debug Tools Go Window Help
Record Fields
Record Type
Num Field Name Type Len Format Short Name Long Name
1 OPRID Char 30 Mixed User User ID
2 QRYNAME Char 30 Upper Query Query Name
3 APPLNAME Char 24 Upper ApplName Name of Appl executing Qry
4 EXECDTTM DtTm 26 McroS EXECDTTM Date and Time of Execution
5 RUNOPRID Char 30 Mixed Oper Id Operator Id
6 EXECTIME Nbr 15.3 EXECTIME Query Execution Time
7 FETCHTIME Nbr 15.3 FETCHTIME Time for Fetching Results
8 NUMROWS Nbr 15 NUMROWS Number of Rows fetched.
9 MAXROWLIMIT Char 1 Upper MAXROWLIMIT Max Rows Limit Reached
10 KILLEDREASON Char 1 Upper Killed Reason Killed Reason

Figure 10-2. *PSQRYEXECLOG as shown by Application Designer*

You could reasonably choose to enable logging for every query in the system. You can do this in the Query Administration component, or you can set the flag on the query definition directly using the SQL in Listing 10-4.

Listing 10-4. *Enabling Query Logging for All Queries (`qrylogall.sql`)*

```
UPDATE pslock
SET    version = version + 1
WHERE  objecttypename IN('SYS','QDM');

UPDATE psversion
SET    version = version + 1
WHERE  objecttypename IN('SYS','QDM');

UPDATE psqrydefn
SET    execlogging = 'Y'
,      version = (SELECT version FROM pslock WHERE objecttypename = 'QDM')
WHERE  execlogging != 'Y';
```

PSQRYEXEC records the Operator ID that ran the query in RUNOPRID, and hence you can find out not only which queries are consuming the most time, but also which operators are spending the most time running queries.

The SQL query in Listing 10-5 produces a similar report to that based on PSQRYSTATS in Listing 10-2; but now you know when the query was run, so you can look at a particular time window, which in this example is the last seven days.

Listing 10-5. Top Ten Queries in the Last Seven Days (top10logqry.sql)

```
SELECT *
FROM   (
       SELECT RANK() OVER (ORDER BY tottime DESC ) as qryrank
       ,      oprid, qryname, totexec, tottime
       ,      100*RATIO_TO_REPORT(tottime) OVER () as pcttime
       FROM   (SELECT oprid, qryname
              ,       COUNT(*) totexec
              ,       SUM(exectime) tottime
              FROM    psqryexeclog
              WHERE   execdttm > SYSDATE - 7
              GROUP BY oprid, qryname
              ) a
       )
WHERE  qryrank <= 10
/
```

Scheduled Queries

Scheduled queries are not logged to PSQRYEXECLOG and are not counted in the metrics on PSQRYSTATS. There are executed in the PSQUERY Application Engine program that is run by the Process Scheduler.

However, the same techniques can be used on PSQUERY as any other batch process. The start and end times of the process are recorded on the Process Scheduler request table PSPRCSRQST. Application Engine batch timings can also be enabled. The name of the query executed by PSQUERY is embedded into the output file name, and the description of the query is used for the content description. Both of these are visible in the View Log/Trace page (see Figure 10-3) below the Process Detail page in Process Monitor.

View Log/Trace

Report

Report ID:	671	**Process Instance:**	850	Message Log
Name:	PSQUERY	**Process Type:**	Application Engine	
Run Status:	Success			

Custom04-Global Employee Listi

Distribution Details

Distribution Node: GO-FASTER-6   **Expiration Date:** 17/10/2011

File List

Name	File Size (bytes)	Datetime Created
AE_PSQUERY_850.log	168	10/10/2011 14:19:34.335000 PDT
CUSTOM04_GLOBAL_EMPLOYEE_LISTI-850.csv	106,710	10/10/2011 14:19:34.335000 PDT

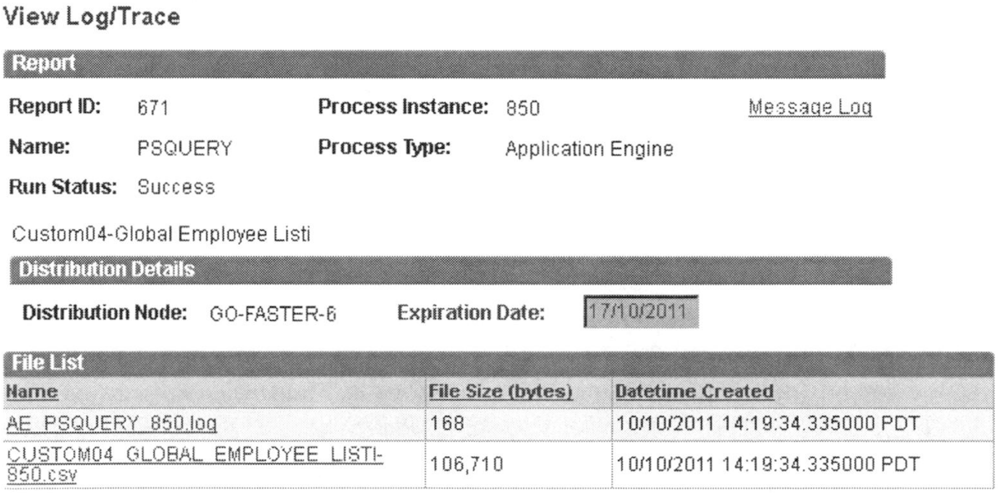

Figure 10-3. View Log/Trace subpage in Process Monitor

The values can also be queried from the PS_CDM_LIST and PS_CDM_FILE_LIST PeopleTools tables using the query in Listing 10-6.

Listing 10-6. *Query Execution Statistics for Scheduled Queries (sched_qry_stats.sql)*

```
column qryname    format a30      heading 'Query Name'
column avg_secs   format 9,999.9 heading 'Average|Exec|(s)'
column sum_secs   format 999,990 heading 'Total|Exec|(s)'
column num_execs format 999,990 heading 'Number|of|Execs'
SELECT qryname
,      AVG(exec_secs) avg_secs
,      SUM(exec_secs) sum_secs
,      COUNT(*) num_execs
FROM (
SELECT SUBSTR(f.filename,1,INSTR(filename,'-'||LTRIM(TO_CHAR(f.prcsinstance))
                                            ||'.')-1) qryname
,      (CAST(p.enddttm AS DATE)-CAST(p.begindttm AS DATE))*86400 exec_secs
FROM psprcsrqst p, ps_cdm_file_list f
WHERE p.prcsname = 'PSQUERY'
AND p.runstatus = 9
AND p.prcsinstance = f.prcsinstance
AND NOT f.cdm_file_type IN('LOG','AET','TRC')
) GROUP BY qryname
ORDER BY sum_secs DESC
/
```

The result of this of query is a profile of the scheduled queries ordered by the cumulative execution time over the period that the output is kept in the report repository (see Listing 10-7).

Listing 10-7. *Top Scheduled Queries by Cumulative Execution Time*

Query Name	Average Exec (s)	Total Exec (s)	Number of Execs
PYRL_SEGMENTATION	3,846.6	38,466	10
PYRL_MISC_ELEMENT	3,363.3	20,180	6
PYRL_ELEMENT_MISC	1,674.8	20,097	12
PYRL_LOAN_BY_PERIOD	2,888.0	5,776	2
Q_ELEMENT_AMOUNTS	1,083.5	2,167	2
...			

PeopleSoft Ping

The PeopleSoft Ping utility was introduced in PeopleTools 8.42 (and was backported to PeopleTools 8.19, although the PIA graph capability was not available in PeopleTools 8.1). It is a PIA component (shown in Figure 10-4) that runs a standard transaction and collects the elapsed times for database, application server, web server, and browser response times.

The PeopleSoft documentation[1] explains how to run Ping. Here I discuss how it can be used, what it tells you, and, more important, what it does not tell you.

■ **Note** Throughout this chapter, unless otherwise stated, *Ping* refers to the PeopleSoft Ping utility, not the network ping utility.

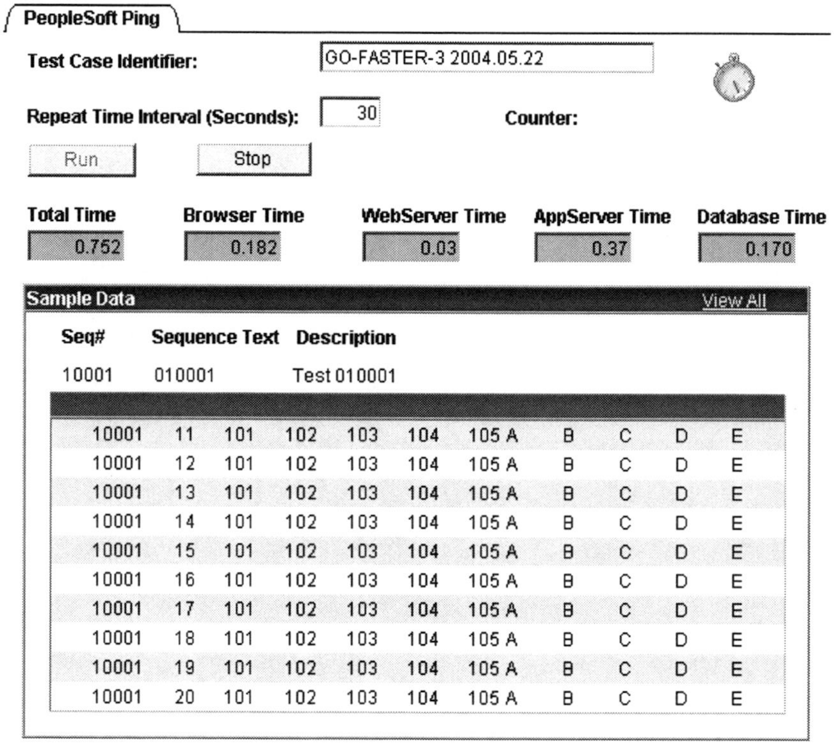

PeopleSoft Ping

Test Case Identifier:	GO-FASTER-3 2004.05.22

Repeat Time Interval (Seconds):	30	Counter:

Run	Stop

Total Time	Browser Time	WebServer Time	AppServer Time	Database Time
0.752	0.182	0.03	0.37	0.170

Sample Data   View All

Seq#	Sequence Text	Description
10001	010001	Test 010001

10001	11	101	102	103	104	105 A	B	C	D	E
10001	12	101	102	103	104	105 A	B	C	D	E
10001	13	101	102	103	104	105 A	B	C	D	E
10001	14	101	102	103	104	105 A	B	C	D	E
10001	15	101	102	103	104	105 A	B	C	D	E
10001	16	101	102	103	104	105 A	B	C	D	E
10001	17	101	102	103	104	105 A	B	C	D	E
10001	18	101	102	103	104	105 A	B	C	D	E
10001	19	101	102	103	104	105 A	B	C	D	E
10001	20	101	102	103	104	105 A	B	C	D	E

Figure 10-4. Ping component

The time between Ping transactions can be set on the page (it defaults to 30 seconds). The page repeatedly pings at that frequency until it is stopped. The times are then stored in the database in the table PS_PTP_TST_CASES, whose structure is described in Table 10-1.

---

[1] See PeopleTools PeopleBook: System and Server Administration ➤ Using PeopleTools Utilities ➤ Using PeopleSoft Ping
(http://download.oracle.com/docs/cd/E24150_01/pt851h2/eng/psbooks/tsvt/book.htm).

Table 10-1. *Columns on PS_PTP_TST_CASES*

Column Name	Description
PTP_TEST_CASE_ID	Test case identifier
PTP_DTTM_A1	Start time of the Ping transaction in PIA JavaScript on the client browser (according to the clock on the client)
PTP_DTTM_A2	End time of the Ping transaction in PIA JavaScript on the client browser (according to the clock on the client)
PTP_DTTM_B1	Start time of the Ping transaction in the application server
PTP_DTTM_B2	End time of the Ping transaction in the application server
PTP_DTTM_C1	Start time of the Ping transaction on the database
PTP_DTTM_C2	End time of the Ping transaction on the database
PTP_TIME_D	Elapsed database server time
PTP_AS_TIME	Elapsed application server time (including database time)
PTP_TOTAL_TIME	Total duration of ping as measured on PIA, including application server time
PTP_WS_TIME	Elapsed web-server duration (including application server time)

You can obtain a graph of the data in PeopleTools; but if it has any large spikes, the scale of the y-axis is automatically adjusted to include the whole range, and you can't see much detail. I prefer to extract the Ping data directly from the database into an Excel spreadsheet and produce a chart (see Figure 10-5). This has the advantage of being able to format the chart and ranges exactly as desired.

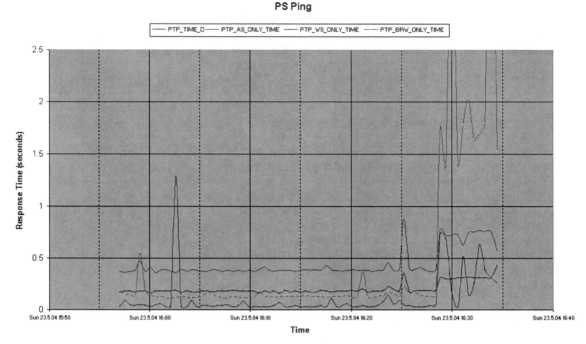

Figure 10-5. *Sample Excel chart of Ping data (*`psping.xls`*)[2]*

What Does Ping Measure?

It is important to understand how, and therefore just what, PeopleSoft Ping measures. Figure 10-6 illustrates the PIA, with the performance measures described in Chapter 9. The four measures collected by the Ping utility have been added.

---

[2] This set of data was produced on a PeopleSoft system running entirely on a stand-alone laptop. At 16.28, a long-running query with a large sort was started. Both the disk and CPU were heavily loaded, so the response time of all components in the system degraded.

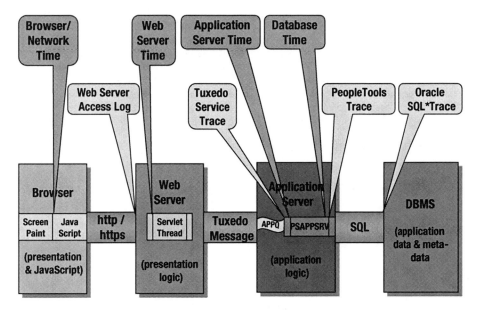

Figure 10-6. Ping measurements on the PIA infrastructure

PeopleSoft has added the instrumentation for Ping without major changes to the underlying technology. As the diagram in Figure 10-6 suggests, Ping does not measure exactly the same thing as the metrics described in Chapter 9. This is best illustrated by examining a single Ping result and comparing the Ping times with the times obtained from the other sources of metrics. These times are collected by a JavaScript script that has been built into the component, and they are then stored in the database in a table called PS_PTP_TST_CASES (see Listing 10-8).

On Oracle, the timestamp columns are of type DATE, so they are accurate only to 1 second. It is necessary to use the time columns for more precise timings.

Listing 10-8. PeopleSoft Ping Data Stored in the Database

```
SELECT * FROM ps_ptp_tst_cases
WHERE ptp_test_case_id = 'GO-FASTER-3 2004.05.22'
AND ptp_dttm_a1 = TO_DATE('20040522 230448','YYYYMMDD HH24MISS');


PTP_TEST_CASE_ID               PTP_DTTM_A1         PTP_DTTM_A2
-----------------------------  ------------------  ------------------
PTP_DTTM_B1         PTP_DTTM_B2         PTP_DTTM_C1         PTP_DTTM_C2
------------------  ------------------  ------------------  ------------------
PTP_TIME_D PTP_AS_TIME PTP_TOTAL_TIME PTP_WS_TIME
---------- ----------- -------------- ----------
GO-FASTER-3 2004.05.22            23:04:48 22/05/2004 23:04:49 22/05/2004
23:04:48 22/05/2004 23:04:49 22/05/2004 23:04:48 22/05/2004 23:04:49 22/05/2004
     .21         .64            .852           .722
```

277

Database Time

The Ping transaction is defined in the DERIVED_PTP.HTMLCTLEVENT.FieldChange PeopleCode (see Listing 10-9). Queries on the records PTP_TABLE1 and PTP_TABLE2 are run and timed in the PeopleCode. The PeopleCode system variable %PerfTime returns the time on the application server, rather than the database server, and is used to calculate the duration of the FILL and SELECT operations.

Listing 10-9. Extract from DERIVED_PTP.HTMLCTLEVENT.FieldChange PeopleCode

```
REM USE ROWSET TO READ RESULTS FROM A JOIN WITH BIND VARIABLE

&nbr = 10001;
&Table1_vw_rs = CreateRowset(Record.PTP_TABLE1_VW);

&startTime = %PerfTime;
&Table1_vw_rs.Fill("WHERE PTP_SEQ_NBR >= :1", &nbr);
&timeTaken = &timeTaken + (%PerfTime - &startTime);

&Rs = GetRowset(Scroll.PTP_TABLE1);
&Rs.Flush();
&startTime = %PerfTime;
&Rs.Select(Record.PTP_TABLE1, "WHERE PTP_SEQ_NBR <= 10010");
&timeTaken = &timeTaken + (%PerfTime - &startTime);

DERIVED_PTP.PTP_TIME_D = &timeTaken;
```

The resultant SQL can be seen in the PeopleTools trace (see Listing 10-10). The queries return 10 and 100 rows, respectively.

Listing 10-10. PeopleSoft Ping SQL

```
PSAPPSRV.2564   1-22899 23.04.49    0.190 Cur#1.2564.HR88 RC=0 Dur=0.000 COM Stmt=SELECT
PTP_SEQ_NBR, PTP_SEQ_CHAR, DESCR, PTP_INT01, PTP_INT02, PTP_INT03, PTP_INT04, PTP_INT05,
PTP_INT06, PTP_INT07, PTP_INT08, PTP_INT09, PTP_INT10, PTP_INT11, PTP_INT12, PTP_INT13,
PTP_INT14, PTP_INT15, PTP_INT16, PTP_INT17, PTP_INT18, PTP_INT19, PTP_INT20, PTP_INT21,
PTP_INT22, PTP_INT23, PTP_INT24, PTP_CHAR01, PTP_CHAR02, PTP_CHAR03, PTP_CHAR04,
PTP_CHAR05, PTP_CHAR06, PTP_CHAR07, PTP_CHAR08, PTP_CHAR09, PTP_CHAR10, PTP_CHAR11,
PTP_CHAR12, PTP_CHAR13, PTP_CHAR14, PTP_CHAR15, PTP_CHAR16, PTP_CHAR17, PTP_CHAR18,
PTP_CHAR19, PTP_CHAR20, PTP_CHAR21, PTP_CHAR22, PTP_CHAR23 FROM PS_PTP_TABLE1 WHERE
PTP_SEQ_NBR <= 10010 ORDER BY PTP_SEQ_NBR
PSAPPSRV.2564   1-22900 23.04.49    0.010 Cur#1.2564.HR88 RC=0 Dur=0.000 COM Stmt=SELECT
PTP_SEQ_NBR, PTP_LINE, PTP_INT01, PTP_INT02, PTP_INT03, PTP_INT04, PTP_INT05, PTP_INT06,
PTP_INT07, PTP_INT08, PTP_INT09, PTP_INT10, PTP_INT11, PTP_INT12, PTP_INT13, PTP_INT14,
PTP_INT15, PTP_INT16, PTP_INT17, PTP_INT18, PTP_INT19, PTP_INT20, PTP_INT21, PTP_INT22,
PTP_INT23, PTP_INT24, PTP_CHAR01, PTP_CHAR02, PTP_CHAR03, PTP_CHAR04, PTP_CHAR05,
PTP_CHAR06, PTP_CHAR07, PTP_CHAR08, PTP_CHAR09, PTP_CHAR10, PTP_CHAR11, PTP_CHAR12,
PTP_CHAR13, PTP_CHAR14, PTP_CHAR15, PTP_CHAR16, PTP_CHAR17, PTP_CHAR18, PTP_CHAR19,
PTP_CHAR20, PTP_CHAR21, PTP_CHAR22, PTP_CHAR23, PTP_CHAR24 FROM PS_PTP_TABLE2 WHERE
EXISTS  (SELECT 'X' FROM PS_PTP_TABLE1  WHERE PTP_SEQ_NBR <= 10010  AND
PS_PTP_TABLE2.PTP_SEQ_NBR = PS_PTP_TABLE1.PTP_SEQ_NBR )  ORDER BY PTP_SEQ_NBR, PTP_LINE
```

There is already a discrepancy in the timings. Ping reports the database time as 0.21s (see Listing 10-8), whereas the trace claims 0.20s (see Listing 10-10) for these two queries. Both of these times include any time spent in the SQL*Net layers and any network layers between the application and database servers.

PeopleSoft Ping is not a good test of database performance: the same rows are read repeatedly by successive Pings, so they are likely to be cached by the database. Therefore, there is unlikely to be any physical I/O for these queries, and their performance is unlikely to be affected by the disk subsystem. If, however, the database server becomes CPU bound, I would expect an increase in database time.

Application Server Time

When a Ping occurs, an ICPanel service runs on a PSAPPSRV server process. The standard transaction copies the data queried into one row set to another (see Listing 10-11). This kind of operation is typical of PeopleSoft 8 applications and so is a reasonable test transaction. This operation does not require any database activity, so it is CPU intensive for the application server process.

Listing 10-11. Extract from DERIVED_PTP.HTMLCTLEVENT.FieldChange PeopleCode Showing a Rowset Copy in PeopleSoft Ping

```
REM  Copy using Rowset function from one RowSet to Another
&Table1_rs.CopyTo(&Table1_cpy_rs);
```

The duration of the service is recorded in the Tuxedo Service trace (see Listing 10-12).

Listing 10-12. Extract from APPQ.stderr

SERVICE	PID	SDATE	STIME	EDATE	ETIME
@ICPanel	3096	1085263488	77964316	1085263489	77964987

The Tuxedo service duration is the difference between the ETIME and STIME,[3] which in this case is 0.671 seconds, whereas Ping reports the application server time as only 0.64 seconds.

The Tuxedo service trace reports the time at which the service starts and completes. This timing information is captured in the Tuxedo libraries that handle the incoming message before unpacking the message and passing it to PeopleSoft code.[4] The PeopleSoft instrumentation must be called from within PeopleSoft's own code, rather than from any Tuxedo code. Hence the PeopleSoft timing must be less than the Tuxedo service time.

The discrepancy in the times must include the time taken to unpack the incoming service message and pass the data to the PeopleSoft functions, and to package the return message before placing it on the return queue. It also implies that the application server time in Ping does not include any time that the request spends on the queue waiting to get onto a server process, because the Tuxedo service time does not either.

---

[3] In this example, the application server was on Windows, so the times are in milliseconds.
[4] It is not clear from the Tuxedo documentation whether the service time includes the time taken to dequeue the incoming request and enqueue the outgoing request.

Web Server Time

The web server response time is reported in the access log (see Listing 10-13) as 0.742 seconds, whereas Ping reports 0.722 seconds.

Listing 10-13. Extract of PIA_access.log

```
2004-05-22   23:04:49   0.742   125316   10.0.0.8   go-faster-3   POST   200
"Mozilla/4.0 (compatible; MSIE 6.0; Windows NT 5.1)"
/psc/ps/EMPLOYEE/HRMS/c/UTILITIES.PTPERF_TEST.GBL
2004-05-22   23:04:49   0.01   1217   10.0.0.8   go-faster-3   GET   200   "Mozilla/4.0
(compatible; MSIE 6.0; Windows NT 5.1)"   /cs/ps/cache/PTPFUNCLIB_1.js   -
2004-05-22   23:04:49   0.0   77   10.0.0.8   go-faster-3   GET   200   "Mozilla/4.0
(compatible; MSIE 6.0; Windows NT 5.1)"   /psc/ps/psping_result.gif
tot=0.852&brt=0.13&wbt=0.082&apt=0.43&dbt=0.210&PpmStateNum=48
```

The results from the previous Ping are encoded as a query string on psping_result.gif. This is so the JavaScript script can make the colors change when the values go over the thresholds that can be defined.

Any time a Tuxedo service request spends on a queue in the application server is not part of the time on the application server process, and so it is included in the web server time.

Browser Time

The browser time is calculated from JavaScript that executes on the client browser itself. It is not clear whether this fully takes into account the time the browser takes to "paint" the screen. Nonetheless, this is certainly a much closer approximation to the end user's actual experience than the access log from either the web server or any proxy server that may be in use.

The browser time is the difference between the browser and web server total response times. It includes the network transmission time between the web server and the browser. It must also include the discrepancy between the web server time as reported by PeopleSoft Ping and the servlet response time as reported in the web server access log.

PeopleSoft Ping Case Study 1: Desktop/Browser Performance

One of the most valuable uses of Ping is to provide an indication of browser and network performance, without the need to introduce third-party measurement software at additional expense.

The graph in Figure 10-7 shows the performance of a 384MHz PC running Microsoft Internet Explorer. It has 64MB of physical memory, but the Task Manager initially indicates that the commit change (total memory usage) is 125MB. Therefore, Windows is likely to be paging memory to and from the page file on the local disk.

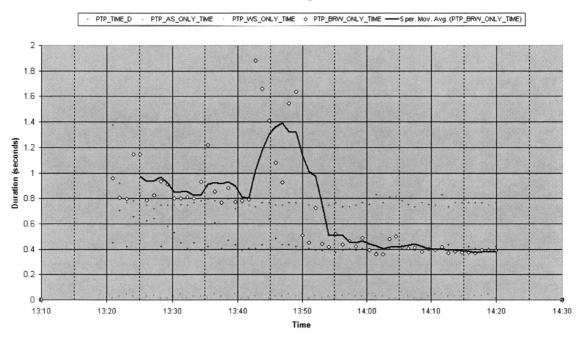

Figure 10-7. Browser-only Ping time

I shut down all other windows and as many services as possible. The act of starting the service management window and shutting down these processes caused Windows to page memory, so there was an increase in browser time. I reduced the commit charge to 89MB, and the browser time fell from 0.8 seconds to 0.4 seconds.

From this, we can reach the following conclusions:

- Paging memory from disk is a slow business and generally degrades Windows performance, not just the browser. Make sure the desktop has enough physical memory.

- PeopleSoft runs in a browser on any PC, but the specification of the PC can significantly affect the user experience.

PeopleSoft Ping Case Study 2: Application Server CPU Speed

Figure 10-8 shows Ping times from two different application servers connected to the same database.

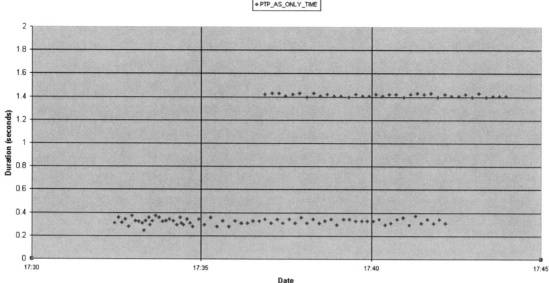

Figure 10-8. Application server–only Ping time

One application server is running on a Unix server with 750MHz processors and reports an average application server Ping time of 1.43 seconds. The other is on a Windows server with 3.2GHz processor and reports an average Ping time of 0.33 seconds. The processors on the Windows server are slightly more that four times faster, and the Ping is slightly more than four times faster.

The part of the Ping transaction that is used to measure application server time copies data from one row set to another. It does not include any database activity, so the application server is simply executing PeopleSoft's C++ code. Therefore it is CPU intensive.

This test indicates that processor speed is important to the performance of the PIA and PeopleCode code (excluding database access) in the application server.

Conclusion

PeopleSoft Ping is not a fundamental indicator of system performance, but it does indicate the presence of contention in the various PIA components. Since all PeopleSoft systems execute the same Ping transaction, it is also a useful standard measure for comparison, either of different desktops within an organization or of different hardware configurations used by PeopleSoft middleware.

Performance Monitor

PeopleTools Performance Monitor (PPM) was first introduced in PeopleTools 8.44. It represents a huge effort by PeopleSoft to fully instrument the application and produce a *timed-event interface*. To put it in terms that an Oracle DBA would recognize, it provides for the application what an Oracle timed event interface (event 10046, level 8) does for the database.

This section provides a brief overview of the utility. I do not explain how to set up and configure every aspect of Performance Monitor. The product documentation in PeopleTools PeopleBook: for Performance Monitor is very detailed,[5] and there is a very useful Red Paper.[6]

Architectural Overview

PeopleSoft uses PeopleTools to monitor PeopleTools. So you don't have learn a completely new technology, it is based on something you are already used to. Performance Monitor is a part of PeopleTools, so it is not separately licensed.

PeopleSoft added instrumentation to the application server processes, the Process Scheduler processes, and the web server servlets. This instrumentation collects performance information and sends it to a new servlet in the web server that in turn sends the data to a new application server process that inserts the data into the database (see Figure 10-9). PeopleSoft also delivered a number of components to retrieve and analyze that data.

---

[5] See http://download.oracle.com/docs/cd/E24150_01/pt851h2/eng/psbooks/tpfm/book.htm.
[6] See My Oracle Support, Document 747510.1.

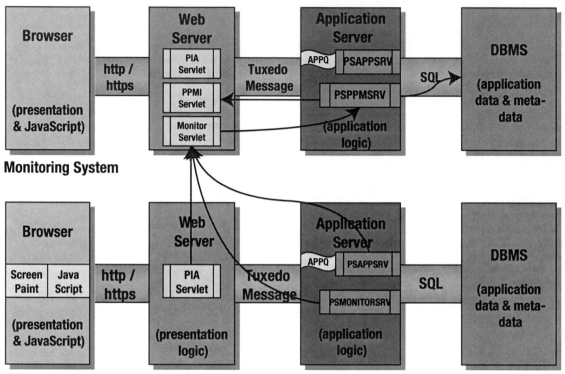

Figure 10-9. Performance Monitor architecture

This architecture separates the job of obtaining the metrics on the system being monitored from the job of storing those metrics in a database. The PeopleSoft documentation talks about a *monitored system* and a *monitoring system:*

- In the monitored system, the only thing instrumented processes have to do is send the data to the monitoring URL as HTTP posts. This minimizes the overhead on the monitored system.

- The monitoring URL is the location of the monitor servlet in the monitoring system. This sends the data on to a new application server process PSPPMSRV, which inserts the data into tables in the database of the monitoring system.

Most of the overhead of Performance Monitor is on the monitoring system. PeopleSoft/Oracle recommends that the monitoring system be placed on a separate stack of hardware from the monitored systems to prevent that overhead from affecting the monitored systems. Although any PeopleSoft system can be used as a monitoring system, PeopleSoft recommends that a PeopleTools-only system database be created for the purpose.

One monitoring system can monitor many monitored systems, regardless of PeopleTools version. Some PeopleSoft customers have more than one PeopleSoft system, and some use PeopleSoft Portal to produce a seamless interface that combines content from more than one system. A single monitoring system can monitor all of these and produce a joined up picture of the systems.

A system can be configured to self-monitor, although there are various warnings against doing so on a production system due to the associated overhead. However, it is useful to configure the monitoring system to self-monitor so that you know it is working correctly. I have also found it useful to be able to use Performance Trace on the self-monitoring system in order to resolve performance problems in the Performance Monitor analytic components. Self-monitoring cannot lead to a recursive loop.

To obtain the metrics from the monitored system, PeopleSoft has added code to the PIA servlet and to the various server processes in the application server and Process Scheduler domains. The monitor server (PSMONITORSRV) was added in PeopleTools 8.44 to collect host resource usage metrics. It also connects to the Tuxedo Bulletin Board to collect information about the Tuxedo domain (see Chapter 2 for a discussion of the Tuxedo architecture). In the Performance Monitor package, these various sources of metrics are referred to as *agents*. The agents send the metrics to the monitor servlet in the monitoring system. The netstat command reports a number of persistent connections established between the agents and the monitoring web server.

Note PeopleSoft systems usually have multiple application servers and multiple web servers. Metrics must be collected from each application server and each web server.

On the monitoring system, the metrics are collected by the monitoring servlet and sent on to the Performance Collator server, PSPPMSRV, which then inserts the metrics into the Performance Monitor PeopleTools tables in that database.

PeopleTools 8.44 was released in 2004. I believe that PeopleSoft intended to enhance and extend Performance Monitor. However, Oracle's acquisition of PeopleSoft at the start of the following year put a stop to that. Apart from a few bug fixes, it has had no development since the initial release, and I do not expect that to change.

For me, Performance Monitor has an unfinished feel to it. It collects metrics, and there are components that let you analyze that data and draw some charts, but they are not particularly sophisticated. I frequently find that I have to go into the underlying tables and work with the data myself. Therefore, an understanding of the structure and meaning of the metrics is very important.

I have always thought that it would be relatively easy to write something using standard PeopleTools workflow functionality to periodically poll the data and send alerts. However, nothing is delivered in Performance Monitor that will proactively alert you to any problem.

Metrics

The metrics collected by Performance Monitor break down into two major groups:

- *Transactions* consist of the activities that occur when the operator does something in the PIA that causes communication between the browser and the web server, such as clicking a Save button in a component.

- *Events* are mostly initiated periodically by the monitoring agents to collect instantaneous metrics, such as CPU or Tuxedo metrics. Some events are generated by errors or exceptions.

Transactions

Transactions are the activities that occur in the web server and application server when a user initiates a conversation between the browser and the web server by clicking a link or button, or navigating between fields in the PIA.

A PIA transaction usually involves a number of operations in the web and application servers. For example, a PIA request can comprise one or more Jolt requests, each Jolt request gives rise to a Tuxedo service, and so on. Each of these elements is a separate Performance Monitor transaction. All of the transactions that occur in response to a single user action are collectively called a *Performance Monitoring Unit* (PMU).[7] The transactions in a PMU exist in a hierarchy and can be displayed as a tree structure in the PIA. Figure 10-10 shows the PMU for a single PeopleSoft Ping. The level of detail in a PMU is controlled by the filtering level, which is discussed later in this chapter.

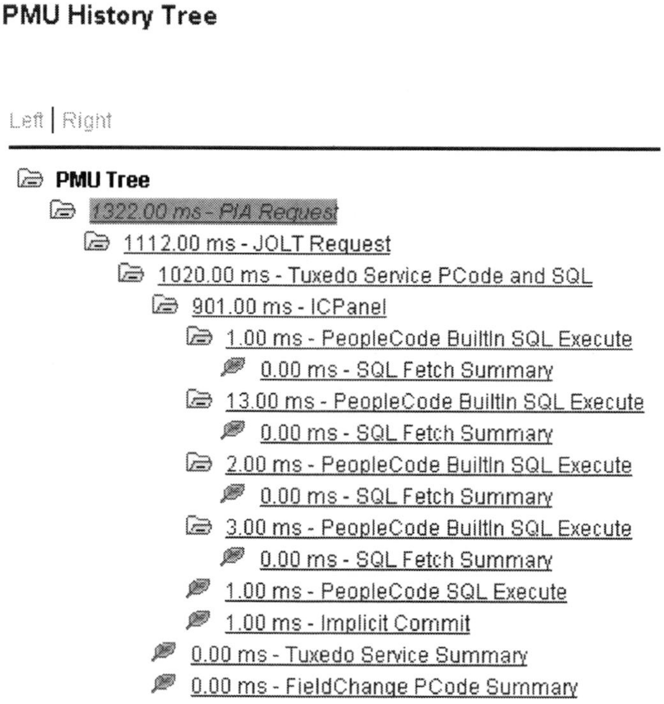

PMU History Tree

Left | Right

PMU Tree
  1322.00 ms - PIA Request
    1112.00 ms - JOLT Request
      1020.00 ms - Tuxedo Service PCode and SQL
        901.00 ms - ICPanel
          1.00 ms - PeopleCode Builtin SQL Execute
            0.00 ms - SQL Fetch Summary
          13.00 ms - PeopleCode Builtin SQL Execute
            0.00 ms - SQL Fetch Summary
          2.00 ms - PeopleCode Builtin SQL Execute
            0.00 ms - SQL Fetch Summary
          3.00 ms - PeopleCode Builtin SQL Execute
            0.00 ms - SQL Fetch Summary
          1.00 ms - PeopleCode SQL Execute
          1.00 ms - Implicit Commit
        0.00 ms - Tuxedo Service Summary
        0.00 ms - FieldChange PCode Summary

Figure 10-10. PMU history tree for a PeopleSoft Ping with verbose agent filtering

Transactions are pieces of processing that take a certain amount of time to execute, so they all have a duration in addition to the various other metrics.

The timings on the various transactions in the PMU show how much time different parts of the technology took to respond. The difference between the duration of parent and child transactions is the time spent in that layer. The PMU in Figure 10-10 took 1322ms on the web server. The Jolt request took 1112ms, so the web server consumed 210ms. The ICPanel service took 901ms, but only 21ms was spent executing SQL; so most of the time is spent executing code on the application server, probably

---

[7] However, in some documentation these two terms are used interchangeably.

PeopleCode. This is very similar to the execution plan for a SQL statement in the extended SQL trace, which reports a duration for each operation.

▓ **Note** A PMU initiated in PeopleSoft Portal may invoke portlets that provide content from different PeopleSoft databases. PPM will represent this as a single PMU containing transactions from different monitored systems.

All the output from Performance Monitor is stored in the database of the monitoring system.[8] Current or open PMUs are temporarily placed in the table PSPMTRANSCURR, and when they are completed they are moved to PSPMTRANSHIST. Old PMUs can be deleted or archived to PSPMTRANSARCH. These three tables have similar structures (see Table 10-2). It is worth taking some time to understand the structure of these tables so you can build your own queries.

Table 10-2. Structure of PSPMTRANS% Tables

Column Name	Description
PM_INSTANCE_ID	Instance. Uniquely identifies a transaction or event.
PM_INSTANCE_SEQ	Only on PSPMTRANSCURR.
PM_TRANS_DEFN_SET	Performance Monitor transaction definition set number. Always 1.
PM_TRANS_DEFN_ID	With PM_TRANS_DEFN_SET, specifies the transaction type defined on PSPMTRANSDEFN, which also holds attributes that describe the contexts and metrics for the transaction.
PM_AGENTID	Specifies the agent (and hence database, application server, and web server) that collected transaction information. The value is looked up on PSPMAGENT.
OPRID	ID of the PeopleSoft operator that generated the transaction.
PM_PERF_TRACE	Name of the Performance Trace. Simply a string attribute set in the user's PIA session that identifies the session so that the transactions for that operator can be easily recovered. Defaults to <OPRID>.
PM_ACTION	Only on PSPMTRANSCURR.

---

[8] An ERD diagram of the performance monitoring tables (PSPM%) is available from the My Oracle Support web site in document 704808.1. There are also two use-case flowcharts for troubleshooting.

Column Name	Description
PM_TRANS_DELETED	Only on PSPMTRANSCURR.
PM_CONTEXT_VALUE1	Identifies what component, PeopleCode, and so on generated the transaction. Not all transactions (such as Tools Controlled Commit) have contexts, and you may need to look at the context of the parent transaction to clarify where the transaction originated.
PM_CONTEXT_VALUE2	Identifies what component, PeopleCode, and so on generated the transaction.
PM_CONTEXT_VALUE3	Identifies what component, PeopleCode, and so on generated the transaction.
PM_CONTEXTID_1	Copied from PSPMTRANSDEFN.PM_CONTEXTID_1. Identifier for PM_CONTEXT_VALUE1 that can be looked up on PSPMCONTEXTDEFN.
PM_CONTEXTID_2	Copied from PSPMTRANSDEFN.PM_CONTEXTID_2. Identifier for PM_CONTEXT_VALUE2 that can be looked up on PSPMCONTEXTDEFN.
PM_CONTEXTID_3	Copied from PSPMTRANSDEFN.PM_CONTEXTID_3. Identifier for PM_CONTEXT_VALUE3 that can be looked up on PSPMCONTEXTDEFN.
PM_AGENT_STRT_DTTM	Timestamp when the agent first updated the transaction.
PM_AGENT_LAST_DTTM	Timestamp when the agent last updated the transaction. Only on PSPMTRANSCURR.
PM_MON_STRT_DTTM	Timestamp when the monitor first received the transaction.
PM_MON_LAST_DTTM	Timestamp when the monitor last received the transaction. Only on PSPMTRANSCURR.
PM_TIMEOUT_DTTM	Timestamp when the transaction timed out. Only on PSPMTRANSCURR.
PM_TRANS_DURATION	Duration of the transaction (milliseconds). Not on PSPMTRANSCURR; only on PSPMTRANSHIST and PSPMTRANSARCH.
PM_PARENT_INST_ID	Transaction instance of the parent transaction. The transaction that spawned this transaction. Zero if this is the top (originating)

Column Name	Description
	transaction.
PM_TOP_INST_ID	Transaction instance that originated the series of transactions.
PM_PROCESS_ID	Operating system process ID of the originating server ID or agent.
PM_METRIC_VALUE1	Transaction metric 1. Metric type defined by PSPMTRANSDEFN.PM_METRICID_1. Description from PSPMMETRICDEFN.PM_METRICLABEL1.
PM_METRIC_VALUE2	Transaction metric 2.
PM_METRIC_VALUE3	Transaction metric 3.
PM_METRIC_VALUE4	Transaction metric 4.
PM_METRIC_VALUE5	Transaction metric 5.
PM_METRIC_VALUE6	Transaction metric 6.
PM_METRIC_VALUE7	Transaction metric 7 (a character string).
PM_ADDTNL_DESCR	Can contain extra information, such as a SQL statement and bind variable values.

CONVERTING LONG COLUMNS TO CLOBS

From PeopleTools 8.48 and Application version 9, columns formerly created as LONG columns in the database are created as CLOBs (see Table 4-8). CLOBs are used in the PeopleTools System database from PeopleTools 8.50.

If you have CLOB columns on PPM tables, you can specify criteria on them if you cast them to VARCHAR2:

```
AND     CAST(c302.pm_addtnl_descr AS VARCHAR2(30)) != '(idle)'
```

However, if you still have LONG columns, this technique doesn't work. Instead, I have created a packaged function that returns the LONG column as a VARCHAR2:

```
create or replace package body SYSADM.longtochar as
function PSPMEVENTHIST(p_rowid ROWID) RETURN VARCHAR2 is
    l_long VARCHAR2(32767):='';
  BEGIN
    SELECT PM_ADDTNL_DESCR INTO l_long
    FROM SYSADM.PSPMEVENTHIST
    WHERE  rowid = p_rowid;
```

```
    RETURN l_long;
end PSPMEVENTHIST;
end longtochar;
/
```

Now the criteria on the LONG column can be specified as follows:

```
AND    longtochar.pspmeventhist(c302.rowid) != '(idle)'
```

Transactions can have up to three contexts, which help to identify the action that generated the transaction. The PM_CONTEXTIDs are stored on the transaction, and the contexts are defined on the table PSPMCONTEXTDEFN.

Each transaction can hold up to seven metrics, one of which can be a character string. The PM_METRICID can be looked up on PSPMMETRICDEFN. Each metric definition has a metric type (PM_METRICTYPE):

- *1: Counter:* For example, metric 4 is "Total servlet request time (ms)". The metric accumulates the time and reports it each time transaction 152 occurs. In order to find the servlet time accumulated since the last transaction 152 occurred, you need to subtract the value of the metric on the last transaction record from the current value.

- *2: Gauge:* For example, metric 102 is "%CPU Used". This type of metric is a scalar quantity. That is to say, it contains a measurement of a particular quantity. The value can be understood in isolation, as opposed to a counter that must be compared.

- *3: Numeric identifier:* For example, metric 20 is the HTTP response code. This is a number that has a meaning, but you don't do any arithmetic with it. However, some type-3 metrics should really be type 2, such as metric 37, "Number of Tuxedo Servers".

- *4: String identifier:* For example, metric 27 is a file name.

The interrelationship of the various tables that hold and describe transactions is shown in Figure 10-11. If you are collecting information for multiple monitored systems on the one monitoring system, then the database name is related to the agent.

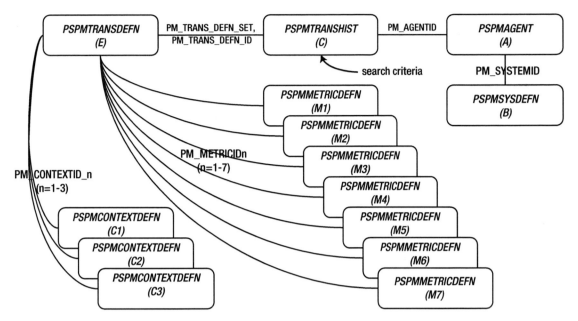

Figure 10-11. *Transaction data structures*[9]

Listing 10-14 shows an example of how to extract that data for a specific transaction. PeopleSoft also delivers a few similar ad hoc queries that interrogate the performance metrics directly.

Listing 10-14. `transaction_metrics.sql`: *SQL Query to Report on Transactions in a PMU*

```
SELECT C.PM_TOP_INST_ID, C.PM_INSTANCE_ID, C.PM_PARENT_INST_ID
,      B.DBNAME
,      A.PM_HOST_PORT, A.PM_DOMAIN_NAME, A.PM_AGENT_TYPE, A.PM_INSTANCE
,      C.PM_AGENT_STRT_DTTM, C.PM_MON_STRT_DTTM
,      C.OPRID, C.PM_PERF_TRACE, C.PM_PROCESS_ID
,      E.PM_TRANS_DEFN_ID, E.DESCR60
,      'Context1:'||c.pm_contextid_1||'-'||C1.PM_CONTEXT_LABEL
                              ||'='||C.PM_CONTEXT_VALUE1
,      'Context2:'||c.pm_contextid_2||'-'||C2.PM_CONTEXT_LABEL
                              ||'='||C.PM_CONTEXT_VALUE2
,      'Context3:'||c.pm_contextid_3||'-'||C3.PM_CONTEXT_LABEL
                              ||'='||C.PM_CONTEXT_VALUE3
,      C.PM_TRANS_DURATION
,      'Metric1:'||M1.PM_METRICLABEL||'='||C.PM_METRIC_VALUE1
,      'Metric2:'||M2.PM_METRICLABEL||'='||C.PM_METRIC_VALUE2
,      'Metric3:'||M3.PM_METRICLABEL||'='||C.PM_METRIC_VALUE3
,      'Metric4:'||M4.PM_METRICLABEL||'='||C.PM_METRIC_VALUE4
,      'Metric5:'||M5.PM_METRICLABEL||'='||C.PM_METRIC_VALUE5
```

[9] PM_CONTREXTID_1, PM_CONTREXTID_2, and PM_CONTREXTID_3 also appear on PSPMTRANSHIST as well as PSPMTRANSDEFN.

```
,       'Metric6:'||M6.PM_METRICLABEL||'='||C.PM_METRIC_VALUE6
,       'Metric7:'||M7.PM_METRICLABEL||'='||C.PM_METRIC_VALUE7
,       C.PM_ADDTNL_DESCR
FROM    PSPMAGENT A, PSPMSYSDEFN B, PSPMTRANSHIST C, PSPMTRANSDEFN E,
        PSPMMETRICDEFN M1, PSPMMETRICDEFN M2, PSPMMETRICDEFN M3,
        PSPMMETRICDEFN M4, PSPMMETRICDEFN M5, PSPMMETRICDEFN M6,
        PSPMMETRICDEFN M7,
        PSPMCONTEXTDEFN C1, PSPMCONTEXTDEFN C2, PSPMCONTEXTDEFN C3
WHERE   B.PM_SYSTEMID = A.PM_SYSTEMID
AND     A.PM_AGENTID = C.PM_AGENTID
AND     C.PM_TOP_INST_ID = 824633721163 /*specify PMU and all child transactions*/
AND     C.PM_TRANS_DEFN_SET = E.PM_TRANS_DEFN_SET
AND     C.PM_TRANS_DEFN_ID = E.PM_TRANS_DEFN_ID
AND     M1.PM_METRICID(+) = E.PM_METRICID_1
AND     M2.PM_METRICID(+) = E.PM_METRICID_2
AND     M3.PM_METRICID(+) = E.PM_METRICID_3
AND     M4.PM_METRICID(+) = E.PM_METRICID_4
AND     M5.PM_METRICID(+) = E.PM_METRICID_5
AND     M6.PM_METRICID(+) = E.PM_METRICID_6
AND     M7.PM_METRICID(+) = E.PM_METRICID_7
AND     C1.PM_CONTEXTID(+) = C.PM_CONTEXTID_1
AND     C2.PM_CONTEXTID(+) = C.PM_CONTEXTID_2
AND     C3.PM_CONTEXTID(+) = C.PM_CONTEXTID_3
;
```

Listing 10-15 shows the output from Listing 10-14 for the root transaction shown in Figure 10-10.

Listing 10-15. Sample Output from `transaction_metrics.sql`

```
PM_TOP_INST_ID PM_INSTANCE_ID PM_PARENT_INST_ID DBNAME
PM_HOST_PORT
PM_DOMAIN_NAME                   PM_AGENT_TYPE
PM_INSTANCE                      PM_AGENT_STRT_DTTM  PM_MON_STRT_DTTM
OPRID                            PM_PERF_TRACE                 PM_PROCESS_ID
PM_TRANS_DEFN_ID DESCR60
'CONTEXT1:'||C.PM_CONTEXTID_1||'-'||C1.PM_CONTEXT_LABEL||'='||C.PM_CONTEXT_VALUE
'CONTEXT2:'||C.PM_CONTEXTID_2||'-'||C2.PM_CONTEXT_LABEL||'='||C.PM_CONTEXT_VALUE
'CONTEXT3:'||C.PM_CONTEXTID_3||'-'||C3.PM_CONTEXT_LABEL||'='||C.PM_CONTEXT_VALUE
PM_TRANS_DURATION
'METRIC1:'||M1.PM_METRICLABEL||'='||C.PM_METRIC_VALUE1
'METRIC2:'||M2.PM_METRICLABEL||'='||C.PM_METRIC_VALUE2
'METRIC3:'||M3.PM_METRICLABEL||'='||C.PM_METRIC_VALUE3
'METRIC4:'||M4.PM_METRICLABEL||'='||C.PM_METRIC_VALUE4
'METRIC5:'||M5.PM_METRICLABEL||'='||C.PM_METRIC_VALUE5
'METRIC6:'||M6.PM_METRICLABEL||'='||C.PM_METRIC_VALUE6
'METRIC7:'||M7.PM_METRICLABEL||'='||C.PM_METRIC_VALUE7
PM_ADDTNL_DESCR
-------------------------------------------------------------------------------
 824633721163   824633721163                    0 HR88
go-faster-3:7201:7202
ps                              WEBSERVER
-1                              16:12:07 14.06.2004 16:12:09 14.06.2004
```

```
PS                          PS: 2004-06-14 16:01:11                    0
            101 Reported at entry and exit of PIA servlet
Context1:3-Session ID=AN7tpzSwpZc4kt9k8QNaCcYUWWh9FaFt!1963244185!1087224685145
Context2:2-IP Address=10.0.0.3
Context3:1-Action=View Page
            1322
Metric1:Response Size (bytes)=17613
Metric2:Response Code=200
Metric3:Static Content Count=0
Metric4:Is this a Pagelet?=0
Metric5:=0
Metric6:=0
Metric7:=
http://go-faster-3:7201/psc/ps/EMPLOYEE/HRMS/c/UTILITIES.PTPERF_TEST.GBL
```

In Listing 10-15, transaction 101 is "Reported at entry and exit of PIA servlet". It is the root transaction of the PMU shown in Figure 10-10. It has three contexts:

- *Context 1:* Action=View Page

- *Context 2:* IP Address=10.0.0.3

- *Context 3:* Session ID=AN7tpzSwpZc4kt9k8 ...

However, the additional description is often more useful. In this case, it is the URL of the component:

http://go-faster-3:7201/psc/ps/EMPLOYEE/HRMS/c/UTILITIES.PTPERF_TEST.GBL

Transaction 101 has 4 metrics:

- *Metric 19:* "Response Size (bytes)"

- *Metric 20:* "Response Code"

- *Metric 22:* "Static Content Count"

- *Metric 23:* "Is this a Pagelet?"

Events

Certain *events* are defined that also cause the monitor agents to collect various related metrics. These events can occur

- On a regular cycle, such as host resource or Tuxedo server metrics

- In response to a user action, such as a PeopleSoft Ping

- On an exception, such as a Jolt exception or query timeout

Events do not have contexts because they are not associated with executing a particular part of the application. Instead, they are related to the agent that collected them: either a web server JVM or an application server or Process Scheduler domain server process. They are stored in the database in PSPMEVENTHIST (described in Table 10-3) and are archived to PSPMEVENTARCH.

Table 10-3. Structure of the PSPMEVENTHIST and PSPMEVENTARCH Tables

Column Name	Description
PM_INSTANCE_ID	Instance. Uniquely identifies a transaction or event.
PM_EVENT_DEFN_SET	Performance Monitor event definition set number. Always 1.
PM_EVENT_DEFN_ID	With PM_EVENT_DEFN_SET, specifies the event type defined on PSPMEVENTDEFN, which also holds attributes that describe the metrics for the event.
PM_AGENTID	Specifies the agent (and hence database, application server, and web server) that collected the transaction information. The value is looked up on PSPMAGENT.
PM_AGENT_DTTM	Timestamp of the event at the agent.
PM_MON_DTTM	Timestamp of the event when received by the monitor process.
PM_PROCESS_ID	Operating system process ID of the originating server ID or agent.
PM_FILTER_LEVEL	Filter level of the agent (see the section "Agent Filter Levels").
PM_METRIC_VALUE1	Transaction metric 1. Metric type defined by `PSPMEVENTDEFN.PM_METRICID_1`. Description from `PSPMMETRICDEFN.PM_METRICLABEL1`.
PM_METRIC_VALUE2	Event metric 2.
PM_METRIC_VALUE3	Event metric 3.
PM_METRIC_VALUE4	Event metric 4.
PM_METRIC_VALUE5	Event metric 5.
PM_METRIC_VALUE6	Event metric 6.
PM_METRIC_VALUE7	Event metric 7 (a character string).
PM_ADDTNL_DESCR	Can contain extra information, such as a SQL statement and bind variable values.

The structure for events (see Figure 10-12) is less complicated than transactions because there are no contexts.

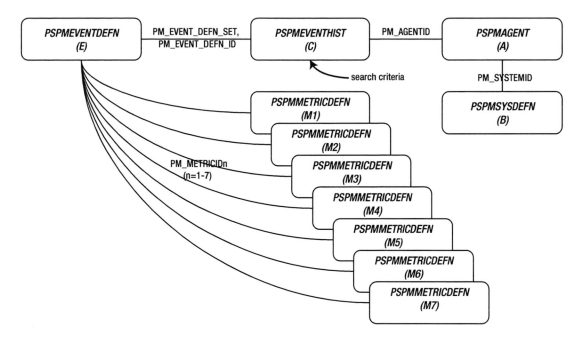

Figure 10-12. Events structure

Listing 10-16 shows a simple query to retrieve the events and metrics that occurred in a particular time window.

Listing 10-16. Extract from event_metrics.sql

```
SELECT B.DBNAME,
       A.PM_HOST_PORT, A.PM_AGENT_TYPE, A.PM_DOMAIN_NAME, A.PM_INSTANCE,
       C.PM_AGENT_DTTM, C.PM_INSTANCE_ID,
       E.PM_EVENT_DEFN_ID, E.DESCR60,
       'Metric1:'||M1.PM_METRICLABEL||'='||C.PM_METRIC_VALUE1,
       'Metric2:'||M2.PM_METRICLABEL||'='||C.PM_METRIC_VALUE2,
       'Metric3:'||M3.PM_METRICLABEL||'='||C.PM_METRIC_VALUE3,
       'Metric4:'||M4.PM_METRICLABEL||'='||C.PM_METRIC_VALUE4,
       'Metric5:'||M5.PM_METRICLABEL||'='||C.PM_METRIC_VALUE5,
       'Metric6:'||M6.PM_METRICLABEL||'='||C.PM_METRIC_VALUE6,
       'Metric7:'||M7.PM_METRICLABEL||'='||C.PM_METRIC_VALUE7,
       C.PM_ADDTNL_DESCR
FROM   PSPMAGENT A, PSPMSYSDEFN B, PSPMEVENTHIST C, PSPMEVENTDEFN E,
       PSPMMETRICDEFN M1, PSPMMETRICDEFN M2, PSPMMETRICDEFN M3,
       PSPMMETRICDEFN M4, PSPMMETRICDEFN M5, PSPMMETRICDEFN M6,
       PSPMMETRICDEFN M7
WHERE  B.PM_SYSTEMID = A.PM_SYSTEMID
AND    A.PM_AGENTID = C.PM_AGENTID
AND    B.DBNAME IN ('HR88' ,'hr88')
AND    C.PM_AGENT_DTTM
            BETWEEN TO_DATE('2004-06-14 16:12:06','YYYY-MM-DD HH24.MI.SS')
                AND TO_DATE('2004-06-14 16:12:11','YYYY-MM-DD HH24.MI.SS')
AND    C.PM_EVENT_DEFN_SET = E.PM_EVENT_DEFN_SET
AND    C.PM_EVENT_DEFN_ID = E.PM_EVENT_DEFN_ID
AND    M1.PM_METRICID(+) = E.PM_METRICID_1
AND    M2.PM_METRICID(+) = E.PM_METRICID_2
AND    M3.PM_METRICID(+) = E.PM_METRICID_3
AND    M4.PM_METRICID(+) = E.PM_METRICID_4
AND    M5.PM_METRICID(+) = E.PM_METRICID_5
AND    M6.PM_METRICID(+) = E.PM_METRICID_6
AND    M7.PM_METRICID(+) = E.PM_METRICID_7
;
```

Listing 10-17 shows a sample of the output from the query in Listing 10-16, the event generated by a PeopleSoft Ping.

Listing 10-17. Sample Output from Event Metrics

```
DBNAME    PM_HOST_PORT
PM_AGENT_TYPE                    PM_DOMAIN_NAME
PM_INSTANCE                      PM_AGENT_DTTM      PM_INSTANCE_ID
PM_EVENT_DEFN_ID DESCR60
'METRIC1:'||M1.PM_METRICLABEL||'='||C.PM_METRIC_VALUE1
'METRIC2:'||M2.PM_METRICLABEL||'='||C.PM_METRIC_VALUE2
'METRIC3:'||M3.PM_METRICLABEL||'='||C.PM_METRIC_VALUE3
'METRIC4:'||M4.PM_METRICLABEL||'='||C.PM_METRIC_VALUE4
'METRIC5:'||M5.PM_METRICLABEL||'='||C.PM_METRIC_VALUE5
'METRIC6:'||M6.PM_METRICLABEL||'='||C.PM_METRIC_VALUE6
'METRIC7:'||M7.PM_METRICLABEL||'='||C.PM_METRIC_VALUE7
```

```
PM_ADDTNL_DESCR
--------------------------------------------------------------------------------
HR88    go-faster-3:7201:7202
WEBSERVER                        ps
-1                               16:12:08 14.06.2004   824633721166
          600 PSPING metrics fowarded from browser
Metric1:Network Latency (ms)=435
Metric2:WebServer Latency (ms)=100
Metric3:AppServer Latency (ms)=561
Metric4:DB Latency (millisecs)=451
Metric5:=0
Metric6:=0
Metric7:IP Address=10.0.0.3
PS;AN7tpzSwpZc4kt9k8QNaCcYUWWh9FaFt!1963244185!1087224685145
```

Metrics of type 1 are numeric counters that increment from event to event. For this type of metric, you need to know the difference between the value of the metric for successive events. The SQL analytic LEAD() function can be helpful. Listing 10-18 shows how you might code a query to do this.

Listing 10-18. Extract from event_metrics2.sql Showing the Use of Analytic Functions for Counters

```
SELECT ...
     PM_METRICLABEL1,
     CASE
       WHEN PM_METRICTYPE1 = '1' AND PM_METRIC_VALUE1<PM_METRIC_LAST1
                           THEN PM_METRIC_VALUE1
       WHEN PM_METRICTYPE1 = '1' THEN PM_METRIC_VALUE1-PM_METRIC_LAST1
       ELSE PM_METRIC_VALUE1
     END AS PM_METRIC_VALUE1,
...
FROM   (
SELECT ...
     M1.PM_METRICLABEL PM_METRICLABEL1 ,C.PM_METRIC_VALUE1,
     LEAD(C.PM_METRIC_VALUE1,1)
         OVER(PARTITION BY E.PM_EVENT_DEFN_SET, E.PM_EVENT_DEFN_ID,
                          C.PM_AGENTID, C.PM_METRIC_VALUE7
         ORDER BY C.PM_AGENT_DTTM DESC) AS PM_METRIC_LAST1,
     M1.PM_METRICTYPE PM_METRICTYPE1,
...
FROM   PSPMAGENT A, PSPMSYSDEFN B, PSPMEVENTHIST C, PSPMEVENTDEFN E,
...
```

Sampling Rates

The way PPM monitors a monitored system, and the quantity of information collected, can be configured in the System Definitions component in the monitoring system. Figure 10-13 shows this component.

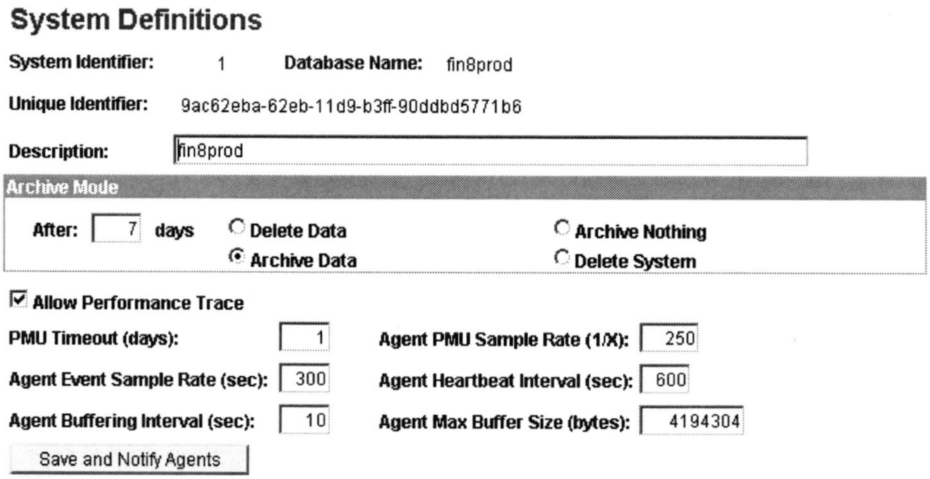

System Definitions

System Identifier: 1	**Database Name:** fin8prod	

Unique Identifier: 9ac62eba-62eb-11d9-b3ff-90ddbd5771b6

Description: fin8prod

Archive Mode

After: 7 **days** ○ **Delete Data** ○ **Archive Nothing**
                    ⊙ **Archive Data** ○ **Delete System**

☑ **Allow Performance Trace**

PMU Timeout (days): 1	**Agent PMU Sample Rate (1/X):** 250	
Agent Event Sample Rate (sec): 300	**Agent Heartbeat Interval (sec):** 600	
Agent Buffering Interval (sec): 10	**Agent Max Buffer Size (bytes):** 4194304	

Save and Notify Agents

Figure 10-13. System Definitions component

A proportion of transactions are captured. It is not possible for me to recommend an appropriate value here. What proportion to capture depends on the activity of the system and how much data you want to work with. I typically use values between 1 in 100 and 1 in 1,000. Generally, I don't want to have more than about 5 million rows in either PSPMTRANSHIST or PSPMEVENTHIST; otherwise the performance of the analytic components and the PPM archiving process degrades. If the web server chooses to sample a transaction, then all the child transactions within that PMU are also sampled.

Events are captured on a regular cycle. Again, the amount of data collected depends on the frequency of collection and the number of middleware components. Each web server, application server, and Process Scheduler process generates metrics. The default sample interval is every 5 minutes (300 seconds), but I have used values between 2 and 10 minutes.

If data has not been received from a web server or Tuxedo domain within the heartbeat interval, the agent is marked as stale on the System Performance component (see Figure 10-16, later in the chapter). Thus this value should be greater than the Agent Sampling Rate.

Each agent maintains its own timer, so you do not get a surge of data simultaneously from each agent. Instead, event metrics arrive at different times from different agents. This can make it difficult to aggregate event statistics across multiple web servers or multiple application servers to build up a complete picture. My solution is to round the timestamps to a multiple of the sampling interval with the PL/SQL packaged function shown in Listing 10-19. This approach is not perfect, but it is good enough for practical purposes.

Listing 10-19. Extract from the PL/SQL Package ppm with Date-Rounding Functions (ppmpkg.sql)

```
CREATE OR REPLACE PACKAGE BODY ppm AS
FUNCTION date_floor(p_datetime DATE,p_roundsecs INTEGER) RETURN DATE IS
```

```
BEGIN
RETURN TRUNC(p_datetime)
+FLOOR(TO_NUMBER(TO_CHAR(p_datetime,'SSSSS'))/p_roundsecs)*p_roundsecs/86400;
END date_floor;

FUNCTION date_round(p_datetime DATE,p_roundsecs INTEGER) RETURN DATE IS
BEGIN
RETURN TRUNC(p_datetime) +
ROUND(TO_NUMBER(TO_CHAR(p_datetime,'SSSSS'))/p_roundsecs,0)*p_roundsecs/86400;
END date_round;
END ppm;
/
```

It is very easy to end up with a lot of PPM data very quickly. As the data accumulates, so the delivered components that query the data slow down. The PPM archive process should be run daily. You can choose to simply delete data, or you can move it to the archive tables (PSPMTRANSARCH and PSPMEVENTARCH). The archive tables have exactly the same structure as the history tables. Once the data has been moved to the archive tables, it is entirely up to the user to use it and manage it. None of the delivered components reference the archive data. There is no delivered process to purge the archive tables.

Agent Filter Levels

Filter levels can be defined in the Agent Filters component (see Figure 10-14) for each type of monitoring agent that controls the metrics that are collected.

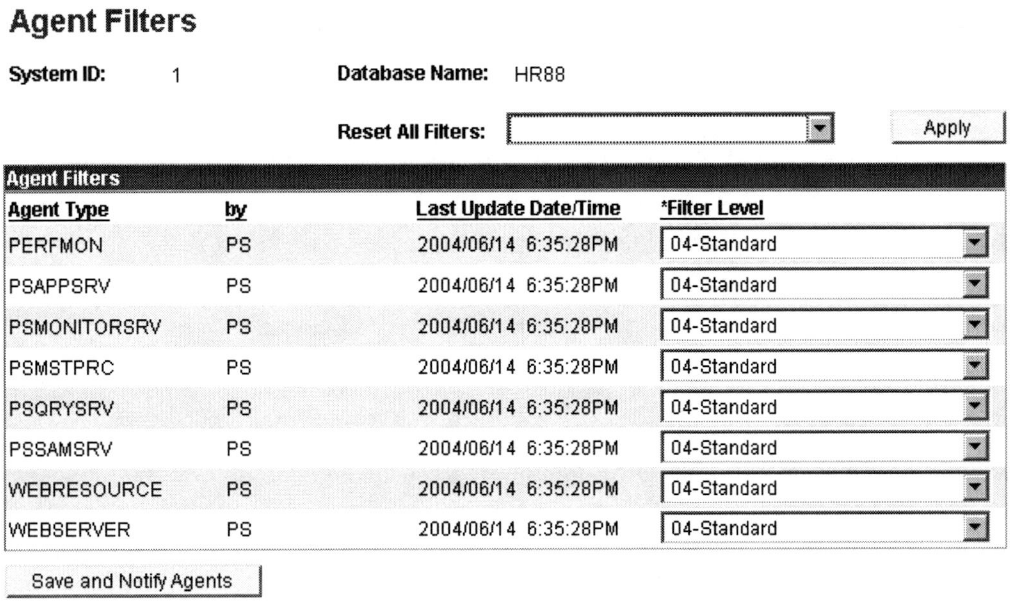

Agent Filters

System ID: 1   **Database Name:**   HR88

Reset All Filters: [▼]   [Apply]

Agent Type	by	Last Update Date/Time	*Filter Level
PERFMON	PS	2004/06/14 6:35:28PM	04-Standard ▼
PSAPPSRV	PS	2004/06/14 6:35:28PM	04-Standard ▼
PSMONITORSRV	PS	2004/06/14 6:35:28PM	04-Standard ▼
PSMSTPRC	PS	2004/06/14 6:35:28PM	04-Standard ▼
PSQRYSRV	PS	2004/06/14 6:35:28PM	04-Standard ▼
PSSAMSRV	PS	2004/06/14 6:35:28PM	04-Standard ▼
WEBRESOURCE	PS	2004/06/14 6:35:28PM	04-Standard ▼
WEBSERVER	PS	2004/06/14 6:35:28PM	04-Standard ▼

[Save and Notify Agents]

Figure 10-14. Agent Filters panel

Event and transaction definitions include a filter level. The agents generate the metrics only if the filter level of the event is less than or equal to the filter level set for the agent. There are seven possible filter levels (see Table 10-4). The default filter level is 4 for all agents.

Table 10-4. Filter Levels

Level	Description
00	No change
01	Standby
02	Error
03	Warning
04	Standard
05	Verbose
06	Debug

Most transaction types are at levels 4 and 5. Events that monitor SQL are defined as level 5. A few transactions at level 6 measure PeopleCode events and some internal aspects of the Component Processor. Most events are defined at filter level 4. There are only a few error events generated on error at level 3, and one at level 6. PPM can effectively be disabled, but without removing the configuration, by setting the filter level to 1 or 2, although Performance Trace still works because it can override these settings.

If the Ping PMU shown in Figure 10-10 had been collected at only the standard filter level, it would not have shown any detail below the ICPanel service. By setting the filter level to 5, the SQL statement and fetch operations were reported.

However, there are warnings in both the Agent Filters component and the documentation that increasing the filter level to 5 or 6 can have a significant performance impact.

I generally recommend using level 4 (standard) to monitor a production system or a performance-test system during a stress test. I would still configure PPM for development and test environments, setting the filter level to less than or equal to 3 so that minimal data is collected; but Performance Trace can still be used.

Performance Trace

Performance Trace is a way to make Performance Monitor collect all the transactions in a user's PIA session.

Access to Performance Trace is controlled by operator security. The link to Performance Trace only appears in the branding if PPM is correctly configured, if Performance Trace is permitted in the system definition (see Figure 10-13), and if the operator has full access to the WEBLIB_PPM web library. Clicking the Performance Trace link causes a Performance Trace Console to appear (see Figure 10-15).

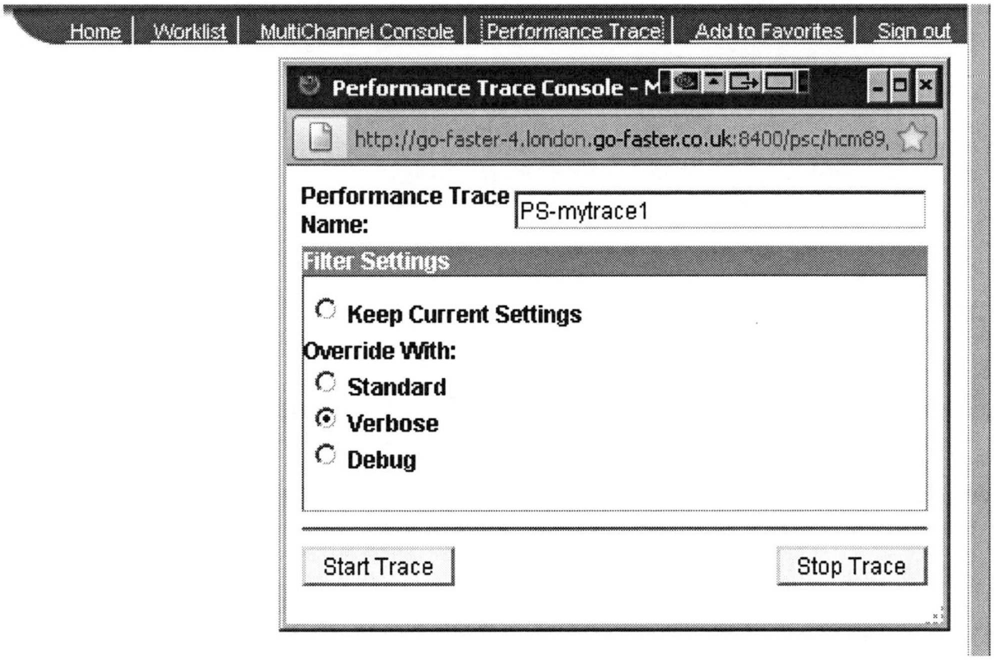

Figure 10-15. Performance Trace Console

The Performance Trace name is stored on the transaction records in PSPMTRANSHIST in the column PM_PERF_TRACE. Transactions can then be queried by trace name. There are two delivered components where this can be done:

- PeopleTools ➤ Performance Monitor ➤ History ➤ Completed PMUs

- PeopleTools ➤ Performance Monitor ➤ Analytics ➤ Performance Trace

The operator can chose to override the filter level set on the agents. If they do so, event 601 is also generated, thus providing an audit of Performance Trace use.

I usually collect Performance Traces at level 5 (verbose) because I want to see how much time I have spent in SQL. That does have a small but usually acceptable runtime overhead. Level 6 (debug) has a very significant overhead, and I have rarely found the additional information to be helpful.

Analytic Components

PeopleSoft delivered a number of analytic components that query the performance metrics collected by PPM and in some cases present the data graphically. A good place to start exploring a system is the System Performance component (see Figure 10-16), which gives an overview of each system by drawing together different events and transactions. From there, you can click the links to other components that look at individual agents in more detail.

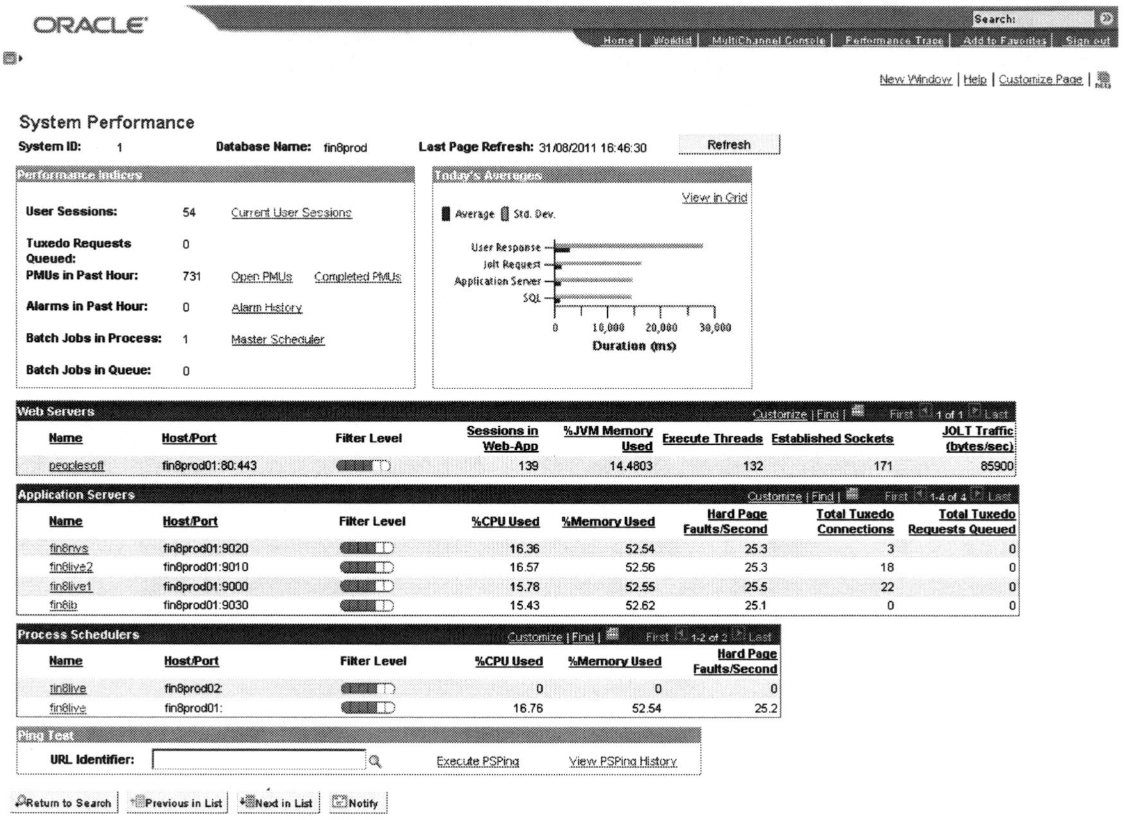

Figure 10-16. PeopleTools ➤ Performance Monitor ➤ System Performance component

I often extract data directly into Excel spreadsheets using MSQuery and an ODBC connection. I can then draw charts on that data. The data in the spreadsheets can easily be refreshed, so the spreadsheets build up to become additional analytic utilities to be used with Performance Monitor. There are examples in the next section.

■ **Note** Toward the end of this chapter is a case study of using Performance Trace to analyze a problem that demonstrates some of the other analytic components.

Transaction and Event Types

Performance Monitor collects and stores some of the same (or at least similar) metrics discussed in Chapter 9, but without the need to process trace files. All the metrics are described in the Performance Monitor PeopleBook, but in this section I want to look at some of those transactions and events and suggest how they can be used.

Transaction ID 115: JOLT Request

The Jolt request transaction (see Table 10-5) shows the size of each incoming and outbound Tuxedo message. It provides an easier way to determine how many Tuxedo messages exceed the Interprocess Communication (IPC) message and queue size limits (see Chapter 13).

Table 10-5. Jolt Request to the Application Server

Metric	Description
Context 1	Session ID
Context 2	IP address
Context 3	Tuxedo service name
Metric 1	Jolt send buffer (bytes)
Metric 2	Jolt receive buffer (bytes)
Metric 3	Jolt return code
Metric 4	Jolt request retried

The Error status code is stored in the additional information column, PM_ADDTNL_DESCR.

Individual transactions and events can also be examined in the PIA by using the components in the PeopleTools Performance Monitor History menu; all contexts and metrics can be viewed (see Figure 10-17).

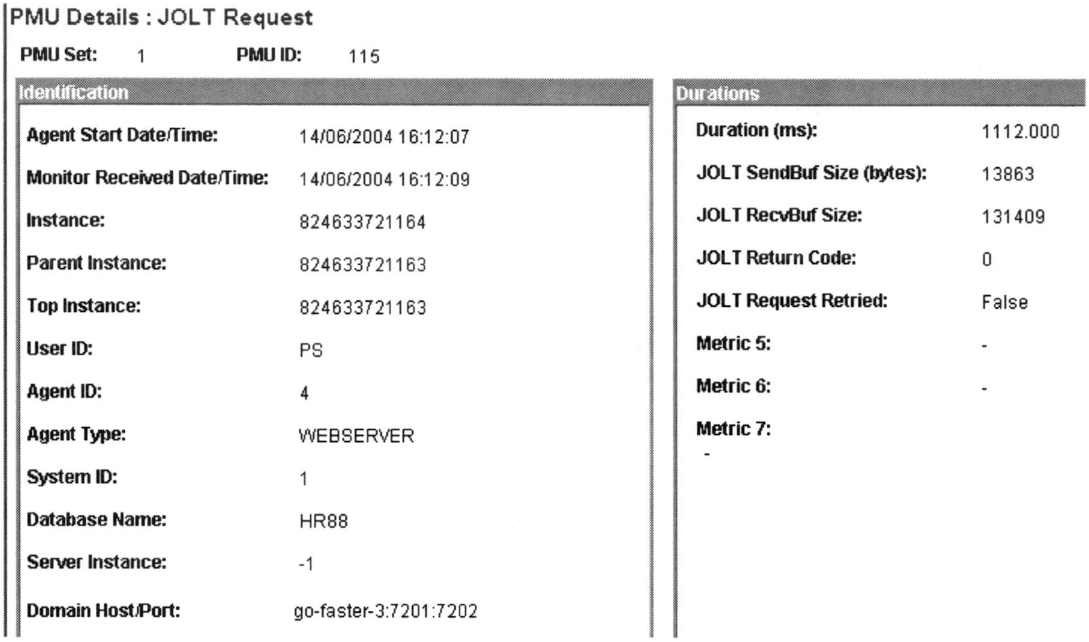

PMU Details : JOLT Request

PMU Set: 1   PMU ID: 115

Identification		Durations	
Agent Start Date/Time:	14/06/2004 16:12:07	Duration (ms):	1112.000
Monitor Received Date/Time:	14/06/2004 16:12:09	JOLT SendBuf Size (bytes):	13863
Instance:	824633721164	JOLT RecvBuf Size:	131409
Parent Instance:	824633721163	JOLT Return Code:	0
Top Instance:	824633721163	JOLT Request Retried:	False
User ID:	PS	Metric 5:	-
Agent ID:	4	Metric 6:	-
Agent Type:	WEBSERVER	Metric 7:	-
System ID:	1		
Database Name:	HR88		
Server Instance:	-1		
Domain Host/Port:	go-faster-3:7201:7202		

Figure 10-17. Jolt request transaction as seen in Performance Monitor's History menu

Previously, the message sizes could be seen only in the enhanced Tuxedo trace, but enabling this trace has a significant performance overhead. You can see that the message sizes reported in the transaction appear as parameters to the Tuxedo service calls in the enhanced Tuxedo log file, as shown in Listing 10-20.

Listing 10-20. Enhanced Tuxedo Log (Edited for Readability)

```
:  { tpservice({"ICPanel", 0x0,0x2413040, 13863, 0, -1, {1087224688, 0, 37}})
:    { tpalloc("CARRAY", "", 8192)
:    } tpalloc = 0x24252e8 [tperrno TPEOS]
:    { tprealloc(0x24252e8, 131072)
:    } tprealloc = 0xfae90e0
:    { tprealloc(0xfae90e0, 196608)
:    } tprealloc = 0xfdca0e0
:    { tpreturn(2, 0, 0xfdca0e0, 131409, 0x0)
:    } tpreturn [long jump]
:  } tpservice
```

Transaction ID 116: Redirect on Login

When an operator logs into PeopleSoft via the PIA, they are redirected from one page to another. This redirection is instrumented at transaction 116. The duration of the transaction is the network round trip from web server to browser and back. This transaction differs from others in that it is not sampled, but is collected for every login.

The transaction has only one metric: the user-agent identifier, as shown in Table 10-6. This metric contains the user-agent string from the HTTP header in the message from the client to the web server, which can also be revealed in the web server access log (see Table 9-1). The string contains information about the client browser and operating system.

Table 10-6. Redirect after Login

Metric	Description
Metric 7	User agent identifier

The second context ID of the transaction is the IP address of the client. However, in most customer systems this is actually the IP address of another piece of network infrastructure in front of the web server, often a load balancer or reverse proxy server.

Case Study: Identifying a Network Problem with Transaction 116

Occasionally, I have used transaction 116 to diagnose a network problem that was affecting PeopleSoft. Figure 10-18 shows a chart of durations for this transaction with respect to time for a single day.

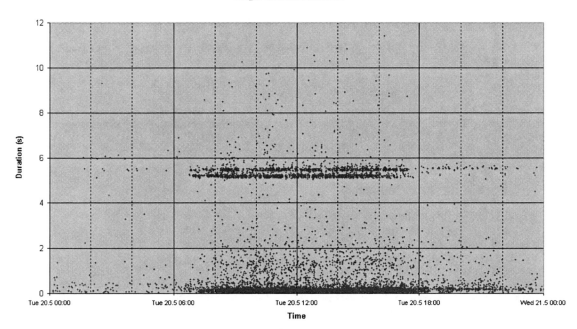

Figure 10-18. Chart of transaction 116 durations for a system

For most of the working day, there were three distinct bands. Many operators were getting good sub-second response, but two bands at around 5.1 and 5.5 seconds were associated with one particular IP address. The operator ID was also recorded on a transaction, so I knew who was logging in. I could get their usual location from the HCM database (not perfect, but right most of the time). I created my own local copy of the location data in the PPM database with the script in Listing 10-21.

Listing 10-21. Obtaining Employee Location from the HCM Database

```
CREATE TABLE dmk_location_tbl AS
SELECT o.oprid, o.emplid, j.empl_rcd, j.effdt, j.location, l.descr, l.city, l.county,
l.country
FROM psoprdefn@hcm o, ps_job@hcm j, ps_location_tbl@hcm l
WHERE j.emplid = o.emplid
AND j.effdt = (
    SELECT max(j1.effdt) FROM ps_job@hcm j1
    WHERE j1.emplid = j.emplid AND j1.effdt <= SYSDATE)
AND j.empl_rcd = (
    SELECT max(j3.empl_rcd) FROM ps_job@hcm j3
    WHERE j3.emplid = j.emplid AND j3.effdt = j.effdt)
AND j.effseq = (
    SELECT max(j2.effseq) FROM ps_job@hcm j2
    WHERE j2.emplid = j.emplid AND j2.empl_Rcd = j.empl_rcd AND j2.effdt = j.effdt)
AND l.setid = j.setid_location
AND l.location = j.location
AND l.effdt = (
    SELECT max(l1.effdt) FROM ps_location_tbl@hcm l1
    WHERE l1.location = j.location AND l1.setid = j.setid_location AND l1.effdt < SYSDATE)
UNION ALL
SELECT o.oprid, o.emplid, 0, sysdate, 'unk', 'unknown', 'unknown', 'unknown', 'unknown'
FROM psoprdefn@hcm o
WHERE O.EMPLID = ' '
ORDER BY 1,2,3
/
```

I was able to profile the duration of transaction 116 by the default location of the employee using the SQL query in Listing 10-22.

Listing 10-22. Query to Profile Transaction 116

```
SELECT L.LOCATION, L.CITY, L.COUNTRY
,       min(C.PM_TRANS_DURATION)/1000 min
,       AVG(C.PM_TRANS_DURATION)/1000 avg
,       median(C.PM_TRANS_DURATION)/1000 med
,       max(C.PM_TRANS_DURATION)/1000 max
,       VARIANCE(C.PM_TRANS_DURATION)/1000 var
--,     VAR_POP(C.PM_TRANS_DURATION)/1000 var_pop
,       COUNT(*) num_events
FROM    PSPMAGENT A, PSPMSYSDEFN B, PSPMTRANSHIST C, DMK_LOCATION_TBL L
WHERE   B.PM_SYSTEMID = A.PM_SYSTEMID
AND     A.PM_AGENT_INACTIVE = 'N' /*exclude Inactive agents*/
AND     A.PM_AGENTID = C.PM_AGENTID
AND     C.PM_TRANS_DEFN_SET = 1
AND     C.PM_TRANS_DEFN_ID = 116
AND     B.DBNAME like '%PRD%' /*Production Databases*/
AND     C.OPRID = L.EMPLID
```

```
AND     C.PM_MON_STRT_DTTM >= TRUNC(SYSDATE)
GROUP BY L.LOCATION, L.CITY, L.COUNTRY
HAVING COUNT(*) >= 10 /*only report if at least 10 transactions*/
ORDER BY avg
/
```

A pattern began to emerge from the transaction profile in Listing 10-23. The external workers in Bangalore and Brno had a much worse experience. I could also see that all the transactions for these operators all one particular client IP address, which was a reverse proxy server.

Listing 10-23. *Transaction 116 Profile*

```
LOCATION    CITY               Cty   MIN    AVG    MED    MAX       VAR EVENTS
----------  -----------------  ---   ------ ------ ------ -------  ---------- ------
EXT-OO-IN   Bangalore          IND   0.109  5.488  5.468  61.321   5,099.0   688
EXT-OO-CZ   Brno               CZE   0.109  4.991  5.218  20.951   2,125.1   555
EXT-MC-UK   Macclesfield       GBR   0.062  0.862  0.281   6.578   3,100.8   224
...
HOME        Home Worker*       GBR   0.031  0.299  0.188   9.109     377.7   489
...
INT-LI      Liverpool          GBR   0.062  0.211  0.110   2.406     140.6    40
INT-MC      Macclesfield       GBR   0.032  0.233  0.078   1.266     114.4    30
INT-WA      Walsall            GBR   0.031  0.086  0.063   0.359       3.5    46
```

This customer uses PeopleSoft CRM as an HR helpdesk. It has outsourced and off-shored its HR helpdesk to a third party. The external operators access the system via a reverse proxy server. This proxy server was the root cause. It was changed, and the problem was resolved.

Event ID 150: JVM Status

The metrics reported by this event (see Table 10-7) are available in the web server console; however, there is no easy way to capture that information.

Table 10-7. *JVM Status*

Metric	Description	Comment
Metric 1	% of JVM memory used	
Metric 2	Max JVM memory available	
Metric 3	Sessions in the web server / application server	This is the actual number of browser sessions concurrently connected to this web server.
Metric 4	Execute threads	
Metric 5	Busy threads	A JVM thread is busy because it is either serving a request from a user itself or waiting for the application server to respond.

Metric	Description	Comment
Metric 6	Domain count	

The printclient command in the Tuxedo tmadmin utility also reports all the clients of the Bulletin Board and their statuses. However, it includes the Tuxedo handler processes and any instances of tmadmin, which this event does not. Hence, it is possible to use printclient to count the number of users connected to the PIA. This is not a perfect measure because the Tuxedo Jolt Listener and the PIA servlet have separate timeout settings. A session may time out on the application server before it does so on the servlet. Therefore, the Performance Monitor metrics provide a better way to determine the number of concurrent users on a system.

Event ID 152: Web Site Status

This event reports metrics for the PIA servlet, as shown in Table 10-8.

Table 10-8. Web Site Status Reported by Web Server Resource Monitor

Metric	Description	Comment
Metric 1	Cumulative number of requests to all servlets	Corresponds to the number of entries found in the access log
Metric 2	Servlet requests (last minute)	
Metric 3	Average request time (last minute)	
Metric 4	Cumulative time in all servlets (ms)	Can be slightly less than the sum of the time taken to serve the requests recorded in the web server access log
Metric 5	Current sessions	Does not match the number of the web/application server session on event 150
Metric 7	Site path	A single web server may host several PeopleSoft systems. Each system has a unique site name in the path to the servlet in the URL.

Event ID 153: Web Servlet Status

This event is similar to event 152, except that the statistics are broken down by servlet (see Table 10-9).

Table 10-9. Web Servlet Status Reported by Web Server Resource Monitor

Metric	Description	Comment
Metric 1	Cumulative request to this servlets	Corresponds to the number of entries found in the access log
Metric 2	Servlet requests (last minute)	
Metric 3	Average request time (last minute)	
Metric 4	Cumulative time in this servlet (ms)	Can be slightly less than the sum of the time taken to serve the requests recorded in the web server access log.
Metric 7	Servlet name	

Events 152 and 153 give a good indication of the total amount of response time consumed in the PIA, although the sum of the durations in the access log may add up to slightly more than the time recorded for the event. For example, Listing 10-24 shows the results of querying, for a five minute interval, the event 153 data for the psc servlet.

Listing 10-24. Details of Part of Event 153

```
DBNAM PM_HOST_PORT          PM_AGENT_DTTM        PM_EVENT_DEFN_ID
----- -------------------- -------------------- ----------------
DESCR60
-----------------------------------------------------------
PM_METRICLABEL1               PM_METRIC_VALUE1
----------------------------- ----------------
PM_METRICLABEL2               PM_METRIC_VALUE2
----------------------------- ----------------
PM_METRICLABEL3               PM_METRIC_VALUE3
----------------------------- ----------------
PM_METRICLABEL4               PM_METRIC_VALUE4
----------------------------- ----------------
PM_METRICLABEL7               PM_METRIC_VALUE7
----------------------------- --------------------
HR88  go-faster-3:7201:7202 16:57:29 24.08.2004           153
Web servlet status reported by WebServer Resource Monitor
Requests to this Servlet                 5
Servlet Requests (last minute)           0
Avg Request Time (last minute)           0
```

```
Time in this Servlet (ms)                  25637
Servlet Name                  /psc
```

Meanwhile, Listing 10-25 shows, for the same period, the entries in the access log for the psc servlet.

Listing 10-25. Corresponding web server access log entries

```
2004-08-24   16:52:35   0.762   3650   10.0.0.8   GO-FASTER-3   GET
/psc/ps/EMPLOYEE/HRMS/s/WEBLIB_PT_NAV.ISCRIPT1.FieldFormula.IScript_PT_NAV_PAGELET
Bodyid=true&c=YN5k5WtxjcM%3d
2004-08-24   16:54:33   0.28   0   10.0.0.8   GO-FASTER-3   GET
200   /psc/ps/EMPLOYEE/HRMS/c/ADMINISTER_WORKFORCE_(GBL).JOB_DATA.GBL...
2004-08-24   16:54:37   2.123   0   10.0.0.8   GO-FASTER-3   POST
200   /psc/ps/EMPLOYEE/HRMS/c/ADMINISTER_WORKFORCE_(GBL).JOB_DATA.GBL   -
2004-08-24   16:54:43   2.984   0   10.0.0.8   GO-FASTER-3   POST
200   /psc/ps/EMPLOYEE/HRMS/c/ADMINISTER_WORKFORCE_(GBL).JOB_DATA.GBL   -
2004-08-24   16:55:06   19.498   0   10.0.0.8   GO-FASTER-3
POST   200   /psc/ps/EMPLOYEE/HRMS/c/ADMINISTER_WORKFORCE_(GBL).JOB_DATA.GBL   -
```

The entries in the web server access log total 25.647 seconds, but Process Monitor reports only 25.637 seconds. It should also be possible to correlate the cumulative servlet time reporting by this event with the CPU consumption recorded in event 300.

If you do configure a system to self-monitor, this event also reports the time spent in the monitoring servlets. It gives an indication of the overhead of self-monitoring.

Event ID 200: Resources per Process

Each instrumented server process generates this event to record operating-system resource consumption by those servers (see Table 10-10).

Table 10-10. Events Sent by All C++ Processes

Metric	Description	Comment
Metric 1	% CPU used	
Metric 2	CPU time (secs)*	Amount of CPU time consumed by the server process since it started
Metric 3	VM (bytes)	
Metric 4	Working set (bytes)	

* CPU time (metric 103) is delivered as type 3 (numeric identifier) when it should actually be type 1 (counter). This does not affect the behavior of Performance Monitor, but counters should be compared with the previously recorded value for the same agent.

Event ID 300: Host Resource Status

The resource status events are generated by the PSMONITORSRV (see Table 10-11). Each application server and Process Scheduler Tuxedo domain includes an instance of this server. If they are all running on the same physical server, then they all report similar data.

Table 10-11. *Host Resource Status*

Metric	Description	Comment
Metric 1	% CPU used	
Metric 2	% memory used	
Metric 3	Hard page faults/second	
Metric 4	Total Tuxedo connections	Closely corresponds to the number of web/application server connections in event 150[10]
Metric 5	Total Tuxedo requests queued[11]	

All operating systems report CPU and memory utilization, but methods to collect and analyze that data vary widely. It is useful to have the data at hand in the PPM repository. The charts in Figures 10-19 and 10-20 are derived from event 300.

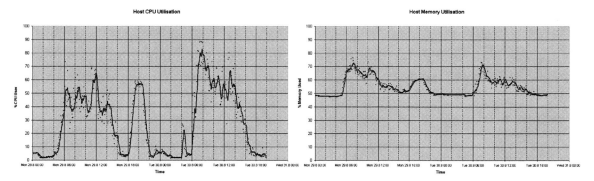

Figure 10-19. *Chart of CPU utilization using Event 300* *Figure 10-20.* *Chart of memory utilization using Event 300*

The total number of connections can also be obtained by counting the rows returned from the printclient command in the Tuxedo tmadmin utility.

---

[10] This metric is also faulty. The number of connections reported appears to be arbitrarily capped, although the value of the cap varies from domain to domain.

[11] As with Event 301, the number of Tuxedo requests queued is always reported as 0.

Event ID 301: Tuxedo pq Row

This event retrieves the same information as the printqueue command in the Tuxedo tmadmin utility[12] (see Chapter 9). One event is written for each queue in the domain for application server and Process Scheduler domains. The PSMONITORSRV server reads this information directly from the Tuxedo Bulletin Board. Table 10-12 contains the metrics and their descriptions.

Table 10-12. *Tuxedo Queuing Reported in Groups to Simulate a Tuxedo Command-Line printqueue*

Metric	Description	Comment
Metric 1	Server count	Number of server processes on the queue.
Metric 2	Queue length	Number of requests currently on the queue.
Metric 3	Average queue length	Not reported by tmadmin unless load balancing is enabled, in which case it returns -1.
Metric 7	Queue name	Name of the Tuxedo queue. If the queue name is not defined in Tuxedo, it defaults to a string containing the Tuxedo group and server IDs.

---

[12] It is critically important to know when services requests are queued in a Tuxedo domain. Unfortunately, this event seems to be broken in every version of PPM that I have used. It reports a zero queue length, even if tmadmin reports prolonged queuing. So, I still use the tuxmon scripts described in Chapter 13.

Event ID 302: Tuxedo psr Row

This event retrieves the same information as the `printserver` command in the Tuxedo `tmadmin` utility (see Chapter 9). One event is written for each server process in the domain for application server and Process Scheduler domains. The PSMONITORSRV server reads this information directly from the Tuxedo Bulletin Board. Table 10-13 contains the metrics and their descriptions.

Table 10-13. Tuxedo Server Process Metrics Reported in Groups to Simulate a Tuxedo Command-Line `printserver`

Metric	Description	Comment
Metric 1	Server instance	Tuxedo server ID. This value is only unique within the queue.
Metric 2	Total requests*	Total number of requests that this server ID has handled.
Metric 3	PID	Operating-system process ID of the server process.
Metric 7	Server name	Name of the server process.

* Total requests (metric 115) is delivered as type 3 (numeric identifier) when it should actually be type 1 (counter). This does not affect the behavior of Performance Monitor, but counters should be compared with the previously recorded value for the same agent.

The additional description shows the name of the Tuxedo service that the server process is currently handling, or "(idle)" if the server process is idle.

I often want to know how busy the application servers in a system are and whether additional server processes have been spawned, so I can make a judgment about the sizing of an application server. This is an example in which analytic components delivered with PeopleTools are not really adequate; I use the query in Listing 10-26 to extract the data into a pivot table in an Excel spreadsheet.

Listing 10-26. Extracting Application Server Process Status information

```
SELECT DISTINCT dbname, pm_host, pm_port, pm_domain_name, pm_agent_dttm
,       pm_instance
,       server_instance
,       process
,       service
FROM (
SELECT b.dbname,
       SUBSTR(a.pm_host_port,1,INSTR(a.pm_host_port,':')-1) pm_host,
       SUBSTR(a.pm_host_port,INSTR(a.pm_host_port,':')+1) pm_port,
       a.pm_instance,
       a.pm_domain_name,
       ppm.date_floor(c.pm_agent_dttm,b.pm_sample_int) pm_agent_dttm,
       c.pm_metric_value1 server_instance,
       c.pm_metric_value7 process,
```

313

```
        CAST(c.pm_addtnl_descr AS VARCHAR2(128)) service
/*      longtochar.pspmeventhist(c.rowid) service*/
FROM    pspmagent a, pspmsysdefn b, pspmeventhist c
WHERE   b.pm_systemid = a.pm_systemid
AND     a.pm_agent_inactive = 'N'
AND     a.pm_agentid = c.pm_agentid
AND     c.pm_event_defn_set = 1
AND     c.pm_event_defn_id = 302 --Tuxedo PSR data
AND     c.pm_metric_value7 LIKE 'PS%' --a PeopleSoft process
AND     a.pm_domain_type = '01' --App Server
)
ORDER BY PM_AGENT_DTTM, pm_host, pm_port, pm_domain_name
```

Figure 10-21 shows a chart of such a pivot table in Excel. It shows the PSAPPSRV processes in a single application server domain for a single day. The system was loaded from 5 a.m. to 6 p.m. The PSAPPSRV processes are arranged in 2 queues.[13] The minimum number of PSAPPSRVs on each queue is three, and the maximum is seven. Around 6 a.m., the load was such that all the application servers were busy, and Tuxedo spawned additional processes up to the full 14. By 1 p.m., the load had subsided such that Tuxedo shut down all the additional servers.

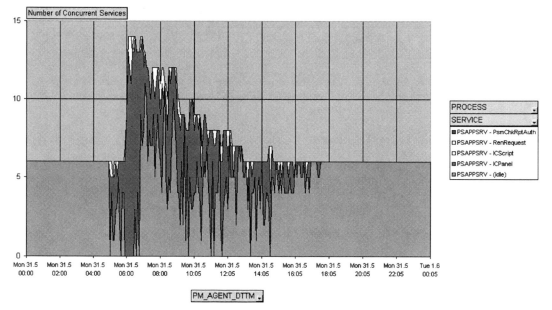

Figure 10-21. *Chart of application server processes by service derived from event 302*
(ev302active_servers.xls)

The chart shows that this application server, having spawned the maximum number of PSAPPSRVs, was still fully loaded between 6 a.m. and 7 a.m. The load was mainly composed of ICPanel services (executing components in the PIA), and some time was spent on ICScript services (mostly navigation

---

[13] Configuring Tuxedo to use multiple queues is described in Chapter 13.

between components). This is normal. I would also want to confirm that there was a queue of service requests.

This chart suggests that the maximum number of PSAPPSRVs could be increased, provided there was free memory and CPU to support them—event 300 could help with that. I would also look at what was running during the peak period, and whether anything could be done to reduce the duration of the Tuxedo services.

The metrics collected by events 150, 300, 301, and 302 effectively contain the same information as the Tuxmon scripts described in Chapter 13.

Event ID 350: Master Scheduler Status

This event provides an overview of each Process Scheduler configured on the database (see Table 10-14).

Table 10-14. Master Scheduler Status

Metric	Description
Metric 1	Active processes
Metric 2	Queued processes
Metric 3	Blocked processes
Metric 4	Unused process slots

Note that the Process Scheduler name is not recorded on this event. It would be advisable to give the Tuxedo domain ID that includes the scheduler name.

Event ID 351: Master Scheduler Detail

An event is generated for each process type configured for each Process Scheduler (see Table 10-15). This event does include the server name.

Table 10-15. Master Scheduler Detail per Process Type

Metric	Description
Metric 1	Active processes
Metric 4	Unused process slots
Metric 7	Server name

Events 350 and 351 provide an indication of the level of batch activity in a system at any time. Users of systems with a significant simultaneous batch and online load sometimes report that online performance degrades when there is a heavy batch load. These metrics should provide the ability to detect any correlation.

Event ID 600: PSPING

When you use the PeopleSoft Ping utility, the Ping also generates an event. The Ping metrics are stored in PS_PTP_TST_CASES on the monitored system by the Ping component itself, but an event is generated and sends the same metrics to the monitoring system as well (see Table 10-16).

Table 10-16. Ping Metrics Forwarded from the Browser

Metric	Description
Metric 1	Network latency (ms)
Metric 2	Web server latency (ms)
Metric 3	Application server latency (ms)
Metric 4	DB latency (ms)
Metric 7	IP address

The Operator ID and Java Session ID are stored in the additional information.

Event ID 601: Override

This event provides a record of the performance monitoring traces performed on the system at more detailed levels (see Table 10-17).

Table 10-17. User Event: Monitoring Level Override

Metric	Description
Metric 1	Agent filter mask
Metric 7	User-initiated PMU name

Instrumentation

Table 10-18 shows all the metrics collected from various sources for the same PeopleSoft Ping transaction shown in Figure 10-10.

Table 10-18. Metrics from a PeopleSoft Ping

Duration (ms)	Description
1547	Total duration of the Ping.
1342	Duration of the servlet request as reported by the web server access log.
1322	Transaction 101: PIA view page request.
1112	Web server duration (including application server and database durations) of the Ping.
1112	Transaction 115: Jolt request. This transaction is produced by the PIA servlet in the web monitor, so you would expect it to correspond to the duration of the Ping as also measured in the servlet. However, sometimes the duration of the Ping can be 10 or 20ms greater than this metric.
1082	Duration of the Tuxedo ICPanel service as reported by the Tuxedo service trace.
1020	Transaction 400: Tuxedo service.
1012	Application server duration of the Ping.
901	Transaction: 401 ICPanel service.
861	Transaction 400: Duration of the PeopleCode component only.
451	Database duration of the Ping.
30	Active database time reported in Oracle SQL Trace.

■ **Note** PeopleTools SQL trace was enabled when these measurements were taken. The overhead of this trace is responsible for the large discrepancy in the time reported by the database and the duration of the database call as measured by the application server.

We can see that nearly all the durations are different from each other. Figure 10-22 shows these metrics superimposed on the now familiar PIA architecture diagram.

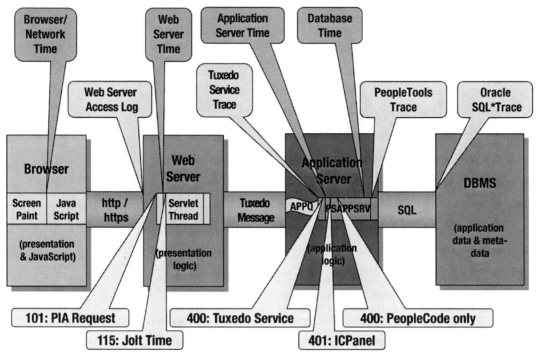

Figure 10-22. *Sources of metrics with Process Monitor transactions added*

The differences indicate that the measurements are collected at slightly different points in the PeopleSoft technology chain. Within the four tiers, the performance measurement instrumentation has been placed in different layers of software. Of course, each of these layers makes its contribution to the overall response time, as seen by the human operator in front of the browser!

Performance Tuning the Performance Monitor

As the volume of data collected by Performance Monitor builds up, you may see some SQL performance problems with some parts of Performance Monitor. I have used Performance Trace on the self-monitoring Performance Monitor to resolve these issues, with the following recommendations.[14]

---

[14] See also http://blog.psftdba.com/search/label/Performance%20Monitor.

Indexes

I recommend changing and adding indexes as shown in Listing 10-27, to improve the performance of some of the queries generated by the delivered analytic components.

Listing 10-27. Custom Indexes for Performance Monitor

```
CREATE INDEX PSDPSPMEVENTHIST ON PSPMEVENTHIST
(PM_EVENT_DEFN_SET, PM_EVENT_DEFN_ID, PM_AGENTID, PM_AGENT_DTTM)
TABLESPACE PSINDEX ... PCTFREE 1 COMPRESS 3
/
CREATE INDEX PSCPSPMTRANSHIST ON PSPMTRANSHIST
(PM_TRANS_DEFN_SET,PM_TRANS_DEFN_ID, PM_PERF_TRACE,PM_METRIC_VALUE7)
TABLESPACE PSINDEX ... PCTFREE 1 COMPRESS 4
/
CREATE INDEX PSDPSPMTRANSHIST ON PSPMTRANSHIST
(PM_TOP_INST_ID, PM_TRANS_DEFN_SET, PM_TRANS_DEFN_ID)
TABLESPACE PSINDEX ... PCTFREE 1 COMPRESS 3
/
CREATE INDEX PSPPSPMTRANSHIST ON PSPMTRANSHIST
(PM_TRANS_DEFN_SET, PM_TRANS_DEFN_ID, PM_CONTEXT_VALUE1, PM_MON_STRT_DTTM)
TABLESPACE PSINDEX … PCTFREE 0 COMPRESS 3
/
```

System Monitor Component

The System Monitor component (Figure 10-16) can be affected by degradation in the performance of the view PSPMSESSIONS_VW. As well as adding index PSPPSPMTRANSHIST, as described in the previous section's Listing 10-27, I suggest rewriting the view as shown in Listing 10-28. A number of changes have been made to simplify the execution of this query without changing it functionally:

- The second subquery is correlated to its grandparent rather than just its parent.

- IN and NOT IN operators have been replaced with EXISTS and NOT EXISTS, respectively.

- The ROWNUM<=1 criteria have been added to restrict the number of rows returned by the subqueries. This also stops them from being merged during SQL transformation.

Listing 10-28. New Version of PSPMSESSIONS_VW

```
SELECT T3.PM_CONTEXT_VALUE1 /*Session ID*/
,      T3.PM_AGENTID
,      T3.PM_AGENT_STRT_DTTM
FROM   PSPMTRANSHIST T3
WHERE  T3.PM_TRANS_DEFN_ID = 116 /*Redirect after login*/
AND    T3.PM_TRANS_DEFN_SET = 1 /*added*/
AND    T3.PM_TRANS_STATUS = '1'
AND    T3.PM_TRANS_DURATION <> 0
AND EXISTS(
```

```
SELECT 'x'
FROM    PSPMTRANSHIST T
WHERE   T.PM_TRANS_DEFN_SET = 1
AND     T.PM_TRANS_DEFN_ID = 109 /*User Session Began*/
AND     T.PM_MON_STRT_DTTM > %TimeAdd(%CurrentDateTimeIn, -720)
AND     T.PM_PARENT_INST_ID <> T.PM_TOP_INST_ID
AND     T.PM_CONTEXT_VALUE1 = T3.PM_CONTEXT_VALUE1
AND NOT EXISTS(
SELECT 'x'
FROM    PSPMTRANSHIST T2
WHERE   T2.PM_TRANS_DEFN_SET = 1
AND     T2.PM_TRANS_DEFN_ID = 108 /*User Session Ended*/
AND     T2.PM_MON_STRT_DTTM > %TimeAdd(%CurrentDateTimeIn, -720)
AND     T2.PM_CONTEXT_VALUE1 = T3.PM_CONTEXT_VALUE1
AND     ROWNUM <= 1)
AND     ROWNUM <= 1)
```

Archive Process

The Performance Monitor archive process is another example of platform-generic design in PeopleSoft. While it runs, metrics are inserted into the tables PSPMTRANSHISTCL and PSPMEVENTHISTCL. This data is moved into the history tables at the end of the process, but agents can be marked as stale while the archive process is running. It repeatedly queries PSPMTRANSHIST and PSPMEVENTHIST for up to 1,000 rows to be purged or archived. Data is archived after a specified number of days. The date criterion is coded as follows using a PeopleCode macro:

```
%DateTimeDiff(X.PM_MON_STRT_DTTM, %CurrentDateTimeIn) >= (PM_MAX_HIST_AGE * 24 * 60)
```

On, Oracle the preceding predicate expands to

```
ROUND((CAST(( SYSDATE) AS DATE) - CAST((X.PM_MON_STRT_DTTM) AS DATE)) * 1440, 0) >=
(PM_MAX_HIST_AGE * 24 * 60)
```

This predicate inevitably results in a full scan of the metrics table. The full scan is repeated for each 1,000 rows archived. Each time the query runs, the system date has moved on. I have seen systems where the scan takes so long to run that more than 1,000 additional rows need to be archived because the system date has moved on. The archive process then runs almost indefinitely.

However, the date criterion can simply be recoded, albeit in an Oracle-specific way, as follows:

```
X.PM_MON_STRT_DTTM <= SYSDATE - PM_MAX_HIST_AGE
```

This substitution needs to be made in two places (once for each history table) in the PSPM_ARCHIVE.ARCHIVE.ARCPCODE.OnExecute PeopleCode called from the PSPM_ARCHIVE Application Engine program.

Performance Monitor Case Study: Diagnosing a SQL Performance Problem

Perhaps the best way to show the value of Performance Monitor is with a practical example from a real production system.[15] To demonstrate the capabilities of Performance Monitor, I configured it to collect metrics from a Financials system.

The Top Components analytic component (see Figure 10-23) reports the top (by default, the top ten) components by number of executions, cumulative execution duration (as measured at the application server), and average execution duration.

---

[15] This example has been heavily anonymized to preserve client confidentiality. Names, dates, and data values have been changed.

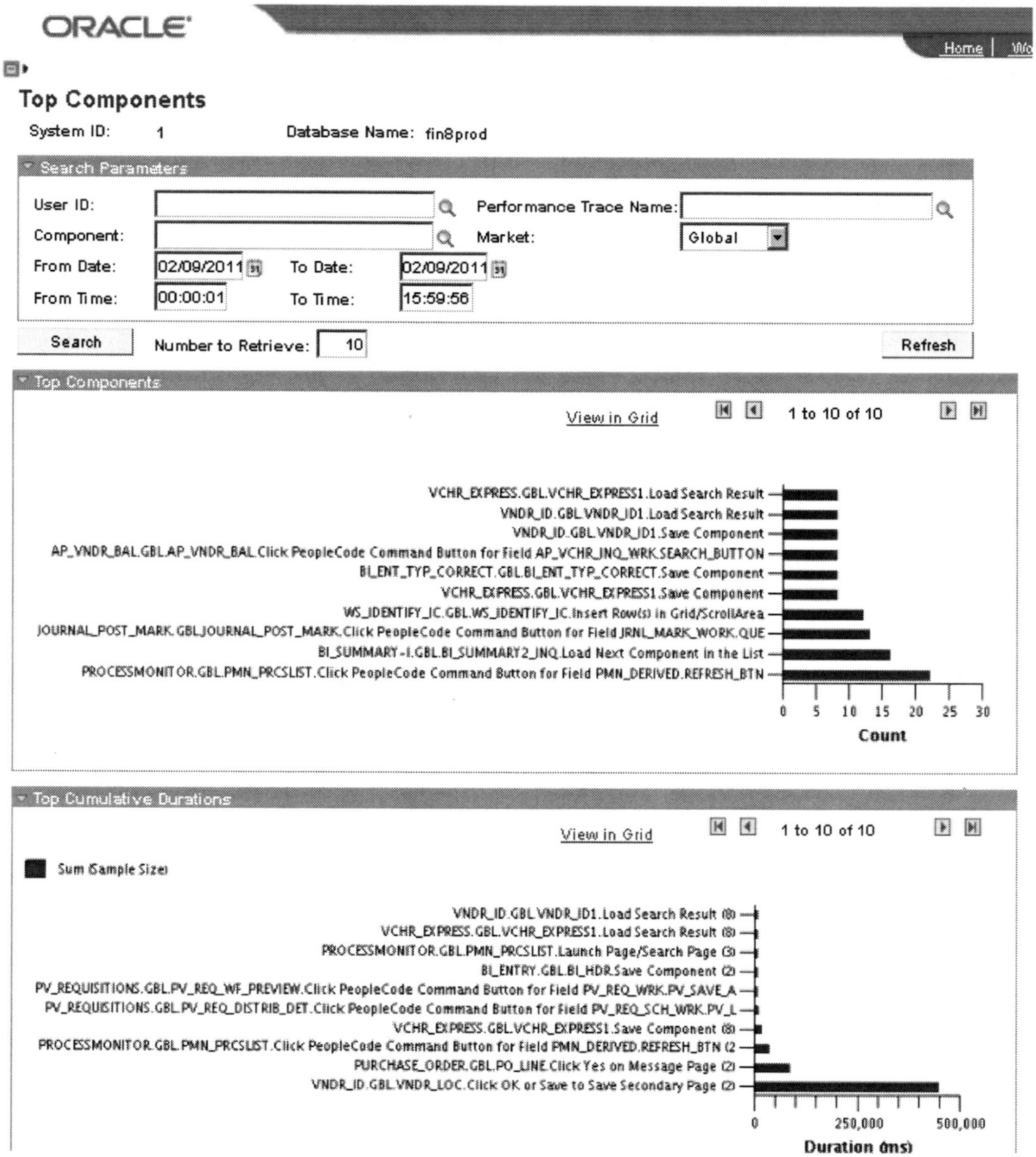

Figure 10-23. Top Components component.

A particular PeopleCode fired by a pushbutton in the VNDR_ID component had a very high cumulative execution time for just two executions (the number of executions is shown in brackets on the Top Cumulative Durations chart). The average execution time (not shown) was half the cumulative time, so it wasn't a just a single execution. I thought this was worth further investigation.

> ▨ **Note** For each chart, the data can be view as a table of numbers on a separate page and can be downloaded to an Excel sheet, as with any component script.

I knew which operator executed this sampled PMU. From the name of the component (the context information on transaction 406 in the PMU, which you see again in the PMU Details page in Figure 10-28), I could also work out where in the application this was and which group of users within the business were affected.

When I spoke to the user who regularly used this component, they confirmed that this component was a big problem for them. I temporarily granted the user access to Performance Trace and walked them through enabling Performance Trace (see Figure 10-15). We used verbose filtering so that we also collected SQL information. Then it was just a matter of going back to the application and demonstrating the problem. Finally, we turned off the trace.

I could then use the Component Trace component (see Figure 10-24) to view the data collected in the trace.

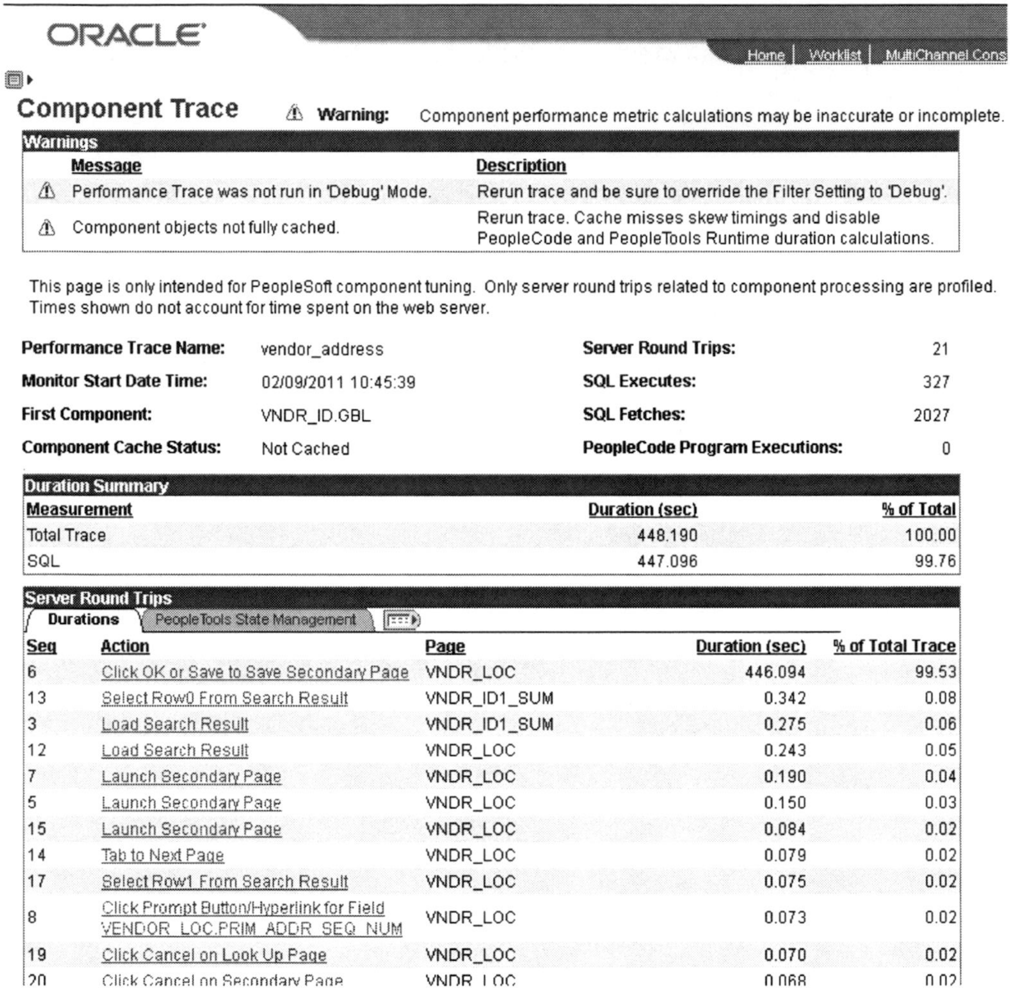

Figure 10-24. *Component Trace component*

In all, the trace contained 448.19s of application server processing time, of which 447.096s was in SQL. I sorted the Server Round Trips by duration by clicking the column title. Nearly all the time, 446.094s, was in a single action (or PMU). I needed to drill into the Round Trip Details subpage (see Figure 10-25) for that action.

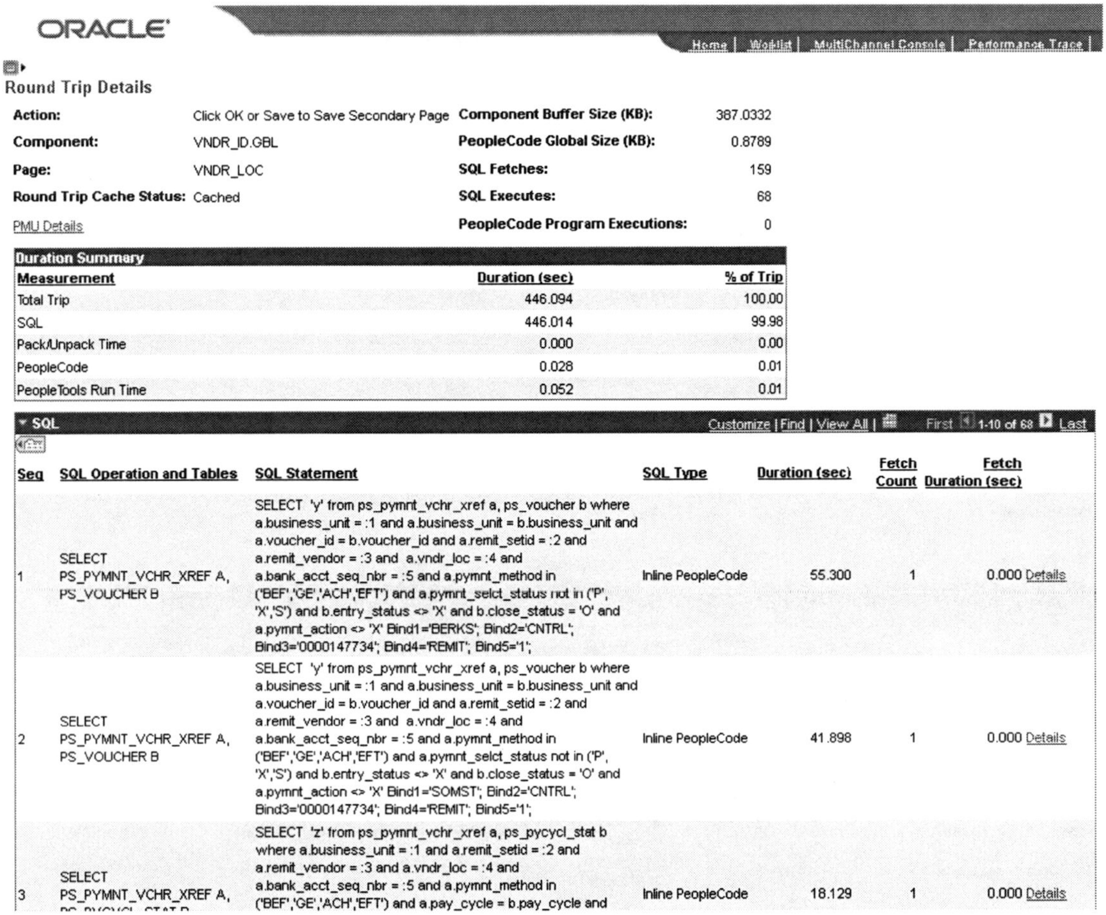

Figure 10-25. Round Trip Details subpage

The 446 seconds were spent executing 68 SQL queries. Each query retrieved a single row. I could see the SQL and the bind variable values. In fact, two SQL queries both queried PS_PYMNT_VCHR_XREF. They were each executed 34 times with different bind variable values each time.

The Details link in the Round Trip Details subpage only appears if you select the All Columns icon in the upper-left corner of the SQL scroll box; it takes you directly to the transaction details (shown in Figure 10-28).

The PMU Details link takes you to the Completed PMUs search dialog (see Figure 10-26). This component can also be accessed directly by choosing PeopleTools   Performance Monitor   History   Complete PMUS.

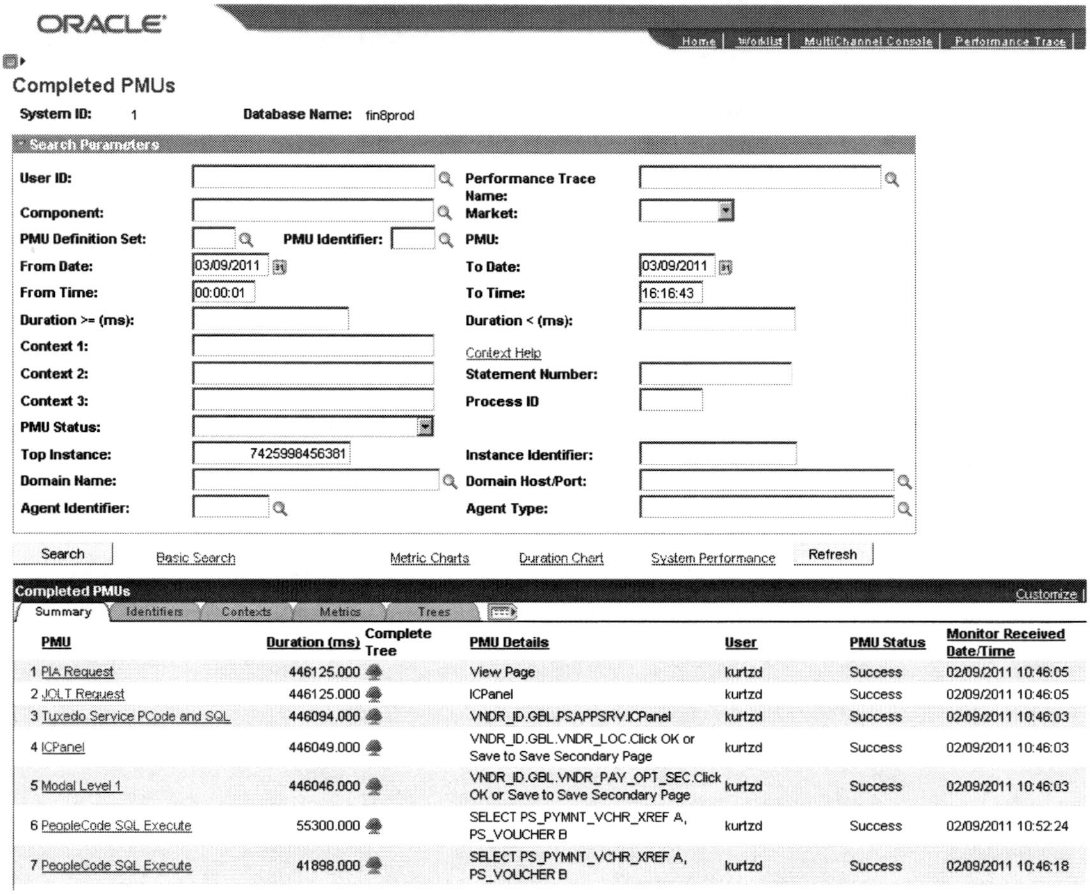

Figure 10-26. Completed PMUs search component

Note that the value of the top instance ID search field was passed in automatically. All the transactions in a PMU have the instance of the top transaction stored in the column TOP_INST_ID.

If you click any of the tree icons (next to the duration in the results), you are taken to the PMU History Tree (see Figure 10-27). In this case, all the transactions come from the same PMU, and so you go to the same tree; but this component is also available directly from the menu so that all transactions can be searched.

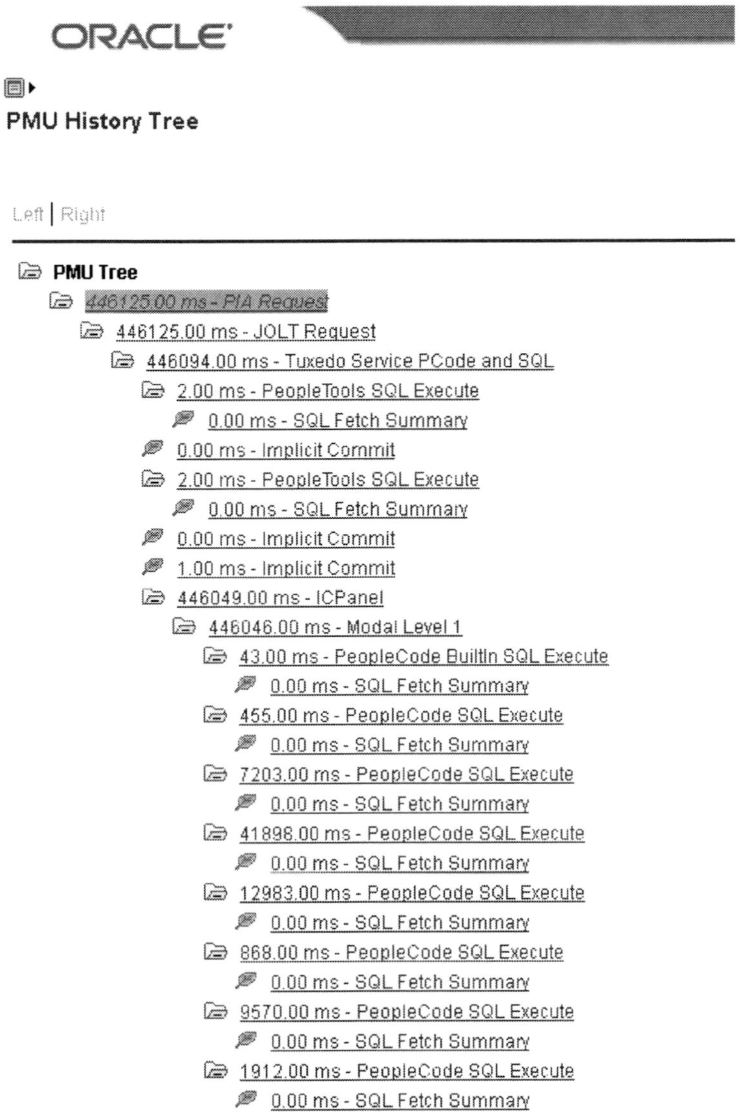

ORACLE

▣▸
PMU History Tree

Left | Right

▱ **PMU Tree**
  ▱ *446125.00 ms - PIA Request*
    ▱ 446125.00 ms - JOLT Request
      ▱ 446094.00 ms - Tuxedo Service PCode and SQL
        ▱ 2.00 ms - PeopleTools SQL Execute
          ⬢ 0.00 ms - SQL Fetch Summary
        ⬢ 0.00 ms - Implicit Commit
        ▱ 2.00 ms - PeopleTools SQL Execute
          ⬢ 0.00 ms - SQL Fetch Summary
        ⬢ 0.00 ms - Implicit Commit
        ⬢ 1.00 ms - Implicit Commit
        ▱ 446049.00 ms - ICPanel
          ▱ 446046.00 ms - Modal Level 1
            ▱ 43.00 ms - PeopleCode BuiltIn SQL Execute
              ⬢ 0.00 ms - SQL Fetch Summary
            ▱ 455.00 ms - PeopleCode SQL Execute
              ⬢ 0.00 ms - SQL Fetch Summary
            ▱ 7203.00 ms - PeopleCode SQL Execute
              ⬢ 0.00 ms - SQL Fetch Summary
            ▱ 41898.00 ms - PeopleCode SQL Execute
              ⬢ 0.00 ms - SQL Fetch Summary
            ▱ 12983.00 ms - PeopleCode SQL Execute
              ⬢ 0.00 ms - SQL Fetch Summary
            ▱ 868.00 ms - PeopleCode SQL Execute
              ⬢ 0.00 ms - SQL Fetch Summary
            ▱ 9570.00 ms - PeopleCode SQL Execute
              ⬢ 0.00 ms - SQL Fetch Summary
            ▱ 1912.00 ms - PeopleCode SQL Execute
              ⬢ 0.00 ms - SQL Fetch Summary

Figure 10-27. PMU History Tree

The tree view of a PMU is a useful way to get a feel for what a transaction consists of and where the time is spent. When PeopleSoft Portal is in use, some PMUs can involve several Jolt requests, possibly from different monitored systems. In this case, you can see all the SQL operations that make up the ICPanel service. You can click any transaction to be taken to the PMU details page (see Figure 10-28), which displays the details for that transaction.

Figure 10-28. PMU Details

Now I had the problem SQL statements and the bind variable values, so I had everything I needed to investigate the statement. I was able to generate an execution plan and decided to add an index to PS_PYMNT_VCHR_XREF (PPM can't do this for itself because it is designed to run on a separate database). I was then able to test the performance with the same data values. The end result was that the action that had taken over seven minutes to respond now returned in under one second.

In this example, the problem was SQL performance. It could have been resolved by the DBA using just database tools, such as ASH or SQL Extended Trace. From PeopleTools 8.50, the PIA registers the component and page names in the module and action attributes of the database session. These values are copied through to the ASH data. The commands that set the values capture in SQL trace files. Thus you know which component and page generated a particular SQL statement, but you cannot localize it to a particular piece of PeopleCode as Performance Monitor does.

Performance Monitor can also identify performance problems in PeopleCode or a different tier of the technology stack. The context information allows you to determine where in the application the problem is located.

The next chapter looks at Active Session History (ASH) in more detail. However, these tools need the skills and sometimes the access privileges of a DBA. Performance Monitor is a tool that can easily be given to a developer or systems administrator. An end user can easily be walked through the process of collecting a Performance Trace, and by doing so they become part of the solution.

Summary

Before the release of PeopleTools 8.4, getting performance metrics out of a PeopleSoft system required the variety of techniques discussed in Chapter 9, involving varying degrees of processing. On Unix systems, this often included writing scripts that were scheduled to run utilities periodically. On Windows, this approach generally was difficult without additional software.

As demonstrated in this chapter, PeopleSoft has made much more performance information readily available in PeopleTools 8.4. The metrics are stored in the database, so it is possible to answer more sophisticated questions by constructing SQL queries.

Performance Monitor represents a huge step forward in measuring, analyzing, and improving the performance of PeopleSoft systems. It is a rich source of performance metrics, yet its overhead can be kept low. It can be used safely in production systems, and it takes all the hard work out of collecting performance metrics for PeopleSoft systems without the need for scripting or assistance from operating-system administrators to schedule tasks. Despite its limitations, mostly due to a lack of continuing development, it is an excellent utility. Even if Oracle does not develop Performance Monitor further, it deserves to be given more publicity so that at least PeopleSoft customers use what is available.

CHAPTER 11

SQL Optimization Techniques in PeopleSoft

The previous two chapters discussed how to obtain the performance metrics that can indicate the most time-consuming processes or activities on your system. In the case of the Application Engine and COBOL processes, traces can identify the particular step in the process that is costing the most time. Although significant amounts of time can be spent executing code in the client or application server processes, you'll often find that the most time-consuming step turns out to involve the execution of SQL.

When SQL performance is not the most significant part of a performance issue, then the problem is likely to be much more complicated to address. It may come down to the design of a process, which may require considerable customization, or it may be a feature of the PeopleSoft supplied program that you either cannot see or cannot change. At least if the issue is SQL performance, then, as the DBA, you can see what is going on, and perhaps you can do something about it, possibly without having to make a code change.

This chapter has several purposes:

- To demonstrate how to use Active Session History to diagnose problems in PeopleSoft

- To demonstrate how to enable Oracle Extended SQL Trace to capture information about the SQL being issued by the application

- To explain how to find where in the application the SQL is defined

- To determine whether, and to what extent, it is possible to change the code

It does not explain how to optimize SQL statements, nor how and why the various techniques for optimization work (there many Oracle-specific books on that subject).

Active Session History

Active Session History (ASH) was introduced in Oracle 10g Enterprise Edition. Every second, it samples information about each session that is currently active. That information is stored in a circular in-memory buffer that is exposed by v$active_session_history. The design goal is to keep about an hour of information in that buffer.

When an Automatic Workload Repository (AWR) snapshot is taken (or when the buffer becomes two-thirds full), one sample in ten is stored in the repository; it can then be queried via DBA_HIST_ACTIVE_SESS_HISTORY.

■ **Note** ASH is enabled by default,[1] but be aware that it is not free. It is a licensed feature as part of the Diagnostic Pack, which is only available on the Enterprise Edition of Oracle. I don't like that either, but that's how it is.

ASH data builds up into a hugely valuable archive of what happened in a system over time. If you were to query all the ASH data for a single session, you would get something a little like a trace of that session. Long-running operations are sampled many times, whereas operations that take less than one second may never be sampled. So, unlike an Extended SQL Trace, the ASH data is not a complete record. However, something that is short-lived but that happens frequently is sampled sometimes. ASH data can then be analyzed statistically.

If you are looking at something that happened recently, you can count one second for each sample in v$active_session_history and derive a profile for set of data that you are analyzing:

```
SELECT    ...
,         SUM(1) ash_secs
FROM      v$active_session_history
WHERE     ...
GROUP BY ...
```

Or, you can go back as far as the AWR retention limit and count ten seconds for each sample in DBA_HIST_ACTIVE_SESS_HISTORY:

```
SELECT    ...
,         SUM(10) ash_secs
FROM      dba_hist_active_sess_history
WHERE     ...
GROUP BY ...
```

Each ASH sample contains various pieces of information about the session. These attributes can be grouped into dimensions, which are used to filter and group the ASH data during analysis:

- *Time:* Sample ID and time

- *Session:* Session ID and serial number, session ID and instance of parallel query coordinator

- *Wait:* Wait event ID, name, and parameters

- *SQL:* SQL_ID, plan hash value, SQL operation code, and SQL execution plan line number (from 11g)

- *Object:* Object, file, and block numbers; row number in the block (from 11g)

- *Application:* Module, action, client ID, and program name

To use ASH data effectively, you need to know what part of the application was being executed in a particular session at a particular time. Oracle provides the dbms_application_info PL/SQL package to set

---

[1] From Oracle 11g, unlicensed features can be disabled by setting the Oracle initialization parameter CONTROL_MANAGEMENT_PACK_ACCESS=NONE.

and read the module, action, and Client ID attributes for a session. These values are exposed on v$session and are sampled by ASH.

Oracle has long recommended that application developers use this package to instrument their applications. Oracle has done so itself in its E-Business Suite applications. Nevertheless, it is rare to find other applications that do so.

If applications set these attributes to meaningful values, then ASH data can be filtered and aggregated by these values, and hence you can work out how much time was spent in which part of an application.

SIMULATING ACTIVE SESSION HISTORY

The data sampled by ASH is available via the dynamic performance views. Much of the data can be obtained from v$session. It is possible to simulate ASH by sampling these views and storing the data captured. An example of this is the S-ASH[2] utility. S-ASH is a PL/SQL procedure that is run by the database job scheduler. This approach has a higher overhead on the database than Oracle ASH and may not be able to support as high a sample rate. However, if you do not have the Diagnostic Pack, it is an alternative.

Module and Action in PeopleSoft

Application Server and Application Engine processes have used dbms_application_info since PeopleTools 7.53.

On startup, module is set to be the same value as the executable program, and client_info is set to a string that starts with the Operator ID used to start the Tuxedo server process (see Listing 9-2).

At the start of each application server service, client_info is set to a string that begins with the ID of the operator logged into the PIA who originated the service request. In Application Engine, it is set to the operator who submitted the Process Scheduler request.

PeopleTools 8.50 on makes additional use of dbms_application_info. module and action are set at the beginning of each application server service:

- Within the PIA, the application server sets module and action to the name of the current component and page within the current components. ClientID is also set to the PeopleSoft Operator's ID.

- For Integration Broker messages, they are set to the service and queue name.

- For Application Engine processes, module is set to PSAE, and action is set to the program name.

_____

[2] See http://ashmasters.com/ash-simulation or http://sourceforge.net/projects/orasash/.

■ **Caution** There is anecdotal evidence that the module and action information may not be entirely reliable on at least PeopleTools 8.50. Existing values may not always be replaced by the new service call. This causes confusion because SQL is wrongly attributed to the previous service.

This information is hugely valuable. It can be seen in Oracle Enterprise Manager, where sessions can be grouped sorted by module or action. For example, Figure 11-1 shows the ASH data for the component RECV_PO. There are actions for two pages in that component: PO_PICK_ORDERS and RECV_WPO_HDR

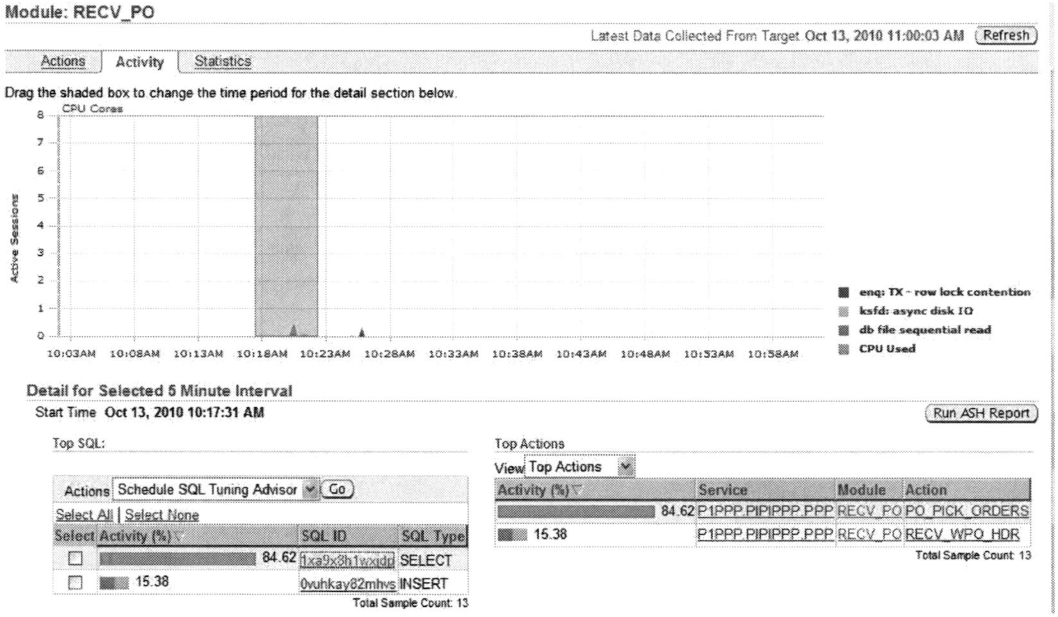

Figure 11-1. Enterprise Manager showing top actions for a particular module in a PeopleTools 8.50 system

It is also possible to query the ASH data directly with SQL to profile which components and pages consume the most time. The query in Listing 11-1 reports the amount of database time spent in each component and page over the last seven days.

Listing 11-1. SQL Query to Profile Top Online Pages

```
SELECT /*+LEADING(x h) USE_NL(h)*/
       h.module, h.action, sum(10) ash_secs
FROM   dba_hist_active_sess_history h,
,      dba_hist_snapshot x
WHERE  x.end_interval_time >= TRUNC(SYSDATE)-7
AND    h.sample_time >= TRUNC(SYSDATE)-7
AND    h.snap_id = x.snap_id
```

```
AND     h.dbid = x.dbid
AND     h.instance_number = x.instance_number
AND     x.instance_number = h.instance_number
AND     UPPER(h.program) like 'PSAPPSRV%'
GROUP BY h.module, h.action
ORDER BY ash_secs DESC
/
```

In Listing 11-2 the action xyzzy is not a component name. It is a dummy value used when the PIA has entered the component but has not opened the page. This usually means that it is in the search dialog defined in the component.

Listing 11-2. Profile of Top Online Pages

```
MODULE                  ACTION                  ASH_SECS
--------------------    --------------------    ----------
RECV_PO                 PO_PICK_ORDERS              240
XXX_REQ_INQUIRY         xyzzy                       170
XXX_REQ_WRKLST          XXX_REQ_WORKLIST            170
VCHR_EXPRESS            VCHR_LINE_RECV_WRK          170
XXX_FIN_WORKLIST        XXX_FIN_WORKLIST            160
VCHR_EXPRESS            VCHR_EXPRESS1               160
PURCHASE_ORDER_EXP      PO_EXPRESS                  140
XXX_HOME_PAGE           XXX_HOME_PAGE               140
RECV_PO                 RECV_WPO                    130
VCHR_EXPRESS            xyzzy                       120
XXX_PUR_WORKLIST        XXX_PUR_WRKLST              120
CDM_RPT                 CDM_RPT_INDEX               100
```

Setting Module and Action for Batch Processes

From PeopleSoft 8.50, Application Engine programs always set module to PSAE and action to the name of the Application Engine program being executed. However, it is still not possible to tie particular ASH samples to particular instances of a program if multiple instances of that program execute concurrently. By default, PeopleTools sets the same values of module and action for all process.

The trigger in Listing 11-3 sets module and action to the name of the scheduler process (as it appears in Process Monitor) and the Process Instance Number, respectively. It can be used in any version of PeopleTools.

Listing 11-3. Database Trigger to set Module and Action for a Scheduled Process[3]

```
CREATE OR REPLACE TRIGGER sysadm.psftapi_store_prcsinstance
BEFORE UPDATE OF runstatus ON sysadm.psprcsrqst
FOR EACH ROW
WHEN ((new.runstatus IN('3','7','8','9','10') OR old.runstatus IN('7','8'))
    AND new.prcstype != 'PSJob')
BEGIN
IF :new.runstatus = '7' THEN
 psftapi.set_prcsinstance(p_prcsinstance => :new.prcsinstance
                         ,p_prcsname     => :new.prcsname);
 psftapi.set_action(p_prcsinstance=>:new.prcsinstance
                   ,p_runstatus=>:new.runstatus
                   ,p_prcsname=>:new.prcsname);
ELSIF psftapi.get_prcsinstance() = :new.prcsinstance THEN
 psftapi.set_action(p_prcsinstance=>:new.prcsinstance
                   ,p_runstatus=>:new.runstatus);
END IF;
EXCEPTION WHEN OTHERS THEN NULL; --deliberately suppress all exceptions
END;
/
```

> ■ **Note** It is generally considered to be poor practice to code EXCEPTION WHEN OTHERS THEN NULL in PL/SQL because it silently suppresses all exceptions and can therefore lead to misleading behavior. However, it is justified in triggers created on PSPRCSRQST because I would rather the trigger doesn't work than cause errors in either batch processes or the Process Scheduler.

Now, it is now easy to determine which database session corresponds to which batch process. The process instance is visible in OEM (see Figure 11-2) if I profile by actions.

---

[3] It may seem a little gratuitous to introduce a packaged procedure to just set the module and action, but the package also stores the process instance in a package global variable so it can be read by audit triggers to suppress auditing on changes made during batch processes. The psftapi package is available from www.go-faster.co.uk/scripts.htm#psftapi.sql.

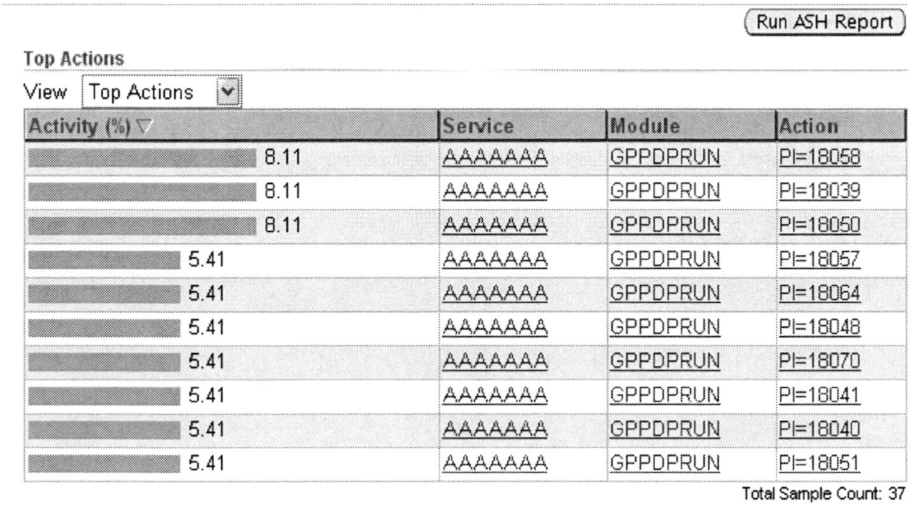

Figure 11-2. Process Instance Number visible in OEM

It is very easy to write simple queries to profile ASH data for specific processes or process instances (for example, Listing 11-4). However, there are a few points to bear in mind:

- The PSPRCSRQST table is used to obtain details about when the process or processes of interest started and finished.

- DBA_HIST_ACTIVE_SESS_HISTORY is filtered by a range of sample times. Module and action must match the PeopleSoft process name and process instance.

- DBA_HIST_ACTIVE_SESS_HISTORY is partitioned by database ID and snapshot ID, so DBA_HIST_SNAPSHOT has been added to the query to determine which AWR snapshots overlap with the period that the process is running.

- The leading hint forces execution of the query to start with the process request table and the snapshot table. The ASH data is last. Thus the unwanted partitions are eliminated from the query. Otherwise, the optimizer tends to start with the ASH data and can spend a long time scanning all the partitions in the table.

Listing 11-4. Query to Profile ASH Data by SQL Statement in Batch Processes

```
SELECT /*+leading(r x h) use_nl(h)*/ h.sql_id, h.sql_plan_hash_value
, (NVL(CAST(r.enddttm AS DATE),SYSDATE)-CAST(r.begindttm AS DATE))*86400 exec_secs
, SUM(10) ash_secs
FROM   dba_hist_snapshot x
,      dba_hist_active_sess_history h
,      psprcsrqst r
WHERE X.END_INTERVAL_TIME >= r.begindttm
AND x.begin_interval_time <= NVL(r.enddttm,SYSDATE)
AND h.snap_id = x.snap_id
AND h.dbid = x.dbid
AND h.instance_number = x.instance_number
```

```
AND h.sample_time BETWEEN r.begindttm AND NVL(r.enddttm,SYSDATE)
AND h.module = r.prcsname
AND h.action LIKE 'PI='||r.prcsinstance||'%'
AND r.prcsname = 'GPPDPRUN'
AND r.prcsinstance BETWEEN 18039 AND 18070
GROUP BY h.sql_id, h.sql_plan_hash_value, r.begindttm, r.enddttm
ORDER BY ash_secs desc
/
```

The profile in Listing 11-5 tells me how much database time was spent in which SQL ID and what execution plan was used.

Listing 11-5. Profile of Time Spent in Each Statement

SQL_ID	sql_plan hash_value	ASH_SECS
bqqf4zfm6rtq4	2651502460	20990
8nmf83f4xu4st	1828647569	8970
0jgk7wnuc91w5	2846503726	4800
f1vsz2xydpa4b	187158194	4590
5vu1u1bzcvwkm	1677726	2160
cq1jdvnftg2gx	1801476215	2000
6uvxmbc46yztd	3033993323	1360
37ddrcg4kcrmv	2653664163	1360
dr4ybtacs2j5a	3071297794	1220
4bnb2875x8wry	4198313841	1060

However, now I want to see the SQL statement and execution plan for the first few statements in the execution plan. Provided the SQL statement was captured by an AWR snapshot, I can use dbms_xplan.display_awr to extract each SQL text and execution plan:

```
SELECT * FROM table(dbms_xplan.display_awr('bqqf4zfm6rtq4', 2651502460,NULL,'ADVANCED'));
```

Cutting and pasting SQL IDs and Plan Hash Values quickly becomes very tedious. I usually want to see the plans for the top statements that have a significant duration. I often generate the commands to call dbms_xplan in an expression, so that I can generate an execution plan for each of the top statements. For example:

```
SELECT 'SELECT * FROM table(dbms_xplan.display_awr('''
||sql_id||''', '||sql_plan_hash_value
||',NULL,''ADVANCED''))/*'||ash_secs||'*/;'
FROM (
```

By grouping and aggregating the data differently, I can answer different questions, but the rest of the query is unchanged. The query in Listing 11-6 obtains a profile by wait event for the same data.

Listing 11-6. Query to Profile ASH Data by Event in Batch Processes

```
SELECT /*+leading(r x h) use_nl(h)*/ h.event
, SUM(10) ash_secs
FROM   dba_hist_snapshot x
,      dba_hist_active_sess_history h
,      psprcsrqst r
```

```
WHERE X.END_INTERVAL_TIME >= r.begindttm
AND x.begin_interval_time <= NVL(r.enddttm,SYSDATE)
AND h.snap_id = x.snap_id
AND h.dbid = x.dbid
AND h.instance_number = x.instance_number
AND h.sample_time BETWEEN r.begindttm AND NVL(r.enddttm,SYSDATE)
AND h.module = r.prcsname
AND h.action LIKE 'PI='||r.prcsinstance||'%'
AND r.prcsname = 'GPPDPRUN'
AND r.prcsinstance BETWEEN 18039 AND 18070
GROUP BY h.event
ORDER BY ash_secs desc
/
```

In this case, the profile (Listing 11-7) tells me that most of the time is spent on single block reads. The blank event indicates time that the session is active but not waiting on any event; in other words, this is time spent on CPU. So, I can get a feel for this program: it spends 70% of its time reading from disk. If I want to improve its performance, I need to look at ways of reducing that time.

Listing 11-7. Profile of ASH Data by Event in Batch Processes

EVENT	ASH_SECS
db file sequential read	44320
	16010
gc cr grant 2-way	1600
db file scattered read	510
gc current block 2-way	90
direct path read temp	80
direct path write temp	70
gc current grant 2-way	20
db file parallel read	20
gc cr multi block request	20
latch: cache buffers chains	10
enq: TT - contention	10
gc current grant busy	10
sum	62770

Performance tuning and optimization is mostly about asking where time was spent in a system. To use ASH effectively,[4] you need to be able to construct queries to answer that question.

ASH vs. Extended SQL Trace

Both ASH and Extended SQL Trace can be used to determine how much time is spent in which SQL statement, but their approaches are very different.

---

[4] I could easily devote a very long chapter just to the use of ASH. I have given some very basic ideas here. I have written a paper on this subject: "Practical Use of Oracle Active Session History"; see www.go-faster.co.uk/Practical_ASH.pdf.

ASH runs all the time and for the whole database. To permit this, it has been built into the database kernel so that it has a low overhead. SQL Trace has to be explicitly enabled. When it also records wait and bind values, it can have a significant overhead, so I usually use it in a targeted manner on specific sessions or modules. You could not afford to enable trace on an entire production database.

Therefore you have to work reactively with trace. You probably will not already be tracing a process when you experience a performance problem, so you need to run the process again and reproduce the poor performance with trace. On the other hand, ASH data is always available to be examined after a problem, or it can be examined to proactively find problems.

A SQL Trace with wait events tells you whether a session was blocked, waiting on a lock. However, it does not tell you what was blocking it. ASH records the session that was holding the blocking lock, and then you can find out what that session was doing while it held the lock.

A SQL Trace file records everything that happens in a session, whereas ASH data samples the session every second. Short-lived events are missed, so the data has to be analyzed statistically.

PeopleSoft is not good at generating sharable SQL. Many SQL statements have literal values rather than bind variables, and (even if Cursor Sharing is enabled) the use of the temporary table instances in Application Engine means similar statements have different SQL IDs and similar execution plans have different hash values. It can be difficult to aggregate such statements in the SQL queries on ASH. Oracle's TKPROF[5] SQL Trace profiler cannot aggregate similar statements.

SQL Trace files contain the full text of the SQL statements and the execution plan, but ASH only records the SQL ID and the hash value of the execution plan. The SQL text and execution plan must be extracted using dbms_xplan package from either the library cache or, more often, the AWR tables.

However, sometimes you cannot find the SQL statement in the AWR tables. This can be because it had already been purged from the library cache at the time of the snapshot, or because the individual statement was not one of the top statements collected by the snapshot. In such cases, you may need to resort to SQL Trace.

■ **Tip** The default AWR snapshot interval is 60 minutes. I usually reduce this to 15 minutes. The snapshot interval, retention time, and number of top SQL statements captured can be set with

dbms_workload_repository.modify_snapshot_settings.

I am fortunate that ASH is licensed by most of the customers whose systems I am asked to examine. For me, ASH has almost completely replaced SQL Trace. But there are still a few occasions when the information collected by ASH is not sufficient to resolve a problem, and I have to go back to trace.

Statspack

If you are not using the Enterprise Edition of Oracle or have not licensed the Diagnostics Pack, then you do not have ASH or AWR and must fall back on other techniques.

---

[5] There are other SQL Trace profilers that can aggregate similar statements, including the Hotsos/Method R Profiler (www.hotsos.com/profiler.html, www.method-r.com/software/profiler) and OraSRP (www.oracledba.ru/orasrp).

Statspack is very similar in concept to AWR, which has superseded it. Both use a packaged procedure to take snapshots of the dynamic performance views, which are then stored in a set of repository tables.

The main differences are that AWR is automatically installed; the database job to collect the snapshots is set up automatically, and old snapshots are automatically purged. AWR is managed with the dbms_workload_repository package; Statspack[6] needs to be installed, set up, and managed by the DBA. Automation and easier management are part of what you pay for in the Diagnostics Pack.

Statspack Trigger

If I cannot use ASH, I generally use SQL Trace with the wait interface enabled, not least because the trace gives me accurate information about just one process, whereas system-wide statistics can be polluted by the background noise of other activity. Later in this chapter, I describe various techniques to enable SQL Trace.

Nonetheless, there are occasions when Statspack is still of use:

- If you suspect that a process is being adversely affected by contention with other activity on the database—in particular, if SQL Trace reports a large discrepancy between CPU and elapsed time that is not accounted for by wait events.

- If you do not have access to the user_dump_dest directory, because you are not the DBA.[7]

- Occasionally I have been in situations in which SQL Trace cannot be used because enabling it has seriously aggravated performance problems.[8]

In any performance tuning exercise, it is important to collect measurements for exactly the thing in which you are interested. That means collecting information for the right process and for the right period of time. It is usual to set up a database job to perform a snapshot on a regular basis. If you are examining the effect of batch processes, it can also be useful to collect additional snapshots when a process starts or finishes. This can be done with a trigger on the process request table.

When PeopleSoft batch processes are initiated by the Process Scheduler, they update their status on the process request record to 7, indicating that they are processing. When they terminate, they again update their status. The trigger created in Listing 11-8 takes a Statspack snapshot when a process starts and ends.

Thus, it is possible to generate a Statspack report for almost exactly the period that a particular process was running.

---

[6] The Statspack documentation has been removed from the Oracle 10g documentation. Refer back to the Oracle9i Database Performance Tuning Guide and Reference, Chapter 21, "Using Statspack" (http://download.oracle.com/docs/cd/B10501_01/server.920/a96533/statspac.htm).

[7] By default on Unix systems, the trace files in user_dump_dest are only readable by a member of the DBA group. However, setting the following undocumented initialization parameter makes them readable by anyone: _trace_files_public = TRUE. This parameter cannot be changed dynamically. MR Trace from Method R (www.method-r.com/software/mrtrace) is an extension for Oracle SQL Developer that transfers extended traces files from the database server to a client workstation.

[8] If you run Oracle on Microsoft Windows, make sure the antivirus software excludes all Oracle files, including trace files!

Listing 11-8. Trigger to Generate Statspack Snapshots When a Process Starts or Ends

```
spool snap_trigger
rollback;
rem requires following grants to be made explicitly by perfstat
rem GRANT EXECUTE ON perfstat.statspack TO sysadm;

CREATE OR REPLACE TRIGGER sysadm.snap
BEFORE UPDATE OF runstatus ON sysadm.psprcsrqst
FOR EACH ROW
WHEN (  (new.runstatus = 7 AND old.runstatus != 7)
    OR (new.runstatus != 7 AND old.runstatus = 7))
DECLARE
 PRAGMA AUTONOMOUS_TRANSACTION;
 l_comment VARCHAR2(160);
 l_level INTEGER;
BEGIN
 IF ( :new.runcntlid LIKE '%SNAP%'
 ----------------------------------------------------------------
 --code conditions for processes for which snapshots to be taken
 ----------------------------------------------------------------
 --  OR (    SUBSTR(:new.prcsname,1,3) = 'TL_'
 --       AND :new.rqstdttm <= TO_DATE('20080509','YYYYMMDD'))
 ----------------------------------------------------------------
    ) THEN
   IF :new.runstatus = 7 THEN
     l_comment := 'Start';
     l_level := 5;
   ELSE
     l_comment := 'End';
     l_level := 6; /*Capture SQL on end snap*/
   END IF;

   l_comment := SUBSTR(:new.prcstype
               ||', '||:new.prcsname
               ||', '||:new.prcsinstance
               ||', '||l_comment
               ||', '||:new.oprid
                  ,1,160);

   perfstat.statspack.snap(
     i_snap_level=>l_level /*SQL captured if level >= 6*/
    ,i_ucomment=>l_comment);
   COMMIT;
 END IF;
EXCEPTION WHEN OTHERS THEN NULL;
END;
/
```

The trigger must use an autonomous transaction because STATSPACK.SNAP() includes a commit.

You would not want two extra snapshots for every process. I have added logic so that the trigger collects snapshots only if the operator runs the process with a run control that contains the string "SNAP".

The snapshot is given a comment that identifies the operator and process that started or ended. The comment can be seen when reports are generated in the usual way with the `$ORACLE_HOME/rdbms/admin/spreport.sql` script. In Listing 11-9, you can see the Statspack snapshots for a particular process as well as the regular snapshots every 15 minutes.

Listing 11-9. List of Statspack Snapshots Produced by `spreport.sql`

```
Listing all Completed Snapshots

                                                    Snap
Instance     DB Name        Snap Id  Snap Started   Level Comment
-----------  ------------   --------  ---------------- ----- --------------------
hcm89        HCM89               153 16 Sep 2011 21:15     6
                                 154 16 Sep 2011 21:30     6
                                 155 16 Sep 2011 21:40     5 SQR Report, SYSAUDIT
                                                             , 5460, Start, PS
                                 156 16 Sep 2011 21:44     6 SQR Report, SYSAUDIT
                                                             , 5460, End, PS
                                 157 16 Sep 2011 21:45     6
```

The snapshot collected at the start of the process was collected at the default level 5. However, the snapshot taken when the process finished was collected at level 6 so that SQL was also captured from the Library Cache, although you can see that the scheduled snapshots are also at level 6.

Extracting Execution Plans from Statspack

The Statspack report (such as in Listing 11-10) may identify a SQL statement that consumed a long time or a lot of resources and that may merit further investigation.

Listing 11-10. Extract from a Statspack Report

```
Elapsed              Elap per          CPU                        Old
Time (s)  Executions Exec (s) %Total  Time (s)  Physical Reads Hash Value
---------- ---------- ---------- ------ ---------- --------------- ----------
    8.73           1     8.73    2.2       1.38             3,224 3312472416
Module: SYSAUDIT
SELECT R.RECNAME, R.RELLANGRECNAME, K.FIELDNAME, 'Base Record
      ', R.OBJECTOWNERID  FROM PSRECDEFN R, PSRECFIELDDB K wh
ere R.RECTYPE in (0, 7) and R.RELLANGRECNAME <> ' ' and K.RECNAM
E = R.RECNAME and TRUNC(K.USEEDIT/2, 0)*2 <> K.USEEDIT and NOT E
XISTS  (select 'X' from PSRECFIELDDB A where A.RECNAME = R.RELLA
```

SQL statements captured by Statspack are stored in `stats$sqltext` but are broken into 64 character chunks. The Statspack report only shows the first five chunks, but the full statement can be queried from this table, as shown in Listing 11-11.

Listing 11-11. Query to Extract the Entire SQL Statement from Statspack

```
column sql_text format a80
SELECT piece, sql_text FROM stats$sqltext s
WHERE old_hash_value = 3312472416

PIECE SQL_TEXT
---- ------------------------------------------------------------------
   0 SELECT R.RECNAME, R.RELLANGRECNAME, K.FIELDNAME, 'Base Record
   1         ', R.OBJECTOWNERID  FROM PSRECDEFN R, PSRECFIELDDB K wh
   2 ere R.RECTYPE in (0, 7) and R.RELLANGRECNAME <> ' ' and K.RECNAM
   3 E = R.RECNAME and TRUNC(K.USEEDIT/2, 0)*2 <> K.USEEDIT and NOT E
   4 XISTS  (select 'X' from PSRECFIELDDB A where A.RECNAME = R.RELLA
   5 NGRECNAME and A.FIELDNAME = K.FIELDNAME and TRUNC(A.USEEDIT/2, 0
   6 )*2 <> A.USEEDIT) UNION SELECT R.RECNAME, R.RELLANGRECNAME, K.FI
   7 ELDNAME, 'Related Language Record', R.OBJECTOWNERID from   PSRECD
   8 EFN R, PSRECFIELDDB K where R.RECTYPE in (0, 7) and R.RELLANGREC
   9 NAME <> ' ' and K.RECNAME = R.RELLANGRECNAME and TRUNC(K.USEEDIT
  10 /2, 0)*2 <> K.USEEDIT and K.FIELDNAME <> 'LANGUAGE_CD' and NOT E
  11 XISTS   (select 'X' from PSRECFIELDDB B where B.RECNAME = R.RECN
  12 AME and B.FIELDNAME = K.FIELDNAME and TRUNC(B.USEEDIT/2, 0)*2 <>
  13  B.USEEDIT) order by 1, 2, 4
```

In the earlier section about ASH, I demonstrated how to extract an execution plan with the dbms_xplan package. This can also be done with the Statspack repository.

The report only shows old_hash_value, and the execution plan held in stats$sql_plan is keyed on plan_hash_value, so you need to look up one from the other on stats$plan_usage. Listing 11-12 shows how to do that.

Listing 11-12. Obtaining plan_hash_value from old_hash_value

```
column sql_id format a16
SELECT DISTINCT u.sql_id, u.hash_value, u.old_hash_value, u.plan_hash_value
FROM stats$sql_plan_usage u
WHERE old_hash_value IN(3312472416)
ORDER BY 1,2,3

SQL_ID           HASH_VALUE OLD_HASH_VALUE PLAN_HASH_VALUE
---------------- ---------- -------------- ---------------
gzrab7jhmbgwz    1630912415    3312472416      1600888416
```

The execution plan can be extracted and formatted using dbms_xplan.display(). The specific plan is chosen by specifying a filter predicate expression using plan_hash_value:

```
SELECT * FROM  table(dbms_xplan.display('perfstat.stats$sql_plan',null,'ADVANCED',
    'plan_hash_value=1600888416'));
```

dbms_xplan.display() produces the execution plan (as showing in Listing 11-13). The original SQL statement is not shown because it is not stored in the plan table.

Listing 11-13. Extract of Execution Plan Produced by dbms_xplan.display()

```
---------------------------------------------------------------------------------------------
| Id  | Operation                   | Name            | Rows  | Bytes |TempSpc| Cost (%CPU)| Time     |
---------------------------------------------------------------------------------------------
|*  0 | SELECT STATEMENT            |                 |       |       |       | 5758 (100)|          |
|*  1 |  SORT UNIQUE                |                 | 20798 | 1949K | 4456K | 5298  (47)| 00:01:04|
|*  2 |   UNION-ALL                 |                 |       |       |       |           |          |
|*  3 |    HASH JOIN ANTI           |                 | 20797 | 1949K | 2552K | 2419   (2)| 00:00:30|
|*  4 |     HASH JOIN               |                 | 35222 | 2132K |       |  827   (2)| 00:00:10|
|*  5 |      TABLE ACCESS FULL      | PSRECDEFN       |  2651 | 74228 |       |  221   (1)| 00:00:03|
|*  6 |      INDEX FAST FULL SCAN   | PSBPSRECFIELDDB |  394K |   12M |       |  604   (2)| 00:00:08|
|*  7 |     INDEX FAST FULL SCAN    | PSBPSRECFIELDDB |  394K |   12M |       |  604   (2)| 00:00:08|
|*  8 |    HASH JOIN ANTI           |                 |     1 |    96 | 2520K | 2418   (2)| 00:00:30|
|*  9 |     HASH JOIN               |                 | 34806 | 2107K |       |  828   (2)| 00:00:10|
|* 10 |      TABLE ACCESS FULL      | PSRECDEFN       |  2651 | 74228 |       |  221   (1)| 00:00:03|
|* 11 |      INDEX FAST FULL SCAN   | PSBPSRECFIELDDB |  390K |   12M |       |  605   (2)| 00:00:08|
|* 12 |     INDEX FAST FULL SCAN    | PSBPSRECFIELDDB |  394K |   12M |       |  604   (2)| 00:00:08|
---------------------------------------------------------------------------------------------
-

Query Block Name / Object Alias (identified by operation id):
-------------------------------------------------------------

   1 - SET$1
   3 - SEL$5DA710D3
   5 - SEL$5DA710D3 / R@SEL$1
...

Predicate Information (identified by operation id):
---------------------------------------------------

   0 - access(0)
       filter(0)
   1 - access(0)
       filter(0)
   2 - access(0)
       filter(0)
   3 - access(0)
       filter(0)
...

Column Projection Information (identified by operation id):
-------------------------------------------------------------

   1 - (#keys=5) STRDEF[15], STRDEF[15], STRDEF[23], STRDEF[18], STRDEF[4]
   2 - STRDEF[15], STRDEF[15], STRDEF[18], STRDEF[23], STRDEF[4]
   3 - (#keys=2) "R"."RELLANGRECNAME"[VARCHAR2,15], "K"."FIELDNAME"[VARCHAR2,18],
       "R"."RECNAME"[VARCHAR2,15], "R"."OBJECTOWNERID"[VARCHAR2,4]
...

Note
```

```
-----
- 'PERFSTAT.STATS$SQL_PLAN' is old version
```

The columns access_predicates and filter_predicates were added to v$sql_plan in Oracle 9*i*. They were also added to the stats$sql_plan table but are not populated by the statspack.snap procedure[9] as delivered. The source code for the Statspack package is delivered in $ORACLE_HOME/rdbms/admin/spcpkg.sql.

The Predicate Information section of the execution plan in Listing 11-13 is blank because the predicate columns are simply set to 0 in spcpkg.sql in the insert into stats$sql_plan (as shown in Listing 11-14).

Listing 11-14. Extract from $ORACLE_HOME/rdbms/admin/spcpkg.sql

```
, 0 -- should be max(sp.access_predicates) (2254299)
, 0 -- should be max(sp.filter_predicates)
```

I have tested replacing the zeros with the expressions in the comments. Statspack successfully collects the predicate information, and dbms_xplan.display() correctly populates the predicate section.

The note at the foot of the execution plan warns that stats$sql_plan is an old version because another column, other_xml, added to v$sql_plan in Oracle 10*g*, has not been added to Statspack.

System and Session Statistics Trigger

One of the problems with Statspack is that it reports only system-wide statistics. The same is true for AWR, but if you have AWR you also have ASH. However, it is also possible to build a pair of triggers that capture database session and system statistics when a process begins and ends. Generally, only a small proportion of the statistics are of interest, and not all statistics report at session level. Nonetheless, in the example in Listing 11-15, I have captured all the statistics.

A Global Temporary Table is used to capture the statistics at the start of the process, and it is only written to the final output directory when the process terminates. This handles the problem of matching start and end statistics, particularly when an Application Engine process has failed and been restarted.

Listing 11-15. Triggers to Collect v$sysstat and v$mystat for a Process: gfc_sysstats.sql

```
rem gfc_sysstats.sql
ROLLBACK;

rem triggers require following grants to be made directly by SYS to SYSADM not via role
GRANT SELECT ON sys.v_$sysstat  TO sysadm;
GRANT SELECT ON sys.v_$mystat   TO sysadm;
GRANT SELECT ON sys.v_$database TO sysadm;
clear screen

DROP TABLE sysadm.gfc_sys_stats_temp
/
CREATE GLOBAL TEMPORARY TABLE sysadm.gfc_sys_stats_temp
(prcsinstance     NUMBER       NOT NULL
,statistic#       NUMBER       NOT NULL
```

---

[9] This was raised with Oracle as Bug 5683955. It was closed as "Not a Bug," but there is no explanation.

```
,db_value            NUMBER        NOT NULL
,my_value            NUMBER        NOT NULL
,begindttm           DATE          NOT NULL)
ON COMMIT PRESERVE ROWS
/
CREATE INDEX gfc_sys_stats_temp
ON gfc_sys_stats_temp(prcsinstance, statistic#)
/

DROP TABLE sysadm.gfc_sys_stats
/
CREATE TABLE sysadm.gfc_sys_stats
(prcsinstance         NUMBER        NOT NULL
,statistic#           NUMBER        NOT NULL
,db_value_before      NUMBER        NOT NULL
,my_value_before      NUMBER        NOT NULL
,begindttm            DATE          NOT NULL
,db_value_after       NUMBER        NOT NULL
,my_value_after       NUMBER        NOT NULL
,enddttm              DATE          NOT NULL)
TABLESPACE users
/
DROP INDEX sysadm.gfc_sys_stats
/
CREATE UNIQUE INDEX sysadm.gfc_sys_stats
ON gfc_sys_stats(prcsinstance, statistic#, begindttm)
/

CREATE OR REPLACE TRIGGER sysadm.psprcsrqst_sys_stats_before
AFTER UPDATE OF runstatus ON sysadm.psprcsrqst
FOR EACH ROW
WHEN (new.runstatus = 7 AND old.runstatus != 7)
BEGIN
 IF ( :new.runcntlid LIKE '%STAT%'
 ----------------------------------------------------------------
 --code conditions for processes for which snapshots to be taken
 ----------------------------------------------------------------
 --  OR (   SUBSTR(:new.prcsname,1,3) = 'TL_'
 --        AND :new.rqstdttm <= TO_DATE('20080509','YYYYMMDD'))
 ----------------------------------------------------------------
 ) THEN
   INSERT INTO sysadm.gfc_sys_stats_temp
   (      prcsinstance, statistic#
   ,      db_value, my_value
   ,      begindttm)
   SELECT :new.prcsinstance, s.statistic#
   ,      S.VALUE, M.VALUE
   ,      NVL(:new.begindttm,SYSDATE)
   FROM   sys.v_$sysstat s
   ,      sys.v_$mystat m
   WHERE  s.statistic# = m.statistic#
   ;
```

347

```
  END IF;
EXCEPTION WHEN OTHERS THEN NULL;
END;
/


CREATE OR REPLACE TRIGGER sysadm.psprcsrqst_sys_stats_after
AFTER UPDATE OF runstatus ON sysadm.psprcsrqst
FOR EACH ROW
WHEN (new.runstatus != 7 and old.runstatus = 7)
BEGIN
 IF ( :new.runcntlid LIKE '%STAT%'
 ----------------------------------------------------------------
 --code conditions for processes for which snapshots to be taken
 ----------------------------------------------------------------
 --  OR (    SUBSTR(:new.prcsname,1,3) = 'TL_'
 --       AND :new.rqstdttm <= TO_DATE('20080509','YYYYMMDD'))
 ----------------------------------------------------------------
 ) THEN
  INSERT INTO sysadm.gfc_sys_stats
  (      prcsinstance, statistic#
  ,      db_value_before, my_value_before, begindttm
  ,      db_value_after , my_value_after , enddttm
  )
  SELECT :new.prcsinstance, s.statistic#
  ,      b.db_value, b.my_value, b.begindttm
  ,      S.VALUE, M.VALUE
  ,      NVL(:new.enddttm,SYSDATE)
  FROM   sys.v_$sysstat s
  ,      sys.v_$mystat  m
  ,      gfc_sys_stats_temp b
  WHERE  s.statistic# = m.statistic#
  AND    b.statistic# = s.statistic#
  AND    b.statistic# = m.statistic#
  AND    b.prcsinstance = :new.prcsinstance
  ;
  --from PT8.4 AE may not shut down
  DELETE FROM gfc_sys_stats_temp
  WHERE  prcsinstance = :new.prcsinstance
  ;
 END IF;
EXCEPTION WHEN OTHERS THEN NULL;
END;
/
```

■ **Note** The Global Temporary Table GFC_SYS_STATS_TEMP must be created ON COMMIT PRESERVE because the update that causes the trigger to fire is always committed so the status can be seen in the Process Monitor and by the Process Scheduler.

The rows in the Global Temporary Table must be explicitly deleted by the trigger PSPRCSRQST_SYS_STATS_AFTER because from PeopleTools 8.4, Application Engine may be managed under Tuxedo and the same processes; hence the same session may handle many requests.

■ **Caution** The warning about frequency of execution on the Statspack trigger applies here too. These triggers can generate a large volume of metrics very quickly.

It is a simple matter to query the data collected by the triggers. Listing 11-16 illustrates.

Listing 11-16. Query to Report Statistic for a Process

```
COLUMN name FORMAT a30
SELECT a.prcsinstance, b.name
,      a.my_value_after-a.my_value_before my_diff
,      a.db_value_after-a.db_value_before db_diff
FROM   sysadm.gfc_sys_stats a
,      v$sysstat b
WHERE  a.statistic# = b.statistic#
AND    (a.db_value_after != a.db_value_before
OR     a.my_value_after != a.my_value_before )
AND    a.prcsinstance = &prcsinstance
/
```

The figures in the DB_DIFF column (see Listing 11-17) are differences in database-wide metrics. These can be matched up with a Statspack report based on snapshots taken at the start and end of a process. The MY_DIFF column shows differences in session statistics that cannot be obtained from Statspack.

Listing 11-17. Extract of the Results of the Query in Listing 11-16

```
PRCSINSTANCE NAME                              MY_DIFF     DB_DIFF
------------ -----------------------------  ----------  ----------
...
        5470 table scans (short tables)            243         378
        5470 table scans (long tables)             46          47
        5470 table scan rows gotten            4565570     4572697
        5470 table scan blocks gotten          126934      127763
        5470 table fetch by rowid              158102      161745
        5470 table fetch continued row            150         193
...
```

Using Oracle Extended SQL Trace with PeopleSoft

Performance metrics may direct you to a particular process and sometimes a particular part of a process. If SQL performance is the problem, then the next question is, which SQL statement or statements are consuming the most time and why?

The timings reports for the COBOL and Application Engine processes can provide valuable information that can direct you to a particular step or statement. Furthermore, for each step, the Application Engine timings can distinguish between time spent on SQL and time spent executing PeopleCode.

The timings reports can sometimes identify a particular SQL statement. You could then use the EXPLAIN PLAN command to generate an execution plan. However, this command may generate a different execution plan from the one that was actually generated and used when the process ran. The reasons for this include, but are not limited to, a change in statistics, environment, or indexing. For instance, PeopleSoft batch processes often truncate and repopulate working storage tables and then refresh cost-based optimizer statistics on those tables.

Extended SQL Trace has been a part of the Oracle database since version 6 and was significantly enhanced to include instructions that do not consume CPU (commonly referred to as *wait events*) in version 7.0.12.

An Extended SQL Trace of a process records all the SQL statements that were issued and how long they took to execute. The execution plan for each SQL statement is written to the trace in the STAT lines when the cursor is closed. It is the only way to know for certain exactly how the SQL was executed when it ran in that process. So, the question is how to enable SQL Trace.

In the sections that follow, I discuss various techniques to enable SQL Trace. There are ways to add code to the application so that it issues the commands to enable and disable tracing. However, in practice, this is rarely helpful because performance problems usually arise in production and final test environments, where code change is not an option. For processes initiated via the Process Scheduler, a trigger can be used to issue the commands to enable SQL Trace. For online processing, it is necessary to identify the database session and enable trace in that session.

Oracle Initialization Parameters and SQL Trace

Before you enable SQL Trace, you need to consider several Oracle initialization parameters:

- TIMED_STATISTICS must be set to TRUE in order to obtain timings in the SQL Trace file or from any of the dynamic performance views (such as V$WAITSTAT). It has been set to TRUE by default since Oracle 9i.

- The trace files are written to the directory specified by USER_DUMP_DEST. If the output directory fills up, no error is generated. Oracle merely stops writing the trace files. However, if that directory is on the same file system as the archive log destination, the database could hang.

- The trace file size is limited by MAX_DUMP_FILE_SIZE. The parameter is expressed in operating system blocks (usually 512 bytes). From Oracle 9, it can also be expressed in kilobytes or megabytes, or it can be set to UNLIMITED. When a trace file exceeds this size, the Oracle process writes the warning message "DUMP FILE SIZE IS LIMITED" and then stops writing to it. PeopleSoft processes can easily produce large trace files. If you work with a truncated trace file, you are not analyzing the whole process, and you may not be working on the biggest performance problem.

- On Unix systems, the trace files can be read only by a member of the dba group. But if you set _TRACE_FILES_PUBLIC to TRUE, the files can be read by any Unix user. However, trace files can contain data values embedded in SQL statements even if bind variables are not logged, so you should be aware of the possible security implications of making these files viewable by anybody with a Unix account on the database server.

- TRACEFILE_IDENTIFIER can be set in a session to a string, which is included in the trace file. If it is set or changed after the tracing is enabled, the trace switches to a new file named with the new identifier. However, be careful when doing this. If you switch trace files while you have open cursors, then tkprof may not generate accurate results for either trace file. Trace files can be joined back together with the Oracle trcsess utility.

Analyzing SQL Trace Files with TKPROF

Oracle provides the tkprof utility to translate raw trace file data into a readable report. It is documented in the *Oracle Performance Tuning Guide*. In most situations, I find it adequate to list the top ten SQL statements in a trace by total execution time and work through them. Listing 11-18 shows a sample tkprof command to produce such a report.

Listing 11-18. tkprof Command

```
tkprof hr88_ora_1748.trc hr88_ora_1748.ela sort=fchela,prsela,exeela print=10 sys=no
```

The various command parameters are as follows:

- SORT: In this case, the SQL statements are sorted by the sum of the elapsed parse, execution, and fetch times for each distinct statement.

- PRINT: The output file lists the top ten statements according to the sort order.

- SYS: Recursive SQL is not reported.

- EXPLAIN: tkprof connects to the database and generates an execution plan with the EXPLAIN PLAN command, in addition to reporting the execution plan in the STAT lines in the trace.

■ **Caution** The EXPLAIN PLAN option makes tkprof generate an additional execution plan at run time. It should be approached with caution, because it may be different from the plan that was used when the SQL was traced and that was recorded in the STAT lines. From Oracle 9.2, this option is all but obsolete because the STAT lines contain the table and index names as well as the object Ids (see Listing 11-19).

Listing 11-19. STAT Lines in an Oracle 9.2.0.5 Trace

```
STAT #15 id=1 cnt=1 pid=0 pos=0 obj=0 op='UPDATE PSPRCSRQST '
STAT #15 id=2 cnt=1 pid=1 pos=1 obj=26955 op='TABLE ACCESS BY INDEX ROWID PSPRCSRQST '
STAT #15 id=3 cnt=1 pid=2 pos=1 obj=27133 op='INDEX UNIQUE SCAN '
```

STAT lines are only emitted to the trace file when the cursor closes. If a session terminates abnormally with open cursors, or if the trace file reaches the MAX_DUMP_FILE_SIZE before a cursor is closed, then the STAT lines will not be in the trace file and tkprof does not report an execution plan for one or more SQL statements.

Enabling SQL Trace by Module, Action, or Client ID

Oracle has provided procedures in the dbms_monitor package to enable trace for particular combinations of service name, module, and action or Client ID. These can be set like watch points in a debugger. When session attributes are set to matching values, session trace is enabled. It is disabled when the attributes are changed.

If you create the trigger in Listing 11-3, this technique can be used to trace specific batch processes—even specific instances of a process, if you know the process instance in advance. You can enable and disable trace as follows:

```
EXECUTE dbms_monitor.serv_mod_act_trace_enable('HCM89', 'SYSAUDIT');
EXECUTE dbms_monitor.serv_mod_act_trace_disable('HCM89', 'SYSAUDIT');
```

From PeopleTools 8.50, module and action are set in the PIA to the component and page name, and in the Integration Broker to the service and queue name. Therefore it is possible to trace individual PIA components or Integration Broker services. For example:

```
EXECUTE dbms_monitor.serv_mod_act_trace_enable('HCM89', 'RECV_PO ', 'PO_PICK_ORDERS');
EXECUTE dbms_monitor.serv_mod_act_trace_disable('HCM89', 'RECV_PO ', 'PO_PICK_ORDERS');
```

■ **Note** The trigger in Listing 11-3 overrides the module and action set by PeopleSoft. If instead the action was set to the run control ID, then trace could be enabled for specific run controls. This would be an alternative method to the trigger described in Listing 11-22.

Also from PeopleTools 8.50, the PeopleSoft Operator ID is set as the Client ID. The client trace procedures can be used to enable trace for a named PeopleSoft operator and capture all the SQL generated by that operator in the PIA. The following example shows how to enable and disable trace for an operator:

```
EXECUTE dbms_monitor.client_trace_enable('kurtzd');
EXECUTE dbms_monitor.client_trace_disable('kurtzd');
```

A PIA session, even within a single component, comprises many Tuxedo services. Different services may be handled by different application server processes and therefore involve different database sessions. Each session generates a separate trace file.

SQL Trace on PeopleTools Windows Clients

PeopleSoft has built its own sophisticated trace facility into all its processes that reports nearly everything that happens. This trace facility was principally intended as a debugging tool, but it also includes the amount of time the operation takes to execute and the time since the last traced operation completed. The timings can be affected by network performance, and some operations are not traced. For example:

- Some SQL statements, such as updates of the operator's password stored in the database, are not logged.

- PeopleTools uses the dbms_application_info PL/SQL package to register the Operator ID with the database. This is not logged in the PeopleTools trace.

Windows clients for only nVision and Query are still delivered with PeopleSoft, although PIA alternatives are provided for both. The Windows run-time client was not a supported run-time option in PeopleTools 8.1, and it has disappeared in PeopleTools 8.4.

It is possible to enable Oracle SQL Trace, usually from another session, on Windows client processes; but since PeopleTools 7.x this has not worked well. The Windows processes are multithreaded and, in two-tier mode, maintain multiple connections to the database. There is also an inactivity timeout that disconnects the client from the database, thus terminating the session and disabling trace. When the user returns, the client silently reconnects to the database, but SQL Trace does not resume, because the client creates a brand new database session.

SQL Trace on Application Server Processes

On startup, each PeopleSoft application server process[10] creates and maintains a persistent database session that is used for every request it handles. Since PeopleTools 8.48, PSAPPSRV processes have created a second session to support the getnextnumberwithgap() PeopleCode function (effectively simulating an autonomous transaction). This can be suppressed by setting DbFlags in the Application Server configuration file, psappsrv.cfg.

To generate a single Oracle SQL Trace of a single PIA client's activity, it is necessary to provide a PIA domain and an application server with only a single PSAPPSRV process exclusively for that one client. Thus all of the activity goes through a single database session.

If you wish to separately trace query or nVision activity, then you should configure the PSQRYSRV process, which is dedicated to running queries from these products. There is now one easily identifiable process for which trace can be enabled and disabled from another session.

---

[10] Except PSWATCHSRV, which was introduced in PeopleTools 8.4.

Enabling Trace in Another Session

You can enable tracing of another session with the Oracle supplied dbms_monitor PL/SQL package:

```
EXECUTE sys.dbms_monitor.session_trace_enable(sid=><sid>,serial=><serial#>
                                              ,waits=>TRUE,binds=>FALSE);
```

It can also be disabled:

```
EXECUTE sys.dbms_monitor.session_trace_disable(sid=><sid>,serial=><serial#>);
```

Note the following:

- SID and SERIAL# are obtained from V$SESSION.

- The package dbms_monitor was introduced in Oracle 10g. It is the supported method of enabling SQL Trace. It is documented in the *PL/SQL Packages Reference*, whereas dbms_support and dbms_system are not.

Listing 11-20 shows a PL/SQL script that enables SQL tracing on the PSAPPSRV processes connected to the database. It identifies application server processes from the client_info string that is written by the application server processes when DBMonitoring (see Chapters 9 and 12) is enabled in the application server configuration file. client_info includes the name of the server program. The script can, of course, be adjusted to further restrict the sessions traced by adding conditions to the driving query. For example, you may wish to trace only the application servers on a particular machine.

Listing 11-20. traceallon.sql: *Enabling Trace on Application Server Processes*

```
set serveroutput on buffer 1000000000 echo on
spool traceallon
DECLARE
  CURSOR c_appsess IS
  SELECT *
  FROM   v$session
  WHERE  type = 'USER'
-- AND    program like '%PSAPPSRV%'
  AND    client_info like '%,PSAPPSRV%';
  p_appsess c_appsess%ROWTYPE;
BEGIN
  OPEN c_appsess;
  LOOP
    FETCH c_appsess INTO p_appsess;
    EXIT WHEN c_appsess%NOTFOUND;
    sys.dbms_monitor.session_trace_enable(sid=>p_appsess.sid, serial=>p_appsess.serial
                                          ,waits=>TRUE ,binds=>FALSE);
    sys.dbms_output.put_line('Enable:'
                              ||p_appsess.sid||','||p_appsess.serial#);
  END LOOP;
  CLOSE c_appsess;
END;
/
```

■ **Note** This only enables trace on the primary connection, not the secondary connection used by the `getnextnumberwithgapscommit()` function to increment sequence numbers, because `client_info` is not set on that session.

Trace can be disabled in a similar way.

Using an AFTER LOGON Trigger

SQL Trace can also be enabled from an `AFTER LOGON` database trigger. However, unless the client program name is properly registered with the database, so that it appears in `V$SESSION.PROGRAM`, it can be difficult to work out what program is connecting to the database. The program name registers for Inter-process Communication (IPC) connections on all platforms and via SQL*Net on Windows and AIX, but not on HP-UX or Solaris.

The trigger in Listing 11-21 trace all processes that are called something that contains "PSAPPSRV", regardless of case.

Listing 11-21. `trace_connect_trigger.sql`: Enabling SQL Trace after Database Logon

```
CREATE OR REPLACE TRIGGER sysadm.connect_trace
AFTER LOGON
ON sysadm.schema
DECLARE
   l_tfid VARCHAR2(64);
BEGIN
-- if this query returns no rows an exception is raised and trace is not set
   SELECT SUBSTR(TRANSLATE(''''
                 ||TO_CHAR(sysdate,'YYYYMMDD.HH24MISS')
                 ||'.'||s.program
                 ||'.'||s.osuser
                 ||''''
         ,' \/','__'),1,64)
   INTO    l_tfid
   FROM    v$session s
   WHERE   s.sid IN(
              SELECT sid
              FROM   v$mystat
              WHERE  rownum = 1)
   AND     UPPER(s.program) LIKE '%PSAPPSRV%';

   EXECUTE IMMEDIATE 'ALTER SESSION SET TIMED_STATISTICS = TRUE';
   EXECUTE IMMEDIATE 'ALTER SESSION SET MAX_DUMP_FILE_SIZE = UNLIMITED';
   EXECUTE IMMEDIATE 'ALTER SESSION SET TRACEFILE_IDENTIFIER = '||l_tfid;
   sys.dbms_monitor.session_trace_enable(waits=>TRUE ,binds=>FALSE);
   EXCEPTION WHEN OTHERS THEN NULL;
END;
/
```

Remember that `client_info` is still `NULL` at connect time because it is set by the application only after the `AFTER LOGON` trigger completes.

Enabling SQL Trace on the Process Scheduler

We have already seen in Chapter 9 how processes that are run via the Process Scheduler log their request record on PSPRCSRQST, with the processes' start and end times and also the processes' status.

When the batch process starts, it updates its own RUNSTATUS on the table PSPRCSRQST to 7, to indicate that it is processing. When the process terminates, it updates the status to 9, indicating success. A trigger configured to fire on this change of status is run in the batch process's own database session. Now you have a way to introduce additional code that runs very close to the start or end of the process, without changing any of the program code.

Enabling SQL Trace for Batch Processes with a Trigger

The trigger shown in Listing 11-22 enables Oracle SQL Trace when a process starts.

Listing 11-22. `trace_trigger.sql`

```
rem requires following grants to be made explicitly by sys
rem GRANT ALTER SESSION TO sysadm;
rollback;

CREATE OR REPLACE TRIGGER sysadm.gfc_set_trace
BEFORE UPDATE OF runstatus ON sysadm.psprcsrqst
FOR EACH ROW
WHEN (new.runstatus = '7' AND old.runstatus != '7' AND new.prcstype != 'PSJob')
DECLARE
 l_waits BOOLEAN := TRUE;
 l_binds BOOLEAN := FALSE;
BEGIN
 --set module and action whether we are tracing or not
 sys.dbms_application_info.set_module(
   module_name => :new.prcsname,
   action_name => SUBSTR('PI='||:new.prcsinstance||':Processing',1,32)
 );

 IF ( :new.runcntlid LIKE 'TRACE%'
 ----------------------------------------------------------------
 --code conditions for enabling trace here instead of when clause
 ----------------------------------------------------------------
 --  OR (    SUBSTR(:new.prcsname,1,3) = 'TL_'
 --       AND :new.rqstdttm <= TO_DATE('20080509','YYYYMMDD'))
 ----------------------------------------------------------------
    ) THEN

    --explicitly set tracefile identifier whether we are tracing or not
    EXECUTE IMMEDIATE 'ALTER SESSION SET TRACEFILE_IDENTIFIER = '''||
      TRANSLATE(:new.prcstype    ,' -','__')||'_'||
      TRANSLATE(:new.prcsname    ,' -','__')||'_'||
```

```
    :new.prcsinstance||'_'||
     TRANSLATE(:new.servernamerun,' -','__')||
     '''';

  EXECUTE IMMEDIATE 'ALTER SESSION SET MAX_DUMP_FILE_SIZE = 2097152'; --1Gb
  EXECUTE IMMEDIATE 'ALTER SESSION SET STATISTICS_LEVEL=ALL';

  ----------------------------------------------------------------
  --logic to determine whether you want to trace binds also
  ----------------------------------------------------------------
  IF :new.runcntlid LIKE 'TRACE%BIND%' THEN
    l_binds := TRUE;
  END IF;
  ----------------------------------------------------------------

  sys.dbms_monitor.session_trace_enable(waits=>TRUE,binds=>l_binds);
  ----------------------------------------------------------------
  --Alternative for Oracle 9i and earlier
  --EXECUTE IMMEDIATE 'ALTER SESSION SET EVENTS ''10046 TRACE NAME CONTEXT FOREVER, LEVEL
12''';
  ----------------------------------------------------------------
 ELSIF :new.prcstype = 'Application Engine' THEN
   --explicitly disable trace if application server process
   sys.dbms_monitor.session_trace_disable;

   --reset max dump file size AFTER disabling trace
   EXECUTE IMMEDIATE 'ALTER SESSION SET MAX_DUMP_FILE_SIZE = 10240';

   --explicitly set tracefile identifier whether we are tracing or not
   EXECUTE IMMEDIATE 'ALTER SESSION SET TRACEFILE_IDENTIFIER = ''''';

 END IF;
EXCEPTION WHEN OTHERS THEN NULL; --deliberately coded to suppress all exceptions
END;
/
```

■ **Note** The Oracle MAX_DUMP_FILE_SIZE parameter is applied individually to each trace file that is generated. The trace file ceases to be written when MAX_DUMP_FILE_SIZE has been reached.

On Windows, when a new TRACEFILE_IDENTIFIER is specified, Oracle starts to write again to a new trace file.

On Unix/Linux platforms, tracing cannot ever be resumed in a session after the maximum size has been exceeded, even if MAX_DUMP_FILE_SIZE is subsequently reset. Thus if a SQL Trace of an Application Engine program exceeds the maximum size, it is not possible to trace any other Application Engine program that runs on that PSAESRV server process. If you set MAX_DUMP_FILE_SIZE=UNLIMITED, the trace is not disabled, but there is an increased risk that the file system could fill up. Furthermore, if MAX_DUMP_FILE_SIZE is set back to a size less than the current trace file size, even after tracing has been stopped, Oracle detects the condition and further tracing is prevented.

The exception at the end of the trigger prevents the UPDATE statement from failing, even if the trigger does not function. Otherwise, it can crash the Process Scheduler.

Logic in the body of the trigger enables trace if the operator uses a run control name that begins with the expression *TRACE*. Thus you can get a trace of a process by choosing a run control ID.

The trigger sets TRACEFILE_IDENTIFIER to be a string made up from the process type, process name, and process instance number. This string is inserted into the trace file name. For example, the trace file hr88_ora_3752_application_engine_prcsyspurge_205.trc was produced when the Application Engine process called PRCSYSPURGE ran on database HR88 as Process Instance 205. The ID of the Oracle shadow process was 3752.

In addition, logic can be added to the trigger so that trace is enabled only for certain processes, operators, process schedulers, time periods, or run controls. For example, using the expression in Listing 11-23, the trigger traces only the GL Journal Edit process when it is run by operator VP1 on the PSUNX Process Scheduler. However, it also traces any process where the run control begins with *TRACE*. Furthermore, the trigger, although still enabled, ceases to enable trace after a specified date.

Listing 11-23. Example of Alternative Criteria to Enable Trace

```
IF ( :new.runcntlid LIKE 'TRACE%'
------------------------------------------------------------------
--code conditions for enabling trace here instead of when clause
------------------------------------------------------------------
OR (:new.prcstype = 'COBOL SQL'
AND :new.prcsname = 'GLPJEDIT'
AND :new.oprid = 'VP1'
AND :new.servernamerqst = 'PSUNX'
AND :new.rqstdttm <= TO_DATE('20110930','YYYYMMDDHH'))
------------------------------------------------------------------
  ) THEN
```

■ **Note** This trigger does not fire on PSJob process types. A PSJob is not an actual process, but a reference to several processes run as a group. The status of the PSJob is updated by the Process Scheduler. The trigger traces the Process Scheduler.

From PeopleTools 8.4, the Process Scheduler is fully integrated with Tuxedo. There are Application Engine server processes, PSAESRV, that respond to Tuxedo service requests from the Process Scheduler server. Like other PeopleSoft Tuxedo processes, each PSAESRV process maintains persistent connections to the database.

If you enable session trace with the trigger on a PSAESRV process, the session continues to trace subsequent Application Engine process requests handled by the same server process.

The trace cannot be disabled when the process updates its status on success or failure because cursors created during execution are still open for which execution plans have not yet been emitted to the trace file, and they would be lost. Instead, we have to wait until the process disconnects from the database. In the case of an Application Engine server process, we have to wait until it starts to handle the next request. Therefore, the trigger explicitly disables trace on startup of any Application Engine process where it has not enabled trace.

Application Engine Database Optimizer Trace

In PeopleTools 8.44, PeopleSoft introduced mechanisms for generating database optimizer information for the SQL submitted by Application Engine programs. The section on Database Optimizer Trace in the Application Engine PeopleBook[11] describes the different behaviors on different databases.

Two new bit values for the TraceAE setting are described in the comments in the Process Scheduler configuration file, psprcs.cfg (see Listing 11-24).

Listing 11-24. Extract from psprcs.cfg

```
;-----------------------------------------------------------------------
; AE Tracing Bitfield
;
; Bit        Type of tracing
...
; 2048       - DB optimizer trace to file
; 4096       - DB optimizer trace to tables
```

I think that if you are going to use either of these features, then in practice you should only enable them for specific processes by appending the trace parameter to the command-line parameter list in the process definition (as shown in Figure 9-8).

DB Optimizer Trace to File: Extended SQL Trace

When PeopleSoft talks about DB Optimizer Trace to File on Oracle, it is referring to the Extended SQL Trace utility. When this option is selected, Application Engine sets two parameters for the current session:

```
ALTER SESSION SET SQL_TRACE = TRUE
ALTER SESSION SET TIMED_STATISTICS = TRUE
```

PeopleTools 8.44 was certified for Oracle 8*i*. At that version of the database, trace could only be enabled by an ALTER SESSION command.[12]

---

[11] See Enterprise PeopleTools 8.51 PeopleBook: Application Engine ➤ Tracing Application Engine Programs (http://download.oracle.com/docs/cd/E24150_01/pt851h2/eng/psbooks/tape/book.htm?File=tape/htm/tape09.htm#H4013).

[12] Prior to the introduction of the dbms_monitor package in Oracle 10*g*, I always used to enable trace by setting event 10046. I could specify a higher level in order to capture wait events and sometimes also

Up to Oracle 8i, the parameter TIMED_STATISTICS was set to false by default, in which case all the timings in the extended trace file and the dynamic performance views were zero. From Oracle 9i, the default changed to true.

The dbms_monitor package was not introduced until Oracle 10g. Although PeopleTools 8.51 is not certified for Oracle 9i, it still invokes trace the same way as PeopleTools 8.44.

There are some problems to consider when using DB Optimizer Trace to File:

- The ALTER SESSION command generates a trace file that does not include wait events or bind variables. Wait events are enabled by default when invoking trace with dbms_monitor.

- The trace files are named according to the standard Oracle naming convention. If you generate a lot of trace files, it can be difficult to work out which trace file relates to which Application Engine program or process instance.

- If the Process Scheduler is configured with the Application Engine server process, PSAESRV (described in Chapter 14), a single persistent database session handles many Application Engine programs. If you invoke SQL Trace for one Application Engine program, then that session continues to trace all subsequent Application Engine programs that it handles.

The database trigger shown in Listing 11-22 does not suffer from these problems. It is a more flexible method of enabling session trace that works for all process types.

DB Optimizer Trace to Table: Explain Plan For

If DB Optimizer Trace to Table is enabled, Application Engine calls the EXPLAIN PLAN FOR command for each statement in a SQL step. Listing 11-25 shows an example of the two extra commands prior to the SQL statement in the application.

■ **Tip** If you use DB Optimizer Trace to Table (4096), then you should also generate the batchtimings report (128 and 1024), and you also need the SQL statement in an Application Engine trace (2). If you trace the SQL, you may as well also trace step execution (1) and temporary table allocation (4). So, you should set the trace to 5255.

The EXPLAIN PLAN FOR command inserts the execution plan for the SQL statement into the table PLAN_TABLE. The plan is given an identifier made from the concatenation of the Application Engine program name, section name, step name, and step type. Unfortunately the step type is converted to an unprintable character. The remarks column is then set to a concatenation of the process instance number, the run control ID, and a sequence number. Listing 11-25 shows an example of the two additional statements generated prior to the application SQL statement. I obtained these statements from an Extended SQL Trace.

---

bind variables to the trace file. It is a pity that PeopleSoft and latterly Oracle didn't choose to encapsulate this and other Oracle database features in a packaged PL/SQL procedure. That would have enabled customers to make better use of new database features as soon as they upgraded their databases.

Listing 11-25. Example SQL Commands with DB Optimizer Trace to Database Enabled

```
EXPLAIN PLAN SET STATEMENT_ID = 'GP_PMT_PREP.XA000.XB009. ' FOR

DELETE FROM PS_GP_PYE_SEG_TMP
WHERE CAL_RUN_ID = 'KL02M12DEC' AND EMPLID BETWEEN 'KUL450' AND 'KUL460'
/
UPDATE PLAN_TABLE SET REMARKS = '6346-1(33)'
WHERE  STATEMENT_ID = 'GP_PMT_PREP.XA000.XB009. ' AND REMARKS IS NULL

/
DELETE FROM PS_GP_PYE_SEG_TMP
WHERE CAL_RUN_ID = 'KL02M12DEC' AND EMPLID BETWEEN 'KUL450' AND 'KUL460'
/
```

From Oracle 10g, PLAN_TABLE is a public synonym for a Global Temporary Table called SYS.PLAN_TABLE$. It is necessary to create a permanent PLAN_TABLE in the PeopleSoft schema. PeopleBooks warns that the column STATEMENT_ID must be 254 characters. As PLAN_TABLE grows, the update of the remark column takes longer. I recommend creating a unique index on the plan table (see Listing 11-26).

Listing 11-26. Creating a Plan Table in the PeopleSoft Schema

```
@?\rdbms\admin\utlxplan.sql
ALTER TABLE sysadm.plan_table MODIFY (statement_id VARCHAR2(254))
/
CREATE UNIQUE INDEX sysadm.plan_table
ON sysadm.plan_table(statement_id, remarks, id) COMPRESS 2
/
```

You need to decide which execution plan is worth looking at. The query in Listing 11-27 profiles statements from the batch timings table cross references to the plan table.

Listing 11-27. SQL Query to Profile Application Engine Steps with Corresponding Entries in PLAN_TABLE

(dbopttrace.sql).

```
column process_instance heading 'Process|Instance' format 9999999
column exec_secs heading 'Exec|Secs'
column execute_count heading 'Execs' format 999999
column remarks format a10
column process_name format a12
column detail_id format a30
column statement_id format a40
column run_cntl_id format a10
SELECT x.process_instance
,      x.statement_id2 statement_id, p.remarks
,      x.exec_secs, x.execute_count
FROM   (
       SELECT  l.process_instance
       ,       l.process_name
       ,       l.run_cntl_id
       ,       d.detail_id
```

```
,        l.process_name||'.'||SUBSTR(d.detail_id,1,LENGTH(d.detail_id)-1)
         ||CASE ASCII(SUBSTR(d.detail_id,-1))
         WHEN 2 THEN 'D' WHEN 4 THEN 'S' ELSE '_' END as statement_id
,        l.process_name||'.'||d.detail_id statement_id2
,        l.process_instance||'-'||l.run_cntl_id||'(%)' remarks
,        d.execute_time/1000 exec_secs
,        d.execute_count
FROM     ps_bat_timings_log l
,        ps_bat_timings_dtl d
WHERE    l.process_instance = d.process_instance
AND      bitand(l.trace_level,4096) = 4096
) x
LEFT OUTER JOIN sysadm.plan_table p
     ON p.statement_id LIKE x.statement_id
     AND p.remarks like x.remarks and p.id = 0
WHERE x.process_instance = &process_instance
ORDER BY exec_secs DESC
/
```

```
Process                                                      Exec
Instance STATEMENT_ID                         REMARKS        Secs   Execs
-------- ------------------------------------ ----------- ---------- -------
   6347 GP_PMT_PREP.BA000.BB004.S                            2.297     1
   6347 GP_PMT_PREP.CHKPOINT                                   .86    58
   6347 GP_PMT_PREP.COMMIT                                    .832    58
   6347 GP_PMT_PREP.DA000.DF001.S             6347-1(24)      .203     1
   6347 GP_PMT_PREP.INSERT PS_GP_NET_PAY2_TMP                 .062    11
   6347 GP_PMT_PREP.ZB100.ZB100C0.H                           .031     2
   6347 GP_PMT_PREP.XA000.XB009.S             6347-1(10)        0      2
...
```

Application Engine does not issue the EXPLAIN PLAN commands for SQL statements from PeopleCode steps, nor from calls to %UpdateStats or %TruncateTable (unless it generates a DELETE statement).

If your Application Engine program spends most of its time in PeopleCode you cannot use this trace technique to obtain execution plans for the statements that took the longest time. PeopleBooks recommends that you use the Trace to File (Extended SQL Trace) instead.

The execution plans can be extracted from the plan table and formatted with the dbms_xplan package as shown in Listing 11-28. The filter predicate parameter is used to choose which execution plan to produce.

Listing 11-28. *Extracting an Execution Plan with dbms_xplan()*

```
SELECT * FROM TABLE(dbms_xplan.display('sysadm.plan_table', NULL, 'ALL',
'statement_id LIKE ''GP_PMT_PREP.XA000.XB009.%'' AND remarks LIKE ''6347-1(%)'''))
/
```

```
-------------------------------------------------------------------------------
| Id  | Operation          | Name            | Rows | Bytes | Cost (%CPU)| Time     |
-------------------------------------------------------------------------------
|   0 | DELETE STATEMENT   |                 |   22 | 1188  |    1   (0)| 00:00:01 |
|   1 |  DELETE            | PS_GP_PYE_SEG_TMP|      |       |           |          |
|*  2 |   INDEX RANGE SCAN | PS_GP_PYE_SEG_TMP|   22 | 1188  |    1   (0)| 00:00:01 |
-------------------------------------------------------------------------------
```

```
Query Block Name / Object Alias (identified by operation id):
-------------------------------------------------------------

   1 - DEL$1
   2 - DEL$1 / PS_GP_PYE_SEG_TMP@DEL$1
```

```
Predicate Information (identified by operation id):
--------------------------------------------------

   2 - access("EMPLID">='KUL450' AND "CAL_RUN_ID"='KL02M12DEC' AND
              "EMPLID"<='KUL460')
       filter("CAL_RUN_ID"='KL02M12DEC')
```

```
Column Projection Information (identified by operation id):
---------------------------------------------------------

   2 - (cmp=2,3) "PS_GP_PYE_SEG_TMP".ROWID[ROWID,10], "EMPLID"[VARCHAR2,11],
       "CAL_RUN_ID"[VARCHAR2,18], "PS_GP_PYE_SEG_TMP"."EMPL_RCD"[NUMBER,22],
       "PS_GP_PYE_SEG_TMP"."GP_PAYGROUP"[VARCHAR2,10],
       "PS_GP_PYE_SEG_TMP"."CAL_ID"[VARCHAR2,18],
       "PS_GP_PYE_SEG_TMP"."ORIG_CAL_RUN_ID"[VARCHAR2,18],
       "PS_GP_PYE_SEG_TMP"."RSLT_SEG_NUM"[NUMBER,22]
```

```
Query Block Name / Object Alias (identified by operation id):
-------------------------------------------------------------
   1 - UPD$1
   2 - UPD$1 / PSPMTABLEMAP@UPD$1
```

```
Column Projection Information (identified by operation id):
---------------------------------------------------------
   2 - (upd=2,3) "PSPMTABLEMAP".ROWID[ROWID,10],
       "PM_TRANS_TBL_NAME"[VARCHAR2,18], "PM_EVENT_TBL_NAME"[VARCHAR2,18]
```

SQL statements are not stored in the plan table and are not emitted by dbms_xplan.display(). If you are using this optimizer trace flag, I also recommend tracing the SQL to the AE Trace file (see Listing 11-29). Thus you can look up the exact SQL that was submitted by a step.

Listing 11-29. AE Trace Showing the SQL for Each Step ID

```
-- 00.35.45 ...(GP_PMT_PREP.XA000.XB009) (SQL)
DELETE FROM PS_GP_PYE_SEG_TMP WHERE CAL_RUN_ID = 'KLO2M12DEC'
AND EMPLID BETWEEN 'KUL450' AND 'KUL460'
```

I think DB Optimizer Trace to Table is of limited use. Automatic Workload Repository and Statspack do a mostly adequate job of capturing SQL statements and execution plans and are not restricted to Application Engine.

Enabling SQL Trace Programmatically

Occasionally you may want to trace a specific part of a batch process rather than use the trigger to trace the entire process. In order to do this, SQL or PL/SQL commands to enable and disable trace must be added to the program in appropriate places.

Application Engine

Any valid SQL command can simply be coded as a free-format SQL statement in an Application Engine SQL step. Thus, it is possible to add code to enable and disable session trace as required within a process.

Figure 11-3 shows an Application Engine program in the Application Designer. In this example, I have added a step to an Application Engine program that calls the dbms_monitor package.

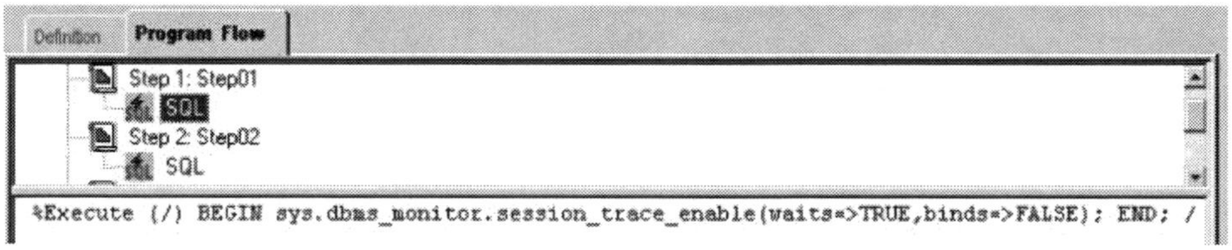

Figure 11-3. Part of an Application Engine program

SQR

For SQR, I have created two procedures in a separate SQC (Listing 11-30) that enable and disable trace. The SQL must be referenced with a #INCLUDE, and then the procedures can be called.

Listing 11-30. sqltrace.sqc: *Standard Procedures to Enable and Disable Trace in SQR*

```
!****************************************
! sqltrace.sqc: oracle session tracing *
!****************************************
!********************************************************************
! Function:    enable_session_trace                               *
!                                                                  *
! Description: enable oracle session trace                        *
!                                                                  *
```

```
!*********************************************************************
begin-procedure enable_session_trace

display 'Enabling Oracle Session Trace'

begin-sql
BEGIN
sys.dbms_monitor.session_trace_enable(waits=>TRUE,binds=>FALSE);;
END;;
end-SQL

end-procedure

!*********************************************************************
! Function:    disable_session_trace                                 *
!                                                                    *
! Description: disable oracle session trace                          *
!                                                                    *
!*********************************************************************
begin-procedure disable_session_trace

display 'Disabling Oracle Session Trace'

begin-sql
BEGIN
sys.dbms_monitor.session_trace_disable;;
END;;
end-SQL

end-procedure
```

These procedures can be called as shown in Listing 11-31.

Listing 11-31. Calling Procedures in an SQR

```
begin-REPORT
 do enable_session_trace
...
...
...
 do disable_session_trace
end-REPORT

#include 'session.sqc'
...
```

PeopleCode

The SQLExec PeopleCode function can be called with either a SQL statement or an anonymous block of PL/SQL. In Figure 11-4, I have created a new step in an application engine that calls dbms_monitor.

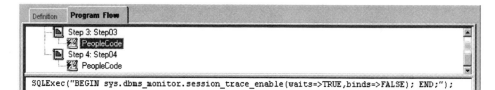

Figure 11-4. *Part of an Application Engine program*

Remote Call

Some batch programs can be initiated synchronously by the PIA. Behind the scenes, the application server initiates the batch process and waits for it to complete. For example, in Financials, a single voucher can be edited and posted online by clicking a button on a page, at which point the application server runs a COBOL process, GLPJEDIT. This is the same process that is run by the Process Scheduler to process many vouchers in a single execution. When a process is executed by remote call, there is no request record for the process on the PSPRCSRQST table to be updated, so the trigger described for scheduled processes (see Listing 11-22) does not fire.

However, when a batch process starts, one of the first things it does is insert a row into the PS_MESSAGE_LOG table; then it commits the insert so that the message can be seen in the Process Monitor. A trigger can be created to execute on this insert (see Listing 11-32).

Listing 11-32. *Trigger to Trace a RemoteCall Process*

```
CREATE OR REPLACE TRIGGER sysadm.trace_remotecall
BEFORE INSERT ON sysadm.ps_message_log
FOR EACH ROW
WHEN (new.process_instance = 0
AND    new.message_seq      = 1
AND    new.program_name     = 'GLPJEDIT'
AND    new.dttm_stamp_sec   <= TO_DATE('200407231500','YYYYMMDDHH24MI')
)
BEGIN
  EXECUTE IMMEDIATE 'ALTER SESSION SET TIMED_STATISTICS = TRUE';
  EXECUTE IMMEDIATE 'ALTER SESSION SET MAX_DUMP_FILE_SIZE = 2048000';
  EXECUTE IMMEDIATE 'ALTER SESSION SET TRACEFILE_IDENTIFIER = '''||
                          replace(:new.program_name,' -','__')||'''';

  sys.dbms_monitor.session_trace_enable(waits=>TRUE,binds=>FALSE);
EXCEPTION WHEN OTHERS THEN NULL;
END;
/
```

There are a number of things to note about this trigger:

- Processes executed by RemoteCall always have a process instance of 0, so the WHEN clause is restricted to this value.

- The trigger fires only on the first message to be inserted, which has a MESSAGE_SEQ of 1.

- The process name is written to the message log, so the trigger can be restricted to particular processes.

- The messages have a timestamp, so the trigger can be restricted to fire in a particular time window.

Where Does This SQL Come From?

Many techniques and tools that are employed in performance tuning are very good at identifying problem SQL statements that consume large amounts of time and resources. Sometimes, a performance problem can be resolved by making changes to the database (parameters, indexes, statistics, or physical storage options). However, in many cases, the solution involves changing the code (hints, FROM clause order, or additional joins). So it is valuable to know where a SQL statement is defined in the application.

PeopleTools Performance Monitor reports SQL statements and their context within the application at a verbose level, but that is generally only used in Performance Trace. Even from PeopleTools 8.50, when the dbms_application_info package is used to set module and action, it can still be difficult to associate a SQL statement with a particular piece of the application.

However, the SQL issued by PeopleSoft applications is stored in various ways and is often generated dynamically. In the following sections, I explain how the way in which a piece of SQL is formatted or structured can give clues as to how you can find it in the PeopleSoft development tools.

If you can find it, you can change it.

Component Processor

As the Component Processor interprets and executes the application stored in the PeopleTools tables, it dynamically generates SQL. The code in Listing 11-33 is an example.

Listing 11-33. PIA Component SQL

```
SELECT EMPLID, PER_STATUS, TO_CHAR(BIRTHDATE,'YYYY-MM-DD'), BIRTHPLACE, BIRTHCOUNTRY,
BIRTHSTATE, TO_CHAR(DT_OF_DEATH,'YYYY-MM-DD'), TO_CHAR(ORIG_HIRE_DT,'YYYY-MM-DD'),
HIGHLY_COMP_EMPL_C, HIGHLY_COMP_EMPL_P FROM PS_PERSON WHERE EMPLID=:1 ORDER BY EMPLID
```

Code generated by the Component Processor has a number of characteristics:

- It is generally all uppercase.

- Each scroll in a page relates to a single PeopleSoft record, and there is a query of the single table or view corresponding to that record.

- There is a WHERE clause condition for each key column, which also appears in the ORDER BY clause.

- Date columns are converted to a character string in the format 'YYYY-MM-DD'.

Component Search Dialog

As you navigate into a component, you normally encounter the component search dialog. This is used to look up the key values of the parent record in the component. Listing 11-34 is an example of the code that is generated.

Listing 11-34. Query Generated by the Component Search Dialog

```
SELECT DISTINCT EMPLID, EMPL_RCD, NAME, LAST_NAME_SRCH, SETID_DEPT, DEPTID,
NAME_AC, PER_STATUS FROM PS_PERS_SRCH_GBL WHERE ROWSECCLASS=:1 AND UPPER(NAME)
LIKE UPPER('Smith') || '%' ESCAPE '\' ORDER BY NAME, EMPLID
```

This SQL has a number of additional characteristics:

- Queries generated from search dialogs are always DISTINCT. This cannot be suppressed.

- It is common to see a criterion on a security column in search dialog SQL, such as ROWSECCLASS, as in the example in Listing 11-34. This criterion is added automatically when one of a number of special columns, such as ROWSECLASS, is present in the search record.

- Anything that the user types into the search criteria, in either a search dialog or a related display search, appears as a literal value in a WHERE clause condition.

- The UPPER() functions are applied (as shown in Listing 11-34) when searching mixed-case fields (as defined in Application Designer) and when case-insensitive searching is permitted in the PeopleTools options (see Chapter 5). The UPPER() function applied to an indexed column can prevent an index from being used for the query.

Prompt Buttons

Prompt buttons are indicated in the PIA by a magnifying glass icon (called a *prompt button* in PeopleTools) that appears next to fields, as show in Figure 11-5. If the user enters something in the field before clicking the magnifying glass icon, that input is carried forward into the Look Up dialog and is used as a search criterion.

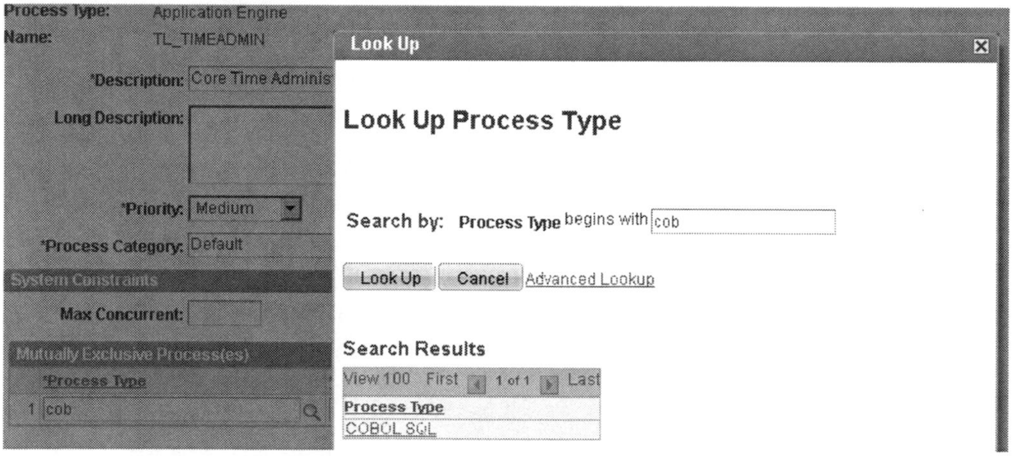

Figure 11-5. Look Up dialog invoked from a prompt button

The construction of the SQL that prompt buttons generate (shown in Listing 11-35) is similar to the component search dialog (shown in Listing 11-34), except only one column is selected and there is no DISTINCT keyword. The user's input is embedded into the SQL as a literal string.

Listing 11-35. Query Generated by a Prompt Button

```
SELECT  PRCSTYPE FROM PS_PRCSTYPE_ALT_VW A
WHERE UPPER(PRCSTYPE) LIKE UPPER('COB') || '%' ESCAPE '\' ORDER BY PRCSTYPE
```

The UPPER() functions are applied when searching fields that are defined in Application Designer as mixed-case. However, a function on a column prevents the database from using the index to look up the value, although it can still scan the index rather than the table. In many cases, such as this example, the lookup tables are quite small, and this does not cause a significant performance problem. However, there are cases, particularly when the prompt looks up application data, in which this can cause a problem.

Type Ahead

Type Ahead is a new feature in PeopleTools 8.50. It applies to both prompt fields and search fields on component search dialogs. If the user starts to type something into a search field, the lookup is performed if they stop typing. Figure 11-6 shows the results of the lookup below the field. The SQL issued to do this is the same as the prompt lookup SQL in Listing 11-35.

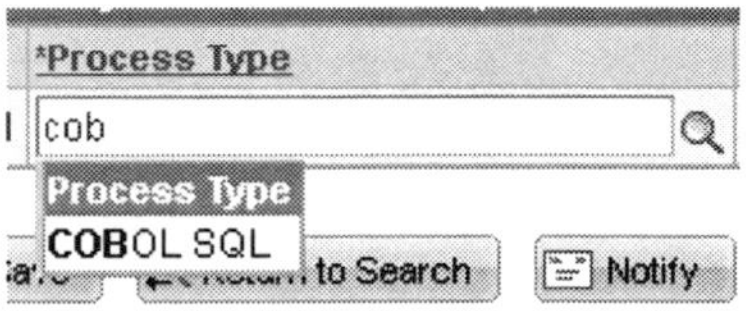

Figure 11-6. Results of Type Ahead lookup on a field with a prompt button

This is a very nice feature for the user, but it has the potential to be a very dangerous feature for the database. Figure 11-7 shows the search dialog for the Job Data component from the HCM application.

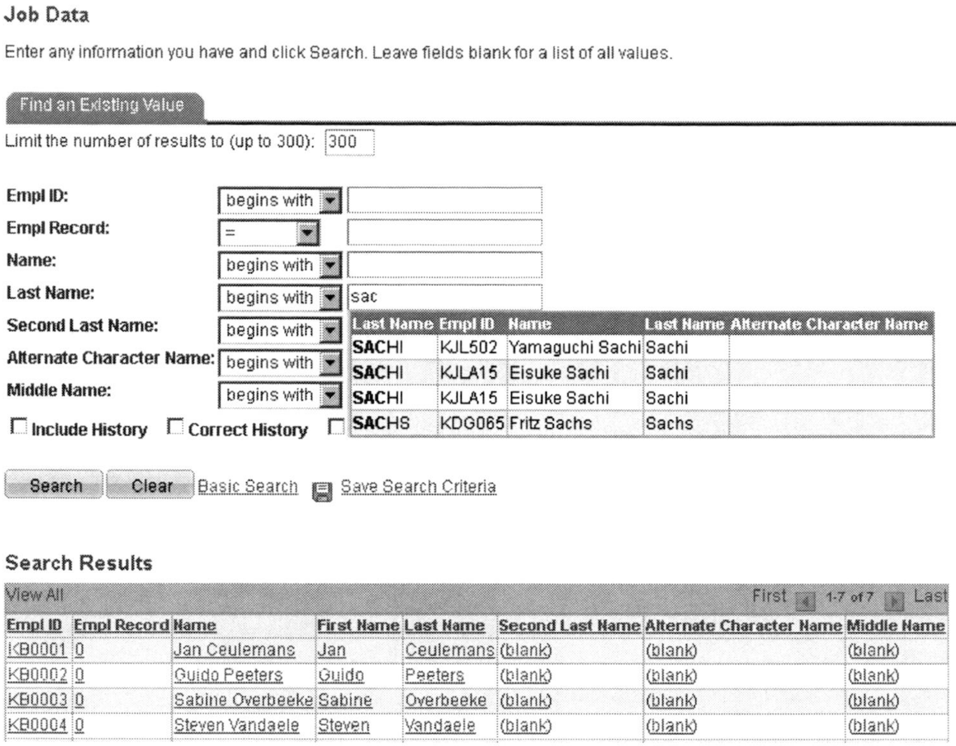

Job Data

Enter any information you have and click Search. Leave fields blank for a list of all values.

Find an Existing Value

Limit the number of results to (up to 300): `300`

Empl ID:	begins with ▼	
Empl Record:	= ▼	
Name:	begins with ▼	
Last Name:	begins with ▼	sac
Second Last Name:	begins with ▼	
Alternate Character Name:	begins with ▼	
Middle Name:	begins with ▼	

Last Name	Empl ID	Name	Last Name	Alternate Character Name
SACHI	KJL502	Yamaguchi Sachi	Sachi	
SACHI	KJLA15	Eisuke Sachi	Sachi	
SACHI	KJLA15	Eisuke Sachi	Sachi	
SACHS	KDG065	Fritz Sachs	Sachs	

☐ Include History ☐ Correct History ☐

Search **Clear** Basic Search 💾 Save Search Criteria

Search Results

View All

First ◄ 1-7 of 7 ► Last

Empl ID	Empl Record	Name	First Name	Last Name	Second Last Name	Alternate Character Name	Middle Name
KB0001	0	Jan Ceulemans	Jan	Ceulemans	(blank)	(blank)	(blank)
KB0002	0	Guido Peeters	Guido	Peeters	(blank)	(blank)	(blank)
KB0003	0	Sabine Overbeeke	Sabine	Overbeeke	(blank)	(blank)	(blank)
KB0004	0	Steven Vandaele	Steven	Vandaele	(blank)	(blank)	(blank)

***Figure 11-7.** A Type Ahead lookup in the component search dialog for the Job Data component*

I typed the letters **sac** into the Last Name field, and when I stopped, the component automatically queried for people whose last name begins with *sac*. When the component search dialog performs a Type Ahead lookup, it queries the component search record with a criteria composed from the contents of the search field (see Listing 11-36).

***Listing 11-36.** Query Generated by Type Ahead in a Search Dialog*

```
SELECT DISTINCT EMPLID, EMPL_RCD, NAME, NAME_DISPLAY_SRCH, LAST_NAME_SRCH, SECOND_LAST_SRCH,
FIRST_NAME, LAST_NAME, SECOND_LAST_NAME, NAME_AC, MIDDLE_NAME FROM PS_EMPLMT_SRCH_COR WHERE
OPRID=:1 AND LAST_NAME_SRCH LIKE 'SAC%' ORDER BY LAST_NAME_SRCH, EMPLID, EMPL_RCD
```

On a small table, such as the process type used in the previous example, this is not a problem. However, on a complex view such as the employee search view, the potential exists to run a query against several large tables with criteria that are not as selective as the user could make them. If the operator pauses while typing, perhaps to check the spelling of a name, PeopleTools starts a Type Ahead lookup.

Type Ahead can be disabled globally for a user in their Navigation Personalization, or it can be disabled for all users for a specific field by disabling the Type Ahead Configuration in the Field Definition.

PeopleCode

PeopleCode is PeopleSoft's proprietary programming language. Explicit SQL statements can be executed in PeopleCode. Certain PeopleCode functions that populate a scroll in a page can accept a WHERE clause that is built into the SQL executed by the command. PeopleCode is executed by the component processor, and from PeopleTools 8.1 it can also be executed by Application Engine.

A mixed-case SQL statement from a PIA trace, such as the one in Listing 11-37, indicates SQL embedded in PeopleCode. This is simply because a lot of PeopleSoft developers are not rigorous about how they write SQL code. However, some SQL embedded in PeopleCode is all uppercase because that is how it was coded, and such SQL can be confused with that generated by the component processor.

Any complex SQL, or SQL that joins several tables, is also likely to be PeopleCode. For example, the SQL shown in Listing 11-37 was extracted from a trace file.

Listing 11-37. SQL Submitted by a SQLExec() Function

```
Select A.BEN_STATUS from PS_ACTN_REASON_TBL A where A.ACTION = :1 and A.ACTION_REASON =
(Select min(AA.ACTION_REASON) from PS_ACTN_REASON_TBL AA where AA.ACTION = A.ACTION) and
A.EFFDT = (Select max(AAA.EFFDT) from PS_ACTN_REASON_TBL AAA where AAA.ACTION = A.ACTION
and AAA.ACTION_REASON = A.ACTION_REASON)
```

The SQL comes from the PeopleCode SQLExec() function shown in Listing 11-38. This function passes the SQL in the string parameter through to the database. What you code is what you get. The statement is also in mixed case and has multicharacter table aliases, both of which suggest a SQLExec() PeopleCode function.

Listing 11-38. SQLExec() Function in PeopleCode

```
    SQLExec("Select A.BEN_STATUS from PS_ACTN_REASON_TBL A where A.ACTION = :1 and
A.ACTION_REASON = (Select min(AA.ACTION_REASON) from PS_ACTN_REASON_TBL AA where AA.ACTION
= A.ACTION) and A.EFFDT = (Select max(AAA.EFFDT) from PS_ACTN_REASON_TBL AAA where
AAA.ACTION = A.ACTION and AAA.ACTION_REASON = A.ACTION_REASON)", &ACTION, &FETCH_STATUS);
```

Uppercase SELECT and FROM statements followed by a mixed-case WHERE clause suggests a function in PeopleCode populating a scroll on a page or a rowset. If the alias of the table is FILL, as in Listing 11-39, it must be a rowset being filled.

Listing 11-39. SQL Generated by a Rowset Fill() Function

```
PSAPPSRV.2564   1-4321   01.52.36    0.551 Cur#1.2564.HR88 RC=0 Dur=0.000 COM Stmt=SELECT
FILL.PNLNAME,FILL.PNLFLDID,FILL.FIELDNUM,FILL.PNLFIELDNAME,FILL.FIELDTYPE,FILL.RECNAME,
FILL.FIELDNAME,FILL.LBLTYPE,FILL.GOTOPORTALNAME,FILL.GOTONODENAME,FILL.GOTOMENUNAME,
FILL.GOTOPNLGRPNAME,FILL.GOTOMKTNAME,FILL.GOTOPNLNAME,FILL.GOTOPNLACTION
FROM PS_CO_PNLFIELD_VW FILL  WHERE PNLNAME = :1 and FIELDTYPE = 16 and LBLTYPE = 7
AND RECNAME = :2 and FIELDNAME = :3
```

The SQL in Listing 11-39 is generated by the PeopleCode shown in Listing 11-40. The table name is obtained from the PeopleSoft record that is the parameter to the CreateRowset() function. The WHERE clause is applied to the Fill() function.

Listing 11-40. Rowset Function in PeopleCode

```
&PnlField_Rs = CreateRowset(Record.CO_PNLFIELD_VW);
  &PnlField_Rs.Flush();
  &PnlField_Rs.Fill("WHERE PNLNAME = :1 and FIELDTYPE = 16 and LBLTYPE = 7 AND
RECNAME = :2 and FIELDNAME = :3", %Page, &LinkRecName, &LinkFieldName);
```

SEARCHING PEOPLECODE

If you are trying to find the PeopleCode in which a particular SQL statement appears, Application Designer provides a utility to search the PeopleCode, as shown in the following image. However, using this utility can be time consuming. Alternatively, you can generate a text file of all the PeopleCode in the system by searching for a semicolon (;) and saving the results to a flat file. You can then search the flat file relatively quickly with a text editor.

Query

The PeopleSoft Query utility is used for ad hoc queries and reporting. The tool is described in the PeopleTools Query PeopleBook. PeopleSoft positions the Query tool for end users as well as developers. Most of these end users are completely non-technical and have probably never heard of SQL. I am not going to comment on the wisdom or otherwise of permitting this, but I have seen PeopleSoft systems brought to their knees by unrestricted access to the ad hoc Query tool!

Each Crystal Report has a corresponding query that feeds data to the report. Queries are also used in nVision and some view definitions in the Application Designer.

The Query utility generates monolithic SQL query statements that frequently join many tables. They can include effective date/sequence and tree subqueries that are automatically generated by PeopleTools. It is relatively easy to write queries that are functionally correct. It is usually more challenging to write a query that generates SQL and also executes efficiently.

The tables' aliases in a query are single letters allocated sequentially along the FROM clause. Gaps can appear in the sequence if a record is deleted from the query. When a record is added to a query, the first unused letter in the alphabet is used as the alias; hence the letter can get out of sequence.

If a record has a query security record defined, then the query security record is automatically added to the query when the record is selected. It is given the same alias as the table it secures, with a 1 appended. A record is joined to its query security records by the key columns they have in common. For example, in Listing 11-41, PERSONAL_DTA_VW is given the alias D. It has a query security record PERS_SRCH_QRY, which is therefore given the alias D1. The two records are joined only by EMPLID, which is the only key column defined on both records in Application Designer (hence the significance of defining key fields on a view, even though there is no corresponding index).

If multiple records have the same query security record, as shown in Listing 11-41, the security record appears only once in the FROM clause after the first table it secures, but it is joined to both tables.

Listing 11-41. Query TRN003_COURSE_WAITING_LIST

```
SELECT A.EMPLID, A.ATTENDANCE, A.COURSE, B.DESCR, D.NAME, A.SESSION_NBR,
TO_CHAR(A.STATUS_DT,'YYYY-MM-DD'),B.COURSE
 FROM PS_TRAINING A, PS_COURSE_TBL B, PS_PERSONAL_DTA_VW D, PS_PERS_SRCH_QRY D1
 WHERE D.EMPLID = D1.EMPLID
   AND D1.ROWSECCLASS = 'HCDPALL'
   AND ( A.COURSE = :1
   AND A.ATTENDANCE IN ('S','W')
   AND A.COURSE = B.COURSE
   AND A.EMPLID = D.EMPLID )
```

Like other PeopleTools objects, queries are stored in the PSQRY% PeopleTools tables. If you have the SQL, it is possible to work out which query you are looking at by querying the PSQRYRECORD table, as shown in Listing 11-42. This table holds one row per record selected in each query.

Listing 11-42. findqry.sql

```
SELECT  a.oprid, a.qryname
FROM    psqryrecord a
,       psqryrecord b
,       psqryrecord d
WHERE   a.oprid = b.oprid
AND     a.qryname = b.qryname
AND     a.oprid = d.oprid
AND     a.qryname = d.qryname
AND     a.corrname = 'A'
AND     a.recname = 'TRAINING'
AND     b.corrname = 'B'
AND     b.recname = 'COURSE_TBL'
AND     d.corrname = 'D'
AND     d.recname = 'PERSONAL_DTA_VW'
/
```

On a demo HR database, this query returns two rows (see Listing 11-43), indicating that there are two queries with at least similar FROM clauses.

Listing 11-43. Results of findqry.sql

```
OPRID                            QRYNAME
-----------------------------    ------------------------------
                                 TRN002__SESSION_ROSTER
                                 TRN003__COURSE_WAITING_LIST
```

Query TRN002__SESSION_ROSTER is shown in Listing 11-44. You can see that the aliases on the tables in the FROM clauses are as specified in the query in Listing 11-41.

Listing 11-44. Query TRN002__SESSION_ROSTER

```
SELECT A.EMPLID, A.COURSE, A.SESSION_NBR, D.NAME, B.DESCR,
TO_CHAR(A.COURSE_START_DT,'YYYY-MM-DD'), A.ATTENDANCE,B.COURSE
 FROM PS_TRAINING A, PS_COURSE_TBL B, PS_PERSONAL_DTA_VW D, PS_PERS_SRCH_QRY D1
WHERE D.EMPLID = D1.EMPLID
   AND D1.ROWSECCLASS = 'HCDPALL'
   AND ( ( A.ATTENDANCE = 'E'
   AND A.COURSE = B.COURSE
   AND D.EMPLID = A.EMPLID
   AND A.COURSE = :1
   AND ( A.SESSION_NBR = :2
   OR A.COURSE_START_DT = TO_DATE(:3,'YYYY-MM-DD'))) )
```

■ **Note** On some systems where operators have the right to develop ad hoc PeopleSoft queries, I have found that they take a public query and save their own private version of it, and possibly adjust it slightly. The result is that when you find one problem SQL statement that is a query, you may discover sets of similar queries that all need to be addressed.

COBOL

SQL statements submitted by PeopleSoft COBOL programs are either read in from the stored statements table, PS_SQLSTMT_TBL, or dynamically generated from COBOL code. Stored statements only use bind variables; the dynamically generated statements may contain literal values.

It can be difficult to distinguish between the two classes in the COBOL statement timings report (see Listing 9-43 in Chapter 9).[13] The point is that it is possible to change or hint the statements on the stored

---

[13] The PeopleTools trace indicates whether a statement is a static statement stored in the database
GETSTMT Stmt=FSPJCOMB_S_COMGRP, length=297 COM Stmt=SELECT A.PROCESS_GROUP
or a dynamic statement:
DYNAMIC Stmt=FSPJECHF_U_CFERROR COM Stmt=UPDATE PS_PSA_ACCTDSTGL SET

statements table, but to change the dynamic statements is likely to require code changes. The PeopleSoft COBOL is extremely complicated, and making changes should be a last resort.

In the Global Payroll engine, some of the dynamic statements are derived from the payroll rules, which are stored in the database as metadata. These statements can be changed to a limited extent by the way the payroll rules are coded.

PeopleSoft delivers the stored statements as Data Mover scripts (in $PS_HOME/src/cbl/base) that are loaded into the database (see Listing 11-45). The scripts should be considered the source for the stored statements. If you make changes and a new version of the script is delivered, you can use file comparison utilities to detect and resolve the differences.

Listing 11-45. Extract from the gppcancl.dms Data Mover Script

```
STORE GPPCANCL_D_WRKSTAT
DELETE FROM PS_GP_PYE_STAT_WRK
WHERE CAL_RUN_ID=:1
  AND EMPLID BETWEEN :2 AND :3
;
```

Identifying Stored Statements

It is often useful to know which stored statement is which. Stored statements are loaded by Data Mover. The trigger in Listing 11-46 adds the name of the statement as a comment to identify it as it is inserted into the stored statement table.

Listing 11-46. gfc_stmtid_trigger.sql: Trigger to Add an Identification Comment to Stored Statements

```
CREATE OR REPLACE TRIGGER gfc_stmtid
BEFORE INSERT ON ps_sqlstmt_tbl
FOR EACH ROW
DECLARE
l_stmt_text CLOB;           /*for stmt text so can use text functions*/
l_stmt_id   VARCHAR2(18); /*PS stmt ID string*/
l_len       INTEGER;      /*length of stmt text*/
l_spcpos    INTEGER;      /*postition of first space*/
l_compos    INTEGER;      /*postition of first comment*/
l_compos2   INTEGER;      /*end of first comment*/
l_idpos     INTEGER;      /*postition of statement id*/
BEGIN
l_stmt_id   := :new.pgm_name||'_'||:new.stmt_type||'_'||:new.stmt_name;
l_stmt_text := :new.stmt_text;
l_spcpos    := INSTR(l_stmt_text,' ');
l_compos    := INSTR(l_stmt_text,'/*');
l_compos2   := INSTR(l_stmt_text,'*/');
l_idpos     := INSTR(l_stmt_text,l_stmt_id);
l_len       := LENGTH(l_stmt_text);
```

Trace has a significant run-time overhead; it is really intended as debugging tool. You would have to search the trace for each statement.

```
IF (l_idpos = 0 AND l_spcpos > 0 AND l_len<=32000) THEN
 /*no id comment in string and its not too long so add one*/
 IF (l_compos = 0) THEN /*no comment exists*/
  l_stmt_text := SUBSTR(l_stmt_text,1,l_spcpos)
||'7*'||l_stmt_id||'*/'||SUBSTR(l_stmt_text,l_spcpos);
 ELSE /*insert into existing comment*/
  l_stmt_text := SUBSTR(l_stmt_text,1,l_compos2-1)||'
'||l_stmt_id||SUBSTR(l_stmt_text,l_compos2);
 END IF;
 :new.stmt_text := l_stmt_text;
END IF;

END gfc_stmtid;
/
```

Every time the COBOL program submits the SQL, it contains the comment (see Listing 11-47); and when you find the statement in a trace, you know where it came from. Dynamic statements can then be easily distinguished because they do not have a comment.

Listing 11-47. Stored Statement with an Identifying Comment

```
DELETE /*GPPCANCL_D_WRKSTAT*/ FROM PS_GP_PYE_STAT_WRK
WHERE CAL_RUN_ID=:1 AND EMPLID BETWEEN :2 AND :3
```

SQR

PeopleSoft uses SQR as both a batch and reporting language. In SQR programs, SQL statements are embedded in the SQR or SQC source files. These files can be edited with any text editor. Finding the SQL is usually just a matter of searching the source code.

It is common for PeopleSoft SQR programs to dynamically generate all or part of a SQL statement in a string variable and then use that string in the SQL statement, as shown in Listing 11-48.

Listing 11-48. Example of SQR Code with a Variable Embedded in the SQL

```
...
FROM  PS_GP_CAL_RUN_DTL A,
      PS_GP_CALENDAR B,
      PS_GP_CAL_PRD C
WHERE A.CAL_RUN_ID = $Cal_Run_ID
[$Paygroup_Where]
AND   B.GP_PAYGROUP = A.GP_PAYGROUP
AND   B.CAL_ID = A.CAL_ID
AND   C.CAL_PRD_ID = B.CAL_PRD_ID
...
```

In Listing 11-48, $Cal_Run_ID is a normal bind variable. However, the square brackets around $Paygroup_Where in Listing 11-49 indicate that the variable is not a bind variable, but that the contents of the variable are to be embedded in the SQL. As in this example, these variables often contain SQL keywords as well as the literal values of variables.

If the values of the variables change with each execution of the statement, the database reparses the statement for each new value.

Listing 11-49. SQR Code to Build the Dynamic Part of a WHERE Clause

```
let $Where = ''
if not isblank($Paygroup)
    let $Where = ' AND GRP.GP_PAYGROUP = ''' || $Paygroup || ''''
    let $Where_B = ' AND B.GP_PAYGROUP = ''' || $Paygroup || ''''
End-If
```

Identifying comments and hints can be added manually to SQL statements in SQR programs. They must be placed in a line on their own, as shown in Listing 11-50.

Listing 11-50. SQR Code with an Embedded Hint and Comment

```
Begin-Procedure Check-Leavers-Float-Balance($Employee_Selection, $Effdt,
$GP_Paygroup, $GP_Cal_Run_ID)
...
Begin-Select On-Error=SQL-Error
/*+LEADING(A) Check-Leavers-Float-Balance*/
A.EMPLID            &EMPLID
...
```

When an SQR process starts, it parses and validates all the static SQL it finds in the program, including any included SQC files, before beginning execution.[14] Hence you may have parsed cursors that are never executed because the SQL is never reached during the SQR program logic.

SQR generates a cursor status report of the static SQL statements if it is run with the -S flag. SQR is not executed directly by the Process Scheduler, but via a PeopleSoft wrapper program called PSSQR. Additional SQR flags can be appended to the SQR command line with the -AP parameter. This can be configured in the Process Type definition, as shown in Figure 11-8.

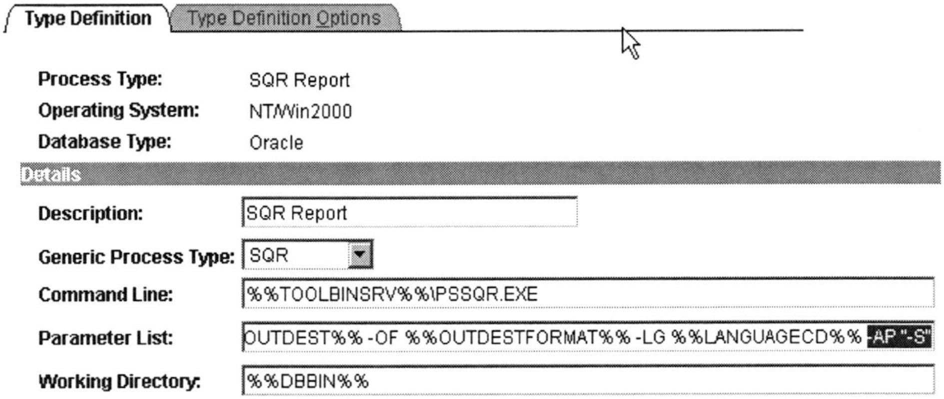

Figure 11-8. Appending the -S parameter to the SQR command line

---

[14] It is possible to compile a run-time version of the SQR. The queries are validated during compilation instead of execution. PeopleSoft does not use this option, and it is not recommended, because compile-time code such as ASK and #IF commands is not executed.

The Cursor Status report (see Listing 11-51) is generated when the SQR program completes.

Listing 11-51. Extract of PTSQRTST_370.out Showing the SQR Cursor Status Report

```
Cursor Status:

Cursor #1:
  SQL = ALTER SESSION SET NLS_DATE_FORMAT='DD-MON-YYYY'
Compiles = 1
Executes = 1
Rows     = 0
…
Cursor #34:
  SQL = SELECT substr(C.PRCSNAME, 1, 5), C.PRCSNAME   FROM PS_PRCSDEFN C
        WHERE C.PRCSTYPE like 'SQR%'
Compiles = 2
Executes = 1
Rows     = 11
```

Application Engine

In Application Engine, SQL is usually explicitly coded, but it can also include PeopleTools macros called *meta-SQL* that either dynamically construct parts of the statement or include blocks of code from elsewhere.

By default, %BIND fields are resolved to literals by Application Engine before the SQL statements are submitted to the database. However, if the ReuseStatement attribute is set to yes on the Application Engine step, then %BIND references to columns in the state record are resolved to Oracle bind variables. In PeopleSoft-delivered applications, ReuseStatement is set to no on the vast majority of steps.

Listing 11-52 shows a SQL statement in an Application Engine step. The %BIND meta-SQL extracts a value from the column SERVERNAMERUN on the state record PRCSPURGE_AET, and %SELECT populates the column SERVERNAME on the same state record with the value selected by the query.

Listing 11-52. PRCSYSPURGE.SchdlSrv.Step01 Do Select

```
%Select(PRCSPURGE_AET.SERVERNAME)
SELECT SERVERNAME
 FROM PSSERVERSTAT
WHERE SERVERNAME <> %Bind(PRCSPURGE_AET.SERVERNAMERUN)
  AND SERVERSTATUS = '3'
  AND ( %DateTimeDiff(LASTUPDDTTM, %CurrentDateTimeIn) < 10)
```

ReuseStatement is not enabled for this set, so it produces the SQL query in Listing 11-53 (as reported by the PeopleTools trace[15]).

---

[15] The %Select macro indicates that the column SERVERNAME is selected into the Application Engine bind variable SERVERNAME on the Application Engine working storage record PRCS_PURGE_AET. A SQL Trace reveals that Application Engine updates the columns on the working storage record unless the restart option is disabled. This allows Application Engine processes to be restarted from the point of their last commit if they crash.

Listing 11-53. PeopleTools Trace of the Application Engine Step `PRCSYSPURGE.SchdlSrv.Step01 Do Select`

```
%Select(PRCSPURGE_AET.SERVERNAME) SELECT SERVERNAME FROM PSSERVERSTAT WHERE
SERVERNAME <> 'PSNT' AND SERVERSTATUS = '3' AND ( ROUND((( SYSDATE) -
(LASTUPDDTTM)) * 1440, 0) < 10)
/
```

From version 8, Application Engine can also execute PeopleCode. Bind variables in PeopleCode are not resolved to literals, even when executed within Application Engine programs.

Techniques for SQL Optimization

Once you have found a piece of problem SQL, you can employ various techniques to improve its performance. This section discusses the techniques you can apply (but without explaining either how or why they work) and then how to apply them to specific PeopleSoft Tools.

Hints

Hints were introduced as a means to give specific instructions to the Oracle cost-based optimizer on how to execute a statement. Oracle has introduced more hints with every release.

A hint is a not just a hint, but a directive to the optimizer.[16] Most hints reduce the options open to the optimizer. The optimizer may appear to ignore the hint either when it is not properly specified or when it chooses an alternate plan that is not precluded by the hint.

In Listing 11-54, a FULL hint has been used to force the optimizer to perform a full table scan on the PS_PERSON table instead of using a FAST FULL SCAN on the PS_PERSON unique index.

Listing 11-54. A FULL *Hint*

```
SELECT EMPLID FROM PS_PERSON A
 INDEX (FAST FULL SCAN) OF 'PS_PERSON' (UNIQUE) (Cost=2 Card=889 Bytes=5334)

SELECT /*+FULL(A)*/ EMPLID FROM PS_PERSON A
 TABLE ACCESS (FULL) OF 'PS_PERSON' (Cost=4 Card=889 Bytes=5334)
```

▨ **Tip** When you add hints to code in PeopleSoft, always use the multiline /* */ notation because the SQL query can be rewrapped by editors or within PeopleSoft.

---

[16] A hint must be a directive because plan stability (stored outlines) works by using a set of hints that guarantees a particular plan for a given SQL statement. See also Oracle Support Document 69992.1: "Why is my hint ignored?"

Indexes

All index changes should be specified in Application Designer (as described in Chapter 5). Otherwise they are likely to be lost if the table is rebuilt by a PeopleTools alter script for any reason.

Disabling Indexes Without Using Hints

It is possible, by use of hints, to make a particular query either use or not use a particular index. However, it is not always possible to add the hint to certain SQL statements in PeopleSoft. An alternative strategy is to disable an index on a particular column by adjusting a SQL query but without changing its function.

Consider the query in Listing 11-55, for example.

Listing 11-55. *A Query Using an Index*

```
SELECT EMPLID, NAME
FROM   PS_NAMES
WHERE  EMPLID >= 'PA001';

Execution Plan
----------------------------------------------------------
SELECT STATEMENT Optimizer=CHOOSE (Cost=4 Card=179 Bytes=3759)
 TABLE ACCESS (BY INDEX ROWID) OF 'PS_NAMES' (Cost=4 Card=179 Bytes=3759)
   INDEX (RANGE SCAN) OF 'PS_NAMES' (UNIQUE) (Cost=3 Card=179)

Statistics
----------------------------------------------------------
       137  consistent gets
```

This query uses the index on PS_NAMES to retrieve the data. However, this might not be desirable. If the query was changed as shown in Listing 11-56, then the index on the column EMPLID could not be used, because there the EMPLID column is part of an expression in the query.

Listing 11-56. *Index Disabled*

```
SELECT EMPLID, NAME
FROM   PS_NAMES
WHERE  ''||EMPLID >= 'PA001';

Execution Plan
----------------------------------------------------------
SELECT STATEMENT Optimizer=CHOOSE (Cost=5 Card=179 Bytes=3759)
 TABLE ACCESS (FULL) OF 'PS_NAMES' (Cost=5 Card=179 Bytes=3759)

Statistics
----------------------------------------------------------
        87  consistent gets
```

The result is that although the full scan of the PS_NAMES table had a higher cost, it required much less logical I/O.

Explicitly Coding Implicit Joins

If A = B and B = C, it implies that A = C. Mathematicians call this *transitive closure*. However, the Oracle optimizer does not work that out for itself on column predicates.[17] Explicitly adding the implicit joins permits the optimizer to consider additional join permutations without changing the function of the statement. Consequently, the optimizer tends to follow the join conditions.

The example in Listing 11-57 is taken from Global Payroll. It became a performance problem because Oracle chose an inappropriate execution plan.

Listing 11-57. Original "Problem" SQL

```
SELECT ...
 FROM PS_GP_PYE_STAT_WRK S
     ,PS_GP_PYE_PRC_STAT P2
     ,PS_GP_RSLT_ACUM RA
WHERE S.RUN_CNTL_ID=:1
  AND S.OPRID=:2
  AND S.EMPLID BETWEEN :3 AND :4
  AND S.EMPLID=RA.EMPLID
  AND P2.EMPLID=RA.EMPLID
  AND S.EMPL_RCD=RA.EMPL_RCD
  AND P2.EMPL_RCD=RA.EMPL_RCD
  AND S.GP_PAYGROUP=RA.GP_PAYGROUP
  AND P2.GP_PAYGROUP=RA.GP_PAYGROUP
  AND S.CAL_ID=RA.CAL_ID
  AND P2.CAL_ID=RA.CAL_ID
  AND P2.CAL_RUN_ID=RA.CAL_RUN_ID
  AND P2.ORIG_CAL_RUN_ID=RA.ORIG_CAL_RUN_ID
  AND S.PRD_TYPE='R'
  AND S.RSLT_SEG_NUM=RA.RSLT_SEG_NUM
  AND S.PRIOR_VER_NUM=P2.RSLT_VER_NUM
  AND S.PRIOR_REV_NUM=P2.RSLT_REV_NUM
  AND RA.ACM_PRD_OPTN='1'
ORDER BY ...
;
```

If you draw out the SQL statement, as shown in Figure 11-9, you can see how the tables are joined. All the selective conditions are on PS_GP_PYE_STAT_WRK, so the optimizer starts with that table. PS_GP_RSLT_ACUM is one of the main payroll result tables and usually holds many millions of rows. PS_GP_PYE_PRC_STAT is also a result table, but it is much smaller than PS_GP_RSLT_ACUM. Each result table has only a single unique index, as shown in Listing 11-58.

Listing 11-58. Index on a Very Large Result Table

```
CREATE UNIQUE INDEX PS_GP_RSLT_ACUM ON PS_GP_RSLT_ACUM
(EMPLID, CAL_RUN_ID, EMPL_RCD, GP_PAYGROUP, CAL_ID, ORIG_CAL_RUN_ID,
```

---

[17] Oracle can do transitive closure on value predicates. If A = 1 and A = B, then adding the condition B = 1 does not make any difference because Oracle does do transitive closure on value predicates. Other databases, such as Sybase and DB2, can do transitive closure on column predicates.

```
RSLT_SEG_NUM, PIN_NUM, EMPL_RCD_ACUM, ACM_FROM_DT, ACM_THRU_DT, SLICE_BGN_DT,
SLICE_END_DT,
SEQ_NUM8) ...
```

The optimizer starts with PS_GP_PYE_STAT_WRK; follows the links on the key columns (see Figure 11-9) and accesses the very large result table PS_GP_RSLT_ACUM second, using the first five columns of the index; and then finally goes to PS_GP_PYE_STAT.

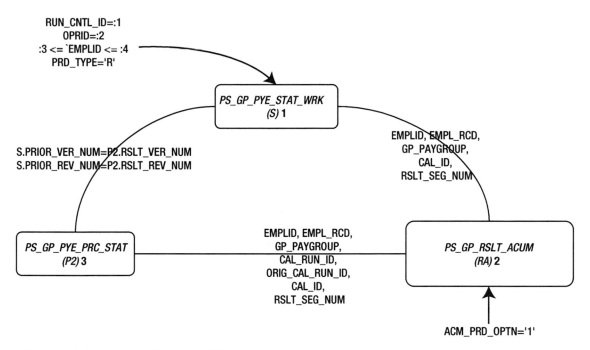

Figure 11-9. Diagram of the original SQL

The joins in Listing 11-59 are implied from other joins in the query.

Listing 11-59. Implied joins

```
AND P2.EMPLID=S.EMPLID
AND P2.EMPL_RCD=S.EMPL_RCD
AND P2.GP_PAYGROUP=S.GP_PAYGROUP
AND P2.CAL_ID=S.CAL_ID
```

By explicitly adding the implicit joins, the optimizer joins the tables in a different order, as shown in Figure 11-10.

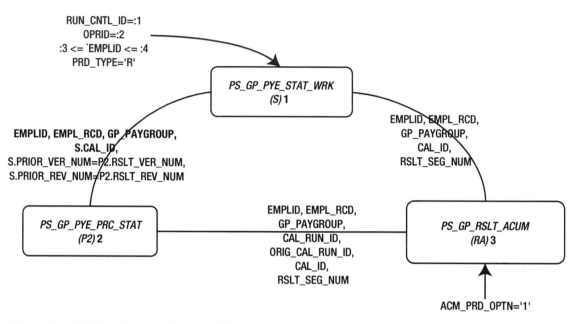

Figure 11-10. SQL with implicit joins added

The optimizer still starts with PS_GP_PYE_STAT_WRK, but it can now join PS_GP_PYE_PRC_STAT second before accessing PS_GP_RSLT_ACUM using the first seven keys of the index. In this case, using the extra two columns on the index produces a dramatic improvement in performance.

▓ **Tip** If you ever have trouble seeing what is going on in a query, or why the optimizer takes a particular path through the tables, draw it in the manner shown in this section. Doing so also helps to identify when implicit joins could be explicitly coded.

Query Block Naming

Occasionally, I need to apply a hint to a table within a view to achieve a particular execution plan. Wherever possible, I avoid putting the hint into the view text because it may not be appropriate for all queries that use the view. Instead, I can give the query block an explicit name by putting a QB_NAME hint into the view and then referring to the named query block.

When I do this, I give the query block the same name as the record in PeopleSoft. This example uses record VAT_TX_AP_I_VW that corresponds to a database view PS_VAT_TX_AP_I_VW. Therefore, I named the query block VAT_TX_AP_I_VW. This naming convention is helpful if the view name is dynamically generated in an Application Engine step. Listing 11-60 shows a view illustrating the approach I've just described.

Listing 11-60. View with Query Block Naming Hint

```
CREATE VIEW PS_VAT_TX_AP_I_VW ... AS
SELECT /*+QB_NAME(VAT_TX_AP_I_VW)*/ B.BUSINESS_UNIT
,B.VOUCHER_ID
,B.UNPOST_SEQ
,B.APPL_JRNL_ID
...
FROM PS_VOUCHER A
,PS_VCHR_ACCTG_LINE B
WHERE A.BUSINESS_UNIT = B.BUSINESS_UNIT
AND A.VOUCHER_ID = B.VOUCHER_ID
AND B.VAT_DISTRIB_STATUS IN (' ', 'N', 'R', 'M')
AND B.DST_ACCT_TYPE IN ('VIR', 'VIWR', 'VIIR', 'VICR')
AND B.PRIMARY_LEDGER = 'Y'
```

I need to use a hint to force this use of an index on the table PS_VCHR_ACCTG_LINE. I can add a hint to the query that references the view and scope the hint to apply to just the named query block, as shown in Listing 11-61.

Listing 11-61. Query with Hint That References a Named Query Block

```
SELECT /*+INDEX(@VAT_TX_AP_I_VW
B@VAT_TX_AP_I_VW(PS_VCHR_ACCTG_LINE.VAT_DISTRIB_STATUS))*/
     C.VAT_ENTITY,…
...
FROM PS_VAT_TX_AP_I_VW A,
PS_VAT_UPD_BU_TAO B
, PS_VAT_ENT_BU_GL C
WHERE B.PROCESS_INSTANCE = 717653
AND B.REQUEST_NBR = 1
AND B.VAT_SOURCE_DEFN = 'AP_VOUCHER'
AND A.BUSINESS_UNIT = B.BUSINESS_UNIT
AND A.BUSINESS_UNIT_GL = C.BUSINESS_UNIT
```

■ **Note** This technique is not infallible. If the optimizer transforms the SQL, the named block may disappear, and any hints using the block name become invalid and cannot be applied.

Plan Stability (or Stored Outlines)

Plan stability is a feature in Oracle that is designed to prevent environmental factors from affecting performance characteristics of the application. The execution plans of SQL statements are held in the database as *stored outlines*. An outline is a set of hints that unambiguously describe a particular execution plan and, if applied to the statement, produces the same execution plan.

Stored outlines provide a way to apply hints to a SQL statement that cannot be changed in the application code. There are various scenarios in PeopleSoft in which a DBA may be tempted to consider introducing plan stability.

A SQL statement may be generated from metadata, and there is no opportunity to edit it directly. This is frequently the case in the component processor. The COBOL batch programs in the Financials product and the Global Payroll module of HCM also dynamically generate SQL within the COBOL.

DBAs might also be tempted to use stored outlines instead of using PeopleSoft development tools to make changes. However, I consider that plan stability is not a generally an effective tuning tool in a PeopleSoft environment, and there are other, better options. The dynamic nature of the SQL generated by PeopleSoft makes it difficult to use stored outlines. The SQL statement stored in the outline must exactly match the one submitted to the database for the outline to be applied.

In Chapter 8, we saw how SQL code generated by the component processor when saving application data changes in the PIA changed depending on which columns were updated by the user. Each combination of columns produced a different SQL statement and required a different outline.

In Chapter 4, I showed how SQL generated by the search dialog includes user input in literal values. Earlier in this chapter, I described how variables referenced by %BIND in Application Engine are also resolved to literal values. Each literal value produces a different SQL statement. If CURSOR_SHARING is set to FORCE or SIMILAR, then the literal values are converted to bind variables, and the statements are considered to be the same.[18]

When Application Engine programs uses non-shared instances of a temporary record, different instances of the program are allocated use different database tables. Such SQL statements can never be shared.

Due to the dynamic nature of the SQL generated by PeopleSoft, stored outlines simply do not work in most situations. They are also an additional administrative overhead. The DBA must manage them outside the PeopleSoft development environment and migrate from database to database in synchronization with program code.

The sole exception that I have found to this is the PeopleSoft Global Payroll engine. It is written in COBOL, so it does use bind variables, it doesn't use multiple tables for working storage, and so it does generate sharable SQL. The problem is that sometimes you run it for a large population and sometimes for a few, or even just a single employee. Due to bind variable peeking, the different data volumes can lead to different execution plans. An execution plan that is fine when processing a single employee can be a disaster when processing an entire company. The problem comes when the small process is run shortly before the large process, and the execution plans generated by the small process are still in the library cache when the large process is run. Oracle reuses the execution plan from last time.

I have been able to collect stored outlines for the large process with a trigger on PSPRCSRQST. Listing 11-62 shows an example of such a trigger. The outlines go into a category that has the same name as the process.

Listing 11-62. Trigger to Collect Stored Outlines on a Specific Process

```
CREATE OR REPLACE TRIGGER sysadm.gfc_create_stored_outlines
BEFORE UPDATE OF runstatus ON sysadm.psprcsrqst
FOR EACH ROW
WHEN (new.prcsname = 'GPPDPRUN' AND (new.runstatus = 7 OR old.runstatus = 7))
DECLARE
l_sql VARCHAR2(100);
```

---

[18] The stored outline contains bind variables if the outline is created by enabling CREATE_STORED_OUTLINES, but not if the CREATE OUTLINE DDL command is used.

```
BEGIN
 l_sql := 'ALTER SESSION SET create_stored_outlines = ';
 IF :new.runstatus = 7 THEN
   EXECUTE IMMEDIATE l_sql||:new.prcsname;
 ELSIF :old.runstatus = 7 THEN
   EXECUTE IMMEDIATE l_sql||'FALSE';
 END IF;
EXCEPTION WHEN OTHERS THEN NULL; --because I dont want to crash the process scheduler
END;
/
```

The outlines can then be applied to that process with a slightly different trigger. Listing 11-63 shows how.

Listing 11-63. Trigger to Use Stored Outlines on a Specific Process

```
CREATE OR REPLACE TRIGGER sysadm.gfc_use_stored_outlines
BEFORE UPDATE OF runstatus ON sysadm.psprcsrqst
FOR EACH ROW
WHEN (new.prcsname = 'GPPDPRUN' AND (new.runstatus = 7 OR old.runstatus = 7))
DECLARE
l_sql VARCHAR2(100);
BEGIN
 l_sql := 'ALTER SESSION SET use_stored_outlines = ';
 IF :new.runstatus = 7 THEN
EXECUTE IMMEDIATE l_sql||:new.prcsname;
 ELSIF :old.runstatus = 7 THEN
   EXECUTE IMMEDIATE l_sql||'FALSE';
 END IF;
EXCEPTION WHEN OTHERS THEN NULL; --because I dont want to crash the process scheduler
END;
/
```

Now all payroll calculation process should[19] do so use the same execution plans. The execution plans for the large process may not be perfect, but on a small data set they are perfectly adequate.

Stored outlines should not be fitted and forgotten. SQL changes caused by upgrade, patch bundles, and fixes are almost certain to result in new SQL statements that do not match the outlines. Data volumes change over time as history accumulates. An outline that was optimal in the past may not be so in the future. Old outlines may need to be removed and replaced with new ones.

Most of the batch-processing source code is accessible either in flat files or via Application Designer. Most of the code generated by the component processor references tables by their primary key columns and is rarely a performance problem.

---

[19] I said the plans *should* be the same. However, I have found plan regressions in statements where a stored outline has been used. The outline is supposed to be a set of hints that if applied to the statement guarantee a specific execution plan. Sometimes, through SQL transformation, the optimizer can find an execution plan in which some of the hints in the outlines are invalid. It has not ignored the hint, but it cannot apply it either. There are also optimizer bugs.

With the one exception of the COBOL in Global Payroll, I have always found that suitable indexes with realistic optimizer statistics, including histograms when necessary and optimizer hints in the source code, are very effective.

Cursor Sharing

Cursor sharing can be effective in reducing the amount of hard parsing in a PeopleSoft system, but it can also prevent the use of histograms, although bind variable peeking, introduced in Oracle9*i*, mitigates this problem. As mentioned in Chapter 5, much of the processing in the Financials product is based on searching for flags set to a particular value, so histograms are needed to make Oracle use indexes on the flag columns.

My own experience is that simply enabling cursor sharing at the instance level causes more problems than it solves. However, I have occasionally enabled it for specific process via a trigger such as the one shown in Listing 11-64.

Listing 11-64. Trigger to Enable Cursor Sharing on a Specific Process

```
CREATE OR REPLACE TRIGGER sysadm.gfc_alter_session
BEFORE UPDATE OF runstatus ON sysadm.psprcsrqst
FOR EACH ROW
WHEN (new.runstatus = 7 AND old.runstatus != 7 AND new.prcstype != 'PSJob'
 AND new.prcsname IN('FS_VATUPDFS'))
BEGIN

 IF :new.prcsname IN('FS_VATUPDFS') THEN
   EXECUTE IMMEDIATE 'ALTER SESSION SET CURSOR_SHARING = SIMILAR';
 END IF;

EXCEPTION WHEN OTHERS THEN NULL; --exception deliberately coded to suppress all exceptions
END;
/
```

Implementing SQL Optimization Techniques

This section discusses how to implement various optimization and other coding tips into SQL generated by PeopleTools. The examples presented here only illustrate the techniques. I am not suggesting that any or all of the changes will actually improve the performance of the specific examples.

Views

Most views in PeopleSoft are defined in Application Designer in the usual way, as a block of SQL. All the standard techniques for improving a query can be brought to bear on views. Some views are defined as a query and have to be edited via the Query design tool, but they can always be changed to normal views.

Views can also be a useful way to introduce a hint via the back door. A reference to one record that is a table can be replaced in PeopleSoft with a different—but identical—record that is a view. That view may simply select the original table (in which case you can still update the table via the view), but now you can add a hint to the view. The scope of the hint is not limited to the view, but it can affect the query that references the view.

▨ **Caution** Use this technique with care because every statement that references the view could be affected by the hint, and that may not be desirable.

Component Processor

There is no way to directly alter the SQL generated by the component processor to load and save data in the PIA. Fortunately, this SQL is rarely a problem. Most of the queries use criteria on the key columns, so the database naturally uses the unique key index. However, it is possible to change the scroll in the page to reference a view instead.

Case-Insensitive Search Dialogs and Function-Based Indexes

The SQL behind the search dialog (shown in Listing 11-65) is generated from the definition of the search record and the fields in the dialog that the user fills in. You cannot change the SQL. In particular, as noted earlier, you cannot remove the DISTINCT keyword.

However, for search records that are tables, indexing usually resolves most problems. When the search record is a view, you can always change the view.

If case-insensitive searching is enabled, a function-based index on a frequently used underlying column is often helpful (also see Chapter 6).

Listing 11-65. Search Dialog SQL and a Suggested Function-Based Index

```
SELECT DISTINCT EMPLID, EMPL_RCD, NAME, LAST_NAME_SRCH, SETID_DEPT, DEPTID,
NAME_AC, PER_STATUS
FROM PS_PERS_SRCH_GBL
WHERE ROWSECCLASS=:1
AND UPPER(NAME) LIKE UPPER('Smith') || '%' ESCAPE '\'
ORDER BY NAME, EMPLID

CREATE INDEX PSZNAMES ON PS_NAMES
(UPPER(NAME)
) ...
/
```

Search Dialog PeopleCode

Sometimes, if you don't like the answer, you should change the question. Search dialogs are sometimes slow because the user has not put in enough data to restrict the amount of data returned (PeopleTools restricts the dialog to show only the first 300 rows queried). PeopleCode can be added to the search record to force at least some of the name to be entered.

In the HCM application, SearchSave PeopleCode on the search record (see Listing 11-66) forces the operator to enter something in the search dialog; otherwise, the operator gets an error message and cannot start the search.

Listing 11-66. Extract of PERS_SGBL_SBR.SearchSave PeopleCode

```
If Not RecordChanged(PERS_SGBL_SBR.EMPLID) Then
  Error MsgGet(1000, 168, "At least one key field must be entered.")
End-If;
```

It is possible to tighten the search restriction a lot more to save users from themselves. In Listing 11-67, the SearchSave PeopleCode has been enhanced to force operators to enter at least the first two characters of the name or last name, or at least five characters of the EMPLID, unless they are also searching by one of the name fields. Forcing operators to put in better search criteria can produce better performance.

Listing 11-67. Additional Validation Added to the PERS_SGBL_SBR.SearchSave PeopleCode

```
/*dmk if searching on a name then at least two characters must be entered*/
If All(PERS_SGBL_SBR.NAME) And
     Len(PERS_SGBL_SBR.NAME) < 2 Then
  Error MsgGet(21000, 28, "Enter at least 2 characters of name");
End-If;
/*dmk if searching on a name then at least two characters must be entered*/
If All(PERS_SGBL_SBR.LAST_NAME_SRCH) And
     Len(PERS_SGBL_SBR.LAST_NAME_SRCH) < 2 Then
  Error MsgGet(21000, 28, "Enter at least 2 characters of last name");
End-If;

/*dmk if entry anything in EMPLID then enter at least 9 characters unless
searching on something else as well */
If All(PERS_SGBL_SBR.EMPLID) And
     Len(PERS_SGBL_SBR.EMPLID) < 5 Then
  If None(PERS_SGBL_SBR.NAME) And
       None(PERS_SGBL_SBR.LAST_NAME_SRCH) Then
    Error MsgGet(21000, 28, "Enter whole of employee ID, not just a part, if not entering any
other search information");
  End-If;
```

PeopleCode

Pieces of PeopleCode are attached to events in the PIA. When a user clicks a link or saves a piece of data, PeopleCode can be coded to fire and perform processing. SQL statements appear in PeopleCode in various forms, as described in the sections that follow.

SQLExec()

What you see is what you get. A SQL statement passed as a string to a SQLExec() function, as shown in Listing 11-68, is passed to the database exactly as coded, although it can use certain PeopleSoft macros to format values.

Listing 11-68. SQL Statement in a SQLExec() PeopleCode Function

```
SQLExec("Select A.BEN_STATUS from PS_ACTN_REASON_TBL A where A.ACTION = :1
and A.ACTION_REASON = (Select min(AA.ACTION_REASON) from PS_ACTN_REASON_TBL AA
where AA.ACTION = A.ACTION) and A.EFFDT = (Select max(AAA.EFFDT) from
PS_ACTN_REASON_TBL AAA where AAA.ACTION = A.ACTION and AAA.ACTION_REASON =
A.ACTION_REASON)", &ACTION, &FETCH_STATUS);
```

Sometimes statements are built dynamically before being submitted, as in Listing 11-69.

Listing 11-69. Dynamically Generated Statement Used in a SQLExec() Function

```
&SEL = "SELECT 'X' FROM PS_" | &RECN | " WHERE PSARCH_ID = :1";
SQLExec(&SEL, PSARCH_ID, &EXIST);
```

Changes to the SQL can be made by simply editing the PeopleCode.

ScrollSelect() and Other Scroll Functions

The PeopleCode scroll functions are used to programmatically load data into scrolls on a page. The **ScrollSelect()** function (see Listing 11-70) queries data from a record into a scroll. The SELECT and FROM clauses of the query are generated automatically by PeopleTools. The fourth parameter of the function is a string, which contains a WHERE clause that is appended to the query generated by the rest of the command.

Listing 11-70. A ScrollSelect() Function

```
ScrollSelect(1, Record.ENCUMB_TRIGGER, Record.ENCUMB_TRIGGER, "Where
TRIGGER_RECORD = 'J' and emplid = :1 and EMPL_RCD = :2 and PROCESSED = 'N'",
&EMPLID, &EMPL_RCD);
```

The scroll function in Listing 11-70 generates the SQL in Listing 11-71.

Listing 11-71. Query Generated by ScrollSelect()

```
Stmt=SELECT SETID, DEPTID, POSITION_POOL_ID, SETID_JOBCODE, JOBCODE,
POSITION_NBR, EMPLID, EMPL_RCD, JOB_REQ_NBR, TRIGGER_RECORD, TIME_STAMP,
TO_CHAR(TIME_STAMP,'YYYY-MM-DD-HH24.MI.SS."000000"'), PROCESSED FROM PS_ENCUMB_TRIGGER
Where TRIGGER_RECORD = 'J' and emplid = :1 and EMPL_RCD = :2 and PROCESSED = 'N'
ORDER BY SETID, DEPTID, POSITION_POOL_ID, SETID_JOBCODE, JOBCODE, POSITION_NBR,
EMPLID, EMPL_RCD, JOB_REQ_NBR, TRIGGER_RECORD, TIME_STAMP
```

You can adjust the WHERE clause of the SQL in PeopleCode, but you need to use a view to control the SELECT or FROM clause.

Rowsets

Scroll functions are still supported in PeopleTools 8 PeopleCode, but they have been superseded by rowset objects (see Listing 11-72).

Listing 11-72. Rowset Methods

```
&Table1_vw_rs = CreateRowset(Record.PTP_TABLE1_VW);
&Table1_vw_rs.Fill("WHERE PTP_SEQ_NBR >= :1", &nbr);
&Rs = GetRowset(Scroll.PTP_TABLE1);
&Rs.Flush();
&Rs.Select(Record.PTP_TABLE1, "WHERE PTP_SEQ_NBR <= 10010");
```

The SQL generated by the Fill() and Select() methods (see Listing 11-73) is similar to that generated by the scroll functions, but it can be distinguished because the table always has the alias FILL.

Listing 11-73. SQL Generated by Rowset Methods

```
PSAPPSRV.3808   1-11990  14.28.59    0.471 Cur#1.3808.HR88 RC=0 Dur=0.000 COM Stmt=SELECT
FILL.PTP_SEQ_NBR,FILL.PTP_SEQ_CHAR,FILL.DESCR,FILL.PTP_INT01,FILL.PTP_INT02,FILL.PTP_INT03
,FILL.PTP_INT04,FILL.PTP_INT05,FILL.PTP_INT06,FILL.PTP_INT07,FILL.PTP_INT08,FILL.PTP_INT09
,FILL.PTP_INT10,FILL.PTP_INT11,FILL.PTP_INT12,FILL.PTP_INT13,FILL.PTP_INT14,FILL.PTP_INT15
,FILL.PTP_INT16,FILL.PTP_INT17,FILL.PTP_INT18,FILL.PTP_INT19,FILL.PTP_INT20,FILL.PTP_INT21
,FILL.PTP_INT22,FILL.PTP_INT23,FILL.PTP_INT24,FILL.PTP_CHAR01,FILL.PTP_CHAR02,
FILL.PTP_CHAR03,FILL.PTP_CHAR04,FILL.PTP_CHAR05,FILL.PTP_CHAR06,FILL.PTP_CHAR07,
FILL.PTP_CHAR08,FILL.PTP_CHAR09,FILL.PTP_CHAR10,FILL.PTP_CHAR11,FILL.PTP_CHAR12,
FILL.PTP_CHAR13,FILL.PTP_CHAR14,FILL.PTP_CHAR15,FILL.PTP_CHAR16,FILL.PTP_CHAR17,
FILL.PTP_CHAR18,FILL.PTP_CHAR19,FILL.PTP_CHAR20,FILL.PTP_CHAR21,FILL.PTP_CHAR22,
FILL.PTP_CHAR23 FROM PS_PTP_TABLE1 FILL  WHERE PTP_SEQ_NBR <= 10001
PSAPPSRV.3808   1-11993  14.28.59    0.000 Cur#1.3808.HR88 RC=0 Dur=0.000 COM Stmt=SELECT
FILL.PTP_SEQ_NBR,FILL.PTP_SEQ_CHAR,FILL.DESCR,FILL.PTP_INT01 FROM PS_PTP_TABLE1_VW FILL
WHERE PTP_SEQ_NBR >= :1
```

Query

The monolithic nature of the SQL generated by PeopleSoft Query not only produces queries that perform poorly, but is also one the main reasons that queries can become a cause of system-wide performance problems.

It is possible to introduce Oracle hints in queries to control execution plans. Outer joins can avoid more complicated constructions. However, other, more esoteric features of SQL are not supported by Query because they are not implemented on all platforms. In such cases, the only option is to create a view as desired and query the view.

Hints in Expressions

For a hint to be recognized in a query, it must appear between the SELECT keyword and the first selected column (see Listing 11-74).

Listing 11-74. PeopleSoft Query with a Hint

```
SELECT /*+ ALL_ROWS*/  A.EMPLID, A.COURSE, A.SESSION_NBR, D.NAME, B.DESCR,
TO_CHAR(A.COURSE_START_DT,'YYYY-MM-DD'), A.ATTENDANCE,B.COURSE
 FROM PS_TRAINING A, PS_COURSE_TBL B, PS_PERSONAL_DTA_VW D, PS_PERS_SRCH_QRY D1
 WHERE D.EMPLID = D1.EMPLID
```

```
AND D1.ROWSECCLASS = 'HCDPALL'
AND ( ( A.ATTENDANCE = 'E'
 AND A.COURSE = B.COURSE
 AND D.EMPLID = A.EMPLID
 AND A.COURSE = :1
 AND ( A.SESSION_NBR = :2
 OR A.COURSE_START_DT = TO_DATE(:3,'YYYY-MM-DD'))) )
```

To achieve this in Query, you need to create an expression, as shown in Figure 11-11, defined the same way as the first selected field it will replace.

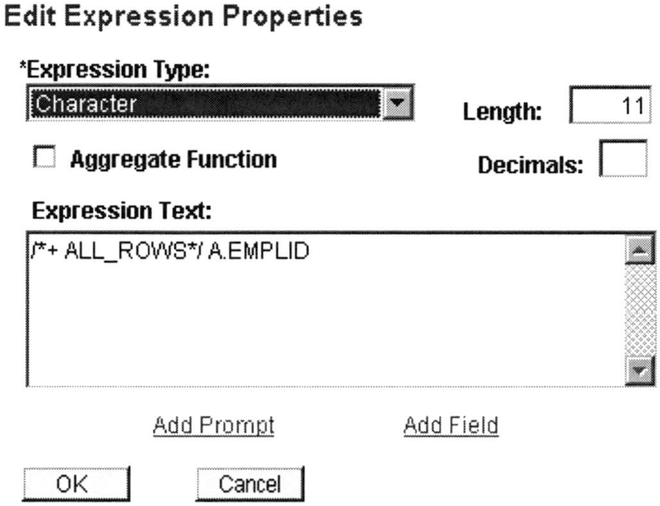

Edit Expression Properties

*Expression Type:

| Character ▼ | **Length:** | 11 |

☐ **Aggregate Function**   **Decimals:** [ ]

Expression Text:

```
/*+ ALL_ROWS*/ A.EMPLID
```

Add Prompt   Add Field

| OK | | Cancel |

Figure 11-11. A Query expression

Then make it the first selected field, as shown in Figure 11-12.

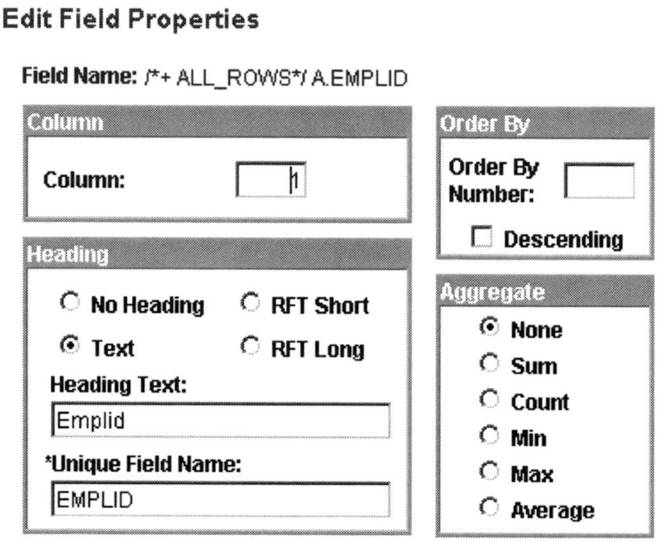

Edit Field Properties

Field Name: /*+ ALL_ROWS*/ A.EMPLID

Column

Column: [1]

Order By

Order By
Number: [   ]

☐ Descending

Heading

○ No Heading   ○ RFT Short

◉ Text   ○ RFT Long

Heading Text:

[Emplid]

*Unique Field Name:

[EMPLID]

Aggregate

◉ None
○ Sum
○ Count
○ Min
○ Max
○ Average

Figure 11-12. Edit Field Properties panel

This technique does not work if the query has been made DISTINCT (see Figure 11-13).

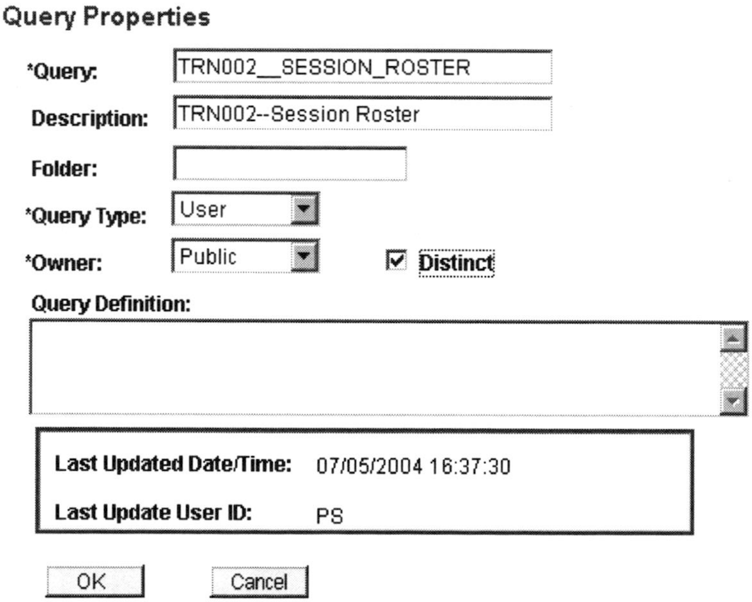

Query Properties

*Query:	[TRN002__SESSION_ROSTER]
Description:	[TRN002--Session Roster]
Folder:	[ ]
*Query Type:	[User ▼]
*Owner:	[Public ▼] ☑ **Distinct**

Query Definition:

[   ]

Last Updated Date/Time:	07/05/2004 16:37:30
Last Update User ID:	PS

[OK]   [Cancel]

Figure 11-13. Query Properties panel

The hint appears after the DISTINCT keyword, and the optimizer ignores it because it is in the wrong place, as shown in Listing 11-75.

Listing 11-75. Hint in the Wrong Place is Just a Comment

```
SELECT DISTINCT /*+ ALL_ROWS*/  A.EMPLID, A.COURSE, ...
```

Instead, the Distinct check box should be unchecked and the DISTINCT keyword put in the expression. The result is shown in Listing 11-76.

Listing 11-76. Hint in the Correct Position

```
SELECT /*+ ALL_ROWS*/ DISTINCT  A.EMPLID, A.COURSE, ...
```

Hints in Views

Optimizer hints can also be introduced into a particular query by adding a view that contains an optimizer hint. The view in Listing 11-77 can be defined in Application Designer (remember to put it on a query tree).

Listing 11-77. Hint in a View

```
CREATE VIEW PS_FIRST_ROWS_VW (DUMMY_FIELD) AS
SELECT /*+ FIRST_ROWS (10)*/
'x' FROM DUAL
```

Then the view can be joined into the query, as shown in Listing 11-78, thus introducing the hint.

Listing 11-78. View with a Hint in a Query

```
SELECT A.EMPLID, A.COURSE, A.SESSION_NBR, D.NAME, B.DESCR,
TO_CHAR(A.COURSE_START_DT,'YYYY-MM-DD'), A.ATTENDANCE,B.COURSE
 FROM PS_TRAINING A, PS_COURSE_TBL B, PS_PERSONAL_DTA_VW D,
    PS_PERS_SRCH_QRY D1, PS_FIRST_ROWS_VW C
 WHERE D.EMPLID = D1.EMPLID
   AND D1.ROWSECCLASS = 'HCDPALL'
   AND ( ( A.ATTENDANCE = 'E'
   AND A.COURSE = B.COURSE
   AND D.EMPLID = A.EMPLID
   AND A.COURSE = :1
   AND ( A.SESSION_NBR = :2
   OR A.COURSE_START_DT = TO_DATE(:3,'YYYY-MM-DD'))) )
```

On systems where some operators are allowed to develop their own queries, this provides a relatively safe and easy way for users to add hints to views.

Outer Joins

There are genuinely occasions when it is necessary for an operator to code an outer join in Query. If it were not possible, the only alternative would be convoluted UNION queries such as the one shown in Listing 11-79.[20]

Listing 11-79. Query Functionally Equivalent to an Outer Join

```
SELECT A.EMPLID, A.NAME, B.COUNTRY, B.CITY, B.COUNTY
FROM   PS_PERSONAL_DATA A, PS_PERS_SRCH_QRY A1, PS_ADDRESSES B
WHERE  A.EMPLID = A1.EMPLID
AND    A1.ROWSECCLASS = 'DPALL'
AND A.EMPLID = B.EMPLID
AND B.EFFDT =
  (SELECT MAX(B_ED.EFFDT) FROM PS_ADDRESSES B_ED
  WHERE B.EMPLID = B_ED.EMPLID
  AND B.ADDRESS_TYPE = B_ED.ADDRESS_TYPE
  AND B_ED.EFFDT <= SYSDATE))
UNION
SELECT C.EMPLID, C.NAME, ' ', ' ', ' '
FROM   PS_PERSONAL_DATA C, PS_PERS_SRCH_QRY C1
WHERE  C.EMPLID = C1.EMPLID
AND    C1.ROWSECCLASS = 'DPALL'
AND NOT EXISTS(
  SELECT 'x' FROM PS_ADDRESSES D
  WHERE  C.EMPLID = D.EMPLID
  AND    D.EFFDT =
    (SELECT MAX(D_ED.EFFDT) FROM PS_ADDRESSES D_ED
    WHERE D.EMPLID = D_ED.EMPLID
    AND D.ADDRESS_TYPE = D_ED.ADDRESS_TYPE
    AND D_ED.EFFDT <= SYSDATE)))
```

Since PeopleTools 8.44, Query optionally generates the SQL92-compliant[21] outer join syntax that Oracle implemented, and now recommends,[22] in release 9*i*.

If you outer join to an effective dated table (in this example, PS_ADDRESSES), then Query automatically adds the effective date subquery. You cannot outer join to a subquery. If the effective date criterion is appropriate, then you need to add the OR B.EFFDT IS NULL criterion manually, as shown in Listing 11-80.

---

[20] This is exactly the kind of thing that PeopleTools does when an operator's language is not the base language for the system. If the translation in the operator's language is not available, PeopleTools retrieves the base language value.

[21] When vendors claim that they are "SQL92 compliant," it is important to know at which level. Oracle 7.0 was certified for SQL92 entry-level compliance in 1993. The left outer join syntax is in the transitional level. There are also intermediate and full levels.

[22] According to the *Oracle9i SQL Reference* (Release 2), "Oracle Corporation recommends that you use the FROM clause OUTER JOIN syntax rather than the Oracle join operator." However, behind the scenes Oracle transforms the SQL back to Oracle's proprietary syntax.

Listing 11-80. Outer Joining an Effective Dated Table

```
SELECT A.EMPLID, A.NAME, B.COUNTRY, B.CITY, B.COUNTY
 FROM (PS_NAMES A LEFT OUTER JOIN  PS_ADDRESSES B ON  A.EMPLID = B.EMPLID ),
PS_PERS_SRCH_QRY A1
 WHERE A.EMPLID = A1.EMPLID
   AND A1.ROWSECCLASS = 'HCDPALL'
   AND ( A.EFFDT =
        (SELECT MAX(A_ED.EFFDT) FROM PS_NAMES A_ED
        WHERE A.EMPLID = A_ED.EMPLID
          AND A.NAME_TYPE = A_ED.NAME_TYPE
          AND A_ED.EFFDT <= SYSDATE)
     AND A.EMPLID LIKE 'KUZ%'
     AND ( B.EFFDT =
        (SELECT MAX(B_ED.EFFDT) FROM PS_ADDRESSES B_ED
        WHERE B.EMPLID = B_ED.EMPLID
          AND B.ADDRESS_TYPE = B_ED.ADDRESS_TYPE
          AND B_ED.EFFDT <= A.EFFDT)
     OR B.EFFDT IS NULL) )
```

Figure 11-14 shows the output of this query in Excel.

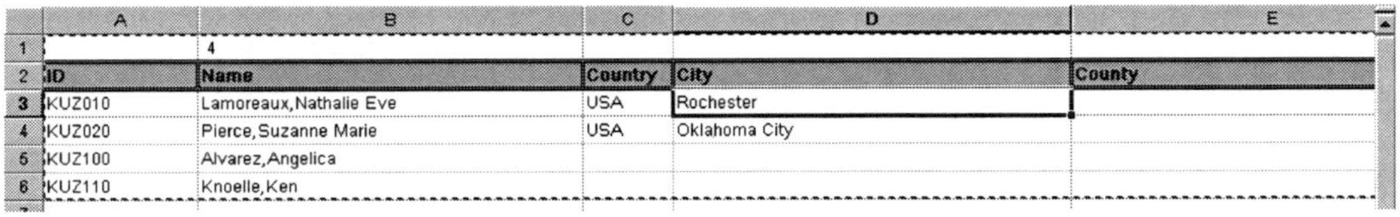

	A	B	C	D	E
1		4			
2	ID	Name	Country	City	County
3	KUZ010	Lamoreaux,Nathalie Eve	USA	Rochester	
4	KUZ020	Pierce,Suzanne Marie	USA	Oklahoma City	
5	KUZ100	Alvarez,Angelica			
6	KUZ110	Knoelle,Ken			

Figure 11-14. Results of Listing 11-80 in Excel

PeopleTools 8.43 and Earlier

Up to PeopleTools 8.43, PeopleSoft Query did not generate any form of outer-join syntax. The only way to introduce an outer join was to manually code the Oracle-specific syntax in an expression, as shown in Figure 11-15. This is still a valid tactic in later versions.

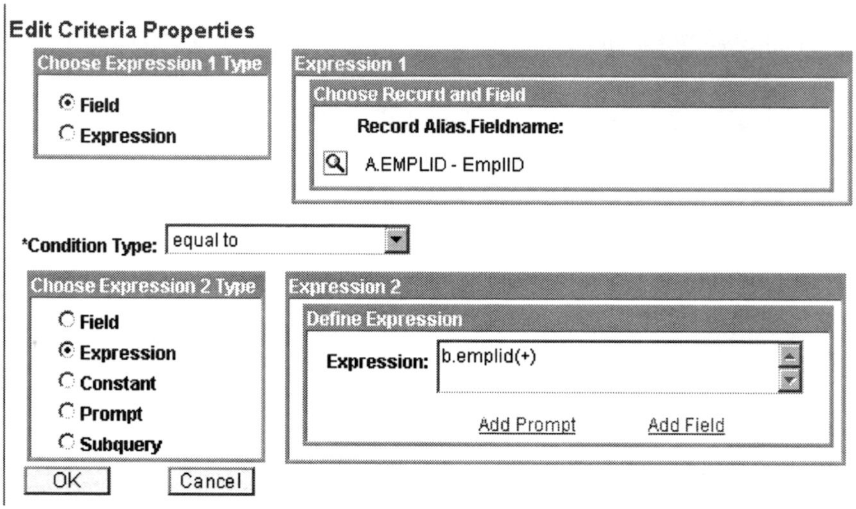

Edit Criteria Properties

Choose Expression 1 Type

- ◉ Field
- ○ Expression

Expression 1

Choose Record and Field

Record Alias.Fieldname:

🔍 A.EMPLID - EmplID

*Condition Type: equal to ▾

Choose Expression 2 Type

- ○ Field
- ◉ Expression
- ○ Constant
- ○ Prompt
- ○ Subquery

Expression 2

Define Expression

Expression: b.emplid(+)

Add Prompt   Add Field

[OK]   [Cancel]

Figure 11-15. PeopleTools 8.1x Query criteria properties with Oracle outer-join syntax

The SQL in Listing 11-81 was generated by Query. It is still necessary to work around the effective date subquery on the outer-joined table by adding the OR … IS NULL condition manually.

Listing 11-81. Query with Oracle-Specific Outer-Join Syntax

```
SELECT A.EMPLID, A.NAME, B.COUNTRY, B.CITY, B.COUNTY
FROM PS_NAMES A, PS_PERS_SRCH_QRY A1, PS_ADDRESSES B
WHERE A.EMPLID = A1.EMPLID
AND A1.ROWSECCLASS = 'DPALL'
AND ( A.EFFDT =
(SELECT MAX(A_ED.EFFDT) FROM PS_NAMES A_ED
WHERE A.EMPLID = A_ED.EMPLID
AND A.NAME_TYPE = A_ED.NAME_TYPE
AND A_ED.EFFDT <= SYSDATE)
AND A.EMPLID = B.EMPLID(+)
AND ( B.EFFDT =
(SELECT MAX(B_ED.EFFDT) FROM PS_ADDRESSES B_ED
WHERE B.EMPLID = B_ED.EMPLID
AND B.ADDRESS_TYPE = B_ED.ADDRESS_TYPE
AND B_ED.EFFDT <= SYSDATE)
OR B.EFFDT IS NULL)
AND A.EMPLID LIKE 'L%' )
```

Outer-Joining Query Security Records

The query security record is an attribute of the record defined in Application Designer. Whenever a record is referenced in Query, it is automatically joined to its query security record, which is also added to the query. If records in a query have the same query security record, the query security record only appears once in the FROM clause of the query.

The newly implemented SQL92 syntax in PeopleTools 8.44 makes it possible to outer join a record with a query security record. In the example in Listing 11-82, both tables are secured by PS_EMPLMT_SRCH_QRY. PeopleTools automatically adds OR B.EMPLID IS NULL to the join to the query security record. The (+) syntax is Oracle specific and so is not used by PeopleTools.

Listing 11-82. SQL92 Outer-Join Syntax

```
SELECT A.EMPLID, A.EMPL_RCD, TO_CHAR(A.EFFDT,'YYYY-MM-DD'), A.EFFSEQ, B.NAME
 FROM (PS_JOB A LEFT OUTER JOIN  PS_EMPLOYEES B
       ON  A.EMPLID = B.EMPLID AND A.EMPL_RCD = B.EMPL_RCD ), PS_EMPLMT_SRCH_QRY A1
WHERE A.EMPLID = A1.EMPLID
  AND A.EMPL_RCD = A1.EMPL_RCD
  AND A1.ROWSECCLASS = 'HCDPALL'
  AND  (B.EMPLID = A1.EMPLID OR B.EMPLID  IS NULL )
  AND  (B.EMPL_RCD = A1.EMPL_RCD OR B.EMPL_RCD  IS NULL )
...
```

This would not have been possible up to PeopleTools 8.43, where the equi-join to the query security table (shown in Listing 11-83) could not be removed.

Listing 11-83. System-Generated Equi-Joins

```
SELECT A.EMPLID, A.EMPL_RCD, TO_CHAR(A.EFFDT,'YYYY-MM-DD'), A.EFFSEQ
 FROM PS_JOB A, PS_EMPLMT_SRCH_QRY A1, PS_EMPLOYEES B
WHERE A.EMPLID = A1.EMPLID
  AND A.EMPL_RCD = A1.EMPL_RCD
  AND A1.ROWSECCLASS = 'HCDPALL'
  AND B.EMPLID = A1.EMPLID
  AND B.EMPL_RCD = A1.EMPL_RCD
...
```

The workaround for this is to outer join the two tables in a view and then use the view with the query security record in Query.

Effective Date and Sequence Processing

This is an appropriate place to talk about a particular behavior of the Query designer that can be a cause of performance problems.

When you add a record to a query that contains the column EFFDT (effective date) or EFFSEQ (effective sequence), Query automatically adds effective date and effective sequence criteria to the query. To be fair, it does warn you that it is doing this, as shown in Figure 11-16.

Figure 11-16. Effective date warning

In this example, I have used the table PS_EMPLOYEES, which has both EFFDT and EFFSEQ columns. The criterion that was automatically added can be seen in the Query Manager (see Figure 11-17).

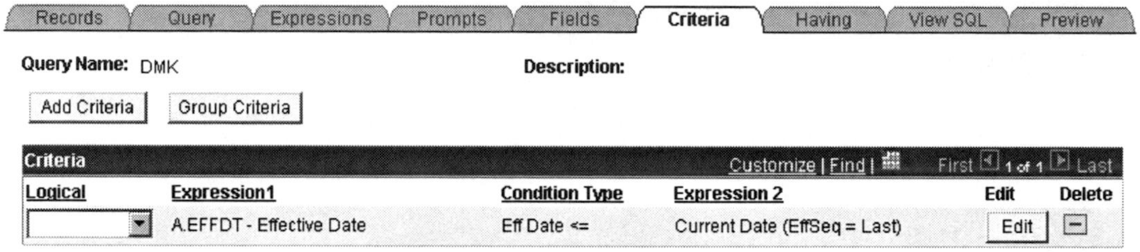

Figure 11-17. Effective-date criteria in the Query Manager

The resulting SQL shown in Listing 11-84 includes two subqueries.

Listing 11-84. Query SQL with Effective-Date and Effective-Sequence Subqueries

```
SELECT A.EMPLID, A.EMPL_RCD, A.NAME
 FROM PS_EMPLOYEES A, PS_EMPLMT_SRCH_QRY A1
 WHERE A.EMPLID = A1.EMPLID
   AND A.EMPL_RCD = A1.EMPL_RCD
   AND A1.ROWSECCLASS = 'HCDPALL'
   AND ( A.EFFDT =
        (SELECT MAX(A_ED.EFFDT) FROM PS_EMPLOYEES A_ED
        WHERE A.EMPLID = A_ED.EMPLID
          AND A.EMPL_RCD = A_ED.EMPL_RCD
          AND A_ED.EFFDT <= SYSDATE)
   AND A.EFFSEQ =
        (SELECT MAX(A_ES.EFFSEQ) FROM PS_EMPLOYEES A_ES
        WHERE A.EMPLID = A_ES.EMPLID
          AND A.EMPL_RCD = A_ES.EMPL_RCD
          AND A.EFFDT = A_ES.EFFDT) )
```

However, the record is not effective dated. There is only one row for each EMPLID/EMPL_RCD value. The key columns are shown in the Query designer (see Figure 11-18).

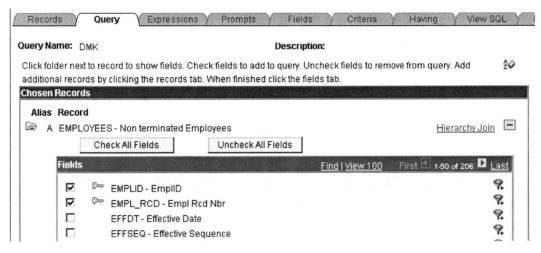

Figure 11-18. Key fields are indicated in the Query designer.

So the subqueries cannot possibly change the result of the query,[23] but they do create additional work. There are two additional accesses of the unique index (because the subqueries are joined on the key columns) and two additional accesses of the table (because the EFFDT and EFFSEQ columns are not in the index, as they are not key fields). The additional accesses are likely to require physical as well as consistent reads, so the unnecessary effective date/sequence criteria has generated unnecessary physical I/O. This degrades the performance of the query; and if there is extensive use of Query and Crystal Reports, it could also impact the performance of the entire system.

■ **Tip** The most efficient way to do anything is not to do it in the first place. You should remove automatically added effective-date/sequence criteria on non-key fields.

Application Engine

SQL statements are coded explicitly within the Application Engine, so all the usual methods can be applied directly. It is simply a matter of editing the step as necessary.

The Application Engine also supports platform-specific sections. PeopleSoft uses this feature to deliver different code on different database platforms, although the code is always functionally equivalent.

In the example in Figure 11-19, you can see that a different version of a step has been coded in an Application Engine program for each database platform.

---

[23] It is my opinion that this is a bug in the Query design tool and that the criteria should be automatically applied only to key fields.

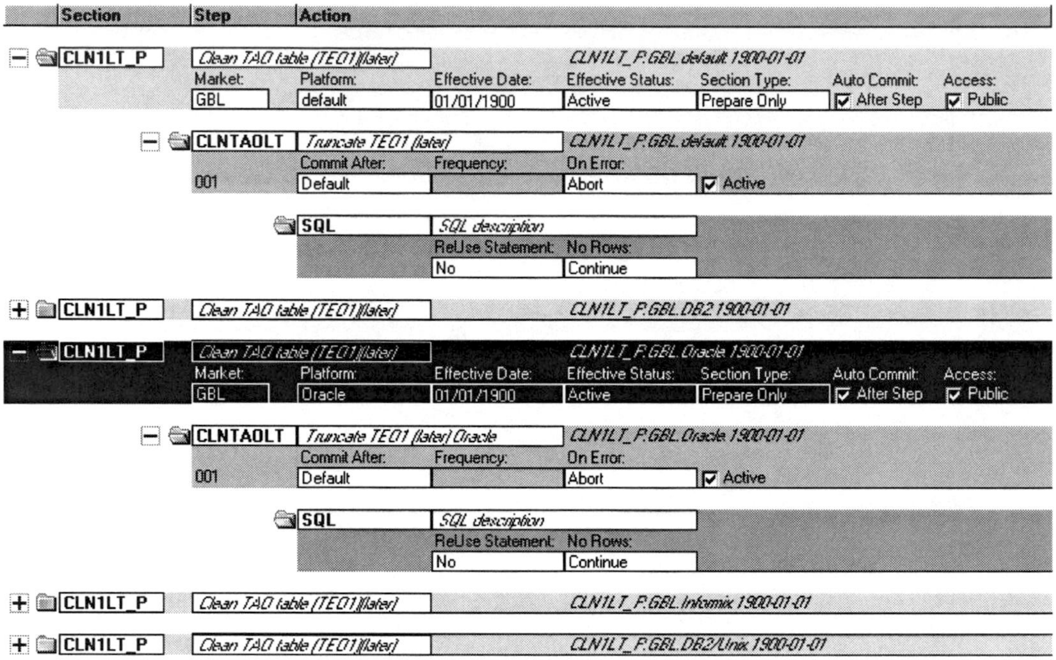

Figure 11-19. Database-specific Application Engine sections

The step does the same thing on all platforms. It removes all the data from a temporary working storage table. Table 11-1 shows the code in the Application Engine steps for each database platform. Oracle and SQL Server support the TRUNCATE TABLE command. The developer has chosen to use the REUSE STORAGE option on Oracle to retain the extents allocated to the table.[24] The TRUNCATE command does not exist on DB2 and Informix, so data simply has to be deleted from the temporary table.

Table 11-1. Application Engine EO_CURRENCY.CLN1LT_P.CLNTAOLT SQL

Database	SQL
Default	%Execute() TRUNCATE TABLE PS_%Bind(TEO1_RECNAME,NOQUOTES)
DB2	DELETE FROM PS_%Bind(TEO1_RECNAME,NOQUOTES)
Oracle	%Execute() TRUNCATE TABLE PS_%Bind(TEO1_RECNAME,NOQUOTES) REUSE STORAGE;
Informix	DELETE FROM PS_%Bind(TEO1_RECNAME,NOQUOTES)

---

[24] If you introduce Global Temporary Tables into a process, make sure it does not attempt to truncate the table with the REUSE STORAGE clause. The command does not raise any error, but it also does not truncate the table.

PeopleSoft develops its applications on Microsoft SQL Server. Where PeopleSoft does deliver database specific sections, as in this example, the default section is SQL Server specific.

If you choose to introduce an Oracle-specific change to a PeopleSoft-delivered Application Engine process, I recommend that you only make the change in the platform-specific section that matches your platform, if it already exists. Otherwise, do not create a platform-specific copy, but work on the default section. That way, when PeopleSoft delivers a patch or upgrade to the process, you can see the differences in the compare report, rather than have to manually compare the default and platform-specific steps.

Stored Statements in COBOL

The stored statements submitted by COBOL are loaded into the database in Data Mover scripts. You can make any change by editing the script and reloading it with Data Mover.

PeopleSoft delivers only a single set of stored statements, so they are all coded in a platform-generic fashion. If you are only running Oracle, then you are free to introduce Oracle-specific changes to performance. However, you must treat that as a customization and compare new versions of the Data Mover scripts when they are delivered.

There are some restrictions you should observe:

- In the query in Listing 11-85, it might be tempting to change the joins in the subquery on PS_EARNINGS_BAL to use the bind variables. The bind variables correspond to specific coding in the programs so that COBOL variables are assigned to the bind variables. Each bind variable should be referenced only once.

- Columns should not be added to nor removed from the SELECT clause, nor should the order or type of the columns be changed. The COBOL programs create cursors for each of the stored statements to read the selected values into program variables.

If the stored statement does not match the coding in the COBOL program, an error occurs.

Listing 11-85. Stored Statement

```
STORE FGPCADJG_S_ERNYTD
SELECT
SUM(A.GRS_YTD)
FROM PS_EARNINGS_BAL A
WHERE A.EMPLID = :1
 AND A.COMPANY = :2
 AND A.BALANCE_ID = :3
 AND A.BALANCE_YEAR = :4
 AND A.BALANCE_PERIOD = (SELECT MAX(B.BALANCE_PERIOD)
                         FROM PS_EARNINGS_BAL B
                         WHERE B.EMPLID = A.EMPLID
                           AND B.COMPANY = A.COMPANY
                           AND B.BALANCE_ID = A.BALANCE_ID
                           AND B.BALANCE_YEAR = A.BALANCE_YEAR
                           AND B.BALANCE_PERIOD <= :5)
...
;
```

SQR

SQL statements are coded in text files that can be altered by any text editor. The SQL passed to the database is exactly as it is coded in the source. All of the standard query tuning methods can be implemented in SQR. However, there are some limitations.

Hints must be placed on lines on their own in BEGIN-SELECT clauses, as shown in Listing 11-86.

Listing 11-86. Hints in SQR

```
Begin-Select On-Error=SQL-Error
/*+ALL_ROWS*/
m.model_statement
m.parmcount
m.statement_type
...
```

Queries are made distinct by adding the DISTINCT keyword to the BEGIN-SELECT keyword. If you try to add the DISTINCT keyword to the main SELECT clause, the SQR errors. Hence, in the SQL submitted to the database, the hint appears after the DISTINCT keyword and is not recognized as a hint by the database.

In the example in Listing 11-87, I have added a comment immediately after the BEGIN-SELECT clause. You can see the resulting SQL in Listing 11-88. The comment appears in the SQL after the DISTINCT keyword. The workaround for hints, also shown in these listings, is to add an in-line view that selects a row from DUAL. This does not functionally alter the query, but you can now put the hint in the in-line view.

Listing 11-87. Extract from sysrecrd.sqc

```
    begin-SELECT DISTINCT on-Error=SQL-Error
/*SYSRECORD-13*/
RECNAME             &Record13_RecName

if (((#current-line + 1) = #sqr-max-lines) and $DetailErrFound = 'Y') or
($DetailErrFound = 'N')
      move 'Y' to $DetailErrFound
      do PrintSectionHeadings
  end-if
  let #rows = #rows +1

    print &Record13_RecName       (+1,#Start1)

FROM PSRECDEFN
, (SELECT /*+ALL_ROWS*/ 'x' FROM DUAL)
WHERE RECTYPE = 7 AND SQLTABLENAME <> ' '
ORDER BY RECNAME
end-SELECT
```

The SQL submitted to the database is shown in Listing 11-88.

Listing 11-88. SQL Generated by Listing 11-87

```
SELECT DISTINCT /*SYSRECORD-13*/ RECNAME
FROM PSRECDEFN
, (SELECT /*+ALL_ROWS*/ 'x' FROM DUAL)
WHERE RECTYPE = 7 AND SQLTABLENAME <> ' '
ORDER BY RECNAME
```

Upgrade Considerations

Every one of the techniques described in this chapter involves making changes to the PeopleSoft application. These must be viewed as customizations. Changes to objects in Application Designer can be seen in the compare reports. Changes to any flat files must be handled manually.

PeopleSoft patches and upgrades frequently rerelease existing programs. Care must be taken to make sure that while the new or fixed functionality is incorporated, the performance improvements are not lost. Therefore, it is essential that all changes be thoroughly documented.

Summary

PeopleSoft is a packaged application, and much of the SQL it generates is buried deep inside the application. To access that code requires some knowledge of PeopleSoft's proprietary design tools, PeopleTools, although it does not require that you have the proficiency of a developer. You are looking for SQL, and most of the time it still looks like SQL.

In this chapter, I discussed how to use ASH, Statspack, and Oracle SQL Trace. Having identified the SQL that needs to be tuned, I demonstrated some techniques that can help you find the source of that SQL in the PeopleSoft application and then implement Oracle tuning techniques.

Resolving SQL performance problems *is* properly a part of the DBA's job. To be effective, the DBA must not simply identify the problem SQL, but must also determine its source and how it can be fixed within the constraints of PeopleTools.

## CHAPTER 12

Configuring the Application Server

This chapter deals with the mechanics of configuring the application server. It explains how the various files are combined and compiled in the Tuxedo configuration file. An understanding of this is necessary before moving on to sizing and configuring the application server for optimal performance, which is discussed in the next chapter. This chapter also discusses the Tuxedo Administration Console, a Java applet shipped with Tuxedo that permits remote administration and some monitoring of the application server.

Naturally, PeopleSoft also provides documentation about the application server. This chapter should be read in conjunction with that documentation.

Overview of Configuration Files

The application server is administered via the psadmin utility in $PS_HOME/appserv. This is a text-mode utility that works exactly the same way on Unix and Windows. The domain configuration process combines and generates a number of files, as shown in Table 12-1.

Table 12-1. Tuxedo Configuration Files

File Name	Description
psappsrv.cfg	Parameter values for both variables in the Tuxedo configuration file psappsrv.ubx and application servers.
psappsrv.val	Validation file for the interactive configuration dialog.
psappsrv.ubx	PeopleSoft Tuxedo template file to specify the layout of psappsrv.ubb and psappsrv.env.
psappsrv.ubb	Tuxedo native domain configuration source file. All of the variables have been resolved to literals.
psappsrv.env	Application server environment file that defines additional environmental variables for server processes.
PSTUXCFG	Compiled binary Tuxedo configuration file.

The application server domain configuration process is an option within the psadmin utility, as shown in Listing 12-1. The domain must be shut down in order to reconfigure it. As a safety precaution, you are asked whether you want to proceed.

Listing 12-1. psadmin Utility

```
--------------------------------
PeopleSoft Domain Administration
--------------------------------
      Domain Name: HCM91SML

 1) Boot this domain
 2) Domain shutdown menu
 3) Domain status menu
 4) Configure this domain
 5) TUXEDO command line (tmadmin)
 6) Edit configuration/log files menu
 7) Messaging Server Administration menu
 8) Purge Cache
 9) Preload Cache
10) Clean IPC resources of this domain
 q) Quit

Command to execute (1-10, q) : 4

This option will shutdown the domain.
Do you want to continue? (y/n) [n] :y
```

From PeopleTools 8.44, a new screen of information, called the Features and Settings report, was introduced. It is displayed before the configuration process is initiated, as shown in Listing 12-2. Selection options 1 to 10 change the value of the corresponding configuration variable for the current psadmin session but do not update psappsrv.ubx.

Listing 12-2. PeopleTools 8.51 Domain Features and Settings Summary

```
-----------------------------------------------
Quick-configure menu -- domain: HCM91SML
-----------------------------------------------
      Features                   Settings
      ==========                 ==========
 1) Pub/Sub Servers    : No   15) DBNAME      :[HCM91]
 2) Quick Server       : No   16) DBTYPE      :[ORACLE]
 3) Query Servers      : No   17) UserId      :[PS]
 4) Jolt               : Yes  18) UserPswd    :[PS]
 5) Jolt Relay         : No   19) DomainID    :[HCM91SML]
 6) WSL                : No   20) AddToPATH   :[C:\app\oracle\product\11.2.0\client32\BIN]
 7) PC Debugger        : No   21) ConnectID   :[people]
 8) Event Notification: No    22) ConnectPswd:[peop1e]
 9) MCF Servers        : No   23) ServerName :[]
10) Perf Collator      : No   24) WSL Port    :[7000]
11) Analytic Servers   : No   25) JSL Port    :[9000]
12) Domains Gateway    : No   26) JRAD Port   :[9100]
```

```
    Actions
    =========
13) Load config as shown
14) Custom configuration
 h) Help for this menu
 q) Return to previous menu

HINT: Enter 15 to edit DBNAME, then 13 to load

Enter selection (1-26, h, or q): 14

Warning:  no changes detected, some configuration files will not be updated.
Loading configuration...
Domain configuration complete.
Performing load prechecks ...
Loading validation table...
```

If you select the Custom configuration option, the reconfiguration process asks whether you want to change any configuration values (as shown in Listing 12-3). The Load config as option skips this section and proceeds to generate the configuration files.

Listing 12-3. Part of the Interactive Configuration Dialog

```
Do you want to change any config values (y/n)? [n]:y
```

If you choose to Change Any Config Values, you are taken through a series of interactive dialogs that give you the opportunity to edit the variables in psappsrv.cfg.

Figure 12-1 illustrates how the various configuration files are used and generated.

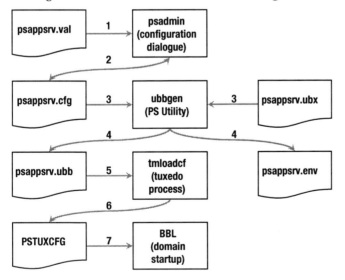

Figure 12-1. Configuration processes and files

The step details are as follows:

1–2. Although most people simply edit the psappsrv.cfg configuration file directly, there is an optional interactive configuration dialog in psadmin. The responses are validated with the instructions in the psappsrv.val file. The passwords in psappsrv.cfg can only be encrypted in the interactive dialog.

3–4. The psappsrv.cfg and psappsrv.ubx files are read by ubbgen, which is a PeopleSoft process that generates the psappsrv.ubb and psappsrv.env files.

5–6. The Tuxedo tmloadcf utility compiles psappsrv.ubb into the binary configuration file PSTUXCFG.

7. When the domain is started, the BBL process is established. This process reads the PSTUXCFG file and starts the rest of the domain.

The ubbgen and tmloadcf processes are run back-to-back, without pause, by psadmin.

■ **Caution** You should never edit psappsrv.ubb. It is an intermediate file generated by the configuration process. However, it is useful to look at it to see what values were used to configure the Tuxedo domain.

The following sections describe each of the configuration files, explaining how they are used and the purpose of some of the parameters. The examples are taken from PeopleTools 8.51, but the essential structure has not changed significantly since PeopleTools 7.0. PeopleSoft has added more servers as it has introduced more functionality.

psappsrv.ubx

This PeopleSoft template file is used to generate the psappsrv.ubb and psappsrv.env files that must conform to Tuxedo formats. It contains variables whose values are specified in the psappsrv.cfg file. The output files contain the literal values of those variables.

In this and the next two chapters, I suggest a number of possible changes to the Tuxedo configuration, some of which require changes to the Tuxedo template files. The following warning message was added in PeopleTools 8.50:

```
# !!!!!!!!!!!!!!!!!!!!!!!!!!!!!!!!!!!!!!!!!!!!!!!!!!!!!!!!!!!!!!!!!!!!!!!!!!!!!!!!!!!!!!!!!!!!!!!!!!
# Oracle does not support creating custom UBX templates nor modifying delivered UBX templates
# !!!!!!!!!!!!!!!!!!!!!!!!!!!!!!!!!!!!!!!!!!!!!!!!!!!!!!!!!!!!!!!!!!!!!!!!!!!!!!!!!!!!!!!!!!!!!!!!!!
```

This warning should not come as a surprise. Oracle does not support any customization. That includes not supporting customization of Tuxedo templates.

RELATIONSHIP BETWEEN THE TUXEDO TEMPLATE AND THE CONFIGURATION FILE

Most domain configuration changes are made in the configuration file psappsrv.cfg. However, there are legitimate reasons to make changes to the template file psappsrv.ubx. Where different domains have different settings, a variable should be set in psappsrv.cfg and referenced in psappsrv.ubx. Thus you can arrange to have a single psappsrv.ubx, common to all domains at the same level of PeopleTools.

For example, you may want to enable the Tuxedo service trace (as discussed in Chapter 9). This requires adding the -r option to the server command line in psappsrv.ubx. I prefer to create a new variable in the trace section of psappsrv.cfg and reference it in psappsrv.ubx. This option can easily be enabled or disabled on different domains by changing a setting in the configuration file.

Any new variables you may have added also appear in the interactive configuration dialog, as shown here:

```
Values for config section - Trace
    TraceSql=0
    TraceSqlMask=12319
    TracePC=0
    TracePCMask=4095
    TracePPR=0
    TracePPRMask=32767
    TracePIA=0
    TracePIAMask=32767
    TraceAE=1152
    TraceAnalytic=9586980
    TraceAnalyticMask=16777215
    TracePPM=0
    DumpMemoryImageAtCrash=NONE
    DumpManagerObjectsAtCrash=Y
    LogErrorReport=N
    MailErrorReport=
```

The new variable is set in the configuration file psappsrv.cfg:

```
;------------------------------------------------------------------------
; when set to -r enables Tuxedo service trace, else set to a single space
TuxedoServiceTrace=-r
```

The variable can be referenced in psappsrv.ubx:

```
CLOPT="{$Trace\TuxedoServiceTrace} -o \"{REL_LOG}{FS}APPQ.stdout\" -e
\"{REL_LOG}{FS}APPQ.stderr\" {$PSAPPSRV\Spawn Server} -s@psappsrv.lst -- -D {$Domain
Settings\Domain ID} -S PSAPPSRV"
```

It duly appears in psappsrv.ubb, including the substitution variable report at the bottom of the file:

```
CLOPT="-r -o \".\LOGS\APPQ.stdout\" -e \".\LOGS\APPQ.stderr\"  -s@psappsrv.lst -- -D
HCM91SML -S PSAPPSRV"
```

Features, Settings, and Ports Sections

The features, settings, and port settings sections, shown in Listing 12-4, were introduced in PeopleTools 8.44. They are used to generate the new features and settings report (shown in Figure 12-2 later in this chapter).

Listing 12-4. Features, Settings, and Port Settings Sections in psappsrv.ubx

```
*FEATURES
{"-label-"},{"-define-"},{"-on-"},{"-servers-"},{"-Oracle Env Manager Label-"}
{Pub/Sub Servers},{PUBSUB},{No},{PSBRK(DSP/HND), PSPUB(DSP/HND),
PSSUB(DSP/HND)},{Publish/Subscribe Server (PUBSUB)}
{Quick Server},{QUICKSRV},{No},{PSQCKSRV},{Quick Server (PSQCKSRV)}
{Query Servers},{QUERYSRV},{No},{PSQRYSRV},{Query Server (PSQRYSRV)}
{Jolt},{JOLT},{Yes},{JSL, JREPSVR},{Jolt Service Listener (JSL)}
{Jolt Relay},{JRAD},{No},{JRAD},{Jolt Relay Adapter (JRAD)}
{WSL},{WSL},{No},{WSL},{WorkStation Listener (WSL)}
{PC Debugger},{DBGSRV},{No},{PSDBGSRV},{PeopleCode Debugger (PSDBGSRV)}
{Event Notification},{RENSRV},{Yes},{PSRENSRV},{Event Notification (PSRENSRV)}
{MCF Servers},{MCF},{No},{PSUQSRV, PSMCFLOG},{Multi-Channel Framework (MCF Servers)}
{Perf Collator},{PPM},{No},{PSPPMSRV},{Performance Collator (PSPPMSRV)}
{Analytic Servers},{ANALYTICSRV},{Yes},{PSANALYTICSRV},{Analytic Servers (PSANALYTICSRV)}
{Domains Gateway},{DOMAIN_GW},{No},{ DMADM, GWADM, GWTDOMAIN },{Domains Gateway (Remote
Search)}
*END
*SETTINGS
{"-label-"},{-formal name-}{"-value-"}
{DBNAME},{Startup/DBName},{ }
{WINDOWS}
{DBTYPE},{Startup/DBType},{MICROSFT}
{WINDOWS}
{UNIX}
{DBTYPE},{Startup/DBType},{}
{UNIX}
{UserId},{Startup/UserId},{QEDMO}
{UserPswd},{Startup/UserPswd},{QEDMO}
{DomainID},{Domain Settings/Domain ID},{PT851}
{WINDOWS}
{AddToPATH},{Domain Settings/Add to PATH},{}
{WINDOWS}
{UNIX}
{AddToPATH},{Domain Settings/Add to PATH},{.}
{UNIX}
{ConnectID},{Startup/ConnectId},{people}
{ConnectPswd},{Startup/ConnectPswd},{peop1e}
{ServerName},{Startup/ServerName},{}
*END
*PORT_SETTINGS
{WSL Port},{Workstation Listener/Port},{7000}
{JSL Port},{JOLT Listener/Port},{9000}
{JRAD Port},{JOLT Relay Adapter/Listener Port},{9100}
*END
```

PS_DEFINES Section

The PS_DEFINES section is the only place where you find any explanation of the ubbgen process and the format of psappsrv.ubx. Essentially, ubbgen substitutes variables delimited by curly brackets ({ }) with literal values from the psappsrv.cfg file. There are four types of variables: environment, configuration, special, and prompted. I discuss each type in detail in the sections that follow.

Environment Variables

Environment variables are read by ubbgen with the genenv() function. However, the psadmin program also sets some environment variables. For example, %TUXDIR%, the directory where Tuxedo was installed, must be set in the environment before executing psadmin, but $PS_SERVDIR, the directory where the domain configuration files are located, is set by psadmin. These variables are then used to set the TUXDIR and APPDIR parameters in the MACHINES section of the Tuxedo configuration:

```
TUXDIR="{$TUXDIR}"                      # Paths cannot end in '\'
APPDIR="{$PS_SERVDIR}"                  # include the database path
```

Configuration Variables

Configuration variables are defined by the Tuxedo template file psappsrv.ubx. ubbgen looks up the value of the variable in the configuration file psappsrv.cfg and substitutes the variable with its value as it writes the Tuxedo configuration file psappsrv.ubb. In the following example, Min Instances is read from the PSAPPSRV section of psappsrv.cfg:

```
PSAPPSRV        SRVGRP=APPSRV
                SRVID=1
                MIN={$PSAPPSRV\Min Instances}
```

Special Variables

A number of *special variables* are generated by ubbgen. These have changed from release to release. The variables generated by ubbgen in PeopleTools 8.44 are set out in Table 12-2.

The values of MAXACCESSERS, MAXSERVERS, MAXSERVICES, and MAXWSCLIENTS are calculated from the number of servers specified in the configuration file psappsrv.cfg, and they are used to set the sizes of table structures in the Bulletin Board to the maximum values that could be used by the domain. This minimizes the use of Inter-process Communication (IPC) resources.

Table 12-2. ubbgen Special Variables

Variable	Description
CFGFILE	Name of the PeopleSoft configuration file. This is always psappsrv.cfg.
ENVFILE	Name of the server environment file. This is always psappsrv.env.
FS	Directory character. / on Unix; \ on Windows. Thus PeopleSoft can deliver the same configuration file for all platforms.
GID	Unix group ID that runs the Tuxedo domain. This is always 0 on Windows.
HI_WSL_PORT	Maximum Workstation Handler (WSH) port number. For use when a firewall exists between the clients and the Workstation Listener (WSL).
IPCKEY	Segment ID for the Bulletin Board. It must be unique across the machine.
LOGDIR	Location of files, generated as $PS_HOME/appserv/<domain name>/LOGS or $PS_CFG_HOME/appserv/<domain name>/LOGS (from PeopleTools 8.50).
LO_WSL_PORT	Minimum WSL port number. For use when a firewall exists between the clients and the WSL.
MACH	Name of the machine. Equivalent to result of uname -n on Unix systems.
MAXACCESSERS	Used to specify the total number of clients of the Bulletin Board, specified in the MACHINES section of the Tuxedo configuration file (see Listing 12-12). It is calculated as follows: = Number of WSH * (number of clients per WSH + 1) + Number of JSLs * (number of clients per JSH + 2), if Jolt configured + Maximum number of PSAPPSRV processes + Maximum number of PSQCKSRV processes, if configured + Maximum number of PSQRYSRV processes, if configured + Maximum number of PSBRKHND_dflt, PSSUBHND_dflt, and PSPUBHND_dflt servers, if publish and subscribe configured + 1, if debug server enabled + 3, if MultiChannel Framework Servers (MCF) enabled + Maximum number of PSPPMSRV servers, if performance collector enabled + 11

MAXSERVERS	Total number of server processes required by Tuxedo to size the Bulletin Board, used in the RESOURCES section of the Tuxedo configuration file (see Listing 12-11). It is calculated as follows: = Maximum number of WSH processes + Maximum number of PSAPPSRV processes + Maximum number of PSQCKSRV processes, if enabled + Maximum number of PSQRYSRV processes, if enabled + 2 * Maximum number of JSH processes, if Jolt configured + Maximum number of PSBRKHND_dflt, PSSUBHND_dflt, and PSPUBHND_dflt servers, if publish and subscribe configured + 1, if debug server enabled + 1, if event notification enabled + 2, if MCF enabled + Maximum number of PSPPMSRV servers, if performance collector enabled + 11
MAXSERVICES	Calculated total number of services advertised across all server processes, used in the RESOURCES section of the Tuxedo configuration file (see Listing 12-11). It is calculated as follows: = 2 * Maximum number of WSH processes + 74 * Maximum number of PSAPPSRV processes + 8 * Maximum number of PSQCKSRV processes, if enabled + 2 * Maximum number of PSQRYSRV processes, if enabled + Number of JSH processes * Number of clients per JSH, if Jolt enabled + Maximum number of PSBRKHND_dflt, PSSUBHND_dflt, and PSPUBHND_dflt servers, if publish and subscribe configured + $2n^2 + 5n$, where n is the number of optimization servers that are enabled + 1, if event notification enabled + 2, if MCF enabled + 31
MAXWSCLIENTS	The sum of the maximum number of clients that the WSH and JSH processes can support, specified in the MACHINES section of the Tuxedo configuration file (see Listing 12-12). It is calculated as follows:~ = Maximum number of WSH * number of clients per WSH + Maximum number of JSH processes * number of clients per JSH
UID	Unix user ID that runs the Tuxedo domain. This is always 0 on Windows.
UNIX	True if running on a Unix platform; otherwise, false.
VERITY_OS	Part of path to Verity product used to search PeopleBooks.
VERITY_PLATFORM	Part of path to Verity product used to search PeopleBooks.
WINDOWS	True if running on a Windows platform; otherwise, false.

If you configure multiple queues for any application server process (see Chapter 13), you need to manually calculate these values, because ubbgen does not take the additional queues into account.

Prompted Variables

All other variables are called *prompted*. They specify a number of yes/no questions that are asked during configuration (see Listing 12-5). These variables, and the Unix and Windows special variables, are used like #ifdef and #endif directives in C or SQR. The default responses to the questions are enclosed in square brackets.

Listing 12-5. Prompted Variables Defined in psappsrv.ubx

```
*PS_DEFINES

...
{PUBSUB} Do you want the Publish/Subscribe servers configured (y/n)? [n]:
{QUICKSRV} Move quick PSAPPSRV services into a second server (PSQCKSRV) (y/n)? [n]:
{QUERYSRV} Move long-running queries into a second server (PSQRYSRV) (y/n)? [n]:
{JOLT} Do you want JOLT configured (y/n)? [y]:
{JRAD} Do you want JRAD configured (y/n)? [n]:
{WSL} Do you want WSL configured (y/n)? [n]:
{DBGSRV} Do you want to enable PeopleCode Debugging (PSDBGSRV) (y/n)? [n]:
{RENSRV} Do you want Event Notification configured (PSRENSRV) (y/n)? [n]:
{MCF} Do you want MCF servers configured (y/n)? [n]:
{PPM} Do you want Performance Collators configured (PSPPMSRV) (y/n)? [n]:
{ANALYTICSRV} Do you want Analytic servers configured (PSANALYTICSRV) (y/n) [n]:
{DOMAIN_GW} Do you want Domains Gateway (External Search Server) configured (y/n)? [n]:

*END
```

For example, if the QUERYSRV special variable is true, then the PSQRYSRV server is configured by including the section between the {QUERYSRV} references, as shown in Listing 12-6.

Listing 12-6. Query Server Definition Inside a Prompted Variable

```
{QUERYSRV}
#
# PeopleSoft Query Application Server
#
PSQRYSRV        SRVGRP=APPSRV
                SRVID=70
                MIN={$PSQRYSRV\Min Instances}
                MAX={$PSQRYSRV\Max Instances}
                RQADDR="QRYQ"
                REPLYQ=Y
                CLOPT="-o \"{REL_LOG}{FS}stdout\" -e \"{REL_LOG}{FS}stderr\" {$PSQRYSRV\Spawn
Server} -s@psqrysrv.lst -- -D {$Domain Settings\Domain ID} -S PSQRYSRV"
{QUERYSRV}
```

■ **Tip** Your responses to the prompted variables are determined by what features you are using. For instance, you only need publish and subscribe servers if you are using that functionality in PeopleSoft. You should set the default values in psappsrv.ubx so that you simply accept the default values when configuring domains.

Main Tuxedo Section

Everything in psappsrv.ubx after the marked end of the PS_DEFINES section until the PS_ENVFILE section is copied by ubbgen to psappsrv.ubb after the variable substitutions have been made. psappsrv.ubb is a Tuxedo format file, as described in the Tuxedo documentation (see the reference section ubbconfig(5)[1]), so the template in psappsrv.ubx must produce that format.

A Tuxedo configuration file consists of a number of sections: RESOURCES, MACHINES, GROUPS, SERVERS, and SERVICES.

Tuxedo RESOURCES Section

The RESOURCES section contains variables that describe the whole Tuxedo domain. The template for this section is shown in Listing 12-7.

Listing 12-7. Template for the Tuxedo RESOURCES Section

```
*RESOURCES
IPCKEY          {IPCKEY}         # ( 32768 < IPCKEY < 262143 )
MASTER          "{MACH}"
DOMAINID        {$Domain Settings\Domain ID}_{IPCKEY}
MODEL           SHM
LDBAL           N
#

...
```

Tuxedo load balancing can be used when there is a choice of queues on which to place service requests (see Chapter 13).

Tuxedo MACHINES Section

A single Tuxedo domain can be split across more than one physical machine to permit load balancing. The Tuxedo machine on each physical server looks similar to an independent Tuxedo domain, but it has additional listener and bridge processes to connect it to the other machines in the domain. Thus, Tuxedo services can be transferred to a different, less heavily loaded Tuxedo machine.

---

[1] See Oracle Tuxedo 10g Release 3 (10.3) ➤ Reference Topics ➤ Section 5 - File Formats, Data Descriptions, MIBs, and System Processes Reference ➤ ubbconfig (http://download.oracle.com/docs/cd/E13161_01/tuxedo/docs10gr3/rf5/rf5.html#wp3370051)

The MACHINES section, the template for which is shown in Listing 12-8, specifies variables that could be set to different values on different physical machines, such as paths or environmental variables. Some of these parameters can be specified in both the RESOURCES and MACHINES sections. The specific value in the MACHINES section overrides the generic value in the RESOURCES section.

Although it is theoretically possible to configure a PeopleSoft application server domain to use the multimachine architecture, PeopleSoft neither uses nor supports this. In practice, you would never want to use multiple machines, because instead you would have multiple, independent application server domains on various physical machines.[2]

Listing 12-8. Template for the Tuxedo MACHINES Section

```
*MACHINES
"{MACH}" LMID="{MACH}"                              # Machine name must be uppercase
        TUXDIR="{$TUXDIR}"                          # Paths cannot end in '\'
{UNIX}
        APPDIR="{$PS_SERVDIR}:{$PS_LIBPATH}"        # Append the PS LLP
{UNIX}
{WINDOWS}
        APPDIR="{$PS_SERVDIR}"
{WINDOWS}
        TUXCONFIG="{$TUXCONFIG}"
        ULOGPFX="{LOGDIR}{FS}TUXLOG"
        ENVFILE="{$PS_SERVDIR}{FS}{ENVFILE}"
        UID={UID}                                   # Has to be 0 at this time.
        GID={GID}                                   # Has to be 0 at this time.
{WINDOWS}
        TYPE="i386NT"
{WINDOWS}
        NETLOAD=0                                   # We are not using multiple machines.
        {MAXWSCLIENTS}
        {MAXACCESSERS2}
```

Tuxedo GROUPS Section

Application servers in a domain are logically divided into groups. The GROUPS section, shown in Listing 12-9, has a default clause that specifies the machine name. Tuxedo groups permit the same service to be configured differently on different servers in different groups.

With successive releases, PeopleSoft has created separate Tuxedo groups for the new server processes, but since PeopleTools 7.57 each service is advertised on only one queue. In the delivered application server configuration, PeopleSoft has not yet used the groups for any practical purpose. At

---

[2] I have seen the multi-machine architecture configured only once in a production PeopleSoft system. That was on PeopleTools 7.5x. Ultimately, it was removed due to instability. The configuration was found to be very sensitive to a problem with the network links between the physical application server nodes. It was found that using round-robin connection and failover between multiple single-machine application servers in the client connection configuration was equally effective and more reliable. I can't imagine needing to configure this in PeopleTools 8. Instead, the PIA can load-balance across multiple single-node application servers.

some point in the future, PeopleSoft could, for instance, apply different Tuxedo parameters to different groups of servers.

Listing 12-9. *Template for the Tuxedo GROUPS Section*

```
*GROUPS

#
# Tuxedo Groups
# For application group numbers for new machines (LMIDs)
# use group numbers 101-199;  201-299;  etc.
#
DEFAULT:        LMID="{MACH}"

BASE            GRPNO=1

{DOMAIN_GW}
{VERITY_TYPE3}
DMADMGRP        GRPNO=101

GWTGROUP        GRPNO=102
{VERITY_TYPE3}
{DOMAIN_GW}

WATCH           GRPNO=10

MONITOR         GRPNO=50

{ANALYTICSRV}
ANALYTICGRP     GRPNO=80
{ANALYTICSRV}

PPMGRP          GRPNO=91

{RENSRV}
RENGRP          GRPNO=92
{RENSRV}

{MCF}
MCFGRP          GRPNO=93
{MCF}

{DBGSRV}
DBGSRV          GRPNO=97
{DBGSRV}

{PUBSUB}
PUBSUB          GRPNO=98
{PUBSUB}

APPSRV          GRPNO=99
```

```
{JOLT}
#
# JOLT Groups
#
JREPGRP          LMID="{MACH}"
                 GRPNO=94
JSLGRP           LMID="{MACH}"
                 GRPNO=95
{JOLT}
```

Some groups (DMADMGRP, GWTGROUP, ANALYTICGRP, RENGRP, MCFGRP, PUBSUB, and JOLT) are defined only if the corresponding prompt variable is true.

Tuxedo SERVERS Section

The list of server processes has continued to grow with each release of PeopleTools. Each of the server processes in a domain is specified in the SERVERS section of psappsrv.ubx.

The default clause, shown in Listing 12-10, specifies default parameters that apply to all servers unless overridden on the server definition. The Tuxedo documentation describes the command-line options parameter (CLOPT) separately in the reference section in servopts(5)[3].

Listing 12-10. Server Defaults Definition

```
*SERVERS

DEFAULT:        CLOPT="-A"       # Advertise all services.
                REPLYQ=N         # Reply queue not needed for our simple setup.
                MAXGEN=3         # Max number of restarts in the grace period.

                GRACE=60         # Grace period in seconds.
                RESTART={$Domain Settings\Restartable}
                SYSTEM_ACCESS=FASTPATH
```

A server can be started six (MAXGEN) times or, if you prefer, restarted five times (MAXGEN - 1) times in the 60-second grace period (GRACE), before it is marked as being in error.

Tuxedo Event Broker

The Tuxedo Event Broker, TMSYSEVT, is the only server process delivered with Tuxedo. It is not configured by default in PeopleSoft application servers, but it is commented out as shown in Listing 12-11. It is useful only if you want to use the Tuxedo Administration Console to administer the domain. It is documented in the Tuxedo tmsysevt(5) reference. Configuration of the console is discussed at the end of this chapter.

---

[3] Oracle Tuxedo 10g Release 3 (10.3) ➤ Reference ➤ File Formats, Data Descriptions, MIBs, and System Processes Reference ➤ Servopts
(http://download.oracle.com/docs/cd/E13161_01/tuxedo/docs10gr3/rf5/rf5.html#wp1003290).

Listing 12-11. Commented-Out Tuxedo Event Broker Definition

```
#
# Tuxedo System Event Server
#
#TMSYSEVT        SRVGRP=BASE
#               SRVID=200
```

Watch Server (PSWATCHSRV)

PSWATCHSRV (see Listing 12-12) was introduced in PeopleTools 8.4. It is unusual in that it does not connect to the database. It does not advertise or handle services. Its job is to kill server processes that are stuck and cannot be shut down.

▨ **Note** Any parameters to the left of the double hyphen in the command-line option are Tuxedo parameters that can be found in the Tuxedo servopts(5) reference. Anything to the right is passed to the tmsvrinit() function defined in the server by PeopleSoft. So, anything to the right of the double hyphen is a PeopleSoft-defined parameter. PeopleSoft does not document these parameters.

IPCKEY, which is the ID of the Bulletin Board shared memory segment, is passed to PSWATCHSRV. Therefore, I infer that the server is making an attachment to the Bulletin Board so it can search for locked servers.

There is only ever one instance of PSWATCHSRV. The minimum and maximum number of instances of the server is hard-coded as one.

Listing 12-12. PSWATCHSRV Server Definition

```
#
# PeopleSoft domain watchdog PSWATCHSRV
#
PSWATCHSRV       SRVGRP=WATCH
                 SRVID=1
                 MIN=1
                 MAX=1
                 RQADDR="WATCH"
                 REPLYQ=Y
                 RESTART=Y
                 CLOPT="-A -- -ID {IPCKEY} -C {CFGFILE} -D {$Domain Settings\Domain ID}
-S PSWATCHSRV"
```

Main Application Server (PSAPPSRV)

The PSAPPSRV server (see Listing 12-13) does the most of the work for online activity in the PeopleSoft application server.

Listing 12-13. PSAPPSRV Server Definition

```
#
# PeopleSoft Application Server
#
PSAPPSRV        SRVGRP=APPSRV
                SRVID=1
                MIN={$PSAPPSRV\Min Instances}
                MAX={$PSAPPSRV\Max Instances}
                RQADDR="APPQ"
                REPLYQ=Y
                CLOPT="{$Trace\TuxedoServiceTrace} -o \"{REL_LOG}{FS}stdout\" -e
\"{REL_LOG}{FS} stderr\" {$PSAPPSRV\Spawn Server} -s@psappsrv.lst -- -D {$Domain
Settings\Domain ID} -S PSAPPSRV"
```

The services advertised by a server process are specified by the -s parameter in CLOPT. There are three formats for this parameter, as shown in Table 12-3. It can be specified more than once, as shown in Listing 12-14, and the effect is cumulative.

The services advertised on the PSAPPSRV process can vary depending on whether the PSQRYSRV and PSQCKSRV servers have also been configured. If they are configured, services are transferred from PSAPPSRV to those servers.

From PeopleTools 8.50, the command-line option for PSAPPSRV is constant, and the psappsrv.lst file is generated by copying the files from $PS_HOME/appserv to the directory for the domain. If PSQRYSRV or PSQCKSRV is not configured the contents of psqcksrv.lst and psqrysrv.lst are appended to psappsrv.lst during domain configuration.

LOCATION OF APPLICATION SERVER AND PROCESS SCHEDULER DIRECTORIES

PeopleTools 8.50 introduced the concept of a configuration home directory ($PS_CFG_HOME), as distinct from the PeopleTools home ($PS_HOME). The directory structure used to hold the application server and Process Scheduler domains is located under $PS_CFG_HOME/appserv; previously it was always under $PS_HOME/appserv. This can be useful if a PeopleTools or application upgrade introduces a new PS_HOME directory.

A consequence is that the service list files are now copied into the same directory as the rest of the application server configuration files. In previous releases, all domains referenced the same files in the relative parent directory:

```
-s@..{FS}psappsrv.lst
```

Table 12-3. Advertise Service Parameter Formats

Format	Description
-s <filename>	Advertises the list of services in the named files. Files that contain lists of services are delivered in $PS_HOME/appserv. From PeopleTools 8.50, there is a file for each type of server except the publish and subscribe servers, even if the server does not advertise any services. In previous versions of PeopleTools, only psappsrv.lst and psqcksrv.lst were used.
-s <service name>	Advertises a named service.
-s <service name:function name>	Normally, the service and function names are the same. This format allows a single function to handle different services. PeopleTools uses this to distinguish between long-running queries (SqlQuery) issued by the query tools and other, quicker queries (SqlRequest). The long-running queries can then be moved to a different server so that they do not block the main application serving server processes.

Up to PeopleTools 8.49, one of four command-line options for PSAPPSRV (shown in Listing 12-14) is used depending on whether separate PSQCKSRV and PSQRYSRV servers are enabled. Substitution variables are used in the ubbgen utility select to both the command line for PSAPPSRV and to enable entire server sections for the optional servers (see Listings 12-14 and 12-15). The substitution variables can be nested two deep but no further. Thus if the optional servers are enabled, then the services that they advertise are no longer advertised by PSAPPSRV.

Listing 12-14. PSAPPSRV Command-Line Definition (Up to PeopleTools 8.49)

```
{QUERYSRV}
{QUICKSRV}
                CLOPT="{$PSAPPSRV\Spawn Server} -s@..{FS}psappsrv.lst -- -C {CFGFILE}
-D {$Domain Settings\Domain ID} -S PSAPPSRV"
{QUICKSRV}
{!QUICKSRV}
                CLOPT="{$PSAPPSRV\Spawn Server} -s@..{FS}psappsrv.lst
-s@..{FS}psqcksrv.lst -- -C {CFGFILE} -D {$Domain Settings\Domain ID} -S PSAPPSRV"
{!QUICKSRV}
{QUERYSRV}
{!QUERYSRV}
{QUICKSRV}
                CLOPT="{$PSAPPSRV\Spawn Server} -s@..{FS}psappsrv.lst -sICQuery
-sSqlQuery:SqlRequest -- -C {CFGFILE} -D {$Domain Settings\Domain ID} -S PSAPPSRV"
{QUICKSRV}
{!QUICKSRV}
                CLOPT="{$PSAPPSRV\Spawn Server} -s@..{FS}psappsrv.lst
-s@..{FS}psqcksrv.lst -sICQuery -sSqlQuery:SqlRequest -- -C {CFGFILE}
-D {$Domain Settings\Domain ID} -S PSAPPSRV"
```

```
{!QUICKSRV}
{!QUERYSRV}
```

Quick Server (PSQCKSRV)

The Quick Server, PSQCKSRV (see Listing 12-15), is now all but obsolete. It was introduced in PeopleTools 7 to separately handle very short duration services, such as simple SQL queries, so they could get through the application server quickly and not have to wait in the queue behind larger and slower services. The concept is rather like a "ten items or less" checkout line at a supermarket.

These services are only used by the Windows three-tier client programs. The PIA does not require this server. There is no requirement to use Application Designer in three-tier mode in a production environment (migrations must be done in two-tier mode). Even if you use Application Designer in three-tier mode in development environments, the number of these quick services is very small.

In short, the Quick Server should never normally be configured on PeopleTools 8.x systems.

Listing 12-15. PSQCKSRV Server Definition

```
{QUICKSRV}
#
# PeopleSoft Quick Application Server
#
PSQCKSRV        SRVGRP=APPSRV
                SRVID=50
                MIN={$PSQCKSRV\Min Instances}
                MAX={$PSQCKSRV\Max Instances}
                RQADDR="QCKQ"
                REPLYQ=Y
                CLOPT="{$PSQCKSRV\Spawn Server} -s@..{FS}psqcksrv.lst -- -C {CFGFILE} -D
{$Domain Settings\Domain ID} -S PSQCKSRV"
{QUICKSRV}
```

Query Server (PSQRYSRV)

PSQRYSRV (see Listing 12-16) handles the long-running queries issued by the PS/Query and nVision tools in both the PIA and Windows-client versions operating in three-tier mode. If Crystal Reports is run in three-tier mode, the PeopleSoft ODBC driver also submits SqlQuery service requests.

Listing 12-16. PSQRYSRV Server Definition

```
{QUERYSRV}
#
# PeopleSoft Query Application Server
#
PSQRYSRV        SRVGRP=APPSRV
                SRVID=70
                MIN={$PSQRYSRV\Min Instances}
                MAX={$PSQRYSRV\Max Instances}
                RQADDR="QRYQ"
                REPLYQ=Y
                CLOPT="{$PSQRYSRV\Spawn Server} -sICQuery -sSqlQuery:SqlRequest
```

```
-C {CFGFILE} -D {$Domain Settings\Domain ID} -S PSQRYSRV"
{QUERYSRV}
```

PSSAMSRV

The PSSAMSRV server (see Listing 12-17) is used only by three-tier clients, mostly when submitting requests to the Process Scheduler. However, it cannot be disabled.

Listing 12-17. PSSAMSRV Server Definition

```
#
# PeopleSoft SQL Access Application Server
#
PSSAMSRV        SRVGRP=APPSRV
                SRVID=100
                MIN={$PSSAMSRV\Min Instances}
                MAX={$PSSAMSRV\Max Instances}
                RQADDR="SAMQ"
                REPLYQ=Y
                CONV=Y
                CLOPT="-A -- -C {CFGFILE} -D {$Domain Settings\Domain ID} -S PSSAMSRV"
```

Performance Collator Server (PSPPMSRV)

The performance collator server, PSPPMSRV, was introduced in PeopleTools 8.44 (see Listing 12-18). It is used by the PeopleSoft Performance Monitor (which is discussed in detail in Chapter 10) to collect metrics and insert them into the database. These servers are configured on the system collecting the performance metrics, not the system being measured.

Listing 12-18. PSPPMSRV Server Definition

```
{PPM}
# Performance Collator. No services, just managed by Tuxedo.
PSPPMSRV        SRVGRP=PPMGRP
                SRVID=100
                MIN={$PSPPMSRV\Min Instances}
                MAX={$PSPPMSRV\Max Instances}
                RQADDR="PPMQ2"
                REPLYQ=Y
                RESTART=Y
                CLOPT="-A -- -C {CFGFILE} -D {$Domain Settings\Domain ID} -S PSPPMSRV"
{PPM}
```

Debug Server (PSDBGSRV)

The debug server process, PSDBGSRV (see Listing 12-19), permits the developer to step through PeopleCode in Application Designer while running a PIA session. Application Designer makes a socket connection to this server. Only one debug server can be configured in an application server.

Listing 12-19. PSDBGSRV Server Definition

```
{DBGSRV}
#
# PeopleCode Debugger PSDBGSRV
#
PSDBGSRV        SRVGRP=DBGSRV
                SRVID=1
                MIN=1
                MAX=1
                RQADDR="DBGQ"
                REPLYQ=Y
                CLOPT="-A -- -C {CFGFILE} -D {$Domain Settings\Domain ID} -S PSDBGSRV"

{DBGSRV}
```

Real-Time Notification Server (PSRENSRV)

The PSRENSRV process (see Listing 12-20) was introduced in PeopleTools 8.4. It is a modified lightweight web server used to send real-time event notifications, such as report notifications, to PIA users. It is also used by the MultiChannel Framework.

Listing 12-20. PSRENSRV Server Definition

```
{RENSRV}
# Event Notification server.
PSRENSRV        SRVGRP=RENGRP
                SRVID=101
                MIN=1
                MAX=1
                RQADDR="RENQ1"
                REPLYQ=Y
                RESTART=Y
                CLOPT="-A -- -C {CFGFILE} -D {$Domain Settings\Domain ID} -S PSRENSRV"
{RENSRV}
```

MultiChannel Framework Servers

The MultiChannel Framework (MCF) was introduced in PeopleTools in 8.4 "to support multiple interaction channels for call center agents or other PeopleSoft users who must respond to incoming requests and notifications on these channels." Listing 12-21 contains a definition of MCF servers.

Listing 12-21. *MCF Servers Definition*

```
{MCF}# MCF Universal Queue server. These are stateful and unique; hence, each needs
# a unique ID on the command line "PSUQSRVn", where 1 <= n <= 9.
PSUQSRV         SRVGRP=MCFGRP
                SRVID=110
                MIN=1
                MAX=1
                RQADDR="UQSRV"
                REPLYQ=Y
                RESTART=Y
                CLOPT="-o \"{REL_LOG}{FS}stdout\" -e \"{REL_LOG}{FS}stderr\" -A -- -D {$Domain
Settings\Domain ID} -S PSUQSRV1"
# MCF Logging server. These are stateful and unique; hence, each needs
# a unique ID on the command line "PSMCFLOGn", where 1 <= n <= 9.
PSMCFLOG        SRVGRP=MCFGRP
                SRVID=120
                MIN=1
                MAX=1
                RQADDR="MCFLG"
                REPLYQ=Y
                RESTART=Y
                CLOPT="-o \"{REL_LOG}{FS}stdout\" -e \"{REL_LOG}{FS}stderr\" -A -- -D {$Domain
Settings\Domain ID} -S PSMCFLOG1"
{MCF}
```

Application Messaging Servers

Up to six different server processes can be configured to support application messaging (also referred to as the *Integration Broker*), as shown in Listing 12-22. It is possible to configure more than one instance of each of the handler servers, but there can be only a single instance of each of the three dispatcher servers.

Listing 12-22. *Application Messaging Servers Definition*

```
##############################################################################
#
# Publish/Subscribe Servers
#
#    THIS SECTION SHOULD NEVER BE EDITED MANUALLY, PSADMIN REQUIRES THIS EXACT FORMAT.
#                      -----
##############################################################################

# DEFAULT Publication broker handler
PSBRKHND        SRVGRP=PUBSUB
                SRVID=101
                MIN={$PSBRKHND_dflt\Min Instances}
                MAX={$PSBRKHND_dflt\Max Instances}
                RQADDR="BRKHQ_dflt"
                REPLYQ=Y
```

```
                    CLOPT="{$Trace\TuxedoServiceTrace} -o \"{REL_LOG}{FS}PUBQ.stdout\"
-e \"{REL_LOG}{FS}Stderr\" {$PSBRKHND_dflt\Spawn Server} -s PSBRKHND_dflt:BrkProcess
-- -D {$Domain Settings\Domain ID} -S PSBRKHND_dflt"

# DEFAULT Publication broker server (dispatcher)
PSBRKDSP        SRVGRP=PUBSUB
                SRVID=100
                MIN=1
                MAX=1
                RQADDR="BRKDQ_dflt"
                REPLYQ=Y
                CLOPT="{$Trace\TuxedoServiceTrace} -o \"{REL_LOG}{FS}PUBQ.stdout\"
-e \"{REL_LOG}{FS}Stderr\" -s PSBRKDSP_dflt:Dispatch -- -D {$Domain Settings\Domain ID}
-S PSBRKDSP_dflt"

# DEFAULT publication contract handler
PSPUBHND        SRVGRP=PUBSUB
                SRVID=201
                MIN={$PSPUBHND_dflt\Min Instances}
                MAX={$PSPUBHND_dflt\Max Instances}
                RQADDR="PUBHQ_dflt"
                REPLYQ=Y
                CLOPT="{$Trace\TuxedoServiceTrace} -o \"{REL_LOG}{FS}PUBQ.stdout\"
-e \"{REL_LOG}{FS}Stderr\" {$PSPUBHND_dflt\Spawn Server} -s PSPUBHND_dflt:PubConProcess
-- -D {$Domain Settings\Domain ID} -S PSPUBHND_dflt"

# DEFAULT Publication contractor server (dispatcher)
PSPUBDSP        SRVGRP=PUBSUB
                SRVID=200
                MIN=1
                MAX=1
                RQADDR="PUBDQ_dflt"
                REPLYQ=Y
                CLOPT="{$Trace\TuxedoServiceTrace} -o \"{REL_LOG}{FS}PUBQ.stdout\"
-e \"{REL_LOG}{FS}Stderr\" -s PSPUBDSP_dflt:Dispatch -- -D {$Domain Settings\Domain ID}
-S PSPUBDSP_dflt"

# DEFAULT subscription contract handler
PSSUBHND        SRVGRP=PUBSUB
                SRVID=301
                MIN={$PSSUBHND_dflt\Min Instances}
                MAX={$PSSUBHND_dflt\Max Instances}
                RQADDR="SUBHQ_dflt"
                REPLYQ=Y
                CLOPT="{$Trace\TuxedoServiceTrace} -o \"{REL_LOG}{FS}PUBQ.stdout\"
-e \"{REL_LOG}{FS}Stderr\" {$PSSUBHND_dflt\Spawn Server} -s PSSUBHND_dflt:SubConProcess
-- -D {$Domain Settings\Domain ID} -S PSSUBHND_dflt"

# DEFAULT Subscription contractor server (dispatcher)
PSSUBDSP        SRVGRP=PUBSUB
                SRVID=300
                MIN=1
```

```
                    MAX=1
                    RQADDR="SUBDQ_dflt"
                    REPLYQ=Y
                    CLOPT="{$Trace\TuxedoServiceTrace} -o \"{REL_LOG}{FS}PUBQ.stdout\"
-e \"{REL_LOG}{FS}Stderr\" -s PSSUBDSP_dflt:Dispatch -- -D {$Domain Settings\Domain ID}
-S PSSUBDSP_dflt"


#_@_APSRV    WARNING: DO NOT MODIFY THIS LINE. Marker for append point used by PSADMIN


##############################################################################
#    END Publish/Subscribe Servers section
##############################################################################
{PUBSUB}
```

In a development environment, the overhead of the application messaging servers can be significant. There is an alternative development template that can be selected when the application server domain is created (see Listing 12-45, later in the chapter), in which there are only two messaging servers, as shown in Listing 12-23.

Listing 12-23. Definition of Application Messaging Servers for a Development Environment

```
{PUBSUB}
# Message Broker
PSMSGDSP        SRVGRP=PUBSUB
                SRVID=100
                MIN=1
                MAX=1
                CLOPT="-o \"{REL_LOG}{FS}stdout\" -e \"{REL_LOG}{FS}stderr\" -
sPSBRKDSP_dflt:Dispatch -sPSPUBDSP_dflt:Dispatch -sPSSUBDSP_dflt:Dispatch -- -D {$Domain
Settings\Domain ID} -S PSMSGDSP"
# Message Broker Handler
PSMSGHND        SRVGRP=PUBSUB
                SRVID=101
                MIN={$PSMSGHND\Min Instances}
                MAX={$PSMSGHND\Max Instances}
                RQADDR="MBHQ"
                REPLYQ=Y
                CLOPT="-o \"{REL_LOG}{FS}stdout\" -e \"{REL_LOG}{FS}stderr\" {$PSMSGHND\Spawn
Server} -sPSBRKHND_dflt:BrkProcess -sPSPUBHND_dflt:PubConProcess -sPSSUBHND_dflt:SubConProcess
-- -D {$Domain Settings\Domain ID} -S PSMSGHND"
{PUBSUB}
```

Performance Monitor Server (PSMONITORSRV)

The PSMONITORSRV server (see Listing 12-24) was introduced in PeopleTools 8.44. It has three functions:

- Measuring host resource usage and Tuxedo performance metrics for the domain being monitored by the Performance Monitor

- Canceling ad hoc queries

- Resolving master/slave failover for the Integration Broker

This server is always configured, and there is only ever one instance it.

Listing 12-24. PSMONITORSRV Server Definition

```
#
# PeopleSoft domain monitor
#
PSMONITORSRV    SRVGRP=MONITOR
                SRVID=1
                MIN=1
                MAX=1
                RQADDR="MONITOR"
                REPLYQ=Y
                RESTART=Y
                CLOPT="-o \"{REL_LOG}{FS}stdout\" -e \"{REL_LOG}{FS}stderr\" -A -- -ID {IPCKEY}
-D {$Domain Settings\Domain ID} -S PSMONITORSRV"
```

Workstation Listener and Handlers (WSL/WSH)

The Workstation Listener (WSL) listens for incoming connections from Windows three-tier clients. There are separate WSL command lines on Unix and Windows, as shown in Listing 12-25. On Unix, a device file is specified with the -d parameter.

Listing 12-25. WSL Server Specification

```
#
# Workstation Listener
#  -I xx   Max time (seconds) for a client connect
#  -T xx   Max time (minutes) for a client to stay idle.
#  -m xx   Min number of workstation handlers
#  -M xx   Max number of workstation handlers
#  -x xxx  Multiplexing, the max number of clients per handler
#
#
{WSL}
WSL             SRVGRP=BASE
                SRVID=20
                CLOPT="-o \"{REL_LOG}{FS}stdout\" -e \"{REL_LOG}{FS}stderr\" -A -- -n
{$Workstation Listener\Address}:{$Workstation Listener\Port} -z {$Workstation
Listener\Encryption} -Z {$Workstation Listener\Encryption} -I {$Workstation Listener\Init
Timeout} {WSL Client Cleanup Timeout} -m {$Workstation Listener\Min Handlers} -M {$Workstation
Listener\Max Handlers} -x {$Workstation Listener\Max Clients per Handler} -c {$Workstation
Listener\Tuxedo Compression Threshold} -p {LO_WSL_PORT} -P {HI_WSL_PORT?"
{WSL}
```

Jolt Servers

The Jolt Server Listener (JSL) listens for incoming connections from the Java servlet (see Listing 12-26). The Jolt Repository server (JREPSVR) translates Java classes to Tuxedo service requests (discussed in Chapter 2).

The -W parameter on JREPSVR permits the jrepository database to be updated. There is no reason for a PeopleSoft customer to do this. The relationships between Java classes and Tuxedo services are closely bound to the coding of PeopleTools. Leaving the jrepository database writable is a security risk, and the -W parameter should be removed.

Listing 12-26. Jolt Listener and Jolt Repository Server Definition

```
{JOLT}
#
# JOLT Listener and Rep Server
#
JSL             SRVGRP=JSLGRP
                SRVID=200
                CLOPT="-o \"{REL_LOG}{FS}stdout\" -e \"{REL_LOG}{FS}stderr\" -A -- -n {$JOLT
Listener\Address}:{$JOLT Listener\Port} -m {$JOLT Listener\Min Handlers} -M {$JOLT
Listener\Max Handlers} -I {$JOLT Listener\Init Timeout} -j {$JOLT Listener\Client Connection
Mode} -x {$JOLT Listener\Max Clients per Handler} {Jolt Encryption} {Jolt Client Cleanup
Timeout} -c {$JOLT Listener\Jolt Compression Threshold} -w JSH"

JREPSVR         SRVGRP=JREPGRP
                SRVID=250
                CLOPT="-o \"{REL_LOG}{FS}stdout\" -e \"{REL_LOG}{FS}stderr\" -A -- -W -P
\"{$PS_SERVDIR}{FS}jrepository\""
{JOLT}
```

Jolt Relay Adapter (JRAD) Server

The Jolt Relay Adapter (JRAD), shown in Listing 12-27, was introduced in PeopleTools 7.5 to permit the Java client applet to be served from a web server on a different node from the application server. Applets can only make socket connections back to the web server that served them. The relay adapter is used to pass the requests from the web server node to the application node. Thus a web server could be placed in a DMZ, and a port could be opened on the firewall through which requests could be passed to the application server.

The PIA does not require JRAD. The servlet can connect to any node.

Listing 12-27. Jolt Internet Relay Server

```
{JRAD}
#
# JOLT Internet Relay (Back End)
#
JRAD            SRVGRP=JSLGRP
                SRVID=2501
                CLOPT="-o \"{REL_LOG}{FS}stdout\" -e \"{REL_LOG}{FS}stderr\" -A -- -l {$JOLT
Relay Adapter\Listener Address}:{$JOLT Relay Adapter\Listener Port} -c {$JOLT
```

```
Listener\Address}:{$JOLT Listener\Port}"
{JRAD}
```

Tuxedo SERVICES Section

The SERVICES section of a Tuxedo file, shown in Listing 12-28, does not define which services are available; rather, it is a method of setting attributes on those services. The list of services that can be advertised by particular servers is hard-coded into the server when it is compiled, although the services actually advertised are controlled by the server command-line options, as seen earlier on PSAPPSRV.[4] Server processes can advertise services that are not described in the SERVICES section. For example, the service RenRequest is advertised on PSAPPSRV, but it does not appear in psappsrv.ubb unless PSRENSRV is configured.

Listing 12-28. Tuxedo SERVICES Section

```
*SERVICES
...
ICPanel         SRVGRP=APPSRV
                LOAD=50 PRIO=50
                SVCTIMEOUT={$PSAPPSRV\Service Timeout}
                BUFTYPE="ALL"
...
ICQuery         SRVGRP=APPSRV
                LOAD=50 PRIO=50
{QUERYSRV}
                SVCTIMEOUT={$PSQRYSRV\Service Timeout}
{QUERYSRV}
{!QUERYSRV}
                SVCTIMEOUT={$PSAPPSRV\Service Timeout}
{!QUERYSRV}
                BUFTYPE="ALL"
...
{RENSRV}
# This timeout determines how long PSRENSRV will wait to boot.
RenRequest      SRVGRP=APPSRV
                LOAD=50 PRIO=50
                SVCTIMEOUT=30
                BUFTYPE="ALL"
# Service on PSRENSRV.
RenDummySvc     SRVGRP=RENGRP
                LOAD=50 PRIO=50
                SVCTIMEOUT={$PSAPPSRV\Service Timeout}
                BUFTYPE="ALL"
{RENSRV}
...
```

---

[4] A server can also dynamically advertise servers, as is the case on startup of the Application Engine server (PSAESRV) in the Process Scheduler in PeopleTools 8.4 (see Chapter 14).

A load and priority are defined for each of the services. These values affect load balancing, spawning of servers, and dequeuing of requests, all of which are discussed in the next chapter. PeopleSoft gives all services the same load and priority. These parameters come into play only if there are multiple queues that can handle the same service and load balancing is enabled in the resources section.

A service timeout variable is defined in psappsrv.cfg for each server type. When a separate PSQRYSRV server is defined, the ICQuery service is no longer advertised on the PSAPPSRV, but on the PSQRYSRV, and the service timeout on the service is taken from the PSQRYSRV section instead.

PS_ENVFILE Section

The PS_ENVFILE section, shown in Listing 12-29, is used by PeopleSoft to generate the server process environment file. The file created by ubbgen is a Tuxedo format file, but this section is a PeopleSoft creation. It is read by each server process as it starts, and it sets environment variables for that server process. The substitutions continue to be made in the same way. You can see that there are different path settings for Windows and additional library paths for Unix.

Listing 12-29. Server Environmental Settings Definition

```
*PS_ENVFILE
TM_BOOTTIMEOUT=120
TM_RESTARTSRVTIMEOUT=120
TM_BOOTPRESUMEDFAIL=Y
FLDTBLDIR32={$TUXDIR}{FS}udataobj
FIELDTBLS32=jrep.f32,tpadm
ALOGPFX={LOGDIR}{FS}TUXACCESSLOG
{WINDOWS}
PATH={$PS_HOME}\bin\server\winx86;{$PS_HOME}\bin\server\winx86\interfacedrivers;{$Domain
Settings\Add to
PATH};{$PS_HOME}\jre\bin\client;{$PS_HOME}\verity\{VERITY_OS}\{VERITY_PLATFORM}\bin;{$PS_HOME}
\jre\bin;{$windir}\system32
INFORMIXSERVER={$Startup\ServerName}
# Set IPC_EXIT_PROCESS=1 to use ExitProcess to terminate server process.
# Set IPC_TERMINATE_PROCESS=1 to use TerminateProcess to terminate server process.
# If both are set, TerminateProcess will be used to terminate server process.
#IPC_EXIT_PROCESS=1
IPC_TERMINATE_PROCESS=1
{WINDOWS}
{UNIX}
LD_LIBRARY_PATH={$LD_LIBRARY_PATH}:{$PS_HOME}/verity/{VERITY_OS}/{VERITY_PLATFORM}/bin
LIBPATH={$LIBPATH}:{$PS_HOME}/verity/{VERITY_OS}/{VERITY_PLATFORM}/bin
SHLIB_PATH={$SHLIB_PATH}:{$PS_HOME}/verity/{VERITY_OS}/{VERITY_PLATFORM}/bin
COBPATH={$PS_HOME}/cblbin
PATH={$PS_HOME}/bin:{$Domain Settings\Add to
PATH}:{$PS_HOME}/verity/{VERITY_OS}/{VERITY_PLATFORM}/bin
INFORMIXSERVER={$Startup\ServerName}
{UNIX}
```

psappsrv.cfg

This file specifies most of the configuration of the application server domain. It is used in two ways:

- It is combined with psappsrv.ubx by ubbgen to produce psappsrv.ubb and psappsrv.env. Variables that appear in psappsrv.ubx are used as part of the Tuxedo configuration, such as the minimum and maximum number of instances of each server process.

- Variables that do not appear in psappsrv.ubx are read directly by the PeopleSoft application server processes: for example, EnableDBMonitoring.

The configuration file is broken into sections. The variables are referenced in psappsrv.ubx by section and variable name. The various sections are documented in PeopleBooks, so I only comment on some parameters in the sections that follow.

Startup

The Startup section, shown in Listing 12-30, specifies how the PeopleSoft application server processes connect to the database. Servername is not used on Oracle.

▪ **Tip** It is a good idea to create a PeopleSoft Operator ID that has only the privilege to start the application server and nothing else. The password then has no use other than to start the application server. The passwords can be encrypted in the interactive configuration dialog.

Listing 12-30. Startup Section of an Application Server Configuration File

```
[Startup]
;========================================================================
; Database Signon settings
;========================================================================
DBName=HCM91
DBType=ORACLE
UserId=PSAPPS
UserPswd=PSAPPS
ConnectId=people
ConnectPswd=people
ServerName=
StandbyDBName=
StandbyDBType=
StandbyUserId=
StandbyUserPswd=
```

The StandbyDB parameters are new in PeopleTools 8.51, which supports Oracle Active Data Guard. Read-only components and queries are submitted via an additional database connection to the standby database.

Database Options

The Database Options section, shown in Listing 12-31, controls how the application servers connect to the database.

Listing 12-31. Database Options Section of an Application Server Configuration File

```
[Database Options]
;=======================================================================
; Database-specific configuration options
;=======================================================================
SybasePacketSize=
UseLocalOracleDB=0
ORACLE_SID=HCM91
EnableDBMonitoring=1
PSDB Maximum Cursors=
```

If UseLocalOracleDB is set to 1, the connect string used by the application servers does not include the TNS service name (which is the same as the DBName). The server processes attempt to make a direct shared-memory connection to the database. This works only if the application server and database are on the same node and the Oracle Server ID environment variable, ORACLE_SID, is set to the name of the database instance.

The same effect can be obtained by defining the TNS service with an IPC key, as shown in Listing 12-32.

Listing 12-32. Extract from tnsnames.ora

```
HCM91 =
 (DESCRIPTION =
   (ADDRESS_LIST =
     (ADDRESS = (PROTOCOL = IPC)(KEY = ora11Gr2))
   )
   (CONNECT_DATA =
     (SERVICE_NAME = hcm91)
   )
 )
```

I prefer this arrangement because it does not rely on the ORACLE_SID variable. If you have application servers on the database server and on another node, then the application server configuration can remain the same on both.

EnableDBMonitoring is described in Chapter 9.

Security

The parameter Validate Signon with Database is left over from PeopleTools 7.x where a database user was created for every PeopleSoft operator. The two-tier login checks that the operator password matches the password to the schema as well as the password stored in operator definition table (PSOPRDEFN). Setting this parameter to 1 causes the application server to do the same when an operator signs in.

In PeopleTools 8, this parameter still enables the same functionality, but the database schemas are no longer created or maintained by PeopleSoft for each user. They have been replaced with ConnectID, described in Chapter 3. If you enable this parameter, user logins fail unless you manually create the corresponding database accounts. The Validate Signon parameter (see Listing 12-33) should never be enabled in PeopleTools 8.

Listing 12-33. Part of the Security Section of a Configuration File

```
[Security]
;=====================================================================
; Security settings
;=====================================================================
Validate Signon with Database=0
DomainConnectionPwd=PS; Use the database for additional signon authentication.
; The default value is 0 (DB signon validation OFF).
Validate Signon with Database=0
```

Workstation and Jolt Listeners

The two listener processes are very similar, so I deal with them together. Their configurations are shown in Listing 12-34.

Listing 12-34. Workstation and Jolt Listener Settings

```
[Workstation Listener]
;=====================================================================
; Settings for Workstation Listener
;=====================================================================
Address=%PS_MACH%
Port=7000
Encryption=0
Min Handlers=1
Max Handlers=2
Max Clients per Handler=10
Client Cleanup Timeout=60
Init Timeout=5
Tuxedo Compression Threshold=5000

[JOLT Listener]
;=====================================================================
; Settings for JOLT Listener
;=====================================================================
Address=%PS_MACH%
Port=9000
Encryption=0
Min Handlers=1
Max Handlers=8
Max Clients per Handler=10
Client Cleanup Timeout=10
Init Timeout=5
Client Connection Mode=ANY
Jolt Compression Threshold=1000000
```

The delivered PeopleSoft default configuration files have 40 clients per handler in both the WSL and JSL. The Tuxedo default parameter for the multiplexing factor (which corresponds to what PeopleSoft calls *clients per handler*) is 10. By reducing the number of clients per handler, more WSH and JSH processes are required, and more return queues to the handler processes are created. This reduces contention on the return queue.

The total number of clients that can connect to the application server via the WSL is the maximum number of handlers multiplied by the multiplexing factor. If you reduce the number of clients per handler, you should increase the maximum number of handlers by the same factor so that the listener supports the same number of concurrent connections.

The timeout parameter is expressed in minutes (all other temporal Tuxedo parameters are expressed in seconds). The PeopleSoft default is 60 minutes before an inactive thread is disconnected. I would suggest reducing this to as little as eight to ten minutes.[5] If the user returns after the application server session has been timed out, then the servlet or Windows client silently reauthenticates to the application server and continues working. The user may experience a momentary pause but does not receive any error message. If the timeout is unrealistically large, then the system must be configured to support more concurrent sessions than are actually needed.

Any message larger than the compression threshold (expressed in bytes) that is sent across the network between the client (either Windows or servlet) and the handler (either WSH or JSH) is compressed. In a good LAN environment, compression is unlikely to be beneficial.

Three-tier clients connected across a WAN may benefit from message compression. However, it is advisable to check with the network administrators to determine whether compression is enabled at a hardware (router) level. It is then at least a waste of CPU resources, if not counterproductive, to have double compression.

The servlet and the application server should always be located physically close to each other, ideally on the same low latency network. Compression is not appropriate in this case. There are two options:

- Set a very large compression threshold so than no messages are large enough to be compressed. The maximum permitted value is 2,147,483,647 bytes.

- Compression is enabled only if the compression threshold is specified, so remove the -c parameter from the JSL section of psappsrv.ubx.

Domain Settings

This section contains some general settings for the application server, as shown in Listing 12-35.

Listing 12-35. Domain Settings

```
[Domain Settings]
;=========================================================================
; General settings for this Application Server.
;=========================================================================


;-------------------------------------------------------------------------
Domain ID=HCM91SML


;-------------------------------------------------------------------------
```

---

[5] Research at one customer site showed that if a user doesn't use a PeopleSoft session within about ten minutes, they are unlikely to come back for a much longer period.

```
Add to PATH=C:\app\oracle\product\11.2.0\client32\BIN

;------------------------------------------------------------------------
Spawn Threshold=1,600:1,1

;------------------------------------------------------------------------
Restartable=Y

;------------------------------------------------------------------------
; Log Directory defaults to the LOGS directory within %PS_SERVDIR%
;Log Directory=
```

In general, the domain ID should be set to the name of the database. However, if you have multiple application servers on the same PeopleSoft database, it is advisable to give each one a different domain ID. When you enable DBMonitoring, the domain ID appears in the column V$SESSION.CLIENT_INFO, and you easily know to which application server the session relates.

If, particularly on a Windows server, you have multiple Oracle homes, you may wish to ensure that a particular application server uses SQL*Net from a particular Oracle home by explicitly setting the path in the application server configuration.

■ **Note** PeopleTools 8.51 on Windows still uses 32-bit processes and thus requires a 32-bit Oracle client. This example comes from an installation on a 64-bit version of Windows running a 64-bit version Oracle.

If you wish to move the application server logs to a different directory, uncomment this parameter and set it accordingly.

Trace

Various trace types can be enabled for the entire server in the configuration file, as shown in Listing 12-36. Trace should be enabled only in a limited test environment. There is a significant overhead to just trace SQL activity. PeopleCode trace can be even heavier.

Masks can be used to restrict the traces that can be enabled, particularly by the user via the PIA.

Listing 12-36. *Trace Settings*

```
[Trace]
;========================================================================
; Server Trace settings
;========================================================================


;------------------------------------------------------------------------
; SQL Tracing Bitfield
;
; Bit        Type of tracing
; ---        ---------------
; 1          - SQL statements
; 2          - SQL statement variables
```

```
;   4          - SQL connect, disconnect, commit and rollback
;   8          - Row Fetch (indicates that it occurred, not data)
;  16          - All other API calls except ssb
;  32          - Set Select Buffers (identifies the attributes of columns
;                  to be selected).
;  64          - Database API specific calls
; 128          - COBOL statement timings
; 256          - Sybase Bind information
; 512          - Sybase Fetch information
; 1024         - SQL Informational Trace
; 4096         - Manager information
; 8192         - Mapcore information
; Dynamic change allowed for TraceSql and TraceSqlMask
TraceSql=03
TraceSqlMask=12319


;-------------------------------------------------------------------------
; PeopleCode Tracing Bitfield
;
; Bit          Type of tracing
; ---          ---------------
;   1          - Trace Evaluator instructions   (not recommended)
;   2          - List Evaluator program         (not recommended)
;   4          - Show assignments to variables
;   8          - Show fetched values
;  16          - Show stack
;  64          - Trace start of programs
; 128          - Trace external function calls
; 256          - Trace internal function calls
; 512          - Show parameter values
; 1024         - Show function return value
; 2048         - Trace each statement in program   (recommended)
; Dynamic change allowed for TracePC and TracePCMask
TracePC=0
TracePCMask=4095
```

Cache Settings

The cache settings parameters disappeared completely in the PeopleTools 8.20 and 8.43 configuration files, but they have reappeared as comments in 8.44, as shown in Listing 12-37.

Listing 12-37. Application Server Cache Settings (PeopleTools 8.51)

```
[Cache Settings]
;================================================================================
; Settings for managed object caching;
; Default EnableServerCaching=2, ServerCacheMode=0
; Default CacheBaseDir=%PS_SERVDIR% if defined else %PS_CFG_HOME/<domain name>/cache
; You can change these values by uncommenting and setting to the desired value
;================================================================================
;--------------------------------------------------------------------
; EnableServerCaching -
;  0        Server file caching disabled
;  1        Server file caching limited to most used classes
;  2        Server file caching for all types
;EnableServerCaching=2
;--------------------------------------------------------------------
; CacheBaseDir = the base file cache directory
;CacheBaseDir=%PS_SERVDIR%
;--------------------------------------------------------------------
; ServerCacheMode
;  0        One file cache directory per app server process
;  1        One file cache directory per domain (shared file cache, needs to be preloaded)
;ServerCacheMode=0
;--------------------------------------------------------------------
; Deprecated cache settings : MaxInMemoryObjects
;--------------------------------------------------------------------
;--------------------------------------------------------------------
; MaxCacheMemory - controls cache memory pruning
;  0        cache memory pruning disabled
;  >0       max size of memory cache in MBytes
MaxCacheMemory=0

;--------------------------------------------------------------------
; EnableDBCache - When set to Y, Cache is accessed from DB, rather than File-System.
; When this setting is enabled, the settings EnableServerCaching, ServerCacheMode and
CacheBaseDir are ignored.
; Y  DB-Cache is enabled
; N  DB-Cache is disabled
;EnableDBCache=

;--------------------------------------------------------------------
; PreloadCache - Preload Cache project for File/DB and in-memory Cache
; PreloadFileCache setting is deprecated but is still supported for backward compatibility
;PreloadCache=
;PreloadMemoryCache=
```

The default value for server caching in PeopleTools 8.1 configuration files was 1, so only some PeopleTools objects were cached in the application server. All versions of PeopleTools 8.x usually benefit from caching all PeopleTools object types.

Remote Call

Remote call is a method of synchronously initiating batch COBOL programs on the application server from the PIA, rather than scheduling processes. It is mainly used for functionality such as online voucher editing and post processing in the Financials product. These batch processes typically take around 10 to 30 seconds to execute, even in a well tuned system. When the application server process initiates the COBOL process, it is in the middle of executing a service routine that must wait for the COBOL process to complete. Meanwhile, it cannot handle any other service. Therefore, there is a risk that if there are many remote calls, and their performance degrades, all the PSAPPSRV processes can be blocked and the application server may appear to hang until a remote call finishes and a service completes.

Up to PeopleTools 7.x, when using the Windows three-tier client there is a dedicated Tuxedo service, RemoteCall, that handles this. It is possible to move this service to a separate set of servers on a different queue. However, from PeopleTools 8 this is no longer possible because in the PIA the remote call is made by the generic ICPanel service, so you cannot distinguish between ordinary component operations and remote calls.

The RCCBL Redirect parameter, shown in Listing 12-38 controls whether the COBOL process generates a trace file on the application server.

Listing 12-38. Remote Call Trace Setting

```
;========================================================================
; Settings for RemoteCall
;========================================================================


;------------------------------------------------------------------------
; RemoteCall child process output redirection
;
; If this parameter is non-zero, the child process output is saved to
; <Domain Settings\Log Directory>\<program>_<oprid>.out, and any error
; output is saved to <program>_<oprid>.err.
; By default, the output is not saved
;
RCCBL Redirect=0
```

PeopleSoft Server Processes

There is a section in psappsrv.cfg for most of the various types of PeopleSoft application server processes. The section for PSAPPSRV is shown in Listing 12-39.

Listing 12-39. Configurable Parameters for the PSAPPSRV Server

```
[PSAPPSRV]
;========================================================================
; Settings for PSAPPSRV
;========================================================================


;------------------------------------------------------------------------
; UBBGEN settings
Min Instances=2
Max Instances=2
Service Timeout=300
```

```
;----------------------------------------------------------------------
; Number of services after which PSAPPSRV will automatically restart.
; If the recycle count is set to zero, PSAPPSRV will never be recycled.
; The default value is 5000.
; Dynamic change allowed for Recycle Count
Recycle Count=1000

;----------------------------------------------------------------------
; Percentage of Memory Growth after which PSAPPSRV will automatically restart.
; Default is 20, meaning additional 20% of memory growth after the process has
; built up its memory cache.
; Uncomment the setting to use memory growth instead of Recycle Count at
; determining the restart point.
; Percentage of Memory Growth=20

;----------------------------------------------------------------------
; Number of consecutive service failures after which PSAPPSRV will
; automatically restart.
; If this is set to zero, PSAPPSRV will never be recycled.
; The default value is zero.
; Dynamic change allowed for Allowed Consec Service Failures
Allowed Consec Service Failures=2

; Max Fetch Size -- max result set size in KB for a SELECT query
; Default is 5000KB. Use 0 for no limit.
Max Fetch Size=5000
; Automatically select prompt, 1 = yes, 0 = no
Auto Select Prompts=1
```

The server definitions contain a number of parameters:

- Some specify the minimum and maximum number of processes, although there are only single instances of some servers.

- Service timeouts are the maximum amount of time a service request can spend either on the queue to the application server or active on the server process before it is timed out by Tuxedo. The timeout parameters appear in the SERVICES section of psappsrv.ubx.

- Some server processes recycle after handling the number of server processes specified. This is essentially a tactic to hide memory leaks and relinquish memory allocated to the server process.

- The maximum fetch size controls the amount of data that can be fetched by the SqlRequest or SqlQuery service executed by PSAPPSRV, PSQCKSRV, or PSQRYSRV. When a query is submitted from the PIA, the entire result set is returned to the servlet in a single Tuxedo message, although only part of it may be displayed.

psappsrv.val

If you use the interactive configuration dialog in psadmin, your responses can be validated according to the specification in the validation file, psappsrv.val, shown in Listing 12-40.

Listing 12-40. Extract from psappsrv.val

```
[Startup]
DBName={string,8}
DBType={string,8}(DB2ODBC,DB2UNIX,INFORMIX,MICROSFT,ORACLE,SYBASE)
...
[Workstation Listener]
Port={int}(1025-65536)
...
```

The code in Listing 12-44 checks the following:

- DBName is a string of up to eight characters.

- DBType is a string of up to eight characters and must be one of the values in the list.

- Port must be a number between 1,025 and 65,536.

psappsrv.ubb

This file, the beginning of which is shown in Listing 12-41, is one of the outputs from ubbgen. All the variables in psappsrv.ubx have been resolved to literal values. This file is then compiled with the Tuxedo tmloadcf utility.

Listing 12-41. Beginning of psappsrv.ubb

```
#####################################################################
#
# This is a skeletal TUXEDO configuration file - "psappsrv.ubb" designed
# to be used for PeopleTools 7.5 app server and the Remote Call mechanism.
# To configure additional resources, machines, servers, services, etc.
# please refer to "ubbconfig" in section 5 of the TUXEDO System Reference
# Manual.
#
# !!!!!!!!!!!!!!!!!!!!!!!!!!!!!!!!!!!!!!!!!!!!!
# Oracle does not support modifying UBB files
# !!!!!!!!!!!!!!!!!!!!!!!!!!!!!!!!!!!!!!!!!!!!!
#####################################################################

*RESOURCES
IPCKEY          35514         # ( 32768 < IPCKEY < 262143 )
MASTER          "GO-FASTER-6"
DOMAINID        HCM91SML_35514
MODEL           SHM
LDBAL           N
...
```

At the end of psappsrv.ubb is a comment section that reports the values of all the ubbgen variables referenced in psappsrv.ubx and the values that were substituted when it was generated, as shown in Listing 12-42. Any variables that you add, such as Trace\TuxedoServiceTrace, are also reported.

Some variables in psappsrv.cfg are not referenced in psappsrv.ubx but are read directly by the server processes. They do not appear in this report.

Listing 12-42. *Configuration Variables and Values Substituted in* psappsrv.ubb

```
#********************************************************************
#   ubbgen substitution values:
#
# [  0]:                                      {IPCKEY}:  35514
# [  1]:                                        {MACH}:  GO-FASTER-6
# [  2]:                  {$Domain Settings\Domain ID}:  HCM91SML
# [  3]:                                  {MAXSERVERS}:  MAXSERVERS        16
# [  4]:                                 {MAXSERVICES}:  MAXSERVICES       200
# [  5]:                              {MAXACCESSERS1}:  MAXACCESSERS      176
# [  6]:                                     {$TUXDIR}:
 c:\app\tuxedo10gR3\tuxedo10gR3_VS2008
# [  7]:                                 {$PS_SERVDIR}:  C:\app\pt\appserv\HCM91SML
# [  8]:                                  {$TUXCONFIG}:
 C:\app\pt\appserv\HCM91SML\PSTUXCFG
# [  9]:                                      {LOGDIR}:  C:\app\pt\appserv\HCM91SML\LOGS
# [ 10]:                                          {FS}:  \
# [ 11]:                                     {ENVFILE}:
 C:\app\pt\appserv\HCM91SML\psappsrv.env
# [ 12]:                                         {UID}:  0
# [ 13]:                                         {GID}:  0
# [ 14]:                                 {MAXWSCLIENTS}:  MAXWSCLIENTS=160
# [ 15]:                               {MAXACCESSERS2}:  MAXACCESSERS=176
# [ 16]:                 {$Domain Settings\Restartable}:  Y
# [ 17]:                 {$Trace\TuxedoServiceTrace}:  -r
# [ 18]:                                     {REL_LOG}:  .\LOGS
# [ 19]:                     {$PSAPPSRV\Min Instances}:  2
# [ 20]:                     {$PSAPPSRV\Max Instances}:  2
# [ 21]:                      {$PSAPPSRV\Spawn Server}:
# [ 22]:                     {$PSSAMSRV\Min Instances}:  1
# [ 23]:                     {$PSSAMSRV\Max Instances}:  1
# [ 24]:                      {$JOLT Listener\Address}:  //GO-FASTER-6
# [ 25]:                         {$JOLT Listener\Port}:  9000
# [ 26]:                 {$JOLT Listener\Min Handlers}:  1
# [ 27]:                 {$JOLT Listener\Max Handlers}:  2
# [ 28]:                 {$JOLT Listener\Init Timeout}:  5
# [ 29]:           {$JOLT Listener\Client Connection Mode}:  ANY
# [ 30]:       {$JOLT Listener\Max Clients per Handler}:  40
# [ 31]:                             {Jolt Encryption}:
# [ 32]:                 {Jolt Client Cleanup Timeout}:  -S 10
# [ 33]:       {$JOLT Listener\Jolt Compression Threshold}:  1000000
# [ 34]:                   {$PSAPPSRV\Service Timeout}:  300
# [ 35]:                   {$PSSAMSRV\Service Timeout}:  300
# [ 36]:                   {$PSQCKSRV\Service Timeout}:  300
# [ 37]:                                     {$PS_HOME}:  c:\app\hcm91
```

```
# [38]:                      {$Domain Settings\Add to PATH}:
 C:\app\oracle\product\11.2.0\client32\BIN
# [39]:                              {VERITY_OS}:  winx86
# [40]:                        {VERITY_PLATFORM}:  _nti40
# [41]:                                {$windir}:  C:\windows
# [42]:                     {$Startup\ServerName}:
# [43]:                       {$PS_SERVDIR){FS}:
# [44]:                               {CFGFILE}:
 C:\app\pt\appserv\HCM91SML\psappsrv.cfg
#*********************************************************************
```

The values of the special variables are also reported, as shown in Listing 12-43.

Listing 12-43. Special Variables and Values Reported in psappsrv.ubb

```
#*********************************************************************
#   ubbgen control values:
#
# [ 0]:                  {UNIX}:  FALSE
# [ 1]:                 {!UNIX}:  TRUE
# [ 2]:               {WINDOWS}:  TRUE
# [ 3]:              {!WINDOWS}:  FALSE
# [ 4]:                {PUBSUB}:  FALSE
# [ 5]:               {!PUBSUB}:  TRUE
# [ 6]:              {QUICKSRV}:  FALSE
# [ 7]:             {!QUICKSRV}:  TRUE
# [ 8]:              {QUERYSRV}:  FALSE
# [ 9]:             {!QUERYSRV}:  TRUE
# [10]:                  {JOLT}:  TRUE
# [11]:                 {!JOLT}:  FALSE
# [12]:                  {JRAD}:  FALSE
# [13]:                 {!JRAD}:  TRUE
# [14]:                   {WSL}:  FALSE
# [15]:                  {!WSL}:  TRUE
...
#*************************************************************************#*******
```

psappsrv.env

The Tuxedo server environment file, shown in Listing 12-44, is generated by ubbgen and is read by each application server process when it starts. The environmental variables specified are set for the application server session.

Listing 12-44. psappsrv.env: Tuxedo Server Environment File

```
TM_BOOTTIMEOUT=120
TM_RESTARTSRVTIMEOUT=120
TM_BOOTPRESUMEDFAIL=Y
FLDTBLDIR32=c:\app\tuxedo10gR3\tuxedo10gR3_VS2008\udataobj
FIELDTBLS32=jrep.f32,tpadm
ALOGPFX=C:\app\pt\appserv\HCM91SML\LOGS\TUXACCESSLOG
PATH=c:\app\hcm91\bin\server\winx86;c:\app\hcm91\bin\server\winx86\interfacedrivers;C:\app\ora
cle\product\11.2.0\client32\BIN;c:\app\hcm91\jre\bin\client;c:\app\hcm91\verity\winx86\_nti40\
bin;c:\app\hcm91\jre\bin;C:\windows\system32
INFORMIXSERVER=
# Set IPC_EXIT_PROCESS=1 to use ExitProcess to terminate server process.
# Set IPC_TERMINATE_PROCESS=1 to use TerminateProcess to terminate server process.
# If both are set, TerminateProcess will be used to terminate server process.
#IPC_EXIT_PROCESS=1
IPC_TERMINATE_PROCESS=1
```

Not all the values in the environment file need to be fully resolved to literals. It is legitimate to dynamically reference other environmental variables, such as $TUXDIR in this example.

Configuration Template Files

A number of template files are delivered in $PS_HOME/appserv as a part of the PeopleTools installation. When a domain is created, you are asked to choose a template (see Listing 12-45), and the appropriate template files are copied to the domain directory.

Listing 12-45. Configuration Template Menu

```
Please enter name of domain to create :HCM91R88NEW

Configuration templates:

  1) developer
  2) large
  3) medium
  4) small


Select config template number:
```

There are four template files: developer.cfx, large.cfx, medium.cfx, and small.cfx. One of these is copied to psappsrv.cfg in the domain directory when the domain is created, depending on the choice made in the preceding menu.

The small, medium, and large configuration templates are intended for use with production application server domains of different sizes. They differ only in the number of servers configured. The developer template has only two application message servers instead of the usual six, as discussed earlier (see Listing 12-23).

There are also two Tuxedo template files. If you choose a developer template, developer.ubx is copied to the domain directory; otherwise, psappsrv.ubx is copied.

New versions of the template files are delivered by PeopleTools upgrades, but existing domains are not affected. Any changes to the template need to be migrated into existing domains. I usually create new domains, compare the new and old configuration files, and resolve any differences manually with a file comparison tool.

Tuxedo Administration Console

The Tuxedo Administration Console, shown in Figure 12-2, is a Java applet that runs in a web browser. It provides a useful graphical overview of the structure of a Tuxedo domain, and it permits remote administration of Tuxedo applications. It also provides some basic remote monitoring of Tuxedo domains.

The console is of limited use in a PeopleSoft system. However, the graphical interface is a useful representation of a Tuxedo domain that can be helpful in understanding Tuxedo architecture.

Administrators usually connect directly to the server where the application server is installed via a terminal emulator to a Unix server or Remote Desktop to a Windows server. However, it is occasionally useful to reconfigure aspects of a domain without shutting it down. Such changes cannot always be made via the `tmadmin` utility. There is an example of this in the next chapter.

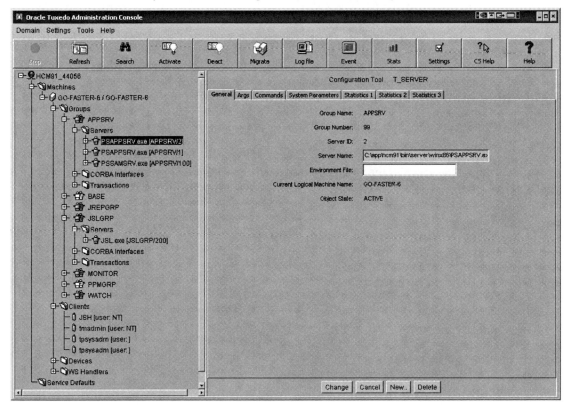

Figure 12-2. *Tuxedo Administrative Console*

The general functionality of the Tuxedo Administration Console is covered thoroughly in the Tuxedo documentation that is delivered with the product in %TUXDIR%\help\guiguide, and it is also available on the Oracle web site.[6]

In addition, the Tuxedo log file can be viewed from the console, which can be useful when a Windows-based application server is behind a firewall and shared files cannot be accessed.

The Tuxedo documentation covers the generic installation process in detail, but in the following sections I explain how to configure the console specifically for PeopleSoft.

Configuring the Tuxedo Administration Console for PeopleSoft

In order to use the Tuxedo Administration Console, you need to run a web server to serve up the Java applet and a listener process to handle communications from the applet once it is running on the client browser, as I explain in the following sections.

Tuxedo Console Listener (wlisten)

The Tuxedo Console Listener process receives incoming connections from console applets and starts a console gateway process (wgated). The listener is started with the command shown in Listing 12-46, and options are read from the parameter file, webgui.ini.

Listing 12-46. Batch Script to Start the Tuxedo Console Listener

```
set TUXDIR=C:\app\tuxedo10gR3\tuxedo10gR3_VS2008
set NLSPATH=%TUXDIR%\locale\C
set LANG=C
set WEBJAVADIR=%TUXDIR%\udataobj\webgui\java

start "wlisten" /min %TUXDIR%\bin\wlisten -i %TUXDIR%\udataobj\webgui\webgui.ini
```

The initialization file specifies the address and port to which wlisten listens for incoming connections, which by default is configured as 4003. At the bottom of the file is a list of the known Tuxedo domains. In this case (see Listing 12-47), HCM91 is an application server.

Listing 12-47. %TUXDIR%\udataobj\webgui\webgui.ini: Tuxedo Console Listener Configuration File

```
# Web GUI initialization file.
# Created 03-Aug-2011 06:27:58 by Oracle software installation program.
#
TUXDIR=c:\app\tuxedo10gR3\tuxedo10gR3_VS2008
INIFILE=c:\app\tuxedo10gR3\tuxedo10gR3_VS2008/udataobj/webgui/webgui.ini
NADDR=//GO-FASTER-6:4003
DEVICE=/dev/tcp
CODEBASE=/java
DOCBASE=http://go-faster-6:8000/doc
```

---

[6] See Oracle Tuxedo 10g Release 3 (10.3) ➤ Installing the Oracle Tuxedo System ➤ Starting the Oracle Tuxedo Administration Console
(http://download.oracle.com/docs/cd/E13161_01/tuxedo/docs10gr3/install/insadm.html)

```
SNAPDIR=c:\app\tuxedo10gR3\tuxedo10gR3_VS2008/udataobj/webgui/java/snapshot
SNAPBASE=/java/snapshot
#not deleivered in PS distribution
ENCRYPTBITS=0
FOLDERS=YNNNYNNNNNNNNNN;YNNNNNYYNNYN;YNYNY;YN;Y;YNN;Y;Y;;;
DETAILS=DETEDIT
SORT=SORTNAME
FOREGROUND=Y
#
# In order to configure one or more domains as part of the Web GUI pull-down
# menu, add lines to this file of the form DOMAIN=domainname;tuxconfig
DOMAIN=HCM91;C:\app\pt\appserv\HCM91\PSTUXCFG
DOMAIN=HCM91PSNT;C:\app\pt\appserv\prcs\HCM91PSNT\PSTUXCFG
```

The listener process runs as a background process unless FOREGROUND is set to Y. The default is N.

Tuxedo Web Server (tuxwsvr)

A simple web server (see Listing 12-48) is delivered for use with the Tuxedo Administration Console, although you could use any HTTP server.

Listing 12-48. Commands to Start the Tuxedo Web Server and Console Listener on Windows

```
start "tuxwsvr" /min %TUXDIR%\bin\tuxwsvr -l //go-faster-6:8000 -F -i
%TUXDIR%\udataobj\tuxwsvr.ini
```

By default, the web server runs as a background process unless the -F parameter is specified.

■ **Tip** The foreground options are useful during testing and until the console is functioning correctly. On Windows, I prefer to run both the listener and web server as foreground processes in minimized windows.

The web server initialization file, shown in Listing 12-49, maps the virtual served directories to directories in the physical file system.

Listing 12-49. %TUXDIR%\udataobj\tuxwsvr.ini: Tuxedo Web Server Configuration File

```
# tuxwsvr initialization file.
# Created 03-Aug-2011 06:27:58 by Oracle software installation program.
#
CGI     /cgi-bin  c:\app\tuxedo10gR3\tuxedo10gR3_VS2008/udataobj/webgui/cgi-bin
HTML    /java  c:\app\tuxedo10gR3\tuxedo10gR3_VS2008/udataobj/webgui/java
HTML    /doc   c:\app\tuxedo10gR3\tuxedo10gR3_VS2008/help
HTML    /      c:\app\tuxedo10gR3\tuxedo10gR3_VS2008/udataobj/webgui
```

Starting the Console

After you start the listener and web server processes, you can access the console from webguitop.html in the root directory of the web server. To continue the example, the URL for this page is http://go-faster-6:8000/webguitop.html. This page presents a button that when clicked runs the CGI gateway to the console, tuxadm (http://go-faster-6: 8000/cgi-bin/tuxadm.exe?TUXDIR=c%3A\app\tuxedo10gR3\tuxedo10gR3_VS2008). You are then presented with the login dialog shown in Figure 12-3.

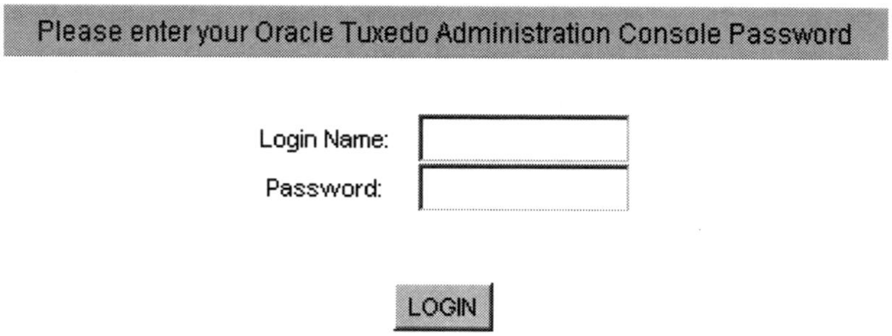

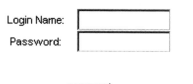

Figure 12-3. *Tuxedo Administration Console applet screen*

The password can be set with the tlistpwd(1) utility, or it can be left blank. It is stored in %TUXDIR%\udataobj\tlisten.pw

If the login is successful, you are taken to the screen shown in Figure 12-2.

Configuring PeopleSoft for the Tuxedo Administration Console

PeopleSoft application server processes rely on two environmental variables, PS_SERVDIR and PS_SERVER_CFG. These variables specify the location of PeopleTools configuration and cache files for a domain, and they are usually set by the psadmin utility. However, if you start either a whole domain or a single server process via the Tuxedo console, psadmin is not used.

The solution is to set the environmental variables in the server environment file, psappsrv.env. As described earlier in this chapter, this file is generated by ubbgen from the Tuxedo template file, psappsrv.ubx. The variables can be specified in the template file as shown in Listing 12-50.

Listing 12-50. *Extract from psappsrv.ubx: Server Environment Variables for the Tuxedo Administration Console*

```
#rem added in order to start domain with Tuxedo Console
PS_SERVDIR={$PS_SERVDIR}
PS_SERVER_CFG={$PS_SERVDIR}{FS}{CFGFILE}
```

The PS_SERVDIR environmental variable is set by psadmin when the domain is configured, so the literal value of the variable is put into psappsrv.env (see Listing 12-51).

Listing 12-51. Extract from `psappsrv.env`: *Server Environmental Variables for the Tuxedo Administration Console*

```
#rem added in order to start domain with Tuxedo Console
PS_SERVDIR=C:\app\pt\appserv\HCM91
PS_SERVER_CFG=C:\app\pt\appserv\HCM91\psappsrv.cfg
```

This advice also applies to the Process Scheduler when run under Tuxedo.

Summary

Chapter 2 explained some of the basic principles of a Tuxedo application server, and this chapter explained how the configuration files are related. It also demonstrated how to configure the Tuxedo Administration Console.

You should now know how to make configuration changes to application servers if the need arises. In the next chapter, we look at how to size an application server and how some of the parameter settings can impact performance.

CHAPTER 13

Tuning the Application Server

Chapters 2 and 12 discussed the underlying architecture of and how to configure the application server. They provide a basis for this chapter, in which I discuss some of the issues that can affect application server performance, including sizing the domain to have an appropriate number of application server processes, setting operating system kernel parameters, and load balancing.

In general, there is little you can do in the application server to improve the performance of a PeopleSoft system, but there are some things that you should consider in order to prevent the application server from becoming a performance bottleneck. Sometimes, application server problems are a symptom of other underlying issues, including database performance problems.

PeopleSoft's official recommendations are set out in its Red Paper[1] titled "Online Performance Configuration Guidelines."

Sizing

The sizing of a PeopleSoft application server can significantly affect the performance of the system as a whole. The use of too many application servers or processes can have just as significant and detrimental an effect as the use of too few.

If you configure too few servers, they may not be able to keep up with the demands made by the users, and you see requests queuing in the application server. Configure too many server processes, and you could either place excessive load on the database server, consume all the CPU on the application server, or cause contention in the application server. All of these could, again, give rise to queuing in the application server.

If the application server is co-resident with the database, and the application server consumes all the CPU, you can expect to see significant degradation of database performance.

The separate query servers put very little load on the application server node but pass additional, relatively heavy, queries through to the database. Permitting too many concurrent report queries degrades database performance.

You can think of the application server as a being like a tap on a pipe. You can open or close the tap to regulate the flow through the pipe. Similarly, you can configure more or fewer application server processes to control the load on the application and database servers.

---

[1] Available from the Oracle Support web site: Online Performance Configuration Guidelines for PeopleTools 8.1x, 8.4, and 8.44 (Doc ID 333300.1).

Spawning

Before looking at how many server processes to configure, it is important to understand the concept of *server spawning* in Tuxedo. Most PeopleSoft server processes are defined in the Tuxedo configuration file (see Listing 13-1) as having a minimum and maximum number of instances. When the domain is started, Tuxedo starts the minimum number of processes and spawns additional instances on demand, up to the maximum number permitted.

Thus spawning releases resources, particularly memory, back to the operating system so that it can be used by other processes. It is common to find PeopleSoft application servers and Process Schedulers collocated on the same servers. Spawning can be used to make the application server shut down server processes to free memory for overnight batch processing. Figure 13-2, later in the chapter, illustrates just such a system. On the other hand, if an application server runs in isolation on a dedicated server, there is no advantage to spawning. It may as well run a constant number of processes all the time.

Listing 13-1. Definition of PSAPPSRV in psappsrv.ubb

```
PSAPPSRV       SRVGRP=APPSRV
               SRVID=1
               MIN=2
               MAX=3
               RQADDR="APPQ"
               REPLYQ=Y
               CLOPT="-o \".\LOGS\stdout\" -e \".\LOGS\stderr\" -p 1,600:1,1 -s@psappsrv.lst -
- -D HCM91 -S PSAPPSRV"
```

Demand is defined in terms of the number of service requests on the queue that leads to the server, or the cumulative load of those service requests. The situation is like a line in a post office or bank, where one line leads to many windows (behind each of which sits an agent). If there is sufficient demand, closed windows may be opened, and if there are idle agents, a window may be closed.

Spawning in Tuxedo is controlled by the -p parameter, which is of this form:

```
-p[L][low_water][,[terminate_time]][:[high_water][,create_time]]
```

The Tuxedo documentation (servopts(5)[2]) states that if the number of service requests per server on the queue exceeds the high_water level for at least create_time seconds, a new server is spawned. If the load drops below low_water for at least terminate_time seconds, a server is deactivated. If the L parameter is specified, the load of the services on the queue is compared to the low_water and high_water thresholds.

In the PeopleSoft application server, the spawning parameter is set to -p 1,600:1,1 for all servers. This means that if a queue of one or more requests per server exists continuously for one second, then another server is spawned (as long as the number of servers is less than the maximum number). Conversely, if there is less than one request per server queued continuously for 600 seconds, and there are more than the minimum number of servers, one is shut down.

However, the spawning algorithm is dependent on the duration services. The logic that Tuxedo uses to check whether a new server should be spawned is in the Tuxedo libraries that are linked into the server-process executables. Each server process autonomously determines whether to spawn another

---

[2] Oracle Tuxedo 10g Release 3 (10.3) ➤ Reference ➤ File Formats, Data Descriptions, MIBs, and System Processes Reference ➤ Servopts
(http://download.oracle.com/docs/cd/E13161_01/tuxedo/docs10gr3/rf5/rf5.html#wp1003290).

server, not the Workstation Handler (WSH) and Jolt Server Handler (JSH) processes that enqueue the service request, nor the Bulletin Board Liaison (BBL) that spawns the restart server, which actually starts the new process.

After processing a message from the queue, a server executes the code that does the server-spawning management. The first time a server process detects that the high water mark is exceeded, it saves the current time. It then processes the next message on the queue. If, when that message has completed, the high water mark is still exceeded, and the difference between the current time and the saved time exceeds the create time, then a new server is spawned.

Hence the time taken to detect that the high water mark has been exceeded may be the time taken for a server process to execute two services. This can lead to some scenarios in which Tuxedo is slow to spawn additional servers:

- It would be a mistake to configure a domain with a minimum of only one PSAPPSRV server and to rely on spawning to initiate sufficient server processes. If the only PSAPPSRV process was occupied with a long-running service, and a queue of requests built up during that time, no server would spawn until that service completed. It is not unusual for some operations to take a long time; for example, an online voucher edit and post process on a Financials system might easily take 60 seconds for the remote call to the COBOL program to complete. So it might take a server process more than one minute to decide to spawn an extra server.

- The PSQRYSRV server executes ad hoc queries that often run for long periods of time. Therefore the servers test for queuing less frequently. If all the servers on a queue are occupied, and a queue of further requests builds up, no additional server process can be spawned until a query service completes.

- Many PeopleSoft sites use a number of small servers to host application servers, rather than a single large server. These smaller servers rarely have more than four CPUs. Therefore, as explained in the discussion in the following sections, the application server domains usually run four to eight PSAPPSRV processes. Smaller domains can be slower to spawn because there are fewer servers. Excessive spawning can also cause performance problems. Therefore, the minimum number of servers configured should be adequate to cope with typical loads, and less reliance should be placed on Tuxedo spawning.

Too Few Server Processes?

If you have too few server processes to handle the incoming requests, then you see requests build up on the queues in the application server. The following sections cover a couple of methods that can be used to determine a reasonable minimum number of server processes for a system.

Concurrency

It is possible to determine how many service requests execute concurrently. The Tuxedo service trace reports the start and end time of each service to an accuracy of $1/100$ of a second on Unix systems and $1/1,000$ of a second on Windows. Hence you can determine how many services were being processed when each service started. I usually do this by loading the Tuxedo service trace into a database table (as described in Chapter 9 in the section "Tuxedo Service Trace (-r Option)") and using PL/SQL to calculate the concurrency. Then I can present that information graphically. If you have several application servers, you can combine the service traces to determine the concurrency across all application servers.

Listing 13-2 shows the PL/SQL code that calculates the concurrency of each request.

Listing 13-2. PL/SQL to Calculate Tuxedo Service Request Concurrency

```
DECLARE
  l_count INTEGER := 0;
  CURSOR    c_txrpt IS
  SELECT    *
  FROM      txrpt t
  WHERE     concurrent = 0
  ORDER BY queue, stime desc, etime desc, stimestamp desc;
  p_txrpt c_txrpt%ROWTYPE;
BEGIN
  OPEN c_txrpt;
  LOOP
      FETCH c_txrpt INTO p_txrpt;
      EXIT WHEN c_txrpt%NOTFOUND;

      UPDATE txrpt a
      SET     concurrent = (
              SELECT COUNT(*)
              FROM    txrpt b
              WHERE   b.stime <= a.stime
              AND     b.etime >= a.stime
              AND     b.stimestamp <= a.stimestamp
              AND     b.stimestamp >= a.stimestamp
                      - ceil((a.etime-a.stime)/1000+1)/86400
              AND     b.queue = a.queue
              )
      WHERE service = p_txrpt.service
      AND   pid = p_txrpt.pid
      AND   stimestamp = p_txrpt.stimestamp
      AND   stime = p_txrpt.stime
      AND   etime = p_txrpt.etime
      ;

      IF l_count <= 1000 THEN
         l_count := l_count + 1;
      ELSE
         l_count := 0;
         COMMIT;
      END IF;
  END LOOP;
  COMMIT;
  CLOSE c_txrpt;
END;
/
```

This SQL is not particularly efficient. It requires an index on the table to satisfy the UPDATE statement:

```
CREATE index txrpt2 ON txrpt(queue,stime,etime,stimestamp);
```

If you are working with a large volume of trace data, then range partitioning the table on stime can be advantageous.

Calculating concurrency shows how many server processes you actually need. If you achieve improvements in performance, the number of server processes that you need may decrease, thus saving resources on both the application and database servers. The graph shown in Figure 13-1 depicts the concurrency of PSAPPSRV requests on a system on two different days. Between these two dates a number of improvements were made to database performance, and so as the service time fell, the number of services that executed concurrently also fell.

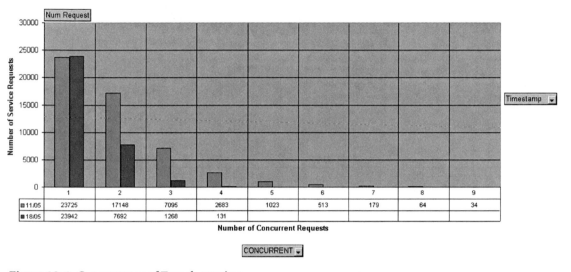

Figure 13-1. Concurrency of Tuxedo services

On the first date (May 11), it would have been appropriate to configure a minimum of five PSAPPSRV processes. This would have ensured that there was a free server process for 98.5% of requests. By the second date (May 18), three PSAPPSRV processes would have been enough for 99.6% of requests, and the system never needed more than four processes.

Application Server Monitoring

Another effective and entirely pragmatic way to assess the required minimum number of server processes is to monitor the number of application server processes and see whether Tuxedo spawns additional server processes and, if so, how many processes and how frequently they should spawn.

It is possible to use tmadmin, the Tuxedo command-line administrative utility, in Unix scripts to poll the application server and collect metrics (as described in Chapter 9). The graph in Figure 13-2 was produced from data collected from the tuxmon.sh script.[3]

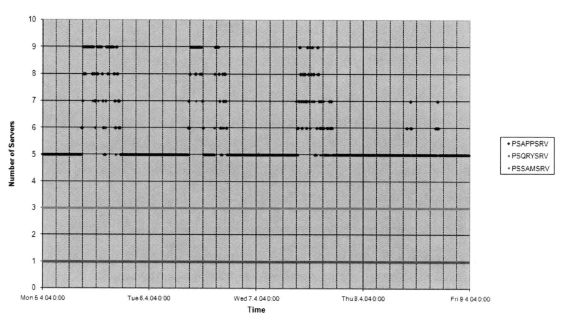

Figure 13-2. Number of application server processes

This system is configured with a minimum of five application server processes and a maximum of nine. On most days, and for much of the working day, Tuxedo spawned additional servers and sometimes all nine available servers. All other factors being equal, it might be worthwhile to increase the minimum number of server processes to at least seven to minimize spawning. However, in this particular case, the minimum was set to five to ensure that sufficient memory was released for the overnight batch processing that runs on the same machine.

The tuxmon.sh script also collects queuing information (not shown), and it does not show significant quantities of queuing on the system, so a maximum of nine server processes is probably enough.

Too Many Server Processes?

There are situations in which you may decide that you have too many server processes configured on a PeopleSoft system. Typically, you are experiencing poor performance in the PIA, and you see that all the application server processes are busy and that there is a queue of requests. It is tempting to decide that you simply need more server processes. After all, Tuxedo spawning works by automatically starting more

---

[3] The tuxmon.sh script can be downloaded from www.go-faster.co.uk.

server processes if there is a queue. However, if the root cause is a resource shortage somewhere in the system, then counter-intuitively the correct action may be to do exactly the opposite. It might be better to reduce the number of application server processes, accept some queuing in the application server, ease the resource shortage, and improve service time in the application server.

The sections that follow describe some of the other symptoms you should look out for.

SPAWNING TOO MANY APPLICATION SERVERS

Tuxedo spawning is a very simple mechanism. If there has been a queue of sufficient requests for sufficient time, Tuxedo spawns additional server processes up to the maximum without considering any other factor.

If the system has spare resource, spawning is a negative feedback mechanism. Starting additional application server processes allows the domain to handle more requests, the queue subsides, and it is not necessary to spawn additional server processes. However, it is possible to reach a tipping point where adding server processes degrades service time. In this case, spawning becomes a positive feedback mechanism. Queuing causes Tuxedo to spawn additional servers. Spawning additional server processes causes more queuing. Tuxedo quickly spawns up to the maximum number of server processes.

Oracle support document 957481.1 proposes a *health check* activity to disable spawning on PSAPPSRV and prevent system overload. The existence of this document implies that overload due to uncontrolled spawning is a common problem. However, I think this document misses the point. The problem isn't spawning. The problem is having too many server processes configured.

If I am going to disable spawning by setting the minimum and maximum number of PSAPPSRV processes to the same value, then I have to choose a value that is sufficient to handle peak activities in the system. If the system has experienced the overload scenario, then I need choose a value close to but not beyond the tipping point I described. If too many server processes are configured, I am almost guaranteed to get the system-overload scenario, probably during the next period of peak activity.

Furthermore, disabling spawning may result in less efficient use of system resources. For example, the application server processes continue to consume memory during quiet periods when it could be used for batch processing, as with the system illustrated by Figure 13-2.

Database Overload

Having too many application server processes can put more load on the database server. I have seen some systems, with a very large amount of online activity, in which all the application server processes were occupied handling existing requests, so new requests were starting to build up on the queues in the application server. In one case, the customer responded by repeatedly adding more physical application servers but did not obtain any improvement in performance. The reason was that, in fact, the application server processes were mostly waiting for responses from the database. In other words, the database had become the bottleneck.

PeopleSoft's ad hoc Query utility can be a particularly significant cause of database overhead. It is a facility that is sold to prospective customers as a major functional benefit. Users can easily build queries to extract data from the system themselves, rather than have a predefined report developed for them.

However, they can also easily generate queries that perform very poorly. There are a couple of common scenarios in which this can happen:

- A query scans large tables and generates a large quantity of physical reads. This leads to contention on the disk subsystem, and the performance of the database as a whole degrades.

- A query uses nested loop joins with an index range scan. The table is accessed by ROWID. There is virtually no physical I/O but a huge amount of logical I/O, which in turn consumes a huge amount of CPU and can result in significant latch contention on the cache buffer chains.

The situation can be aggravated by the user resubmitting the query, should it time out. The Oracle shadow process can continue to process the first query, and now you have two (or more, for especially insistent users) sessions consuming resources.

In most cases, I suggest that the correct response to either scenario is to reduce the number of application server processes to a level where the database can cope with the load, and accept that requests builds up on the application server queues. In particular, you should restrict the number of query server (PSQRYSRV) processes and other batch-reporting activity to preserve online activity. Then you can address the causes of poor database performance, thus increasing throughput through the existing server processes and perhaps permitting more process to be configured.

Oracle Resource Manager can be used to restrict resource consumption for sessions. Sessions can be automatically allocated to a consumer group by various attributes including program name and user name. Thus database sessions created by PSQRYSRV processes can easily be allocated to a restricted consumer group by program name. Additionally, PSQRYSRV can be made to use a different configuration file, and so ultimately connect to a different Oracle user (described in Chapter 3). Therefore, queries can use a different temporary tablespaces.

Running Out of CPU

When executing PeopleCode, the PSAPPSRV processes are heavy consumers of CPU. The PeopleSoft Ping case studies (see Chapter 10) show that the application server service time is closely related to CPU speed. If no free CPU is available to an application server, then processes have to wait to run on a processor, and this degrades PeopleCode performance.

In terms of the overall performance of a system, it is better for the number of application server processes to be restricted such that the CPU on the application server is almost, but not quite, fully utilized. Thus the PSAPPSRV processes do not contend for CPU, and the application server service time does not increase due to CPU contention. If the number of application server processes is increased, the same amount of CPU may have to be shared between more concurrently executing processes.

■ **Note** In general, it is better that any queuing should occur as high up the application stack as possible. The lower in the stack queuing occurs, the more processes are affected. In this case, once the CPU is fully utilized, it is better for application server service requests to wait on a Tuxedo Inter-process Communication (IPC) queue than to contend with other service requests for CPU and end up on the operating system run queue.

When there is a CPU shortage, increasing the number of application server processes can cause increased contention on the shared memory queues. When a request is either enqueued or dequeued by an application server process, it needs to acquire an exclusive lock on the queue. This can cause additional contention (see the section "Multiple Queues," later in this chapter).

Analysis based on Tuxedo Service Trace

The following steps are a method for estimating the maximum number of application server processes that you can use before the CPU is fully utilized:

1. On a Unix server, collect CPU statistics with the sar (system activity reporter) or sadc (system activity data collector) commands, and generate a simple tabular report. On Windows, use the Windows Performance Monitor to collect CPU statistics that can be exported to a comma-separated file. I suggest collecting the information on a one-minute cycle.

2. Use the Tuxedo service trace to report the time and duration of each Tuxedo service.

3. Load both sets of statistics into a database (using SQL*Loader, as described in Chapter 9). From this, you can determine how much service time was expended in each one-minute sample for which you have CPU statistics.

4. Produce a graph of CPU utilization against Tuxedo service time (see Figure 13-3).

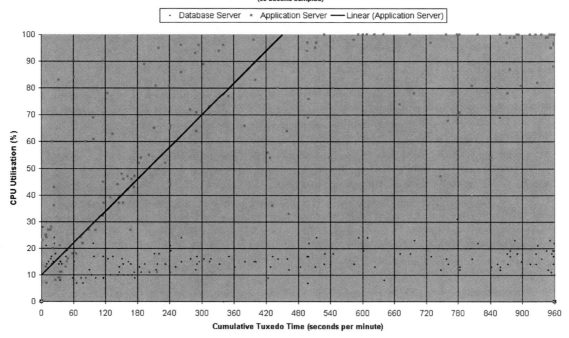

Database and Application Server: CPU Utilisation -v- Cumulative Tuxedo Service Time
(60 second samples)

Figure 13-3. CPU utilization versus Tuxedo service time

The graph shows the results from a system where the database and application server were on separate physical servers. CPU utilization for both servers has been plotted against Tuxedo service time. The database CPU utilization rarely exceeds 20%, whereas the application server is fully CPU utilized at about 450 seconds of Tuxedo service time per minute. The application server clearly becomes the bottleneck first.

The solid line on the graph is a linear regression to the application server CPU utilization up to the point at which the CPU on the application server is fully utilized. As noted, it reaches 100% CPU utilization at around 450 seconds of Tuxedo service time per minute.

There are also some data points that indicate up to 960 seconds per minute of service time. These are consistent with long-running SQL queries, where the database is active and the application server is waiting for a response and consuming less CPU.

Four hundred and fifty seconds (which is 7.5 minutes) of Tuxedo service time per minute suggests that 7.5 concurrently actively PSAPPSRV processes would fully consume all the CPU on the application server. Therefore, the absolute maximum number of PSAPPSRV processes that should be used for this physical application server node is seven. That estimate makes no allowances for any other activity on that server, in which case the maximum number of application server processes may need to be further reduced.

Analysis based on PeopleSoft Performance Monitor Data

A similar analysis can be performed using data in two events collected by Performance Monitor (PPM):

- Event 300 contains CPU and memory consumption for the host server (see Listing 10-11).

- Event 302 simulates the Tuxedo printserver (or psr) command (see Listing 10-13). The number of currently active servers can be determined by counting the number of PSAPPSRV servers that are not idle.

It is easy to extract and correlate the two sets of PPM events in a single SQL query because for each domain both are collected by the PSMONITORSRV process and are given the same timestamp.

In the previous section, I obtained the number of seconds per minute of Tuxedo service time from the Tuxedo service trace. Thus, for example, 90 seconds per minute of Tuxedo service time is the same thing as an average of 1.5 active application servers. Using PPM data, the number of active servers can only be an integer value. Rather than drawing a scatter of data points where all the points are on integer values on the x-axis, I have calculated the median and standard deviation of the CPU consumption for each value of active sessions. The SQL query to do all this is in Listing 13-3.

Listing 13-3. Correlations of orintserver to CPU (cputrend.sql)

```
SELECT * FROM (
SELECT y.*
,       num_active*cpu_m+cpu_c cpu_y
,       num_active*mem_m+mem_c mem_y
FROM    (
SELECT  num_active
,       MEDIAN(cpu_pct) med_cpu_pct, STDDEV(cpu_pct) cpu_std_dev
,       MEDIAN(mem_pct) med_mem_pct, STDDEV(mem_pct) mem_std_dev
,       COUNT(*) num
,       avg(cpu_m) cpu_m, avg(cpu_c) cpu_c
,       avg(mem_m) mem_m, avg(mem_c) mem_c
FROM    (
SELECT  e302.num_active, e300.cpu_pct, e300.mem_pct
,       REGR_SLOPE(e300.cpu_pct, e302.num_active) OVER () as cpu_M
,       REGR_INTERCEPT(e300.cpu_pct, e302.num_active) OVER () as cpu_C
,       REGR_SLOPE(e300.mem_pct, e302.num_active) OVER () as mem_M
,       REGR_INTERCEPT(e300.mem_pct, e302.num_active) OVER () as mem_C
FROM    (SELECT c300.pm_agentid, c300.pm_agent_dttm
        ,       c300.pm_metric_value1 cpu_pct
        ,       c300.pm_metric_value2 mem_pct
        FROM    pspmeventhist c300
        WHERE   c300.pm_event_defn_set = 1
        AND     c300.pm_event_defn_id = 300 /*host CPU*/
        ) e300
,       (SELECT c302.pm_agentid, c302.pm_agent_dttm, COUNT(*) num_active
        FROM    pspmeventhist c302, pspmagent b, pspmsysdefn a
        WHERE   a.pm_systemid = b.pm_systemid
        AND     b.pm_agentid = c302.pm_agentid
```

```
        AND     c302.pm_event_defn_id = 302 /*PSR*/
        AND     a.dbname IN(<database name>)
        AND     c302.pm_event_defn_set = 1
        AND     c302.pm_metric_value7 = 'PSAPPSRV'
/*      AND     longtochar.pspmeventhist(c302.rowid) != '(idle)'⁴*/
        CAST(c302.pm_addtnl_descr AS VARCHAR2(30)) != '(idle)'
        GROUP BY c302.pm_agentid, c302.pm_agent_dttm
     ) e302
WHERE   e300.pm_agentid = e302.pm_agentid
AND     e300.pm_agent_dttm = e302.pm_agent_dttm
) x GROUP BY num_active ) y )
ORDER BY 1
```

The results of the query in Listing 13-3 have been extracted into an Excel sheet and used to produce the graph in Figure 13-4. I can't just use Excel to draw a trend line because each of the data points represents a different number of event samples. Instead, I calculated a linear regression for all the database points using the SQL functions REGR_SLOPE() and REGR_INTERCEPT() and drew my own trend line based on those values. The point at which the trend line meets 100% CPU utilization marks the upper limit on the number of application server processes that should be configured.

---

[4] In PeopleTools 8.50, Oracle LONG columns were replaced with CLOBs. Thus it became possible to specify criteria on them. If you still have LONG columns, then use the longtochar() function shown in a comment in this code and described in Chapter 10 see Converting Long Columns to CLOBs.

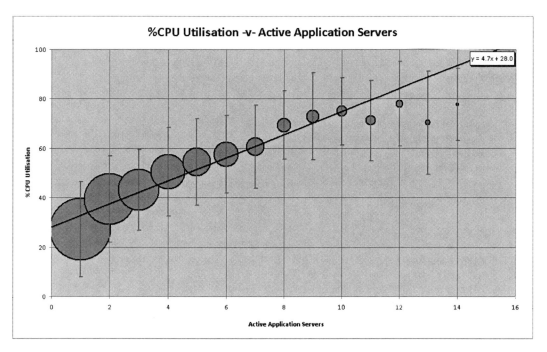

Figure 13-4. Correlation of CPU utilization and number of active application servers (cputrend.xls).[5] The area of the bubbles indicates the number of samples.

Multiple Queues

Application server processes on a single queue contend because it is necessary to briefly take out a lock on the queue in order to enqueue or dequeue a request. The contention increases as the number of servers increases, and by the time there are ten servers, the contention can become significant. Therefore, Oracle recommends that you do not have more than ten server processes per queue. This is likely to be necessary only on large, highly active online systems (usually CRM or self-service HR) and where the application servers have sufficient CPUs to support more than ten PSAPPSRV processes.

One option to avoid overloading a queue would be to simply configure a second application server on the same node. The servlet would randomly connect to one server or the other, and the load would roughly balance between the servers. The downside, of course, is that there would be two servers to maintain, administer, and monitor. There would also be two sets of Tuxedo processes to run.

An alternative is to configure a second queue for the same type of server process. If, for example, you need to run up to 16 application server processes, you can have two queues serving PSAPPSRV processes, each with up to 8 processes. To create the additional queue, it is only necessary to add a second PSAPPSRV section in psappsrv.ubx, as shown in Listing 13-4.

---

[5] This chart does not depict the same system as Figure 13-3.

Listing 13-4. Two APPQs queues configured in psappsrv.ubx

```
#
# PeopleSoft Application Server
#
PSAPPSRV        SRVGRP=APPSRV
                SRVID=1
                MIN={$PSAPPSRV\Min Instances}
                MAX={$PSAPPSRV\Max Instances}
                RQADDR="APPQ"
                REPLYQ=Y
                CLOPT="{$Trace\TuxedoServiceTrace} -o \"{REL_LOG}{FS}APPQ.stdout\" -e
\"{REL_LOG}{FS}APPQ.stderr\" {$PSAPPSRV\Spawn Server} -s@psappsrv.lst -- -D {$Domain
Settings\Domain ID} -S PSAPPSRV"
#
# PeopleSoft Application Server on 2nd Queue
#
PSAPPSRV        SRVGRP=APPSRV
                SRVID=11
                MIN={$PSAPPSRV\Min Instances}
                MAX={$PSAPPSRV\Max Instances}
                RQADDR="APPQ"
                REPLYQ=Y
                CLOPT="{$Trace\TuxedoServiceTrace} -o \"{REL_LOG}{FS}APPQ2.stdout\" -e
\"{REL_LOG}{FS}APPQ2.stderr\" {$PSAPPSRV\Spawn Server} -s@psappsrv.lst -- -D {$Domain
Settings\Domain ID} -S PSAPPSRV" #
```

There are two changes in the second PSAPPSRV server definition:

- The server ID must be unique for each server process within a group, so I have added ten to the server ID, because there should never be more than ten server processes on a queue.

- The queue has been given a unique name of APPQ2. This is visible in the tmadmin interface.

All configuration variables have been used for both servers. This ensures that the two queues have the same configuration and handle approximately the same load. The maximum number of instances of PSAPPSRV, in psappsrv.cfg, now means the number of server processes per queue. So, to have 16 PSAPPSRV processes, Max Instances must be set to 8.

The additional queues and servers require additional resources to be allocated in the Tuxedo configuration. The sizes of the Bulletin Board internal tables are determined by the Tuxedo parameters MAXACCESSERS, MAXSERVERS, and MAXSERVICES. The values for these parameters are calculated by ubbgen (see Table 12-2), but ubbgen does not take the second queue into account. The values must be calculated manually; and I recommend replacing the existing special variables in psappsrv.ubx with new configuration variables, as shown in Listing 13-5, which are then defined in psappsrv.cfg.

■ **Tip** The easiest way to calculate the new values for Bulletin Board resources is to take values calculated by ubbgen for a single queue before reconfiguring the domain and then add adjustments for an additional queue. Add the maximum number of servers on each additional queue to MAXACCESSERS and MAXSERVERS, and add 74 times maximum number of PSAPPSRVs on each additional queue. If you change the maximum number of servers on any queue or any listener parameter, you must remember to recalculate these values.

Listing 13-5. Replacing Special Variables in psappsrv.ubx

```
*RESOURCES
...
#-------------------------------------------------------------------------
#Manually defined Tuxedo bulletin board sizing parameters
#required because multiple APPQs defined
#{MAXSERVERS}
#{MAXSERVICES}
#{MAXACCESSERS1}
MAXSERVERS      {$Domain Settings\MAXSERVERS}
MAXSERVICES     {$Domain Settings\MAXSERVICES}
MAXACCESSERS    {$Domain Settings\MAXACCESSERS}
#{MAXSERVERS}
...
# ------------------------------------------------------------------

*MACHINES
"{MACH}" LMID="{MACH}"                          # Machine name must be uppercase
...
#       {MAXACCESSERS2}
        MAXACCESSERS={$Domain Settings\MAXACCESSERS}
```

The literal values can then be seen in psappsrv.ubb (see Listing 13-6).

Listing 13-6. Corresponding Extract from psappsrv.ubb

```
[Domain Settings]
...
#-------------------------------------------------------------------------
#Manually defined Tuxedo bulletin board sizing parameters
#required because multiple APPQs defined
#{MAXSERVERS}
#{MAXSERVICES}
#{MAXACCESSERS1}
MAXSERVERS      39
MAXSERVICES     1542
MAXACCESSERS    199
...
#**********************************************************************
#   ubbgen substitution values:
```

```
#
...
# [ 3]:                      {$Domain Settings\MAXSERVERS}:   39
# [ 4]:                      {$Domain Settings\MAXSERVICES}:   1542
# [ 5]:                      {$Domain Settings\MAXACCESSERS}:   199
...
```

■ **Note** Only variables that are referenced in lines other than comments in `psappsrv.ubx` are included in the `ubbgen` substitution report in `psappsrv.ubb`.

Kernel Configuration

Whether you are running Tuxedo on Unix or Windows, you need to consider the kernel parameters that control the amount of IPC resources that are available to the system.

Tuxedo makes extensive use of IPC queues. IPC resources are global to the entire machine and are shared by all Tuxedo domains. It is necessary to make sure there are sufficient resources to support all the queues created by all the application server and Process Scheduler domains (as described in Chapter 2 in the section "IPC Resources"). Otherwise, you get run-time errors when Tuxedo can't create additional queues when starting additional servers.

On Unix systems, you may have to take other applications into account when determining kernel parameters. On Windows, the kernel is simulated by the Tuxedo IPC helper service, so it is only necessary to consider the Tuxedo domains.

On Windows, Oracle delivers a Control Panel utility to configure Tuxedo. One of the tabs defines IPC resources, as shown in Figure 13-5.

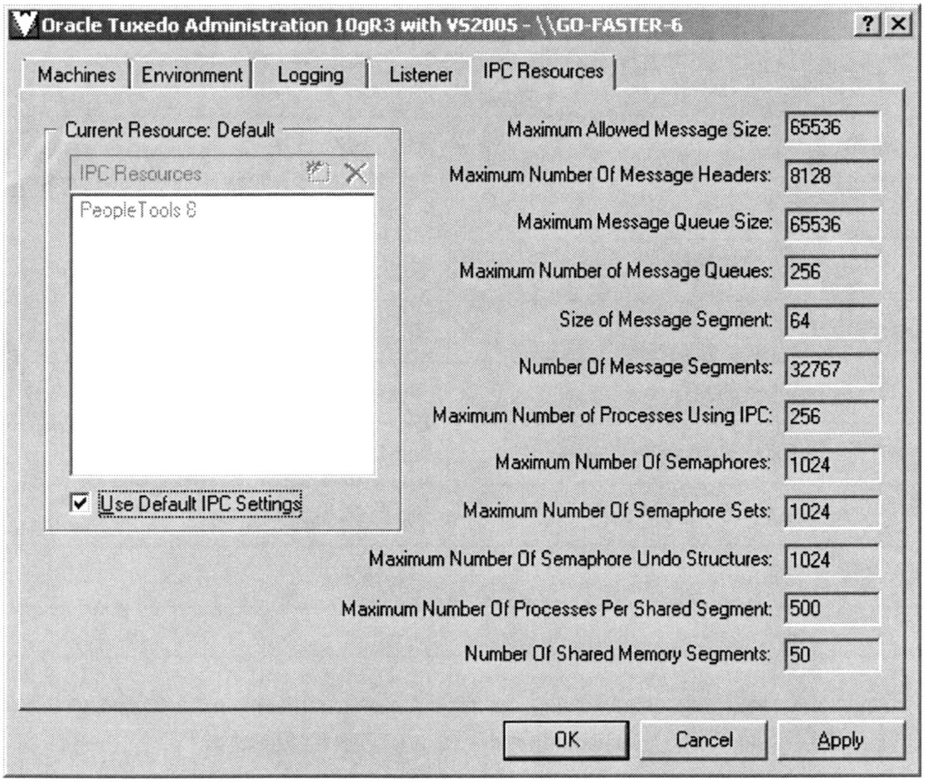

Figure 13-5. Tuxedo IPC configuration on Windows

Most of these parameters correspond directly to Unix kernel parameters. The mapping is described in Table 13-1.

Table 13-1. IPC Resource Name Mappings Between Windows and Unix[6]

Windows Name	Traditional Unix Name
Maximum Allowed Message Size	MSGMAX
Maximum Number Of Message Headers	No matching name
Maximum Message Queue Size	MSGMNB

---

[6] See Using Oracle Tuxedo ATMI on Windows ➤ Configuring Oracle Tuxedo ATMI for Windows Server 2003 (http://download.oracle.com/docs/cd/E13161_01/tuxedo/docs10gr3/nt/ntadmin.html).

469

Windows Name	Traditional Unix Name
Maximum Number of Message Queues	MSGMNI
Size of Message Segment	MSGSSZ
Number Of Message Segments	MSGSEG
Maximum Number of Processes Using IPC	NPROC
Maximum Number Of Semaphores	SEMMNS
Maximum Number Of Semaphore Sets	SEMMNI
Maximum Number Of Semaphore Undo Structures	SEMMNU
Maximum Number Of Processes Per Shared Segment	No matching name
Number Of Shared Memory Segments	SHMMNI

■ **Note** The Tuxedo documentation makes recommendations for setting these parameters in the sections "IPC Resource Configuration on a UNIX System" and "Configuring Oracle Tuxedo ATMI for Windows."

IPC Queue Sizing

The following warning appears in all versions of the Tuxedo manual, and it applies to all operating systems:

> If the limit specified by any of [the IPC] parameters is exceeded, then a blocking condition occurs. There is one exception to this rule: MSGMAX. Messages that exceed 75 percent of MSGMNB, or that are larger than MSGMAX, are placed in a UNIX file. A very small message containing the filename is then sent to the recipient. Because this mode of operation results in a severe reduction in performance, [Oracle] strongly recommend that you avoid it.[7]

---

[7] See Oracle Tuxedo Documentation ➤ Installing the Oracle Tuxedo System ä IPC Resource Configuration on a Unix System ➤ Message Queues and Messages (http://download.oracle.com/docs/cd/E13161_01/tuxedo/docs10gr3/install/insappd.html).

When this occurs, especially in a highly active online system, the time taken to enqueue or dequeue requests increases because a physical disk access is required, leading to increased contention on the queues.

It is possible to see evidence of this phenomenon on some Unix systems. The temporary files are created in directories whose names begin with tx, located in the temporary directory, but sometimes Tuxedo does not delete all of these directories.

So the next question is, just how big are Tuxedo messages in PeopleSoft?

Jolt Message Size Analysis using Tuxedo Log

The Tuxedo log can be enhanced to show every Tuxedo function call by either setting an environmental variable, TMTRACE=on, or issuing the tmadmin command changetrace on. This additional information is intended to assist debugging by the Tuxedo developer, but it does show the sizes of messages sent to and from the application server processes.

Table 13-2 shows the functions that are of interest in a PeopleSoft system. There are other functions, and they are explained in more detail in the Tuxedo documentation.

Table 13-2. *Tuxedo Service Functions*

Function	Description
tpalloc	This function allocates memory to a buffer returning a pointer to it. The last parameter is the number of bytes requested.
tprealloc	This function changes the size of an existing buffer, usually to extend it. The pointer to the memory and the new buffer size are passed as parameters.
tpfree	This function releases the memory from use as a buffer. The pointer allocated by tpalloc is passed in as a parameter.
tpservice	This function is the call for the service routine. The first parameter of the structure is the name of the service, and the fourth parameter is the size of the message passed to the server.
tpreturn	This function returns the result from a service routine. The fourth parameter is the size of the message returned from the service.

The size of the messages passed within the application server varies with the PeopleTools release, the complexity of the PIA components (or panel groups), and the amount of application data involved. Listing 13-7 shows an example of the additional trace information in the Tuxedo log. It shows a single ICPanel service call. The incoming message is 10,817 bytes in length. The service returns a message of 49,514 bytes.

Listing 13-7. Sample of a Tuxedo Log with Trace Information[8]

```
:  { tpservice({"ICPanel", 0x0, 0x27a20e0, 10817, 0, -1, {1082411157, 0, 29}})
:    { tpalloc("CARRAY", "", 8192)
:    } tpalloc = 0x35e0c48
:    { tprealloc(0x35e0c48, 65536)
:    } tprealloc = 0x4a0d020
:    { tprealloc(0x4a0d020, 131072)
:    } tprealloc = 0x4af40e0
:    { tpreturn(2, 0, 0x4af40e0, 49514, 0x0)
:    } tpreturn [long jump]
:  } tpservice
```

It is possible to analyze this trace and determine the number and sizes of the messages.

■ **Caution** Enabling this trace can have a noticeable impact on performance. It should not usually be used for long periods. It generates a lot of trace files very quickly. I generally find that a sample from a few minutes of activity is sufficient to demonstrate the message sizes.

There are two approaches to analyzing the trace file. The Unix shell and awk script in Listing 13-8 can be used to extract the distribution of message sizes.

Listing 13-8. `msglen.sh`: Script to Analyze Tuxedo Message Sizes

```
TUXLOG=$PS_HOME/appserv/DEVP8/LOGS
for i in $TUXLOG/TUXLOG.[0-1][0-9][0-3][0-9][0-9][0-9]
 do
    FILE=`basename $i`
    echo "$FILE \c"
    egrep -h "tpservice\(|tpreturn\(" $i | \
awk '{
        elements=split($4,var1,"(");
        if(var1[1]=="tpservice") {
            dir="c->s"
            elements=split($4,var1,"\"");
            service=var1[2]
        }
        if(var1[1]=="tpreturn") {
            dir="s->c"
        }
        elements=split($7,var1,",")
        size=var1[1]
```

---

[8] Edited for readability.

```
            print dir, service, size
}' | \
    sort -k3n,3 | \
    awk '{
        lineno++
        totsize+=$3
        print lineno, $1, $2, $3, totsize
    }' | \
    sort -rn | \
    awk 'BEGIN{
        printf("Message direction,Service name,Message size (bytes),")
        printf("Proportion of messages not larger than this message,")
        printf("Proportion of traffic in messages not larger than this message\n")
    }{
        if(lines==0) {
            lines=$1
            totsize=$5
            sizeleft=totsize
        }
        if($4>0) {
            printf("%s,%s,%d,%f,%f\n", $2, $3, $4, $1/lines, $5/totsize)
        }
    }' | \
    tee $FILE.msglen |\
    wc -l
done
```

Alternatively, the tuxlog file can be loaded into a database table, created by Listing 13-9, with SQL*Loader.

Listing 13-9. tuxlog_pre.sql

```
CREATE TABLE tuxlog
(timestamp  DATE            NOT NULL
,nodename   VARCHAR2(20) NOT NULL
,prcsname   VARCHAR2(20) NOT NULL
,prcsid     VARCHAR2(20) NOT NULL
,funcname   VARCHAR2(20) NOT NULL
    CONSTRAINT funcname CHECK (funcname IN('tpservice','tpreturn'))
,service    VARCHAR2(20) NOT NULL
,msg_size   NUMBER(8)
);
```

The funcname constraint on the table limits the rows loaded to just the two Tuxedo functions that report message sizes. By careful control of termination characters, it is possible to load the Tuxedo log directly into the database with SQL*Loader with the control file in Listing 13-10, without the need to reformat it.

Listing 13-10. `tuxlog.ldr`

```
LOAD DATA
INFILE 'TUXLOG.041904'
REPLACE
INTO TABLE tuxlog
FIELDS TERMINATED BY WHITESPACE
TRAILING NULLCOLS
(timestamp TERMINATED BY '.' "TO_DATE(:timestamp,'HH24MISS')"
,nodename   TERMINATED BY '!'
,prcsname   TERMINATED BY '.'
,prcsid     TERMINATED BY ':'
,dummy1     FILLER
,dummy2     FILLER
,funcname   TERMINATED BY '(' --function name
,service    TERMINATED BY ',' --"TRANSLATE('{','')"
,dummy3     FILLER TERMINATED BY ','
,dummy4     FILLER TERMINATED BY ','
,msg_size   TERMINATED BY ','
)
```

The data can then be extracted from the database into an Excel spreadsheet to produce a graph, as shown in Figure 13-6.

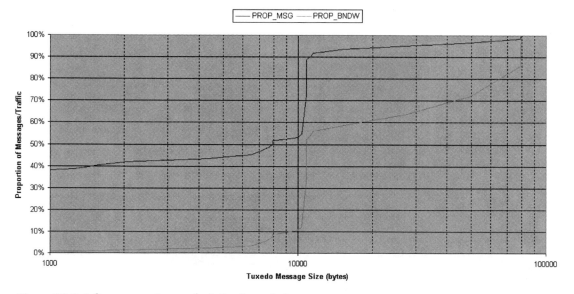

Figure 13-6. Jolt message size analysis (tuxlog.xls)

In the case of a few tests run on a demo HCM8.8/PeopleTools 8.44 database, most of the messages are under 11KB, so they would definitely fit in the default-sized 64KB queues. Just 4% of messages are over 48KB, and these account for 28% of the total message volume. You can't tell from this measurement that this is a performance problem. All you can say is that a potential problem exists.

Jolt Message Size Analysis Using PeopleSoft Performance Monitor

Performance Monitor Transaction 115 also records the size of the Jolt messages sent to and from the Jolt Server Listener (JSL) process (see Table 10-4). Message metrics can be queried and profiled with a single SQL statement using analytic functions (as shown in Listing 13-11). This query combines metrics from sent and received messages into a single profile.

Listing 13-11. Query to Profile Jolt Message Size Data (jolt_msg_anal_comb_115.sql)

```
SELECT jolt_bytes, cum_prop_msg, cum_prop_vol, num_messages
FROM (      SELECT z.*
    ,       SUM(prop_message) OVER (ORDER BY jolt_bytes
                                    RANGE UNBOUNDED PRECEDING) AS cum_prop_msg
    ,       SUM(prop_volume)  OVER (ORDER BY jolt_bytes
                                    RANGE UNBOUNDED PRECEDING) AS cum_prop_vol
    FROM    (   SELECT y.*
        ,       RATIO_TO_REPORT(num_messages) OVER () AS prop_message
        ,       RATIO_TO_REPORT(sum_bytes) OVER () AS prop_volume
        FROM    (   SELECT x.*, COUNT(*) num_messages, SUM(jolt_bytes) sum_bytes
            FROM    (
                SELECT c.pm_metric_value1 jolt_bytes
                FROM    pspmtranshist c, pspmagent b, pspmsysdefn a
                WHERE   a.pm_systemid = b.pm_systemid
                AND     b.pm_agentid = c.pm_agentid
                AND     c.pm_trans_defn_set = 1 AND c.pm_trans_defn_id = 115
                AND     c.pm_trans_status = 1
/*              AND     a.dbname IN(<list of database names>)
                AND     c.pm_agent_strt_dttm >= SYSDATE - 3*/
                UNION ALL
                SELECT c.pm_metric_value2 jolt_bytes
                FROM    pspmtranshist c, pspmagent b, pspmsysdefn a
                WHERE   a.pm_systemid = b.pm_systemid
                AND     b.pm_agentid = c.pm_agentid
                AND     c.pm_trans_defn_set = 1 AND c.pm_trans_defn_id = 115
                AND     c.pm_trans_status = 1
/*              AND     a.dbname IN(<list of database names>)
                AND     c.pm_agent_strt_dttm >= SYSDATE - 3*/
            ) x GROUP by jolt_bytes ) y ) Z
) ORDER BY jolt_bytes
/
```

This query can be used to extract the data into an Excel spreadsheet, in which it then can be graphed. Figure 13-7 shows a graph of data from a live PeopleTools 8.49 system. Only 6% of messages exceed the 48KB default limit on the IPC queues, but this accounts for 35% of messages by volume. The messages appear to be larger than the result obtain using the Tuxedo log in the previous section. Messages contain the application data loaded into PIA components. Therefore, their sizes vary from system to system depending on product, both application and PeopleTools versions and customization, and vary with time.

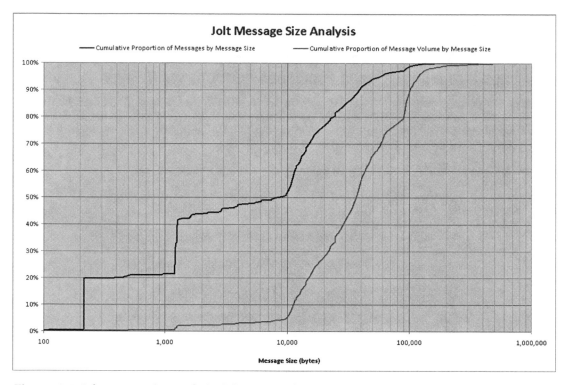

Figure 13-7. Jolt message size analysis (jolt_msg_anal_comb_115.xls)

Information from this analysis, using either source of metrics, can be used to justify a change to the Unix kernel parameters that control IPC queue sizing. In this case, increasing the queue size from 64KB to 128KB, and therefore increasing the maximum message size to 96KB, reduces the number of messages pinging to disk from 6% to 1.5%. More significantly, the total volume of messages pinged to disk falls from 35% to 12%.

Recommended IPC Parameter Changes

Messages of up to 100KB are typical in PeopleTools. Where possible, I suggest increasing the maximum message size to at least 128KB and possibly as far as 256KB if sufficient memory is available. There are always a few messages that don't fit in the queues. Ad hoc queries that are run online in the PIA and that generate large result sets can easily exceed this limit.

On Windows, it is possible to save tuned sets of IPC parameters (see Figure 13-8).

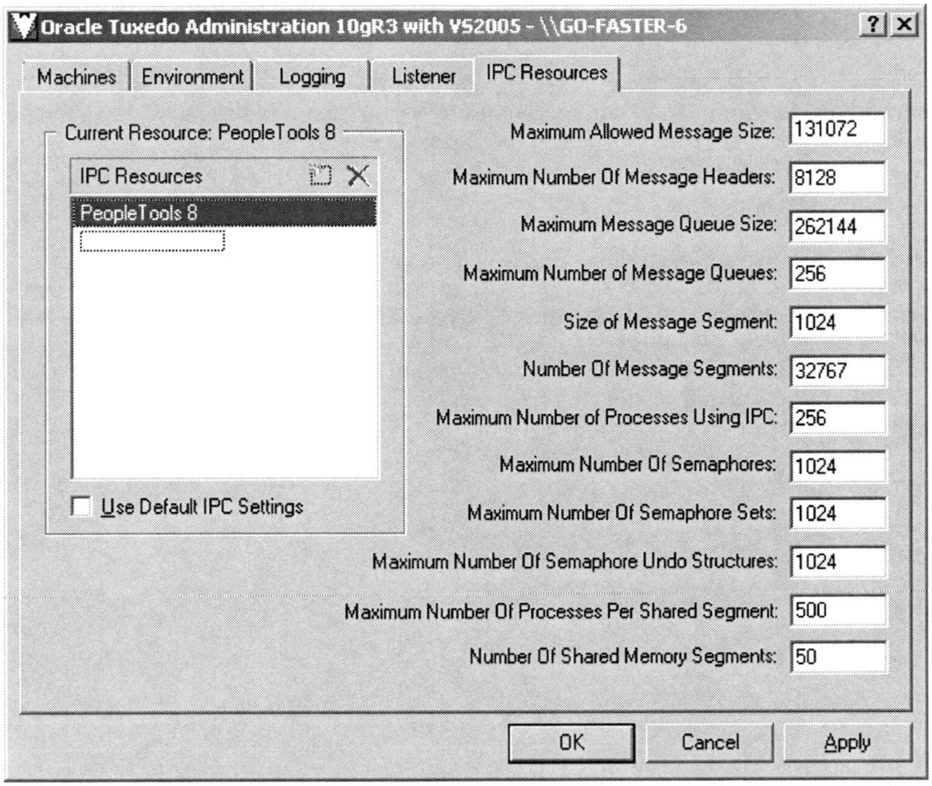

Figure 13-8. IPC settings tuned for PeopleSoft 8

On both Unix and Windows, the Message Size kernel parameter is a global setting and affects all messages in all Tuxedo domains.

The increase in the maximum message size increases the total amount of shared memory that could be used. Either additional message segments must be provided, or the size of the message segments should be increased. I have done both in order to satisfy the following formula:

```
Maximum Number of Message Queues * Maximum Message Queue Size
    = Number of Message Segments * Size of Message Segment
    = Total Memory Overhead of Message Queues
```

■ **Note** Not all of the kernel parameters can be set on all of the supported flavors of Unix, and sometimes they cannot be set as desired. For example, on HP-UX 11, the maximum message size that can be set is 64KB, although a larger value would be desirable.

Other Tuxedo Options

In the sections that follow, I describe a number of other Tuxedo features and options that PeopleSoft does not use in its delivered application server configurations. However, they can be easily incorporated; and, if used appropriately, they can improve or at least preserve system performance.

Operating System Priority

On Unix systems, the operating system scheduling priority of a process can be lowered with the nice command. Only the superuser (root) can increase the priority. When a server has no free CPU, processes with a lower priority get less time on the CPU. Where there is free CPU, the scheduling priority does not affect the amount of CPU the process can utilize.

When Tuxedo is run on Unix, the priority of server processes can be adjusted using the -n server option, as shown in Listing 13-12. The parameters to this option are simply passed through to the nice(2) function. Hence, this option does not work on Windows.

Listing 13-12. Extract from psappsrv.ubb

```
PSAPPSRV        SRVGRP=APPSRV
                SRVID=1
                MIN=2
                MAX=3
                RQADDR="APPQ"
                REPLYQ=Y

                CLOPT="-n 5 -o \"./LOGS/stdout\" -e \"./LOGS/stderr\" -p 1,600:1,1 -
s@psappsrv.lst -- -D HCM91 -S PSAPPSRV"
```

There are a number of potential uses for the -n server option:

- The operating system priority of a process is inherited from its parent. The priority of the Process Scheduler running under Tuxedo can be lowered so that batch processes also run with a lower priority. In PeopleTools 8.4, the priority of the Application Engine server processes can be lowered directly. This is discussed in more detail in Chapter 14.

- If the application server is co-resident with the database server, then the application server can be run at a lower priority to prevent it from starving the database of CPU. This is another example of keeping any queuing as high as possible in the application stack.

- A company running HR and Payroll has two web sites and two application servers connected to the same database: one for self-service HR and the other for the back-office HR department. The self-service application server is run at a lower priority.[9]

---

[9] The example is in production and has been put to the test. In the early days of the system, an e-mail was sent to all 30,000 employees telling them that they could see their pay slips online in the self-service HR application. A large proportion of them promptly tried it. This far exceeded the design specification

Load Balancing

Load balancing in a Tuxedo domain is relevant only if the same service is advertised on more than one queue. This is not the case in a PeopleTools 8 application server domain[10] unless multiple queues have been configured for the same application server, as described earlier in this chapter. Only larger systems, where more than ten PSAPPSRV processes are required, need to consider the load-balancing option.

In this section, I want to look at what Tuxedo does if there is a choice as to where a service request can be enqueued (see Figure 13-9).

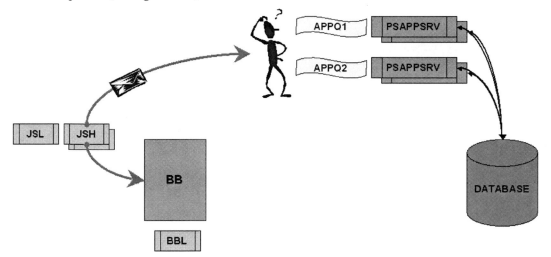

Figure 13-9. *Where to enqueue?*

If load balancing is not enabled, the request is placed on the first available queue. This can result in the queues receiving a significantly unequal load.

Load balancing is enabled in the RESOURCES section of the Tuxedo configuration file, as shown in Listing 13-13. In the delivered PeopleSoft configuration, it is disabled.

Listing 13-13. *Tuxedo RESOURCES Section from psappsrv.ubx with Load Balancing Enabled*

```
*RESOURCES
IPCKEY          {IPCKEY}        # ( 32768 < IPCKEY < 262143 )
MASTER          "{MACH}"
DOMAINID        {$Domain Settings\Domain ID}_{IPCKEY}
MODEL           SHM
LDBAL           Y
```

---

of the system. The self-service application server was completely overwhelmed, and performance was severely affected, but the back-office HR function was able to continue almost unaffected.

[10] Until PeopleTools 7.57, the services advertised on the PSQCKSRV were also advertised on PSAPPSRV. Tuxedo could enqueue requests for the quick services on either queue.

If load balancing is enabled, then Tuxedo places the request on a queue where there is an idle server process. If there is no idle server, then for each queue on which the request could be enqueued, the sum of the load of each of the service requests of the queue is calculated. The request is enqueued on the queue with the lower total load.

A useful analogy is a row of supermarket checkouts. Each checkout represents a queue offering a checkout service. The shoppers with their baskets represent the messages requesting the service. When you have finished shopping, how do you choose which checkout line to join? What most people do is look at the lines and make a judgment as to which line will take the shortest amount of time to get through. To put it a different way, which queue has the least load queued on it? That judgment is more sophisticated than simply counting the number of baskets; it involves an estimate of how many items are in the baskets.

This is exactly what Tuxedo does. It uses the definition of the service in the SERVICES section of the Tuxedo configuration file to obtain the load value for the service, and so sums the loads of all the service requests in the queue.

Unfortunately, all the services in a PeopleSoft domain are delivered with a load of 50 (see Figure 13-10). That is like saying all baskets in the supermarket take the same amount of time to get through the checkout. This is demonstrably not the case in both supermarkets and Tuxedo application servers.

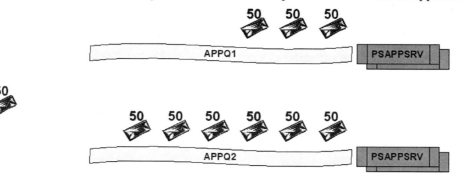

Figure 13-10. All PeopleSoft services are delivered with the same loads.

If you choose your supermarket checkout line simply on the basis of the number of baskets in the line, then you may get in a line behind three baskets filled to overflowing, in preference to six almost empty baskets in another line.

If load balancing is to be used, then realistic loads must be applied to the services.

■ **Note** If load balancing is enabled, you may find that the printqueue command in tmadmin incorrectly reports requests on the queue when in fact there are none.[11] This inaccuracy may have an effect on load balancing. It occurs because the shared memory–based statistics accuracy in Tuxedo defaults to "approximate." Setting it to "exact" (with the sstats ex command) prevents the inaccuracy, but at the cost of a small performance hit.

---

[11] See Oracle Support Document 765783.1: Tuxedo CR017477, "Shared memory–based statistics accuracy may influence the load balancing."

Calculating Service Loads

If the Tuxedo service trace (the -r option described in Chapter 9) is enabled, you get a log of every service that passes through an application server and the time it took to execute. The trace file can be processed directly with the Tuxedo txrpt utility to produce a summary report of performance (see Listing 13-14) that includes an average service time.

Listing 13-14. txrpt Report

```
SERVICE SUMMARY REPORT


SVCNAME          7a-8a      ...    14p-15p      TOTALS
                 Num/Avg    ...    Num/Avg      Num/Avg
---------------- --------   ...    --------     -------
ICPanel          471/0.64   ...    490/0.36     15875/0.53
ICScript         207/0.27   ...    94/0.29      4644/0.25
PortalRegistry   120/0.09   ...    27/0.09      1758/0.08
GetCertificate   23/0.24    ...    13/0.19      625/0.18
HomepageT        30/0.27    ...    7/0.24       464/0.25
PsmChkRptAuth    3/0.01     ...    0/0.00       211/0.01
FileAttach       0/0.00     ...    0/0.00       7/0.05
ICWorkList       1/0.55     ...    0/0.00       4/0.48
---------------- -------    ...    -------      -------
TOTALS           855/0.45   ...    631/0.34     23588/0.42
```

If the load on the queue is to be a measure of how long it is likely to take to get onto the server, then the load for a service should be proportional to the average execution time. So set the service load in the SERVICES section of psappsrv.ubx to be the duration of the service, as shown in Listing 13-15.

Listing 13-15. Extract from psappsrv.ubx

```
PortalRegistry  SRVGRP=APPSRV
                LOAD=8 PRIO=50
                SVCTIMEOUT={$PSAPPSRV\Service Timeout}
                BUFTYPE="ALL"

ICPanel         SRVGRP=APPSRV
                LOAD=53 PRIO=50
                SVCTIMEOUT={$PSAPPSRV\Service Timeout}
                BUFTYPE="ALL"

ICScript        SRVGRP=APPSRV
                LOAD=25 PRIO=50
                SVCTIMEOUT={$PSAPPSRV\Service Timeout}
                BUFTYPE="ALL"

HomepageT       SRVGRP=APPSRV
                LOAD=25 PRIO=50
                SVCTIMEOUT={$PSAPPSRV\Service Timeout}
                BUFTYPE="ALL"
```

Figure 13-11 shows a contrived but entirely plausible scenario. The load of three ICPanel requests on APPQ1 is 159, but the load of six services on APPQ2 is only 154. The new request is enqueued on APPQ2, then, because although there are more requests, their total load is lower, and the request should reach the server process more quickly.

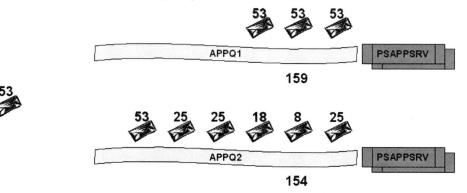

Figure 13-11. Load balancing with realistic loads

The load of a service can also be changed dynamically in the tmadmin utility with the changeload (or chl) command, as shown in Listing 13-16.

Listing 13-16. Dynamically Changing the Load of a Service in tmadmin

```
> help scp
serviceparms (scp) -g groupname -i srvid -s service
----------------------------------------------------
Print the parameters associated with the specified service.

> scp -g APPSRV -i 1 -s ICPanel
    Service Name: ICPanel
   Function Name: ICPanel
            Load: 50
        Priority: 50
         Address: 0xa

> help chl
changeload (chl) [-m machine] {-q qaddress [-g groupname] [-i srvid]
        [-s service] | -g groupname -i srvid -s service |
        -I interface [-g groupname]} newload
---------------------------------------------------------------------------
Change the load associated with the specified service or interface.

> chl -g APPSRV -i 1 -s ICPanel 53
2 entries changed.

> scp -g APPSRV -i 1 -s ICPanel
    Service Name: ICPanel
   Function Name: ICPanel
```

```
          Load: 53
      Priority: 50
       Address: 0xa

> scp -g APPSRV -i 2 -s ICPanel
  Service Name: ICPanel
 Function Name: ICPanel
          Load: 53
      Priority: 50
       Address: 0xa
```

So performance improvements can be attempted by adjusting service loads without downtime, and they can be reversed if they are not successful. If they are successful, they can be added to the domain configuration. The load can also be changed dynamically via the Administration Console.

Even though you have to specify a server in the changepriority (or chp) command on which to change the load of a service, it applies to all the servers on that queue. The queue is identified in terms of the server ID.

If the service is advertised on several queues in the same group, the serviceparams (or scp) command only changes the load of the service for the one queue where the specified server ID resides. Note that the Tuxedo configuration permits only the service load to be specified for all the queues and servers in a group.

Service Priority

The priority of a service controls how it is dequeued by the server processes. Higher priority requests are dequeued first (see Figure 13-12). However, a lower priority message does not remain forever enqueued, because every tenth message is also retrieved from the front of the queue.

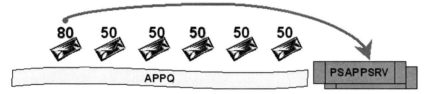

Figure 13-12. Service dequeuing priority

As noted previously, PeopleSoft delivers all services with a priority of 50, so it is always the request at the front of the queue that is dequeued. Adjusting service priorities is unlikely to be beneficial to configure in PeopleSoft systems, and I have included it mainly to distinguish load and priority.

A possible use might be to give ICScript services a higher priority so that navigation responds more quickly. A user might make have to make a number of selections to navigate the menu hierarchy before entering a panel. If a system is exhibiting queuing in the application server, menu accesses also degrades. Menu-navigation performance would be improved at the expense of component response.

The priority of a service can also be changed dynamically in the tmadmin utility with the changepriority command, as shown in Listing 13-17, or via the Administration Console.

Listing 13-17. Dynamically Changing the Priority of a Service in tmadmin

```
> scp -g APPSRV -i 1 -s ICScript
   Service Name: ICScript
  Function Name: ICScript
           Load: 50
       Priority: 50
        Address: 0xc

> help chp
changepriority (chp) [-m machine] {-q qaddress [-g groupname] [-i srvid]
      [-s service] | -g groupname -i srvid -s service |
      -I interface [-g groupname]} newpri
--------------------------------------------------------------------
Change the dequeuing priority associated with the specified service
or interface.

> chp -g APPSRV -i 1 -s ICScript 80
2 entries changed.

> scp -g APPSRV -i 2 -s ICScript
   Service Name: ICScript
  Function Name: ICScript
           Load: 50
       Priority: 80
        Address: 0xc
```

The comments made in the previous section about the scope of the changeload command and service load also apply to the changepriority command and service priority.

Other Tips

Finally, I would like to mention a few configuration options that can make administration of the PeopleSoft application server a little easier, particularly in an environment with a requirement of high availability.

Unix User Accounts

It is common for a single physical Unix server to run several application server domains, especially in development environments. It is advisable to have each Tuxedo domain running under a different Unix user account. The IPC resources created by the domain are owned by the Unix user running the domain, and the owner can be seen in the output of the ipcs command. Hence it is easy to associate IPC resources with a particular domain.

Occasionally, a Tuxedo domain can lock up, and you need to kill the IPC resources associated with that domain. PeopleSoft even provides a script, killipc.sh, to do that. It finds and deletes all the IPC resources owned by a particular Unix user and group.

The situation is complicated if several domains are running as the same Unix user. Although it is possible to work out which process belongs to which domain from the process's command line that can be seen from the ps command, it is only possible to identify IPC resources from the process ID of the last process to access them. However, some of the IPC queues (described in Chapter 2) may not have been used by any process. It is then impossible to determine the domain to which they belong. You then have no alternative but to shut down all the Tuxedo domains running under that Unix account and kill any outstanding IPC resources. This loss of service would be bad enough in a development system, but in production environment it could be much more serious.

Multiple Domains on Small Production Systems

If you operate with only a single application server domain in production, it is still useful to configure the servlet to reference a second server so that you can make configuration changes to the application server without requiring system downtime.

A second application server domain can be started, and then the first can be shut down and reconfigured. The users are automatically reconnected to the surviving application server without any error message. There is no loss of service, although the users might experience a temporary loss of performance.

Cycling the Application Server Without Shutting It Down

Occasionally (usually after an application upgrade) it may be necessary to recycle the PSAPPSRV processes in order to clear the in-memory cache of PeopleTools objects, so the application change that was upgraded is recognized and loaded. Instead of recycling the whole application server, you can use the stop and boot commands of the tmadmin interface to stop and restart individual server processes. As long as you start with more than a single PSAPPSRV process, there is no loss of service for the users, although again they may experience some loss of performance.

It is possible to automate this process with a Unix shell script, as shown in Listing 13-18.

Listing 13-18. Extract from tuxcycle.sh Showing Recycling of PSAPPSRV Processes

```
tuxcmd() {
(
$TUXDIR/bin/tmadmin -r <<! 2>/dev/null
psr
!
) | grep "PSAPPSRV" | grep "APPQ" | sort  |\
awk '
{
    printf("stop -g %s -i %s\n",$3,$4);
    printf("boot -g %s -i %s\n",$3,$4);
}'
}
)
$TUXDIR/bin/tmadmin <<! 2>&1
`tuxcmd`
!
```

The procedure tuxcmd() lists the PSAPPSRV processes and formats the commands with awk; they are then piped into another tmadmin session that executes them.

Reconfiguring Tuxedo with the Administration Console

You can make changes to various settings, such as service loads and priorities, in both the Tuxedo Administration Console and the tmadmin interface. Other settings can be changed only in the Administration Console, such as server command-line options. You can see in Figure 13-13 that I have changed the name of the Tuxedo standard error file to APPQ_HR88.stderr2 in the executable options.

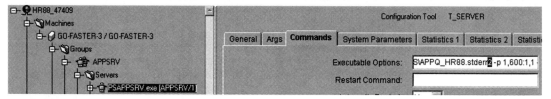

Figure 13-13. *Setting a server command line in the Tuxedo Administration Console*

■ **Caution** There is a significant difference between tmadmin and the Tuxedo Administration Console when making dynamic configuration changes. Changes made via tmadmin persist only until the domain is shut down, and they are lost when the domain is restarted. The Tuxedo Administration Console not only changes the current settings for the server, but also updates the compiled Tuxedo configuration file, PSTUXCFG—but not any other file! Therefore, the setting persists until the domain is reconfigured in psadmin, at which point the change is lost because the configuration file is compiled from psappsrv.ubb.

The PSTUXCFG file can be decompiled with the Tuxedo tmunloadcf utility,[12] as shown in Listing 13-19.

Listing 13-19. *tmunloadcf Decompiling the Tuxedo Configuration File PSTUXCFG*

```
rem tmunloadcf.bat
set PS_SERVDIR=D:\ps\hr88\appserv\HR88
set TUXCONFIG=%PS_SERVDIR%\PSTUXCFG
set TUXDIR=D:\ps\bea\Tuxedo8.1
set PATH=%TUXDIR%/bin;%PATH%
%TUXDIR%\bin\tmunloadcf > tmunloadcf.txt
```

The output from tmunloadcf is similar to psappsrv.ubb, but it includes all default values and excludes any comments. The new definition for the command-line options for PSAPPSRV that were set in the console (as shown in Figure 13-13) can be seen in Listing 13-20.

---

[12] See Oracle Tuxedo 10g Release 3 (10.3) ➤ Reference Topics ➤ Command Reference ➤ Section 1 - Commands ➤ tmunloadcf
(http://download.oracle.com/docs/cd/E13161_01/tuxedo/docs10gr3/rfcm/rfcmd.html#wp1001507).

Listing 13-20. Decompiled Tuxedo Configuration File

```
"PSAPPSRV"    SRVGRP="APPSRV"    SRVID=1
  CLOPT="-r -e D:\ps\hr88\appserv\HR88\LOGS\APPQ_HR88.stderr2 -p 1,600:1,1
-s@..\psappsrv.lst -s@..\psqcksrv.lst -sICQuery -sSqlQuery:SqlRequest -- -C psappsrv.cfg
-D HR88 -S PSAPPSRV"
  RQADDR="APPQ"
  RQPERM=0660    REPLYQ=Y    RPPERM=0660    MIN=1    MAX=3    CONV=N
  SYSTEM_ACCESS=FASTPATH
  MAXGEN=6    GRACE=60    RESTART=Y
  MINDISPATCHTHREADS=0    MAXDISPATCHTHREADS=1    THREADSTACKSIZE=0
  SICACHEENTRIESMAX="500"
```

If you want to permanently retain any configuration changes that you have made with the console, they must be manually transferred into psappsrv.ubx and psappsrv.cfg.

■ **Tip** It is helpful to keep a decompiled version of the Tuxedo configuration before making any changes in the console. If, having made changes, you decompile the configuration file again, you can compare the two files to identify any Tuxedo changes.

Summary

This chapter completes the final piece of the application server jigsaw. You should now be able to monitor the application server, and size and adjust it so that it is not causing a performance bottleneck. In which case, you should be left with SQL performance issues that should be easier to diagnose.

CHAPTER 14

The Process Scheduler

The Process Scheduler is an agent that initiates batch and report processes on a server. Although this element of PeopleSoft infrastructure is only of limited direct interest to the DBA, there are some aspects of the Process Scheduler of which you should be aware.

In this chapter, I describe the architecture and configuration of the Process Scheduler, and the data that is set up when a process is scheduled to be run by an operator in the PIA. I also discuss some configuration options and administrative tasks that can prevent the overhead of the Process Schedulers and batch programs from affecting the performance of the whole system.

When a process is scheduled to run, a number of request records are inserted into various tables in the database. Process Schedulers regularly poll these tables looking for work. The polling frequency is configured in the Server Definition (see Figure 14-4, later in the chapter).

A number of Process Scheduler definitions for different operating systems are delivered with PeopleTools. Most installations configure Process Schedulers to use these delivered definitions before creating further definitions.

It is usual to configure schedulers for the same PeopleSoft database on at least two separate physical servers in order to avoid a single point of failure, and sometimes more if demand requires. Sometimes, it is also necessary to configure more than one Process Scheduler on the same server.

A process may be scheduled to run on a specific scheduler or on any scheduler that is available. From PeopleTools 8.4, process requests can be load balanced across schedulers. A process may be scheduled to run at a particular time in the future and to recur on a regular schedule.

Processes can be grouped into jobs. A job (the process type is PSJob) can be configured to run its processes either sequentially or in parallel. *Schedule JobSets* contain processes and jobs in a hierarchical structure. They also specify a schedule, recurrence, and run control for a process. They are a more robust alternative to scheduling a recurring process. Process Scheduler request records are created for jobs and JobSets as well as the processes within them.

Some process types, such as nVision and Crystal Reports, can run only on Windows. Unix-based systems often require a Process Scheduler on a Windows server. Other process types, including Application Engine, SQR, and COBOL, can run on any platform

As with the application server, the configuration of the Process Scheduler can be used to restrict the workload on the database. The Process Scheduler workload can be restricted in various ways. Each scheduler can be configured to run concurrently no more than a maximum number of processes and not more than a maximum number of a particular type of process (including not running that type at all). Processes can be grouped into categories, and a maximum number of concurrent processes can be defined for the category.

Process Scheduler Architecture

From PeopleTools 8.4, the Process Scheduler became a fully -fledged Tuxedo domain (as depicted in Figure 14-1). In earlier versions, the Process Scheduler was a single stand-alone process. Tuxedo provides a more robust way to manage and start the Process Scheduler process and the other processes that have been added:

- The Tuxedo domain is collectively called the Process Scheduler, but the Process Scheduler itself is just the PSPRCSRV server process. Processes are initiated by the PSPRCSRV process.

- The Distribution Agent, another Tuxedo server process called PSDSTSRV, transfers report, log, and other output files to the Report Repository. The Report Repository is a shared filesystem accessible to the web servers. The Distribution Agent is usually configured to post files via HTTP to the Report Repository servlets that write to the shared filesystem. The Distribution Agent can also transfer files via FTP or XCOPY directly to the shared filesystem.

- The Master Process Scheduler, PSMSTSRV, is an optional server process. It balances the load between the various Process Schedulers on a system by assigning queued requests to different Process Schedulers.

- Application Engine can run either as a Tuxedo server processes or as a stand-alone processes initiated by the Process Scheduler.

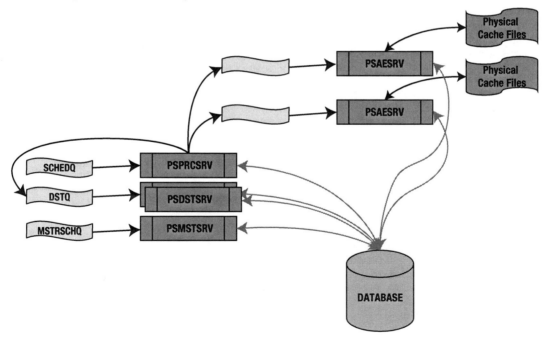

Figure 14-1. *Process Scheduler Tuxedo domain*

The configuration process for the Tuxedo domain for the Process Scheduler is very similar to that of the application server described in Chapter 12. Whereas most of the application file names are psappsrv.*, the Process Scheduler files are called psprcsrv.*, with the same extensions. The exception is that the configuration file is psprcs.cfg. PeopleSoft's ubbgen utility is used to merge the configuration file and the Tuxedo template to generate a Tuxedo configuration file (psprcsrv.ubb).

However, the Process Scheduler domain has some significant differences from the application server domain described in Chapters 2, 12, and 13. First, the Process Scheduler domain has no external clients and so has no listener processes. Instead, server processes in the Process Scheduler domain respond to Tuxedo service requests issued by the Process Scheduler server process, PSPRCSRV.

In the application server, the Tuxedo service calls to the PSAPPSRV and PSQRYSRV processes are synchronous because they have to send a message back to the PIA user session. However, this is not the case with the Process Scheduler domain. When report output and log files have to be transferred to the Report Repository, the Process Scheduler generates a PostReport service call, which is routed by Tuxedo via the DSTQ queue to the Report Distribution Agent, PSDSTSRV. In the Tuxedo trace in Listing 14-1, you can see that the Process Scheduler submits the service asynchronously, with the tpacall() function.[1]

Listing 14-1. Tuxedo Trace for the PostReport Service Call

```
185104.GO-FASTER-6!PSPRCSRV.3180.6600.-2: TRACE:at
  :  { tpacall("PostReport", 0x06F61190, 48, 0x7)
185104.GO-FASTER-6!PSPRCSRV.3180.6600.-2: TRACE:at
  :  } tpacall = 0 [CLIENTID {0, 0, 0}]
...
185104.GO-FASTER-6!PSDSTSRV.5352.5652.0: TRACE:at
  :  { tpservice({"PostReport", 0x4, 0x06EBAD70, 48, 0, -2147483648, {0, 0, 0}})
```

Once the PostReport message is successfully enqueued, the Process Scheduler does not wait for a reply. The PostReport service continues to process after tpacall() returns a response.

Master Process Scheduler

The Master Process Scheduler permits different processes within the same job to run on different Process Schedulers and therefore on different operating systems. For example, you might have a job consisting of a COBOL process followed by a Crystal Reports process. If you only have a COBOL compiler on Unix, the COBOL process must be run on Unix, but the Crystal Reports process can run only on Windows.

Although optional, the Master Process Scheduler should always be configured if you have more than one Process Scheduler. You should always configure more than one domain with a Master Process Scheduler process so that you do not have a single point of failure. Only one of the Master Process Scheduler processes acts as the master. Another automatically takes over if the active master process terminates.

---

[1] The tpcall() function sends a service request and waits for a reply message, but tpacall() does not wait for the reply message. These functions are defined in the BEA documentation "ATMI C Function Reference, Section 3c" (see
http://docs.oracle.com/cd/E13161_01/tuxedo/docs10gr3/rf3c/rf3c.html#wp1037129).

Application Engine

Up to PeopleTools 8.1, the Application Engine was only a stand-alone executable initiated by the Process Scheduler. From PeopleTools 8.4, it was also delivered as a Tuxedo server process. If PSAESRV is used, the Tuxedo domain should be configured to run as many PSAESRV processes as the Process Scheduler can run concurrent Application Engine programs. Otherwise, you get a warning message in the Process Scheduler log file similar to the one shown in Listing 14-2.

Listing 14-2. Extract from SCHDLR_<mmdd>.LOG[2]

```
PeopleTools Release 8.51 (WinX86) starting. Tuxedo server is BASE(1)/101
Cache Directory being used: C:\app\pt\appserv\prcs\HCM91PSNT\CACHE\CACHE\PSPRCSRV_101\
    Log Fence is set to 3 = Display detailed message
Max Server Setting for Server: PSAESRV, Server Group AESRV, Server ID: 1, Group No: 101
Validating Application Engine Server Setup....
        Processes with Generic Process Type of Application Engine:
                Application Engine      :   3
                XML Publisher           :   3
                Optimization Engine     :   2
                Total:                      8
        Server Max Concurrent Task Allowed    5
        Application Engine Max Instances:     2
Warning:  System has detected the Process Scheduler Server is not set with the required
minimum Application Engine Tuxedo Server needed to run the maximum concurrency based on
Process Scheduler Server Setting.  It is recommended to have PSAESRV instance in the Process
Scheduler Config file set to 5. The current max max instance setting for the Application
Engine is 2.
```

Nothing untoward happens in this situation. The Process Scheduler attempts to run only as many concurrent Application Engine programs as there are PSAESRV processes.

■ **Note** If you manually shut down one of the PSAESRV processes, the service that it advertises is no longer available. The Process Scheduler may still attempt to run a program on the deactivated process by requesting that service. The request fails, and the NET.334 error message is found in the scheduler's error log, SCHDLR_<mmdd>.log. The process scheduler then tries another PSAESRV process until successful.

```
(NET.334): Tuxedo cannot find the service RunAeAsync1.  Make sure the application server
advertising this service is booted.

        Process Scheduler encountered an error sending the request to the AE Tuxedo Server

(NET.113): Client RunAeAsync2 service request succeeded
```

---

[2] This and other traces in this chapter have been edited for readability.

A separate inbound Tuxedo message queue is created for each PSAESRV process. Each PSAESRV server dynamically advertises two routines as services on startup,[3] as shown in the Tuxedo trace in Listing 14-3. The server ID, in this case 2, is appended to the routine name to form the service name.

Listing 14-3. Tuxedo Trace of a PeopleTools 8.51 PSAESRV Process Startup

```
{ tpsvrinit(24, "PSAESRV -C dom=PSNT_62503 -g 101 -i 2 -u GO-FASTER-6 -U
C:\app\pt\appserv\prcs\HCM91PSNT\LOGS\TUXLOG -m 0 -o .\LOGS\stdout -e .\LOGS\stderr -- -CD
HCM91 -S PSAESRV")
...
  { tpadvertise("RunAeAsync2", 0x00402BF0)
  } tpadvertise = 1 [tperrno TPENOENT]
  { tpadvertise("ChkAeStatus2", 0x00402D30)
  } tpadvertise = 1 [tperrno TPENOENT]
} tpsvrinit = 0 [tperrno TPENOENT]
```

Therefore, each Application Engine service is advertised on only a single server process. By choosing the service name, the Process Scheduler effectively chooses which Application Engine server process handles the request. PSPRCSRV submits a RunAEAsyncn service request to a PSAESRV server to initiate an Application Engine program on the server.

The service is submitted synchronously via tpcall() so that the Process Scheduler knows when the service has reached a server process, but the service routine completes immediately on the server although the Application Engine program continues to run. From PeopleTools 8.44, the Process Scheduler periodically checks that the Application Engine program is running with the CheckAEStatusn service. This implies that PSAESRV is a threaded process, where one thread runs the CheckAEStatusn service while another runs the Application Engine program.

Process Monitor

PeopleSoft provides a PIA component called the Process Monitor to enable users to view the Process Scheduler requests and to retrieve reports and log files via the browser. This page, shown in Figure 14-2, is essentially a view of the table PSPRCSRQST.

---

[3] Earlier versions of PeopleTools 8.4 also advertised a third function, CnclAeProg, as a service.

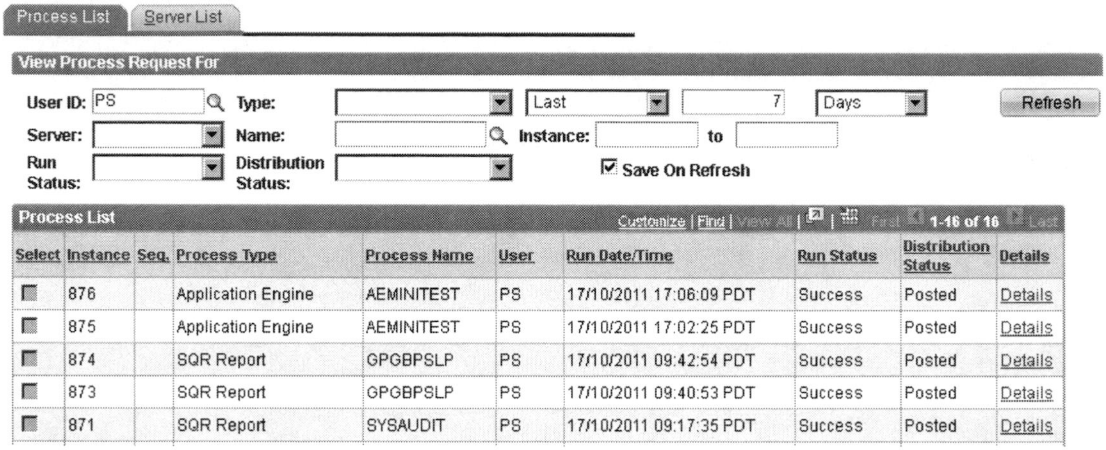

Figure 14-2. *Process Monitor*

DBA Issues

Several aspects of the Process Scheduler are of concern to the DBA. I discuss a number of these issues in the sections that follow.

What Happens When a Process Is Scheduled?

In this section, I walk through the SQL that is generated when a report process is scheduled via a component in the PIA. This explains the information the Process Scheduler needs in order to run a batch process. The SQL can be extracted with the PeopleTools trace. The following SQL was generated when I scheduled the Print GBR Payslips SQR report GPGBPSLP, and it was captured in a PeopleTools trace of the SQL. For clarity, I have replaced the bind variables with the literal values.

The PIA component HC_GPGB_PSLIP, shown in Figure 14-3, is used to create a request to schedule the GPGBPSLP report (and other processes).

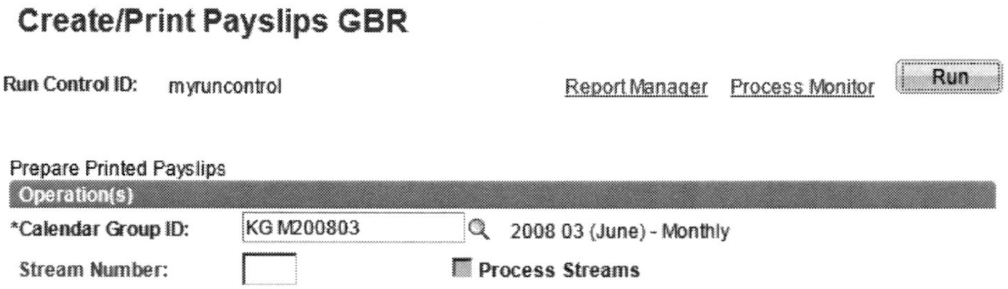

Figure 14-3. *Component to schedule a Payslips report*

The component sets up *run control records* that are used to pass parameters to the scheduled process. Different processes can either share or have different run control records, depending on what parameters need to be passed to them. In Listing 14-4, the table PS_GPGB_PSLIP is specific to the payslip process and is used to pass parameters specific to the process.

Listing 14-4. Setting Up Process-Specific Run Control Records

```
INSERT INTO PS_GPGB_PSLIP
(RUN_CNTL_ID,OPRID,CAL_RUN_ID,STRM_NUM,RUN_CALC_IND,RUN_FINAL_IND)
VALUES('myruncontrol' ,'PS', 'KG M200803' ,0 ,' ' ,'N')
```

Next, a row to hold the output destination options for the report is inserted (see Listing 14-5). For now, it only holds dummy values; the values are updated later (see Listing 14-11).

Listing 14-5. Destination Operations

```
INSERT INTO PS_PRCSRUNCNTLDTL
(OPRID, RUNCNTLID, PRCSTYPE, PRCSNAME, OUTDESTTYPE, OUTDESTFORMAT, OUTDEST
, PSRF_FOLDER_NAME,  PRCSFILENAME, EMAIL_WEB_RPT, EMAIL_LOG_FLAG, PT_RETENTIONDAYS)
VALUES ('PS' ,'myruncontrol' ,'SQR Report' ,'GPGBPSLP' ,'1' ,'1' ,' ' ,' ' ,' ' ,'0' ,'0' ,0)
```

PeopleSoft has separate sequence numbers for scheduled processes and report output. Sequence numbers are incremented and then selected, as shown in Listing 14-6.

▒ **Note** PeopleSoft does not use Oracle sequences.

Listing 14-6. Obtaining the Next Process Request and Content Sequences Numbers

```
UPDATE PS_PRCSSEQUENCE
SET    SEQUENCENO = SEQUENCENO + 1
WHERE  PRCSSEQKEY = 0
```

Distribution and content request records are inserted as shown in Listing 14-7. By convention, tables with *PRCS* in their name are related to the process, and tables with *CDM* in their name are related to the distribution of process and report output and log files. PeopleSoft sometimes refers to report output as *content*. The acronym CDM stands for *Content and Distribution Management*.

Listing 14-7. Creating the Distribution Request and Content Records

```
RCSINSTANCE,DISTID,DISTIDTYPE) VALUES (874, 'PS', 2);
INSERT INTO  PS_CDM_AUTH ( PRCSINSTANCE,CONTENTID,DISTID,DISTIDTYPE) VALUES
(874, 8, 'PS', 2);
INSERT INTO  PS_CDM_LIST (PRCSINSTANCE, CONTENTID, PRCSNAME, PRCSTYPE,
CONTENT_DESCR, OUTDESTFORMAT, RQSTDTTM, ENDDTTM, EXPIRATION_DATE, DISTSTATUS,
DISTNODENAME, OUTPUTDIR, ADMIN_FILENAME, TRANSFERINSTANCE, PRCSOUTPUTDIR,
GENPRCSTYPE, LOGFILEONLY_FLAG, FILENAME, PSRF_FOLDER_NAME, PRCSBURSTRPT)
VALUES (874, 695, 'GPGBPSLP', 'SQR Report', ' Printed Payslip ', 2
, CAST(SYSTIMESTAMP AS TIMESTAMP), TO_TIMESTAMP('','YYYY-MM-DD-HH24.MI.SS.FF')
, TO_DATE('2011-10-24','YYYY-MM-DD'), 1, 'GO-FASTER-6', ' ', 'index.html', 0
, ' ', 1, 0, ' ', ' ', 0);
```

The PSPRCSPARMS table holds the parameters for the process request. These mostly come from the process-type definition. You can see in Listing 14-8 that environmental variables and the access ID and password (explained in Chapter 3) are left as variables, which are substituted by the Process Scheduler at run time.

Listing 14-8. *Inserting a Run-Time Parameter Record*

```
INSERT INTO PSPRCSPARMS (PRCSINSTANCE, PARMLIST, WORKINGDIR, CMDLINE, OUTDEST
, ORIGPARMLIST, ORIGOUTDEST, PRCSOUTPUTDIR, PRCSPARMEXTFLAG, PRCSFILENAME )
VALUES
(874, '-CT ORACLE -CS %SERVER% -CD HCM91 -CA %ACCESSID% -CAP %ACCESSPSWD% -RP
SYSAUDIT -I 874 -R myruncontrol -CO PS -OT 6 -OP "%LOG/OUTPUT DIRECTORY%" -OF 2
-LG ENG', '%DBBIN%', '%TOOLBINSRV%\PSSQR.EXE', '%%Log/Output Directory%%', '-CT
ORACLE -CS %SERVER% -CD HCM91 -CA %ACCESSID% -CAP %ACCESSPSWD% -RP GPGBPSLP -I
868 -R myruncontrol -CO PS -OT 6 -OP "%LOG/OUTPUT DIRECTORY%" -OF 2 -LG ENG',
'%%Log/Output Directory%%', ' ', '0', ' ')
```

The table PSPRCSQUE was added in PeopleTools 8.1[4] (see Listing 14-9). It holds information needed to schedule the request and to check that it is still running. The Process Scheduler uses PSPRCSQUE while the processes themselves update PSPRCSRQST.

When the process is initiated, the operating system process ID of the client process is stored in the column SESSIONIDNUM on this table.[5] This information is needed should the Process Scheduler need to kill the process.

Listing 14-9. *Creating a New Process Request Record*

```
INSERT INTO PSPRCSQUE (PRCSINSTANCE, JOBINSTANCE, PRCSJOBSEQ, PRCSJOBNAME,
PRCSTYPE, PRCSNAME, RUNLOCATION, OPSYS, SERVERNAMERQST, SERVERNAMERUN, RUNDTTM,
RECURDTTM, RECURNAME, OPRID, PRCSPRTY, SESSIONIDNUM, RUNSTATUS, RQSTDTTM,
LASTUPDDTTM, RUNCNTLID, PRCSRTNCD, CONTINUEJOB, USERNOTIFIED, INITIATEDNEXT,
OUTDESTTYPE, OUTDESTFORMAT, ORIGPRCSINSTANCE, GENPRCSTYPE, RESTARTENABLED,
TIMEZONE, MAINJOBNAME, MAINJOBSEQ, MAINJOBINSTANCE, PRCSITEMLEVEL,
EMAIL_WEB_RPT, EMAIL_LOG_FLAG, PSRF_FOLDER_NAME, SERVERASSIGN, SCHEDULENAME,
PRCSWINPOP, MCFREN_URL_ID, RECURORIGPRCSINST, RETRYCOUNT, P_PRCSINSTANCE,
PRCSCATEGORY, PRCSCURREXPIREDDTTM, DISTSTATUS, RUNSERVEROPTION, PT_RETENTIONDAYS,
PRCSRUNNOTIFY, TUXSVCID, PTNONUNPRCSID)
VALUES (874, 0, 0, ' ', 'SQR Report', 'GPGBPSLP', '2', '2', 'PSNT', ' ',
TO_TIMESTAMP('2011-10-17-09.42.54.000000','YYYY-MM-DD-HH24.MI.SS.FF'), NULL,
' ', 'PS', 5, 0, '5', CAST(SYSTIMESTAMP AS TIMESTAMP),  CAST(SYSTIMESTAMP AS
TIMESTAMP), 'myruncontrol', 0,  0, 0, 0, '6', '2', 874, '1', '0', ' ', ' ', 0,
0, 0, '0', '0', ' ',  'PSNT', ' ', '0', ' ', 874, 0, 0, 'Default', NULL, '1',
```

---

[4] I believe this was done by PeopleSoft to mitigate the effect on Microsoft SQL Server where updates would block queries in Read Committed mode. However, this has not been an issue since the introduction of the Read Committed Snapshot isolation level (which is similar to Oracle's statement-level read consistency) in SQL Server 2005. This shows how decisions made to work around problems on one database platform get into the product for all platforms, and once in the product they tend to stay there.

[5] When an SQR is run, PSPRCSQUE.SESSIONIDNUM contains the process ID of the PSSQR wrapper program, which calls the SQR program, and not the SQR program itself. From PeopleTools 8.4, the server ID of the Application Engine server process is stored in PSPRCSQUE.SESSIONIDNUM, and not the PID of the server process.

```
'1', 7, '0' ,0 , ' ')
```

Before PSPRCSQUE was added, all the information needed to schedule the process was held on PSPRCSRQST (see Listing 14-10). So, for historical reasons, there is some duplication of information between these two tables.

Only PSPRCSRQST holds the start and end times for each process, which can be viewed via the Process Monitor component. Therefore, this table is of interest when trying to quantify batch performance.

Listing 14-10. Creating a Process Request Record

```
INSERT INTO PSPRCSRQST (PRCSINSTANCE, JOBINSTANCE, PRCSJOBSEQ, PRCSJOBNAME,
PRCSTYPE, PRCSNAME, RUNLOCATION, OPSYS, DBNAME, DBTYPE, SERVERNAMERQST,
SERVERNAMERUN, RUNDTTM, RECURNAME, OPRID, PRCSVERSION, RUNSTATUS, RQSTDTTM,
LASTUPDDTTM, BEGINDTTM, ENDDTTM, RUNCNTLID, PRCSRTNCD, CONTINUEJOB,
USERNOTIFIED, INITIATEDNEXT, OUTDESTTYPE, OUTDESTFORMAT, ORIGPRCSINSTANCE,
GENPRCSTYPE, RESTARTENABLED, TIMEZONE, MAINJOBNAME, MAINJOBSEQ, MAINJOBINSTANCE,
PRCSITEMLEVEL, PSRF_FOLDER_NAME, SCHEDULENAME, RETRYCOUNT, P_PRCSINSTANCE, RECURORIGPRCSINST,
DISTSTATUS, PRCSCATEGORY, PRCSCURREXPIREDTTM, RUNSERVEROPTION, PT_RETENTIONDAYS, CONTENTID,
PTNONUNPRCSID) VALUES
(874, 0, 0, ' ', 'SQR Report', 'GPGBPSLP', '2', '2', 'HCM91', '2', 'PSNT', ' ',
TO_TIMESTAMP('2011-10-15-23.19.48.000000_,'YYYY-MM-DD-HH24.MI.SS.FF'), ' ',
'PS', 0, '5', CAST(SYSTIMESTAMP AS TIMESTAMP),  CAST(SYSTIMESTAMP AS TIMESTAMP),
NULL, NULL, 'myruncontrol', 0,  0, 0, 0, '6', '2', 874, '1', '0', ' ', ' ', 0,
  0, 0, ' ', ' ', 0, 0, 868, '1', 'Default', NULL, '1', 7, 689, ' ')
```

The output destination parameters are updated, as shown in Listing 14-11. I have no idea why these values were not set when the record was inserted by the SQL statement shown in Listing 14-5.

Listing 14-11. Updating Output Destination Parameters

```
UPDATE PS_PRCSRUNCNTLDTL
SET OUTDESTTYPE='6', OUTDESTFORMAT='5',  OUTDEST=' ',  PSRF_FOLDER_NAME=' ',
PRCSFILENAME=' ', EMAIL_WEB_RPT='0', EMAIL_LOG_FLAG= '0', PT_RETENTIONDAYS= 7
WHERE OPRID='PS' AND RUNCNTLID='myruncontrol'
  AND PRCSTYPE = 'SQR Report' AND PRCSNAME = 'SYSAUDIT'
```

The run control distribution record is replaced, as shown in Listing 14-12.

Listing 14-12. Deleting and Reinserting the Run Control Distribution Record

```
DELETE FROM PS_PRCSRUNCNTLDIST
WHERE OPRID='PS' AND RUNCNTLID='myruncontrol'
AND PRCSTYPE = 'SQR Report' AND PRCSNAME = 'SYSAUDIT'
```

Process Scheduler Activity

The Process Scheduler periodically queries the request tables, looking for work. The frequency of these queries is determined by the Sleep and Heartbeat times specified in the server definition. The PeopleSoft delivered settings are shown in Figure 14-4 (select Process Scheduler ► Servers ► Server Definition).

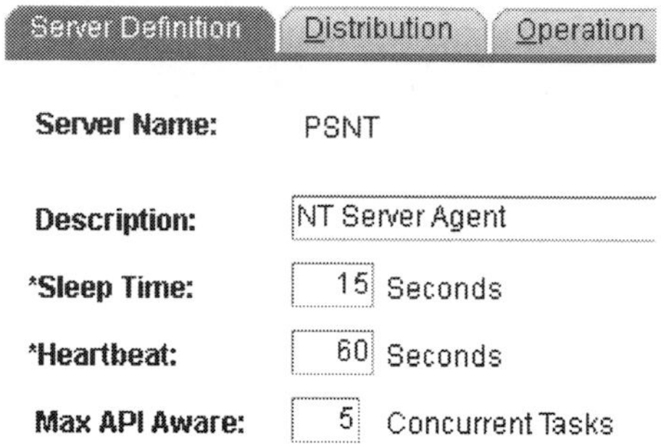

Figure 14-4. Server Definition page

Processing Between Sleeps

After each "sleep," the Process Scheduler (or the Master Process Scheduler if configured) performs a number of checks. For example, Listing 14-13 shows the query to determine which process requests (that are not PSJobs) are due to be scheduled, and which can be scheduled given the load characteristics of the server, in descending order of priority.

Listing 14-13. Checking for Processes, but Not PSJobs, That Are Due to Be Scheduled

```
SELECT  R.PRCSINSTANCE ,R.ORIGPRCSINSTANCE ,R.JOBINSTANCE ,R.MAINJOBINSTANCE
,R.MAINJOBNAME ,R.PRCSITEMLEVEL ,R.PRCSJOBSEQ ,R.PRCSJOBNAME ,R.PRCSTYPE ,R.PRCSNAME
,R.PRCSPRTY ,TO_CHAR(CAST((R.RUNDTTM) AS TIMESTAMP),'YYYY-MM-DD-HH24.MI.SS.FF') ,R.GENPRCSTYPE
,R.OUTDESTTYPE ,R.RETRYCOUNT ,R.RESTARTENABLED ,R.SERVERNAMERQST ,R.OPSYS ,R.SCHEDULENAME
,R.PRCSCATEGORY ,R.P_PRCSINSTANCE,C.PRCSPRIORITY ,S.PRCSPRIORITY ,R.PRCSWINPOP
,R.PRCSRUNNOTIFY ,R.MCFREN_URL_ID ,R.PT_RETENTIONDAYS
FROM PSPRCSQUE R
     ,PS_SERVERCLASS S
     ,PS_SERVERCATEGORY C
WHERE R.RUNDTTM <= CAST(SYSTIMESTAMP AS TIMESTAMP)
AND R.SERVERASSIGN = :1
AND R.RUNSTATUS = :2
AND S.SERVERNAME = :3
AND R.PRCSTYPE = S.PRCSTYPE
AND R.PRCSCATEGORY = C.PRCSCATEGORY
AND S.SERVERNAME = C.SERVERNAME
AND C.MAXCONCURRENT > 0
AND R.PRCSTYPE NOT IN ('PSJob')
ORDER BY C.PRCSPRIORITY DESC, R.PRCSPRTY DESC
        , S.PRCSPRIORITY DESC, R.RUNDTTM ASC
```

Processing on Heartbeat

On each heartbeat, the Process Scheduler server performs other tests. In particular, it checks its status record (as shown in Listing 14-14) to determine whether it has been instructed to suspend or shut down.

Listing 14-14. Checking the Process Scheduler Status Record

```
SELECT SERVERSTATUS,SERVERACTION
FROM   PSSERVERSTAT
WHERE SERVERNAME = :1
ORDER BY 1
```

The Process Scheduler also updates its own status and a timestamp column (as shown in Listing 14-15).

Listing 14-15. Updating the Process Scheduler Status Record

```
UPDATE PS_SERVERACTVTY
SET    SERVERSTATE = :1
,      LASTUPDDTTM = CAST(SYSTIMESTAMP AS TIMESTAMP)
WHERE SERVERNAME = :2
  AND  SERVERACTIVITYTYPE = :3
```

The timestamp can be seen in the Server List tab of the Process Monitor component (see Figure 14-5).

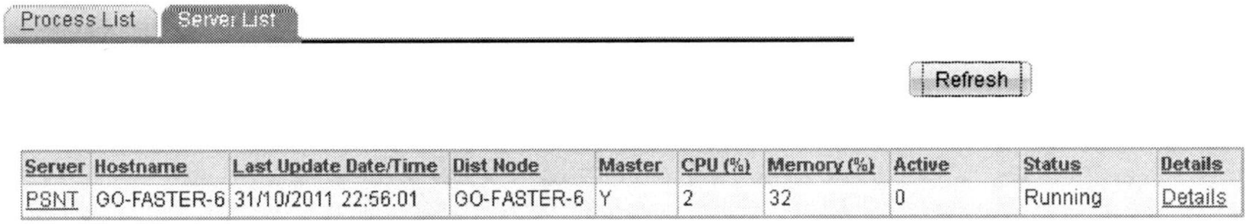

Server	Hostname	Last Update Date/Time	Dist Node	Master	CPU (%)	Memory (%)	Active	Status	Details
PSNT	GO-FASTER-6	31/10/2011 22:56:01	GO-FASTER-6	Y	2	32	0	Running	Details

Figure 14-5. Process Scheduler status on the Server List tab of the Process Monitor component

When the Process Scheduler is shut down in an orderly fashion, the status is set to Down. However, if the Process Scheduler crashes, the status is still Running but the timestamp is not updated. If the Last Update Date/Time is older than a sleep and a heartbeat (by default 75 seconds), then it is likely that the Process Scheduler is not running.

Prioritization of Process Scheduler Requests

The query in Listing 14-13 shows the Process Scheduler looking for requests that are due for processing. The order by clause of this statement is significant because it determines the order in which requests are initiated by the Process Scheduler. Process requests are sorted by three process priorities (highest to lowest) before they are sorted by the run date (oldest to newest):

- PS_SERVERCATEGORY.PRCSPRIORITY: Process Categories are defined for all Process Schedulers in a system. A server category is specified as a part of the process definition. A priority is specified for the category on the server. The maximum number of concurrent processes that a Process Scheduler can run is specified on the Server Definition. A category can be disabled on a particular Process Scheduler by setting the maximum concurrency to 0.

- PSPRCSQUE.PRCSPRTY: The priority of a process on the Process Scheduler is specified on the Process Definition. This value is then copied from PS_PRCSDEFN.PRCSPRIORITY to the PSPRCSQUE when the request is submitted.

- PS_SERVERCLASS.PRCSPRIORITY: This is also specified on the Server Definition. It assigns a priority to a type of process and also limits the number of concurrent instances on a Process Scheduler.

I have found the priorities defined on the Server Category and the Process Definition to be useful in managing batch processing in systems where a backlog of queued requests can build up on the Process Scheduler at peak periods. In these cases, I ask the business users to identify any high priority processes and to organize them into a hierarchy. I then specify Process and Process Category priorities to match.

With just three delivered priorities (1-low, 5-medium, 9-high), process priority on its own is often not sufficiently granular. Combining process priority with Process Categories of different priorities produces nine priorities. The delivered priorities are defined as translate values on the field PRCSPRIORITY. It is possible to add custom translate values to this field.[6] Figure 14-6 shows the Field Properties dialog in Application Designer. I have added six priorities to fill in the gaps and adjusted the descriptions on the delivered priorities.

---

[6] See also http://blog.psftdba.com/2011/03/more-process-priority-levels-for.html.

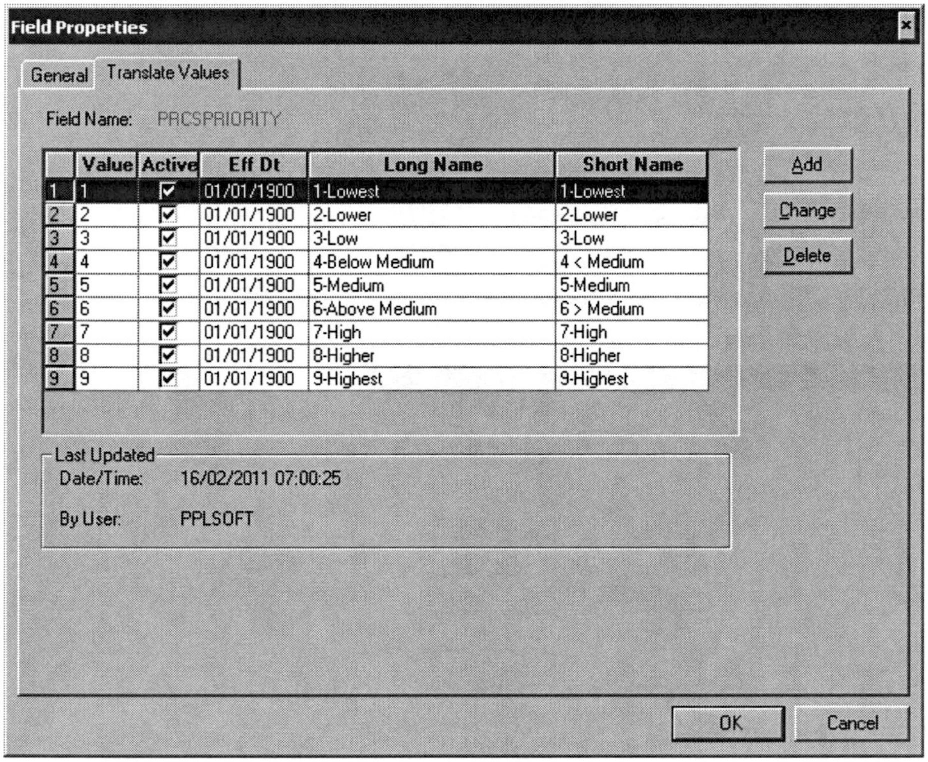

Figure 14-6. Additional translate values on field PRCSPRIORITY

I can then create additional Process Categories and assign them to the Process Scheduler with different priorities (as shown in Figure 14-7).

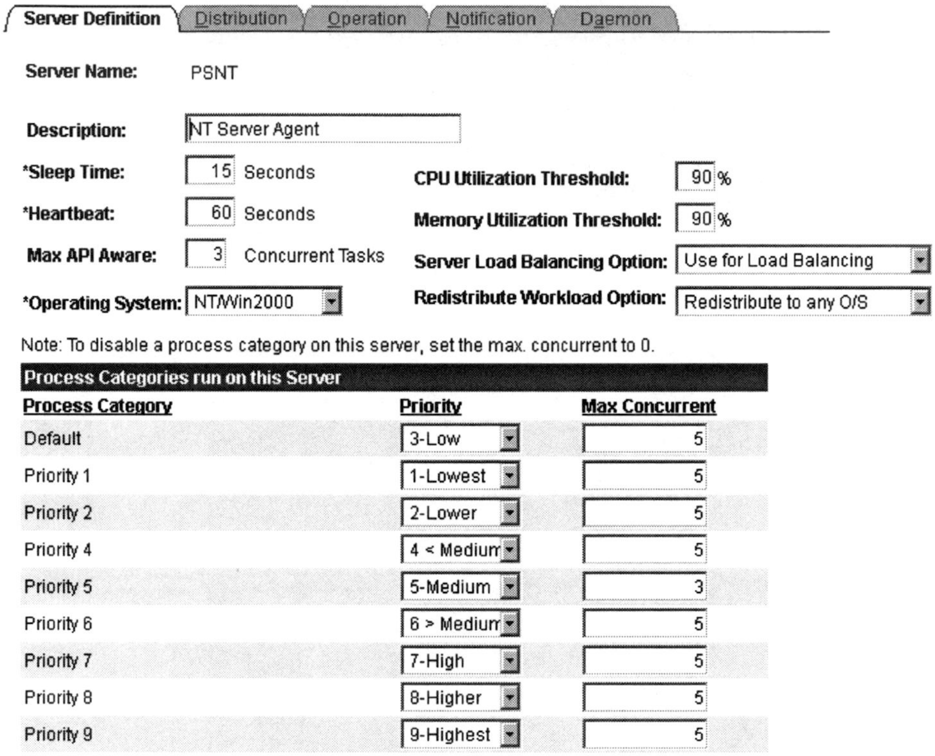

Server Definition	Distribution	Operation	Notification	Daemon

Server Name: PSNT

Description: NT Server Agent

*Sleep Time:	15 Seconds	**CPU Utilization Threshold:**	90 %
*Heartbeat:	60 Seconds	**Memory Utilization Threshold:**	90 %
Max API Aware:	3 Concurrent Tasks	**Server Load Balancing Option:**	Use for Load Balancing
*Operating System:	NT/Win2000	**Redistribute Workload Option:**	Redistribute to any O/S

Note: To disable a process category on this server, set the max. concurrent to 0.

Process Categories run on this Server

Process Category	Priority	Max Concurrent
Default	3-Low	5
Priority 1	1-Lowest	5
Priority 2	2-Lower	5
Priority 4	4 < Medium	5
Priority 5	5-Medium	3
Priority 6	6 > Medium	5
Priority 7	7-High	5
Priority 8	8-Higher	5
Priority 9	9-Highest	5

Figure 14-7. Server Definition Component

I have also reduced the priority on the default Process Category from the delivered default of 5 to 3. I find that users tend to be better at identifying processes as needing higher priority than lower!

Processes Categories can be assigned to a Process in the Process Definition Component (see Figure 14-8).

■ **Caution** Only the three delivered priorities (1, 5, and 9) should be used for Process Definition priorities. Although nothing in the Process Definition component stops you from using one of the additional priorities, there is logic in the Process Scheduler server that checks explicitly for requests with the delivered priorities. Process requests with one of the additional priorities are executed, but they may not be executed in the correct order. Sometimes the Process Scheduler can wait for process with delivered priorities to complete before scheduling any with custom priorities.

It is now possible to define up to 27 levels of priority.

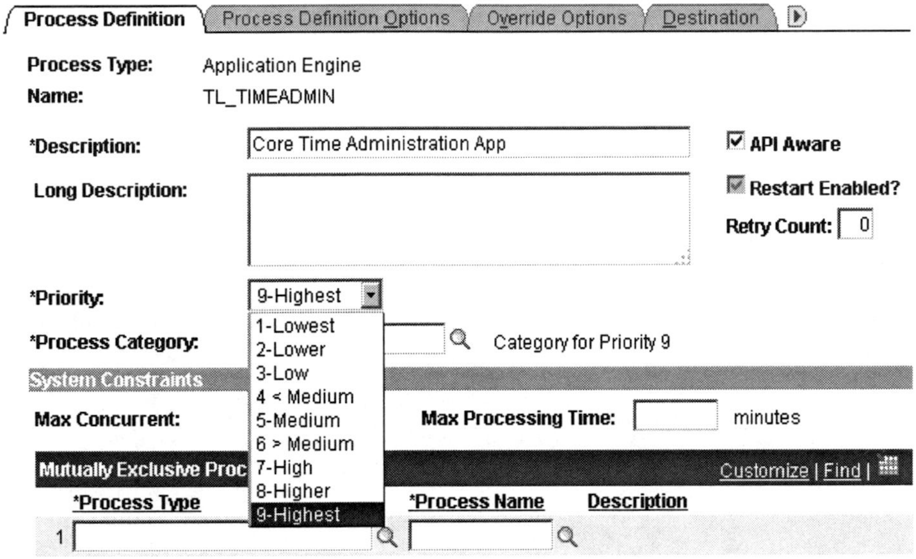

Figure 14-8. Assigning priorities in the Process Definition Component

CASE STUDY: USING PROCESS SCHEDULER PRIORITIZATION

Let me illustrate how to use priorities with an example taken from an HCM system with both Time & Labor and Global Payroll. I configured priorities as follows:

- TL_TIMEADMIN, the main Time & Labor administration batch process, was given the highest possible priority. Both the Process Category and Process Definition have a priority of 9.

- GPPDPRUN, the Global Payroll calculation process, was also put into the Process Category with a priority of 9 because Payroll is a critically important process. The process priority was only set to 5 because TL_TIMEADMIN calculates payable time that is an input into the payroll calculation, and so takes precedence over GPPDPRUN.

- Some one-off processes that are run in special cases were also put into category Priority 9 so that when they are scheduled, they run as soon as possible.

- A number of other processes that are important to the business were put into the category Priority 8. These include some overnight processes and some daytime T&L processing. These processes take precedence over general processing, but they do not take precedence over the main T&L batch and payroll calculation.

The charts in the following figures show the amount of the time Process Scheduler requests spend queuing between submission and execution against start time, before and after the introduction of prioritization. The higher and lower priority processes are shown in different series with different colors.

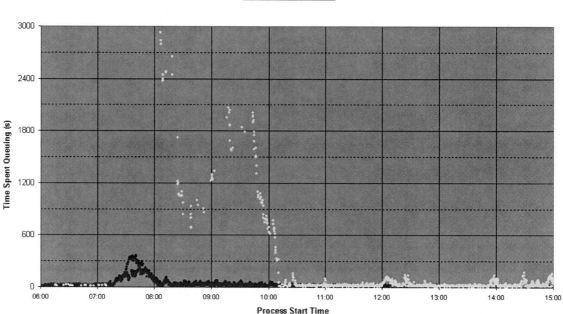

Process Scheduler queuing before the introduction of prioritization

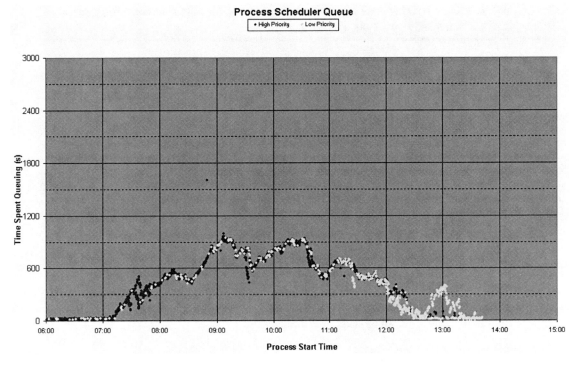

Process Scheduler queuing after the introduction of prioritization

The users of this system have to run high and lower priority processes as part of their jobs. They do the high priority Time & Labor work first in order to meet a payroll deadline and then move on to the lower priority work. Inevitably, some users start on the lower priority work while other users are still on the higher priority work.

If prioritization is not defined, the processes are run in the order of the time at which they were scheduled to run, which generally defaults to the time at which the user submitted the request. Lower priority processes consume the limited number of concurrent process that the Process Scheduler can execute and thus delay the high priority processes. The number of concurrent processes is limited to prevent the Process Scheduler from overloading the physical server.

In the first chart, without prioritization, users can wait up to 15 minutes for their processes to start.

With prioritization, the high priority processes are run before any lower priority processes on the queue and are rarely queued for more than a minute before they are initiated. Between 7 a.m. and 8 a.m., there is a queue of high priority processes, and processing of low priority processes ceases. There is no such thing as a free lunch. The low priority processes pay the price by queuing for up to 50 minutes. Nevertheless, the total amount of time that process requests spend queuing has fallen to about a third of what it was before.

> The business as a whole considers that it is getting better performance from the system because it completes all the high priority work more than an hour earlier.

The configuration of the various priorities must be suitable for all times. In practice, it is not possible to have different sets of priority configurations that can be used for different time windows.

Process Scheduler Overhead

The Process Scheduler tables can become quite large, even if they are regularly purged. It is not unreasonable to see in excess of 1,000 requests per day on a busy Financials system. The overhead of the queries submitted by the Process Scheduler can become significant.

It is not uncommon for several schedulers to run on several different servers on a single system. Each scheduler submits these queries according to its own sleep and heartbeat times. A number of options can be considered:

- *Purging the Process Scheduler request tables:* This is discussed in the next section.

- *Increasing the heartbeat, and particularly the sleep, times to reduce the frequency of these queries:* Be aware that this might result in users waiting longer before their report is scheduled.

- *Tuning SQL queries, but without changing the SQL:* Additional indexes can be helpful. Partitioning can be used in extreme cases.

Purging the Process Scheduler Tables

Unless the Process Scheduler request tables are regularly purged, they grow, as processes either are scheduled by users or recur automatically. The Process Scheduler scans the request tables looking for work. Listing 14-16 shows one such query that has to scan the PSPRCSQUE table looking for recurring processes that have completed and should be rescheduled.

Listing 14-16. A Process Scheduler Query

```
SELECT R.PRCSINSTANCE ,R.ORIGPRCSINSTANCE ,R.RECURORIGPRCSINST
,R.MAINJOBINSTANCE ,R.PRCSJOBSEQ ,R.PRCSJOBNAME ,R.PRCSNAME ,R.PRCSTYPE
,R.RECURNAME ,R.TIMEZONE ,R.PT_RETENTIONDAYS ,R.PTNONUNPRCSID
FROM PSPRCSQUE R ,PS_PRCSRECUR S
WHERE ((R.RUNSTATUS IN ('9', '17')
        AND S.INITIATEWHEN = 1 -- schedule next on current complete successfully
        )
   OR  (R.RUNSTATUS IN ('3','6', '7', '9','10','12', '17')
        AND S.INITIATEWHEN = 0 -- schedule next when current initiated
        ))
AND R.INITIATEDNEXT = 0        -- next occurrence not initiated
AND R.RUNLOCATION = '2'        -- run on server(2)
AND R.RECURNAME > ' '          -- a recurring process
AND R.PRCSJOBSEQ = 0           -- not part of a job
AND R.RECURNAME = S.RECURNAME  -- join to recurrence definition record
```

It is a feature of human nature that when users schedule a report, they often follow the link from the component that scheduled the process to the Process Monitor and sit there repeatedly clicking the Refresh button (see Figure 14-2) to see whether the report has completed. However, every click generates and runs a query like the one in Listing 14-17 on PS_PMN_PRCSLIST, which is a view on PSPRCSRQST.

Listing 14-17. *Query Generated by the Process Monitor*

```
SELECT ...
FROM   PS_PMN_PRCSLIST
WHERE  PRCSJOBSEQ = 0
AND    OPRID = 'PS'
AND    (  SERVERNAMERUN  = 'PSNT'
       OR SERVERNAMERQST = 'PSNT')
AND    RQSTDTTM >=
             TO_DATE(SUBSTR('2004-07-06-23.43.47.000000',
 0, 19),'YYYY-MM-DD-HH24.MI.SS')
ORDER BY SEQUENCENO DESC, PRCSJOBSEQ
```

The query is generated dynamically by the component using the parameters in the View Process Request For part of the component. So every query is slightly different, and the database must parse every one each time, unless CURSOR_SHARING is enabled.

As in the previous example, this query is likely to use a full scan of the request table. You are unlikely to find any of these individual statements in an Oracle Automatic Workload Repository (AWR) or Statspack report or a tkprof report, because each has a relatively small overhead. The problem is the cumulative effect of many similar queries. Some PeopleSoft customers have made the decision to customize the Process Monitor and disable the Refresh button, I know one that used the JavaScript timer function to refresh the page at a fixed rate.

In systems where the Process Scheduler tables are not regularly purged, these queries can become some of the heaviest statements in the system, and I have sometimes seen them impact the performance of the entire database, not just the Process Scheduler and Process Monitor. In the case of the Process Monitor, the issue is not just that the component performs poorly, but also that the application server processes are blocked by long-running queries that are generating physical I/O to the data files.

The Process Scheduler can be configured to purge the requests after a number of days. I suggest setting this option to as small a number as the business requirements permit, to keep the Process Scheduler request tables as small as possible. When purging is enabled, the first purge may be exceptionally large, in which case it is advisable to rebuild the Process Scheduler tables and indexes in order to repack the data and reset the high-water marks.

The Process Scheduler requests on PSPRCSRQST are a valuable source of batch process performance metrics and should be retained in an archive table. Chapter 9 illustrates how to copy purged data into an archive table with a trigger. The built-in Process Scheduler archive process controls the purging of physical files from the report repository and uses the table PSPRCSRQSTARCH.

Lowering Operating System Priority of Batch Processes

Some of the PeopleSoft batch processes can consume large amounts of CPU. On Unix systems, it is possible to lower the operating system priority of the Process Scheduler, which is then inherited by the processes it initiates. In some scenarios, this may be desirable in order to prevent batch processing contending with other processes for CPU:

- PeopleSoft is delivering less processing in COBOL and SQR and is moving toward increased use of the Application Engine. From PeopleTools 8, the Application Engine is also capable of executing PeopleCode. PeopleSoft applications make widespread use of this facility to perform sequential processing in Application Engine programs. PeopleCode is also executed by the component interface, which loads data from a flat file into the system via a component as if it had been typed into a component in the PIA, executing all validation PeopleCode. As illustrated by the discussion of PeopleSoft Ping in Chapter 10, PeopleCode execution is CPU intensive.

- Many PeopleSoft-delivered SQR programs dynamically generate SQL statements in string variables. The CPU overhead of variable handling in SQR also appears to have increased in the versions shipped with PeopleTools 8.x.

The principle of lowering the operating system priority of batch processes is the same as lowering the priority of an application server process, as discussed in the last chapter. There are two architectural configurations where you are likely to want to consider this:

- The Process Scheduler is on the same server as the application server, and you do not want batch processing to contend for CPU with the application server because online performance would be degraded.

- The Process Scheduler is on the same server as the database, and you do not want to starve the database of CPU.

■ **Caution** The UseLocalOracleDB feature should not be used in conjunction with lowering the operating system priority of the client process. Otherwise, the Oracle shadow process will inherit the priority of the client, and it will be more likely to be taken off the processor run queue while holding a database latch. This can significantly increase contention. If batch processes are run on the same server as the database, then configure an IPC SQL*Net connection instead. The client processes still make an IPC connection, but now the priority of the Oracle shadow process is inherited from the Oracle Listener.

On Unix systems only, you can use Tuxedo to lower the priority of the Process Scheduler and Application Engine server processes using the -n server option (described in Chapter 13). Rather than put the setting directly into the Tuxedo template file (psprcsrv.ubx), I prefer to create additional variables in the configuration file (psprcs.cfg), as shown in Listing 14-18, and then reference them in the template.

Listing 14-18. New Parameter in the Process Scheduler Configuration File, psprcs.cfg

```
[Process Scheduler]
;=====================================================================
; General settings for the Process Scheduler
;=====================================================================
PrcsServerName=PSUNX
;---------------------------------------------------------------------
```

```
;Reduce priority of Process Scheduler server process, set to 0 if not needed
Niceness=4
...
```

From PeopleTools 8.4, the Application Engine can be configured to run as a number of Tuxedo server processes in the Process Scheduler domain. The priority of these processes can be controlled independently by creating an additional variable in the PSAESRV section of the configuration file, as shown in Listing 14-19.

Listing 14-19. New Parameter in the PSAESRV Section of psprcs.cfg

```
[PSAESRV]
;========================================================================
; Settings for Application Engine Tuxedo Server
;========================================================================
;------------------------------------------------------------------------
;Reduce priority of application engine server process, set to 0 if not needed
Niceness=5
...
```

The new variable can then be added to the Tuxedo template (psprcsrv.ubx), as shown in Listing 14-20.

Listing 14-20. Extract from psprcsrv.ubx

```
{APPENG}
#
# PeopleSoft Application Engine Server
#
PSAESRV         SRVGRP=AESRV
                SRVID=1
                MIN={$PSAESRV\Max Instances}
                MAX={$PSAESRV\Max Instances}
                REPLYQ=Y
                CLOPT="-n {$PSAESRV\Niceness} -o \"{REL_LOG}{FS}stdout\"
-e \"{REL_LOG}{FS}stderr\" --  -CD {$Startup\DBName} -S PSAESRV"
```

When the domain is configured, the variables are resolved in the Tuxedo configuration file (psprcsrv.ubb), and the nice command can be seen in the server command-line options (CLOPT) in Listing 14-21.

Listing 14-21. Extract from psprcsrv.ubb

```
#
# PeopleSoft Application Engine Server
#
PSAESRV         SRVGRP=AESRV
                SRVID=1
                MIN=1
                MAX=1
                REPLYQ=Y
                CLOPT="-n 5 -o \"./LOGS/stdout\" -e \"./LOGS/stderr\" --
```

```
-CD HCM91 -S PSAESRV"
```

Mutually Exclusive Processing

It may be desirable to prevent the Process Scheduler from initiating certain processes while certain other processes are already running. This may simply be because one process changes data that the other relies on. Sometimes batch processes can also fail when Oracle detects a deadlock.

From[7] PeopleTools 8.4, Process Definition has been enhanced to specify

- The number of instances of a particular process that can run concurrently across all schedulers

- Mutually exclusive processes—that is, processes that if already running prevent this process from being initiated

Figure 14-9 shows how the Global Payroll banking process, GP_PMT_PREP, can be specified in PeopleTools 8.4. I have chosen to permit only a single instance of this process to run at the same time; otherwise, one process could corrupt or lock data required by another. Thus the banking process cannot start while the Global Payroll calculation, GPPDPRUN, is running. This is sensible because the banking process needs the result generated by the payroll calculation.

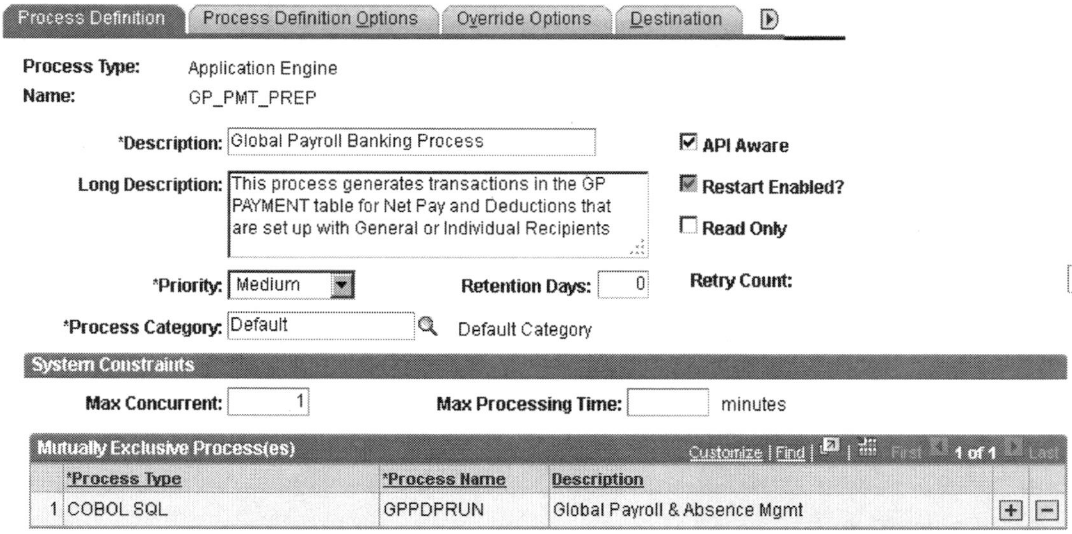

Figure 14-9. Process definition in PeopleTools 8.4

---

[7] In PeopleTools 8.1 and earlier, a similar effect could be achieved by putting the mutually exclusive processes that were of the same process type into a new process class with an occurrence level of 1. Thus, only one process in that class could run at a time.

Application Engine Server Considerations

Application Engine programs can be run as stand-alone executables that can be initiated by the Process Scheduler, or from the command line, in the same way as all other batch process. The psae executable connects to the database, does its work, and then disconnects and terminates.

In PeopleTools 8.4, an Application Engine Tuxedo server process was introduced into the Process Scheduler domain as an alternative. Like most other PeopleSoft Tuxedo server processes, PSAESRV maintains a persistent connection the database, so the same database session may be used for several Application Engine programs. By default, the Process Scheduler is configured with PSAESRV processes. If the PSAESRV server process is not configured, the Process Scheduler instead launches the stand-alone psae process.

Although PSAESRV is enabled by default, I generally recommend disabling it and using the stand-alone psae process, unless your application uses lots of short-lived Application Engine programs. The PeopleTools Performance Guidelines White Paper[8] suggests that ten seconds or less is short-lived:

> *The benefits of PSAESRV versus PSAE are a popular topic of discussion. Our studies have shown that PSAE is as good as PSAESRV for most practical purposes.*
> *If you have an application engine job that runs longer than 10 seconds, PSAE is equivalent to PSAESRV. PSAE has the added advantage of being recycled at the end of each application engine job, cleaning up any outstanding SQL cursors to the database that may have been left behind. Because PSAE recycles after each use, PSAE does not have any possible memory leakage problem that may occupy the precious system memory. In short, PSAE is a cleaner workhorse.*

In an extreme case, I have created additional Process Schedulers with PSAESRV processes to run alongside other Process Schedulers running psae processes. I configured a Process Scheduler Server Category so that only the one frequently executed short-lived Application Engine program executes only on the Process Schedulers running PSAESRV.

The non-shared instances of PeopleTools Temporary Records, used by Application Engine programs as temporary working storage, can be created as Global Temporary Tables, provided the restart facility is disabled for the Application Engine programs. In any version of PeopleTools, the Global Temporary Tables must be created as ON COMMIT PRESERVE because Application Engine programs generally commit at intermediate points. These tables are not automatically cleared out of the temporary segment when the Application Engine program executing on a PSAESRV server completes, because the PSAESRV server process, and therefore the database session, does not terminate. This may result in increased and longer-lasting demands for space in the temporary tablespace. It may be helpful to add additional statements to truncate these tables as the Application Engine program terminates.

Application Engine programs automatically truncate non-shared instances of Temporary Records as the records are allocated to the Application Engine, usually as it starts.

It is tempting to set the recycle count on the PSAESRV processes to 1, so they restart after every service request. However, the server is threaded, and the Application Engine program is called asynchronously and continues to execute after the service has completed. While it executes, the Process Scheduler periodically makes other synchronous service calls to the server to check the status of the program. These services are counted toward the recycle count. Hence if a recycle count is specified, the

---

[8] Oracle Support Document 747389.1.

server may try to recycle while an Application Engine program is executing.[9] Therefore, recycling should be disabled by setting the recycle count to 0.

Summary

As explained in this chapter, the Process Scheduler is of importance to the DBA because it can affect areas of the system for which the DBA is properly responsible. Just as the application server can be used to regulate online activity, so the configuration of the Process Scheduler can be used to regulate the load that batch and report processing can place on the database. The Process Scheduler tables need to be aggressively and regularly purged to prevent the Process Scheduler itself from becoming a source of database performance problems.

---

[9] I have found that this caused the process to lock up itself, its queue, and the Tuxedo Bulletin Board.

Index

CPSIA information can be obtained at www.ICGtesting.com
Printed in the USA
LVOW120221280112

265993LV00004B/1/P